THE LAW OF TUPE TRANSFE

THE LAW OF TUPE TRANSFERS

CHARLES WYNN-EVANS LL.B (BRIS), B.C.L (OXON)

Solicitor, Partner, Dechert LLP; a fee paid Employment Judge

OXFORD
UNIVERSITY PRESS

OXFORD
UNIVERSITY PRESS

Great Clarendon Street, Oxford, OX2 6DP,
United Kingdom

Oxford University Press is a department of the University of Oxford.
It furthers the University's objective of excellence in research, scholarship,
and education by publishing worldwide. Oxford is a registered trade mark of
Oxford University Press in the UK and in certain other countries

First Edition published in 2013

Impression: 1

British Library Cataloguing in Publication Data

Data available

ISBN 978–0–19–966169–5

Printed and bound in Great Britain by
Ashford Colour Press Ltd, Gosport, Hampshire

For Alex, Catherine and David

FOREWORD

If it were not that an 'organised grouping of employees' can by Regulation 2(1) of TUPE include a single employee, one would have doubts that this *magnum opus* was indeed the work of one man! It is a masterly exposition of the law of TUPE Transfers, set out in a very clear and logical order. He has not simply carried out a transfer of the undertaking of the education of his readers seamlessly from one book to another, but he has thoroughly reconsidered, reordered and updated the content of his previous excellent publication, now six years on from the inception of what were then the new Regulations. Whereas his 2006 work was Charles Wynn-Evans' important contribution to our understanding of much that was relatively new, now by 2012 he has been able to take a long hard look at how it has all worked out in practice. No one in the employment field, transferor, transferee, employer, trade union or lawyer should be without a copy of this invaluable work at his side.

Sir Michael Burton
High Court Judge, Chairman of the Central Arbitration Committee,
President of the Employment Appeal Tribunal (2002–2005).

PREFACE

Since coming into force in 1982, TUPE has been one of the most important aspects of the domestic statutory employment law regime, having immense practical, commercial, and financial significance for employers and employees in the private and public sectors in relation to transactions such as outsourcings, contract retenderings, and business sales. Whether considering employees' rights on a transaction out of insolvency, addressing what happens to employees on an outsourcing or the retendering of a service contract, or assessing the employment-related liabilities associated with the sale of a business, TUPE issues are often closely scrutinized by, and affect the interests of, a variety of interested parties.

The commercial consequences of applying an incorrect interpretation of TUPE can be significant for all concerned, quite apart from the consequent potential prejudice to employees' legal rights and livelihoods. Assuming incorrectly that TUPE does not apply to a given situation can lead to an employer facing penalties for failure to inform and consult employee representatives, and taking responsibility for the payment of potentially avoidable redundancy and other termination costs. In addition, the transferee may face unfair dismissal claims from those employees whom it does not take into its employment. Incorrectly adopting the position that TUPE does apply in a particular scenario not only leaves an employer with termination costs (in terms of notice and redundancy entitlements) but also with potential liabilities arising from the dismissal of the employees in question where the employer, rather than, for example, conducting a redundancy exercise, wrongly argues that the relevant employees transfer automatically to the supposed transferee.

The first incarnation of this work, as *Blackstone's Guide to the New Transfer Legislation*, focused upon the changes made to TUPE in 2006. Not least due to constraints of space, this edition is unashamedly private sector in focus and parochial in scope, only addressing the wider EU jurisprudence to the extent considered necessary to discuss the provisions and effect of TUPE, and does not explore every last nook and cranny of the legislation. To that extent, in relation to this book does not pretend to be exhaustive and inevitably therefore reflects the author's assessment of the most important issues arising in practice in relation to the legislation. Nonetheless, it is intended to provide a relatively concise but reasonably thorough introduction to and review of the legislation and its attendant case law as a whole, reflecting the various case law developments since 2006 and expanding upon certain areas which received less detailed treatment in the previous work.

After a general introduction in Chapter 1, Chapters 2 and 3 address the key issue of the events and transactions which fall within the scope of TUPE. Chapter 2 summarizes what constitutes a transfer of an undertaking whilst Chapter 3 describes the concept of a service provision change which addresses the specific application of TUPE to outsourcing, retendering, and in-housing. After Chapter 4 considers the position with regard to those individuals who fall within the scope of the legislation, Chapter 5 then addresses the preservation by TUPE of individual and collective rights. The ability (albeit limited) validly to amend employees' terms and conditions of employment in connection with a TUPE transfer is dealt with in Chapter 6 against the background of the case law invalidating transfer-related contract changes.

Following a discussion of the protection provided by TUPE in respect of transfer-related dismissals in Chapter 7, Chapter 8 addresses the obligation imposed on transferors to provide to transferees prescribed employee liability information about the transferring employees in advance of transfer. Chapter 9 details the obligations to which transferors and transferees are subject requiring them to inform and consult with appropriate representatives of the affected employees in relation to TUPE transfers.

The next two chapters review the operation of TUPE in certain specific contexts. Chapter 10 summarizes the relaxation of the application of TUPE in certain insolvency situations which, by permitting appropriate representatives of the transferring employees to agree changes to those employees' terms and conditions of employment and excusing the transferee from responsibility for certain of the debts owed by the transferor to transferring employees and which it would otherwise inherit, seeks to facilitate the 'rescue culture'. Chapter 11 addresses the exclusion of certain occupational pension scheme rights from the protective scope of TUPE and the separate pension protection provided for transferring employees who enjoyed pension entitlements prior to the transfer under an occupational pension scheme operated by the transferor. Finally, Chapter 12 briefly addresses some miscellaneous yet important issues, including the prohibition of contracting out of the application and effects of TUPE, its territorial aspects, and certain aspects of the interaction of TUPE with taxation, immigration, and equal pay legislation. A brief overview is also offered of some of the drafting and commercial points which need to be considered by those negotiating contracts involving TUPE transfers.

The law is stated as I understand it to be as at 31 December 2012. Whilst this book has been finalized in the shadow of potential TUPE reform leading on from the 'Call For Evidence' issued by BIS in 2012, it is hoped that this edition will remain of value whatever degree of amendment to TUPE might follow. In its response to the Call for Evidence on the effectiveness of TUPE BIS confirmed that the issues that it will be considering in terms of potential TUPE reform will include:

- whether the provisions with regard to service provision changes should be retained or repealed;
- whether, generally, liability should pass entirely to the transferee as now, or be held jointly and severally by transferee and transferor;
- whether employee liability information should be provided earlier to the transferee than is currently required; and
- whether it would be possible to provide that a change of location of the workplace following a relevant transfer can constitute an economic, technical, or organizational reason entailing changes in the workforce, thereby potentially avoiding the automatic unfairness of any dismissal related to the transfer.

I have numerous debts to acknowledge in the production of this book. This edition would never have seen the light of day without the efforts of my indefatigable secretary, Sam Hewitt, whose ever cheerful word-processing support, as well as her ability to decipher my hieroglyphics and correct my typing errors, has been absolutely invaluable. I am enormously grateful to Sir Michael Burton for being so kind as to be willing again to provide a foreword.

Chris Long from Dechert's library has been of invaluable assistance with locating source materials. The employment team at Dechert have been remarkably supportive of the project and uncomplaining about any distraction the writing process may have caused. Eleanor Walter, Roxanne Selby, and their colleagues at OUP have managed the process of getting this book to publication with their customary skilful blend of exhortation and encouragement and have been very accommodating in allowing me to include at a very late stage material on the numerous decisions on service provision changes which came out after the supposedly final manuscript was delivered. I am also grateful to Alex Lock, formerly the Editor of *ELA Briefing*, Jackie Le Poidevin, the Editor of the *Employment Law Journal*, and Professor Simon Deakin, the Editor-in-Chief of the *Industrial Law Journal*, for their indulgence in permitting me to draw upon and incorporate into this work some material previously published in their respective publications (as indicated in the relevant footnotes). Any infelicities, inaccuracies, and misunderstandings of course remain entirely my own responsibility.

I would also like to take this opportunity to thank a number of people from whose support and guidance I have benefited professionally including Toby Landau, Paul Nicholls, Ivan Hare, Nicholas Robertson, Geoffrey Mead, Jason Butwick, all the past and present members of the Dechert employment team, and my colleagues at the Birmingham Employment Tribunal including, in particular, Colin Goodier, David Dimbylow, Pauline Hughes, Fiona Monk, and—not least for unwittingly spurring me finally to get started on the project of a new edition—David Kearsley. Finally, to Alex, Catherine, and David go my heartfelt thanks for their patience with this project and all their love and support.

Charles Wynn-Evans
31 December 2012

CONTENTS

Table of Cases   xvii
Tables of Legislation   xxiv
Table of Abbreviations and Terms   xxix
Note to Readers   xxxi

1. Introduction

    A. Overview   1.01
    B. Legislative History   1.26
    C. Share-based Transactions   1.40
    D. Public Sector Issues   1.45

2. The Transfer of an Undertaking

    A. Identifying an Undertaking and its Transfer   2.01
    B. Labour-intensive Activities   2.94
    C. The *Cheesman* Guidance   2.126
    D. Miscellaneous   2.127

3. Service Provision Changes

    A. Introduction   3.01
    B. The Definition of an SPC   3.11
    C. Interpretation of the SPC Provisions   3.19
    D. Activities and their Similarity Post Transfer 3.25
    E. Multiple Transferees and Fragmentation   3.42
    F. Activities Must Transfer—Work in Progress?   3.59
    G. Who is the Client?   3.63
    H. Client Must Remain the Same   3.67
    I. An Organised Grouping of Employees   3.78
    J. Principal Purpose   3.93
    K. One-off Service Contracts   3.98
    L. Supply of Goods   3.112
    M. Professional Business Services   3.119
    N. Summary   3.125

4. Who Transfers?

    A. Automatic Transfer   4.01

B. Who Transfers?   4.08

C. Electing not to Transfer and Consequent Claims   4.71

5. What Transfers?

A. Individual Rights   5.01

B. Collective Agreements   5.73

C. Trade Union Recognition   5.88

D. Other Representative Structures   5.96

6. Changes to Employees' Contracts

A. Invalidity of Transfer-related Contract Changes   6.01

B. Permissible Contract Changes   6.27

7. Transfer-related Dismissals

A. Introduction   7.01

B. Automatic Unfairness   7.10

C. Economic, Technical, or Organisational Reasons Entailing
Changes in the Workforce   7.43

D. Liability and Fairness   7.72

8. Employee Liability Information

A. Introduction   8.01

B. Employees   8.07

C. Information   8.09

D. Delivery and Updating   8.30

E. Instalments   8.34

F. Indirect Provision   8.35

G. Timing   8.37

H. Remedy   8.41

I. Due Diligence Exercises   8.52

J. Contracting Out   8.61

9. Collective Information and Consultation

A. Overview   9.01

B. Affected Employees   9.06

C. Information   9.14

D. Consultation   9.48

E. Representation of Employees   9.61

F. Remedies for Breach   9.89

G. Interaction with Other Consultation Requirements   9.139
H. Planning for Compliance   9.153

10. **TUPE and Insolvency**
A. Introduction   10.01
B. Bankruptcy and Analogous Insolvency Proceedings   10.18
C. Administration   10.24
D. Transferor's Debts   10.37
E. Opening/Instituting Insolvency Proceedings   10.50
F. Permitted Contract Variations   10.54
G. Misuse of Insolvency Proceedings   10.84
H. Hiving Down   10.85

11. **TUPE and Pensions**
A. Overview   11.01
B. The Pensions Exclusion   11.06
C. TUPE Pension Provisions   11.10
D. Occupational Pension Schemes   11.14
E. The Limits of the Pensions Exclusion   11.21
F. Pension Communications   11.48
G. PA 2004 and PPR 2005   11.56

12. **Miscellaneous**
A. Contracting Out   12.01
B. Territoriality   12.12
C. Tax and Employee Transfer   12.38
D. Immigration   12.41
E. Equal Pay   12.43
F. Drafting and Commercial Issues   12.51

Appendix 1 Transfer of Undertakings (Protection of Employment)
            Regulations 2006   319
Appendix 2 Pension Act 2004, ss 257 and 258   331
Appendix 3 Transfer of Employment (Pension Protection) Regulations 2005 333
Appendix 4 Council Directive 2001/23/EC   335

Index   343

TABLE OF CASES

ADI (UK) Ltd v Willer [2001] IRLR 542, CA 2.30, 2.38, 2.51, 2.114
Abellio London Ltd v Musse et al (1) Centrewest London Buses Ltd (2) [2012]
    IRLR 360, EAT. 4.130, 5.54
Abels v Administrative Board of the Bedrijfsvereniging voor de Metaalindustrie
    en de Electrotechnische Industrie. 10.01, 10.02, 10.10
Abernethy v Mott [1974] IRLR 213, CA. 7.20
Abler v Sodexho MM Catering Gessellschaft [2004] IRLR 168, ECJ 2.15, 2.79, 3.113
Adams v Lancashire County Council and BET [1997] IRLR 436, CA 11.09
Addison and ors v Denholm Ship Management (UK) Ltd [1997] IRLR 389, EAT 12.23
Adult Learning Inspectorate v Beloff UKEAT/0238/07 . . . . 1.56
Alamo Group (Europe) Ltd v Tucker and anor [2003] IRLR 266, EAT. 9.05
Albron Catering BV v FNV Bondgenoten [2011] IRLR 76, ECJ. 4.23
Alemo-Herron and ors v Parkwood Leisure Ltd [2009] IRLR 322, EAT; [2011] IRLR 696,
    SC; [2010] IRLR 298, CA 5.55, 5.59, 5.63, 5.65, 5.70, 5.72
Allen and ors v Amalgamated Construction Co Ltd [2000] IRLR 119, ECJ. 2.21, 2.62, 2.78, 2.126
Allen v Amalgamated Construction Co Ltd [2000] IRLR 119, ECJ. 1.43
Amicus v City Building (Glasgow) LLP [2007] IRLR 253, EAT. 9.59, 9.60
Amicus v Dynamex Friction Ltd [2005] IRLR 724, QBD 9.138
Amicus v GBS Tooling Ltd (in administration) [2005] IRLR 683, EAT 9.114
Anderson v Kluwer Publishing Ltd COIT 15068/85 . . . . 4.40
Angel Services (UK) Ltd v Hambley and ors [2008] IRLR 682, EAT 3.45
Arab Bank plc v Mercantile Holdings Ltd [1994] 2 All ER 74 . . . . 12.30
Argyll Coastal Services Ltd v Stirling and ors UKEATS/0012/11 . . . . 3.28, 3.78, 3.88, 3.95, 12.17
Argyll Training Ltd v Sinclair [2000] IRLR 630, EAT. 2.38
Askew v Governing Body of Clifton Middle School and ors [1999] IRLR 708, CA 1.23
Astle v Cheshire County Council and anor [2005] IRLR 12, EAT. 2.117
Astley and ors v Celtec Ltd [2002] IRLR 629, CA 2.130, 2.133, 5.46
Atos Origin UK Ltd v Amicus and ors UKEAT/0566/03 . . . . 2.116
Ayse Süzen [1997] IRLR 255, ECJ 2.17, 2.47, 2.84, 2.97–2.111, 2.124

BSG Property Services v Tuck [1996] IRLR 134, EAT. 5.11, 7.65
Bakers Union v Clarks of Hove Ltd [1978] IRLR 366, CA 9.132, 9.134
Balfour Beatty Power Networks Ltd & anor v Wilcox & ors [2006] IRLR 258, EAT. 2.09, 2.31,
    2.41, 2.92
Banking Insurance and Finance Union v Barclays Bank plc [1987] ICR 495, EAT. 9.34
Barnes and ors v Brush Transformers Ltd and anor UKEAT/256/99 . . . . 7.79
Baxter v Marks and Spencer UKEAT/162/05 . . . . 9.57
Beckmann v Dynamco Whicheloe Macfarlane Ltd [2002] IRLR 578, ECJ. 11.24, 11.28–11.31,
    11.44, 11.46, 11.47, 11.58
Berg & Busschers v Besselsen [1989] IRLR 447, ECJ 2.13, 2.135, 4.72
Bernadone v Pall Mall Services Group and ors [2000] IRLR 487, CA 5.18, 5.25, 5.26, 11.52
Berriman v Delabole State Ltd [1985] IRLR 305, CA 6.47, 7.51, 7.55
Betts v Brintel Helicopters Ltd and KLM ERA Helicopters (UK) Ltd [1997] IRLR 361,
    HC; [1997] IRLR 311, CA 2.45, 2.99, 7.01
Birch v Sports and Leisure Management [1995] IRLR 518, EAT. 2.23
Boor v Ministre de la Fonction Publique [2005] IRLR 61, ECJ. 5.72, 6.17
Bork International A/S [1989] IRLR 41, ECJ 2.13
Botzen v Rotterdam Sche Droogdok Maatschappij BV [1985] ECR 519, ECJ. 3.50, 4.38
Brennan and ors v Sunderland City Council and ors UKEAT/0286/11 . . . . 9.127
British Aerospace v Green [1995] IRLR 433, CA 7.82

Brooks and ors v Borough Care Services and CLS Care Services Ltd [1998] IRLR 636, EAT 1.41

Buchanan-Smith v Schleicher & Co International Ltd [1996] IRLR 547, EAT 4.41

Burke v Royal Liverpool University Hospital [1997] ICR 730, EAT 2.06

CAB Automotive Ltd v Blake and ors UKEAT/0298/07. . . . . 7.29, 7.33

CPL Distribution v Todd [2003] IRLR 28, CA 4.47

CWW Logistics v Ronald EAT, 1/12/98 . . . . .2.30

Cable & Wireless plc v P Muscat [2006] EWCA Civ 220, CA 4.13

Cable Realisations Ltd v GMB Northern UKEAT/0538/08 . . . . 9.43, 9.46

Canning v (1) Niaz (2) McLaughlin [1983] IRLR 431, EAT 7.45

Capita Health Solutions Ltd v BBC and McLean [2008] IRLR 595, CA. 4.02, 4.07, 4.75, 4.83

Carisway Cleaning Consultants Ltd v Richards & anor UKEAT/629/97 . . . . .4.62, 5.01

Carlisle Facilities Group v Matrix Events & Security Services and ors
    UKEAT/0380/04 . . . . 2.121, 3.18

Castle View Services Ltd v Howes and ors (29.2.00 Inner House). 2.136

Catamaran Cruises Ltd v Williams [1994] IRLR 386, EAT. 6.02

Celtec Ltd v Astley [2005] IRLR 647, ECJ. 4.01–4.04, 4.35

Chambers v QCR Motors Ltd (in voluntary liquidation) & ors UKEAT/0549/09 . . . . 4.05, 4.35, 4.75

Chapman and Elkin v CPS Computer Group plc [1987] IRLR 462, CA. 5.35, 5.37

Charlton v Charlton Thermosystems (Romsey) Ltd [1995] IRLR 79, EAT 2.22, 10.23

Cheesman and ors v Brewer Contracts Ltd [2001] IRLR 144, EAT 2.08, 2.31, 2.50, 2.64,
                                           2.126, 3.22

Clark v Nomura International plc [2000] IRLR 766, QBD 11.47

Clearsprings Management Ltd v Ankers and anor UKEAT/0054/08 . . . . 3.54, 3.55

Clece SA v Valor [2011] IRLR 251, EAT 2.100

Clifton Middle School Governing Body v Askew [1999] IRLR 708, CA. 1.51

Collino and Chiappero v Telecom Italia SpA [2000] IRLR 788, ECJ 1.47, 5.46

Commercial Motors (Wales) Ltd v Howley UKEAT/0491/11 . . . . 2.135

Computacenter (UK) Ltd v Swanton and ors UKEAT/0256/04. . . . . .3.18

Connor and anor v the Secretary of State for Trade & Industry UKEAT/0589/05 . . . . 10.44

Council of the Isles of Scilly v Brintel Helicopters Ltd [1995] ICR 249, EAT 2.26

Cowell v Quilter [1989] IRLR 392, CA 4.12

Crawford v Swinton Insurance Brokers Ltd [1990] IRLR 42, EAT 6.47, 7.53

Credit Suisse First Boston (Europe) Ltd v Lister [1998] IRLR 700, CA. 6.16, 6.25, 6.26, 6.55,
                                           6.58–6.60

Credit Suisse First Boston (Europe) Ltd v Padiachy [1998] IRLR 504, QBD. 6.26, 6.58

Cross v British Airways plc [2005] IRLR 423, EAT 5.39

Curr v Marks & Spencer plc [2003] IRLR 74, CA 4.13

D36 Ltd v Castro UKEAT/0853/03. . . . . 5.06, 5.45

DJM International Ltd v Nicholas [1996] IRLR 76, EAT. 5.08

Daddy's Dance Hall [1988] IRLR 315, ECJ 2.13, 2.18, 4.02, 4.72, 5.03, 5.40, 6.06, 6.12–6.17,
                        6.21, 6.25–6.27, 6.30, 6.34, 6.54–6.57, 10.56

Danmols Inventar [1985] ECR 2639, ECJ 1.24

Department for Education v Huke and anor UKEAT/0080/12. . . . . .3.32, 3.41

Derrick Cyffin Jones t/a the Barley Mow Public House v Beardmore
    UKEAT/0392/09 . . . . .2.25

Dillon and ors v Todd and anor UKEAT/0010/11 . . . . 9.126, 9.128, 9.129

Dines and ors v Initial Health Care Services Ltd and anor [1994] IRLR 336, CA. 2.17, 2.18

Dowling v ME Ilic Haulage & anor [2004] ICR 1176, EAT 4.67, 9.83

Dr Sophie Redmond Stichting v Bartol [1992] IRLR 366, ECJ. .1.26, 2.27

Dudley Bower Building Services Ltd v Lowe and Ors [2003] IRLR 260, EAT 2.35

Duncan Web Offset (Maidstone) Ltd v Cooper [1995] IRLR 184, EAT 4.21, 4.39, 4.43, 4.49

D'Urso and ors v Ercole Marelli Elettromeccanica Generale SpA (in special administration)
    and ors [1992] IRLR 136, ECJ 10.01, 10.38

Dynamex Friction Ltd and anor v Amicus and ors [2008] IRLR 515, CA 7.35, 7.41

ECM v Cox [1998] IRLR 416, EAT; [1999] IRLR 559, CA 2.45, 2.106, 2.112, 2.119
Eddie Stobart Ltd v Moreman and ors [2012] IRLR 356, EAT 1.25, 3.81, 3.88, 4.37
Edinburgh Home–Link Partnership and ors v The City of Edinburgh Council and ors
    UKEATS/0061/11 . . . . 4.38
Eidesund v Stavanger Catering A/S [1996] IRLR 684, ECJ. 11.09
Enterprise Managed Services Ltd v Dance UKEAT/0200/11 . . . . 6.43
Enterprise Management Services Ltd v Connect-Up Ltd and ors [2012] IRLR 190, EAT 3.32,
    3.56, 3.65, 3.125
Euro-Die (UK) Ltd v Skidmore UKEAT/1158/98. . . . . 4.124

Fairhurst Ward Abbotts v Botes Building Ltd and ors [2004] IRLR 304, CA 2.65, 2.72, 3.43, 4.51
Farmer v Danzas UKEAT 858/93. . . . . 2.58
First Scottish Searching Services Ltd v McDine & anor UKEATS/0051/10 . . . . 7.82
Franklin v BPS Public Sector Ltd [1999] IRLR 212, EAT 11.22

G4S (Justice Services) Ltd v Anstey and ors [2006] IRLR 588, EAT 4.64
GEFCO UK Ltd v Oates (1) Car & Delivery Co Ltd UKEAT/0014/05 . . . . 2.90
Gabriel v Peninsula Business Services Ltd and anor UKEAT/0190/11 . . . . 1.08
Glendale Managed Services v Graham 5.61
Green v Fraser [1985] IRLR 55, EAT 7.81
Gutridge and ors v Sodexo Ltd and anor [2009] IRLR 721, CA 5.08, 12.44, 12.46

H Rooke and Sons Ltd [1978] IRLR 204, EAT. 9.132
Hagen v ICI Chemicals and Polymers Ltd [2002] IRLR 31, EAT 5.06, 11.13, 11.48
Hairsine v Kingston upon Hull C.C. [1992] ICR 212, EAT 9.85
Hamish Armour v ASTMS [1979] IRLR 24, EAT 9.136
Harrison Bowden Ltd v Bowden [1994] ICR 186, EAT 7.26, 7.29, 7.32, 7.33
Hartlebury Printers Ltd (in liquidation), Re [1992] IRLR 516, HC. 9.132
Hassard v McGrath and ors [1996] NI 586, NICA 2.68, 2.69, 4.45
Hay v George Hanson (Building Contracts) Ltd [1996] IRLR 427, EAT 4.79, 4.80, 4.88
Head Entertainment Ltd v Walker and ors [2011] IRLR 272, CA 10.01
Henke v Gemeinde Schierke and Verwaltungsgemeinschaft 'Brocken'
    [1996] IRLR 701, ECJ 1.39, 1.53
Holis Metal Industries Ltd v GMB (1) Newell Ltd (2) [2008] IRLR 187, EAT. 2.54, 4.131,
    12.24, 12.27, 12.29, 12.33, 12.36
Honeycombe 78 Ltd v Cummins and anor UKEAT/100/99. . . . . 7.42
Hope v PGS Engineering UKEAT/0267/04 . . . . 4.82
Horkulak v Cantor Fitzgerald International [2004] IRLR 942, CA 11.47
Howard v Millrise Ltd (1) SG Printers (2) UKEAT/0658/04. . . . . 9.74
Hunt v Storm Communications Ltd and ors ET Case No 2702546 . . . . 3.85
Hunter v McCarrick [2012] IRLR 274, EAT 3.63, 3.71–3.75, 3.107
Hynd v Armstrong [2007] IRLR 338, CSIH 7.66

I Lab Facilities Ltd v Metcalfe and ors UKEAT/441/10 . . . . 2.10
Ibex Trading Co Ltd v Walton [1994] ICR 907; [1994] IRLR 564, EAT 7.27, 7.29, 7.33
Imperial Group Pension Trust Ltd and Ors v Imperial Tobacco Ltd and Ors
    [1991] 1 WLR 589 . . . . 11.35
Independent Insurance Company Ltd v Aspinall [2011] IRLR 716, EAT. 9.93, 9.95
Institute of Chartered Accountants of England & Wales v Customs and Excise
    Commissioners [1997] STC 1115, CA. 1.50
Institution of Professional Civil Servants v Secretary of State for Defence [1987]
    IRLR 373, Ch 9.14, 9.20, 9.45, 9.46, 9.135

Jackson v Computershare Investor Services PLC [2008] IRLR 70, CA 5.22, 5.24
John Brown Engineering Ltd v Brown & ors [1997] IRLR 90, EAT 7.82
Johnson Controls Ltd v Campbell and anor UKEAT/0041/12 . . . . 3.32, 3.37

Jones v Darlow Estate Agency UKEAT/1038/97. . . . . .4.55
Jowett (Angus) & Co Ltd v National Union of Tailors and Garment Workers
    [1985] IRLR 426, EAT 5.15
Jules Detlier Equipement v Dassy and Sovramspral (in liquidation) [1998]
    IRLR 266, ECJ 10.04, 10.38
Juuri v Amica Oy [2009] 1 CMLR 33, ECJ 4.108, 4.112

KLT Water Engineering Ltd v Irvine and ors UKEATS/0005/09 . . . . 7.34, 7.84
Katsikas v Konstantinidis [1993] IRLR 179, ECJ 4.72
Kelman v Care Services Ltd [1995] ICR 260, EAT 2.12
Kenny v South Manchester College [1993] IRLR 265, EAT 2.55
Kerry Foods Ltd v Creber [2000] IRLR 10, EAT 7.08, 9.05
Key2Law LLP v d'Acquis[2011] IRLR 272, CA 10.01, 10.34
Kimberley Group Housing Ltd v Hambley [2008] ICR 1030;
    [2008] IRLR 682, EAT 3.24, 3.45, 3.52, 3.54
King's College v Clark UKEAT/1049/02 . . . . 12.49
Kingston v Darlows Estate Agency [1995] IRLR 623, CA. 4.46
Klarenberg v Ferrotron Technologies GmbH [2009] IRLR 301, ECJ 2.59
Kuehne and Nagel Drink Logistics Ltd and ors v the Commissioners for Her Majesty's
    Revenue and Customs [2012] EWCA Civ 34, CA 12.38

LOM Management Ltd v Sweeney UKEATS/0058/11 . . . . .2.49
Law Society of England and Wales v the Secretary of State for Justice and the
    Office for Legal Complaints [2010] IRLR 407, QBD. 1.57, 2.50
Lightway (Contractors) Ltd v Associated Holdings Ltd [2000] IRLR 247, CS 2.11, 2.104
Litster v Forth Dry Dock & Engineering Co. Ltd [1989] IRLR 161, HL 1.18, 1.35, 3.80, 4.25,
                           4.27, 4.30, 4.127, 5.30, 7.14, 10.86
London Borough of Hackney v Sivanandan [2011] IRLR 740, EAT 9.127
London Metropolitan University v Sackur and ors UKEAT/0286/06. . . . . 6.38, 7.23, 7.55
Longden and anor v Ferrari Ltd and anor [1994] IRLR 157, EAT 2.128, 4.31, 7.21

MSF v Refuge Assurance plc [2002] IRLR 324, EAT 9.136
McCarrick v Hunter [2013] IRLR 26, CA 2.56, 3.13, 3.24, 3.33, 3.74
McCormack and Ors v Scottish Coal Company Ltd [2005] All ER (D) 104 . . . . .2.88
McGrath v Rank Leisure Ltd [1985] IRLR 323, EAT 1.17, 7.45
Mackie v Aberdeen City Council UKEATS/0095/04. . . . . .2.39
Mackinnon v Donaldson, Lufkin & Jenrette [1986] 1 All ER 613 . . . . 12.30
McLeod Ingram t/a Phoenix Taxis and Rainbow Cars Ltd t/a Rainbow
    Cars UKEAT/1344/01. . . . . .2.91
Manchester College v Hazel and anor UKEAT/0642/1. . . . . .7.59
Marcroft v Heartland (Midlands) Ltd [2011] IRLR 599, CA. 4.53, 4.70, 5.12
Marleasing S.A. v Comercial Internacional De Alimentacion S.A. [1992] 1
    CMLR 305, ECJ. 1.19
Martin and ors v South Bank University [2004] IRLR 74, ECJ. 6.10, 11.27, 11.30, 11.31,
                           11.44, 11.46, 11.47, 11.58
Mathieson v United News Shops Ltd UKEAT/554/95. . . . . .2.56
Mayeur v Association Promotion de l'Information Messine (APIM) [2000] IRLR 783, ECJ. 1.45
Meade and Baxendale v British Fuels Ltd [1996] IRLR 541, EAT; [1997] IRLR 505, CA;
    [1998] IRLR 706, HL 6.09, 12.05
Merckx and Neuhuys v Ford Motors Belgium SA (C-171/94 & C-172/94)
    [1996] IRLR 467, ECJ. 2.14, 2.15, 2.52, 4.114, 4.115
Meter U Ltd v Ackroyd and ors [2012] IRLR 367, EAT 7.60
Metropolitan Resources Ltd v Churchill Dulwich Ltd (in liquidation) and ors [2009]
    IRLR 190, EAT 2.134, 3.02, 3.19, 3.20, 3.32, 3.66, 3.68
Michael Peters Ltd v Farnfield (1) and Michael Peters Group plc (2) [1995] IRLR 190, EAT 4.19
Mikkelsen [1989] ICR 330, ECJ 4.10

Millam v The Print Factory (London) 1991 Ltd [2007] IRLR 526, CA 1.42–1.44
Milligan v Securicor [1995] IRLR 288, EAT. 7.74
Ministry of Defence v Jeremiah [1979] IRLR 436, CA 9.77
Mitie Managed Services Ltd v French [2002] IRLR 521, CA. 5.32, 5.52
Morris Angel & Son Ltd v Hollande [1993] IRLR 169, CA. 5.29
Morris v John Grose [1998] IRLR 499, EAT. 7.28
Mowlem Technical Services v King [2005] CSIH 46 . . . . 4.40

National Coal Mining v NUM UKEAT/0397/06 . . . . 9.118
Nationwide Building Society v Benn and ors [2010] IRLR 922, EAT 4.118, 7.55, 7.63, 9.92
New ISG Ltd v Vernon and ors [2008] IRLR 115, Ch 4.86, 4.90, 4.91
Newns v British Airways plc [1992] IRLR 575, CA. 1.06
Nokes v Doncaster Amalgamated Collieries Ltd [1940] AC 1014. . . . . 1.06, 1.08
Norris v Brown and Root Ealing Technical Services Ltd UKEAT/386/00 . . . . 7.21
Northern General Hospital NHS Trust v Gale [1994] ICR 426, CA 4.39
Northgate HR Ltd v Mercy [2008] IRLR 222, CA. 9.91
Nottinghamshire Healthcare NHS Trust v Hamshaw and ors
     UKEAT/0037/11 . . . . 2.56, 3.32, 3.64, 3.67
Numast v P&O Scottish Ferries Ltd [2005] ICR 1270, EAT. 2.43, 2.86, 2.88
Ny Mølle Krø [1989] IRLR 37, ECJ. 2.13, 2.49, 2.61

OCS Group UK Ltd v Jones and anor UKEAT/0038/09 . . . . 3.32, 3.34
OTG Ltd v Barke and ors; Olds v Late Editions; Key2Law (Surrey) Ltd v Antiquis and ors;
     Secretary of State for Business, Innovation and Skills v Coyne and ors;
     Head Entertainment Ltd v Walker and ors [2011] IRLR 272, EAT 10.01, 10.24, 10.33
Oakland v Wellswood (Yorkshire) Ltd [2009] IRLR 250, EAT; [2010]
     IRLR 82, CA. 5.47, 10.25, 10.26, 10.29
Onwuka v Spherion & ors UKEAT/0523/06 . . . . 4.50
Oy Liikenne [2001] IRLR 171, ECJ 1.45, 1.46, 2.15, 2.74, 2.82–2.87

P&O Trans European Ltd v Initial Transport Services Ltd [2003] IRLR 128, CA 2.82, 2.85
P Bork International A/S v Foreningen af Arbejdsledere i Danmark [1989]
     IRLR 41, ECJ 2.61, 6.56, 7.26
Page and anor v Lakeside Collection Ltd and anor UKEAT/0216/10. . . . . 7.21
Pannu v Geo W King Ltd and ors [2012] IRLR 193, EAT 3.116
Perry's Motor Sales Ltd & anor v Lindley UKEAT/0616/07 . . . . 7.76
Perth & Kinross Council v Donaldson and ors [2004] IRLR 121, EAT 2.40, 10.10
Photostatic Copiers (Southern) Ltd v Okuda [1995] IRLR 11, EAT. 4.69
Pickstone v Freemans plc [1989] IRLR 161, HL 1.21
Porter and Nanayakkara v Queen's Medical Centre [1993] IRLR 486, QBD 2.20, 2.53, 7.50
Power v Regent Security Services Ltd [2007] IRLR 226, EAT. 6.16, 6.52, 6.56, 6.59
Powerhouse Retail v Burroughs [2006] IRLR 381, HL 12.45
Pressure Coolers Ltd v Molloy [2011] IRLR 630, EAT 10.48
Procter & Gamble Company v Svenska Cellulosa Aktiebolagetsca SCA Hygiene Products
     Manchester Ltd [2012] IRLR 733, Ch 5.10, 5.19, 11.31, 11.35, 11.36, 11.44

RCO Support Services Ltd v Unison [2002] IRLR 401, CA 2.109, 2.111, 2.115
R v British Coal Corporation and Secretary of State for Trade and Industry ex parte Price
     [1994] IRLR 72, CA 9.55
R v Secretary of State for Trade and Industry ex parte Unison [1996] IRLR 439. . . . . 9.75
Ralton v Havering College of Further Education [2001] IRLR 738, EAT 6.15
Rask and Christensen v ISS Kantineservice A/S [1993] IRLR 133, ECJ 1.26, 2.27, 6.08
RCO Support Services and Aintree Hospital Trust v UNISON and ors [2000]
     IRLR 624, EAT. 2.34
Redmond Stichting (Dr Sophie) v Bartol [1992] IRLR 366, ECJ 1.26, 2.27
Roberts v West Coast Trains Ltd [2005] ICR 254, EAT 4.65, 4.66

Rossiter v Pendragon plc and Crosby-Clarke v Air Foyle Ltd UKEAT/243/00;
  [2002] IRLR 483, CA 4.94, 4.95
Royal Mail Group Ltd v Communication Workers Union [2009] IRLR 108, EAT;
  [2009] IRLR 1046, CA 4.03, 4.55, 9.30, 9.33
Royden and ors v Barnetts Solicitors ET Case No 2103451/07 . . . . .3.124, 7.58
Rygaard v Stø Mølle Akustik A/S [1996] IRLR 51, ECJ. 2.28, 2.36, 2.38, 2.41, 2.42

SNR Denton LLP v Kirwan and anor [2012] IRLR 966, EAT 3.39, 3.75, 3.108, 3.109
SO Bernicia [1989] 1 AC 643 . . . . .3.49
Sainsbury v Savage [1981] ICR 1, CA 4.66
St. John of God (Care Services) Ltd v Brooks [1992] IRLR 546, EAT .6.02
Sanchez Hidalgo v Asociacion de Servicios Aser [1999] IRLR 136, ECJ. 1.45, 2.14, 2.126, 5.46
Scattolon v Ministero dell'Istruzione, dell'Universita et della Ricerca [2011]
  IRLR 1020, ECJ 1.48, 1.58, 2.100
Schmidt v Spar und Leihkasse der Früheven Ä mter Bordesholm, Kiel und
  Cronshagen [1994] IRLR 302, ECJ 2.13, 2.33, 2.95, 2.108, 2.126
Seawell Ltd v Ceva Freight (UK) Ltd and anor [2012] IRLR 802, EAT 3.87, 3.88, 3.92,
                                                                                                    3.97, 4.44, 4.61
Secretary of State for Business, Innovation and Skills v Coyne and ors [2011]
  IRLR 272, CA. 10.01
Secretary of State for Employment v Spence [1986] IRLR 248, CA. 4.26
Secretary of State for Trade & Industry v Cook [1997] IRLR 150, EAT 4.69, 4.89
Secretary of State for Trade and Industry v (1) Slater and ors and (2) CGF Nationwide
  Site Services Ltd [2007] IRLR 928, EAT 10.17, 10.21, 10.42, 10.51
Securiplan v Bademosi [2003] All ER (D) 435, EAT 4.59
Senior Heat Treatment Ltd v Bell [1997] IRLR 614, EAT 4.81, 5.49, 6.23
Serco Ltd v Lawson [2006] IRLR 289, HL. 12.15, 12.33
Shamoon v Royal Ulster Constabulary [2003] IRLR 285, HL 4.116
Sidney Smith v Hill EAT 17 February 1998. . . . . .7.29
Sita (GB) Ltd v Burton [1997] IRLR 501, EAT. 4.129
Skillbase Services Ltd v King [2005] All ER (D) 106, CS 4.48
Skills Development Scotland Co Ltd v Buchanan and anor UKEATS/0042/10. . . . . 12.48, 12.49
Small and ors v The Boots Co PLC and anor [2009] IRLR 328, EAT 5.24, 5.34
Smith and anor v Cherry Lewis Ltd [2005] IRLR 86, EAT. 9.111
Smith and ors v Trustees of Brooklands College UKEAT/028/11. . . . . .6.39
Solectron Scotland Ltd v Roper [2004] IRLR 4, EAT. 6.19, 12.08
South Durham Health Authority v UNISON [1995] IRLR 407, EAT 9.103
Spaceright Europe Ltd v Baillavoine [2012] IRLR 111, CA. 7.15, 7.30, 7.34, 7.49, 7.62
Spano v Fiat Geotech [1995] ECR 1-4321, ECJ. 10.38
Spijkers v Gebroeders Benedik Abbatoir [1986] ECR 1119; [1986] CMLR 296, ECJ 2.44–2.47,
                                                                             2.55, 2.82, 2.94, 2.97, 2.100, 2.107, 2.111, 2.115, 2.126
Sunley Turriff Holdings Ltd v Thompson [1995] IRLR 633, EAT. 4.20, 4.23
Susie Radin v GMB and ors [2004] ICR 893, CA. 9.111, 9.116, 9.117
Sweetin v Coral Racing [2006] IRLR 252, EAT 9.108, 9.116
Swissport *See* TGWU v Swissport Ltd (in administration)

TGWU v James McKinnon, JR Haulage Ltd and ors [2001] IRLR 597, EAT 9.05
TGWU v Swissport (UK) Ltd (in administration) [2007] ICR 1593, EAT 10.11
Tapere v South London & Maudsley NHS Trust [2009] IRLR 972, EAT 4.101, 4.113, 4.116,
                                                                                                    5.33, 5.51, 7.58
Taurus Group Ltd v Crofts and anor UKEAT/0024/12. . . . . .3.72
Taylor v Connex South Eastern Ltd UKEAT/1243/99 . . . . 6.38, 7.22
Temco Service Industries SA v Imzilyen and ors [2002] IRLR 214, ECJ 2.104
Thomas v Ewar Stud Farm Ltd (1) the Lord Tryon (2) UKEAT/934/01 . . . . .4.127
Thomas-James v Cornwall County Council ET Case Nos 1701021-22, 1701230-31,
  1701051 & 1701059/07. . . . . .3.53

Thompson and ors v Walton Car Delivery and BRS Automotive [1997] IRLR 343, EAT 12.10

Thompson v SCS Consulting Ltd [2001] IRLR 801, EAT. 7.73

Todd v Strain and ors [2011] IRLR 11, EAT. 9.23, 9.27, 9.58, 9.60, 9.115–9.118, 9.127

Trafford v Sharpe and Fisher (Building Supplies) Ltd [1994] IRLR 325, EAT 7.08

Transport & General Workers Union v Brauer Coley [2007] ICR 226, EAT. 9.94

Transport and General Workers Union v Morgan Platts Ltd (in administration)
    UKEAT/0646/02 . . . . 9.113

Transport and General Workers' Union v Swissport Ltd and anor [2007] ICR 1593, EAT . . . 2.70, 2.73

Tsangacos v Amalgamated Chemicals [1997] IRLR 4, EAT 7.83

Unicorn Consultancy Services v Westbrook [2000] IRLR 80, EAT. 5.09

UNISON v Somerset County Council and ors [2010] IRLR 207, EAT. 9.09, 9.10, 9.132, 9.134

University of Oxford v Humphreys [2000] IRLR 183, CA 4.125, 4.128, 4.132, 12.36, 12.59

Vernon *See* New ISG Ltd v Vernon and ors. 4.90, 4.91

Vidal (Francisco Hernandez) SA v Gomez Perez and ors [1999] IRLR 132, ECJ 2.19, 2.29, 2.126

Vigano v Red Elite de Electrodomesticos SA [2009] 1 CMLR 428, ECJ .5.16

von Colson and Kamann v Land Nordrhein Westfalen [1984] ECR 1891, ECJ 1.20

Waite v GCHQ [1983] 2 AC 714, HL 5.42

Walden Engineering Co Ltd v Warrener [1993] ICR 967, EAT. 11.08

Ward Hadaway v Love and ors UKEAT/0471/09 . . . . .3.29, 3.32, 3.59, 3.63

Warner v Adnet [1998] IRLR 394, CA. 7.08, 7.21

Wendelboe v LJ Music ApS [1986] 1 CMLR 476, ECJ 4.10

Werhof v Freeway Traffic Systems Gmbh [2006] IRLR 400, ECJ 5.59, 5.62, 5.64, 5.66, 5.68, 5.69

West Midlands Co-Operative Society Ltd v Tipton [1986] ICR 192, HL. 4.66

Wheeler v Patel & anor [1987] IRLR 211, EAT. 7.48

Whent v T Cartledge Ltd [1997] IRLR 153, EAT 5.59, 5.61, 5.63

Whitehouse v Charles A. Blatchford and Sons Ltd [1999] IRLR 492, CA 5.21, 7.47, 7.56

Whitewater Leisure Management Ltd v Barnes [2000] IRLR 456, EAT 2.07, 2.113

Whitney v Monster Worldwide Ltd [2011] Pens LR 1, CA. 11.54

Williams v Advance Cleaning Services (1) Engineering & Railway Solicitors Ltd
    (In liquidation) UKEAT/0838/04 . . . . .4.49

Wilson v St. Helen's Borough Council [1996] IRLR 320, EAT; [1997] IRLR 505, CA;
    [1998] IRLR 706, HL 1.20, 1.24, 6.09, 6.11, 6.14, 6.37, 7.03, 12.05

Wood v Caledon Social Club Ltd UKEAT/0528/09. . . . . 2.63, 2.64

Worrall and ors v Wilmott Dixon Partnerships Ltd and anor UKEAT/0521/09. . . . . .5.70, 6.17

Wynnwith Engineering Co Ltd v Bennett [2002] IRLR 170, EAT 2.32

Zaman and Ors v Kozee Sleep Products Ltd t/a Dorlux Beds UK [2011] IRLR 196, EAT. 9.107

TABLES OF LEGISLATION

Paragraph numbers in **bold** indicate that the text is reproduced in full.

STATUTES

Aliens Restriction (Amendment) Act 1919,
   s. 5 . . . . 7.16

Civil Liability (Contribution) Act 1978 . . . 9.127
Company Directors' Disqualification
   Act 1986 . . . . 10.84
Contracts of Employment Act 1963, Sch. 1,
   para 10. . . . . 1.05
Contracts (Rights of Third Parties)
   Act 1999 . . . . .12.10

Data Protection Act 1998(DPA 1998). 8.20,
                          8.25
   s. 2 . . . . 8.22
   Sch 1 . . . . 8.24
   Sch 3, para 2(1) 8.22
Disability Discrimination Act 1995, s 9 . . . 12.03

Employment Act 2002 . . . . 1.34
European Communities Act 1972 . . . .1.04, 6.60
   s. 2(2) 1.30, 1.38
Employers' Liability (Compulsory
   Insurance) Act 1969 . . . . 5.25
   s. 1(1). 5.26
   s. 3 . . . . 5.27
   s. 3(1)–(c) 5.27, 5.28
Employment Protection (Consolidation)
   Act 1978, s 81(2) 5.38
Employment Relations Act 1999
   s. 38 . . . . .1.37, 1.38, 6.60
   s. 38(2) 3.74
Employment Rights Act 1996 (ERA 1996)
   Pt I (ss 1–12). 1.05
   s. 1. . . . . 8.09, 8.11, 8.12, 8.13
   s .1(4) 8.12
   s. 1(5) 8.13
   s. 23 . . . . .5.34, 6.18
   s. 47. . . . . 9.80
   s. 47(1). .9.76, 9.77
   s. 47(1A) 9.77
   s. 49(1)–(5) 9.79
   s 61 . . . . 9.85
   Pt X (ss 94–134A) 7.05, 7.10
   s. 94 . . . . 5.41, 7.18
   s. 95(1). 9.106
   s. 95(1)(c) 4.94, 4.96, 11.12
   s. 95(2) 9.106

s. 97 . . . . 9.106
s. 98. . . . . 7.86
s. 98(1). 7.44
s. 98(2)(c) 7.44
s. 98(4) 6.02, 7.44, 7.79, 7.81, 7.86
s. 102 . . . . 10.45
s. 103 . . . . 9.81
s. 104 . . . . 7.75, 7.76, 7.78
s. 105 . . . . 9.81
s. 108(3)(f) 9.82
s. 109 . . . . 5.41, 6.53
Pt XI (ss 135–181). 10.30
s. 135 . . . . 7.44
s. 139 . . . . 9.106
s. 155 . . . . 9.106
ss. 166–170 . . . . 10.43
Pt XII (ss 182–190). 10.43, 10.48, 10.49
ss. 184–186 . . . . 10.44
s. 203 . . . . .12.02, 12.11
s. 203(2) 12.03
s. 203(2)(d) 12.03
s. 203(2)(e) 12.03
s. 205(1). 9.89
s. 210(5). 6.23
s. 212(1). 6.23
s. 212(3). 6.23
s. 214(2) 5.50
s. 218(2) 5.46, 5.47, 6.23, 10.28
s. 218(3)–(9) 5.48
ss. 220–228. . . . . 9.106
s. 230 . . . . .4.11
Employment Tribunals Act 1996,
   s. 18. . . . . .7.18, 8.41, 9.89, 12.03, 12.04
   s. 35. . . . . 9.129
Equal Pay Act 1970 . . . .
   s. 1(3) 12.48
   s. 2ZA 12.44
Equality Act 2010 . . . . 12.44
   s. 147 . . . . 12.03

Human Rights Act 1998
   Sch 1 European Convention on Human
     Rights, Art 11. . . . . 5.64

Immigration, Asylum and Nationality
   Act 2006 . . . . .12.41
Income Tax (Earnings and Pensions)
   Act 2003, s 401 . . . . 9.105

Insolvency Act 1986. . . . . 10.84
  Pt XIII (ss 390–398) (IA 1986). 10.19
  s. 388. . . . . 10.50
  s. 388 (1)(a) 10.19
  s. 389 (2). 10.19
  ss. 390–398 . . . . .10.19
Interpretation Act 1978 . . . . 3.76
  s. 6 . . . . 3.47

Merchant Shipping Act 1894 . . . . 2.138
Merchant Shipping Act 1970 . . . . 2.138

National Health Service and Community
  Care Act 1990 . . . . 5.27
  s. 4(3) 2.20
National Minimum Wage Act 1998,
  s. 49(3) 12.03

Pensions Act 1995, s 124(1). 11.62
Pensions Act 2004 (PA 2004) 6.61, 6.63,
  9.28, 9.29, 11.04, 11.10, 11.45, 11.56–11.83
  s. 7 . . . . .11.75
  s. 10. . . . . .11.75
  s. 17. . . . . .11.75
  s. 239. . . . . 11.17, 11.18
  s. 256(6) 11.77
  s. 257. . . . . 11.57, 11.62, App 2
  s. 257(1)(a). 11.61
  s. 257(1)(b) 11.61
  s. 257(1)(c)(i). 11.61
  s. 257(5) 11.76
  s. 257(7) 11.70
  s. 257(8) 11.61
  s. 258. . . . . 11.57, 11.65, App 2
  s. 258(1). 11.65, 11.74
  s. 258(2)(c) 11.71
  s. 258(3) 11.65
  s. 258(6) 6.64
  s. 258(7) 11.65, 11.66
  s. 318(1). 11.62
Pensions Act 2008
  s. 8 . . . . .11.82
  s. 29 . . . . .11.79
Pensions Schemes Act 1993 . . . . 11.10
  s. 1. . . . . 11.16, 11.20

Race Relations Act 1976, s 72. . . . . 12.03

Sex Discrimination Act 1975, s 77 . . . . 12.03

Trade Union and Labour relations
  (Consolidation) Act 1992
  s. 154. . . . . 9.84
  s. 168. . . . . 9.87
  s. 168(3) 9.88
  s. 169. . . . . 5.95

s. 178(1) 5.81
s. 178(2). 5.81
s. 179. . . . . .5.74, 5.84
s. 179(1)–(3). 5.85
s. 180. . . . . .5.74, 5.84
s. 188. . . . . . . 5.07, 5.15, 6.03, 7.71, 9.08, 9.35,
     9.50, 9.56, 9.93, 9.109, 9.132, 9.139,
        9.140, 10.44, 12.11, 12.27
s. 188(7). 9.133
s. 189(1). 9.91
s. 237. . . . . 7.18
s. 237(1A) 9.82
s. 238(2A) 9.82
Trade Union Reform and Employment
  Rights Act 1993
  s. 33. . . . . 2.27
  s. 33(1). 1.26
  s. 33(2) 1.26
  Sch 10 . . . . 1.26
Treaty on the Functioning of the
  European Union, Art 267 . . . . 5.69
Welfare Reform and Pensions
  Act 1999 . . . . .11.19

SECONDARY LEGISLATION

Statutory Instruments

Agency Workers Regulations 2010
  (SI 2010/93) 9.17

Collective Redundancies and Transfer of
  Undertakings (Protection of Employment)
  (Amendment) Regulations 1995
  (SI 1995/2587) 1.26
Collective Redundancies and Transfer of
  Undertakings (Protection of Employment)
  (Amendment) Regulations 1999
  (SI 1999/1925). 1.26, 9.63

Employers Duties (Implementation)
  Regulations 2010 (SI 2010/4),
  reg 5 . . . . .11.79
Employment Protection Code of Practice
  (Time Off for Trade Union Duties
  and Activities) Order 2009
  (SI 2009/3223) 9.88
Employment Equality (Sexual Orientation)
  Regulations 2003 (SI 2003/1661),
  reg 35 . . . . 12.03
Employment Rights (Increase of Limits)
  Order 2011 (SI 2011/3006). 9.107
Employment Tribunals (Extension of
  Jurisdiction) (England and Wales)
  Order 1994 . . . . 5.34
Equality (Religion or Belief) Regulations
  2003 (SI 2003/1660), reg 35 . . . . 12.03

Fixed-Term Employees (Prevention of
    Less Favourable Treatment) Regulations
    2002 (SI 2002/2034), reg 10 . . . . . . 12.03

Information and Consultation of
    Employees Regulations 2004
    (SI 2004/3426) 5.97, 9.142
    reg 9 . . . . 12.03
    reg 20 . . . . 9.143–9.149
    reg 20(1)(b) 9.148
    reg 20(5) 9.148
    reg 20(5)(b) 9.146

Local Government (Early Termination
    of Employment) (Discretionary
    Compensation) (England and Wales)
    Regulations 2000 (SI 2000/1410) 5.70

Occupational Pension Schemes
    (Contracting-Out) Regulations 1996
    (SI 1996/1172) 11.72

Part-time Workers (Prevention of Less
    Favourable Treatment) Regulations
    2000 (SI 2000/1551), reg 9 . . . . 12.03

Transfer of Employment (Pension
    Protection) Regulations 2005
    (SI 2005/649) 6.61, 6.63, 6.64,
                        9.28, 9.29, 11.04, 11.45,
                        11.56–11.83, **App 3**
    reg 2(1)(a) 11.73
    reg 2(1)(b) 11.73
    reg 3(1)(a) 11.70
    reg 3(1)(b) 11.70
    reg 3(2)(a) 11.70
    reg 3(2)(b) 11.70
    reg 3(3) 11.70
Transfer of Undertakings (Protection
    of Employment) Regulations
    1981 . . . . .1.01, 1.26
    reg 2(2) 2.136, 2.137
    reg 4(1) 10.85
    reg 5 . . . . 4.127, 5.43, 11.23, 12.08, 12.47
    reg 5(1) 4.27, 4.32, 4.33, 4.36, 4.92,
                        5.58, 5.68
    reg 5(2) 5.68
    reg 5(3) 4.66
    reg 5(4) 5.49
    reg 5(4A) 4.82, 4.88, 4.92, 4.125
    reg 5(4B) 4.82, 4.88, 4.89, 4.125
    reg 5(5) 4.89, 4.92, 4.93, 4.95, 4.96,
                        4.103, 4.119, 11.13
    reg 7 . . . . .11.01, 11.09, 11.22, 11.52
    reg 8 . . . . .12.14
    reg 8(1) 7.08, 7.28

reg 8(2) 7.08, 7.67
reg 8(2)(b) 7.45
reg 8(4) 7.16
reg 10 . . . . .9.45, 11.52, 12.14
reg 10(2)(d) 9.42
regs 10–12 . . . . 9.143
reg 11 . . . . .9.109, 12.14
reg 12 . . . . 6.27, 6.54, 6.57, 12.08, 12.09
reg 13 . . . . 12.23
reg 13(2) 12.14
Transfer of Undertakings (Protection of
    Employment) Regulations 2006 (SI 2006/246)
    reg 2(1) 3.16, 3.84, 4.11, 4.15, 4.16, 5.81,
                        9.06, **App 1**
    reg 2(2) 9.65
    reg 2(3) 12.17
    reg 3(1) 3.62, 4.22
    reg 3(1)(a) 1.55, 2.01–2.03, 2.06, 2.10,
                        2.12, 2.14, 2.26, 2.32, 2.42, 2.43, 2.50,
                        2.51, 2.56, 2.61–2.65, 2.69, 2.74,
                        2.94, 2.100, 2.109, 2.113, 2.116, 2.117,
                        2.125–2.127, 2.134, 2.135, 3.14, 3.17, 3.18,
                        3.22, 3.30, 3.43, 3.46, 3.47, 3.101, 3.116,
                        3.119, 4.16, 4.22, 7.76, 10.14, 12.16, 12.37
    reg 3(1)(b) 1.25, 1.39, 1.55, 2.14, 2.42,
                        2.56, 2.94, 2.123, 2.125, 2.134, 3.01, 3.11,
                        3.13–3.23, 3.27, 3.28, 3.30, 3.34, 3.35,
                        3.43, 3.45, 3.49, 3.53, 3.61, 3.63, 3.67,
                        3.72, 3.74, 3.78–3.80, 3.92, 3.98, 3.101,
                        3.103, 3.104, 3.106, 3.115–116,
                        3.123–3.125, 4.18, 4.22, 10.14, 12.17, 12.37
    reg 3(1)(b)(ii) 3.68–3.70, 3.85
    reg 3(2) 2.02, 2.14, 2.26, 2.28
    reg 3(3) 3.12, 3.23
    reg 3(3)(a) 3.12
    reg 3(3)(a)(i) 3.28, 3.78, 3.80, 3.81,
                        3.83, 3.87, 3.90, 3.92, 3.97, 4.37, 12.17
    reg 3(3)(a)(ii) 3.15, 3.98, 3.100–3.102,
                        3.109–3.111
    reg 3(3)(b) 3.15, 3.112, 3.113, 3.117, 3.118
    reg 3(4) 2.128, 12.20
    reg 3(4)(a) .1.49, 2.03
    reg 3(4)(b) 12.20
    reg 3(5) 1.49, 1.54, 1.55, 2.05, 2.50
    reg 3(6) 3.14
    reg 3(6)(a) 2.127, 3.14
    reg 3(6)(b) 3.14
    reg 3(7) 2.138
    reg 4 . . . . .3.81, 4.30, 4.35, 6.62, 7.14,
                        7.84, 7.86, 10.16–10.18, 10.20, 10.22,
                        10.24–10.29, 10.37, 11.10, 11.35, 11.78
    reg 4(1) 4.08, 4.09, 4.14, 4.15, 4.18,
                        4.22, 4.27, 4.36, 4.44, 4.122,
                        5.23, 5.31, 5.68, 5.74, 8.08
    reg 4(2) 4.131, 5.04, 5.05, 5.14, 5.43,
                        5.45, 5.54, 5.68, 7.86

reg 4(2)(a) 5.10, 5.35, 7.86, 11.41
reg 4(2)(b) 5.10, 7.71, 7.77, 7.78, 7.86
reg 4(3) 4.24, 4.25, 4.27, 4.31, 4.66,
7.15, 7.86, 8.29
reg 4(4) 4.120, 5.31, 6.04, 6.10,
6.28–6.35, 6.39–6.41, 6.48–6.51, 6.60,
6.63, 9.60, 10.56, 10.59, 10.77, 12.07
reg 4(5) 4.120, 5.31, 6.04, 6.10,
6.28–6.35, 6.48–6.51, 6.60, 6.63, 9.60,
10.56, 10.59, 10.77, 12.07
reg 4(5)(b) 10.77
reg 4(6) 5.14
reg 4(7) 4.34, 4.71, 4.73–4.76, 4.78,
4.82, 4.90, 4.125, 4.128, 5.49
reg 4(8) 4.34, 4.74, 4.82, 4.122, 4.125
reg 4(9) 4.71, 4.74, 4.78, 4.93,
4.97–4.108, 4.113, 4.117–4.123, 4.128,
4.130, 4.132, 5.17, 5.92, 7.64, 7.66, 7.67,
8.17, 11.13, 12.36
reg 4(10) 4.78, 4.104, 4.112, 4.122
reg 4(11) . . . 4.71, 4.74, 4.122, 4.131, 7.10, 8.17,
10.82, 12.36
reg 5 . . . . . . 5.74–5.81, 5.86, 8.09, 11.10, 11.78
reg 5(3) 2.128, 4.65, 4.66
reg 6 .5.91, 5.92, 5.96
reg 6(2) 5.90, 5.91
reg 6(2)(b) 5.92
reg 7 . . . . . . 4.28–4.30, 6.43, 7.07, 7.10–7.16,
7.74, 7.84, 10.16–10.18, 10.20,
10.22, 10.24–10.29
reg 7(1) 4.107, 7.05, **7.10**, 7.15–7.19, 7.32,
7.33, 7.59, 7.73, 7.86, 10.40
reg 7(2) 7.43, 7.55, 7.60, 7.61, 7.68,
7.71, 7.73, 7.86
reg 7(3) 7.43, 7.44
reg 7(3)(a) 7.86
reg 7(3)(b) .7.45, 7.86
reg 7(4) 7.12
reg 7(5) 7.16
reg 7(6) 7.16, 7.17
reg 8 . . . . .5.02, 10.14, 10.17, 10.28, 10.51
reg 8(2) 7.79, 10.16, 10.40
reg 8(2)(a) 10.40
reg 8(2)–(6) 10.38, 10.39, 10.47, 10.48,
10.57
reg 8(3) 10.42, 10.45
reg 8(4) 10.41
reg 8(5) 10.41, 10.42
reg 8(6) 10.17, 10.21, 10.37, 10.50–10.52
reg 8(7) 10.12, 10.16, 10.18, 10.20–10.37,
10.50, 10.51, 10.52
reg 9 . . . . .5.02, 10.08, 10.14, 10.17, 10.20,
10.54, 10.57, 10.59, 9.61, 10.63,
10.67, 10.71, 10.79–10.83
reg 9(1) 10.58
reg 9(2) 10.62
reg 9(2)(a) 10.64
reg 9(2)(b)(i) 10.67
reg 9(3) 10.66
reg 9(4) 10.70
reg 9(5) 10.71–10.73
reg 9(6) 10.75, 10.78, 10.82
reg 9(7) 10.76
reg 10 . . . . 6.61, 6.63, 8.10, 9.04
reg 10(1) 11.01, 11.10
reg 10(2) 11.11
reg 10(3) 4.122, 11.12, 11.13
reg 11 . . . . . .8.05, 8.06, 8.09, 8.13, 8.20–8.22,
8.30, 8.33, 8.34, 8.36, 8.41, 8.46,
8.52–8.55, 9.04
reg 11(1) 8.08
reg 11(2) 8.09, 8.12, 8.21, 8.23, 8.29,
8.47, 8.55
reg 11(2)(d) 8.10
reg 11(2)(d)(ii) 8.16–8.18
reg 11(2)(d)(iii) 8.17
reg 11(3) 8.37
reg 11(4) 8.28
reg 11(5) 8.32, 8.48
reg 11(7)(a) 8.34
reg 11(7)(b) 8.35
reg 12 .8.06, 8.41, 8.51
reg 12(1) 8.41
reg 12(2) 8.41
reg 12(4) 8.43, 8.46
reg 12(5) 8.49
reg 12(6) 8.51
reg 12(7) 8.41
reg 13 . . . . . . 4.11, 4.70, 8.49, 9.01, 9.05–9.08,
9.14, 9.29, 9.30, 9.51, 9.54–9.56, 9.60,
9.61, 9.66, 9.67, 9.70–9.73, 9.89–9.93,
9.99, 9.101–9.104, 9.198, 9.111, 9.119, 9.122,
9.123, 9.138–9.141, 9.146–9.150, 10.44,
10.65, 10.67–10.70, 11.78, 12.04,
12.11, 12.27, 12.34
reg 13(1) 8.49, 10.66
reg 13(2) 9.02, 9.17, 9.19, 9.35, 9.43,
9.44, 9.46, 9.50
reg 13(2)(a) 9.15–9.17
reg 13(2)(b) 9.15, 9.18
reg 13(2)(d) 9.39, 9.42, 9.46, 9.52
reg 13(2A) 9.17
reg 13(3) 9.61
reg 13(3)(b)(i) 9.70
reg 13(4) 9.27, 9.40, 9.42, 9.101, 9.124
reg 13(5) 9.37, 9.38
reg 13(6) 9.02, 9.11, 9.43, 9.44,
9.46–9.48, 9.59
reg 13(7) 9.53
reg 13(8) 9.69
reg 13(9) 9.130, 9.131
reg 13(10) 9.73

reg 13(11) 9.74
reg 13(12). 9.133
regs 13–16 . . . . 8.44
reg 14. . . . . . 9.01, 9.02, 9.62, 9.67, 9.70, 9.90,
9.147
reg 14(1). 9.61, 9.71–9.73
reg 15. . . . . . 4.70, 9.01, 9.89, 9.93, 9.98, 9.109,
9.127, 12.04
reg 15(1). 9.90
reg 15(2) 9.131
reg 15(3) 9.68
reg 15(5) 9.02, 9.27, 9.41, 9.101
reg 15(7) 9.104
reg 15(8) 9.101, 9.128, 9.129
reg 15(8)(a) 9.119, 9.127
reg 15(9) 9.119, 9.125, 9.126
reg 15(10). 9.128
reg 15(10)(b) 9.129
reg 15(12). 9.60, 9.102, 9.128, 9.129
reg 15(12)(b) 9.129
reg 16. . . . . 4.70
reg 16(1). 9.89
reg 16(2) 9.89
reg 16(3) 9.105
reg 16(4) 9.106
reg 16(10). 12.04
reg 17(1)(a). 5.28
reg 17(1)(b) 5.28
reg 17(2) 5.27, 5.28
reg 18. . . . . 6.27, 12.01, 12.08
Transfer of Undertakings (Protection of
    Employment) (Rent Officer Service)
    Regulations 1999 (SI 1999/2511) 1.39
Transfer of Undertakings (Protection of
    Employment) (Transfer to OFCOM)
    Regulations 2003 (SI 2003/2715) 1.39
Transfer of Undertakings (Protection of
    Employment) (RCUK Shared Services
    Centre Limited) Regulations 2012 (SI
    2012/2043) 1.39
Transitional Information and Consultation
    of Employees Regulations 1999
    (SI 1999/3323) 9.151
    reg 41. . . . . 12.03

Unfair Dismissal and Statement of Reasons
    for Dismissal (Variation of
    Qualifying Period) Order 1999
    (SI 1999/1436). 7.05
Unfair Dismissal and Statement of Reasons
    for Dismissal (Variation of Qualifying
    Period) Order 2012 (SI 2012/989) 7.05

Working Time Regulations 1998
    (SI 1998/1833), reg 35 . . . . 12.03

EU Regulation

Reg 44/2001 Jurisdiction Regulation 12.26

EU Directives

Dir 75/129/EEC Collective Redundancies
    OJ [1975] L48/29 . . . . .1.01
Dir 77/187/EEC First Acquired Rights
    Directive 1.01, 1.32, 1.46, 2.16, 2.77,
    2.80, 2.115, 4.38, 6.07, 7.29, 10.02
    Art 1 . . . . 2.81
    Art 3(1) 11.29
    Art 3(3). 11.29
Dir 80/97/EEC Insolvency OJ [1980]
    L283/23 . . . . .1.01
Dir 92/50/EC standard forms in the
    publication of public contract
    notices. 1.46, 2.16
    Art 1(1)(c) 1.52, 1.54
Dir 94/45/EC 9.151
Dir 96/71/EC Posted Workers Directive. . . 12.30
Dir 98/50/EC Acquired Rights Directive
    (ARD 1998). 1.27, 1.32
    Art 4A 10.05
Dir 2001/23/EC Acquired Rights Directive
    OJ [2001] L82/16 . . . . . . .1.27, 1.32, **App 4**
    Recital 3 . . . . .1.01
    Art 1(1)(a) 2.01, 2.02, 2.12
    Art 1(1)(b) 2.01, 2.02, 2.27
    Art 1(1)(c) 1.53
    Art 1(2) 12.12
    Art 2(1)(a) 4.17
    Art 2(1)(d). 4.10
    Art 2(2). 4.10
    Art 3 . . . . 5.75, 6.08, 6.29
    Art 3(1) 5.16, 5.19, 5.27, 5.68, 5.69,
    9.122, 11.35, 11.37
    Art 3(2). 5.63, 6.10, 8.01, 8.02, 8.03
    Art 3(3). 5.73
    Art 4 . . . . 11.01, 11.06–11.08
    Art 4(1) 6.33
    Art 4(2). 4.71, 4.92, 4.96, 4.108–4.110,
    6.17, 7.02, 7.05
    Art 5 . . . . 10.28
    Art 5(1) 10.05, 10.12, 10.15–10.17, 10.20,
    10.21, 10.27, 10.31
    Art 5(2). 10.06, 10.07, 10.14, 10.15, 10.21,
    10.37, 10.54
    Art 5(2)(a). 10.48
    Art 5(4). 10.84
    Art 6 . . . . 12.26
    Art 6(1) 5.88
    Art 7(2). 9.60
    Art 7(3). 9.59
    Art 7(4). 9.133
    Art 8 . . . . 1.37

TABLE OF ABBREVIATIONS AND TERMS

2001 Consultation	Transfer of Undertakings (Protection of Employment) Regulations 1981, Government Proposals for Reform, Detailed Background Paper, Employment Relations Directorate, Department of Trade and Industry, September 2001, URN 01/1158
2005 Consultation	TUPE, Draft Revised Regulations, Public Consultation Document, Employment Relations Directorate, Department of Trade and Industry, March 2005, URN 05/926
2006 Guidance	Employment Rights on the Transfer of an Undertaking, A Guide to the 2006 TUPE Regulations for Employees, Employers and Representatives, Employment Relations Directorate, Department of Trade and Industry, January 2006
2009 Guidance	Employment Rights on the Transfer of an Undertaking, A Guide to the 2006 TUPE Regulations for Employees, Employers and Representatives, Department for Business, Innovation and Skills, June 2009 URN 09/1013
ARD 1977	Council Directive 77/187/EEC OJ L 061
ARD 1998	Council Directive 98/50/EC OJ L 201/88
ARD 2001	Council Directive 2001/23/EC OJ L 82/16
BIS	Department for Business, Innovation and Skills
CA	Court of Appeal
CAC	Central Arbitration Committee
CJEU	Court of Justice of the European Union
CS	Court of Session
Consultation Response	TUPE, Draft Revised Regulations, Government Response to the Public Consultation, Department of Trade and Industry, February 2006
DPA 1998	Data Protection Act 1998
DTI	Department of Trade and Industry
EAT	Employment Appeal Tribunal
ECJ	European Court of Justice
EA 2010	Equality Act 2010
ELCIA 1969	Employers' Liability (Compulsory Insurance) Act 1969
EqPA 1970	Equal Pay Act 1970
ERA 1996	Employment Rights Act 1996
ERA 1999	Employment Relations Act 1999
ET	Employment Tribunal
ETOR	an 'economic, technical or organisational reason entailing changes in the workforce'
EU	European Union
EWC	European Works Council
HL	House of Lords
IA 1986	Insolvency Act 1986
ICE	Information and Consultation of Employees Regulations 2004 SI 2004/3426
NJC	National Joint Council for Local Government Services
PA 2004	Pensions Act 2004

PA 2008	Pensions Act 2008
PPR 2005	Transfer of Employment (Pension Protection) Regulations 2005 SI 2005/649
PSA 1993	Pension Schemes Act 1993
SC	Supreme Court
SPC	service provision change
Schedule B1	Schedule B1 to the Insolvency Act 1986
TEC	Training and Enterprise Council
TFEU	Treaty on the Functioning of the European Union
TULRCA 1992	Trade Union and Labour Relations (Consolidation) Act 1992
TUPE 1981	Transfer of Undertakings (Protection of Employment) Regulations 1981 SI 1981/1974
TUPE 2006/ 2006 Regulations	Transfer of Undertakings (Protection of Employment) Regulations 2006 SI 2006/246
TURERA 1993	Trade Union Reform and Employment Rights Act 1993
UKBA	UK Border Agency

NOTE TO READERS

Since they are the terms deployed in TUPE 2006, the concepts of 'transferor' and 'transferee' have been used throughout this book (as opposed to terms which might, in a particular context, better describe the parties involved, such as acquirer, buyer, seller, etc.). The term 'transferor' denotes the original owner or operator of the business or activity which is the subject of TUPE and the term 'transferee' denotes the party which acquires or takes over the conduct of that business or activity. Where reference is made in this book to the domestic transfer of undertakings legislation generally, whether in its 1981 or 2006 incarnation, references are simply to 'TUPE'. Similarly, where reference is made to the European transfer of undertakings legislation generally, whether in its 1977, 1998, or 2001 incarnation, references are simply to 'the Directive'. All references in this book to 'regulations' are to regulations of TUPE 2006 and to 'Articles' are to Articles of ARD 2001.

DISCLAIMER

This book is not intended to and does not give any advice in relation to any particular circumstance whatsoever.

1

INTRODUCTION

A.	**Overview**	1.01		3. TUPE 2006	1.34
	1. Introduction	1.01		4. Employment Relations Act 1999, s. 38	1.37
	2. The impact of TUPE	1.05	C.	**Share-based Transactions**	1.40
	3. Purposive interpretation	1.17	D.	**Public Sector Issues**	1.45
B.	**Legislative History**	1.26		1. Transfers in and out of the public sector	1.45
	1. TUPE 1981 and subsequent			2. Economic Activity	1.50
	amendments	1.26		3. Public sector reorganisations	1.52
	2. The Revised Acquired Rights			4. Public sector codes of practice	1.59
	Directive	1.32			

A. Overview

1. Introduction

The Transfer of Undertakings (Protection of Employment) Regulations 2006 implement **1.01** into domestic law the requirements of Council Directive 2001/23/EC of 12 March 2001 on the Approximation of the Laws of Member States relating to the Safeguarding of Employees' Rights in the Event of Transfer of Undertakings, Businesses or Parts of Businesses, the so-called 'Acquired Rights Directive'. The primary purpose of the Directive is 'to provide for the protection of employees in the event of a change of employer, in particular, to ensure that their rights are safeguarded'.[1] The predecessor of the 2006 Regulations, TUPE 1981, was originally enacted in order to implement into domestic law the predecessor of ARD 2001, Council Directive 77/187/EEC which formed part of the 1974–76 Social Action Programme aimed at addressing the social consequences of economic change[2] along with Directive 75/129 in relation to collective redundancies[3] and Directive 80/97 in relation to insolvency.[4]

As Deakin and Morris put it,[5] TUPE constitutes 'a major limitation on both the principle of **1.02** freedom of contract and the power of employers to arrange their commercial and corporate

---

[1] Recital (3) of ARD 2001.

[2] See Barnard, *EC Employment Law*, 4th Edition, Oxford: OUP, 2012 p. 577 *et seq.* and, more generally, Chapter 13.

[3] OJ [1975] L48/29.

[4] OJ [1980] L283/23 and as subsequently amended.

[5] Deakin and Morris, *Labour Law*, 6th Edition, Oxford: Hart, 2012 p. 234.

affairs in such a way as to minimise or fragment their employment law liabilities' and, as Barnard notes, critics of the Directive argue that it:

> interferes with free enterprise [and] severely restricts contractors in their ability to restructure their workforces or to devise new performance-related arrangements or to introduce innovative ways of doing the work, thus interfering with any anticipated increase in efficiency [and] dissuades a potential transferee from acquiring the undertaking.[6]

1.03 The European Commission's view is unsurprisingly somewhat different:

> Generally speaking, as far as legislation is concerned, the effectiveness in social terms of the protection afforded by the Directive is beyond dispute. The Directive has proved to be an invaluable instrument for the protection of workers in the event of the reorganisation of an undertaking, by ensuring peaceful and consensual economic and technological restructuring and providing minimum standards for promoting fair competition in the context of such changes.[7]

1.04 TUPE 1981 was made under the European Communities Act 1972 and was only implemented after considerable delay and the commencement of infraction proceedings against the United Kingdom. Famously, the then Government explicitly acknowledged its 'remarkable lack of enthusiasm' in implementing the Directive.[8]

2. The impact of TUPE

1.05 In implementing the Directive into domestic law, supplemented by provisions relating to the preservation of continuity of employment for statutory purposes,[9] TUPE establishes a legal regime for the protection of employees' employment and related entitlements when the ownership of or responsibility for the operation of the business or business function in which they work transfers from their employer to a third party.

1.06 A central objective of TUPE is to protect employees from the consequences at common law of a disposal or other transfer by their employer of the business in which they work. Since the contract of employment is a contract personally to provide services, it cannot at common law transfer to a new owner or operator of the relevant business without the consent of that new owner/operator and indeed of the employee in question. Transfer to a third party of the business in which an employee works leads at common law to a dismissal of the employee by the pre-transfer employer.[10] As was said in *Newns v British Airways plc*[11] '[i]t is ... basic to contract law that a contract of employment cannot be transferred without the consent of both parties to it. But that is the common law position before the intervention of statute'. This reflects the following observations of Lord Atkin in *Nokes v Doncaster Amalgamated Collieries Ltd*,[12]:

> It appears to me astonishing that apart from overriding questions of public welfare power should be given to a court or to anyone else to transfer a man without his knowledge and

---

[6] See Barnard, above n. 2, at p. 580.

[7] As set out in the Commission memorandum on Acquired Rights of Workers in Cases of Transfers of Undertakings.

[8] HC Deb, 6 Ser., Vol. 691, Col. 680, David Waddington for the Government—see Davies and Freedland, *Labour Legislation and Public Policy*, Oxford: OUP, 1993, pp. 577–80.

[9] Originally contained in the Contracts of Employment Act 1963, Sch. 1, para. 10, the relevant provisions are now set out in ERA 1996, Pt I, Chapter XIV. See Chapter 5, para. 5.45 *et seq.* for further discussion.

[10] See *Brace v Calder* [1895] 2 QB 253 and *Nokes v Doncaster Amalgamated Collieries Ltd* [1940] AC 1014.

[11] [1992] IRLR 575, CA at para. 11.

[12] [1940] AC 1014.

possibly against his will from the service of one person to the service of another. I had fancied that ingrained in the personal status of a citizen under our laws was the right to choose for himself whom he would serve; and that this right of choice constituted the main difference between a servant and a serf.[13]

In similar vein in the same case Viscount Simon LC described the position thus: **1.07**

It will be readily conceded that the result contended for by the respondents in this case would be at complete variance with a fundamental principle of our common law—the principle, namely, that a free citizen, in the exercise of his freedom, is entitled to choose the employer whom he promises to serve, so that the right to its services cannot be transferred from one employer to another without his assent.[14]

A more modern reminder of the fact that the identity of an employee's employer cannot be **1.08** changed without either the employee's consent or by operation of law pursuant to TUPE is *Gabriel v Peninsula Business Services Ltd and anor*.[15] There was no suggestion of a TUPE transfer in circumstances where an employee, in contrast to other colleagues, had not received an email notifying her of the intended change to the identity of her employer from one group company to another. As HHJ Peter Clark noted, by reference to *Nokes*, 'at common law a contract of service cannot be novated by substituting a new employer without the express or implied consent of the employee'.[16]

Against this background, the mischiefs which TUPE seeks to address are that at common **1.09** law, as a consequence of a transfer of the business in which he or she works, an affected employee:

- is left with no entitlement to continued employment in the business in which he or she was employed prior to the transfer in question;
- has no right to be employed on his or her previous contractual terms (even if the new owner/operator is willing to engage the employee); and
- has no entitlement to any information about, or consultation in relation to, the transfer and its consequences.

In establishing a regime of protection for employees in relation to business transfers and **1.10** implementing the requirements of the Directive, TUPE has three principal effects:

- the contracts of employment of those employees working in the relevant undertaking automatically pass to the transferee of the undertaking along with associated liabilities, rights, and powers (save for certain categories of pension entitlement);
- unless a legitimate economic, technical or organisational reason entailing changes in the workforce (an 'ETOR') provides a justification, neither the pre- nor the post-transfer employer may dismiss the relevant employees without potential unfair dismissal consequences; and
- the pre-transfer employer is required to provide prescribed information to 'appropriate representatives' of the employees who are affected by a relevant transfer about the impending transfer and, where action is anticipated in connection with the transfer (by way, for example, of dismissals and changes to terms and conditions), to consult those representatives about those anticipated steps.

---

[13] Ibid. at 1026.
[14] Ibid. at 1020.
[15] UKEAT/0190/11.
[16] Ibid. at para. 12.

1.11 The range of transactions and events to which TUPE can apply is wide. Examples include:

- the sale of the whole or part of the assets and undertaking of a business, whether by the owner or operator of the business, or, in an insolvency situation, by administrators or administrative receivers;
- an internal group reorganization pursuant to which assets and activities are transferred between different companies within a group (which may be desirable for a variety of reasons such as tax planning, organizational convenience, or as a precursor to a sale of a corporate entity);
- the outsourcing of a specific business activity or business support function such as information technology support and administration, payroll management, or the manufacture of components;
- the award of a contract to an external service provider for the provision of services such as security, catering, cleaning, refuse collection, and property management; and
- the retendering of outsourced services leading to the award of a contract to a replacement service provider ('second generation contracting') or its being brought back in-house ('in-housing').

1.12 There are two forms of 'relevant transfer' for the purposes of TUPE. These are not mutually exclusive so may both apply to the same set of circumstances. The first form of relevant transfer is a 'transfer of an undertaking', which some describe as a 'traditional' or 'classic' transfer since until 2006 it was the only form of relevant transfer under TUPE.

1.13 The most straightforward example of a transfer of an undertaking is where there is a sale of an ongoing business which the purchaser will continue to operate in more or less the same way, with the same premises, equipment, and machinery following the transfer. TUPE can also apply to an internal reorganization where employees and the part of a business in which they work are transferred from one group company to another. The decisive criterion in assessing whether TUPE applies to a given scenario by way of a transfer of an undertaking is whether there is a stable and identifiable economic entity which retains its identity after the transfer. When deciding whether a transfer of an undertaking for the purposes of TUPE has occurred, account will be taken of the type of business or undertaking, the transfer of tangible assets such as buildings or stocks, the value of intangible assets at the date of transfer, whether the majority of the staff are taken over by the new employer, the transfer of customers, the degree of similarity of activities before and after the transfer, and the duration of any interruption in those activities.

1.14 The second form of relevant transfer is a 'service provision change' (SPC), which was introduced by the 2006 Regulations. An SPC arises in the three situations of outsourcing, retendering, and in-housing where there is, prior to the event in question, an organised grouping of employees whose principal purpose is the conduct of particular activities and those activities:

- cease to be carried on by a person ('a client') on his own behalf and are carried out instead by another person on the client's behalf ('a contractor'); or
- cease to be carried out by a contractor on a client's behalf and are carried out instead by another person ('a subsequent contractor') on the client's behalf; or
- cease to be carried out by a contractor or a subsequent contractor on a client's behalf and are carried out instead by the client on his own behalf.

TUPE does not, however, apply by way of an SPC to cover the transfer of activities to con-   **1.15**
tractors who are engaged to provide services on an occasional basis, or to groups of employees
who carry out services on behalf of a number of clients. Nor is there an SPC where the client
appoints a contractor to provide services on a one-off basis for a limited period without any
intention of creating an ongoing relationship with the client.

The SPC provisions also do not apply to situations where the arrangement is for the procure-   **1.16**
ment of goods, rather than services (such as, for example, an arrangement to supply food and
drink to a staff canteen as opposed to catering services).

3. Purposive interpretation

Over the years during which it has been in force much concern has been expressed about the   **1.17**
uncertainty of the application and scope of TUPE and the consequent volume of litigation
to which TUPE has given rise. In *McGrath v Rank Leisure Ltd*,[17] for example, the respondent's description of TUPE 1981 was 'a Pandora's box of ambiguities'.[18] Nonetheless, in light
of its EU law parentage, the EAT considered that:

> Fairness to the draftsman requires us, however, to bear in mind the almost insuperable dif-
> ficulties which faced him when he was required to patch new Flemish broadcloth upon the
> fine weave of our domestic employment law—with instructions to do the minimum damage
> to either fabric.[19]

The EU law basis of the transfer of undertakings legislation (save with regard to the UK   **1.18**
specific form of relevant transfer, the SPC) is the reason that so much of the relevant case
law guidance has been provided by the ECJ when addressing the proper application and
interpretation of the domestic transfer of undertakings legislation of the EU Member States.
Cases such as *Litster v Forth Dry Dock & Engineering Ltd*[20] demonstrate the readiness of the
domestic courts and tribunals to apply (and the necessity of their applying, so far as is possible) a purposive interpretation to the domestic legislation in order to ensure compliance
with the Directive and its objectives in relation to the application of the concept of a transfer
of an undertaking as distinct from that of an SPC.

To apply a purposive interpretation to the provisions of TUPE relating to transfers of under-   **1.19**
takings in order to ensure compliance with the Directive, and, if necessary, to imply words
into the legislation to achieve that result, follows the principle established in *Marleasing S.A.
v Comercial Internacional De Alimentacion S.A.*[21] to the effect that:

> in applying national law, whether the provisions in question were adopted before or after the
> Directive, the national court called upon to interpret it is required to do so, as far as possible,
> in the light of the wording and the purpose of the Directive in order to achieve the result
> pursued by the latter.[22]

Likewise, in *von Colson and Kamann v Land Nordrhein Westfalen*[23] the ECJ commented that   **1.20**
'national courts are required to interpret their national law in the light of the wording and

---

[17] [1985] IRLR 323, EAT.
[18] Ibid. at para. 2 per Waite J.
[19] Ibid.
[20] [1989] IRLR 161, HL.
[21] [1992] 1 CMLR 305, ECJ.
[22] Ibid. at p. 322.
[23] [1984] ECR 1891, ECJ at para. 26.

the purpose of the Directive...' and, as Lord Slynn of Hadley said in *Wilson v St. Helen's Borough Council*:

> [i]t is common ground that, both under English law and under community law, the national court should construe a regulation adopted to give effect to a Directive as intended to carry out the obligations of the Directive and as not being inconsistent with it if it is reasonably capable of bearing such a meaning.[24]

1.21 More particularly in relation to TUPE, the need to apply a purposive interpretation has been remarked upon on many occasions. As Lord Keith of Kinkel said in *Lister* in relation to the provisions of TUPE 1981 effecting the transfer of contracts of employment on a relevant transfer:

> it is the duty of the court to give regulation 5 a construction which accords with the decisions of the European Court upon the corresponding provisions of the Directive to which the regulation was intended by Parliament to give effect. The precedent established by *Pickstone v Freemans plc* indicates that this is to be done by implying the words necessary to achieve that result.[25]

1.22 In similar vein in the same case, Lord Oliver of Aylmerton said as follows:

> If the legislation can reasonably be construed so as to conform with those obligations— obligations which are to be ascertained not only from the wording of the relevant Directive but from the interpretation placed upon it by the European Court of Justice at Luxembourg— such a purposive construction will be applied even though, perhaps, it may involve some departure from the strict and literal application of the words which the legislature has elected to use.[26]

1.23 In *Askew v Governing Body of Clifton Middle School and others* Peter Gibson LJ reinforced this point with the warning that:

> English courts have constantly to be on their guard against too insular an approach to the construction of European legislative instruments and of statutes and regulations giving effect to European obligations. As Advocate-General Sir Gordon Slynn said in Spijkers v Benedik [1986] ECR 1119 at p 1112 in the context of transfers of undertakings, 'Technical rules are to be avoided and the substance matters more than the form...A realistic and robust view must be taken and all the facts be considered.'[27]

1.24 Nonetheless, it is important to appreciate that the Directive is only intended to effect partial harmonization and not a uniform level of protection throughout the Community on the basis of common criteria.[28] National law determines a variety of specific issues for the purposes of the domestic law of the relevant Member State such as defining an employee, establishing the consequences of an objection by an individual to transfer, and the penalties for failure to inform and consult appropriate representatives of the affected employees. In the specific context of the question of the validity of a transfer-related dismissal, which is in principle prohibited in the absence of an economic, technical or organisational reason entailing changes in the workforce for the dismissal, Lord Slynn described the position as follows in *Wilson v St. Helen's Borough Council*:

> The object and purpose of the Directive is to ensure in all Member States that on a transfer an employee has against the transferee the rights and remedies which he would have had against

---

[24] [1998] IRLR 706, HL at para. 4.
[25] [1989] IRLR 161, HL at para. 5.
[26] Ibid. at para. 21.
[27] [1999] IRLR 708, CA at para. 23.
[28] *Danmols Inventar* [1985] ECR 2639, ECJ at para. 26.

the original employer. To that extent it reduces the differences which may exist in the event of a change of employers as to the enforcement by employees of existing rights. They must all provide for enforcement against the transferee of rights existing against the transferor at the time of transfer. It seems to me that the Court has clearly recognised that the precise rights to be transferred depend on national law. But neither the Regulations nor the Directive nor the jurisprudence of the Court create a Community law right to continue employment which does not exist under national law.[29]

Nonetheless, the purposive approach to the interpretation of those aspects of TUPE derived **1.25** from the Directive is not unlimited in its application. As Underhill P put it in *Eddie Stobart Ltd v Moreman and others* in an observation which applies equally to a regulation 3(1)(a) transfer of an undertaking as to a regulation 3(1)(b) SPC:

No doubt the broad purpose of TUPE is to protect the interests of employees by ensuring that in the specified circumstances they 'go with the work' (though the assumption that in every case that will benefit, or be welcome to, the employees transferred is not universally true). But it remains necessary to define the circumstances in which a relevant transfer will occur, and there is no rule that the natural meaning of the language of the Regulations must be stretched in order to achieve transfer in as many situations as possible.[30]

B. Legislative History

1. TUPE 1981 and subsequent amendments

TUPE 1981 came into force on 1 May 1982. Amendments were made in 1993[31] to remove **1.26** the exception from the scope of TUPE 1981 of undertakings not in the nature of a commercial venture. These amendments reflected the ECJ decisions in *Dr Sophie Redmond Stichting v Bartol*[32] and *Rask and Christensen v ISS Kantineservice*.[33] The explicit individual right to object to transfer was also introduced by TURERA 1993. Amendments were also made pursuant to the Collective Redundancies and Transfer of Undertakings (Protection of Employment) (Amendment) Regulations 1995[34] and 1999[35] updating the provisions of TUPE 1981 concerning the obligation to conduct collective information and consultation. However, more fundamental statutory reform came onto the agenda in due course prompted both by domestic debate and the amendments made to ARD in its revised versions introduced in 1998 and 2001. Proposals to amend and update TUPE 1981 were a considerable time in their gestation and implementation. The Government's 'Fairness at Work' White Paper in 1998 confirmed the intention to reform TUPE 1981. As the Government put it:

As business becomes more open and competitive the pressures on businesses to trim down through redundancies, more flexible contracting out arrangements or to develop through merger and acquisition will intensify.... The existing provisions have been widely criticised and the Government intends to amend them. Employers will in future have clearer obligations to inform and consult recognised trade unions or, in their absence, independent

---

[29] [1998] IRLR 706, HL at para. 71.
[30] [2012] IRLR 356, EAT at para.19. In contrast, in *OTG v Barke* [2011] IRLR 272, EAT the EAT took the view (at para. 21) that TUPE's primary purpose of employee protection 'in any doubtful case must prevail'.
[31] Pursuant to TURERA 1993, s. 33(1) and (2) and Sch. 10.
[32] [1992] IRLR 366, ECJ.
[33] [1993] IRLR 133, ECJ.
[34] SI 1995/2587.
[35] SI 1999/1935.

employee representatives. Where businesses are transferred the law will strike the right balance between safeguarding employees' existing rights and enabling businesses to adapt to changing circumstances.[36]

1.27 ARD 1998 and ARD 2001 amended the provisions of the Directive so that Member States had new alternatives open to them in terms of the domestic legislation which they could adopt. This provided further impetus to and opportunity for reform of TUPE 1981.

1.28 Although in the 2001 Consultation[37] it was anticipated that a 'new TUPE' would be laid before Parliament in the summer of 2002, it was March 2005 before revised draft regulations were issued for consultation.[38] Implementation slipped from the initially targeted 1 October 2005 to enable consideration of the representations received as part of the consultation process on the initial draft of what was to become the 2006 Regulations. The final version of the 2006 Regulations was made on 6 February 2006, laid before Parliament on 7 February 2006, and came into force with effect from 6 April 2006.[39]

1.29 Guidance on the 2006 Regulations was issued by the DTI[40] as was the Government's response to the responses to the consultation process which was conducted in relation to the new regulations.[41] Neither of those documents are of legal force but they both provide some useful insights into the intention behind the drafting of certain aspects of the 2006 Regulations. The Guidance was updated and reissued by BIS in 2009.[42]

1.30 TUPE 2006 was introduced pursuant to the ERA 1999, s. 38[43] as well as the European Communities Act 1972, s. 2(2), reflecting the fact that in certain respects (such as the new concept of an SPC) the 2006 Regulations provide greater protection for employees than the Directive requires.

1.31 Further amendments were made to TUPE in 2009 to reflect the repeal of the statutory disciplinary and grievance provisions put in place pursuant to the provisions of the Employment Act 2002[44] and in 2010 to add to the information to be supplied by the relevant employer to the appropriate representatives of employees affected by a transfer falling within TUPE certain prescribed information about the use of agency workers.[45]

---

[36] Cm 3968, May 1998.

[37] *Transfer of Undertakings (Protection of Employment) Regulations 1981, Government Proposals for Reform, Detailed Background Paper*, Employment Relations Directorate, Department of Trade and Industry, September 2001, URN 01/1158.

[38] *TUPE, Draft Revised Regulations, Public Consultation Document*, Employment Relations Directorate, Department of Trade and Industry, March 2005, URN 05/926.

[39] Regulation 21 set out the applicable transitional provisions which are not addressed in this work.

[40] *Employment Rights on the Transfer of an Undertaking, A Guide to the 2006 TUPE Regulations for Employees, Employers and Representatives*, Employment Relations Directorate, Department of Trade and Industry, January 2006.

[41] *TUPE, Draft Revised Regulations, Government Response to the Public Consultation*, Department of Trade and Industry, February 2006.

[42] *Employment Rights on the Transfer of an Undertaking, A Guide to the 2006 TUPE Regulations for Employees, Employers and Representatives*, Department for Business, Innovation and Skills, June 2009, URN 09/1013.

[43] Whose effect is in essence to permit regulations to be implemented to extend the protection of TUPE beyond the strict scope of the Directive. See also para. 1.37 *et seq.*

[44] The Transfer of Undertakings (Protection of Employment)(Amendment) Regulations 2009 SI 2009/592.

[45] Agency Workers Regulations 2010 SI 2010/93. See Chapter 9, para. 9.17.

2. The Revised Acquired Rights Directive

As was noted in the 2001 Consultation,[46] the Government made it a social affairs priority **1.32**
for the United Kingdom Presidency of the EU in 1998 to secure the revision of ARD 1977.
The twin objectives of this process were, first, to clarify the application of the legislation
by reference to jurisprudence of the ECJ and, second, to give the Member States increased
flexibility in tailoring their national implementing legislation to domestic circumstances. As
a result of this process, ARD 1998[47] was adopted. ARD 2001[48] subsequently consolidated
ARD 1977 and ARD 1998.

The principal amendments to ARD 1977 made as a result of this process were the introduc- **1.33**
tion of the following options for Member States in their implementing legislation, all of
which were taken up in the 2006 Regulations:

- trade union or appropriate representative of the employees can be permitted by domestic
  legislation to negotiate changes to the terms and conditions of employment of the transferring employees in order to save jobs on the transfer of the undertaking of an insolvent
  employer;[49]
- it can be provided by domestic legislation that, in order to assist the preservation of jobs on
  the transfer of an insolvent company's undertaking, certain of the transferor's outstanding
  debts to its employees do not pass to the transferee;[50]
- the transferor can be required by domestic legislation to provide to the transferee prescribed
  information about the transferor's rights, powers, duties, and liabilities to the transferring
  employees of which the transferor is or should be aware.[51]

3. TUPE 2006

In approaching the reformulation of TUPE in the 2006 Regulations, the Government con- **1.34**
sidered TUPE to be based on the positive principle of combining flexibility for business with
fairness for employees.[52] The objective of the reform process which led to the introduction of
the 2006 Regulations was to ensure that TUPE should operate effectively for all concerned
including employers, employees, contractors, and local authorities who use it as a framework
for contracting.[53] As the DTI (as it then was) put it:

> Failure to introduce the revised Regulations would mean that their shortcomings remained
> unaddressed, contrary to the Government's commitment to review and where necessary reform
> outdated and deficient regulation that imposes undue burdens on business [and] would mean
> that the valuable new flexibilities in the revised Directive, successfully negotiated by the UK
> in 1998, were not taken advantage of.[54]

The approach adopted in formulating the 2006 Regulations was not to amend TUPE **1.35**
1981 unless the intention was to bring about a specific substantive change or amendments
were considered to be useful in order to reduce or eliminate confusion or deliver 'increased

---

[46] At para. 9.
[47] Council Directive 98/50/EC OJ L 201/88.
[48] Council Directive 2001/23/EC OJ L 82/16.
[49] Article 5(2)(b).
[50] Article 5(2)(a).
[51] Article 3(2).
[52] 2001 Consultation para. 12.
[53] 2005 Consultation para. 13.
[54] 2005 Consultation Partial Impact Assessment para. 8.

user-friendliness'.[55] In addition to the introduction of the concept of the SPC, the 2006 Regulations made a number of important changes to TUPE, including:

- updating the identification by the legislation of who transfers from the transferor to the transferee on a relevant transfer by providing that an employee falls within the scope of TUPE 2006 if he or she is 'employed by the transferor and assigned to the organised grouping of resources or employees that is subject to the relevant transfer';
- codifying into the legislation the principle established by the House of Lords in *Litster v Forth Dry Dock Engineering Co Ltd*[56] in order to ensure that the legislation provides protection for those dismissed before and in connection with a relevant transfer but who therefore are not actually employed immediately before transfer;
- seeking to enable a change to an employee's terms of employment which is by reason of or connected to a TUPE transfer to be valid where an ETOR exists to justify that change;
- providing that liability for an award made in respect of a failure to comply with the requirements imposed under TUPE to provide information to and to consult with appropriate representatives of the affected employees is borne jointly and severally by the transferor and the transferee;
- introducing the obligation upon the transferor to provide to the transferee specified 'employee liability information' relating to matters such as the age and identities of the transferring employees, their employment particulars, disciplinary and grievance issues, applicable collective agreements, and actual and potential claims on the part of the transferring employees;
- adopting the ability provided by ARD 2001 to modify the effect of the transfer legislation in relation to certain insolvency situations in order to facilitate the 'rescue culture';
- removing the exclusion of employees working abroad from its scope and making some specific provisions concerning the location of the undertakings and activities to which TUPE applies; and
- providing that, where the transferor does not have a statutory obligation to maintain employers' liability insurance, the transferor and transferee are jointly and severally liable for any employers' liability claim which a transferring employee may have arising from employment by the transferor prior to the transfer.

1.36 During the gestation of what was to become the 2006 Regulations, specific provisions preserving pension rights on a TUPE transfer were introduced. The Pensions Act 2004 and the Transfer of Employment (Pension Protection) Regulations 2005 were introduced, with effect from 6 April 2005, the combined effect of which in this context is to require transferees to provide a specific minimum level of pension provision in respect of those transferring employees who were active members or were eligible or contingently eligible to be members of occupational pension schemes operated by the transferor during their pre-transfer employment.

4. Employment Relations Act 1999, s. 38

1.37 Member States are entitled under their domestic legislation to adopt provisions which are wider in scope or more favourable than those of the Directive. Article 8 provides that the Directive 'shall not affect the right of Member States to apply or introduce laws, regulations

---

[55] 2005 Consultation para. 10.
[56] [1989] IRLR 161, HL.

or administrative provisions which are more favourable to employees or to promote or permit collective agreements or agreements between social partners more favourable to employees'.

Consistent with this, ERA 1999, s. 38 empowers the Secretary of State to make provision by statutory instrument, subject to the negative resolution procedure, for employees to be given the same or similar treatment in specified circumstances falling outside the scope of the EU transfer legislation to that which they are given under the domestic legislation. ERA 1996, s. 38 provides as follows: **1.38**

> (1) This section applies where regulations under section 2(2) of the European Communities Act 1972 (general implementation of Treaties) make provision for the purpose of implementing, or for a purpose concerning, a Community obligation of the United Kingdom which relates to the treatment of employees on the transfer of an undertaking or business or part of an undertaking or business.

> (2) The Secretary of State may by regulations make the same or similar provision in relation to the treatment of employees in circumstances other than those to which the Community obligation applies (including circumstances in which there is no transfer or no transfer to which the Community obligation applies).

> (3) Regulations under this section shall be subject to annulment in pursuance of a resolution of either House of Parliament.

As the 2001 Consultation noted[57] the Secretary of State can therefore confer 'TUPE-equivalent' protection on employees affected by public sector transfers which would otherwise fall outside the scope of the transfer legislation on the basis of the *Henke* decision.[58] Examples of regulations to this effect include the Transfer of Undertakings (Protection of Employment) (Rent Officer Service) Regulations 1999,[59] the Transfer of Undertakings (Protection of Employment) (Transfer to OFCOM) Regulations 2003,[60] and the Transfer of Undertakings (Protection of Employment) (RCUK Shared Services Centre Limited) Regulations 2012.[61] This power was also the means by which the SPC provisions established by regulation 3(1)(b) were introduced. **1.39**

C. Share-based Transactions

TUPE does not apply to transfers of shares per se, i.e. to transactions solely comprising the transfer (whether by sale or otherwise) of all or part of the share capital of a corporate entity. In a share-based transaction, in contrast to a business sale, the ownership of all or part of the share capital of the employer changes but the contracts of employment of the relevant employees are unaffected. As the change of ownership is share-related, there is no change of employer. The employees engaged in the company's business remain employed by the relevant entity to whose shares the relevant transaction relates. This is the case regardless of whether the company in question is a private or public company. **1.40**

---

[57] At paras 18–23.
[58] See para. 1.52 *et seq*.
[59] SI 1999/2511.
[60] SI 2003/2715.
[61] SI 2012/2043.

1.41 An example of this principle in operation is *Brookes and others v Borough Care Services and CLS Care Services Ltd,*[62] where TUPE 1981 was held not to apply to a transfer of a company limited by guarantee and where it was noted that it is widely recognized that a transfer of shares, as distinct from a transfer of business, is outside the scope of TUPE and, indeed, ARD.[63] The argument was rejected that TUPE should have applied to an arrangement which it was argued had been structured around the transfer of ownership of a company in order to evade the application of TUPE. As the EAT put it:

> The Regulations and the Directive refer quite specifically to the change of employer and to a transfer and transferee being any natural or legal person. They could have addressed, but did not, the circumstance in which there was no transfer from a legal person to another legal person, but the shareholding membership of the legal person changed though its separate legal identity remained untouched.[64]

1.42 In *Millam v The Print Factory (London) 1991 Ltd,*[65] despite there being a share sale in respect of the employee's employer, the claimant employee was told that his employment continued in accordance with TUPE. After the acquisition, the acquiring company took over control of the activities of the employee's employer to a significant extent—it paid the employee, managed the employee's pension arrangements, managed the employer's sales function, and conducted joint meetings of the boards of directors of the acquirer and the employee's employer. However, as the transaction pursuant to which the acquiring company acquired the employee's original employer was a share sale, the EAT disagreed with the conclusion that the ET had reached—to the effect that there had been a TUPE transfer of the employer's business to the acquiring company. The Court of Appeal overturned the decision of the EAT on the basis that the ET was entitled to make the finding of fact that there had been a TUPE transfer in these particular circumstances. Having acquired the shares of the employee's employer, the acquirer then proceeded to take over the operation of the business of the company whose shares it had acquired such that there was then a transfer of the undertaking of the acquired company to the acquirer. As Buxton LJ put it, 'the legal structure is of course important, but it cannot be conclusive in deciding the issue of whether, within that structure, control of the business has been transferred as a matter of fact'.[66]

1.43 *Millam* therefore demonstrates that it can be dangerous to discount the transfer legislation from consideration merely on the basis that the transaction in question relates to the share capital of the acquired entity. It may be that a transfer of an undertaking falling within the scope of the transfer of undertakings legislation is a precursor to, or is an ancillary part of, an otherwise share-based corporate transaction. A TUPE transfer may occur separately from but effectively in parallel with a share-based transaction to which TUPE does not apply. For example, a group reorganization which entails a transfer or transfers falling within the scope of TUPE may be implemented in order to transfer the requisite assets and business activities to the particular corporate entity whose shares are the subject of a sale transaction.[67]

---

[62] [1998] IRLR 636, EAT.
[63] Ibid. at para. 55 per Kirkwood J.
[64] Ibid. at para. 67.
[65] [2007] IRLR 526, CA.
[66] Ibid. at para. 9.
[67] See *Allen v Amalgamated Construction Co Ltd* [2000] IRLR 119, ECJ—discussed further at Chapter 2, para. 2.21—where a transfer of business between group companies was confirmed as falling within the scope of the transfer of undertakings legislation.

Alternatively, a function which has been outsourced (externally or to other group companies) by a corporate entity being disposed of may be brought back in-house by the new owner when it acquires the shares of the target company. Another scenario to which TUPE may apply is where an internal group reorganization is effected by a purchaser after acquisition of the shares of a target company, as was the case in *Millam*.

It is therefore important to be alert to the potential for a TUPE transfer to arise in conjunction or connection with a share-based transaction to which TUPE does not apply. Whether TUPE applies by way of a transfer prior, collateral, or subsequent to a share sale will essentially be an evidential matter for the ET to determine. As Moses LJ said in *Millam*:   **1.44**

> The proposition that the transfer of shares in one company to another is not the same as the transfer of the business of the one to the other gives rise to the difficulty apparent in the instant case. Where, following a transfer of shares, a subsidiary is 100 per cent owned by a parent, how can one tell whether the business has been transferred to the parent for the purposes of the TUPE Regulations? It is that, sometimes difficult, question of fact which must be resolved deploying the experience and expertise of the Employment Tribunal.

> The mere fact of control, which will follow from the relationship between parent and subsidiary, will not be sufficient to establish the transfer of the business from subsidiary to parent. There will often be little to distinguish between the case of transfer of control on acquisition by a new parent and transfer of the business to a new parent. Faced with such difficulties, the Employment Tribunal is not entitled to indulge in the industrial equivalent of a Gallic shrug.[68]

D. Public Sector Issues

1. Transfers in and out of the public sector

Transfers to and from the public sector can fall within the scope of the Directive and TUPE.   **1.45**
By way of example, in *Sanchez Hidalgo*[69] the contracting out of home help services by a local authority fell within the scope of the Directive. That the transfer of undertakings legislation can also apply where a public authority assumes responsibilities for a particular function previously conducted in the private sector was demonstrated by *Mayeur v Association Promotion de l'Information Messine (APIM)*.[70] The Directive applied where a tourist information function conducted by a private non-profit-making organization was taken over by a public authority.

In *Oy Liikenne*[71] the ECJ held that the fact that a contract was awarded following a public   **1.46**
procurement procedure[72] does not of itself preclude the application of the Directive which does not provide for any such exception to its scope.[73] As the ECJ put it:

> The fact that the provisions of Directive 77/187 may in certain cases be applicable in the context of a transaction which comes under Directive 92/50 cannot be seen as calling into question the objectives of the latter Directive. Directive 92/50 is not intended to exempt contracting authorities and service providers who offer their services for the contracts in question

---

[68] *Millam*, above n.65, at para. 13.
[69] [1999] IRLR 136, ECJ.
[70] [2000] IRLR 783, ECJ.
[71] [2001] IRLR 171, ECJ.
[72] In this case conducted in accordance with Directive 92/50.
[73] Nor indeed did Directive 92/50.

from all the laws and regulations applicable to the activities concerned, in particular in the social sphere or that of safety, so that offers can be made without any constraints. The aim of Directive 92/50 is that, in compliance with those laws and regulations and under the conditions it lays down, economic operators may have equal opportunities, in particular for putting into practice their rights of freedom of establishment and freedom to provide services.

In such a context, operators retain their room to manoeuvre and compete with one another and submit different bids. In the field of passenger transport by scheduled bus services they may, for instance, adjust the standard of facilities of the vehicles and their performance in terms of energy and ecology, the efficiency of the organisation and methods of contact with the public, and, as with any undertaking, the profit margin desired. An operator who makes a bid must also be able to assess whether, if his bid is accepted, it will be in his interests to acquire significant assets from the present contractor and take over some or all of his staff, or whether he will be obliged to do so, and, if so, whether he will be in a situation of a transfer of an undertaking within the meaning of Directive 77/187.[74]

1.47 Another example of the Directive applying in a public sector context is *Collino and Chiappero v Telecom Italia SpA*,[75] where the Directive was held to apply to the transfer of a concession in respect of telecommunications activities from state-owned to private sector responsibility— there was a transfer of an economic entity regardless of whether or not the relevant activities were carried on for profit prior to the putative transfer.

1.48 Consistent with this, in *Scattolon v Ministero dell'Istruzione, dell'Universita et della Ricerca*[76] the ECJ held that the transfer of staff providing auxiliary cleaning and maintenance services from certain Italian local authorities to the employment of the State constituted a transfer of an undertaking for the purposes of the Directive. That the decision to effect this transfer was made unilaterally by a public authority rather than by a contractual agreement did not take the transfer out of the scope of the Directives consistent with the principle that the decisive criterion is the change in the person responsible for operating the undertaking, not the existence of a contractual agreement.

1.49 That said, there are two particular limitations to the applicability of TUPE in the public sector context. First, regulation 3(4)(a) makes clear that TUPE (only) applies to public (as well as private) undertakings 'engaged in economic activities whether or not they are operating for gain'. A public sector activity may fall outside the scope of the legislation because it does not constitute an economic activity. Second, TUPE may not apply because of the specific exclusion from its scope by regulation 3(5) of internal public sector reorganisations.

2. Economic Activity

1.50 In determining whether there is a transfer of an undertaking, the question may therefore arise of what constitutes an economic activity. In *Institute of Chartered Accountants of England & Wales v Customs and Excise Commissioners*,[77] in which the operations of the Institute of Chartered Accountants were considered to be a regulatory public service and therefore not to be an economic activity, Beldam LJ commented that:

[t]he concept of an economic activity is an activity which typically is performed for consideration and is connected with economic life in some way or other. It is not an essential

---

[74] *Oy Liikenne*, above n. 71, at paras 22 and 23.
[75] [2000] IRLR 788, ECJ.
[76] [2011] IRLR 1020, ECJ.
[77] [1997] STC 1115, CA.

characteristic that it should be carried on with a view to profit or for commercial reasons but it must be an activity which is analogous to the activities so carried on. An activity which consists in the performance of a public service to which the idea of commercial exploitation with a view to profit or gain is alien is not of an economic nature particularly where the activity is one typically of a public authority.

In *Clifton Middle School Governing Body v Askew*,[78] a middle school was transferred between governing bodies and it was found that a state-funded school could conduct an economic activity even if it were non-profit-making. **1.51**

3. Public sector reorganisations

Article 1(1)(c) provides that: **1.52**

> An administrative reorganisation of public administrative authorities, or the transfer of administrative functions between public administrative authorities is not a transfer within the meaning of this Directive.

This provision codifies the view of the ECJ as to the proper analysis of the effect of the Directive in *Henke v Gemeinde Schierke and Verwaltungsgemeinschaft 'Brocken'*.[79] Administrative tasks relating to the exercise of public authority were considered to be outside the scope of the Directive, which focuses on concepts of business and enterprise. The ECJ held as follows: **1.53**

> 13. As appears from the preamble to the Directive, in particular the first recital, the Directive sets out to protect workers against the potentially unfavourable consequences for them of changes in the structure of undertakings resulting from economic trends at national and Community level, through, inter alia, transfers of undertakings, businesses or parts of businesses to other employers as a result of transfers or mergers.

> 14. Consequently, the reorganisation of structures of the public administration or the transfer of administrative functions between public administrative authorities does not constitute a 'transfer of an undertaking' within the meaning of the Directive.

> 15. This interpretation, moreover, is borne out by the terms used in most of the language versions of the Directive in order to designate the subject of the transfer (virksomhed, Unternehmen, entreprise, impresa, onderneming, empresa, yritys, företag; and bedrift, Betrieb, business, établissement, stabilimento, vestiging, estabelecimento, centro de actividad) or the beneficiary of the transfer (indehaver, Inhaber, chef d'entreprise, imprenditore, ondernemer, empresário, empresario) and is not contradicted by any of the other language versions of the text.

Consistent with Article 1(1)(c), regulation 3(5) provides that an administrative reorganisation of public administrative authorities or the transfer of administrative functions between public administrative authorities is not a relevant transfer for the purposes of TUPE. The exception from the scope of TUPE of administrative reorganisations of public administrative authorities and transfers of administrative functions between public administrative authorities effectively establishes an exclusion zone with regard to transfers internal to the public sector of administrative functions and administrative reorganisations. **1.54**

Regulation 3(5) applies equally in respect of the possibility of there being a transfer of an undertaking for the purposes of regulation 3(1)(a) and an SPC for the purposes of regulation 3(1)(b) and there are two further important aspects of the application of regulation 3(5). **1.55**

---

[78] [1999] IRLR 708, CA.
[79] [1996] IRLR 701, ECJ. This principle was specifically incorporated into ARD 2001 in Article 1(1)(c).

First, the parties involved must be public administrative authorities. Second, the subject matter in question must constitute administrative functions.

1.56 In *Adult Learning Inspectorate v Beloff*[80] the EAT considered what constitutes a public administrative body and upheld both the ET's decision that OFSTED was such a body and its statement that 'a public body whose functions involve the exercise of public authority would be a public administrative authority for the purposes of TUPE'.[81] OFSTED was viewed as a public administrative body by virtue of its regulatory functions but public and private sector education providers were not.

1.57 *Law Society of England and Wales v the Secretary of State for Justice and the Office for Legal Complaints*[82] concerned the abolition of the Legal Complaints Service and its replacement by the Office for Legal Complaints. The Law Society sought a High Court declaration as to various issues including whether the cessation of the function of the Legal Complaints Service and the establishment of the Office of the Legal Complaints was a transfer of administrative functions between public administrative authorities for the purposes of regulation 3(5). Even though it was not necessary for the purposes of these proceedings to determine the issue—because it was held that there was no relevant transfer in any event[83]—the High Court did address the regulation 3(5) question and concluded that the changes in question did constitute a transfer of an administrative function between administrative authorities. Whilst there was no statutory definition to rely on in this regard, the High Court considered that the Legal Complaints Service was a public administrative body on the basis that, following the EAT in *Adult Learning Inspectorate v Beloff*,[84] it was a public body whose functions involved the exercise of public authority. The Legal Complaints Service's regulatory function was viewed as an administrative function which was being transferred to the Office of Legal Complaints. As Akenhead J put it,[85] 'regulatory activity designed to protect the public by bringing to account practitioners whose service falls below an acceptable standard can be said to be administrative rather than anything else'.

1.58 By way of contrast in *Scattolon v Ministero dell'Istruzione, dell'Universita et della Ricerca*[86] the ECJ held that the Directive can apply to the transfer between public authorities of auxiliary cleaning and maintenance services. Cleaning and maintenance auxiliary services did not constitute activities involving the exercise of public authority and were an economic activity for the purposes of the Directive which applied to their transfer.

4. Public sector codes of practice

1.59 In light of concerns over employee protection following outsourcing from the public sector, transfers relating to the public sector have been governed (as a matter of guidance rather than legally binding obligations) by a variety of codes of practice which were intended to regularize the approach adopted to public sector staff transfers and protect transferring employees

---

[80] UKEAT/0238/07.
[81] Ibid. at para. 30.
[82] [2010] IRLR 407, QBD.
[83] See Chapter 2, para. 2.50.
[84] See above, n. 80.
[85] *Law Society of England and Wales v the Secretary of State for Justice and the Office for Legal Complaints*, above n 82, at para. 69.
[86] [2011] IRLR 1020, ECJ

as well as those separately employed by organizations to which public sector functions were outsourced. The principal guidance comprised:

- Staff Transfers in the Public Sector (2000);
- Staff Transfers from Central Government—A Fair Deal for Staff Pensions (1999);
- Code of Practice on Workforce Matters in Local Authority Service Contracts (2003); and
- Code of Practice on Workforce Matters in Public Sector Service Contracts (2005).

1.60 The detailed provisions of these Codes of Practice are outside the scope of this work not least because on 13 December 2010 the Public Sector Service Contracts Code of Practice was withdrawn and on 21 March 2011 its local authority equivalent was also withdrawn. The so-called 'Two Tier' Codes had been introduced to address the concern that, following a contracting-out from the public sector, suppliers and contractors would employ new staff to work alongside those who had transferred into their organizations in the public sector on less generous terms and conditions. This would have the consequence of rendering the employees formerly engaged in the public sector less attractive and at greater risk of redundancy. Moreover, the concern was that private sector providers would be able to undercut the public sector by employing staff on less favourable terms.

1.61 A particular aspect of concern was occupational pensions which are not protected by TUPE.[87] The Two Tier Codes required new employees who were engaged by private sector employers in relation to outsourced functions falling within their scope to be engaged on overall no less favourable terms and conditions than the transferred employees and to be provided with reasonable pensions arrangements either by way of a final salary scheme or a defined contribution scheme with the employer matching employee contributions up to at least 6 per cent of salary. The provisions of the Two Tier Codes were often incorporated into the terms of service contracts between the relevant public sector organization and the private sector supplier and often the service provided was required under the relevant contractual arrangements on request to supply information about the terms of employment provided to new employees. The Government's view of the Two Tier Codes as expressed when it withdrew the Public Sector Service Contracts Code of Practice was that it had done 'little to protect staff while deterring responsible employers from delivering public service contracts'. The Statement of Practice on Staff Transfers in the Public Sector and Fair Deal on Pensions currently remain in place. The Fair Deal requires private sector suppliers to offer a broadly comparable pension scheme to the existing public sector arrangements. Space constraints do not permit detailed commentary on this statement of practice or the other codes of practice which are or have been in operation in the public sector.[88]

---

[87] See Chapter 11.
[88] Such as those affecting the National Health Service and Ministry of Defence.

2

THE TRANSFER OF AN UNDERTAKING

A. **Identifying an Undertaking and its**		10. Break in activities	2.61
Transfer	2.01	11. Transfer of part of an undertaking	2.65
1. Article (1)(1)(a) and regulation 3(1)(a)	2.01	12. Asset transfer	2.74
2. The components of a transfer of an		B. **Labour-intensive Activities**	2.94
undertaking	2.06	1. *Schmidt* and *Ayse Süzen*	2.94
3. What is a transfer?	2.12	2. Subsequent case law	2.106
4. What is an economic entity?	2.26	3. The transferee's motives	2.112
5. One-person undertakings	2.33	C. **The *Cheesman* Guidance**	2.126
6. Specific works contracts and		D. **Miscellaneous**	2.127
unstable contracts	2.36	1. Series of transactions and timing of	
7. Retention of identity	2.43	transfer	2.127
8. Changes to the operation	2.51	2. Ships	2.136
9. Post-transfer integration	2.58		

A. Identifying an Undertaking and its Transfer

1. Article 1(1)(a) and regulation 3(1)(a)

2.01 The Directive sets out its application to transfers of undertakings by way of the following provisions. Article 1(1)(a) provides that the provisions of the Directive apply to 'any transfer of an undertaking, business, or part of an undertaking or business of another employer as a result of the legal transfer or merger'. Expanding on this definition, Article 1(1)(b) provides that 'there is a transfer within the meaning of this Directive where there is a transfer of an economic entity which retains its identity, meaning an organised grouping of resources which has the objective of pursuing an economic activity, whether or not that activity is essential or ancillary'.

2.02 TUPE implements these provisions into domestic law by way of regulations 3(1)(a) and 3(2). Following Article 1(1)(a), a transfer of an undertaking is defined by regulation 3(1)(a) as 'a transfer of an undertaking, business or part of an undertaking or business situated immediately before the transfer in the United Kingdom to another employer where there is a transfer of an economic entity which retains its identity'. Reflecting Article 1(1)(b), a separate definition of an 'economic entity' is provided in regulation 3(2), consistent with the terms of ARD 2001—' "economic entity" means an organised grouping of resources which has the objective of pursuing an economic activity, whether or not that activity is central or ancillary'. Naturally the jurisprudence relating to ARD 2001 and its predecessors is highly relevant to the interpretation of regulation 3(1)(a) and the definition of an economic entity for the purposes of regulation 3(2).

Regulation 3(4)(a) provides that, with regard to a transfer of an undertaking for the pur- **2.03** poses of regulation 3(1)(a) or an SPC pursuant to regulation 3(1)(b), the legislation applies to 'public and private undertakings engaged in economic activities whether or not they are operating for gain'. Provided that it constitutes an economic activity, the relevant activity need not be conducted on a commercial basis in order to fall within the scope of TUPE nor indeed be of any particular scale.[1]

As the 2009 Guidance puts it: **2.04**

> [t]he Regulations can apply regardless of the size of the transferred business: so the Regulations equally apply to the transfer of a large business with thousands of employees or of a very small one (such as a shop, pub or garage). The Regulations also apply equally to public or private sector undertakings and whether or not the business operates for gain, such as a charity.[2]

These provisions should be read in conjunction with the provisions of regulation 3(5) exclud- **2.05** ing public sector reorganisations from the scope of TUPE.[3]

2. The components of a transfer of an undertaking

The definition of a transfer of an undertaking in regulation 3(1)(a) comprises the following **2.06** components:

- there must be a transfer;
- that transfer must be of an undertaking, business, or part thereof;
- the undertaking, business, or part transferred must be situated in the United Kingdom immediately before the transfer;[4]
- the transfer must be to another employer;[5]
- there must be a transfer of an 'economic entity'; and
- the economic entity transferred must retain its identity.

In relation to the issue of whether a set of circumstances fall within the scope of regulation 3(1) **2.07** (a), two issues must be determined. The undertaking which it is contended has transferred within the scope of the legislation must be identified and it must be established whether the undertaking in question was actually transferred. In *Whitewater Leisure Management Ltd v Barnes*[6] it was made clear by the EAT that:

> a Tribunal should consider these questions separately and in turn, for different considerations relate to each. It will normally be best and clearest for an employment tribunal to deal first with the question of whether there was a relevant and sufficiently identifiable economic entity, and then proceed, whatever be the answer to that question, to ask and answer whether there

---

[1] See Chapter 1, para. 1.50 *et seq.* for discussion of what can constitute economic activities.
[2] At p. 4.
[3] See Chapter 1, para. 1.52 *et seq.*
[4] See Chapter 12, para. 12.12 *et seq.* for discussion of the territoriality issues arising in relation to TUPE.
[5] An example of this requirement in practice is *Burke v Royal Liverpool University Hospital* [1997] ICR 730, EAT, where TUPE did not apply in circumstances in which an in-house bid was successful in a council's tendering process and so the operation continued to be operated by the same legal person—the employer of the staff affected remained the same, i.e. the Council.
[6] [2000] IRLR 456, EAT.

was (or would have been, if such hypothetical question can be answered, in the event of a conclusion that there was no such entity) a relevance transfer of any such entity.[7]

2.08 In a similar vein, the EAT put the point as follows in *Cheesman and others v Brewer Contracts Ltd*[8]—'whilst we do not say that it is invariably an error of law not to raise those two questions as separate questions or to fail to deal with them in that order, a tribunal which so fails runs a real risk of error'.[9]

2.09 The ET is the master of fact in determining the fact-sensitive application of TUPE. Langstaff J described the respective roles of the EAT and ET in this context as follows in *Balfour Beatty Power Networks Ltd and anor v Wilcox and others*:

> 13. We may not substitute our own view of the facts, however convinced we may be of their righteousness, for those of the Tribunal if the factual finding below fell within the remit of that Tribunal; and we have to remind ourselves that whether or not there was an undertaking, is essentially a finding of fact as the European Court of Justice has emphasised in case after case. We also have to remind ourselves that whether there has been a transfer of such an undertaking, again involves a factual assessment. This is not the occasion for a rehearing of fact. We may only interfere if there is an error of law. We recognise that an Employment Tribunal does not have to deal with every argument which is presented to it. It is common experience that Tribunals sometimes appear to fear that if they do not deal with every argument, however small, and every disagreement, however immaterial, which is put before them, they may be subject to criticism. The criticism which we would make, however, is that approach itself tends to a complete lack of clarity.
>
> 14. Some arguments may even appear central before a Tribunal but on a logical approach, applying appropriate principles, are of no real relevance. Although we hope and expect Employment Tribunals to deal with an argument which had appeared to the parties before it to be central, we do not consider it to be an error of law if the Tribunal does not do so. The Tribunal's decision is not required to be one which is the product of elaborate draftsmanship. It needs simply and preferably, as briefly as the circumstances properly permit, to deal with the issues before it and its conclusions.[10]

2.10 That the ET must nonetheless address and reach relevant findings of fact on the issue of whether there is a transfer of an undertaking was made clear in *I Lab Facilities Ltd v Metcalfe and others*.[11] No material findings of fact had been made by the ET upon which the finding that there had been a relevant transfer for the purposes of regulation 3(1)(a) was founded. Consequently, an appeal was allowed and the matter was remitted to a fresh ET.

2.11 While far from being a decisive factor, the parties' view as to the application of the legislation can be taken into account, both with regard to the parties' intentions and what they anticipate will be the consequence of the relevant scenario. As Lord Hamilton put it in *Lightways (Contractors) Ltd v Associated Holdings Ltd*:

> A declared intention that TUPE will apply, made prior to the transaction by the alleged transferee, may make even easier an inference of transfer.
>
> Quite apart from any anti-avoidance strategies, the anticipations of the alleged transferee may shed light on the true nature of the transaction. If, as here, the evidence discloses that

---

[7] Ibid. at para. 7 per Burton J.
[8] [2001] IRLR 144, EAT.
[9] Ibid. at para. 19.
[10] [2006] IRLR 258, EAT.
[11] UKEAT/441/10.

it was anticipated that persons previously employed in the relevant lighting maintenance work would be available, either transferred under TUPE or employed under fresh contracts of employment, to carry on the same class of work, that is a strong indicator, in my view, of identity of the undertaking. That aspect of the employment tribunal's reasoning is not open to valid criticism.[12]

3. What is a transfer?

(a) Nature of a transfer

Article 1(a) requires that the transaction or event to which the Directive applies by way of a transfer of an undertaking must entail 'a legal transfer or merger', a specific qualification which is not carried across into TUPE. Determining whether an undertaking has been transferred for the purposes of regulation 3(1)(a) is an employment test rather than a corporate, property, or conveyancing test. As the EAT stated in *Kelman v Care Services Ltd*,[13] 'the theme running through all the recent cases is the necessity of viewing the situation from an employment perspective, not from a perspective conditioned by principles of property, company or insolvency law'. A transfer for the purposes of regulation 3(1)(a) arises where a change of responsibility for or of management of the relevant undertaking occurs.

2.12

As the ECJ indicated in *Daddy's Dance Hall*,[14] the transfer legislation 'applies as soon as there is a change, resulting from a conventional sale or from a merger, of the natural or legal person responsible for operating the undertaking... and it is of no importance to know whether the ownership of the undertaking is transferred'.[15] This point has been made repeatedly in the jurisprudence. In *Berg and Busschers v Besselsen*[16] the ECJ stated that:

2.13

> [the Directive] applies as soon, because of a contractual agreement or merger, as a change occurs in the natural or legal person operating the undertaking who, in that capacity, has obligations vis-a-vis the employees employed in the undertaking and... it is of no importance whether the ownership of the undertaking has been transferred.[17]

Consistent with this in *Schmidt v Spar-und Leihkasse der früheren Ämter Bordesholm, Kiel und Cronshagen*,[18] the ECJ held as follows:

> According to the case law of the Court (judgment in *Rask and anor v ISS Kantineservice* A/S, C-209/91 [1993] IRLR 133 at paragraph 15) the Directive is applicable where, following a legal transfer or merger, there is a change in the legal or natural person who is responsible for carrying on the business and who by virtue of that fact incurs the obligations of an employer vis-à-vis the employees of the undertaking, regardless of whether or not ownership of the undertaking is transferred.

---

[12] [2000] IRLR 47, CS at paras 23 and 24. The issue of motive in relation to whether employees transfer or not is discussed in further detail at para. 2.112 *et seq.*

[13] [1995] ICR 260, EAT at para. 268A.

[14] *Foreningen af Arbejdsledere i Danmark v Daddy's Dance Hall A/S* [1988] IRLR 315, ECJ at para. 9.

[15] This principle has been reiterated in a number of decisions such as *Ny Mølle Krø* [1989] IRLR 37, ECJ and *Bork International A/S* [1989] IRLR 41, ECJ.

[16] [1989] IRLR 447, ECJ.

[17] Ibid. at para. 18.

[18] [1994] IRLR 302, ECJ.

(b) Relationship between transferor and transferee

2.14   While regulation 3(1)(b) in its provisions with regard to SPCs specifically addresses the replacement of one contractor by another in relation to services,[19] regulation 3(1)(a) contains no equivalent provision in its definition of a transfer of an undertaking. Nonetheless, there can be a transfer of an undertaking for the purposes of the Directive, and by extension regulation 3(1)(a), even where there is no direct contractual link between the transferor and transferee, for example where an operation is transferred between contractors at the behest of the ultimate client.[20] There need be no formal legal agreement for there to be a transfer of an undertaking for the purposes of regulation 3(1)(a) nor indeed any legal relationship between transferor and transferee.[21] For example, in *Merckx*[22] an economic entity comprising a Ford car dealership transferred within the scope of the legislation when the dealership was awarded by Ford to a new contractor. In *Sanchez Hildalgo*[23] it was stated that 'there is no need, in order for the Directive to be applicable, for there to be any direct contractual relationship between the transferor and the transferee'.[24]

2.15   The transfer may take place in stages through an intermediary or third party. This has been confirmed in decisions such as *Abler*[25] and *Oy Liikenne*.[26] In *Abler* the ECJ said as follows:

> . . . as has been held on several occasions, Directive 77/187 is applicable whenever, in the context of contractual relations, there is a change in the natural or legal person responsible for carrying on the business and entering into the obligations of an employer towards employees of the undertaking. Thus there is no need, in order for Directive 77/187 to be applicable, for there to be any direct contractual relationship between the transferor and the transferee: the transfer may take place through the intermediary of a third party such as the owner or the person putting up the capital (see, inter alia, joined cases C-171/94 and C-172/94 *Merckx and Neuhuys* [1996] IRLR 467, paragraphs 28 to 30, *Süzen*, paragraph 12, and case C-51/00 *Temco* [2002] IRLR 214, paragraph 31).[27]

2.16   In *Oy Liikenne* the ECJ reiterated the point that:

> Directive 77/187 can therefore apply where there is no direct contractual link between two undertakings successively awarded a contract, following procedures for the award of public service contracts in accordance with Directive 92/50, for a non-maritime public transport service, such as the operation of scheduled local bus routes, by a legal person governed by public law.[28]

2.17   *Dines and others v Initial Health Care Services Ltd and anor*[29] considered this issue in the context of TUPE. The employees in question were cleaners employed by Initial Health Care at a hospital and, after a competitive tendering exercise run by the relevant health authority,

---

[19]   Regulation 3(1)(b)(ii).

[20]   See *Sanchez Hidalgo* [1999] IRLR 136, ECJ.

[21]   TUPE 2006 does not contain an equivalent to TUPE 1981 regulation 3(2), which provided that TUPE 1981 applied 'whether the transfer is effected by sale or by some disposition or by operation of law'. It is presumed that such a provision was not considered necessary as the point is clearly established by the case law.

[22]   *Merckx v Ford Motors Co Belgium SA* [1996] IRLR 467, ECJ.

[23]   [1999] IRLR 136, ECJ.

[24]   Ibid. at para. 23.

[25]   [2004] IRLR 168, ECJ.

[26]   [2001] IRLR 171, ECJ.

[27]   Ibid. at para. 39.

[28]   Ibid. at para. 30.

[29]   [1994] IRLR 336, CA, a decision which insofar as it concerned labour-intensive activities should be read subject to the case law in *Ayse Süzen* and a number of other decisions—see para. 2.94 *et seq*.

the relevant contract was awarded to Pall Mall Services whereupon the employees were dismissed by Initial on grounds of redundancy. The Court of Appeal held that it was clear from the ECJ jurisprudence that the fact that another company takes over the provision of certain services as a result of competitive tendering does not mean that the first business or undertaking necessarily comes to an end.

In *Dines* there was a transfer of an undertaking analysed to have been effected in two **2.18** phases—the handing back to the awarding client by Initial of the cleaning services and their handing over to Pall Mall the next day. In so finding reliance was placed[30] on indications in *Daddy's Dance Hall*[31] and elsewhere that a transfer may take place in two phases. As the ECJ put it in *Daddy's Dance Hall*,[32] addressing the scenario where a transfer of an undertaking occurred when the transferee took over the lease of the premises at which the transferor had operated the restaurant activities in question and which it proceeded to continue:

> The fact that in such a case the transfer takes place in two phases, in the sense that as a first step the undertaking is transferred back from the original lessee to the owner who then transfers it to the new lessee, does not exclude the applicability of the Directive as long as the economic unit retains its identity. This is the case in particular when, as in the instant case, the business continues to be run without interruption by the new lessee with the same staff that was employed in the undertaking before the transfer.

In *Vidal*,[33] the ECJ observed that a transfer of an undertaking for the purposes of the Directive **2.19** may occur on an undertaking deciding to take specific functions such as cleaning work back in-house—this 'cannot have the effect of excluding the operation from the scope of [the Directive]'.[34] However, the other requirements of the Directive must be satisfied. Hence, '[t]he mere fact that the maintenance work carried out first by the cleaning firm and then by the undertaking owning the premises is similar does not justify the conclusion that a transfer of [an economic] entity has occurred'.[35]

(c) Commissioning under statutory provisions

Porter and Nanayakkara v Queen's Medical Centre[36] concerned circumstances where the ulti- **2.20** mate responsibility for provision of paediatric services remained with the relevant health authority but the relevant provider was changed. It was held that TUPE applied to a change in the person responsible for operating the undertaking in question. In *Porter* the change was to the actual provision of the relevant services rather than to the responsibility for arranging and ensuring their provision. The question of whether the change to the arrangements in question constituted a legal transfer such as to support the contention that there was a transfer of an undertaking for the purposes of TUPE centred the National Health Service and Community Care Act, s. 4(3), pursuant to which the change of provider was made and which provides that an NHS contract is not to be regarded for any purpose as giving rise to contractual rights or liabilities. Consequently, it was argued that the entry into

---

[30] Ibid. at para. 48 per Neill LJ.
[31] [1988] IRLR 315, ECJ.
[32] Ibid. at para. 10.
[33] *Francisco Hernandez Vidal SA v Gomez Perez and others* [1999] IRLR 132, ECJ.
[34] Ibid. at para. 33.
[35] Ibid. at para. 35.
[36] [1993] IRLR 486, QBD.

such a contract could not give rise to a relevant transfer. Sir Godfray Le Quesne, sitting as a Deputy High Court Judge, took the view that:

> A transfer of an undertaking accomplished by an NHS contract results from a process established by law and is enforceable, not indeed by the courts, but by persons authorised by the Act to enforce it. This, in my view, is a legal transfer.

(d) Intra-group transfers

2.21 In *Allen and others v Amalgamated Construction Co Ltd*,[37] a case which concerned the subcontracting by one company of driveage works in mines to another company in the same group, the ECJ held that the Directive can apply to a transfer between two legally distinct subsidiary companies in the same group, notwithstanding the fact that the two entities have the same management and operate from the same premises and are engaged in the same works.[38] To find otherwise would exclude intra-group transfers from the scope of the Directive, which would be contrary to the objective of the Directive of safeguarding employees' rights.[39]

(e) Lack of formality

2.22 In *Charlton v Charlton Thermosystems (Romsey) Ltd*[40] TUPE applied, despite the lack of any formal transfer, where the directors of a dissolved company continued its trade. Mr and Mrs Charlton argued[41] that, as they were no longer directors of the company, since it had ceased to exist, they had no authority to effect a transfer to themselves or to deal with the company's undertaking, property, or assets and that what in fact they had done was unlawfully use the name and assets of the company and wrongfully held themselves out as having authority to trade in the company's name. Whilst this might render them liable to claims for trespass, conversion, and breach of warranty of authority, they contended that none of those matters made them transferees of the company's undertaking. Mummery J disagreed with this analysis:

> In our view, the underlying fallacy in [counsel]'s submissions is that, although they may constitute a correct analysis of the legal position in terms of company law, contract law and the law of tort, they do not address the essential question of the interpretation of the Directive and the Regulations in the context of the protection of the rights of the company's employees in the event of a change of employer. The issue in this case is confined to that point. It is not concerned with other consequences which may flow from the intermeddling of Mr and Mrs Charlton in the affairs and property of the company after dissolution. As pointed out above, the relevant decisions of the European Court of Justice on the interpretation of the Directive make it clear that a transfer of an undertaking has occurred in this case by virtue of the fact that the undertaking of the company retained its identity, including the identity of the employees, in Mr and Mrs Charlton's hands. That is sufficient to protect the rights of the employees.[42]

(f) Retention of control

2.23 The existence of a transfer of an undertaking falling within regulation 3(1)(a) will not necessarily be prejudiced by some degree of retention of control over the relevant operation by the

---

[37] [2000] IRLR 119, ECJ.
[38] Ibid. at paras 17, 21, and 34.
[39] Ibid. at para. 20.
[40] [1995] IRLR 79, EAT.
[41] Ibid. see para. 13.
[42] Ibid. at para. 15.

transferor. In *Birch v Sports and Leisure Management*,[43] a council retained some control over contracted-out sports facilities but TUPE nevertheless applied.

(g) Property transfer

Regulation 3(6)(b) makes clear that there may be a relevant transfer 'whether or not any property is transferred to the transferee by the transferor'. The absence of any transfer of assets is not therefore of itself a determining factor (although the issue of asset transfer can be relevant where the activities in question are asset reliant).[44]   **2.24**

(h) Transfer of more than just employment

That there needs to be a transfer of an economic entity for TUPE to apply to a given set of circumstances under regulation 3(1)(a), rather than merely the transfer of an employment, was demonstrated by *Derrick Cyffin Jones trading as the Barley Mow Public House v Beardmore*.[45] An employee worked part-time on a farm collecting and grading eggs and was paid hourly. She was employed by Mr Jones and his father in partnership. When egg production was reduced, the employee performed increasing amounts of work at the brewery and pub operated by Mr Jones as a separate operation. When she eventually became employed full-time by Mr Jones (as distinct from the partnership by which she had been previously been employed) at the brewery and pub, there was no relevant transfer in these circumstances. No activities had been transferred—rather, the employee had taken a new job with a new employer.   **2.25**

4. What is an economic entity?

A transfer of an undertaking for the purposes of regulation 3(1)(a) must entail the transfer of an economic entity. Regulation 3(2) defines an economic entity for the purposes of identifying a transfer of an undertaking falling within regulation 3(1)(a) as 'an organised grouping of resources which has the objective of pursuing an economic activity, whether or not that activity is central or ancillary'. The use of the specific term 'economic entity' in the 2006 Regulations reflects the ECJ jurisprudence. The observations of the EAT in *Council of the Isles of Scilly v Brintel Helicopters Ltd*[46] emphasize the need to focus on the statutory and case law guidance as: **2.26**

> 'business' implies an activity which is being carried on commercially for profit: that is not a requirement. The use of the word 'business' may well lead a tribunal into error, simply because it is associated with the idea that there must be a transfer of a business 'as a going concern' with an emphasis on an examination of whether there has been a transfer of outstanding orders and goodwill....[W]e would respectfully suggest that by using the language of the Court of Justice, [employment] tribunals will find it easier to put aside some of the old caselaw...which has now been overtaken by more recent cases.

The key points to note in relation to the definition of an economic entity in regulation 3(2) are as follows: **2.27**

- The objective of the entity must be the pursuit of an economic activity—as already noted,[47] the nature of the activity must be economic even if not pursued for commercial purposes.[48]

---

[43] [1995] IRLR 518, EAT.
[44] See para. 2.74 *et seq.* below.
[45] UKEAT/0392/09.
[46] [1995] ICR 249, EAT at para. 255.
[47] See Chapter 1, para. 1.50 *et seq.*
[48] See also *Dr Sophie Redmond Stichting v Bartol* [1992] IRLR 366, ECJ which applied ARD 1977 to the transfer of a subsidy by a local authority from one charitable foundation to another. TURERA 1993, s. 33 removed from TUPE 1981 the exclusion of non-commercial ventures from its scope.

- The activity in question need not be the primary purpose of the organization in question. As the ECJ put it in *Rask and Christensen v ISS Kantineservice A/S*,[49] 'the fact that . . . the activity transferred is only an ancillary activity of the transferor undertaking not necessarily related to its objects cannot have the effect of excluding that transaction from the scope of the Directive'. Thus, IT, security, catering, cleaning, payroll, back office, and other functions may be ancillary to an organization's primary objectives or *raison d'être* but can nonetheless of themselves constitute an economic entity for the purposes of regulation 3(1)(a).
- The entity must be constituted by an 'organised group of resources'—this requirement derives from the ECJ case law in relation to the Directive and reflects Article 1(b).

2.28 The requirement of regulation 3(2) that there be an organised group of resources entails a stable structure which renders the relevant function more than a mere activity. Autonomy and stability of the operation in question are crucial. As the Advocate General commented in *Rygaard*,[50] '[i]t will be for the National Court to examine, inter alia, whether the activity transferred in the given case is autonomous from an organizational point of view in the sense that persons and possibly materials have been allocated for its completion'.

2.29 In relation to an activity which is asset reliant, the transfer of assets can be relevant in determining whether there has been a relevant transfer.[51] However, it is clear from *Sanchez Hildalgo*,[52] in the context of the prior question of identifying whether an economic entity exists, that:

> [w]hilst such an entity must be sufficiently structured and autonomous, it will not necessarily have significant assets, material or immaterial. Indeed, in certain sectors, such as cleaning and surveillance, these assets are often reduced to their most basic and the activity is essentially based on manpower. Thus, an organized grouping of wage earners who are specifically and permanently assigned to a common task may, in the absence of other factors of production, amount to an economic entity.

The ECJ made the same point in *Vidal*[53] in relation to cleaning activities which had been taken back in house by the putative transferee from a service provider.

2.30 A more succinct approach was adopted in *ADI v Willer*[54] where Burton J described the use of the expression 'distinct cost centre'[55] as 'notwithstanding the resort to modern jargon, . . . a helpful thought process' in identifying an economic entity for those purposes.[56]

---

[49] [1993] IRLR 133, ECJ at para. 17.
[50] *Rygaard v Stø Mølle Akustik A/S* [1996] IRLR 51, ECJ at para. 978.
[51] See para. 2.74 *et seq.* below.
[52] [1999] IRLR 136, ECJ at para. 26.
[53] *Francisco Hernandez Vidal SA v Gomez Perez and others* [1999] IRLR 132, ECJ at para. 27.
[54] UKEAT/11/99.
[55] An expression, quoted at para. 10 of *ADI v Willer*, which had been utilized by the ET in *CWW Logistics v Ronald* EAT, 1/12/98.
[56] Ibid.

In *Cheesman and others v R. Brewer Contracts Ltd*[57] Lindsay J provided an invaluable sum- **2.31**
mary of the ECJ and domestic case law as to whether there is an economic entity for the
purposes of TUPE,[58] the principal aspects of which are as follows:

- There needs to be a stable economic entity whose activity is not limited to performing one
  specific works contract, an organised grouping of persons and of assets enabling (or facilitating) the exercise of an economic entity which pursues a specific objective.
- In order to be such an entity, it must be sufficiently structured and autonomous but will
  not necessarily have significant assets, either tangible or intangible.
- In certain sectors such as cleaning and surveillance the assets are often reduced to their
  most basic and the activity is essentially based on manpower.
- An organised grouping of wage earners who are specifically and permanently assigned to a
  common task may, in the absence of other factors of production, amount to an economic
  entity.
- An activity of itself is not an entity—the identity of an entity emerges from other factors
  such as its workforce, management staff, the way in which its work is organized, its operating methods and, where appropriate, the operational resources available to it.

Wynnwith Engineering Co Ltd v Bennett[59] is a further example of the requirement of stability **2.32**
and structure for there to be an economic entity for the purposes of what is now regulation
3(1)(a) in a given situation. A group of employees who had ceased employment by way of
voluntary early retirement were re-engaged by the employer. The employees were subsequently required to transfer their employment from the original employer to a third party
employment agency. This transfer of the employment of the relevant employees from the
original employer to the employment agency was held to fall outside the scope of TUPE. The
employees in question were not devoted to a specific common activity but were deployed
across various parts of the original employer's business. Those employees did not constitute
an economic entity merely on the basis that they were treated in the same way in employment terms. In this context it was the organization and structure of the operation that was
central to the determination of whether there was an economic entity in a given situation
rather than the contractual relationship with the employer.

5. One-person undertakings

Schmidt[60] indicates that an activity conducted by one person can constitute an economic **2.33**
entity for the purposes of the Directive and therefore, by extension, TUPE. In that case, a
cleaning contract performed by one employee was outsourced by a bank and the Directive
was held by the ECJ to apply. As the ECJ put it:

> Nor is the fact that the activity in question was performed, prior to the transfer, by a single
> employee sufficient to preclude the application of the Directive, since its application does
> not depend on the number of employees assigned to the part of the undertaking which is the
> subject of the transfer. It should be noted that one of the objectives of the Directive, as clearly
> stated in the second recital in the preamble thereto, is to protect employees in the event of a

---

[57] [2001] IRLR 144, EAT at para. 10. This guidance was referred to approvingly by the Court of Appeal in
Balfour Beatty Power Networks Ltd v Wilcox [2007] IRLR 63, CA.
[58] Reproduced in full at para. 2.126 below.
[59] [2002] IRLR 170, EAT.
[60] *Schmidt v Spar und Leihkasse der Frühren Ämter Bordesholm, Kiel und Cronshagen* [1994] IRLR 302,
ECJ.

change of employer, in particular to ensure that their rights are safeguarded. That protection extends to all staff and must therefore be guaranteed even where only one employee is affected by the transfer.

2.34 As Lindsay J subsequently observed:

> *Schmidt* still stands as a reminder of how very little is required to amount to something capable of being an undertaking... once due regard is paid to the safeguarding of employees' rights, the subject-matter of the Directive.[61]

2.35 In *Dudley Bower Building Services Ltd v Lowe and others*[62] a reactive maintenance programme was substantially performed by one employee. The EAT considered that there was no reason in principle why work performed by a single employee could not form a stable economic entity for the purposes of TUPE. Structure and autonomy were seen as key factors. As the EAT put it, while there might not be an economic entity for these purposes where an activity consists of a cleaning lady and her mop,[63] there could be such an entity where a single employee conducts a complex and sophisticated task requiring planning, specification, and costings. The question was viewed as one of fact and degree with relevant factors including the organization of work, any operational resources deployed, and the operating methods utilized.[64]

6. Specific works contracts and unstable contracts

2.36 *Rygaard*[65] held that the award of a contract for the completion of a specific works contract may fall outside the scope of the Directive and, by extension, TUPE. The building works in question had already started before the award of the contract for the completion of those works was made. The ECJ concluded that, in relation to the award of the contract for completion of the relevant building works, the performance of those works did not constitute the stable economic entity required for there to be a transfer of an undertaking for the purposes of the Directive because the relevant activity was limited to performing the completion of one specific works contract.

2.37 As the ECJ put it:

> 20. The authorities cited above presuppose that the transfer relates to a stable economic entity whose activity is not limited to performing one specific works contract.
>
> 21. That is not the case of an undertaking which transfers to another undertaking one of its building works with a view to the completion of that work. Such a transfer could come within the terms of the Directive only if it included the transfer of a body of assets enabling the activities or certain activities of the transferor undertaking to be carried on in a stable way.
>
> 22. That is not so where, as in the case now referred, the transferor undertaking merely makes available to the new contractor certain workers and material for carrying out the works in question.
>
> 23. The reply to the question submitted must therefore be that the taking over—with a view to completing, with the consent of the awarder of the main building contract, works started by another undertaking—of two apprentices and an employee, together with the materials

---

[61] *RCO Support Services and Aintree Hospital Trust v UNISON and others* [2000] IRLR 624, EAT at para. 28.
[62] [2003] IRLR 260, EAT.
[63] Despite the finding that the Directive applied to such a person in *Schmidt*.
[64] See *Dudley Bower Building Services Ltd v Lowe and others*, above n. 62 at para. 53.
[65] *Ledernes Hovedorganisation, acting for Rygaard v Dansk Arbejdsgiverforening, acting for Strø Mølle Akustik A/S* [1996] IRLR 51, ECJ.

assigned to those works, does not constitute a transfer of an undertaking, business or part of a business, within the meaning of Article 1(1) of the Directive.

In the domestic context, in *ADI v Willer*, Burton J described *Rygaard* as entailing 'the trans- **2.38** fer of the fag-end, or run-off, of a particular construction sub-contract'.[66] In *Argyll Training Ltd v Sinclair*[67] the EAT took a narrow view of the scope of the argument that, pursuant to *Rygaard*, single contracts can lack the autonomy and stability to fall within the scope of TUPE. The EAT considered that there was no basis for automatically excluding what were described as single-contract undertakings from the potential application of TUPE. It was not accepted that single contracts necessarily lack the autonomy and stability to come within the scope of the transfer legislation. As the EAT saw it, 'there is no reason to give *Rygaard* an extended meaning and the proposition we have cited from it must thus be taken to be restricted to single specified works contracts for building works'.[68]

The application of the exclusion from the scope of the concept of a transfer of an undertak- **2.39** ing of single works contracts on the basis of a lack of the requisite stability is necessarily fact specific. In *Mackie v Aberdeen City Council*[69] the claimant employee's role had been to set up an operational smart card system for one of her employer's clients. When the client of the employee's original employer offered employment to her in a role involving administration of the relevant system, the new employer treated the transfer of employment as falling within TUPE. Nonetheless the original employer's contract was considered to be for a fixed price for a fixed task and defined product, and therefore as a one-off contract on the termination of which nothing was left to transfer. Accordingly, TUPE did not apply to the change of the employee's employer, despite the new employer's view of the position at the relevant time. TUPE did not apply and the employee's continuity of employment for statutory purposes was not preserved on the change of employer.

Perth & Kinross Council v Donaldson and others[70] also demonstrates the importance of stabil- **2.40** ity in the relevant operation for it to fall within the scope of what is now regulation 3(1)(a) by virtue of constituting the requisite economic entity. The EAT held that, inter alia, there was no stable economic entity capable of transfer to a council, after the insolvency of a housing maintenance contractor, when the council took the relevant activities in-house. In circumstances where the relevant work was handed out on an ad hoc basis, the contractor had no contractual entitlement to work, and the operation could be terminated at any time, there was no stable economic entity. Lord Johnston could not 'contemplate that an opera-tion which depends for its existence from a day-to-day effective handout of work to which it is not contractually entitled, such as could be terminated or ceased at any time, should be determined as a stable entity'.[71] In his view, it was not the case that:

> there was anything left to transfer to the council at the time of the cessation of business brought about by the appellants declining to offer any more work. There was simply nothing to transfer. The fact that in due course the work has been taken up by the original employer,

---

[66] UKEAT/11/99 at para. 8.
[67] [2000] IRLR 630, EAT.
[68] Ibid. at para. 18.
[69] UKEATS/0095/04.
[70] [2004] IRLR 121, EAT.
[71] Ibid. at para. 21.

ie the appellants, is nothing to the point. Nothing passed between the parties. The liquidator simply brought the business to an end because there was no more work for it to do.[72]

2.41 A distinction can be drawn between situations where, as it has been put, there is nothing left to transfer and situations where the regularity of work is unpredictable or precarious. In *Balfour Beatty Power Networks Ltd & anor v Wilcox & others*,[73] the fact that the work in question was 'capable of collapsing at short notice . . . being dependent as it was upon a single contract'[74] was not sufficient for the *Rygaard* principle to apply. Whilst, on the facts of *Balfour Beatty*, there was no guarantee of work, the fact that the contract was (as the appellants had described it) 'defeasible' did not take the transfer of the relevant functions outside the scope of TUPE. The relevant contract could be terminated at will or others brought in to perform the relevant work as substitutes but the EAT considered that the facts of *Balfour Beatty* were 'so far removed from those which operated in the Rygaard case that not only would that defeat the purpose of the regulations . . . but it makes no practical sense'.[75] Moreover, to apply *Rygaard* in such circumstances 'would encourage would-be employers who wished to avoid any TUPE consequences to ensure that contracts were "defeasible" even if the expectation of the parties was that they would be honoured in a practical way'.[76] As Buxton LJ put it when the case reached the Court of Appeal, 'an enterprise may be stable as a matter of practical and industrial reality, even though its long-term future is not secured'.[77]

2.42 The transfer of contracts for the provision of services in respect of single specific events or tasks of short-term duration is explicitly excluded from the scope of the provision of regulation 3(1)(b) relating to SPCs.[78] Accordingly, an approach similar to that adopted in *Rygaard* is effectively codified into domestic law as part of the test of whether there is an SPC for the purposes of regulation 3(1)(b). Regulation 3(1)(a) does not, however, address the issue explicitly. Accordingly, *Rygaard* and the associated case law remain relevant to the issue of whether there is a transfer of undertaking for the purposes of regulation 3(1)(a).

7. Retention of identity

2.43 That the economic entity transferred must retain its identity on transfer is a crucial and explicit requirement of the definition of a transfer of an undertaking set out in regulation 3(1)(a) and one which reflects the ECJ jurisprudence in relation to the Directive. In *Numast v P&O Scottish Ferries Ltd*[79] Bean J indicated that the question of whether an economic entity has been transferred depends on two questions—whether the entity had retained its identity; and whether it has been transferred as a going concern.

2.44 The leading case on retention of identity in relation to the Directive (and therefore by extension TUPE) is *Spijkers*[80] which stated the relevant test to be 'whether the business was disposed of as a going concern, as would be indicated inter alia by the fact that its operation was either continued or resumed'.[81] The context in which this test was established was the

---

[72] Ibid. at para. 22.
[73] [2006] IRLR 258, EAT.
[74] Ibid. at para. 33.
[75] Per Langstaff J at para. 34.
[76] Ibid.
[77] [2007] IRLR 63, CA at para. 39.
[78] Regulation 3(3)(ii). See Chapter 3, para. 3.98 *et seq.*
[79] [2005] ICR 1270, EAT at para. 25.
[80] *Spijkers v Gebroeders Benedik Abbatoir* [1986] CMLR 296, ECJ.
[81] Ibid. at para. 15.

putative transferor ceasing to conduct its activities, dissipating its goodwill, and then selling its assets—a slaughterhouse and related goods and premises—to the putative transferee which resumed the same activities for new customers after a six-week gap having re-engaged all but two of the employees of the putative transferor.

In *Spijkers* the ECJ made clear that in the assessment of whether a transfer of an undertaking **2.45** has occurred it is necessary to consider all the factual circumstances relating to the situation in question. The '*Spijkers* factors' adumbrated by the ECJ set out the range of issues to be considered in the factual determination of whether the Directive (and by extension TUPE) apply to a given situation. Similarity of pre- and post-transfer activities is only one of these factors, being variously described in subsequent decisions as 'necessary but not sufficient'[82] and 'relevant but not critical'.[83]

The '*Spijkers* factors' articulated by the ECJ are as follows: **2.46**

- the type of undertaking or business concerned;
- whether tangible assets, such as buildings and movable property, are transferred;
- whether or not the majority of the employees assigned to the undertaking are taken over by the new employer;
- whether or not the customers of the business are transferred;
- the degree of similarity between the activities carried on before and after the transfer;
- the period, if any, for which the activities of the undertaking are suspended in connection with the putative transfer.

The *Spijkers* factors were described by the ECJ[84] as 'merely single factors in the overall assess- **2.47** ment' to be conducted by the relevant court in its factual appraisal. Whether there is a transfer of an undertaking is inevitably specific to the particular context. As the ECJ put it in *Ayse Süzen*, 'it follows that the degree of importance to be attached to each criterion for determining whether or not there has been a transfer within the meaning of the Directive will necessarily vary according to the activity carried on'.[85]

As the analysis of the case law which follows indicates, a distinction has often been drawn in **2.48** applying the *Spijkers* factors between asset-reliant and labour-intensive activities. Absence of asset transfer in relation to an asset-reliant activity could be a contra-indication of the relevant economic entity retaining its identity and there being a TUPE transfer, as could, in relation to a labour-intensive activity, the putative transferee not taking on the relevant staff. However, the dichotomy often deployed in the cases between asset-reliant and labour-intensive activities, as argued below, is only a gloss on the central test of retention of identity which rests on the 'multifactorial' *Spijkers* considerations.

That the court or ET must address whether an economic entity has been transferred and **2.49** retained its identity on transfer is also demonstrated by *LOM Management Ltd v Sweeney*.[86] In that case the ET had found there to be, as it had put it, 'a classic transfer of undertakings situation'[87] where the lease of certain licensed premises were transferred to the respondent.

---

[82] Per Morison J in *ECM v Cox* [1998] IRLR 416, EAT at para. 21.
[83] Per Kennedy LJ in *Betts v Brintel* [1997] IRLR 361, CA at para. 43.
[84] *Spijkers*, above n. 80, at para. 13.
[85] [1997] IRLR 255, ECJ at para. 18.
[86] UKEATS/0058/11.
[87] Ibid. para. 8, quoting para. 61 of the judgment of the ET.

Even if there has been an assignment of a lease of commercial property, for there to be a transfer of an undertaking there needs also to be 'a business also transferred which was intrinsically linked to the property and satisfied the definition of economic entity'.[88] The ET had erred by basing its finding that there was a transfer of an undertaking on the assignment of the lease alone and without consideration of the wider test of whether there was an economic entity which was transferred and which retained its identity on transfer.

2.50 In *Law Society of England and Wales v Secretary of State for Justice and Office for Legal Complaints*[89] the Law Society sought a declaration that the transfer to the newly created Office of Legal Complaints of the regulatory functions of the Legal Complaint Service on the abolition of the latter body was a transfer of an undertaking for the purposes of regulation 3(1)(a). The High Court concluded that there was no such relevant transfer. The Legal Complaints Service was an undertaking (by virtue of having a relatively autonomous identity) and was an economic entity (by virtue of pursuing an economic activity of providing redress for complainants about the provision of legal services). Nonetheless, by reference to the multifactorial test set out in *Cheesman*,[90] there was no transfer of an undertaking—no tangible or intangible assets or indeed any of the Legal Complaints Service's case load were to transfer and the Legal Complaints Service was not to retain its identity post-transfer in light of the Office of Legal Complaints' independence, wider powers and obligations and (in the court's view) probable different culture. As Akenhead J put it:

> From all the evidence that I have seen and heard, the independence of OLC, actual and perceived, functional as well as structural, coupled with the wide range of powers and obligations granted to and imposed upon it are such that the probability is that 'the culture and approach of OLC will be very different' from that of LCS. It follows from this that it is improbable that the identity of LCS will or could remain.[91]

8. Changes to the operation

(a) General

2.51 Changes to the relevant operation in the period after transfer may affect whether an economic entity retains its identity after the putative transfer as is required by regulation 3(1)(a). If, for example, the transferee changes the location or methods of work of the undertaking in question or integrates it with its own existing operations, can it be argued that TUPE does not apply on the basis that the undertaking does not retain its identity by virtue of the pre- and post-transfer activities being different? As May LJ said in *ADI (UK) Ltd v Willer*:[92]

> The decisions stress that the decisive criterion for a transfer is whether the business in question retains its identity, and an important consideration is whether the operation is continued by the new employer with the same or similar activities.[93]

---

[88] Ibid. at para. 13, referring to *Ny Mølle Krø* [1989] IRLR 137, ECJ.
[89] [2010] IRLR 407, QBD. See Chapter 1, para. 1.57 for commentary on the consideration by the High Court in this case of the application of regulation 3(5).
[90] See para. 2.126.
[91] *Law Society*, above n. 89, at para. 61.
[92] [2001] IRLR 542, CA.
[93] Ibid. at para. 29.

(b) Location

A change of location may not of itself preclude the application of the Directive and by exten-   **2.52**
sion TUPE. In *Merckx*[94] a transfer of an undertaking between motor dealerships entailed a
change of location and the ECJ said as follows:

> The purpose of an exclusive dealership for the sale of motor vehicles of a particular make in a
> certain sector remains the same even if it is carried on under a different name, from different
> premises and with different facilities. It is also irrelevant that the principal place of business
> is situated in a different area of the same conurbation provided that the contract territory
> remains the same.[95]

In *Porter and Nanayakkara v Queen's Medical Centre*[96] the location of the provision of pae-   **2.53**
diatric services changed when a new provider was appointed. The way in which the services
were to be provided also changed. Neither factor precluded TUPE from applying. The EAT
recognized that an economic entity could retain its identity even though its location might
change and its mode of delivery might evolve (as was acknowledged as inevitable in the medical context). A change in location of the performance of some of the functions in question
did not prevent there being a relevant transfer.

Nonetheless, in *Holis Metal Industries Ltd v GMB (1) Newell Ltd (2)*[97] HHJ Ansell made   **2.54**
the following comments about the potential relevance of a relocation overseas of an economic entity to the question of whether the entity retained its identity on transfer:

> Even if it can be held that TUPE has extra-territorial application there will still be an issue as
> to whether the entity to be transferred has retained its identity as required under reg.3(1)(a).
> There must be an issue of fact, not for this decision, as to whether it is possible for an entity to
> retain its identity when that entity moves from one country to another. The various factors set
> out in the seminal ECJ case of *Spijkers* [1986] 2 CMLR will come into consideration such as
> transfer of assets, staff or customers. In this case there was a transfer of plant and/or machinery
> that would clearly be a factor.[98]

(c) Manner of operation

In *Porter,* Sir Godfray Le Quesne, sitting as a Deputy High Court Judge, quoted a passage   **2.55**
from Advocate-General Slynn's opinion in *Spijkers*[99] to the effect that 'the fact that the business is carried on in a different way is not conclusive against there being a transfer—new
methods, new machinery, new types of customer are relevant factors but they do not of
themselves prevent there being in reality a transfer of a business or undertaking'. He also
cited, as an example of this principle, *Kenny v South Manchester College*[100] 'in which Sir
Michael Ogden held that there was a transfer of the undertaking of providing prison education services at a young offender institution, notwithstanding the fact that some of the teaching materials used by the transferors would no longer be used and the transferees would use

---

[94] [1996] IRLR 467, ECJ.
[95] Ibid. at para. 21.
[96] [1993] IRLR 486, QBD.
[97] [2008] IRLR 187, EAT.
[98] Ibid. at para. 9.
[99] Above, n. 80, at p. 299.
[100] [1993] IRLR 265, EAT.

their own teaching materials and open learning packs'.[101] The specific nature of the activities in question was also relevant:

> One factor which is always to be taken into account is the type of undertaking in question. Here it is an undertaking for the provision of medical services. Medical science does not stand still. As it advances, methods of giving neonatal and paediatric care are naturally modified and improved. This process is going on all the time. It does not mean that the object of the undertaking is changing but only that new means of achieving it are being adopted. In the language of the hospital general manager in his letter of 28 January 1993, it means that 'the care to children presently provided is being developed'. We are therefore dealing with a type of undertaking in which it is particularly likely that different ways of carrying on the undertaking may be adopted without destroying its identity.
>
> In my judgment, the undertaking of providing neonatal and paediatric care has retained its identity through the change of provider and there has been a transfer of the undertaking.[102]

2.56 By contrast, in *Mathieson v United News Shops Ltd*[103] a hospital shop's replacement by an operation which stocked a far wider variety of items did not constitute a transfer of an undertaking because the undertaking had changed so much that it did not retain its identity.[104]

(d) Change to the identity of the client to whom a service is provided

2.57 In relation to the regulation 3(1)(b) concept of a service provision change it has been established that for there to be a relevant transfer the client must remain the same before and after the putative SPC.[105] The case law has not considered specifically whether this is the case in relation to a putative transfer of an undertaking for the purposes of regulation 3(1)(a) by way of a change to the provider of services. As Elias LJ put it in *McCarrick v Hunter*,[106] in the context of a factual matrix where regulation 3(1)(b) did not engage because the client was not the same before and after the putative SPC:

> The appellant has assumed that if he can show that there was a regulation 3(1)(a) transfer, it would not matter that there had been a change in the client receiving the service. He may be right about that, but it seems to me that the point is arguable. I am not aware of any authority on it, and we were not shown any. It may be that where the business is in the nature of a service provided to a particular client, the identity of the client is an essential element in the description of the undertaking. If that is so, the services carried on for the new client would constitute a different undertaking and there would be no transfer. But that is an argument for another day.

9. Post-transfer integration

2.58 That the economic entity transferred may be absorbed into the transferee's existing operations does not of itself preclude TUPE from applying. Otherwise, the legislation could be too easily avoided by virtue of the integration which is the natural consequence of many business acquisitions. For example, in *Farmer v Danzas*[107] the integration of the transferor's

---

[101] Ibid. at para. 38.
[102] Ibid. at paras 49 and 50.
[103] UK EAT/554/95.
[104] See also *Nottinghamshire Healthcare and NHS Trust v Hamshaw and others* UKEAT/0037/11 discussed in more detail at Chapter 3, para. 3.36.
[105] See *McCarrick v Hunter* [2013] IRLR 26, CA discussed in relation to the EAT and Court of Appeal decisions at para. 3.67 *et seq.*
[106] Ibid. at para. 48.
[107] UKEAT/858/93.

business with the transferee's existing operations (by removing its trading name) was held not to preclude the operation of TUPE on the basis that, immediately after the transfer but before the integration took place, the economic entity retained its identity.

The requirement that the economic entity in question retain its identity after an alleged **2.59** transfer for its transfer to fall within the scope of the Directive, and by extension TUPE, need not, according to the case law on the Directive, entail the retention of the entity's pre-transfer organizational structure. In *Klarenberg v Ferrotron Technologies GmbH*[108] the ECJ held that the Directive may apply to a transfer of a part of an undertaking even where the part transferred does not retain its organizational autonomy after the transfer in question has taken place. As the ECJ put it:

> It cannot be accepted that the identity of the economic entity depends entirely upon organisational autonomy, having regard to the objective of the Directive to ensure the effective protection of employees' rights in the event of a transfer. Otherwise, the Directive could not apply where the transferee decided to break down the part of the undertaking or business which it has acquired and to integrate it into its own structure, with the result that the employees concerned would be deprived of the protection afforded by the Directive.[109]

However, for there to be a transfer of an undertaking in such circumstances, it must be the **2.60** case, as assessed by the domestic court, that 'the functional link between the various elements of production transferred is preserved, and that that link enables the transferee to use those elements to pursue an identical or analogous economic activity'.[110] The ECJ rejected the argument put forward by the putative transferee, Ferrotron, to the effect that an economic entity only retains its identity for the purposes of the Directive if the organizational link which connects all of the staff and/or all of the elements is preserved—which would not be the case where, as in this instance, the transferring part was integrated into the transferee's operations. Although precisely what is meant by the 'functional link' to which the ECJ refers and how this is to be assessed on the facts of a given case will be a matter for the relevant national court to determine, it appears clear that, whilst post-transfer integration may lead to justifiable dismissals for an ETOR,[111] it does not of itself preclude there being a transfer of an undertaking.

10. Break in activities

A suspension of the relevant activities at or around the point of a putative transfer is one of the **2.61** potentially relevant *Spijkers* factors but various cases have demonstrated that an interruption to the relevant activity will not necessarily avoid there being a transfer of an undertaking for the purposes of regulation 3(1)(a). The ET or court will look at why the suspension occurred and whether that had any impact on the retention (or otherwise) by the relevant operation of its identity. As the ECJ put it in *P Bork International A/S v Foreningen af Arbejdsledere i Danmark*:[112]

> . . . as the court already decided in its judgment of 17.2.87 (*Ny Molle Kro*, 287/86 [1989] IRLR 37), that the fact that the undertaking in question was temporarily closed at the time of the transfer and therefore had no employees certainly constitutes one factor to be taken

---

[108] [2009] IRLR 301, ECJ.
[109] Ibid. at para. 54.
[110] Ibid.
[111] See Chapter 7.
[112] [1989] IRLR 41, ECJ.

into account in determining whether a business was transferred as a going concern. However, the temporary closure of an undertaking and the resulting absence of staff at the time of the transfer do not of themselves preclude the possibility that there has been a transfer of an undertaking within the meaning of Article 1 of the Directive. That is true, in particular, in circumstances such as those of this case, where the undertaking ceased to operate only for a short period which coincided, moreover, with the Christmas and New Year holidays.[113]

2.62 *Allen and others v Amalgamated Construction Co Ltd*[114] concerned driveage functions in mines where the timing of the engagement by the new contractor (AMS) of certain employees formerly employed by the previous contractor (ACC) did not precisely match the end of the outgoing contractor's work. The ECJ observed as follows:

> As regards the fact that the re-engagement of ACC's employees by AMS did not coincide with the beginning or end of the contracts, it must be observed that, as the Commission points out, a transfer of an undertaking is a complex legal and practical operation which may take some time to complete. Furthermore, according to the order for reference, the dismissal of ACC's employees and their engagement by AMS was clearly connected with ACC's decision to subcontract the work in question to AMS. Moreover, when ACC itself took on the driveage work again, it re-engaged the employees who had been with AMS. Accordingly, no particular importance can be attached to the lack of contemporaneity between the start of the work of the work subcontracted to AMS and its re-engagement of ACC's employees.

> Moreover, even if a temporary suspension of the undertaking's activity does not itself preclude the possibility that a transfer has taken place . . . , the fact that the work was performed continuously with no interruption or change in the manner of performance, is none the less a normal feature of transfers of undertakings.[115]

2.63 In *Wood v Caledon Social Club Ltd*,[116] the EAT considered whether the economic entity referred to in regulation 3(1)(a) must retain its identity at the point of transfer for there to be a transfer of an undertaking or whether it may be sufficient that the operation resumes at some later date. In this case, a parish council had leased a building to a community association which subleased various parts of the building to the social club for which the claimant employee worked as a bartender. Following the withdrawal of the premises' alcohol licence, the social club's lease was surrendered to the parish council and the employee dismissed. Some time later, a personal alcohol licence was granted to a councillor and the bar reopened but without a full-time bar steward.

2.64 The ET found that, if there were a transfer, it took place when the licence for the club premises was surrendered. However, it held that there was no relevant transfer because, even if there was an economic entity before that date, the operation in question did not retain its identity once it ceased to have the alcohol licence which formed an essential element of the entity in question. On appeal, the EAT held that there was a temporary cessation of the bar operations such that regulation 3(1)(a) applied and there was a transfer of an undertaking from the social club to the new bar operator. In reaching this conclusion the EAT was strongly influenced by the fact that, at the time when the property licence was surrendered to the council, the council already intended to obtain a fresh alcohol licence and subsequently to

---

[113] Ibid. at para. 16. In *Ny Mølle Krø* [1989] IRLR 37, ECJ the Directive was held to apply to circumstances where a lease was rescinded and the relevant business only resumed after a period of some three months, which coincided with its usual seasonal closure.

[114] [2000] IRLR 119, ECJ.

[115] Ibid. at paras 32 and 33.

[116] UKEAT/0528/09.

open the bar and operate it precisely in the way that it had been previously. Specific reference was made to the guidance of Lindsay P in *Cheesman*[117] to the effect that an indication that an entity retains its identity is the fact that its operation is actually continued or resumed. The resumption of the activities in question was central to there being a relevant transfer in this situation, especially since that resumption was (already) planned at the time when the original operator ceased to have control over the relevant premises. The plans of the putative transferee are clearly relevant to an assessment which can, as *Wood* indicates, be assessed by reference to an unfolding series of events.

11. Transfer of part of an undertaking

Regulation 3(1)(a) can apply to the transfer of part of an undertaking as distinct from the **2.65** transfer of the whole undertaking. The application of what is now regulation 3(1)(a) to transfers of parts of undertakings was considered in *Fairhurst Ward Abbotts Ltd v Botes Building Ltd and others*.[118] A contract for the carrying out of maintenance works and alterations to domestic residences for a three-year period was contracted out by a London Borough Council. On this retendering, the original contract area of Southwark was divided into two separate areas. The ET found that the area which had been awarded to Fairhurst Ward Abbotts did not constitute a discrete economic entity prior to the end of the original contract. However, on award of a contract to the new contractor, there was held nonetheless to have been a relevant transfer for the purposes of TUPE 1981. The ET rejected the putative transferee's argument that part of the undertaking in question could not have been transferred to it within the scope of TUPE on the basis that the part undertaking had not existed as a discrete economic entity prior to the alleged transfer. The ET held that there was a transfer of part of the undertaking in question on the basis that:

> 57. There was a similarity of the undertaking before and after the change of contractor. On a partial basis, defined geographically, the support, administration and premises dedicated to the original contract related to the whole of Southwark were continued.

> 58. Having regard to the factors which we have set out and having regard to the overall picture which they create, we find that there was an undertaking which was transferred in two parts, to areas one and two.[119]

The EAT held that there could be a transfer of part of an undertaking falling within the scope **2.66** of TUPE even if that part was not a separate economic entity prior to the transfer (i.e. in this case the re-tendering) and the Court of Appeal rejected an appeal against the EAT's decision. As Mummery LJ explained:

> This case is concerned with the effect of partitioning the borough into two separate areas. As already explained, the Directive and TUPE are capable of applying to the transfer of 'part of an undertaking', as well as to the transfer of an entire undertaking. A part of an undertaking is simply something less than the whole of an undertaking. Neither the legislation nor the case law expressly requires that the particular part transferred should itself, before the date of the transfer, exist as a discrete and identifiable stable economic entity. Nor do I think that such a requirement is implicit in the need to identify a pre-existing stable economic entity. In my judgment, it is sufficient if a part of the larger stable economic entity becomes identified for the first time as a separate economic entity on the occasion of the transfer separating a part from the whole.[120]

---

[117] See para. 2.126.
[118] [2004] IRLR 304, CA.
[119] Quoted by the Court of Appeal at para. 16.
[120] Ibid. at para. 32.

2.67 His conclusion was that:

> The fact that the two areas were previously one entire area covered by one contract prior to April 1999 did not prevent the tribunal from concluding in the circumstances that part of the larger economic entity in the hands of Botes and covered by area two was capable of being transferred to Fairhurst, in whose hands it then retained its identity as a part of the larger economic entity.[121]

2.68 That said, Mummery LJ also noted that fragmentation of the undertaking on the putative transfer might be relevant to the issue of whether an economic entity retained its identity for the purposes of establishing whether or not there was a transfer of an undertaking and quoted with approval[122] the decision of the Northern Ireland Court of Appeal in *Hassard v McGrath and others*[123] which concerned a situation where an undertaking was divided into four. In that case it was acknowledged that 'there must of course be a point at which the fragmentation is so great that the fragments could not be regarded as distinct parts of the transferor's undertakings'.[124]

2.69 Even if on division of an undertaking there are separate transfers of different parts of the undertaking falling within the scope of regulation 3(1)(a), the question may then arise of to which of the transferees (if any) the affected employees should transfer, given that only those assigned to the relevant undertaking transfer. The point was made in *Hassard v McGrath and others*[125] that 'the question of fragmentation would also be material to the second issue in this appeal, namely whether the employee was assigned to the part or parts transferred'.

2.70 Whether an economic entity needs to be shown to have existed prior to a putative transfer of an undertaking was further considered in *Transport and General Workers' Union v Swissport Ltd and anor* in the particular context of insolvency.[126] In this case, there was a claim for breach of the obligation to inform and consult appropriate representatives as required by regulation 13[127] and therefore it needed to be established whether there was a relevant transfer by reference to which such a claim could be based. Swissport, which provided ground handling services for a number of airlines including Aer Lingus, went into administration, whereupon Aer Lingus proceeded to conduct the service itself for six months using the equipment and premises of the insolvent provider and engaging its former employees (who subsequently resigned, were made redundant, or transferred elsewhere). The ET held that there was no relevant transfer for the purposes of TUPE 1981 on the basis that there was no identifiable economic entity providing ground handling services specifically to Aer Lingus before it took on the provision of the services itself.

2.71 The EAT allowed an appeal and remitted the matter to the ET for rehearing. The parties against whom the claims were brought maintained that there was no relevant transfer on the basis of a lack of tangible asset transfer (as only some minor office equipment was transferred), the majority of employees not transferring and no intangible assets transferring (by way of debts, goodwill, licences, and leases). In addition, the management of the operation significantly changed on the basis that after the putative transfer it related only to

---

[121] Ibid. at para. 36.
[122] Ibid. at para. 35.
[123] [1996] NI 586, NICA.
[124] Ibid. at p. 596.
[125] Ibid. With regard to the issue of assignment see Chapter 4, para. 4.36 *et seq.*
[126] [2007] ICR 1593, EAT.
[127] See Chapter 9 for detailed discussion of regulation 13.

the activities then performed by Aer Lingus rather than all Swissport's previous customers. In arguing that there was a relevant transfer, the trade union which brought the complaint pointed to the continuity of the relevant work without interruption, the use of the same ground handling equipment and some office equipment and the fact that certain staff categories had been specifically or mainly dedicated to Aer Lingus.

The EAT acknowledged that it might be difficult to identify a stable economic entity prior to **2.72** transfer in circumstances where what was transferred was only part of the putative transferor's operations and where the part transferred had not been self-contained so as to form a stable economic entity of itself. However, the lack of a 'bundle of resources' being dedicated to the part of the undertaking contended to transfer within the scope of TUPE prior to the putative transfer was not sufficient on its own to dispose of the matter. The ET had failed to address the situation properly applying the test as a matter of fact as at the point of transfer. This conclusion was considered to be entirely consistent with *Fairhurst Ward Abbotts Ltd*[128]—'a stable economic entity can exist prior to transfer or fragmentation provided that the part argued to be transferred within TUPE could be identified at the time of transfer as a stable economic entity even if such identification could only be made by or on the transfer'.[129] That said, the EAT recognized that the issue is fact sensitive and that the *Spijkers* criteria should be relied upon to determine whether a stable economic entity can be identified.

It is therefore clear that TUPE cannot necessarily be avoided by an argument that there was **2.73** no separate identifiable stable economic entity prior to the putative transfer. An inchoate economic entity may become an actual stable economic entity on transfer and may emerge from what was described in *Swissport* as the 'primordial soup'.[130] As HHJ Serota QC said in *Swissport*:[131]

> As a matter of practicality it may be more difficult to recognise a stable economic entity after transfer of part of an undertaking if that part undertaking is not self contained in some way so as to constitute itself as a stable economic entity. In particular... there may be difficulty in defining and delimiting the part of the undertaking said to be transferred. Consideration will also need to be given as to the extent to which administrative and managerial structures have been changed. However these are all matters of fact and as a matter of principle I conclude that the Employment Tribunal is bound to consider whether what was not recognised as being a stable economic entity before transfer was capable of being one as at the time of the alleged transfer.

12. Asset transfer

Whether TUPE applies by way of a transfer of an undertaking where the relevant activity is **2.74** 'labour-intensive' and needs few or no assets to be operated is considered below.[132] But what if assets are a key component of the conduct of the activity in question and are not transferred? Regulation 3(6)(b) provides that no property need transfer for there to be a relevant transfer. However, whether there is a transfer of assets can still be relevant to whether there is a transfer of an undertaking for the purposes of regulation 3(1)(a). In *Oy Liikenne*,[133] on

---

[128] Above, n. 118.
[129] *Transport and General Workers' Union v Swissport Ltd & anor*, above n.126, at para. 46.
[130] Ibid. at para. 35.
[131] Ibid. at para. 48.
[132] See para. 2.94 *et seq.*
[133] [2001] IRLR 171, ECJ.

transfer of a contract to supply bus services, a majority of the relevant employees but none of the buses used to fulfil the relevant services transferred to the new contractor. There was held to be no transfer of an undertaking for the purposes of the Directive in the absence of the transfer of those assets which contributed significantly to the operation and conduct of the relevant activity. The ECJ considered that bus transport could not be regarded as an activity based on manpower in view of the need for assets to conduct the relevant operation. Accordingly, in the absence of asset transfer, the transfer of employees was not of itself sufficient to establish the application of the Directive.

2.75   In terms of the general approach to be adopted, the ECJ indicated that:

> the national court, in assessing the facts characterising the transaction in question, must take into account among other things the scope of undertaking or business concerned. It follows that the degree of importance to be attached to the various criteria for determining whether or not there has been a transfer within the meaning of the Directive will necessarily vary according to the activity carried on, and indeed the production or operating methods employed in the relevant undertaking, business or part of a business.[134]

2.76   In the context of this particular case the ECJ's conclusion was that:

> bus transport cannot be regarded as an activity based essentially on manpower, as it requires substantial plant and equipment.... The fact that the tangible assets used for operating the bus routes were not transferred from the old to the new contractor therefore constitutes a circumstance to be taken into account.[135]

2.77   The ECJ also made the following points:

> However, in a sector such as scheduled public transport by bus, where the tangible assets contribute significantly to the performance of the activity, the absence of a transfer to a significant extent from the old to the new contractor of such assets, which are necessary for the proper functioning of the entity, must lead to the conclusion that the entity does not retain its identity.
>
> Consequently, in a situation such as that in the main proceedings, Directive 77/187 does not apply in the absence of a transfer of significant tangible assets from the old to the new contractor.[136]

2.78   In contrast, in *Allen and others v Amalgamated Construction Co Ltd*[137] the lack of asset transfer was not fatal to there being a transfer of an undertaking in the context of the subcontracting by one company (ACC) of driveage works in mines to another company in the same group (ACM). As the ECJ put it:

> Although, as far as this case is concerned, the driving of underground tunnels cannot be considered to be an activity based essentially on manpower since it requires a significant amount of plant and equipment, it is clear from the order for reference that, in the mining sector, it is common for the essential assets required for driveage work to be provided by the mine owner himself. For instance, AMS, as subcontractor, was able to use the equipment which RJB previously made available to ACC. The fact that ownership of the assets required to run the undertaking did not pass to the new owner does not preclude a transfer.... In the circumstances, the fact that there was no transfer of assets between AMS and ACC is not of decisive importance.[138]

---

[134] Ibid. at para. 35.
[135] Ibid. at para. 39.
[136] Ibid. at para. 42.
[137] [2000] IRLR 119, ECJ.
[138] Ibid. at para. 30.

Lack of asset transfer also did not preclude the application of the Directive in *Abler v Sodexho* **2.79**
MM Catering Gessellschaft,[139] in which an orthopaedic hospital retendered catering services
which it had previously contracted out. Meals were prepared for patients and staff on the
hospital premises. It was the contractor's responsibility to draw up menus, purchase, store,
produce, portion, and transport meals to various hospital departments, serve meals in the
dining room, wash the crockery, and clean the premises used. However, the premises themselves, as well as water, energy, and equipment, were provided by the management authority
for the hospital. The new contractor refused to take over the materials, stock, and employees
of its predecessor contractor who dismissed the catering staff whom it employed at the hospital. The equipment upon which the performance of the relevant contract was dependent
remained the property of the client hospital throughout.

Since the relevant function was considered to be asset reliant, the transfer (or not) of employ- **2.80**
ees was not of itself a decisive factor. Even though the new contractor did not acquire move-
able assets, it used a variety of assets provided by the relevant hospital. It was also relevant, as
a factor indicating the existence of a transfer falling within the scope of the Directive, that
the new contractor provided its service to the same group of customers (hospital patients) as
the old contractor. The lack of specific transfer of assets or employees did not preclude the
application of the Directive. As the ECJ put it:

> Catering cannot be regarded as an activity based essentially on manpower since it requires a
> significant amount of equipment. In the main proceedings, as the Commission points out,
> the tangible assets needed for the activity in question—namely, the premises, water and energy
> and small and large equipment (inter alia the appliances needed for preparing the meals and
> the dishwashers)—were taken over by Sodexho. Moreover, a defining feature of the situation
> at issue in the main proceedings is the express and fundamental obligation to prepare the meals
> in the hospital kitchen and thus to take over those tangible assets. The transfer of the premises
> and the equipment provided by the hospital, which is indispensable for the preparation and
> distribution of meals to the hospital patients and staff is sufficient, in the circumstances, to
> make this a transfer of an economic entity. It is moreover clear that, given their captive status,
> the new contractor necessarily took on most of the customers of its predecessor.
>
> It follows that the failure of the new contractor to take over, in terms of numbers and skills,
> an essential part of the staff which its predecessor employed to perform the same activity is
> not sufficient to preclude the existence of a transfer of an entity which retains its identity
> within the meaning of Directive 77/187 in a sector such as catering, where the activity is based
> essentially on equipment. As the United Kingdom and the Commission rightly point out, any
> other conclusion would run counter to the principal objective of Directive 77/187, which is to
> ensure the continuity, even against the wishes of the transferee, of the employment contracts
> of the employees of the transferor.[140]

The ECJ therefore concluded that: **2.81**

> The answer to the question of the referring court must therefore be that Article 1 of Directive
> 77/187 must be interpreted as applying to a situation in which a contracting authority which
> had awarded the contract for the management of the catering services in a hospital to one con-
> tractor terminates that contract and concludes a contract for the supply of the same services
> with a second contractor, where the second contractor uses substantial parts of the tangible
> assets previously used by the first contractor and subsequently made available to it by the

---

[139] [2004] IRLR 168, ECJ.
[140] Ibid. at paras 36 and 37.

contracting authority, even where the second contractor has expressed the intention not to take on the employees of the first contractor.[141]

2.82 That *Oy Liikenne* did not establish an absolute principle that the transfer legislation cannot apply to the transfer of an asset reliant activity where the relevant assets do not change hands—and that asset transfer is just one of the *Spijkers* factors—is further demonstrated by *P&O Trans European Ltd v Initial Transport Services Ltd*.[142] Shell operated petroleum delivery activities by way of a combination of an in-house function and the use of P&O and Initial as external contractors. Shell awarded a comprehensive contract to P&O which was treated as a transfer for TUPE purposes. Initial contended that the transfer legislation also applied to the service which it provided to Shell and that therefore four administrative staff who worked on that service should have transferred to P&O. Against this interpretation stood the facts that the relevant activity was asset reliant, P&O took none of Initial's vehicles, and there was no transfer of assets.

2.83 The Court of Appeal considered that in *Oy Liikenne* the ECJ did not establish a principle that, in relation to asset-intensive activities, the lack of transfer of significant assets would indicate that there was no relevant transfer. The ET was held to have been entitled to conclude that TUPE applied in these circumstances, having applied the appropriate multifactorial test. Particularly relevant matters were the facts that all the other employees involved in the operation transferred, that the core service remained the same, and that there was a dedicated workforce of which the relevant administrators were a part.

2.84 It was argued on the basis of *Oy Liikenne* that in an asset-intensive industry, such as the delivery of petroleum products by tanker, the absence of a transfer of such assets or a significant part of them is decisive in that, in such circumstances, the entity does not retain its identity. As Nelson J clarified,[143] *Oy Liikenne* itself, however, 'makes it plain that the 'multifactorial' approach remains' and referred to the ECJ's statement[144] in that decision that:

> to determine whether the conditions for the transfer of an economic entity are satisfied, it is also necessary to consider all the factual circumstances characterising the transaction in question, including in particular the type of undertaking or business involved, whether or not its tangible assets such as buildings and movable property are transferred, the value of its intangible assets at the time of the transfer, whether or not the core of its employees are taken over by the new employer, whether or not its customers are transferred, the degree of similarity between the activities carried on before and after the transfer, and the period, if any, for which those activities were suspended. These are, however, merely single factors in the overall assessment which must be made, and cannot therefore be considered in isolation (see in particular *Spijkers* paragraph 13 and *Süzen* paragraph 14).

2.85 The view taken of the approach of the ECJ in *Oy Liikenne* was as follows:

> In our opinion, the Court of Justice was not laying down a principle that in all cases of asset-intensive industries the absence of a transfer, to a significant extent, of such assets would always lead to the conclusion that no transfer had taken place. When the judgment is read as a whole, it is apparent that the Court of Justice was reaffirming the principle that all relevant factors had to be weighed in assessing whether a transfer had taken place or not, and that the

---

[141] Ibid. at para. 44.
[142] [2003] IRLR 128, CA.
[143] Ibid. at para. 35.
[144] At para. 33 of *Oy Liikenne*.

weight to be given to particular factors would vary in accordance with the facts of the case. Thus, in an asset-intensive industry, the fact that assets were not transferred will be 'a circumstance to be taken into account'. In some cases of this type the absence of a transfer will be decisive; in some it will not. On the facts of the case before them relating to 'scheduled public transport by bus', they concluded that the absence of a transfer of assets was such an important circumstance that it must lead to the conclusion that no transfer had taken place.

The relative significance of assets in relation to manpower and how each contributes to the performance of the particular activity will vary according to the facts of the particular case. The whole of the transaction has to be looked at in order to see whether one particular factor is decisive; that includes all the circumstances of the transaction.[145]

In *Numast and anor v P&O Scottish Ferries and others*[146] the EAT considered *Oy Liikenne* in **2.86** the context of the retendering of a ferry service from Scotland to the Northern Isles. None of the outgoing contractors' ships were acquired by the new contractor due to health and safety requirements which required new vessels. The vast majority of seafaring staff did, however, transfer. Workshop maintenance staff did not transfer as this work was subcontracted by the new contractor.

The EAT held that the ET had been entitled to find there to have been a relevant transfer **2.87** and that both the seafarers and maintenance staff had been employed in the undertaking (or parts thereof) transferred. *Oy Liikenne* was again viewed as not laying down a principle that 'in all cases of asset intensive industries the absence of a transfer to a significant extent of such assets would always lead to the conclusion that no transfer had taken place'.[147] On the basis of the multifactorial test, the ET's decision was sound, based as it was on the strong correlation between the premises and piers used by the transferor and transferee (which constituted the significant asset transfer absent in *Oy Liikenne*), the transfer of the intangible asset of the applicable government subsidy, the transfer of 90 per cent of the transferor's seafarers, the transfer of customers, and the high degree of similarity between the pre- and post-transfer activities. *Oy Liikenne* was therefore easily distinguished. As the EAT put it, '[i]n an asset-intensive industry the fact that assets were not transferred will be a circumstance to be taken into account. But the whole of the transaction has to be looked at in order to see whether one particular factor is decisive'.[148]

The approach adopted in *Numast* was echoed in *McCormack and others v Scottish Coal* **2.88** *Company Ltd*,[149] a decision which largely addressed the adequacy of the ET and EAT's reasoning but which also considered the weight to be given to the transfer or otherwise of assets. The majority of the relevant employees became employed by the putative transferee/respondent when it took over certain coal mining activities and the relevant activities essentially remained the same. The ET finding that TUPE 1981 applied was challenged on the basis that it failed to follow the ECJ guidance with regard to the transfer of plant or lack thereof.

Whilst it was held by the Court of Session that the position with regard to assets had been **2.89** inadequately explored and analysed by the ET, it was made clear that the issue of asset transfer is contextual rather than the crucial determining factor—'it does not necessarily flow from use, even intensive use, of plant by an entity that the plant employed before transfer is

---

[145] *P&O Trans European Ltd v Initial Transport Services Ltd,* above n. 142, at paras 39 and 40.
[146] [2005] ICR 1270, EAT.
[147] Ibid. at para. 28.
[148] Ibid.
[149] [2005] All ER (D) 104.

definitive of the identity of the entity'.[150] With regard to the correct approach to be adopted, the Court of Session took the view that:

> In assessing the degree of importance to be given to plant, and the transfer or non-transfer of it as part of the transaction, the national court must have regard to all the circumstances and must take into account the type of undertaking or business transferred, having regard in particular to the sector of activity in which it operates. That requires a close examination of the wider industry context, and the activities of the predecessor entity within that context. It is in the light of that enquiry that the national court must determine what are the essential and indispensable elements required in order for the economic entity to carry on operating and establish whether these elements have been taken over by [the] transferee.[151]

2.90 *GEFCO UK Ltd v Oates (1) Car & Delivery Co Ltd*[152] addressed similar ground where a contract for car transportation was held to fall within the scope of TUPE despite the lack of transfer of any tangible or intangible assets. Acknowledging that similarity of pre- and post-transfer activities was insufficient on its own to establish a TUPE transfer, the EAT held that continuity of customers entitled the ET properly to find that TUPE applied.

2.91 An example of where there was a transfer neither of assets nor of employees but nonetheless a relevant transfer is *McLeod Ingram t/a Phoenix Taxis and Rainbow Cars Ltd t/a Rainbow Cars*.[153] A taxi company agreed to make a payment to purchase the goodwill and telephone numbers of another taxi company and this was held to constitute a transfer of an undertaking in light of the payment for an identifiable business notwithstanding the lack of transfer of tangible assets or indeed of employees.

2.92 These decisions are a useful reminder that, while the categorization of an undertaking as asset-reliant or labour-intensive can be of assistance in applying the *Spijkers* criteria, it can present a potentially false dichotomy. The need to apply a fact-specific approach was noted by Langstaff J in *Balfour Beatty Power Networks and anor v Wilcox and others*:

> It seems to us that... the factual assessment of the importance of the balance between the significance of equipment, plant, premises, goodwill, tangible and intangible assets, and the question whether the identity of the labour force is a significant part of the undertaking, will necessarily vary. If one were to regard it as a spectrum, then if at one end of the spectrum were activities which would be regarded as almost entirely labour-intensive (the example used in argument was cleaning) and at the other an undertaking which was almost completely reliant upon heavy plant, machinery and premises (such perhaps as heavy manufacturing requiring no skilled labour input), there would be a sliding scale between them in which the relevant importance of the number and skills of the workforce engaged would necessarily vary.[154]

2.93 It can therefore be seen from the jurisprudence that the multifactorial approach applies just as much in relation to asset-reliant activities as others and that, while usage of assets may well be an important factor to take into account, the absence of their transfer will not necessarily be fatal to the application of TUPE.

---

[150] Ibid. at para. 30.
[151] Ibid. at para. 32.
[152] UKEAT/0014/05.
[153] UKEAT/1344/01.
[154] [2006] IRLR 258, EAT at para. 25.

B. Labour-intensive Activities

1. *Schmidt* and *Ayse Süzen*

The *Spijkers* principles have led to particular difficulty and uncertainty in cases where the relevant activities are 'labour-intensive' even though in principle, dependent upon the factual matrix, a transfer of labour-intensive activities may constitute a transfer of an undertaking for the purposes of regulation 3(1)(a).[155] The term 'labour-intensive' is used to describe activities (such as security and cleaning) which depend principally on the deployment of the efforts of individuals and do not require particular assets to pass over for the activities to be capable of being carried on by a new contractor. **2.94**

In *Schmidt*[156] the ECJ held that there was a transfer of an undertaking for the purposes of the Directive where no assets had been transferred on the contracting out of the relevant cleaning services from the transferor bank to the transferee cleaning contractor. As the ECJ indicated: **2.95**

> The fact that in its case law, the Court includes a transfer of such assets among the various factors to be taken into account by a national court to enable it, when assessing a complex transaction as a whole to decide whether an undertaking has in fact been transferred does not support the conclusion that the absence of these factors precludes the existence of a transfer.[157]

In this case the ECJ found there to be a transfer of an undertaking, commenting that: **2.96**

> the similarity in the cleaning work performed before and after the transfer, which is reflected, moreover, in the offer to re-engage the employee in question is typical of an operation which comes within the scope of the Directive and which gives the employee whose activity has been transferred the protection afforded to him by that Directive.

Despite the potentially expansive interpretation applied in *Schmidt*, in *Ayse Süzen*[158] the ECJ indicated that more was required for the Directive to apply than merely the transfer from one contractor to another of a service contract. Acknowledging the *Spijkers* principles and that each case must be assessed on its own facts—and indeed approving of *Schmidt*—the ECJ nonetheless held in *Ayse Süzen* that a transfer of significant tangible or intangible assets or a major part of the relevant employees in terms of numbers or skills would be necessary for the Directive to apply to a transfer of a (labour-intensive) service contract. Transfer of a service contract without more would not suffice. As the ECJ put it: **2.97**

> The mere fact that the service provided by the old and the new awardees of a contract is similar does not therefore support the conclusion that an economic entity has been transferred. An entity cannot be reduced to the activity entrusted to it. Its identity also emerges from other factors, such as its workforce; its management staff; the way in which its work is organised; its operating methods, or indeed, where appropriate, the operational resources available to it.[159]

The ECJ also counselled: **2.98**

> caution against jumping to the conclusion that the mere fact that the service provided by the old and new undertaking is similar does not justify the conclusion that there has been a

---

[155] As well as an SPC pursuant to regulation 3(1)(b).
[156] [1994] IRLR 302, ECJ.
[157] Ibid. at para. 16.
[158] [1997] IRLR 255, ECJ.
[159] Ibid. at para. 15.

transfer of an economic entity by the one to the other. There is of course a logic in that because, if one business ceases to function for one reason or another and coincidentally another business is set up and seeks to perform the same activities, it is difficult to say from this factor alone that there has been a transfer of an economic entity from one to the other. It might of course be different if a controlling organisation or public body shuts down the business being carried out by X and starts it up again to be carried out by Y.[160]

2.99   The *Ayse Süzen* approach was applied in relation to TUPE in *Betts v Brintel Helicopters Ltd and KLM ERA Helicopters (UK) Ltd*[161] which concerned the retendering of a contract to provide helicopter services to oil rigs. The original contractor's operation had constituted an undertaking consisting of helicopters, infrastructure, staff, and a contractual right to land on oil rigs and use the relevant facilities. However, all that transferred was the right to land on the relevant oil rigs. As the decisive criterion for determining there to be a transfer of such an undertaking is that the economic entity retained its identity after the putative transfer, transfer of only such a limited part of the original undertaking could not amount to the transfer of the undertaking such that it retained its identity in the hands of the second contractor. There could be no transfer, on the termination of one fixed-term contract for services and the commencement of another such contract to provide essentially similar services, unless there was also a transfer of significant assets or taking over by the new employer of the major part of the workforce. With no staff or equipment transferred, TUPE was held not to apply.

2.100   That the mere transfer of a service contract—without the transfer of employees—can fall outside the scope of the Directive (and by extension regulation 3(1)(a)) and the continuing relevance of *Ayse Süzen* are demonstrated by the decision of the ECJ in *Clece SA v Valor*.[162] In this case, the ECJ held that the Directive did not apply where a municipal authority took back in-house the cleaning of its premises which had been contracted out to a private company and hired new staff to perform that function. Whilst the ECJ adopted the *Spijkers* approach—that in order to determine whether such an entity retains its identity, it is necessary to consider all the facts characterizing the transaction in question and that the relevant circumstances are merely single factors in the overall assessment and cannot be considered in isolation—certain additional observations were made consistent with the restrictive approach adopted in *Ayse Süzen*.

2.101   The ECJ indicated that, in certain sectors, an economic entity is able to function without any significant tangible or intangible assets and that therefore the maintenance of identity following the putative transaction in question cannot depend on the transfer of such assets. Cleaning services were seen as an activity essentially based on manpower such that the group of employees permanently assigned to the common task of cleaning may amount to an economic entity. However, that entity's identity must nonetheless be retained after the transfer in question for the Directive to apply. According to the ECJ, where the transferee employs

---

[160] Ibid. at para. 48.

[161] [1997] IRLR 311, CA.

[162] [2011] IRLR 251, EAT. In contrast in *Scattolon v Ministero dell'Istruzione, dell'Universita et della Ricerca* [2011] IRLR 1020, ECJ the ECJ held that the transfer of staff providing auxiliary cleaning and maintenance services from certain Italian local authorities to the employment of the State was a transfer of an undertaking for the purposes of the Directive. The transferred employees were an economic entity (despite the absence of assets being transferred) as the activity being carried out was labour-intensive. The economic entity retained its identity after the transfer because the State took over the employees previously assigned to the cleaning and maintenance activities.

new staff to carry out the relevant activities and does not take on the employees who previously conducted the relevant work or take over any tangible or intangible assets, then the only link between the activities carried out by transferor and transferee is cleaning. The mere fact that activities conducted by the transferor and transferee are similar or even identical does not lead to the conclusion that an economic entity has retained its identity—an entity cannot be reduced to the activity entrusted to it. The identity of an entity was considered to be referable to several 'indissociable' factors such as the workforce, management, the way in which work is organized, operating methods, and, where appropriate, relevant resources. In particular, the ECJ indicated that the identity of an economic entity essentially based on manpower cannot be retained if the majority of its employees are not taken on by the alleged transferee.

The approach adopted in *Ayse Süzen*—to the extent that it established that lack of staff   **2.102** transfer would be a strong contra-indication of and therefore could preclude there being a transfer of an undertaking in the context of labour-intensive activities—has been subject to considerable criticism. As Barnard put it:

> since an adviser may need to know whether the Directive applies in order to determine whether the transferee ought to take the employees of the transferor into its employ, it is unhelpful to try to answer that question by application of the test whether the transferee has in fact done that very thing.[163]

Davies and Freedland described the approach adopted by the ECJ authorities in relation   **2.103** to the application of the Directive to labour-intensive activities as 'somewhat circular and unsatisfactory'.[164] Moreover, there was concern that the approach adopted in *Ayse Süzen* would not only deny the protection of the Directive to those engaged in labour-intensive activities such as cleaning and security but would also enable parties to avoid the application of the concept of a transfer of an undertaking to labour-intensive activities by electing not to transfer the relevant employees.

This concern was attenuated—but only to an extent—by the fact that a relevant transfer can   **2.104** take place when the major part of the relevant employees in terms of skills (as opposed to numbers) transfers. In *Lightway (Contractors) Ltd v Associated Holdings Ltd*[165] a minority of the relevant staff were taken on by the transferee but there was nonetheless a relevant transfer since those that transferred were mostly skilled. A subsequent ECJ decision which adopted the same approach and held there to be a transfer of an undertaking for the purposes of the Directive on a switch of cleaning contractors is *Temco Service Industries SA v Imzilyen and others*,[166] in which the conclusion on one of the questions posed by the national court was as follows:

> ...Article 1(1) of the Directive must be interpreted as applying to the situation in which a contractor which has entrusted the contract for cleaning its premises to a first undertaking, which has that contract performed by a subcontractor, terminates that contract and enters into a new contract for the performance of the same work with a second undertaking, where the transaction does not involve any transfer of tangible or intangible assets, between the first undertaking or the subcontractor and the second undertaking, but the

---

[163] Barnard, *EC Employment* Law, 4th Edition, Oxford: OUP, 2012 p. 597, referring to Davies (1997) 26 ILJ 193 who described the test as having 'a peculiar 'boot strap' quality about it'.
[164] Davies and Freedland, *Towards a Flexible Labour Market*, Oxford: OUP, 2007 p. 92.
[165] [2000] IRLR 247, CS.
[166] [2002] IRLR 214, ECJ.

second undertaking has taken on, under a collective labour agreement, part of the staff of the subcontractor, provided that the staff thus taken on are an essential part, in terms of their number and their skills, of the staff assigned by the subcontractor to the performance of the subcontract.[167]

2.105 Moreover, the domestic case law subsequent to *Ayse Süzen* mitigated or reduced its impact in relation to labour-intensive activities in two important respects—first, *Ayse Süzen* does not exclude the multifactorial approach in relation to labour-intensive activities; second, a putative transferee's motives in not accepting the affected employees into its employment can be relevant to the assessment of whether there is a transfer of an undertaking.

2. Subsequent case law

2.106 Notwithstanding the concerns noted above, it has been made clear in subsequent cases that in the domestic context *Ayse Süzen* does not, as a matter of general principle, disapply the multifactorial *Spijkers* factors and automatically preclude their being a transfer of a labour intensive undertaking where the putative transferee does not take on the putative transferor's staff. In *ECM (Vehicle Delivery) Ltd v Cox*[168] the employees were employed by Axial Ltd as drivers and yardmen servicing a contract with VAG Ltd to deliver cars imported into the UK. When ECM was appointed in place of Axial, the location where the work was conducted was changed, a different system of delivery was introduced and the arrangements for administering the contract were altered. ECM did not offer employment to any of the employees who had worked on the contract prior to the change of contractor. The ET held (in a decision reached before the *Ayse Süzen* decision was handed down by the ECJ) that this was because the employees were claiming through their trade union representatives that TUPE applied and were threatening an action for unfair dismissal if they were not employed by ECM.

2.107 The ET concluded that there was a transfer of an undertaking to ECM, identifying the undertaking which was transferred as the VAG contract itself and the activities that surrounded that contract. The Court of Appeal held that the ET had correctly considered the *Spijkers* factors and was entitled to conclude that the identity of the economic entity in the hands of Axial was retained in the hands of ECM, in that the customers were essentially the same and the work going on was essentially the same. The Court of Appeal also held that the ET had been entitled to have regard to the reason why the employees of the transferor were not taken on by the transferee.[169]

2.108 As Mummery LJ put it, making clear that the ECJ had not in *Ayse Süzen* overruled the prior authorities:

> In my judgment, this appeal fails on the ground that there is no error of law in the decision of the employment tribunal. In reaching its conclusion that the 1981 Regulations applied, the employment tribunal had regard to all those factors which were held by the European Court of Justice in *Spijkers* to be relevant to the determination of the issue whether there was a transfer of an undertaking. The employment tribunal considered the factors on each side. They noted the differences in the way that ECM carried out the VAG contract, but pointed out that the customers were essentially the same and that the work that was going on was essentially the same ie cars were unloaded at Grimsby, were put onto transporters and were driven to VAG dealers. The result was the same. The employment tribunal were entitled to conclude that,

---

[167] Ibid. at para. 33.
[168] [1999] IRLR 559, CA.
[169] The relevance of the putative transferee's motives on not taking on the putative transferor's employees is expanded upon in para. 2.112 *et seq*.

even though ECM did not take on any Axial staff, the identity of the economic entity in the hands of Axial was still retained in the hands of ECM after the loss of the VAG contract. This justified the finding of a transfer.

The employment tribunal applied the correct test, as laid down by the European court in *Spijkers* and followed in other cases, such as *Schmidt* [1994] IRLR 302. Although the *Süzen* [1997] IRLR 255 decision has been described as involving a shift of emphasis or a clarification of the law, nothing was said in *Süzen* [1997] IRLR 255 which casts doubts on the correctness of the interpretation of the Directive in the earlier decisions cited to and applied by the employment tribunal in the extended reasons.

In my judgment, it is clear that, but for the argument about the scope and effect of the later decision in *Süzen* [1997] IRLR 255, there would be no possible ground of appeal in this case. ECM's case has to be that *Süzen* [1997] IRLR 255 makes all the difference. It does not in this case. The importance of *Süzen* [1997] IRLR 255 had, I think, been overstated.[170]

RCO Support Services Ltd v Unison[171] also demonstrates how there may still, notwithstanding **2.109** *Ayse Süzen*, be a transfer of an undertaking for the purposes of regulation 3(1)(a) in relation to labour-intensive activities. In *RCO*, in-patient care at Walton Hospital was phased out and increased at Fazakerly Hospital which was some three miles away and run by the same NHS Trust. There was ward-for-ward, theatre-for-theatre equivalence of the functions conducted at the new location. RCO successfully tendered for the cleaning contract at Fazakerly and already held the catering contract there. Claims were brought against RCO by cleaners previously employed by Initial at Walton Hospital—on the basis that their dismissal was unfair by reason of a relevant transfer and constituted unfair selection for redundancy—as well as by catering staff originally employed by the NHS Trust itself at Walton and who were not offered employment by RCO or rejected employment on RCO's terms. The ET had held that there was a relevant transfer for the purposes of what is now regulation 3(1)(a) on the basis that the cleaning services in question remained the same:

> It was no more than a change of location for the same business carried on by a different firm. Here was a labour-intensive business: the transfer of tangible assets was of little significance, for there was not much that might be transferred... there was the same need for cleaning, some of it rather specialised, as before.[172]

The EAT[173] held that the ET had not erred in law in its conclusions and made the follow- **2.110** ing observations which further demonstrate the point that *Ayse Süzen* does not establish an absolute rule against TUPE applying where the operation is labour-intensive and employees do not in actual fact transfer:

> There is a real danger, were *Süzen* given the unqualified force that has been argued for it, that in labour-intensive areas of employment such as cleaning and catering where contracting out is now common and where significant assets are often either unnecessary or unlikely to be moved, an incoming contractor would be able to avoid the Directive by the simple expedient, often easy of achievement, of ensuring that he took on none of the previous contractor's workforce. The protection of employees' acquired rights, a basic object of the Directive, would not only be jeopardised but... would be jeopardised in relation to perhaps the most vulnerable of all classes of workers, those with only relatively simple and commonly available skills which,

---

[170] *ECM*, above n. 168, at paras 21–3.
[171] [2002] IRLR 401, CA.
[172] Quoted by Mummery LJ at para. 14.
[173] [2000] IRLR 624, EAT.

on that account, the incoming contractor could readily choose to supply by way of others in the labour market.[174]

2.111 In dismissing a further appeal and upholding the ET's decision, Mummery LJ's comments[175] in a similar vein when *RCO* reached the Court of Appeal are instructive:

> 25. I am, however, unable to accept *RCO*'s submissions that the limits on the application of the Directive set in *Süzen* mean that, as a matter of Community law, there can never be a transfer of an undertaking in a contracting-out case if neither assets nor workforce are transferred; that the only legally permissible conclusion on the facts of this case was that, as none of the workforce were taken on by *RCO*, no transfer could have taken place; and that the employment tribunal must have erred in law in concluding that there were in fact transfers within the meaning of TUPE.
>
> 26. I do not read *Süzen* as singling out, to the exclusion of all other circumstances, the particular circumstance of none of the workforce being taken on and treating that as determinative of the transfer issue in every case. That interpretation of the Directive would run counter to what is described . . . as the 'multifactorial approach' to the retention of identity test in *Spijkers*. Whether or not the majority of employees are taken on by the new employer is only one of all the facts, which must be considered by the national court in making an overall assessment of the facts characterising the transaction. Single factors must not be considered in isolation . . .
>
> 27. There was no misdirection or misapplication of the law by the employment tribunal. *Spijkers* is still good law . . . (T)he employment tribunal was entitled to characterise the facts found by it as involving retention of the identity of the economic entities of cleaning and catering previously carried on at Walton Hospital. The finding of retention of identity was based on more than just a comparison of the similarity in the activities undertaken by the contractors before and after the move. It was reached by a consideration of all the circumstances. There was significantly more to this case than Initial losing a contract and *RCO* winning a contract covering the same activities in a different location. The entities . . . had a discrete organisation for the exercise of special and important support skills, including established operating methods and training and they were an integral part of the distinctive inpatients infrastructure.

3. The transferee's motives

2.112 In *ECM* Mummery LJ described the role of the putative transferee's motive in not taking on the putative transferor's employee's in determining whether a particular situation constituted a transfer of an undertaking in relation to labour-intensive activities as follows:

> The tribunal was entitled to have regard, as a relevant circumstance, to the reason why those employees were not appointed by ECM. The Court of Justice has not decided in *Süzen* or in any other case that this is an irrelevant circumstance or that the failure of the transferee to appoint any of the former employees of the transferor points conclusively against a transfer.[176]

2.113 A deliberate decision not to take staff on with the objective of evading the application of TUPE is a relevant matter for the ET or court to take into account in determining whether there has been a transfer of an undertaking within regulation 3(1)(a), but what weight should be attached to such an evidential matter? In *Whitewater Leisure Management Ltd v Barnes*[177] Burton J made the following observations about the proper application of the

---

174 Ibid. at para. 29 per Lindsay J.
175 [2002] IRLR 401, CA at paras 25–27.
176 *ECM*, above n. 168, at para. 23.
177 [2000] IRLR 456, EAT.

approach in *ECM* to the transferee's motives in not taking on the relevant staff, making clear that an intention to evade TUPE does not automatically mean that there was a transfer of an undertaking:

15.1 ... but what the Court of Appeal in *Betts* did not say, and indeed the Court of Appeal in *ECM* did not say, is that if there be a finding of fact by a tribunal that there was a deliberate decision by a possible transferee not to take on any of the possible transferor's staff, in order that, or with the intended result that, [TUPE] should not apply, then in such a circumstance all the employees are deemed to have been transferred.

15.2 In any event, if the 'reason why the employees were not appointed by *ECM*' is to be left to be considered as a factor by the employment tribunal, the interpretation and the weight must also be for them. Is subjective intention or motive, or objective purpose or effect to be judged? It may be difficult if not impossible to differentiate—if it is relevant to do so—between a decision not to take on any staff because it is desired to avoid, or not to trigger, the Regulations of 1981, a decision not to take on any staff with the effect that the Regulations do not apply and a decision that, because it is not intended to take on any staff, the Regulations do not apply.... On the one hand there will no doubt be scrutiny by the employment tribunal of the transactions, on the other hand the fact that there is not a transfer, because no transfer of staff, cannot itself lead to a conclusion that there is a transfer.

15.3 Mummery LJ in the Court of Appeal in *ECM* ... [at] 561–562 is at pains to point out, not only, as Morison P himself had done in the Appeal Tribunal, that the issue arose out of a finding by the employment tribunal, but also that, again as Morison P had concluded ... [at] 419, such factor did not, on the facts of *ECM*, stand alone as the only basis for the conclusion that there had been a transfer. *ECM* is thus not itself a case which would support, or at any rate exemplify, a proposition that, in the absence of a transfer of any assets or any staff, or of any other material factor indicating a transfer, the *ECM* point alone would be determinative of the issue of transfer.

16. It is in all those circumstances that Mummery LJ's guidance remains, at 562 paragraph 23(6), simply that 'the tribunal was entitled to have regard, as a relevant circumstance, to the reason why those employees were not appointed by *ECM*'.

In similar vein, May LJ made the following observations in *ADI (UK) Ltd v Willer*: **2.114**

35. Consideration does, however, have to be given to the *ECM* point. As Mummery LJ said in that case, it is necessary to have regard, as a relevant circumstance, to the reason why Firm Security Group [the putative transferee] did not take on the nine security officers. Granted that, as is constantly stressed in the authorities, no one factor is determinative of whether there is a transfer for the purpose of the 1981 Regulations, in a labour-intensive case where the work or services are substantially the same and performed in the same place for the same person, questions relating to the taking on of employees may tip the scales one way or the other.

36. In my judgment, [counsel] was correct to accept that there would have been a transfer in the present case for the purpose of the 1981 Regulations if the nine security officers had been taken on by Firm Security Group, and that there would also be a transfer if the reason why they were not taken on was in order to avoid the application of the Regulations. More generally, it seems to me that if, as in the present case, the economic entity is labour-intensive such that, applying *Süzen*, there is no transfer if the workforce is not taken on but there would be if they were, there will be a transfer if, although the workforce is not taken on, it is established that the reason or principal reason for this was in order to avoid the application of the Regulations.[178]

---

[178] [2001] IRLR 542, CA.

2.115 That the motive of the putative transferee is but one of the factors to be considered in assessing whether there is a transfer of an undertaking in any given situation was reiterated by Mummery LJ in *RCO Support Services Ltd v Unison*:

> 35. In RCO's submissions, the *ECM* point was treated as a matter of subjective motive of the putative transferee, which was condemned as obviously irrelevant, patently circular and plainly proving too much: the putative transferee has no obligations, unless there is a transfer and, as *Süzen* makes clear, a transfer cannot take place unless either assets or the workforce transfer. In a labour-intensive case the employees are the undertaking and the undertaking cannot be said to have transferred, if they have not. The putative transferee, who does not receive the benefit of the employees, should not be saddled with the burden of the employment liabilities. The applicants and Unison were, for policy reasons, relying on circumstances in which there was no transfer to establish that there was a deemed transfer. There was no support for that approach in Directive 77/187 or in the decisions of the Court of Justice.
>
> 36. ...I have reached the conclusion that, as I have attempted to indicate in *ECM*... this is not in truth a separate point. I am inclined to accept the submissions of RCO that a subjective motive of the putative transferee to avoid the application of the Directive and the 1981 Regulations is not the real point. The relevant exercise is that in *Spijkers*... ie objective consideration and assessment of all the facts, including the circumstances of the decision not to take on the workforce.[179]

2.116 An alternative description of the proper approach to be adopted to the assessment of the effect of an intention to evade regulation 3(1)(a) by not taking on staff who would otherwise transfer was suggested by the EAT in *Atos Origin UK Ltd v Amicus and others*,[180] where it was considered to be 'manifest common sense for the tribunal to consider what impact that policy had by considering what would have happened but for that policy. That is a matter of evidence and, no doubt in some cases, the drawing of an inference.'[181]

2.117 *Astle v Cheshire County Council and anor*[182] considered circumstances where the parties to what was contended to be a transfer of an undertaking had genuine commercial reasons for implementing arrangements which they appreciated might have the collateral consequence of precluding the application of what is now regulation 3(1)(a). The EAT considered that, whilst there must be more than a transfer of an activity for there to be a transfer of an undertaking and the reason for employees not transferring can be relevant, an intention to evade the application of TUPE of itself is not relevant unless there would have been a TUPE transfer had the employees actually transferred. If there would have been a transfer of an undertaking had employees been taken on by the transferee, TUPE may apply where employees are not taken on by the transferee in order to seek to avoid the application of the legislation.

2.118 In *Astle* the council in question established a panel of consultants to replace a supplier of outsourced architectural services which had been terminated for performance reasons. The local authority viewed this structure as a way to 'thwart' TUPE so that the relevant employees would not pass back to the council. Ultimately, the way in which the relevant panel was appointed was varied due to advice that TUPE might apply. The council did take over the relevant service for a short period after the incumbent contractor had been terminated. Despite this, TUPE was held not to apply on the basis that the panel system, which caused

---

[179] [2002] IRLR 401, CA.
[180] UKEAT/0566/03.
[181] Ibid. at para. 22 per HHJ Wilkie QC.
[182] [2005] IRLR 12, EAT.

the operation not to retain its identity post-transfer, was found to have been implemented for genuine commercial reasons rather than the purposes of TUPE avoidance.

In reaching this conclusion, Burton J described the proper approach to the *ECM* point concerning the motive of the putative transferee in not taking on relevant staff as follows: **2.119**

> 21.1 If it is not the reason or principal reason of the transferee to avoid the application of TUPE, then the question is not relevant and does not arise.
>
> 21.2 If it is, then it is a relevant factor to take into account in the *Spijkers* exercise, and may be decisive.[183]

Burton J also observed that: **2.120**

> May LJ's test may be appropriate in many factual circumstances, ie that one assumes that the workforce, or that part of it which was deliberately not taken on for an *ECM* reason, is transferred, and then asks, on that assumption, whether there is a TUPE transfer (ie 'there would be if they were'). However that may not be apt in all factual circumstances, for example if the structure is so different that the assumed transfer of a workforce makes no sense.

The issue of the motive of the transferee in not taking on the transferor's staff falls into particularly sharp relief where the unsatisfactory performance of the relevant staff has led to the putative relevant transfer in the first place. The EAT addressed such a scenario in *Carlisle Facilities Group v Matrix Events & Security Services and others*.[184] Sea France decided for a variety of reasons, including the poor performance of the staff of its contractor, Carlisle, which provided guarding services, that it wished to replace Carlisle by a new contractor, Matrix. Whilst the relevant activities remained similar, none of the relevant employees transferred from Carlisle to Matrix.   **2.121**

The ET determined that, whilst the security guards comprised an undertaking for the purposes of TUPE, the lack of any transfer of employees or assets and the fact that there was no intention on the part of Matrix to evade TUPE by not taking on Carlisle's staff led to the conclusion that there was no transfer of an undertaking and therefore that TUPE did not apply.   **2.122**

An appeal against this decision failed. The ET was entitled to find that the decision not to take on the Carlisle staff was not motivated by an intention to evade TUPE but to comply with the ultimate client's wishes with regard to the staffing of the contract. Accordingly, the non-transfer of employees was properly taken into account as indicating that there was no relevant transfer in these circumstances.[185]   **2.123**

The proper approach to be adopted by ETs in assessing whether a given scenario constitutes a transfer of an undertaking can be summarized as follows: **2.124**

- In relation to a labour-intensive function, following *Ayse Süzen*, whether a major part of the workforce (in terms of numbers and skills) transfers will be an important factor.
- Given that a multifactorial approach must be adopted, the lack of transfer of employees will not necessarily debar TUPE from applying.

---

[183] Ibid. at para. 21.
[184] UKEAT/0380/04.
[185] That the facts of this case appear potentially to fall squarely within regulation 3(1)(b) demonstrates how the SPC concept was intended to simplify the application of TUPE in relation to the change of service providers.

- The motive of the employer in not taking on staff can be relevant but cannot lead to there being a relevant transfer where there would not have been one even if the employees had transferred.

2.125 It should also be noted in passing and contra-distinction that in relation to SPCs regulation 3(1)(b) entails different considerations of motive than apply in relation to regulation 3(1)(a). What matters for the purposes of regulation 3(1)(b) is the pre-transfer existence of an organised grouping of employees whose principal purpose is the conduct of the relevant activities and a switch in the conduct of those activities (relating to the provision of services rather than goods) where the intention is to create a relationship which is not one-off and of short duration. Motive is only relevant to the intended nature of the relationship between supplier and recipient of services. The parties' motivation in relation to their decisions as to transfer (or otherwise) of employees is irrelevant to the issue of whether particular circumstances give rise to an SPC.

C. The *Cheesman* Guidance

2.126 To conclude this review of the application of regulation 3(1)(a), it is worthwhile noting in full the comprehensive summary provided by Lindsey P in *Cheesman and others v Brewer Contracts Ltd*[186] of the test of whether there has been a transfer of an undertaking in which he sought to 'divide considerations between those going to whether there is an undertaking and those, if there is an undertaking, going to whether it has been transferred' His analysis was as follows:

> 10 . . . (i) As to whether there is an undertaking, there needs to be found a stable economic entity whose activity is not limited to performing one specific works contract, an organised grouping of persons and of assets enabling (or facilitating) the exercise of an economic activity which pursues a specific objective—*Sanchez Hidalgo* [1999] IRLR 136 paragraph 25; *Allen* [2000] IRLR 119 paragraph 24 and *Vidal* [1999] IRLR 132 paragraph 6 (which, confusingly, places the reference to 'an economic activity' a little differently). It has been held that the reference to 'one specific works contract' is to be restricted to a contract for building works—see *Argyll Training* [2000] IRLR 630, infra, EAT at paragraphs 14–19.
>
> (ii) In order to be such an undertaking it must be sufficiently structured and autonomous but will not necessarily have significant assets, tangible or intangible—*Vidal* [1999] IRLR 132 paragraph 27; *Sanchez Hidalgo* [1999] IRLR 136 paragraph 26.
>
> (iii) In certain sectors such as cleaning and surveillance the assets are often reduced to their most basic and the activity is essentially based on manpower—*Sanchez Hidalgo* [1999] IRLR 136 paragraph 26.
>
> (iv) An organised grouping of wage-earners who are specifically and permanently assigned to a common task may in the absence of other factors of production, amount to an economic entity—*Vidal* [1999] IRLR 132 paragraph 27.
>
> (v) An activity of itself is not an entity; the identity of an entity emerges from other factors such as its workforce, management staff, the way in which its work is organised, its operating methods and, where appropriate, the operational resources available to it—*Vidal* [1999] IRLR 132 paragraph 30; *Sanchez Hidalgo* [1999] IRLR 136 paragraph 30; *Allen* [2000] IRLR 119 paragraph 27.

---

[186] [2001] IRLR 144, EAT at paras 10 and 11.

11 As for whether there has been a transfer:

(i) As to whether there is in any relevant sense a transfer, the decisive criterion for establishing the existence of a transfer is whether the entity in question retains its identity, as indicated, inter alia, by the fact that its operation is actually continued or resumed—*Vidal* [1999] IRLR 132 paragraph 22 and the case there cited; *Spijkers v Gebroeders Benedik Abattoir CV* [1986] ECR 1119 ECJ; *Schmidt v Spar-und Leihkasse* [1994] IRLR 302 ECJ paragraph 17; *Sanchez Hidalgo* [1999] IRLR 136 paragraph 21; *Allen* [2000] IRLR 119 paragraph 23.

(ii) In a labour-intensive sector it is to be recognised that an entity is capable of maintaining its identity after it has been transferred where the new employer does not merely pursue the activity in question but also takes over a major part, in terms of their numbers and skills, of the employees specially assigned by his predecessors to that task. That follows from the fact that in certain labour-intensive sectors a group of workers engaged in the joint activity on a permanent basis may constitute an economic entity—*Sanchez Hidalgo* [1999] IRLR 136 paragraph 32.

(iii) In considering whether the conditions for existence of a transfer are met it is necessary to consider all the factors characterising the transaction in question but each is a single factor and none is to be considered in isolation—*Vidal* [1999] IRLR 132 paragraph 29; *Sanchez Hidalgo* [1999] IRLR 136 paragraph 29; *Allen* [2000] IRLR 119 paragraph 26. However, whilst no authority so holds, it may, presumably, not be an error of law to consider 'the decisive criterion' in (i) above in isolation; that, surely, is an aspect of its being 'decisive', although, as one sees from the 'inter alia' in (i) above, 'the decisive criterion' is not itself said to depend on a single factor.

(iv) Amongst the matters thus falling for consideration are the type of undertaking, whether or not its tangible assets are transferred, the value of its intangible assets at the time of transfer, whether or not the majority of its employees are taken over by the new company, whether or not its customers are transferred, the degree of similarity between the activities carried on before and after the transfer, and the period, if any, in which they are suspended—*Sanchez Hidalgo* [1999] IRLR 136 paragraph 29; *Allen* [2000] IRLR 119 paragraph 26.

(v) In determining whether or not there has been a transfer, account has to be taken, inter alia, of the type of undertaking or business in issue, and the degree of importance to be attached to the several criteria will necessarily vary according to the activity carried on—*Vidal* [1999] IRLR 132 paragraph 31; *Sanchez Hidalgo* [1999] IRLR 136 paragraph 31; *Allen* [2000] IRLR 119 paragraph 28.

(vi) Where an economic entity is able to function without any significant tangible or intangible assets, the maintenance of its identity following the transaction being examined cannot logically depend on the transfer of such assets—*Vidal* [1999] IRLR 132 paragraph 31; *Sanchez Hidalgo* [1999] IRLR 136 paragraph 31; *Allen* [2000] IRLR 119 paragraph 28.

(vii) Even where assets are owned and are required to run the undertaking, the fact that they do not pass does not preclude a transfer—*Allen* [2000] IRLR 119 paragraph 30.

(viii) Where maintenance work is carried out by a cleaning firm and then next by the owner of the premises concerned, that mere fact does not justify the conclusion that there has been a transfer—*Vidal* [1999] IRLR 132 paragraph 35.

(ix) More broadly, the mere fact that the service provided by the old and new undertaking providing a contracted-out service or the old and new contract-holder are similar does not justify the conclusion that there has been a transfer of an economic entity between predecessor and successor—*Sanchez Hidalgo* [1999] IRLR 136 paragraph 30.

(x) The absence of any contractual link between transferor and transferee may be evidence that there has been no relevant transfer but it is certainly not conclusive as there is no need for any such direct contractual relationship—*Sanchez Hidalgo* [1999] IRLR 136 paragraphs 22 and 23.

(xi) When no employees are transferred, the reasons why that is the case can be relevant as to whether or not there was a transfer—*ECM* [1999] IRLR 559 p. 561.

(xii) The fact that the work is performed continuously with no interruption or change in the manner or performance is a normal feature of transfers of undertakings but there is no particular importance to be attached to a gap between the end of the work by one subcontractor and the start by the successor—*Allen* [2000] IRLR 119 paragraphs 32–33.

D. Miscellaneous

1. Series of transactions and timing of transfer

(a) Series of transactions

2.127 A relevant transfer, whether by way of a transfer of an undertaking pursuant to regulation 3(1)(a) or an SPC for the purposes of regulation 3(1)(b), can occur as a result of the combination of a number of transactions which are linked and entered into by a variety of parties. Regulation 3(6)(a)[187] provides that a relevant transfer may be effected by a series of two or more transactions. A variety of connected transactions or a series of sequential transactions may have the cumulative effect of constituting a relevant transfer. This provision ensures the application of the legislation even if a complex series of transactions implements the actual transfer.

2.128 As Mummery J put it in *Longden and anor v Ferrari Ltd and anor*[188] in relation to the corresponding provisions of what was then TUPE 1981:

> The obvious case at which regulations 3(4) and 5(3) are aimed is that of an attempt to disguise the fact that there is a transfer of an undertaking within the meaning of the Regulations and the Directive. The parties to the proposed transfer of an undertaking may... arrange for the transfer to be effected in a series of two or more transactions dealing with separate assets, none of which, taken individually, could be regarded as the transfer of an undertaking. A composite plan of sub-division or fragmentation of a transfer may be adopted for no sensible commercial purpose, other than to avoid the consequence of the application of Regulations enacted for the protection of employees. These Regulations direct the tribunal to treat as a single transfer of an undertaking a transfer which is effected by such a series of transactions. Although these Regulations do not define a transfer, they direct a Tribunal to treat what might in form be a series of separate transactions as, in substance, a single transfer.[189]

(b) Timing of transfer

2.129 The timing of a transfer is of course of importance for a variety of reasons. In particular, it determines when the transferee commences employment obligations, by reference to what date the parties should provide the required information to appropriate employee representatives, when consultation with those representatives (if required) should commence, and the timeframe for the provision by the transferor to the transferee of the required employee liability information. The key point is that, regardless of the structure which the parties may adopt in any commercial documentation, what matters is when management or responsibility for the operation changes.

2.130 *Astley and others v Celtec Ltd*[190] addressed a situation where a transfer of an undertaking was initially found to have occurred over a considerable period of time. Training and Enterprise

---

[187] Which restates TUPE 1981, regulation 3(4).
[188] [1994] IRLR 157, EAT.
[189] Ibid. at para. 16.
[190] [2002] IRLR 629, CA.

Councils (TECs) were established to take over the management of training and enterprise facilities from the Department of Employment. The relevant organizations were staffed by seconded civil servants. At the end of a three-year secondment period, the relevant staff were given the choice of returning to the Department of Employment for redeployment or resigning from the civil service and taking up employment with the relevant TEC.

The Court of Appeal held that the ET was justified in concluding that the Directive preserved **2.131** the continuity of employment for statutory purposes of those employees who transferred to a TEC on the basis that they were employed in the relevant undertaking by the transferor (the Department of Employment) 'at the time of transfer'. The wording of the Directive was considered to be sufficiently wide to embrace a transfer of an undertaking which takes place over a period of time. Once it was accepted that an undertaking can be transferred over a period of time, it was a matter of fact to establish the precise timing of the transfer.

Accordingly, the Court of Appeal considered that the ET was entitled to find as it did. There **2.132** was a relevant transfer commencing when the TEC started business—the transfer took place over a period of years until the last secondments from the civil service ended. Each time a seconded employee became directly employed by the TEC, there was another part transfer immediately before which the employee was employed by the transferor such that the employee's employment and associated rights passed to the transferee under TUPE. The ET saw no reason in principle why such a very long period should not be found to constitute the transfer when that was the plan from the outset.

The subsequent ECJ decision in the same litigation held that this approach was incorrect.[191] **2.133** The ECJ considered that the date of transfer for the purposes of the Directive is the particular moment when responsibility as employer for carrying on the business of the undertaking transferred moves from the transferor to the transferee. The ECJ took the view that the Directive intended to create certainty by applying its protection at the date of transfer. This has the consequence that the workers who are to benefit from the Directive's protection should be identified at a particular moment in time. The date of a transfer is therefore 'the date on which responsibility as employer for carrying on the business of the unit transferred moves from the transferor to the transferee. That is a particular point in time which cannot be postponed to another date at the will of the transferor from the transferee.'[192] With regard to the issue of the date of a transfer of an undertaking, *Celtec* therefore requires the ET or court to determine one specific date on which the TUPE transfer in question occurs. It is not clear how this analysis interacts with regulation 3(6)(a) which envisages a transfer over a period of time by virtue of a series of transactions.

Celtec was considered in *Metropolitan Resources Ltd v Churchill Dulwich Ltd (in liquida-* **2.134** *tion) and others*,[193] albeit a case concerning regulation 3(1)(b) rather than regulation 3(1)(a). The ET had determined that the relevant transfer took place on 26 January 2007 and Metropolitan Resources argued that in reaching this conclusion the ET had failed properly to consider the fact that the employees had continued to work for the transferor after that date and Churchill Dulwich had continued to provide accommodation to asylum seekers—the activity which was the subject of the SPC—as it was commissioned to do until 31 March

---

[191] [2005] IRLR 647, ECJ.
[192] Ibid. at para. 44.
[193] [2009] IRLR 190, EAT.

2007. In terms of the timing of the transfer itself, the EAT considered that the continued presence of some asylum seekers following the transfer date at Churchill Dulwich's premises could properly be viewed by the ET as not detracting from the fact that the core activities had been transferred to Metropolitan Resources on an earlier date. HHJ Burke QC took the view that:

> It is unlikely that a service provision change will in practice always be entirely achieved in one day; and I have no doubt that the law is not such as to require that it should be so achieved.... I accept [the] argument that Celtec requires the Tribunal to find one date on which any type of TUPE transfer occurred on the facts before them but does not require that all the steps which constitute such a transfer must take place on the same day.... The tribunal, in the case in which the date of the alleged transfer is an issue must, in my judgement, determine the date at which the essential nature of the activity carried on by the alleged transferor ceased to be carried on by him and is instead carried on by the transferee.[194]

2.135 That the transfer date for the purposes of regulation 3(1)(a) is a factual matter determined by reference to the change to the responsibility for carrying on the relevant business was demonstrated by *Commercial Motors (Wales) Ltd v Howley*.[195] In this case, the ET found that the date of the relevant transfer was 2 February 2009 when the transferee took over the running of the relevant business and took over responsibility for paying the wages of the relevant staff. This was the case notwithstanding the fact that the relevant contract of sale relating to the transfer of the business in question was not completed until 6 March 2009. The EAT considered this decision to be perfectly permissible as it was consistent with the principle set down by the ECJ in *Berg & Busschers v Besselsen*[196] to the effect that:

> If the purchaser of an undertaking becomes the employer, the transfer must be considered as the transfer of an undertaking as a result of the legal transfer within the meaning of Article 1(1) of the Directive even when the purchaser only acquires the ownership of the undertaking at the moment when he has paid the complete purchase price.[197]

2. Ships

2.136 As the 2005 Consultation noted,[198] the 2006 Regulations do not contain a provision equivalent to TUPE 1981, regulation 2(2) which provided that a transfer of a ship without more did not constitute a relevant transfer. The reason for the absence of such a provision is the Government's view that the TUPE 1981 provision was 'declaratory only' and added nothing of substance to the operation of the legislation. Only if a ship, even with its crew, were sold as part of a business, would the legislation apply.[199]

2.137 The transfer of ships was excluded from the scope of TUPE 1981 by its regulation 2(2). However, no provision to this effect is included in TUPE 2006. This is the case notwithstanding Article 1(3) of the Directive which states that it does not apply to sea-going vessels.

---

[194] Ibid. at para. 38.
[195] UKEAT/0491/11.
[196] [1989] IRLR 447, ECJ.
[197] Cited at para. 19 of *Howley*, above n. 195.
[198] At para. 13.
[199] As para. 13 of the 2005 Consultation noted, this interpretation was confirmed by the Court of Session in *Castle View Services Ltd v Howes and others* (29.2.00 Inner House).

Regulation 3(7) makes specific provision to deal with the situation where ships[200] registered **2.138** in the United Kingdom cease to be so. The right of seamen to be discharged from the relevant ship's crew when it ceases to be registered in the United Kingdom[201] is not affected by the fact that such a change in registration may take place in connection with a transaction which otherwise falls within TUPE.

---

[200] Within the meaning of the Merchant Shipping Act 1894.
[201] Conferred by the Merchant Shipping Act 1970.

3

SERVICE PROVISION CHANGES

A. Introduction	3.01	I.	An Organised Grouping of Employees	3.78
B. The Definition of an SPC	3.11		1. General	3.78
C. Interpretation of the SPC provisions	3.19		2. A group is not necessarily an organised grouping	3.81
D. Activities and their Similarity Post Transfer	3.25		3. Groupings of one	3.84
E. Multiple Transferees and Fragmentation	3.42	J.	Principal Purpose	3.93
F. Activities Must Transfer—Work in Progress?	3.59	K.	One-off Service Contracts	3.98
		L.	Supply of Goods	3.112
G. Who is the Client?	3.63	M.	Professional Business Services	3.119
H. Client Must Remain the Same	3.67	N.	Summary	3.125

A. Introduction

3.01   Regulation 3(1)(b) establishes, as a form of relevant transfer for the purposes of TUPE, the service provision change (SPC). TUPE can therefore apply to a given situation by way of an SPC for the purposes of regulation 3(1)(b) as an alternative to (or indeed as well as by virtue of being) a transfer of an undertaking for the purposes of regulation 3(1)(a).

3.02   As HHJ Burke QC put it in *Metropolitan Resources Ltd v Churchill Dulwich Ltd (in liquidation) and others*[1] the SPC was, when introduced, 'a wholly new statutory concept. It is not defined in terms of economic entity or of other concepts which developed under TUPE 1981 by Community decisions upon the Acquired Rights Directive prior to April 2006 when the new Regulations took effect.'[2] The purpose of the SPC provisions, HHJ Burke QC went on to say, was:

> to remove or at least alleviate the uncertainties and difficulties created, in a variety of familiar commercial settings, by the need under TUPE 1981 to establish a transfer of a stable economic entity which retained its identity in the hands of the alleged transferee, particularly in the case of a labour-intensive operation.[3]

3.03   An SPC occurs on a change (other than on a one-off or short-term basis or in relation to the supply of goods) to the identity of the person who has the conduct of activities to

---

[1] [2009] IRLR 190, EAT.

[2] Ibid. at para. 26.

[3] Ibid. at para. 27.

which an organised grouping of employees has principally been dedicated for a particular client. According to the 2009 Guidance SPCs 'concern relationships between contractors and the clients who hire their services'.[4] The Consultation Response indicated that the term 'describes situations where a contract to provide a business service to a client is let, re-let or ended by bringing it in house'.[5]

For there to be an SPC certain other requirements must be satisfied—first, there must be an **3.04** organised group of employees principally dedicated to that contract or activity prior to the transfer for there to be an SPC and, second, the contract award must be on an ongoing rather than on a one-off and short-term basis and not relate to the supply of goods. This additional and alternative concept of a relevant transfer was introduced with the objective of ensuring clarity in the application of the transfer legislation to situations such as outsourcing, in-housing, and the retendering of contracts from one contractor to another. As the DTI put it,[6] in the absence of further ECJ jurisprudence to resolve what it saw as the case law conflict with regard to the application of the transfer legislation to labour-intensive activities,[7] it was considered to be a 'moot point' to what extent the Directive and TUPE 1981 already applied to such problem cases.

From the Government's perspective, the introduction of the concept of the SPC was intended, **3.05** by way of the comprehensive application of TUPE to the transactions which it covers which was its objective, to reduce insecurity and help to 'take the fear out of transfer' by smoothing the transfer process, thereby improving workplace relationships and partnership and promoting business flexibility.[8] Davies and Freedland, who had described the approach adopted by the ECJ authorities to the application of the Directive to labour-intensive activities as 'somewhat circular and unsatisfactory',[9] considered that the Government's decision to make more certain the application of TUPE to outsourcing, retendering and in housing by introducing the SPC concept was taken 'in the name of clarity and protecting vulnerable groups of workers'[10] and that '[t]he Government's overall strategy seems to have been to promote the acceptability of contracting out, in both the public and the private sectors, by reducing the potential for claims that the reconfiguration was being done at the expense of the employees'.[11]

The 2001 Consultation considered that the introduction of the concept of the SPC would **3.06** be a significant extension of the scope of TUPE.[12] Basing the application of TUPE, by way of an SPC, on the dedication of staff to an activity which is taken over by a new operator is to the effective exclusion of the other factors to be considered when determining whether there is a transfer of an undertaking in terms of identifying an economic entity, and its retention of identity.[13] To adopt the SPC concept was viewed as giving TUPE a wider scope than the Directive requires in terms of employee protection.

---

[4] At p. 6.
[5] At para. 2.1.
[6] 2005 Consultation Annex D para. 3.
[7] Described in detail in Chapter 2 at para. 2.94 *et seq.*
[8] 2005 Consultation Annex D, para. 7.
[9] Davies and Freedland, *Towards a Flexible Labour Market*, Oxford: OUP, 2007 p. 92.
[10] Ibid.
[11] Ibid. p. 93.
[12] At para. 28. Notwithstanding this, the Consultation Response stated (at para. 2.5) that '[m]any service provision changes are also in fact business transfers and are thus already covered by TUPE'.
[13] See Chapter 2 generally.

3.07 The concept of the SPC was also seen as of value by virtue of the improved predictability of the application of TUPE which it would produce and which would create a 'level playing field'[14] for contractors competing for contracts to provide services. In the light of the obligation on the transferor to notify the transferee of prescribed employee information,[15] the more predictable application of TUPE in these circumstances could therefore be catered for and dealt with adequately by those affected in their commercial arrangements. The desirability of the introduction of the concept of the SPC was not, it has to be said, accepted unanimously—the Engineering Employers' Federation, for example, argued that the introduction of the SPC concept would 'create inflexibility in contract provision and reduce competition and innovation at the same time as creating new areas of legal uncertainty'.[16]

3.08 That the comprehensive application of TUPE to contracting out, retendering, and in-housing by way of the SPC provisions introduced in TUPE 2006 would create a level playing field was also seen as promoting competition in line with, for example, the Government's best value framework for local authority services. An expanded and clarified TUPE was expected to remove a significant disincentive for potential bidders[17] from becoming involved in service contracting.[18] The SPC concept would also assist in ensuring that the principles set out in the Government's statement of practice on staff transfers in the public sector were fully observed within local government and the non-central government public sector.[19]

3.09 The 2001 Consultation also noted that excluding the application of the new concept from arrangements which were 'one-off' task-specific contracts would ensure that the legislation did not go beyond the scope of the Directive in terms of the stability of the activity in question.[20] The view was also taken that employees providing the kind of 'commodity services' which were perceived as being purchased on such a one-off basis are less likely to be at risk of redundancy as a result of the awarding of contracts for the supply of such services. They were therefore less likely to be in need of statutory employment protection by TUPE. These employees would be likely to remain part of the workforce of the provider of such commodity services which would presumably deploy such staff to its remaining variety of clients and customers. In effect, an ongoing relationship as between client and supplier is required to attract the application of employment protection for the employees affected by a contract award by way of there being an SPC.

3.10 Critics of the SPC concept will argue that, quite apart from the litigation which the SPC concept has prompted, one of the perceived advantages of the regime introduced in 2006—the more predictable application of the legislation to changes of contractor—does not actually deliver the intended level playing field. Lack of cooperation from an incumbent contractor may make planning and tendering difficult. The incumbent contractor may end up with an enhanced position compared to other bidders given that the assigned staff would transfer to a new contractor—this may act as a disincentive to clients from retendering and to new potential contractors from bidding. A new contractor may have to deal with the logistical

---

[14] 2005 Consultation para. 18.
[15] See Chapter 8.
[16] Consultation Response para. 2.5.
[17] And particularly smaller firms.
[18] 2001 Consultation para. 29.
[19] See Chapter 1, para. 1.59 *et seq.*
[20] 2001 Consultation para. 30.

and financial burdens of relocation and consequent redundancy liabilities when it takes over a contract and then services it from another site and cannot, on the basis of the current case law, straightforwardly arrange for redundancy dismissals before the new contract begins and the relevant staff actually transfer to its employment.[21] These difficulties are only exacerbated by uncertainties over the proper interpretation of regulation 3(1)(b) which detract from its objective of clarity and certainty.

B. The Definition of an SPC

For the purposes of regulation 3(1)(b), an SPC arises in the following situations: **3.11**

- 'Activities cease to be carried out by a person ("a client") on his own behalf and are carried out instead by another person on the client's behalf ("a contractor").'[22] This essentially covers outsourcing.
- 'Activities cease to be carried out by a contractor on a client's behalf (whether or not those activities had previously been carried out by the client on its own behalf) and are carried out instead by another person ("a subsequent contractor") on the client's behalf.'[23] This essentially covers a re-tendering or contractor change.
- 'Activities cease to be carried out by a contractor or a subsequent contractor on a client's behalf (whether or not those activities had previously been carried out by the client on its own behalf) and are carried out instead by the client on his own behalf.'[24] This essentially covers in-housing.

The conduct of the activities in question must, however, also be of the requisite stability and   **3.12**
structure before transfer. Accordingly, pursuant to regulation 3(3), immediately before an SPC:

- There must be an 'organised grouping of employees situated in Great Britain which has as its principal purpose the carrying out of the activities concerned on behalf of the client'.[25]
- The client must also intend 'that the activities will, following the service provision change, be carried out by the transferee other than in connection with a single specific event or task of short-term duration'.[26]

Essential elements of the application of regulation 3(1)(b) are therefore the existence imme-   **3.13**
diately prior to the putative SPC of an organised grouping of employees, its dedication to one client, and the change of service provider. The transfer of assets or employees, so integral to the test of whether there is a transfer of an undertaking for the purposes of regulation 3(1)(a),[27] is not relevant to the test of whether there is an SPC. Nor are the motives of a putative transferee in not taking employees on post-transfer or any break in activities to be

---

[21] Because the transferor cannot rely on the transferee's reason for dismissal to establish an ETOR—see Chapter 7, para. 7.65 *et seq.*
[22] Regulation 3(1)(b)(i).
[23] Regulation 3(1)(b)(ii).
[24] Regulation 3(1)(b)(iii).
[25] Regulation 3(3)(a)(i).
[26] Regulation 3(3)(a)(ii).
[27] See Chapter 2, para. 2.74 *et seq.*

considered, again in contrast to the approach of regulation 3(1)(a).[28] As Elias LJ noted in *McCarrick v Hunter*,[29] as between a transfer of an undertaking for the purposes of regulation 3(1)(a) and an SPC for the purposes of regulation 3(1)(b), 'the principal distinction, therefore, is that the economic entity is constituted by an organised grouping of resources, whilst a service provision only requires an organised grouping of employees'.

3.14 Despite the fact that there is no express statement to that effect, regulation 3(1)(b) presumably applies regardless of whether the transfer is voluntary or involuntary and whether there is any contractual relationship between the parties. This would be consistent with the approach in relation to regulation 3(1)(a). As is the case in relation to regulation 3(1)(a),[30] regulation 3(6) confirms that no property need transfer for there to be a relevant transfer by way of an SPC[31] and that an SPC can be effected by a series of two or more transactions.[32]

3.15 Two key elements of regulation 3(1)(b)—the reference to 'service' in the descriptive term 'service provision change' and the concept of 'activities'—are not specifically defined in TUPE. The drafting approach was not to define these aspects of regulation 3(1)(b) but rather to exclude specific matters from its scope. Accordingly, the SPC concept does not apply, pursuant to regulation 3(3)(a)(ii), where 'the client intends that the activities will, following the service provision change be carried out by the transferee other than in connection with a single specific event or task of short-term duration'.[33] In addition, an SPC only arises where the relevant activities 'do not consist wholly or mainly of the supply of goods for the client's use'.[34]

3.16 Concern had been expressed by some commentators in relation to the earlier drafting of the SPC provisions that regulation 3(1)(b) might not cover the subcontracting of activities by a client's contractor or changes of subcontractor. This concern was addressed by the inclusion in regulation 2(1) of the specific provision that 'references to 'contractor' in regulation 3 shall include a subcontractor'. As indicated in the Consultation Response,[35] it was 'decided to make it explicit (rather than implicit) that sub-contractors are in the same position as contractors when activities are performed by them'. Transactions involving awards and retendering of subcontracts are therefore be equally susceptible to the application of regulation 3(1)(b) as contract awards by the ultimate client.

3.17 Regulation 3(1)(b) does not address expressly whether an interruption or temporary cessation of activities will take what would otherwise be an SPC outside its scope. The jurisprudence on regulation 3(1)(a) in this regard may be prayed in aid but can be argued not to be strictly relevant to this domestic, rather than Directive derived, concept of an SPC.[36]

3.18 An example of a decision under TUPE 1981 in relation to whether there was a transfer of an undertaking which might well be decided differently under regulation 3(1)(b)

---

[28] See respectively, Chapter 2, paras 2.112 *et seq.* and 2.61 *et seq.*
[29] [2013] IRLR 26, CA at para. 14.
[30] See Chapter 2, para. 2.24.
[31] Regulation 3(6)(b).
[32] Regulation 3(6)(a); see Chapter 2, para. 2.127 *et seq.* for further discussion of the timing of a relevant transfer.
[33] Regulation 3(3)(a)(ii).
[34] Regulation 3(3)(b).
[35] At para. 27.
[36] See Chapter 2, para. 2.61 *et seq.*

is *Computacenter (UK) Ltd v Swanton and others*.[37] A dedicated team of employees were engaged in servicing a subcontract from IBM repairing Lloyds TSB computers. This arrangement constituted an economic entity in the view of the ET. The subcontract was awarded to a new subcontractor and no staff transferred. The ET found that there was no relevant transfer on the basis of the lack of any transfer of assets or employees, the lack of any relationship between the two subcontractors, and the fact that the arrangements had not been structured deliberately to avoid TUPE. The EAT rejected an appeal. Given the presence of the key factors of a dedicated team of employees and the transfer of the relevant activities between contractors, the ET might well, had it been required to consider regulation 3(1)(b), have found there to have been an SPC, despite the fact that the requirements of what is now regulation 3(1)(a) were not satisfied.

C. Interpretation of the SPC Provisions

The concept of the SPC is a purely domestic one which is not as susceptible to, nor indeed **3.19** required where appropriate to be subjected to, a purposive interpretation unlike the regulation 3(1)(a) concept of a transfer of an undertaking, based as it is on the Directive and its jurisprudence. In *Metropolitan Resources Ltd v Churchill Dulwich Ltd (in liquidation) and others*[38] HHJ Burke QC considered the proper approach to be adopted when considering whether there has been an SPC and commented as follows: '[t]he circumstances in which service provision changes are established are, in my judgment, comprehensively and clearly set out in regulation 3(1)(b) itself and regulation 3(3)'.[39] In his view, a purposive interpretation to regulation 3(1)(b) was not appropriate.[40] The ET should, in considering whether there has been an SPC, almost exclusively be focused on the situation before the putative transfer and therefore not be influenced by what happens to the transferor's assets or employees after the transfer.[41]

In *Metropolitan Resources*, the Home Office had a contract with a charitable organization, **3.20** Migrant Helpline, for the accommodation of asylum seekers. The charitable organization in turn had contracts with a number of providers of accommodation including Churchill Dulwich. Churchill Dulwich provided its services on a series of six-month contracts which were regularly renewed and the relevant employees were employed by Churchill Dulwich at its hostel for asylum seekers, Barry House. Metropolitan Resources began to provide accommodation to Migrant Helpline on the basis of a short-term contract in the Christmas and New Year period of 2006/7 and Migrant Helpline decided to divert new asylum seekers to Metropolitan Resources' operation instead of to Churchill Dulwich, even though the current contract with Churchill Dulwich was allowed to continue to the end of its then six-month term.

The contract between Migrant Helpline and Metropolitan Resources was almost identical to **3.21** the contract with Churchill Dulwich. The only differences were the location and the fact that

---

[37] UKEAT/0256/04. *Carlisle Facilities Group v Matrix Events & Security Services* discussed in Chapter 2 at para. 2.121 is another example of a situation to which regulation 3(1)(b) could apply but where what is now regulation 3(1)(a) did not.

[38] [2009] IRLR 190, EAT at para. 26.

[39] Ibid. at para. 27.

[40] Ibid. at para. 28.

[41] Ibid. at para. 43.

accommodation was to be provided only for one or two nights. In the subsequent period, the number of asylum seekers accommodated by Churchill Dulwich reduced to zero despite the ongoing contractual obligations to provide bed spaces. After expiry of Churchill Dulwich's contract with Migrant Helpline, the claimant employees presented themselves for work at Metropolitan Resources' Croydon site on the basis that their employment had transferred across by way of an SPC pursuant to regulation 3(1)(b). They were then sent home and effectively dismissed, either by Metropolitan Resources Ltd or Churchill Dulwich.

3.22 As a preliminary issue, the ET held that there had been a relevant transfer by way of an SPC from Churchill Dulwich to Metropolitan Resources. On appeal, it was submitted that the ET had erred by not applying the multifactorial approach set out in *Cheesman and others v Brewer Contracts*,[42] i.e. considering a formal list of factors before deciding whether there was a relevant transfer. Even though *Cheesman* concerned the transfer of an undertaking under TUPE 1981,[43] it was argued that the same approach should be applied to the issue of whether there was an SPC for the purposes of regulation 3(1)(b). The ET had determined that the relevant transfer took place on 26 January 2007 and Metropolitan Resources argued that in reaching this conclusion the ET had failed properly to consider the fact that the employees had continued to work after that date and Churchill Dulwich had continued to provide accommodation until 31 March 2007.[44]

3.23 The EAT held that the ET had not erred in law in finding that there had been an SPC. There was no need for a formal list of factors to be drawn up and considered before the decision can be made. In HHJ Burke QC's view the (then new) SPC provisions are straightforward and their application to an individual case essentially one of fact. There was no need to adopt a purposive construction to the SPC provisions nor indeed any need for a multifactorial approach to its application. The ET should ask itself simply whether, on the facts, one of the three situations laid out in regulation 3(1)(b) existed and whether the conditions set out in regulation 3(3) are satisfied.

3.24 That this is in general terms the correct approach to the interpretation of regulation 3(1)(b) was confirmed by the Court of Appeal in *McCarrick v Hunter*,[45] subject, however, to the point that a broad interpretation of the SPC provisions may be appropriate in relation to certain aspects of their operation. Elias LJ adopted the following analysis:

> I do not dispute that there may be issues where a purposive interpretation is appropriate with respect to service transfer provisions and where the courts should approach matters as they would similar issues relating to transfers of undertakings. For example, it may be necessary not to be too pedantic with respect to the question whether the activities carried on before and after the transfer are sufficiently similar to amount to the same service; or to take a broad approach to the question whether an employee is employed in the service transferred: see *Kimberley Group Housing Ltd v Hambley* [2008] ICR 1030. But I agree with HH Judge Burke QC that there is no room for a purposive construction with respect to the scope of regulation 3(1)(b) itself. So far as that is concerned, there is in my view no conflict between a straightforward construction and a purposive one: the natural construction gives effect to the draftsman's purpose. There are no underlying EU provisions against which the statute has to be measured. The concept of a change of service provision is not complex and there is no reason to think that

---

[42] [2001] IRLR 144, EAT; see Chapter 2, para. 2.126.
[43] i.e. what is now regulation 3(1)(a).
[44] On this particular point, see Chapter 2, para. 2.134.
[45] [2013] IRLR 26, CA.

the language does not accurately define the range of situations which the draftsman intended to fall within the scope of this purely domestic protection.[46]

D. Activities and their Similarity Post Transfer

In formulating the reforms to TUPE which led to the introduction of the 2006 Regulations, **3.25** the possibility was considered by the Government of providing expressly that regulation 3(1)(b) should not apply where the relevant service is to be provided in a new or innovative manner by the new service provider.[47] It was ultimately concluded that such an exemption would not be included in TUPE 2006. The rationale for this decision was as follows. If new methods of working (such as computerization) are introduced as part of a change of service provider, the employees engaged in relation to the relevant service might be redundant as regards the transferee if those employees do not have the requisite skills relative to those new methods of working. To apply the SPC provisions in such circumstances, thereby transferring responsibility for the relevant employees to the new service provider, was considered to be in line with the employment protection objectives of TUPE—perhaps optimistically it was considered that to do so would maximize the possibility of those employees who do not have the relevant skills retaining their jobs by having the opportunity to be retrained or reallocated elsewhere in the new contractor's business.

On this analysis, a transferee inheriting employees (or liability for them) in such circum- **3.26** stances would, not least in order to minimize the risk of unfair dismissal claims and liability for termination payments, seek alternative positions for those employees or provide training in order to avoid or reduce the termination costs associated with the transfer and related technological or other changes. Moreover, a level playing field would be created in relation to retendering exercises thereby increasing 'certainty and confidence for all concerned'.[48]

Whilst the 2006 Regulations did not incorporate a specific provision dealing with the appli- **3.27** cation of regulation 3(1)(b) to so-called innovative bids, the case law on regulation 3(1)(b) has nonetheless allowed for changes to the method of delivery of the activities in question potentially to take a change of service provider outside the scope of regulation 3(1)(b) where the activities in question are no longer essentially or fundamentally the same.

A question central to the issues of whether there is the requisite organised grouping of **3.28** employees, whether the relevant activities cease to be conducted by one person and are then conducted by another person, and the application of the exclusions from the scope of the SPC provisions of TUPE in relation to the supply of goods, single specific events, or tasks of short-term duration is the proper identification of the activities which are the subject of a putative SPC. As the EAT commented in *Argyll Coastal Services Ltd v Stirling and others*:

> it seems plain from the terms of both regulation 3(1)(b) and 3(3)(a)(i) that Parliament, by using the word 'activities' had in mind considering what it was that the client required of the transferor or employer. What exactly was the service that was contracted for?[49]

---

[46] Ibid. at para. 22.
[47] 2005 Consultation paras 27 and 28.
[48] Ibid.
[49] UKEATS/0012/11 at para. 20 per Lady Smith.

3.29 This question is a factual matter for the ET. As the EAT put it in *Ward Hadaway v Love and others*,[50] 'the judgment as to the character and the quantity of the work and the nature of the service [are] all matters of fact for [the Tribunal] to decide'.

3.30 Leaving aside the exceptions in respect of one-off short-term contracts and the supply of goods,[51] the test of whether there is an SPC in a given situation is based principally upon there being an organised grouping of employees principally dedicated to servicing the relevant function and there being a change to the identity of the person performing or providing the activities in question. Regulation 3(1)(b) and its supplementary provisions do not expressly require that the activities which are the subject of an alleged SPC retain their identity on transfer. This is in contrast to the position in relation to a transfer of an undertaking for the purposes of regulation 3(1)(a) where the economic entity must retain its identity.[52] The decision not to exclude innovative bids[53] from the scope of regulation 3(1)(b) could be argued to indicate that changes to the mode of operation or delivery of the relevant activities should not take the contract award in question outside the scope of regulation 3(1)(b). Moreover, the Consultation Response set out the Government's view that '[t]here is no implied requirement for... activities to be carried out by the transferee in an identical manner'.[54] Against this background, it could be argued that to interpret the SPC provisions to entail a strict requirement of retention of identity of the relevant activities post transfer was not what was intended when regulation 3(1)(b) was formulated.

3.31 No specific definitions of the concepts of services or activities are provided in TUPE 2006 from which guidance can be gleaned as to whether the activities in question must remain identical after the putative transfer for there to be an SPC. However, it is the need for the activities which are the subject of the putative SPC to be conducted before and after the relevant event which has enabled it to be argued that there is no SPC where the activities in question are not fundamentally or essentially the same or similar after the putative SPC, or where the services are fragmented sufficiently during the process of transferring them to various new service providers to take the relevant arrangements outside the scope of the SPC provisions.

3.32 In *Metropolitan Resources Ltd v Churchill Dulwich Ltd (in liquidation) and others*[55] HHJ Burke QC expressed the view that ETs will inevitably be faced with arguments that the activities carried on by the alleged transferee are not identical to those carried on by the alleged transferor because there are detailed differences in the manner in which the service is performed. Nonetheless, he took the view that it cannot have been intended that minor differences between the nature of the tasks carried on or the way in which they are performed should disapply the application of the SPC provisions. More particularly, HHJ Burke QC indicated that a difference in location is highly unlikely on its own to be determinative against the existence of an SPC. Similarly unlikely to disapply the SPC provisions is the addition of some new duty or function unless the addition is of such substance that the activity is no longer essentially the same as before. Whether, in relation to the SPC provisions, the

---

[50] UKEAT/0471/09 at para. 28.
[51] See paras 3.98 and 3.109 respectively.
[52] See Chapter 2, para. 2.43 *et seq.*
[53] See para. 3.24 above.
[54] At para. 2.7.
[55] [2009] IRLR 190, EAT at para. 26.

putative transferee is performing essentially the same activity as the putative transferor is a question of fact for the ET to assess on the evidence before it in each case. As HHJ Burke QC said:

> A common sense and pragmatic approach is required to enable a case in which problems of this nature arise to be appropriately decided, and as was adopted by the Tribunal in this case. The Tribunal needs to ask itself whether the activities carried on by the alleged transferee are fundamentally or essentially the same as those carried out by the alleged transferor. And the answer to that question will be one of fact and degree to be assessed by the Tribunal on the evidence of the individual case before it.[56]

This approach is consistent with the analysis of Elias LJ in *McCarrick v Hunter*[57] where he **3.33** stated that 'it may be necessary not to be too pedantic with respect to the question whether the activities carried on before and after the transfer are sufficiently similar to amount to the same service'.[58]

An example of where a change to the activities in question took a retendering exercise outside **3.34** the scope of regulation 3(1)(b) is *OCS Group UK Ltd v Jones and anor.*[59] OCS provided a catering service at BMW's Cowley site consisting of a central restaurant, four satellite food outlets, and a shop. After unsuccessful attempts at a renegotiation of the contract, BMW appointed MIS to provide food at the plant in place of OCS. The new arrangement involved the provision of five dry goods kiosks with no requirement to provide hot food at the satellites, in contrast to OCS's obligations. The claimant, a chef/supervisor at one of the satellites, argued that there was an SPC from OCS to MIS.

The ET found that the service which MIS provided was materially different from that pro- **3.35** vided by OCS—the claimant's role had changed from the chef providing a full canteen service to a sales assistant in a kiosk. The changes in the service were not minor (such as changes to menu options or the style of food). The service provided by MIS was sufficiently different that the requirements of regulation 3(1)(b) were not satisfied and therefore there was no SPC from OCS to MIS. The EAT found that the ET was entitled, in determining whether there was an SPC, to adopt the approach whereby it assessed the differences between the OCS contract and the MIS contract rather than take a more general view of whether the activities fitted into the same broad general category. An essential question in relation to an SPC is therefore 'whether the activities carried on by the transferee are fundamentally or essentially the same as those carried out by the alleged transferor, the question being one of fact and degree'.[60]

The issue of retention of identity in relation to SPCs was also addressed by the EAT in **3.36** *Nottinghamshire Healthcare and NHS Trust v Hamshaw and others*[61]. The ET had held that there

---

[56] *Metropolitan Resources Ltd*, above n.55, at para. 30. As was noted by Lady Smith in *Department for Education v Huke and anor* UKEAT/0080/12 in a footnote to para. 21, this approach has been followed in cases such as *OCS Group UK Ltd v Jones and anor* UKEAT/0038/09, *Ward Hadaway Solicitors v Love and others* UKEAT/0471/09, *Nottinghamshire Healthcare NHS Trust v Hamshaw and others* UKEAT/0037/11, *Enterprise Management Services Ltd v Connect-Up Ltd and others* [2012] IRLR 190, EAT and *Johnson Controls Ltd v Campbell and anor* UKEAT/0041/12, which decisions are discussed below.

[57] *McCarrick v Hunter* [2013] IRLR 26, CA.

[58] Ibid. at para. 22.

[59] UKEAT/0038/09.

[60] Ibid. at para. 21.

[61] UKEAT/0037/11.

was no SPC where residents of an NHS Trust care home were rehoused in individual homes and the care workers previously employed at the care home were offered employment by the second or third respondents, mostly to sleep at the homes of the users of the care service. Continuing care provision was delivered by what was described as a 'multi-agency commission led model' service. This constituted what the ET found to be fundamental changes from the care home regime operated prior to the putative transfer—each resident was moved from an institutional setting to their own house, structured and personally focused care plans were introduced, and each resident was discharged from the care of the NHS Trust. The services provided before and after the reorganization were not fundamentally or essentially the same. The EAT held that the ET had been entitled to reach this decision.

3.37 *Johnson Controls Ltd v Campbell and anor* [62] concerned a situation where a centralized taxi booking administration service was taken back in-house by the client and thereafter was no longer conducted on a centralized basis. Before the change the claimant employee was an administrator who by way of his duties had taken bookings, advised on taxi timings, reviewed bookings dates, ensured efficient allocation of pick-ups, allocated jobs to subcontractors, checked and entered onto his employer's database the cost of subcontractors, checked suppliers, and assigned security passes to suppliers. After the change, secretaries employed by the alleged transferee dealt with the booking of taxis directly rather than utilizing the services of the taxi booking service administrator.

3.38 The EAT held that the ET had been entitled to find that the service as operated after the change was essentially a different activity, not least as the centralized nature of the service no longer continued. Consequently, the finding that there was therefore no SPC (back to the client) in these circumstances was upheld. The secretaries who now dealt with taxi-related matters for the alleged transferee did not conduct the activity which the administrator had—his activity no longer existed and was not retained by the client. A service can, as the ET had indicated, be 'more than the sum total of the list of activities or tasks'[63] and the EAT noted that:

> identifying what an activity is involves a holistic assessment by the Tribunal. The Tribunal is trusted to make that assessment. Its evaluation will be alert to possibilities of manipulation, but it is not simply to be decided by enumerating tasks and identifying whether the majority of those tasks quantitatively is the same as the majority was prior to the putative transfer.[64]

3.39 In *SNR Denton LLP v Kirwan and anor*,[65] a putative transferee argued that the purpose of the activities needed to be taken into account when considering whether the activities in question remained the same after an alleged SPC. In this case the legal work conducted by the employee was transferred from her employer to a firm of solicitors instructed by the joint administrators of the employer. The fact that the relevant activities were now being conducted in the context of an administration was argued to colour the nature of the activities as the administrator acts in the interests of the creditors rather than the company itself. It was therefore contended that, in its consideration of whether there was an SPC, the ET had been in error in only looking at the nature of the legal work in question before and after the

---

[62] UKEAT/0041/12.
[63] Ibid. at para. 19.
[64] Ibid. at para. 18.
[65] UKEAT/0158/12.

putative transfer and not taking into account the changed purpose of the activities and the service provider engaged to perform them.

This ground of appeal was rejected on the basis that the ET had reached a decision which was **3.40** open to it as a matter of fact to the effect that the activities in question were the same following the putative transfer, although Langstaff P did observe as follows:[66]

> As to 'activities', the common use of the word is to describe what is being done. If there is a relevant distinction between the nature of activities and the purpose of them, it is to the nature of the activities that the statute primarily looks. There may be some cases in which the purpose of the activities is such that the whole nature of the activities is shaped by that purpose, such that activities with that purpose may be said to be distinct from similar activities with a very different purpose, but it cannot in my view be said that this is necessarily such a case; the conclusion to which the Tribunal came in respect of activities was a conclusion of fact, it was within the scope of permissible findings of fact and degree, and there seems to be nothing wrong in concluding that the activity of disposing of the contracts was the same essentially whether performed by the Claimant in-house or by Dentons outsourced. I therefore reject that ground of appeal.

Diminution in the volume of work may also be a contra-indication of the relevant activities **3.41** remaining fundamentally or essentially the same and therefore of there being an SPC. As the EAT put it in *Department for Education v Huke and anor*[67] 'changes in volume of work are relevant when considering whether or not "the activities" carried out by the client on his own behalf from the point of change are "the activities" which were, immediately before the change, being carried out by the "organised grouping of employees"'. More particularly, 'where the volume of work undergoes a substantial diminution, it may lead to the conclusion that the activities being carried out are not essentially the same as before, even if the same categories of work apply'.[68]

E. Multiple Transferees and Fragmentation

Where an outsourcing or retendering entails the conduct of activities being transferred to **3.42** more than one new service provider the crucial factual question will be whether there is an SPC or SPCs of identifiable parts of the relevant activities to the new service providers or whether the activities become so fragmented that the SPC provisions do not apply.

Regulation 3(1)(b) does not explicitly address the situation where activities are divided between **3.43** new service providers on what would otherwise be an SPC. While it was not expressly stated by the DTI (as it then was) that it considered there can still be an SPC where pre-transfer activities are divided on a contract award, that view was implicit in the position adopted in the Consultation Response. In defending its use of the term 'activities' in formulating regulation

---

[66] Ibid. at para. 22.
[67] UKEAT/0080/12 per Lady Smith at para. 32.
[68] Ibid. at para. 35. A contrasting decision is *London Borough of Islington v Bannon and anor* UKEAT/0221/12. The EAT held that the ET was entitled to have found that there was an SPC, even if not all the activities carried out by the transferor were carried out after the putative SPC because of lack of resources or the fact that the transfer occurred at short notice. HHJ McMullen QC, who considered that the situation where the activities in question were not precisely the same after an alleged SPC as before is as 'not uncommon', observed that '[w]hen a canteen changes hands, the work may decline because people may not want to go to the new provider; it does not change the character of the service being provided or of the activities being provided just because on accepting the change not all of the activities can be carried out' (at para.34).

3(1)(b),[69] the DTI indicated that it considered that the approach adopted in *Fairhurst Ward Abbotts v Botes Building Ltd and others*[70] in relation to transfers of undertakings[71] was equally applicable to SPCs. Whilst not argued in detail, it seems that the DTI's view was that, if on a transfer of an undertaking for the purposes of regulation 3(1)(a) a separate economic entity can emerge for the first time, there is no reason why divided activities cannot lead to SPCs to the various contractors who take over different parts of the pre-transfer activities carried on by the relevant organized grouping of employees.[72]

3.44 The 2009 Guidance further indicates the view of BIS that this is the correct interpretation, stating[73] that the SPC provisions also potentially cover situations where just some of those activities in the original service contract are retendered and awarded to a new contractor, or where the original service contract is split into two or more components, each of which is assigned to a different contractor. On this analysis, in each of these cases, the key test is whether an organized grouping has as its principal purpose the carrying out of the activities that are transferred.

3.45 The case law on SPCs has nonetheless established that on an outsourcing or retendering the relevant activities can become so fragmented amongst various service providers that there is no SPC. The application of regulation 3(1)(b) when activities transfer to more than one new employer was considered in *Kimberley Group Housing Ltd v Hambley and others*[74] in which the claimant employees had been employed by an organization, Leena, which provided accommodation for asylum seekers pursuant to a Home Office contract. Leena provided some 140 properties in Middlesbrough and fifty in Stockton. On losing the relevant contract, the services in question were awarded to and conducted by two different organizations, Kimberley Group Housing and Angel Services. As between the two new providers, 97 per cent of the operations in Stockton and 71 per cent of the Middlesbrough function transferred to Kimberley and the balance to Angel Services. Neither potential transferee organization accepted that regulation 3(1)(b) applied to their assumption of the relevant part of the functions previously conducted by Leena. This decision demonstrates the proper approach to be taken in assessing the position of the employees where a service is divided between transferees in relation to an SPC, and also paved the way for subsequent arguments that the fragmentation of a service can mean that there is no SPC.

3.46 The ET concluded that there was no transfer of undertaking for the purposes of regulation 3(1)(a) not least by virtue of the lack of asset transfer as between the outgoing and incoming service providers. However, the ET did hold that these circumstances did constitute SPCs to the two new contractors. The activities in question were found to be 'the provision of suitable accommodation and related support to asylum seekers in Middlesbrough and separately in Stockton'. Comments in the EAT's judgment indicate that there might have been scope for greater argument over the identification of the relevant activities and indeed that the result might have been different had, for example, the relevant activities been analysed/identified as 'maintenance functions'.[75] However, this aspect of the ET's judgment was not challenged before the EAT.

---

[69] As opposed to other concepts which consultees had suggested such as 'function' or 'service' (see Consultation Response para. 2.6).

[70] [2004] IRLR 304, CA—see Chapter 2, para. 2.65 *et seq.*

[71] For the purposes of what is now regulation 3(1)(a).

[72] See Consultation Response para. 2.7.

[73] At p. 6.

[74] *Kimberley Group Housing Ltd v Hambley and others; Angel Services (UK) Ltd v Hambley and others* [2008] IRLR 682, EAT; see Wynn-Evans, 'Service Provision Fragmentation and the Limits of TUPE Protection' (2008) 37 ILJ 371.

[75] Ibid. at para. 28.

On appeal, the EAT rejected the argument that regulation 3(1)(b) can only apply where **3.47** there is one transferee. By reference to the case law relating to transfers of undertakings and the Interpretation Act 1978, s. 6,[76] the EAT held that there could be an SPC where functions are divided to more than one transferee. It should be uncontroversial that an SPC can arise on a division of activities which otherwise falls within the scope of regulation 3(1)(b). As well as enabling avoidance, to find otherwise would be inconsistent both with the prior case law in relation to transfers of undertakings and the Government's indication in the 2006 Guidance that regulation 3(1)(b) applies where an original service contract is divided into two or more components and its statement[77] that the SPC concept would 'potentially cover situations . . . where the original contract is split up into two or more components, each of which is assigned to a different contractor'.

The question then arose of the position of the employees in relation to an SPC to more than **3.48** one transferee, especially where the employees had not been taken on by any transferee and therefore sought to claim unfair dismissal. The EAT reviewed a number of possible approaches which had been considered by the ET as to the proper resolution of the issue of how employment liabilities should be allocated when an SPC is to more than one trans- feree. One approach identified by the ET was to make an arbitrary allocation of the affected employees as between the two potential transferees. The ET (understandably) considered this approach to be absurd, a view with which the EAT tended to agree, although the argu- ment was not pursued on appeal. Another possible analysis was that the transferee which took over the greater part of the transferor's activities could be held to be responsible for all the employees in question. The ET considered this to be an unfair approach that would be stifling of competition and enterprise as well as only being operable retrospectively. The analysis which the ET did actually adopt was to the effect that, while the employees and their contracts of employment could not be 'split', the associated liabilities with regard to their dismissals could be divided on a percentage basis by reference to the proportion of the relevant functions which each new contractor took over.

In allowing an appeal against this finding, the EAT gave short shrift to what it described **3.49** as the ET's 'creative option', intended to achieve an equitable distribution of liabilities, of allocating dismissal-related liabilities on a percentage basis as between the new operators of the relevant functions. The EAT viewed this 'proportionate' approach as 'truly novel', unwarranted in statute and common law terms and without precedent. In its view there could be no justification for treating the application of regulation 3(1)(b) to liabilities for transfer-related dismissals differently from its application to employees who were retained by the transferee or transferees. The ET's analysis was viewed as entirely inconsistent with the established principle[78] that an employee cannot be the servant of two masters at the same time, especially where those employers are in competition. Just as employees cannot be split between transferee employers, dismissal-related liabilities cannot be so divided.

The EAT concluded that, once an SPC has been established to have taken place, the proper **3.50** approach is to apply the test of assignment in order to establish to which of the contractors who have assumed the relevant activities employees should transfer. The guidance provided

---

[76] Which provides that in any Act, unless the contrary intention appears, words in the singular include the plural.
[77] 2006 Guidance at p. 7, a statement repeated in the 2009 Guidance at p. 6.
[78] See *SO Bernicia* [1989] 1 AC 643.

by the ECJ in *Botzen v Rotterdamsche Droogdok Maatschappij BV*[79] and its associated cases might be difficult to apply in particular cases but provided the basis for establishing which transferee would inherit the relevant employees and/or liabilities. The EAT considered the overall principle to be clear—what is to be focused upon is essentially the link between the employee and the work or activities which are to be performed. Had this approach been adopted, the relevant employees would have been found to have transferred to Kimberley Group Housing on the basis of the relevant percentages of work transferred. The EAT accordingly substituted a finding to this effect.

3.51 In reaching these conclusions, the EAT considered that for the ET to have criticized the assignment approach, on grounds of unfairness in terms of its effect on competition and enterprise, was erroneously to focus on the effect of the legislation on employers, as opposed to on employees, and to fail to recognize the protective nature of the legislation. In addition, to argue that the test could only be applied with hindsight was also seen as untenable given, as was the case in these proceedings, the fact that specific functional responsibilities are often allocated as between particular successful contractors at the point of contracting.

3.52 Presaging the arguments deployed in subsequent cases, the EAT also made the point that there may be circumstances in which a service is 'in the event so fragmented that nothing which one can properly determine as a service provision change has taken place'.[80]

3.53 That fragmentation of the activities in question may lead to there being no SPC is demonstrated by *Thomas-James v Cornwall County Council*.[81] In this case, seventeen contractors provided free legal advice to telephone callers under contracts awarded by the Legal Services Commission. On a retendering exercise, the number of contractors was reduced to nine. The issue before the ET was whether any of the employees who were engaged by a contractor whose services were dispensed with transferred to one of the remaining contractors pursuant to regulation 3(1)(b). Although an organised grouping of employees was held to have existed for the purposes of regulation 3(1)(b) prior to the putative transfer, the ET considered that there was no SPC because it was not possible to identify to which new service providers specific functions conducted by predecessor contractors had transferred. It has to be said that this ET decision reflects a materially different situation from that in *Hambley* where it was clear that the major proportion of work had transferred to Kimberley Group Housing, thereby enabling a transferee to be identified and the assignment test to be operated. By contrast, in *Thomas-James*, there was, as the ET put it, no nexus between any of the transferors and any particular transferee. Factors indicating this lack of connection to a particular transferee included the facts that telephone calls were allocated randomly between contractors, the percentage of the service provided pre and post transfer could not be compared directly due to the change in number of contractors, and the allocation of hours was not uniform amongst the outgoing and incoming contractors. As the ET put it, had the activities been defined by location or alphabetically or in some other way and been allocated to the new contractors according to that definition then the answer might have been different.

---

[79] [1985] ECR 519, ECJ—see Chapter 4, para. 4.36 *et seq* for further discussion.
[80] *Kimberley Group Housing*, above n. 74, at para. 35.
[81] ET cases numbers 1701021-22, 1701230-31, 1701051, and 1701059/07.

A further example of fragmentation of the relevant activities leading to there being no SPC is *Clearsprings Management Ltd v Ankers and anor*.[82] As was the case in *Kimberley*, the case concerned the provision of accommodation and support services to asylum seekers. On a retendering exercise, three new contractors were awarded contracts for the provision of such services in the north-west of England in place of the previous incumbent contractor, Clearsprings. The question was whether the employment of seventeen of the employees of the outgoing contractor, Clearsprings, was protected by TUPE by way of an SPC. **3.54**

The EAT dismissed an appeal against the ET's decision that the activity carried out by *Clearsprings* was so fragmented as a result of the retendering that there was no SPC. The fact pattern was materially different from that in *Kimberley* where the bulk of the relevant activities previously carried on by the transferor had transferred to one of the two potential transferees, thereby constituting an SPC. In *Clearsprings*, it was not possible to determine to which new contractor the work carried on by Clearsprings' employees had been transferred. The EAT commented as follows: **3.55**

> The allocation of [service users] to individual Claimants...showed no discernible pattern of re-allocation to the incoming contractors. In short, we accept the submissions...that on their findings of primary fact this Employment Tribunal was entitled to conclude that the activity carried on by Clearsprings was so fragmented that no relevant transfer took place, applying Regulation 3(1)(b) read with Regulation 3(3).[83]

Another example of circumstances in which a change in the nature of the activities in question and their fragmentation meant that there was no SPC is *Enterprise Management Services Ltd v Connect-Up Ltd and others*.[84] In 2004 Leeds City Council put out to tender the IT support services which it supplied to schools for which it had responsibility and granted preferred provider status to Enterprise. During the currency of the contract, the number of schools utilizing the service offered by Enterprise reduced to some 80 per cent and only twenty of 240 opted for the total maintenance support option offered as distinct from the option offered of full support for management information systems software. On expiry of the initial framework agreement, Enterprise declined to bid and Connect-Up successfully tendered, entering subsequently into a new framework agreement on the day before the new contract went into effect. In the ensuing period a variety of providers were appointed by schools within the scope of the framework agreement. Enterprise dismissed the claimants. **3.56**

The ET found that the omission from the scope of the new contract of curriculum work, representing some 15 per cent of the work done by the Enterprise staff who had been dedicated to the service provided to the relevant Leeds County Council Schools, meant that the activities carried out by Connect-Up were not essentially or fundamentally the same as those carried out by Enterprise. Moreover, even though Connect-Up was appointed as a preferred supplier in place of Enterprise, the ET found that the provision of the relevant services was, under the new arrangements, so spread out between Connect-Up and five other suppliers who over time were appointed by schools to provide services that there was no SPC. The EAT rejected an appeal against this finding on the basis that the ET had been entitled to make these findings by way of its factual determinations and that, taking the issues of altered **3.57**

---

[82] UKEAT/0054/08.
[83] Ibid. at para. 18.
[84] [2012] IRLR 190, EAT.

activities and fragmentation together, the ET's decision that there was no SPC was not perverse. HHJ Judge Peter Clark was:

> satisfied that the Judge was entitled to conclude, as a matter of fact and degree, that the omission of curriculum work, representing, it is common ground, some 15 per cent of the work done by the organised grouping of Enterprise employees dedicated to the LCC schools service, meant that the activities carried out by Connect were not essentially or fundamentally the same as those carried on by Enterprise[85]

and held that '. . . the Employment Judge was entitled to conclude that post [the transfer] the provision of services formerly provided by Enterprise were so spread amongst other providers as well as Connect that no SPC had taken place on that basis'.[86]

3.58   It has been suggested that this decision does not fit easily with the Government guidance on TUPE 2006 which suggests that there will be a SPC even where only part of the relevant activities transfer. This critique arguably fails to appreciate that the ET's decision in cases of this sort is inevitably fact-sensitive and that in this decision it was the combined effect of the issues both of materially changed activities and fragmentation which led to there being no SPC. Nonetheless, it is important to appreciate that the issue of whether pre- and post-transfer activities are the same or essentially the same is one of fact for the ET to determine and may provoke attempts to categorize an outsourcing, retendering, or in-housing as one of two distinguishable types of situations depending on the relevant party's interest in the outcome—a transfer of part of the activities which constitutes an SPC or a fragmentation which does not.

F. Activities Must Transfer—Work in Progress?

3.59   *Ward Hadaway v Love and others*[87] addressed the operation of the SPC concept in the specific context of where, by way of transition to a new service provider, the client refers or awards discrete pieces of work to the outgoing and incoming service providers. When the Nursing and Midwifery Council (NMC) awarded a new contract for future solicitors' regulatory work to the solicitors' firm Capsticks in place of Ward Hadaway, there was found to be no SPC because none of Ward Hadaway's existing work in progress was transferred. The EAT upheld the ET's decision to this effect.

3.60   The contract in question entailed the relevant solicitors being the recipients of referrals of legal work from the NMC—there being no obligation upon the NMC to award work to the firm or for the firm to accept it. In one six-month period, for example, no work had been provided to Ward Hadaway. When Capsticks was appointed as a single provider of the relevant services to the NMC, to an extent the work to be done was different to that carried on by Ward Hadaway in that much 'post-preparation work' previously conducted by Ward Hadaway and other panel firms was taken in-house by the NMC. Moreover, despite the cessation of its contract with the NMC in 2007, Ward Hadaway retained some 100 to 140 cases which entailed work for at least six months following Capsticks' appointment as preferred

---

[85]   Ibid. at para. 15.
[86]   Ibid. at para. 16.
[87]   UKEAT/0471/09.

providers. Some time after the alleged SPC, two major cases were still being handled by Ward Hadaway.

It was accepted that, for the purposes of regulation 3(1)(b), there was, prior to the putative **3.61** SPC, an organised grouping of employees at Ward Hadaway whose principal purpose was carrying out the relevant activities on behalf of the NMC. In relation to the identification of the relevant activities, the ET distinguished between work in progress and the expectation of future work. Only the work in progress constituted activities actually conducted by Ward Hadaway prior to the putative SPC and it was these activities which did not transfer. There was therefore no SPC because no activities conducted by the putative transferor were then conducted by the putative transferee.

In a decision which demonstrates the need carefully to analyse and identify the activities in **3.62** question as well as the need for them to transfer—in the sense of there being a change in the person who conducts them—the EAT put it as follows:

> The first issue is to decide what the Tribunal was doing when it was looking at the activities. There is some uncertainty in paragraph 60 of its Judgment for on its own it indicates that the Tribunal regarded the activities as including both work in progress and expected work. The clear findings in the succeeding paragraphs put that beyond doubt. The Tribunal was here deciding a question of fact. It had already decided one important fact. Ward Hadaway had been able to carry out the work in progress in 2005 while not expecting or taking new work. Although the Tribunal's finding on this simply says no new cases were allocated, we have been told it was beyond its capacity to deal with any more work during that six month period. Thus, if it were true that the activities carried on by Ward Hadaway included the availability for new work, the activity of doing the work in progress continued unabated when the availability dried up temporarily. That was a fact which the Tribunal had in its mind when looking at the expectation of work. We did give anxious consideration to the possibility that this was, like the *OCS* case, a question of law. The application of regulation 3(1) to those facts was a matter of law. But it was open to the Tribunal to conclude that activities were not so extensive. Indeed, the proposition that the activity includes, however loosely it is put, the availability of Ward Hadaway to do work for NMC, pointed towards an economic entity on the lines of old TUPE. We can see that a firm of solicitors would provide solicitors to do work, office equipment, professional indemnity insurance, CPD, access to legal resources and so on, in the hope that they might attract work, or even where there is a strong relationship, as there is here, that they might expect work. That could itself be an activity which could be transferred, but it looks to us more like an economic entity than a service provision. It is at most the opportunity to be on standby should NMC refer a case. We hold that, while it is arguable that that constituted part of the activities, the Tribunal cannot be faulted in its clear decision that the activities for the purposes of a service provision change were the work in progress.[88]

G. Who is the Client?

As can be seen from cases like *Ward Hadaway*, where the awarding client for the purposes of **3.63** the SPC provisions was the NMC, as opposed to the recipients of the legal services in question, a potentially crucial issue in determining whether there is an SPC in any given set of circumstances will be the correct identification of the client for the purposes of regulation 3(1)(b). The identification of the client is also crucial to the issue of whether the client

---

[88] Ibid. at para. 27.

remains the same, which *McCarrick*[89] clarifies is required for there to be an SPC following the change to the identity of the person conducting the relevant activities.

3.64 In *Nottinghamshire Healthcare and NHS Trust v Hamshaw and others*[90] a care home was closed and residents rehoused in properties provided by a housing association. The ET identified the client for the purposes of considering whether there was an SPC as the residents of the home—the beneficiaries of the relevant activities. The EAT considered that this was incorrect:

> [T]he client is the person who is carrying out the activities before or after the transfer as the case may be and on whose behalf (not 'for whose benefit') the activities are carried out. Moreover…the 'client' is the person who makes the decision about transfer since by regulation 3(3)(b) it is necessary for a service provision change that the client must intend that the activities, following the change, will be carried out by the transferor.[91]

3.65 Similarly, in *Enterprise Management Services Ltd v Connect-Up Ltd*,[92] the transferor and transferee provided IT support to schools pursuant to framework agreements which they had entered into with Leeds County Council. The client was held to be the Council awarding the contracts rather than the schools to which the relevant services were ultimately provided.[93]

3.66 Likewise, in *Metropolitan Resources v Churchill Dulwich Ltd (in liquidation) and others*,[94] the client was the charitable organization, Migrant Helpline, which entered into contracts with providers of accommodation for asylum seekers rather than the asylum seekers themselves who received the accommodation or indeed the Home Office with whom Migrant Helpline had a contract to provide the relevant accommodations.

H. Client Must Remain the Same

3.67 A potentially crucial aspect of the proper interpretation of regulation 3(1)(b) was addressed in *Hunter v McCarrick*[95]—whether the SPC provisions can apply in the situation where the client and the service provider change simultaneously. In *Nottinghamshire Healthcare and NHS Trust v Hamshaw and others*[96] the possibility had been canvassed but not determined that there might be no SPC in such circumstances and the EAT and a Court of Appeal agreed with this proposition in *Hunter*. By way of a simplistic overview of a complex set of facts, the employee had been employed to manage a property portfolio. Receivers were appointed by the mortgagee of the relevant properties and then took over control of that property portfolio. At the same time a replacement property manager was appointed.

3.68 The EAT held that, for there to be an SPC within the meaning of regulation 3(1)(b)(ii) by way of a retendering, the activities carried out by different contractors before and after the putative transfer must be carried out for the same client. A decision of the ET that there had

---

[89] [2012] IRLR 274, EAT; [2013] IRLR 26, CA; see para. 3.67 *et seq.*
[90] UKEAT/0037/11.
[91] Ibid. at para. 25.
[92] [2009] IRLR 190, EAT, discussed in relation to the issue of change of activities at para. 3.56.
[93] Ibid. at para. 8.
[94] [2009] IRLR 190, EAT.
[95] Above n. 89.
[96] UKEAT/0037/11 at paras 25–7.

been an SPC where there was a change of client as well as a change of contractor was overturned on appeal. In reaching this conclusion, the EAT noted the prior lack of authority on the issue of whether the references in regulation 3(1)(b) to 'a client' and the client are (or, for there to be an SPC, must be) to the same person and approvingly referred to the analysis of the purpose of regulation 3(1)(b) set out by the HHJ Burke QC in *Metropolitan Resources Ltd v Churchill Dulwich Ltd (in liquidation) and others*[97] in declining to adopt purposive interpretation of the SPC provisions.[98]

The EAT rejected the contention that regulation 3 is intended to preserve employees' terms **3.69** and conditions and continuity of employment in circumstances in which the activities in relation to which they are engaged by one contractor are carried out by a different contractor and for a different client. There was no indication of that being the intention of regulation 3(1)(b). The reference to the client in regulation 3(1)(b)(ii) was seen as referring back to the specific client, i.e. the client for whom the previous contractor carried out the relevant activities. The transferring activities must be performed for the same client before and after the putative transfer, i.e. the specific client on whose behalf the contractor originally carried out the activities. The EAT considered that there was no authority for arguing that 'a client' and 'the client' in regulation 3(1)(b)(ii) could refer to different persons.

As the EAT put it in *Hunter*: **3.70**

> In our judgment 'the client' in regulation 3(1)(b)(ii) refers back to a specific client. The specific client referred to earlier in the provision is the client on whose behalf the transferor contractor carried out activities. The use of the definite article 'the' must refer back to 'any client'. Regulation 3(1)(b)(i) applies to contracting out activities which were carried out by the client himself, 'a client', and are to be carried out on 'the client's' behalf by another person. Similar wording, 'a client' and 'the client', is used in Regulation 3(1)(b)(iii) dealing with contracting in. There is no warrant for giving the words 'a client' and 'the client' different meanings in the different subparagraphs of regulation 3(1)(b). As in regs 3(1)(b)(i) and (iii), 'the client' in reg 3(1)(b)(ii) is the same client as 'a client'.[99]

In *Hunter* the ET had found there to have been two SPCs affecting the claimant and his **3.71** colleagues. The property management services which they provided were the subject of an SPC in February 2009—this much was uncontroversial. The ET also held that there was a second SPC when the ownership of the properties in relation to which the claimants worked transferred to new ownership and the new owner engaged new property managers. As the client (the owner of the properties) changed as well as the property management contractor, the EAT held that the ET had erred in finding that there had been an SPC at this (second) stage. The principle established by *Hunter* limits the scope of SPCs significantly, for example in the property arena, where management agreements are replaced on change of ownership of the relevant properties.[100]

Hunter was followed and applied in *Taurus Group Ltd v Crofts and anor*,[101] a case which **3.72** considered the application of regulation 3(1)(b) in the context of the change of ownership of a building at which security services were provided. Mr Crofts was one of two security staff

---

[97] [2009] IRLR 190, EAT.
[98] See para. 3.19 *et seq.*
[99] *Hunter*, above n. 89, at para. 25.
[100] See 3.74 et seq. for consideration of the Court of Appeal decision.
[101] UKEAT/0024/12.

employed by a company called Reliance to provide security services at a building called the Glasshouse in Nottingham. Following the insolvency of the original owner of the property, the new owner appointed a new security contractor, Taurus. The ET accepted the employee's contention that, for regulation 3(1)(b) to apply, the client did not have to stay the same on a change of service providers, the rationale for the decision appearing to be that to require the client to remain the same would cause individuals in circumstances such as those in which Mr Crofts found himself to lose the protection of TUPE, thereby undermining its purpose of employee protection.

3.73   Before the EAT, Taurus, as the putative transferee, relied on *Hunter* as disposing of the issue while Mr Crofts argued that *Hunter* was wrongly decided and at the rights of employees would not be protected in a straightforward scenario where the SPC concept would have been expected to apply given its objective of introducing clarity and certainty.[102] The EAT held that it should follow *Hunter* on the basis that '[a]s a general rule, the Appeal Tribunal will follow its own decisions, particularly where they are considered decisions after argument on the point, and where there are no conflicting appellate decisions'.[103] Mr Crofts' attempt to distinguish *Hunter* also failed. Put shortly, on the facts as found by the ET, the new owner did not (as Mr Crofts sought to argue) become the client prior to the putative SPC which it was contended occurred when Reliance was replaced by Taurus—if the client had changed before the change of contractor then the *Hunter* principle would not have engaged.[104]

3.74   In any event, the approach adopted by the EAT to the interpretation of regulation 3(1)(b) in *Hunter* was approved by the Court of Appeal on a further appeal in that case. As Elias LJ put it, '[t]he language of regulation 3(1)(b) is only consistent with the situation where there is the same client throughout; and regulation 3(3), which focuses on the intention of the client, is premised on that same assumption.'[105] The appellant had argued that a purposive interpretation should be applied to regulation 3(1)(b) on the basis that it was a provision adopted under ERA 1999, s. 38[106] which enables regulations to be put in place making 'the same or similar provision in relation to the treatment of employees in such cases as are affected where business transfers occur'.[107] Consequently, it was argued that a broad interpretation of regulation 3(1)(b) was required to achieve the objective of ERA 1999, s. 38. In rejecting this argument the analysis of Elias LJ was as follows:

> I can see no basis for giving the language of regulation 3(1)(b) an artificial or expanded meaning. It would be quite illegitimate to rewrite the statutory provisions in the very broad way suggested by the appellant. This is domestic legislation and is not giving effect to EU law. Section 38(2) of the Employment Relations Act 1999 confers a power to make the regulations to provide the same or similar provision 'in relation to the treatment of employees in circumstances other than those to which the Community obligation applies'. That is precisely what the regulations do. The section does not, however, identify which employees should be afforded that treatment, and nothing in section 38 has any bearing at all on that question. The section does not advance the appellant's case.[108]

---

[102]   Ibid. para. 27.
[103]   Ibid. para. 28.
[104]   Ibid. paras 29–33.
[105]   *McCarrick v Hunter* [2013] IRLR 26, CA at para. 37.
[106]   See Chapter 1, para. 1.37 *et seq.*
[107]   *Hunter*, above n.105, at para. 21.
[108]   Ibid. at para. 37.

The proper identification of the client for the purposes of the SPC provisions is essential to   **3.75**
the proper application of the approach required by *Hunter*[109] and this point was considered
in the context of an administration in *SNR Denton LLP v Kirwan and anor.*[110] A solicitor
working for a facilities management company, the majority of whose work latterly involved
the disposal of service contracts due to the employer's financial difficulties, argued that there
was an SPC when the employer went into administration and the its joint administrators
appointed SNR Denton as solicitors to handle, inter alia, the work previously conducted by
the employee. The ET was found to have erred in finding that the client had remained the
same. It had not and therefore the principle in *Hunter* applied such that the ET's decision
that there was an SPC could not stand.

Determination of this issue necessitated the consideration of the precise basis of the   **3.76**
retainer of the solicitors instructed by the joint administrators. At the risk of oversimplify-
ing an analysis which involved detailed consideration of the relevant provisions of the IA
1986, and the agency basis upon which administrators make appointments, the question
was whether the firm of solicitors which was argued to be the transferee for the purposes
of the putative SPC was acting for the joint administrators (in which case it could be
argued that the client had changed) or whether they were acting for the company, albeit
engaged by the joint administrators as the company's agents (in which case the client had
not changed). The distinction which the putative transferee urged upon the EAT was
'between the administrators arranging by contract with a firm of solicitors for that firm of
solicitors to convey property on behalf of a company in administration (those solicitors
instructed by the administrators for the company would be acting on behalf of the company) and those solicitors appointed to advise and act for the administrators as administrators who ... would be acting on behalf of the administrators and not the company in
receivership or administration'.[111]

Langstaff P accepted 'that for solicitors engaged by retainer to act for the administrators to   **3.77**
be held to be acting on behalf of the company because the administrators are in the exercise
of many of their functions acting so as to bind the company could potentially bring those
solicitors into a situation of conflict that militates against the proposition being correct'.[112]
The ET was held to have erred in finding that the client had remained the same following the
putative SPC on the basis, as Langstaff P put it, that:

> on the facts of this case on this appeal the Tribunal was in error in concluding that merely
> because the administrator could act as agent, and in exercise of its functions as admin-
> istrator did act as agent, for the company, it meant that the solicitors retained by the
> administrator were themselves acting on behalf of the company when they acted in the
> administration. They might have been, but it could not be assumed that they necessarily
> did.[113]

---

[109] to the effect that the client must remain the same.
[110] [2012] IRLR 966, EAT.
[111] Ibid. at para. 39.
[112] Ibid. at para. 38.
[113] Ibid. at para. 39.

I. An Organised Grouping of Employees

1. General

3.78 In order for there to be an SPC for the purposes of regulation 3(1)(b), the relevant activity or activities must, before the putative SPC, be conducted by an 'organised grouping of employees situated in Great Britain which has as its principal purpose the carrying out of the activities concerned on behalf of the client'.[114] As the 2005 Consultation indicated,[115] this requirement confines the application of the concept of an SPC to situations where the incumbent service provider (which includes the client, where a service is being contracted out) operates the relevant activities by way of an identifiable team of employees that is essentially dedicated to meeting one particular client's needs. By way of overview, in *Argyll Coastal Services Ltd v Stirling and others*,[116] the EAT commented that:

> the phrase 'organised grouping of employees' connotes a number of employees which is less than the whole of the transferor's entire workforce, deliberately organised for the purpose of carrying out the activities required by the particular client contract and who work together as a team.[117]

3.79 Where there is no identifiable and organised group of employees assigned to a function or contract conducted for a particular client, an SPC for the purposes of regulation 3(1)(b) will not arise even if the identity of the provider of the service changes. Accordingly, adopting the example used by the 2005 Consultation,[118] courier services provided by various different couriers on an ad hoc basis to various clients would not fall within regulation 3(1)(b) but a permanently assigned team of couriers working for a particular client would transfer should a replacement contractor be appointed by that client.

3.80 The requirement that there be an organised grouping of employees not only in principle ensures that the relevant activities are sufficiently structured, stable, and identifiable that they can predictably fall within the general scope of the legislation consistent with its objectives. This requirement also renders the concept workable in terms of which employees should transfer on a change of service provider. As the 2009 Guidance noted, 'it would be unclear which employees should transfer in the event of a change of contractor, if there was no such grouping'.[119] The test of whether there is an organised grouping of employees for the purposes of regulation 3(1)(b) is applied immediately before the change.[120] That said, purposive arguments analogous to those deployed in *Litster*[121] would presumably be deployed by employees seeking to establish that they are protected by TUPE in relation to an SPC were, for example, a client to disband a dedicated group of staff in advance of an outsourcing deliberately in order to seek to avoid the application of regulation 3(1)(b). Whether it would be feasible to run such an argument in the face of the case law on SPCs which precludes a purposive interpretation remains to be seen.[122]

---

[114] Regulation 3(3)(a)(i).
[115] At para. 22.
[116] UKEATS/0012/11.
[117] Ibid. at para. 18 per Lady Smith.
[118] Ibid.
[119] At p. 9.
[120] Regulation 3(3)(a)(i).
[121] [1989] IRLR 161, HL. See Chapter 4, para. 4.25.
[122] See para. 3.19 *et seq.*

2. A group is not necessarily an organised grouping

In *Eddie Stobart Ltd v Moreman and others*[123] thirty-five employees worked for Eddie Stobart **3.81**
Ltd at its site in Manton, Nottinghamshire and claimed that on closure of that site their
contracts of employment transferred pursuant to regulation 4 to FJG Logistics Ltd, a logistics business which had taken over the work previously conducted by Eddie Stobart Ltd and
in relation to which the employees worked. By the time of closure, Eddie Stobart serviced
two clients, ASDA and Vion, from the Manton site and believed that Vion had arranged
for FJG Logistics to take over all the work done at the site. The ET determined that there
was no organised grouping of employees for the purposes of regulation 3(3)(a)(i). Whilst
the employees in question were spending all or most of their time on tasks necessitated by
the Vion contract, the organization of work at the site was based on a shift system and job
function rather than being referable to specific clients. This did not mean that there was an
organised grouping of employees—merely working for most of the time for a particular client did not satisfy this essential ingredient of an SPC.

The EAT held that the fact that a necessary precondition of an SPC is the existence of an **3.82**
organised grouping of employees whose principal purpose is the carrying out of the activities which transfer 'necessarily connotes that the employees be organised in some sense by
reference to the requirements of the client in question'.[124] That a group of employees 'may
in practice but without any deliberate planning or intent, be found to be working mostly on
tasks which benefitted a particular client'[125] does not satisfy the requirement that there be
such an organised grouping of employees. Part of the rationale for interpreting regulation
3(3)(a)(i) in this way was, as Underhill P put it, that:

> [i]f the putative grouping does not reflect any existing organisation or unit there are liable to be
> real practical difficulties in not identifying which employees belong to it. It is important that
> on a transfer employees should, so far as possible, 'know where they stand'.[126]

This decision demonstrates that a group of employees does not of itself necessarily constitute **3.83**
a grouping, let alone an organised grouping, of employees for these purposes. That said, the
EAT did note that regulation 3(3)(a)(i) can be satisfied where the identification or the relevant grouping is less explicit than what was described as the 'paradigm' where employees are
organised as 'the [Client's A] team'.[127] For these purposes, organization is required but can
exist without explicit client identification. Nonetheless, Underhill P's comments in *Eddie
Stobart* suggest that, for there to be an organised grouping of employees for these purposes,
there must be some design or intent behind the relevant employees' deployment to provide
services to the relevant client rather than it just being accidental or customary.

3. Groupings of one

Regulation 2(1) provides that 'references to "organised grouping of employees" shall include a **3.84**
single employee'.[128] As the Consultation Response put it,[129] '[s]ome contractual services—for

---

[123] [2012] IRLR 356, EAT.
[124] Ibid. at para. 18.
[125] Ibid.
[126] At para. 20.
[127] Ibid.
[128] This provision was not included in the original draft of what became TUPE 2006 but was added to
remove the uncertainty which would otherwise have resulted.
[129] At para. 2.8.

example, the cleaning of a relatively small office—are sometimes undertaken by just one person, and the Government accepts it would be unfair to deny rights to such individuals simply because they are single employee units'.

The 2009 Guidance echoed this point—'it should be noted that a "grouping of employees" can constitute just one person, as may happen, say, when the cleaning of a small business premises is undertaken by a single person employed by a contractor'.[130]

3.85   *Hunt v Storm Communications Ltd and others*[131] was an early ET decision with regard to SPCs which demonstrates the potential application of the SPC legislation to activities conducted by just one employee. Storm Communications lost an account to provide specialist PR services when the client took those services back in-house on a caretaker basis until a new agency was, only a couple of months later, appointed in its stead. An SPC was found to have occurred by way of a retendering for the purposes of regulation 3(1)(b)(ii). The claimant employee was found to satisfy the requirement that there be an organised grouping of employees as her principal purpose was the provision of the relevant services to the client. The SPC was held to have taken place on the date when the client dispensed with Storm's services, even though there was then a brief interregnum until the new agency was appointed.

3.86   The fact that there can be an SPC in relation to the activities carried out by an organised grouping of employees constituted by just one employee raises the prospect of there being SPCs in respect of separate individual employees who are dedicated to particular separate sets of activities where there is no wider organised grouping for the purposes of regulation 3(3)(i). Just because an employee works exclusively or predominantly on activities which transfer does not necessarily mean that the individual alone constitutes the requisite organised grouping, especially if the individual is in reality part of wider team which services a variety of clients. However, whether this is the case in a given situation entails the proper identification of the organised grouping of employees in question. Apparent assignment to a client's activities should not automatically be equated with the individual on his or her own constituting the requisite organised grouping. The test of whether there is an organised grouping of employees should not be conflated with the question of whether an employee is assigned to the relevant activities.

3.87   This point is demonstrated by *Seawell Ltd v Ceva Freight (UK) Ltd and anor*[132] in which Seawell was one of the clients of Ceva, a freight forwarding and management logistics business, and took in-house the service delivered to it by that service provider. The employee in question, Mr Moffat, was part of Ceva's 'outbound' team of eight staff and spent 100 per cent of his time on the relevant activities taken back in-house by Seawell, whereas certain of his colleagues spent between 10 per cent and 30 per cent of their time on those activities. The ET held that Mr Moffat himself was an organised grouping for the purposes of regulation 3(3)(i) on the basis that he was in charge of the activity in question and was responsible for ensuring that the service was provided effectively. Since there can be an organised grouping of one person, it was therefore not necessary to include in the organised grouping those colleagues who also worked on the relevant activity.

---

[130]   At p. 7.
[131]   ET case no. 2702546.
[132]   [2012] IRLR 802, EAT.

In the judgment of the EAT allowing an appeal, Lady Smith referred to her own comments **3.88** in *Argyll Coastal Services*[133] and those of Underhill P in *Eddie Stobart Ltd v Moreman and others*[134] and reiterated her view 'that the description "organised grouping of employees" connotes a deliberate putting together of a group of employees for the purpose of the relevant client work—it is not a matter of happenstance'.[135] As Lady Smith made clear, logically the identification of the organised grouping of employees comes before the question of whether an employee is or was assigned to it.[136]

The EAT allowed an appeal against the ET's finding that there was an SPC in these circum- **3.89** stances since the group of employees in which Mr Moffat worked conducted activities for a variety of clients—'whilst it does appear to have been a deliberately organised grouping of employees, there are no findings to indicate that it was organised for the purposes of the Seawell contract or that Seawell work was its principal purpose'.[137]

The EAT also concluded that it was not sufficient for the purposes of regulation 3(3)(i)— **3.90** and therefore for Mr Moffat to constitute the requisite organised grouping on his own— that he spent all his time on Seawell work. First, there was no indication, despite the fact that he worked exclusively on the relevant activities, that Ceva 'specifically formed a grouping consisting of Mr Moffat to carry out the Seawell work'.[138] Second, the ET was considered 'in effect [to have] concluded that because Mr Moffat spent 100 per cent of his time on Seawell work, he carried out 100 per cent of that work and [to be] illogical'.[139] As Lady Smith put it:[140]

> Reg 3(3)(i) requires that the organised grouping of employees carried out 'the activities concerned' which, in the circumstances of this case, is a reference back to reg 3(1)(iii); the 'activities concerned' are whatever activities are, after the change, carried out by the client on his own behalf instead of by the contractor. Here, Seawell took 'in-house' the whole of the receipt, storage and supply to the oil platforms of goods and materials. That is, they took over all aspects of the work that they had formerly had carried out for them by Ceva, not just those aspects of it which were carried out by Mr Moffat. Accordingly, the 'activities concerned' in this case comprised the entirety of the work carried out by Mr Moffat, the General Manager, the Manager and the two warehousemen. Mr Moffat was not carrying out 'the activities concerned' albeit that he was carrying out part of them. Rather, the activities concerned were carried out by several people, one of whom did only Seawell work.

In addition, to the extent that the ET treated Mr Moffat's responsibility for ensuring **3.91** that the relevant service was provided effectively as relevant to determining the correct organised grouping of employees, the ET was seen to have erred—'[t]he task for the Tribunal was to apply the terms of TUPE and nowhere do the regulations provide for such a test'.[141]

---

[133] See para. 3.78.
[134] See para. 3.81 *et seq.*
[135] *Seawell Ltd v Ceva Freight (UK) Ltd and anor*, above n. 132 at para. 17.
[136] Ibid.
[137] Ibid. at para. 41.
[138] Ibid. at para. 43.
[139] Ibid. at para. 45.
[140] Ibid. at para. 44.
[141] At para. 46.

3.92   *Seawell* serves as a reminder that the issues of establishment of the requisite organised grouping of employees for the purposes of regulation 3(3)(a)(i) and assignment to the that organised grouping are analytically distinct and should not be conflated. Those seeking to establish that regulation 3(1)(b) applies to a given situation cannot confine the activities by reference to which an organised grouping is to be identified for these purposes to a particular individual where that does not reflect the reality of how the putative transferor organizes its staffing for the purposes of conducting the relevant activities or more generally. In considering the regulation 3(3)(a)(i) requirement of an organised grouping of employees, a proper assessment is required of whether, in relation to the activities which are the subject of the putative SPC, there is a grouping of employees, its organization (or otherwise), and its principal purpose.

J. Principal Purpose

3.93   For there to be an SPC not only must there be an organised grouping of employees, its principal purpose must also be to carry out the relevant activities for the particular client. An established team of staff providing services to a variety of clients or customers will fall outside the scope of the concept of the SPC. It is on this basis that many service contracts will fall outside the scope of the legislation, such as where a contractor's cleaners work for various clients.

3.94   In considering whether the requisite organised grouping of employees existed at the relevant time, it is not necessary for the ET to undertake a quantitative comparison of the service after the putative SPC with that conducted beforehand—it is to decide whether the purpose of the organised grouping of employees is an ancillary or principal purpose.[142]

3.95   That said, the test is that the organised grouping of employees in question must have the principal (rather than exclusive) purpose of carrying out the relevant activities on behalf of the client. As the EAT commented in *Argyll Coastal Services Ltd v Stirling and others*:

> there seems to be no reason why the words should not bear their ordinary meaning. Thus, the organised grouping of employees need not have as its sole purpose the carrying out of the relevant client activities, that must be its principal purpose.[143]

3.96   Percentage tests as to the amount of time spent by a group of employees on a relevant client's business or the revenue which is attributable to a client may well be evidentially important but may not be determinative of what should be, it is submitted, a test to be determined as a matter of fact by reference to all the circumstances.

3.97   *Seawell Ltd v Ceva Freight (UK) Ltd and anor*[144] demonstrates this principle in operation. As an alternative finding to its decision that Mr Moffat was an organised grouping of employees by himself, the ET considered that Mr Moffat transferred to Seawell by virtue of an SPC on the basis that he and his colleagues formed an organised grouping of employees for the purposes of regulation 3(3)(a)(i), and that Mr Moffat was assigned to the conduct of the activity which was the subject of the SPC—indeed he was the only person so assigned, given that the other members of the organised grouping spent considerably less than 50 per cent

---

[142] See *Kimberley Group Housing*, n. 70 at paras 29–30.
[143] UKEATS/0012/11 at para. 19.
[144] [2012] IRLR 802, EAT.

of their time on the relevant activity. An appeal was allowed against this finding on the basis that 'whilst it does appear to have been a deliberately organised grouping of employees, there are no findings to indicate that it was organised for the purposes of the Seawell contract or that Seawell work was its principal purpose'.[145]

K. One-off Service Contracts

Regulation 3(3)(a)(ii) has the effect of excluding from the scope of an SPC for the purpose of regulation 3(1)(b) situations where a client obtains services from a contractor on a basis which it intends to be one-off and short-term as opposed to entering into an ongoing relationship with that contractor. The 2005 Consultation anticipated that, where a one-off contract is awarded, it is unlikely that the transfer legislation would apply in any event in such circumstances. The basis for this assessment was the view that an organised grouping of employees with the principal purpose of meeting the particular client's needs would be unlikely to exist prior to the relevant contract award.[146] However, in situations where the nature of the project in question entails the establishment of a team of employees, the Government considered that it was appropriate to provide this express exception in order clearly to exclude from the scope of the SPC provisions contracts (intended to be) for single specific events or tasks of short-term duration. **3.98**

The 2006 Guidance explained the position as follows: **3.99**

> the Regulations should not be expected to apply where a client engaged a contractor to organise a single conference on its behalf, even though the contractor had established an organised grouping of staff—e.g. a 'project team'—to carry out the activities involved in fulfilling that task. Thus, were the client subsequently to hold a second conference using a different contractor, the members of the first project team would not be required to transfer to the second contractor.[147]

Moreover, the Government's intention[148] was that, even if a client engages a particular contractor on a number of separate occasions to provide one-off services, the exclusion established by regulation 3(3)(a)(ii) should still apply provided that the series of engagements is 'coincidental or fortuitous' and the client has no intention of establishing an ongoing relationship with the contractor. It is for that reason that the client's intention is specifically referred to as an essential requirement for there to be a service provision change in regulation 3(3)(a)(ii)—'the client intends that the activities will, following the service provision change be carried out by the transferee other than in connection with a single specific event or task of short-term duration'. An ongoing relationship is intended to be caught by the SPC concept. One-off unrelated and short-term contract awards are not. **3.100**

There was initial concern in relation to their first draft that the SPC provisions would not apply to large projects, which might otherwise be expected to attract the application of the legislation, simply because they were 'one-off'. Unless regulation 3(1)(a) applied in any event, very significant but one-off service contracts would then fall outside the scope of TUPE due to their specific exclusion from the scope of regulation 3(1)(b) by virtue of regulation 3(3)(a)(ii) **3.101**

---

[145] Ibid. at para. 41.
[146] 2005 Consultation para. 24.
[147] At p. 10, repeated in the 2009 Guidance at p. 7.
[148] Ibid. para. 25.

as originally drafted. On this analysis, the employment protection objectives of the legislation would not necessarily be best served by the blanket exclusion of single specific events and tasks from the scope of the SPC provisions.

3.102   This point was addressed by the addition of the words 'of short-term duration' to regulation 3(3)(a)(ii). As noted in the Consultation Response, the original wording was accepted not to have been sufficiently precise, as was the scope for litigation over whether a particular contract concerned a specific, overarching task or a series of interlinked tasks.[149] The Government therefore determined that it should make clear that the exemption applies to tasks or events of short-term duration.

3.103   The 2009 Guidance explains the requirement that a one-off service contract must also be of short-term duration to fall outside the scope of regulation 3(1)(b) as follows:

> To illustrate the point take the example of two hypothetical contracts concerning the security of an Olympic Games or some other major sporting event. The first contract concerns the provision of security advice to the event organisers and covers a period of several years running up to the event; the other concerns the hiring of security staff to protect athletes during the period of the event itself. Both contracts have a one-off character in the sense that they both concern the holding of a specific event. However, the first contract runs for a significantly longer period than the second; therefore, the first would be covered by the TUPE Regulations (if the other qualifying conditions are satisfied) but the second would not.[150]

3.104   Whether a contract is intended to relate to a single specific event or task of short-term duration will be determined as a matter of fact. Despite the inclusion of the requirement that an excluded one-off contract be 'of short duration', it may not always be the case that ETs will find it easy to assess a client's intention with regard to the award of an initial contract which employees seek to argue falls outside the exclusion of one-off short-term contracts from the scope of regulation 3(1)(b). Specific evidence may not be available of an intention to establish an ongoing business relationship with the relevant contractor in such circumstances, let alone an intention to structure the parties' commercial arrangements by way of ostensibly one-off contracts to seek to avoid regulation 3(1)(b). An anti-avoidance mechanism based on intention may be difficult to apply in practice at the time when it is most needed to be effective in order to protect employees (i.e. at the point of the initial contract award). Being able to establish that an initial contract was not one-off by reference to subsequent contract awards may come too late to provide protection to employees whose employment did not transfer to the initial contractor because at the time it was considered that the one-off contract exclusion applied.

3.105   The same challenge may arise in determining whether successive contracts are fortuitous and therefore that each still relates to a 'single specific event or task of short-term duration'. Conversely, as a contractor relationship develops over time, the risk increases of retrospective claims (perhaps directed particularly at issues of continuity of employment for statutory purposes) that TUPE applied to the original contract awards or extensions.

3.106   This risk was acknowledged in the Consultation Response which noted the possibility of misuse of the exemption of contracts of short-term duration from the scope of regulation 3(1)(b) by parties 'deliberately break[ing] up longer term contracts into a series of smaller

---

[149] At para. 2.13.
[150] At p. 7.

contracts of a short-term duration'.[151] The Government felt confident that the ET would be able to deal with such issues, being 'accustomed to assessing the motivation of parties when considering cases put before it'.[152]

One issue which has arisen in respect of the interpretation of regulation 3(3)(a)(ii) is the precise application of the qualification of short term duration. Regulation 3(3)(a)(ii) could be construed to mean that the qualification of short term duration applies to tasks but not to single specific events - in which case the award of contracts for single specific events, however that term might be interpreted, would fall outside the SPC regime regardless of their duration and even if lasting for a considerable period. On the other hand, the qualification of short term duration could apply both to tasks and to single specific events such that only short term contract awards in respect of either type of activity would be excluded from the scope of the SPC provisions. In *Hunter v McCarrick*[153] the EAT was asked to determine whether a single specific event must be of short-term duration (in the same way as a task must) to fall outside the scope of the SPC provisions. The EAT declined to express a view on the point as it was not necessary to do so, although the 2009 Guidance is clear in the Government's view that the requirement of short-term duration applies equally to tasks and single specific events.[154]

3.107

Whether the qualification of short-term duration applies to both single specific events and to tasks was described by Langstaff P in *SNR Denton LLP v Kirwan and anor*[155] as 'an interesting but somewhat theological question'[156] but one in respect of which his preference was that the qualification apply to both concepts, the point being in his view 'essentially one of time and permanence'.[157] Langstaff P also provided the following useful guidance on the application of the qualification that the relevant situation be of short-term duration:[158]

3.108

> First, what is short-term or long-term is inevitably a matter of perspective. Perspective depends entirely upon the viewer. The view to be taken here in what is an avowedly employment context is, it seems to me, that of the employee and not that of the historian for whom short-term duration may be a very much longer period. It cannot be so short-term as to suggest that it is of no great relevance to consider whether there should be a transfer under TUPE or not; that suggests that a length of time of more than a few weeks will undoubtedly still be capable of falling within 'short-term duration'. But it seems to me that the broader context is that of employment relationships as a whole, in which such guidelines, as they are, are that at the time that the Regulations were made it would take a year for an employee to obtain employment rights other than those in respect of automatic dismissals, but similarly an employee might expect to receive at the most 12 weeks' notice from his employer and could in some circumstances give as little as 1 week to him. He would have three months within which to appeal a finding of unfair dismissal.

> All these are capable of creating a context within which 'short term' may be judged, but it seems to me that there is more than just the general employment context; there is necessarily the context of the particular employment and the particular relationships. That must vary, inevitably, from case to case. It will be, inevitably, therefore to some extent a matter of fact and degree, and, providing the Tribunal has regard to the words of the paragraph and the general context within which to place the particular facts of the case, a finding of fact and degree is unlikely ever to be wrong.

---

[151] At para. 2.13.
[152] Ibid.
[153] [2012] IRLR 274, EAT.
[154] See para. 3.98 *et seq.*
[155] [2012] IRLR 966, EAT.
[156] Ibid. at para. 41.
[157] Ibid.
[158] Ibid. at paras 43–4.

3.109 The application of regulation 3(3)(a)(ii) was also considered in *Liddell's Coaches v Cook and ors*[159]. In this case the client contract in question was for the transportation of schoolchildren for a fixed period of one year – the children in question were being 'decanted' from their school while it was rebuilt. The ET had concluded that TUPE did not apply to the award of this contract because it related to a single specific event and was of short term duration. More particularly, as transport contracts were found typically to be for between three and five years, the one year contract was held to be short term. The EAT considered the comments of Langstaff P in *SNR Denton UK LLP v Kirwan and anor*[160] and agreed with his view that whether the task in question is short term is a question of fact and degree which will inevitably vary from case to case. The ET was entitled to make the finding it did to the effect that the one year contract was short term.

3.110 That said, as a matter of interpretation, Lady Smith appeared to disagree with Langstaff P's view that the qualification of short term duration applies to both tasks and single specific events for the purposes of the disapplication of the SPC provisions effected by regulation 3(3)(a)(ii).[161] She took the view that:[162]

> [a]n 'event' is a single happening or occurrence; in philosophical terms, it is an occurrence involving a qualitative or quantitative change or complex of changes located in a restricted portion of time. Further, "event", of itself, connotes short duration; to refer to a single specific event of short term duration is, we consider, tautologous. There was no need for the draughtsman to apply the phrase "of short term duration" to "single specific event".

3.111 Also, the EAT appeared to take the view, in contrast to the DTI guidance, that activities related to a single specific event could still fall outside the scope of the SPC provisions even if not of themselves short term. The example referred to was security services at the Olympics which would be longer in duration than the Games themselves but still activities relating to a single event. As the EAT put it, 'whatever problems there may be with the wording of reg 3(3)(a)(ii), on no view can it be read so as to qualify the word "activities" with the phrase "of short term duration". The grammar used does not permit that interpretation.'[163]

L. Supply of Goods

3.112 Regulation 3(3)(b) excludes from the scope of the SPC provisions those situations where the contractor's engagement by the client is wholly or mainly for the supply of goods for the client's use. It will be important, in considering the potential application of this exclusion, to identify precisely the activities in question and their scope to ascertain if the exclusion of the supply of goods from the scope of the SPC provisions applies. A function may have elements which are goods related and some which are service related. Given that the test of the exclusion in regulation 3(3)(b) is that the activities should not 'wholly or mainly' consist of the supply of goods, key factual issues will include identifying the nature of the services, whether they are separable from the supply of goods (functionally and in terms of whether there is an

---

[159] UKEATS/0025/12.
[160] See above para. 3.108.
[161] Ibid. at para. 41.
[162] Ibid. at para. 29.
[163] *Liddell's Coaches*, above n. 159 at para. 29.

organised grouping of employees principally conducting them), and whether, if not entirely separable, the function is wholly, mainly, or only partially related to the supply of goods.

The example given in the 2005 Consultation[164] of the application of regulation 3(3)(b) is **3.113** where a client engages a contractor to supply sandwiches and drinks to a canteen for the client to sell on to its own staff. If the contract were for the running of the canteen, then its award to a new contractor could well constitute a relevant transfer by virtue of being a transfer of an undertaking or as an SPC, provided that the applicable conditions were satisfied.[165] In that case, the main activities involved in the contract would be to deal with managing facilities, serving customers, washing crockery, etc. In contrast, the supply of food and drink would be ancillary to these main activities and the goods would not be for direct sale—a contract simply for supply of such goods would not constitute an SPC for these purposes.

Whilst the distinction between a contract to run a canteen and a contract simply to supply **3.114** food to a canteen is superficially straightforward, the application of this exception of what can be termed 'goods-only supply contracts' from the concept of an SPC may not always be simple, especially where a team of staff is dedicated to the supply of goods to a client.

It should be noted that, in the initial draft of the SPC provisions, the 'procurement' of goods **3.115** was also excluded from their scope. The reference to 'procurement' was deleted from the final version of the provision, not least as it might have meant that the outsourcing of a client's procurement department would have fallen outside the scope of regulation 3(1)(b), 'an effect which the Government did not want to achieve as such departments clearly provide a service function'.[166]

The application of this exclusion was considered by the EAT in *Pannu v Geo W King Ltd* **3.116** *and others*.[167] The claimants worked for the first respondent, Geo W King Ltd, on its axle assembly line, manufacturing products which were supplied to the third respondent, IBC Vehicles Ltd. The claimants were dismissed by the first respondent when its production terminated (whereupon the first respondent went into liquidation). After the first respondent's axle production operation ceased, the third respondent entered into a contract with the second respondent, Premier, for the assembly of the parts previously manufactured by the first respondent. The ET rejected the claimant's claims that there was any form of relevant transfer, whether under regulation 3(1)(a) or regulation 3(1)(b), from Geo W King Ltd to either Premier or IBC.

The ET held that regulation 3(3)(b) applied to deny the relevant employees the protection **3.117** of TUPE by way of an SPC. The activities in question were not simply the assembly of the relevant modules (i.e. the provision of a service) but also the sourcing and acquisition of the relevant component parts. Whilst there was an organised grouping of employees which had the principal purpose of assembling the modules, the relationship between Geo W King and its client IBC was analysed as being the supply and sale of the relevant goods to the client. Assembly of the relevant goods was performed for the purposes of their supply and sale. That IBC, the ultimate client, paid some of Geo W King's suppliers direct for parts was not seen as

---

[164] Ibid. at para. 26.
[165] An example of there being a transfer of undertaking in such circumstances is *Abler*—see Chapter 2, para. 2.79 *et seq.*
[166] Consultation Response at para. 2.7.
[167] [2012] IRLR 193, EAT.

undermining this conclusion by demonstrating that Geo W King was performing a service for IBC by way of assembling the relevant parts, rather than supplying goods. Instead, payments were made, reflecting Geo W King's financial difficulties, to ensure that the supply chain was maintained. In these particular circumstances, the payments to component suppliers by the ultimate client did not indicate that the client's supplier was supplying services rather than goods.

3.118 The EAT held that the ET's decision should stand. Whilst there was an organised grouping of employees which provided services—in the sense that they provided their services to their employer Geo W King—the ET was entitled to find that the activity for these purposes was the supply of the finished goods to IBC. As HHJ Peter Clark noted:

> [i]dentifying an organised grouping of employees carrying out the activities concerned on behalf of the client is a pre-requisite of an SPC. . . . However, the fact that that organised group provide a service (directly to their contractor employer) cannot answer, of itself, the separate reg. 3(3)(b) question.[168]

M. Professional Business Services

3.119 During the course of formulating the reforms to TUPE which led to the adoption of the 2006 Regulations, the Government received representations from some employers' organizations that 'white collar' professional business services should be exempted from the scope of the SPC provisions.[169] The argument in favour of this proposed exemption[170] was principally that professionally qualified employees 'by virtue of having skills that are generally highly sought after by employers' are less in need of additional legal protection than those engaged in routine manual work. In practice, changes of provider in relation to professional services such as accountancy, legal advice, and software design were considered rarely to give rise to difficulties for the relevant employees.

3.120 Those who favour a professional services exemption argue that the qualities and performance of employees providing professional services are central to the engagement of service providers providing professional services and that it is therefore not appropriate for there to be an SPC where a client wishes to change professional advisers and therefore by extension the personnel involved. The previous provider's staff should not, on that analysis, move across with the retainer to the new provider whom the client wishes to service its needs with different and presumably in its view higher-quality and more appropriate staff. Nevertheless, identifying what constitutes a professional service—and the precise scope of such an exemption—could be challenging.

3.121 The opposing view[171] argues that a professional services exemption should not be established for a variety of reasons including its perceived lack of regular practical relevance, the inappropriateness of distinguishing between 'white collar' and 'blue collar' workers in terms of the application of employment protection legislation, and the legal and practical difficulties of drawing a distinction between professional business services and other types of services. With regard to that latter point, the Government considered[172] establishing a professional

---

[168] Ibid. at para. 21.
[169] 2005 Consultation para. 30.
[170] Ibid. para. 31.
[171] Ibid. para. 32.
[172] Ibid. paras 35 and 36.

business services exception by reference to either a 'generic description' of such services or, as was its preference (if the proposal were to have proceeded), a list of specified services meriting exceptional treatment by reference to their distinctive features.

In any event the likelihood of a business services exemption having practical relevance was considered to be low. It was seen as likely only to apply[173] in cases of a change of an ongoing arrangement to which an organized grouping of employees was dedicated pre-transfer and the award of the relevant contract did not also constitute a traditional transfer of an undertaking pursuant to regulation 3(1)(a). Cases in which there would not be a 'traditional' transfer of an undertaking but the requirements for there to be an SPC would be satisfied were considered likely to be rare.[174]   **3.122**

The Government also took the view that banks, solicitors, and accountants would rarely in practice service their major clients by way of dedicated teams which would fall within the scope of regulation 3(1)(b) in the absence of a business services exemption, especially in the context of what were styled 'high street' providers of services. It was considered that any team of staff which is devoted to a particular client will normally carry out tasks for a number of clients even if this is done on an 'irregular or ad hoc basis'. Ultimately the Government decided not to proceed with the proposal for a professional services exemption in the light of what were described as the strong arguments against the exclusion and the fact that most consultees considered that these disadvantages outweighed the potential benefits.[175]   **3.123**

Royden and others v Barnetts Solicitors[176] is an ET decision demonstrating that regulation 3(1)(b) can apply to the transfer of activities constituting the provision of professional services. Certain staff employed in the conveyancing department of the solicitors' firm Lees Lloyd Whitley argued that there was an SPC when another firm, Barnetts, was appointed by the Britannia Building Society to replace their employer as the firm of solicitors to which that building society referred its customers for the provision of legal services in respect of the relevant property transactions. That the building society was the client for the purposes of regulation 3(1)(b) was conceded. The relevant activities were considered to be the branch referrals of the relevant legal work. The requirements of regulation 3(1)(b) were held to have been satisfied and there was therefore an SPC in the circumstances of that case.   **3.124**

N. Summary

In *Enterprise Management Services Ltd v Connect-Up Ltd and others*[177] HHJ Peter Clark summarized the analysis to be conducted when considering regulation 3(1)(b). To adopt the key points of that analysis: **3.125**

(a) The expression 'activities' is not defined in TUPE. The first task of the ET is to identify the relevant activities carried out by the original contractor.

---

[173] 2005 Consultation para. 33.
[174] Ibid. para. 34, a comment which was somewhat at odds with the view expressed at para. 28 of the 2001 Consultation that the introduction of the service provision change concept would represent a significant extension of the legislation.
[175] Consultation Response para. 2.12.
[176] ET case numbers 2103451/07 and others.
[177] [2012] IRLR 190, EAT.

(b) The next (critical) question is whether the activities carried on by the subsequent contractor after the relevant date are fundamentally or essentially the same as those carried on by the original contractor. Minor differences may be disregarded. This is essentially a question of fact and degree for the ET.

(c) Cases may arise where the division of services after the relevant date, known as fragmentation, amongst a number of different contractors means that the case falls outside the SPC regime.

(d) Even where the activities remain essentially the same before and after the putative transfer date, as performed by the original and subsequent contractors, an SPC will only take place if the following conditions are satisfied:

(i) there is an organised grouping of employees in Great Britain which has as its principal purpose the carrying out of the activities concerned on behalf of the client;

(ii) the client intends that the putative transferee will not carry out the activities in connection with a single event of short-term duration;

(iii) the activities are not wholly or mainly the supply of goods (rather than services) for the client's use.

(e) Finally, the ET must decide whether each claimant was assigned to the organised grouping of employees.[178]

---

[178] Ibid. at para. 8.

4

WHO TRANSFERS?

A. Automatic Transfer	4.01	10. Knowledge of transfer and collective consultation	4.68
B. Who Transfers?	4.08	C. Electing not to Transfer and Consequent Claims	4.71
1. Regulation 4(1)	4.08	1. Introduction	4.71
2. Employment	4.10	2. Objection to transfer	4.72
3. By transferor	4.14	3. Effecting the objection	4.80
4. Immediately before the transfer	4.24	4. Secondment or objection?	4.83
5. Employee's contract would otherwise terminate	4.32	5. Ignorance of transfer and subsequent objection	4.85
6. Assignment	4.36	6. Changes to working conditions	4.92
7. Absence and assignment	4.51	7. Constructive dismissal	4.122
8. Redeployment and temporary or artificial assignments	4.55	8. Claims against the transferor	4.125
9. Appeals against dismissal and interim relief	4.64	9. Change of location	4.130

A. Automatic Transfer

TUPE operates to transfer from the transferor to the transferee the contract of employ-   **4.01**
ment of an employee who falls within its scope and this transfer is automatic and without
regard to the parties' intentions—save where the employee is dismissed prior to the transfer
or exercises the right to object to transfer. As the ECJ made clear in *Celtec Ltd v Astley* the
date of transfer 'cannot be postponed to another date at the will of the transferor or the
transferee'.[1] The sole exception to this rule of automatic transfer is the ability, following a
freely taken decision, of employees to opt 'not to continue the employment relationships
with the transferee'.[2]

Consistent with of this rule of automatic transfer, in *Capita Health Solutions Ltd v BBC and*   **4.02**
McLean[3] Lady Smith held[4] that legally an employee's employment could not continue with
the transferor without interruption simply by virtue of the parties' agreement—such an
agreement is ineffective consistent with authorities such as *Daddy's Dance Hall*.[5] In reaching

---

[1] [2005] IRLR 647, ECJ at para. 44.
[2] Ibid. at para. 37.
[3] [2008] IRLR 595, CA.
[4] Ibid. at para. 42.
[5] [1988] IRLR 315, ECJ, see Chapter 6, para. 6.06 *et seq.*

this conclusion, Lady Smith quoted the analysis of Lord Hope in *Celtec Ltd v Astley*[6] to the following effect:

> it is a fundamental right of the employee to be free to choose his employer. So he cannot be obliged to work for an employer whom he has not freely chosen: Katsikas, paragraph 32. From this it follows that it is open to an employee whose contract of employment would otherwise be transferred automatically from the transferor to the transferee on the date of the transfer of his own free will to withdraw from this arrangement by declining to enter the employment of the transferee: Mikkelson, paragraph 16, Berg paragraph 37. That then is the sole reservation referred to in paragraph 37 [of the ECJ judgment in *Celtec*]. It does not, as my noble and learned friend Lord Mance suggests, work the other way round. It does not enable effect to be given to an employee's wish to continue to be employed by the transferor while continuing to be employed in the unit to which he has been assigned after its transfer to the transferee. But the application of the rule that he can withdraw from the arrangement depends on two things; first that the employee is in a position to choose whether or not to enter the employment of the transferee after the date of the transfer; and second, that he in fact exercises that choice by deciding of his own free will not to do so.

4.03 TUPE therefore has the effect that an employee who is within its scope transfers automatically unless the individual elects to object to transfer in which case his or her employment terminates. That position has been queried judicially, most notably by Lord Mance in *Celtec Ltd v Astley*,[7] who in his judgment 'saw no sensible reason why an inflexible rule should be adopted which would deny employees the right to remain with the transferor, even on terms that they would be seconded to the transferee'.[8] In similar vein in *Royal Mail Group v Communication Workers Union*,[9] Elias J said as follows:

> We find it difficult to understand why a law designed to favour employees should have the effect of preventing them from remaining with the transferor and being seconded to the transferee, but that is how the House [of Lords] has construed the European jurisprudence and we are obliged to follow it.

4.04 Regulation 4(3) provides that, where a transfer is effected by a series of two or more transactions, an employee is within the scope of the legislation if assigned to the relevant undertaking or activities immediately before any of those transactions. This renders the scope of TUPE wider in its potential application than the approach required by *Celtec Ltd v Astley* of there being one date only on which a transfer occurs as a matter of law. The application of *Celtec Ltd v Astley* to situations where a relevant transfer is genuinely effected over a period of time, perhaps by way of a staged and scheduled migration of services or functions, remains unclear.

4.05 HHJ McMullen QC also considered the automatic transfer of employment effected by TUPE, and the proper analysis of situations where parties are ignorant of the true effect of TUPE, in *Chambers v QCR Motors Ltd (in voluntary liquidation) & others*[10] In this case the relevant transfer was held to have occurred when QCR lost a painting contract which was awarded to Paintbox. The date of transfer was held to be 7 August 2007. However, on 24 August 2007, the relevant employees were told to attend work at QCR when they would be given a letter and from that date be employed by Paintbox. The letter was found to have

---

[6] [2006] IRLR 635, HL at para. 55.
[7] See above, n. 1.
[8] Per Elias J in *Royal Mail Group v Communication Workers Union* [2009] IRLR 108, EAT at para. 102.
[9] Ibid. at para. 117.
[10] UKEAT/0549/09.

constituted an assurance that the employees would continue to be paid until the end of the notice period served on QCR by the ultimate client to terminate its appointment, i.e. until 12 September 2007.

The EAT analysed what had happened as follows in the context of the (unappealed) finding **4.06** that as a matter of fact the transfer had occurred at the earlier date of 7 August 2007. Since TUPE transfers the contracts of employment of the relevant employees automatically by operation of law, the relevant employees transferred to Paintbox from QCR on 7 August 2007. Their continued work for, and receipt of pay from QCR 'could only have been under new contracts for employment'.[11] They had therefore been dismissed by Paintbox (after employment by Paintbox for what was described as a nanosecond[12]) and then employed by QCR until 12 September 2007 when their contracts came to an end pursuant to the notice on 28 August 2007 that they would continue to be paid until then.

As HHJ McMullen QC put it, that was the 'way of explaining the apparent conundrum **4.07** of the employees being at the same time employed by competitors'.[13] This 'extraordinarily artificial' analysis was seen[14] as consistent with that adopted by Lady Smith in *Capita Health Solutions Ltd v BBC and McLean*[15] and further demonstrates the need to appreciate not only that the date of a relevant transfer is a matter of fact independent of the parties' intentions or understanding but also that transferors can assume liabilities by engaging staff who would otherwise transfer elsewhere as a consequence of a mistaken understanding of the effect of TUPE.

B. Who Transfers?

1. Regulation 4(1)

Regulation 4(1) effects the transfer of the relevant employees and provides as follows: **4.08**

> Except where objection is made under paragraph (7), a relevant transfer shall not operate so as to terminate the contract of employment of any person employed by the transferor and assigned to the organised grouping of resources or employees that is subject to the relevant transfer, which would otherwise be terminated by the transfer, but any such contract shall have effect after the transfer as if originally made between the person so employed and the transferee.

There are various elements to regulation 4(1) including employment, employment by the **4.09** transferor, such employment being immediately before the transfer, the employee's contract of employment otherwise terminating by virtue of the relevant transfer, and the issue of assignment, each of which elements will now be examined in turn.

2. Employment

The protection of the Directive only extends to employees as that category of person is **4.10** determined in accordance with the applicable national law of the Member State in question.

---

[11] Ibid. at para. 38.
[12] Ibid. at para. 40.
[13] Ibid.
[14] Ibid. at para. 39.
[15] See above n. 3.

As provided by Article 2.1(d), for these purposes an employee is 'any person who, in the Member State concerned, is protected as an employee under national employment law'.[16] This provision is supplemented by Article 2.2 which provides that the Directive is 'without prejudice to national law as regards the definition of contract of employment or employment relationship'. As the ECJ confirmed in *Wendelboe v LJ Music ApS*:

> [t]he existence or otherwise of a contract of employment or an employment relationship on the date of transfer within the meaning of [the Directive] must be established on the basis of the rules of national law, subject however to observance of the mandatory provisions of the Directive, and more particularly... the protection of employees against dismissal by the transferor or the transferee by reason of the transfer.[17]

4.11 Consistent with the Directive, TUPE operates on a relevant transfer, whether by way of a transfer of an undertaking or an SPC, to transfer to the transferee the employment of, or to render the transferee responsible for liabilities in respect of, only those who satisfy the technical requirements of status as an employee as that term is defined by regulation 2(1). Regulation 2(1) defines an employee as 'any individual who works for another person whether under a contract of service or apprenticeship or otherwise but does not include anyone who provides services under a contract for services and references to a person's employer shall be construed accordingly'. The definition of an employee under regulation 2(1) is subtly different from the definition utilized in ERA 1996, s. 230, which provides that the term 'employee' means an individual who has entered into or works under (or, where the employment has ceased, worked under) a contract of employment and that the term 'contract of employment' means 'a contract of service or apprenticeship, whether express or implied, and (if it is express) whether oral or in writing'.[18] That TUPE extends to those engaged under a 'contract of service or apprenticeship or otherwise' suggests that those who are 'workers' in employment law terms may be covered by TUPE provided they are not independent contractors who are engaged under a contract for services. Whilst only employees for the purposes of ERA 1996 have unfair dismissal rights,[19] the wider category of employee for the purposes of TUPE needs to be considered both in terms of the transfer of contractual liabilities and identification of the affected employees in respect of whom information and consultation pursuant to regulation 13 must be conducted.[20]

4.12 The engagement of non-employees therefore does not automatically transfer to the transferee as a consequence of a TUPE transfer nor is the panoply of other transfer-related obligations triggered in respect of such persons (such as the transferor's obligation to provide employee liability information to the transferee, the obligation to provide information to and consult with employee representatives, and so on[21]). A transferee that wishes to engage persons who fall outside the scope of the transfer of undertakings legislation must conduct separate discussions with those parties effectively in order to agree the novation of their contracts. An example of an individual falling outside the scope of TUPE is *Cowell v Quilter*[22] in which it

---

[16] See also *Mikkelsen* [1989] ICR 330, ECJ.
[17] [1986] 1 CMLR 476, ECJ, at para. 16.
[18] Under ERA 1996, s. 230(2).
[19] See Chapter 7.
[20] See Chapter 9.
[21] Although details concerning agency workers must be supplied to the relevant appropriate representatives pursuant to regulation 13—see Chapter 9, para. 9.17.
[22] [1989] IRLR 392, CA.

was held that an equity partner in a partnership was not an employee for these purposes on the basis that his or her contract is 'for services' rather than 'of service'.

The complexity of the issue of what constitutes employment status for the purposes of domes- **4.13** tic employment law[23] renders the application of TUPE uncertain in difficult cases of status categorization. The status of agency workers may, for example, present particular problems and therefore the position of such individuals needs to be considered carefully.[24] Whether those on career breaks remain employed and therefore in scope to transfer to the transferee on a relevant transfer may also need to be considered.[25] The length of an employee's service is irrelevant to the application of TUPE to transfer the individual's contract of employment to the transferee although it will of course be relevant to the individual's ability to claim unfair dismissal if not retained by the transferee.[26]

3. By transferor

Regulation 4(1) provides that the relevant employees' contracts of employment shall have **4.14** effect after the relevant transfer in question as if originally made between the individual and the transferee. This implements the requirement of Article 3.1 that '[t]he transferor's rights and obligations arising from a contract of employment or from an employment relationship existing on the date of a transfer shall, by reason of such transfer, be transferred to the transferee'.

The category of person whose contract of employment transfers to the transferee as a con- **4.15** sequence of a relevant transfer is defined by regulation 4(1) as 'any person employed by the transferor'. One issue which can arise as a result of this formulation is the position where the employees who work in the business or activity which is the subject of a relevant transfer are not actually directly employed by the transferor.

The definition of 'relevant transfer' in regulation 2(1) provides that 'transferor' is a term to be **4.16** construed in connection with the relevant transfer. In relation to a transfer of an undertaking for the purposes of regulation 3(1)(a), the concept of the transferor in domestic law is gener- ally considered to denote the owner or operator of the relevant undertaking which disposes or divests itself of that undertaking. In the context of an SPC, the transferor is expressly stated to be the person 'who carried out the activities prior to the service provision change' and the transferee to be 'the person who carries out the activities as a result of the service pro- vision change'.[27] In either case the actual employer, in terms of the relevant direct contractual relationship, of the employees who work in the business or activity which is potentially the subject of the relevant transfer could be a different legal person from the person from whom the relevant undertaking or activities transfer.

---

[23] A detailed treatment of which issue is outside the scope of this work.
[24] Although overtaken by subsequent case law in relation to employee status, *Cable & Wireless plc v P Muscat* [2006] EWCA Civ 220, CA demonstrated the potential relevance of this issue in the TUPE context. A telecom- munications specialist who was engaged through an employment agency was held to have been the employee of the end-user client after the acquisition, by way of a TUPE transfer, of the business of a company by which he had originally been engaged as an employee and subsequently a contractor.
[25] See *Curr v Marks & Spencer plc* [2003] IRLR 74, CA.
[26] See Chapter 7.
[27] Regulation 2(1).

4.17   By contrast, the wording of the Directive focuses on the employees' employer rather than the party which transfers the relevant undertaking or conducts the relevant activities prior to a relevant transfer. Article 2.1(a) defines the transferor as 'any natural or legal person who, by reason of a transfer . . . , ceases to be the employer in respect of the undertaking, business or part of the undertaking or business'.[28] The Directive therefore identifies those employees whose employment transfers from transferor to transferee by reference to the identity of the relevant employees' employer rather than the person conducting the relevant business or activities.

4.18   The reference in regulation 4(1) to its applying to those employed by the transferor raises the issue of how TUPE operates in circumstances where the transferor of the business (in terms of the party transferring or disposing of the undertaking in question or ceasing to conduct activities which fall within the scope of an SPC) is not the company or other legal person which actually employs the employees who work in the relevant business or on the relevant activities. In group situations, the relevant employees may be employed by a central management services company in which case they will therefore not formally be employed by the transferor. Therefore, on a literal interpretation of TUPE, those employees would not fall within the scope of TUPE so as to transfer to the transferee. This would hardly be the intention of the legislation in terms of its employment protection objectives. A number of cases have considered this issue, albeit in the context of what is now the regulation 3(1)(a) concept of the transfer of an undertaking in respect of which, given the European law basis of the relevant provisions, a purposive interpretation is more easily justifiable than in relation to SPCs for the purposes of regulation 3(1)(b).

4.19   In *Michael Peters Ltd v Farnfield (1) and Michael Peters Group plc (2)*[29] the EAT overturned the finding of the industrial tribunal (as it then was) that the chief executive of a group who was employed by its parent company could argue that he was protected by TUPE 1981 when the business of four of its subsidiaries were sold. Quite apart from the point that the employee was found not to have been wholly or mainly assigned to the undertakings disposed of, the EAT considered that the tribunal had been wrong to pierce the corporate veil and to conclude that the business of the subsidiaries was the business of the parent company so that the parent company was the transferor and the employee therefore fell within the scope of TUPE.

4.20   By way of contrast, in *Sunley Turriff Holdings Ltd v Thompson*[30] the EAT upheld a decision to take the 'exceptional step' of lifting the veil of incorporation. Even though the contracting party in respect of the sale of the business was a group company by which the employee in question was not employed, TUPE was held to apply to transfer the employee's employment to the transferee. Part of the business disposed of was that of his employer. He devoted some of his time to the remainder. It was found that what was transferred was in reality not only the undertaking of a group company by which the employee was not employed but also a substantial part of the undertaking of his actual employer, thereby bringing his employment within the scope of TUPE.

---

[28] Article 2.1(b) defines 'transferee' as 'any natural or legal person who, by reason of a transfer . . . becomes the employer in respect of the undertaking, business, or part of the undertaking or business'.

[29] [1995] IRLR 190, EAT.

[30] [1995] IRLR 633, EAT.

In *Duncan Web Offset (Maidstone) Ltd v Cooper*[31] it was observed that '[i]ndustrial tribunals **4.21** will be astute to ensure that the provisions of the regulations are not evaded by devices such as service companies, or by complicated group structures which conceal the true position'.[32] The EAT raised the possibility that, in a group context, a service company could in appropriate circumstances be viewed as employing the relevant employees on behalf of and as agent for the operating company—the transferor —for whom the employees in reality performed their services. Rather more speculatively, it is submitted, the EAT also raised the possibility that the ET might, in its assessment of the factual matrix, regard the service company employing the employees as effectively a party to the transfer (thereby becoming a/the transferor), even if it were not a signatory to any commercial agreement recording the arrangements.

It is therefore clear that, whilst regulation 4(1) maintains the requirement that an employee **4.22** be employed by the transferor in order for his or her contract of employment to transfer to the transferee on a relevant transfer, the ET may, where possible, construe the relevant arrangements in a way which will ensure that the objectives of the legislation are met, in terms of protecting those working in businesses which are transferred at the very least in relation to transfers of undertaking for the purposes of regulation 3(1)(a).

That it is potentially permissible in appropriate circumstances to go behind the 'corporate veil' **4.23** and apply the transfer legislation to those who are engaged in a particular business which is the subject of a relevant transfer but who are not employed by the actual transferor—at least for the purposes of the Directive and, by extension, regulation 3(1)(a)—was reinforced by *Albron Catering BV v FNV Bondgenoten*.[33] The relevant staff were employed by a services company within the Heineken group whilst the catering business in which they worked was operated by a different entity within that group. The relevant employee sought a declaration that his employment transferred to the transferee when the catering function was transferred out of the Heineken group to a new provider. The ECJ held that the Directive can apply to what it described as non-contractual (as well as contractual) employment relationships. Consequently, those staff who were assigned to the business of the transferor were protected by the Directive, even if they had no direct contractual relationship with the transferor entity which operated and disposed of the relevant businesses. The relationship of the relevant staff with the transferor need not be contractual for the Directive to apply to protect their position—Article 3(1) transfers to the transferee the 'transferor's rights and obligations arising from a contract of employment or from an employment relationship'. Moreover, the ECJ considered that, where there could be seen to be more than one employer, the 'contractual employer' does not take precedence over the non-contractual or 'relationship' employer. The *Albron* decision reinforces the argument that the approach in decisions such as *Sunley Turriff* can be appropriate to ensure that those assigned to the relevant business or activities are protected by TUPE.

4. Immediately before the transfer

Regulation 4(3) further refines the process of the identification of the employees whose con- **4.24** tracts of employment and associated liabilities transfer to the transferee. It provides that:

> any reference . . . to a person employed by the transferor and assigned to the organised grouping of resources or employees that is subject to a relevant transfer, is a reference to a person so

---

[31] [1995] IRLR 184, EAT.
[32] Ibid. at para. 16.
[33] [2011] IRLR 76, ECJ.

employed immediately before the transfer or [who] would have been so employed if he had not been dismissed in the circumstances described in regulation 7(1) including, where the transfer is effected by a series of two or more transactions, a person so employed and assigned or who would have been so employed and assigned immediately before any of those transactions.

4.25 As the 2005 Consultation noted,[34] regulation 4(3) updated the legislation in this regard to reflect the decision in *Litster v Forth Dry Dock & Engineering Co Ltd*.[35] This ensures that the transferee inherits liabilities in respect of those who would have transferred to it pursuant to TUPE had they not been dismissed prior to transfer for a transfer-related reason. The crucial point to note is that for an employee's contract of employment to transfer to the transferee by virtue of a relevant transfer, the employee must be employed immediately before the transfer. The contract of employment of an employee who would have been so employed but for a transfer-related dismissal not justified by an ETOR does not transfer to the transferee but the liabilities associated with the dismissal of that employee do so transfer.

4.26 In *Secretary of State for Employment v Spence*[36] the employees were dismissed at 11 a.m. on a particular day, the relevant business was sold some three hours later and the employees were found for the purposes of TUPE 1981 not to have been employed by the transferor immediately before the transfer. On this basis dismissal prior to a relevant transfer would deny employees the protection of TUPE because they would not then be employed immediately before transfer. This was a potentially serious limitation on the protection of TUPE.

4.27 In *Litster* the House of Lords applied a purposive interpretation to the requirement that an employee be employed by the transferor 'immediately before the transfer' in order to fulfil the protective purposes of the legislation. Dismissal effected before the transfer and solely because of it could not be effective to avoid transfer to the transferee of liabilities in respect of that automatically unfair dismissal. As Lord Keith put it in *Litster*,[37] to find otherwise would have driven a 'coach and four' through what was regulation 5(1) of TUPE 1981 and is now regulation 4(1) of TUPE 2006. Regulation 4(3) encapsulates that principle.

4.28 Accordingly, if there is no ETOR justifying dismissal,[38] then a dismissal connected with a transfer, even if it results in the employee ceasing to be employed some time before the transfer, does not preclude the transferee from inheriting liability for that dismissal under TUPE. Regulation 4(3) operates in such circumstances to transfer the liabilities associated with the employee's contract to the transferee and the provisions with regard to transfer-related dismissals then come into play.[39]

4.29 Some respondents to the 2005 Consultation had been concerned that regulation 4(3) would have the unintended effect of transferring to the transferee the actual employment or contracts of employees dismissed prior to transfer.[40] This concern (which was also raised in relation to regulation 7) was rejected on the basis in part that domestic law does not render

---

[34] At para. 43.
[35] [1989] IRLR 161, HL.
[36] [1986] IRLR 248, CA. This considered the position under TUPE 1981 whose regulation 5(1) referred only to employment 'immediately before' the transfer.
[37] *Litster v Forth Dry Dock & Engineering Co Ltd* [1989] IRLR 161, HL at para. 3.
[38] See Chapter 7 for further discussion of the inheritance by the transferee of liability for pre-transfer dismissals.
[39] Regulation 7.
[40] See Consultation Response para. 3.9.

a transfer-related dismissal a nullity.[41] Accordingly, all that can transfer to the transferee are the liabilities associated with a pre-transfer dismissal which is not justified by an ETOR as opposed to the employee's (terminated) contract.

The fact that *Litster* operates to provide protection to those dismissed before the transfer does **4.30** not, however, alter the principle that the transfer of employment (as distinct from the inheritance by the transferee of employment claims) only applies to those employed immediately before the transfer. As Balcombe LJ put it in *Spence*:

> If a person is dismissed because of the transfer, either the impending transfer or one which has already taken place, then he is given specific rights under Regulation 8.[42]Applying that construction of Regulation 5[43] to the facts of the present case, it is clear that the employees, the applicants, were dismissed before the relevant transfer. Their contracts of employment were not existing at the point of transfer. There was nothing on which Regulation 5 could bite.[44]

Regulation 4(3) also clarifies that a series of transactions, pursuant to which, for example, the **4.31** relevant undertaking passes through various hands over a period of time, does not disqualify employees employed in the relevant undertaking or activities at the outset of the relevant series of transactions from the protection of the legislation. In *Longden and anor v Ferrari Ltd and anor*[45] Mummery J observed that in determining whether a person is employed in an undertaking or part of one immediately before the transfer the ET must ask itself, first, whether the transfer was effected by a series of two or more transactions and, if so, second, whether the person was employed in the undertaking immediately before any of those transactions.

5. Employee's contract would otherwise terminate

TUPE 1981, regulation 5(1) identified the employees whose employment transferred to the **4.32** transferee on a relevant transfer as those employed under a contract 'which would otherwise have been terminated by the transfer'. The rationale for that wording was presumably the fact that at common law a transfer of the business in which an employee works constitutes a termination by the employer of that employee's contract of employment.[46] The objective of the transfer legislation is to address that very consequence in order to protect the employment of those employees whose employment would terminate at common law on a transfer of an undertaking.

The reference to transferring employees being those whose contracts would otherwise ter- **4.33** minate as a result of the transfer was omitted from the initial draft of what became the 2006 Regulations. The language which was removed was viewed as adding nothing of value.[47] Moreover, the wording of TUPE 1981, regulation 5(1) was seen as presenting a potential and unintended loophole. If a transferor determined that it would retain employees who might otherwise fall within the scope of TUPE then their employment would not terminate by reason of the transfer because the transferor was content to and did continue to employ them. Accordingly, since they would not terminate as a consequence of the transfer, the contracts

---

[41] See Chapter 7.
[42] Now regulation 7.
[43] Now regulation 4.
[44] Above para. 4.26 at para. 18.
[45] [1994] IRLR 157, EAT at para. 16.
[46] See Chapter 1, para. 1.06 *et seq.*
[47] 2005 Consultation para. 42.

of those employees could be argued not to transfer automatically to the transferee (as is the objective of the transfer legislation). This could be to the prejudice of the employees (who might wish to be able to transfer with the relevant undertaking and activities) and indeed the transferee (who might well wish to inherit the employees central to the operation of the relevant undertaking or activities).

4.34 The removal from TUPE 1981 of the qualification 'which would otherwise have been terminated by the transfer' could have removed this possibility. Retention by the transferor of employees who would otherwise transfer to the transferee would then have been solely a matter of the employees in question exercising their right to refuse to transfer[48], with the transferor in relation to their continued employment by it.

4.35 Despite having adopted such a firm view, as a result of its consultation about the amendments to be made by what became the 2006 Regulations, the Government concluded that it would not dispense with the requirement that an employee falling within the scope of regulation 4 be one whose contract would terminate as a result of the transfer.[49] Although the proviso in question had been omitted from the initial draft of the new legislation on grounds that it was unnecessary and encouraged the transferor to pick and choose which employees to transfer, it was retained presumably to reflect the views of those respondents to the 2005 Consultation who favoured the retention of the relevant wording in order to provide some scope for transferors to retain employees who would otherwise transfer.[50]

6. Assignment

4.36 Regulation 4(1) provides for the transfer of the contract of employment 'of any person employed by the transferor and assigned to the organised grouping of resources or employees that is subject to the relevant transfer'. As the 2005 Consultation noted,[51] the 2006 Regulations expanded upon the equivalent provision in TUPE 1981[52] which had simply made reference to 'any person employed by the transferor in the undertaking or part transferred'. The additional wording included in regulation 4(1) incorporates by reference the assignment test established by the ECJ case law and which, as the 2005 Consultation noted,[53] is a question of fact in each case.

4.37 Assignment is a matter which can easily overlap with the issue—which is central to establishing whether or not there is an SPC in a given scenario—of whether there is prior to the putative SPC an organised grouping of employees whose principal purpose is the conduct of the relevant activities for the purposes of regulation 3(3)(a)(i). As Underhill P put it in *Eddie Stobart v Moreman & others*:[54]

> I accept that the issues of whether there existed an organised grouping satisfying the requirements of regulation 3(3)(a)(i) and of whether, if so, all or any of the claimants were assigned to that grouping are analytically distinct, and that the evidence before the Judge was addressed

---

[48] Pursuant to regulations 4(7) and 4(8). See para. 4.71 *et seq.* below.

[49] Although slightly rephrased as regulation 4(1) refers to a contract which would otherwise 'be terminated' rather than 'have been terminated'.

[50] See Consultation Response para. 3.7. This analysis does not sit easily with the approach in the *Celtec* and *QCR* cases discussed at para. 4.01 *et seq.*

[51] At paras 38–41.

[52] TUPE 1981, regulation 5(1).

[53] At para. 39.

[54] [2012] IRLR 356, EAT.

only to the latter issue. But the two points nevertheless self-evidently overlap to a very considerable extent, since for the purposes of considering who is assigned to a putative 'organised grouping' it is necessary to identify what that grouping consisted of.

The approach to be adopted in respect of assignment for the purposes of the Directive and by **4.38** extension TUPE was articulated in *Botzen v Rotterdam Sche Droogdok Maatschappij BV*.[55] That said, in *Edinburgh Home–Link Partnership and others v The City of Edinburgh Council and others*[56] Lady Smith did comment that 'it is difficult to see that what was determined in [*Botzen*] can properly be described as a test', a comment reflecting the fact sensitive nature of the issue of assignment.[57] The ECJ established the principle that the employees whose contracts of employment transfer to the transferee pursuant to the Directive, and by extension TUPE, are those who are assigned to the relevant part of the undertaking or business. The ECJ held that:

> [a]n employment relationship is essentially characterised by the link existing between the employee and the part of the undertaking or business to which he is assigned to carry out his duties. In order to decide whether the rights and obligations under an employment relationship are transferred under Directive No 77/187 by reason of a transfer within the meaning of Article 1(1) thereof, it is therefore sufficient to establish to which part of the undertaking or business the employee was assigned.[58]

By way of a gloss on this approach, *Northern General Hospital NHS Trust v Gale*[59] advanced **4.39** a 'human stock' concept based around integration into the relevant business. In *Duncan Web Offset*[60] the EAT indicated that a variety of factors should be borne in mind by the ET in assessing whether employees are assigned to the undertaking (or activities) and Morison J described the assignment test as follows:

> There will often be difficult questions of fact for industrial tribunals to consider when deciding who was 'assigned' and who was not. We were invited to give guidance to industrial tribunals about such a decision, but declined to do so because the facts will vary so markedly from case to case. In the course of argument a number were suggested such as the amount of time spent on one part of the business or the other; the amount of value given to each part by the employee; the terms of the contract of employment showing what the employee could be required to do; how the cost to the employer of the employee's services had been allocated between different parts of the business. This is, plainly, not an exhaustive list; we are quite prepared to accept that these or some of these matters may well fall for consideration by an industrial tribunal which is seeking to determine to which part of his employers' business the employee had been assigned.[61]

A percentage test of involvement in the relevant undertaking (or activities) is often relied **4.40** upon in negotiations or by parties to litigation as evidentially relevant to or even determinative of the assignment issue. Such an approach was applied in *Anderson v Kluwer Publishing Ltd*.[62] In that case the employee in question was found to be assigned to the undertaking transferred when he dedicated 80 per cent of his time to it. However, the danger of relying on a percentage test in determining who is assigned to the undertaking or the activities

---

[55] [1985] ECR 519, ECJ.
[56] UKEATS/0061/11.
[57] Ibid. footnote to para. 23.
[58] *Botzen*, above n. 55.
[59] [1994] ICR 426, CA.
[60] [1995] IRLR 184, EAT.
[61] Ibid. at para. 15.
[62] COIT 15068/85.

transferred was demonstrated by *Mowlem Technical Services v King*[63] in which the Inner House of the Court of Session rejected an appeal against a decision of an ET that only one of two employees transferred, notwithstanding the fact that they both spent 80 per cent of their time on the undertaking which was the subject of the relevant transfer in question. Nonetheless, a percentage test may be viewed as just one of the various potentially relevant factors.

4.41 In *Buchanan-Smith v Schleicher & Co International Ltd*[64] the employee in question was a director and company secretary dealing with both some of the transferor's shredding machine sales and its service business. The service side of the business was disposed of and the sales function ceased. The employee transferred to the acquirer of the service business and argued that this transfer of employment fell within the scope of TUPE, thereby preserving the employee's continuity of employment for statutory purposes.

4.42 The EAT noted that '[t]he test for whether a person is employed in an undertaking or part is simply: was he assigned to that undertaking or part? That is a question of fact to be determined by considering all the relevant circumstances.'[65] Allowing an appeal against the ET's decision that the employee was not assigned to the service side of the business transferred, the EAT found that, since at the time of transfer one part of the business in which she worked was to cease, the employee was assigned to the (remaining) transferred sales operation. An employee could be assigned to one of two undertakings operated by an employer even if he or she is engaged to some extent in the other. Whilst exclusivity was not required for the *Botzen* requirement of assignment to be satisfied, some small degree of involvement in an undertaking or work for its benefit would in contrast not suffice for assignment to be established.

4.43 *Duncan Web Offset*[66] also made the point that the terms of the relevant employees' contracts can be taken into account in determining the assignment issue. However, this is just one factor. In *Securicor v Fraser Security Services Ltd*[67] the relevant employees had mobility clauses in their contracts pursuant to which the employer could require them to work at any of its branches. Nonetheless, the fact that there was a mobility clause did not mean that for the purposes of TUPE, assessing the circumstances as a whole, the employees in question were not assigned to the relevant site at which they had been working for two years prior to the relevant transfer.

4.44 In *Seawell Ltd v Ceva Freight (UK) Ltd and anor*[68] the need to assess the assignment issue rigorously by reference to factual findings was reiterated by Lady Smith. In *Seawell*, the EAT held that the conclusion in that case by the ET that the employee in question was assigned to the activities transferred from the putative transferor to the putative transferee, Seawell, 'because he spent 100 per cent of his time on Seawell work' did not necessarily follow:

> Whether or not an employee was 'assigned' in terms of reg 4(1) is a question of fact. There require to be specific findings in fact about that matter. That an employee happens to have

---

[63] [2005] CSIH 46.
[64] [1996] IRLR 547, EAT.
[65] Ibid. at para. 21.
[66] [1995] IRLR 184, EAT.
[67] [1996] IRLR 552, EAT.
[68] [2012] IRLR 802, EAT.

been doing particular work does not, of itself, show that the employer assigned him to a group-ing which was organised for the purpose of carrying it out.[69]

That the issue of assignment cannot lead to the splitting of an employment between employ-   **4.45**
ers on a relevant transfer was noted by the Northern Ireland Court of Appeal which made the
following observations in *Hassard v McGrath and others*:[70]

> The tribunal [found] that the employee was assigned to both groups of modules on which he
> worked. If this were correct, it would follow that his contract of employment with the execu-
> tive became two contracts of employment, and he was after the transfer employed by both
> contractors in differing proportions. We do not consider that such a situation is envisaged by
> the directive or the regulations, and it seems to us wholly at odds with the *Botzen* decision.
> Indeed it might give rise to insuperable difficulties. If his employment were split in such a
> fashion, the new employers could find themselves unable to agree over the allocation of his
> time between them. One of them might terminate his employment, and one would have to
> ask then whether that employer's proportion of the employee's time automatically passed
> to the other. These considerations seem to us strongly to support the proposition that an
> employee is only protected under the directive or the 1981 regulations if before the transfer he
> was assigned solely to one part of the undertaking transferred to a transferee. Whether he was
> so assigned is a question of fact, and may well give rise to difficult questions. But the tribunal
> was not in our opinion entitled to find as it did, that the employee was assigned to two separate
> parts of the undertaking and when those parts were transferred to two separate transferees his
> contract of employment had effect after the transfer as if it had been originally made between
> the employee and the two separate contractors.[71]

In view of the fact-specific nature of the issue of assignment test, it is worthwhile briefly   **4.46**
reviewing in summary form some of the scenarios which the case law has considered. In
Kingston v Darlows Estate Agency[72] the Court of Appeal rejected an appeal against an ET decision that two senior estate agent employees who had respectively managerial and administrative responsibilities covering the relevant organization's Wales and West region as a whole
were not assigned to a particular part of the undertaking. When a number of Welsh branches
were sold to a transferee, the two employees in question did not transfer as they were not
assigned to the particular part of the business transferred.

In *CPL Distribution v Todd*[73] the employee in question worked as personal assistant to a   **4.47**
manager who had responsibility for a contract to distribute coal (to which contract most of
her typing related) but who also had other responsibilities. The personal assistant was found
(on the basis of her overall, rather than just typing, duties) not be assigned to the coal distribution part of the employer's undertaking which was transferred.

---

[69] Ibid. at para. 47.
[70] [1996] NICA 586, NICA at pp. 601–2.
[71] The rejection by the NICA of the possibility of a transferring employee's employment being split upon
a relevant transfer between transferees is consistent with the position adopted by the EAT with regard to the
suggestion that employment liabilities could be apportioned between transferees in *Kimberley Group Housing
Ltd v Hambley and others; Angel Services (UK) Ltd v Hambley and others* [2008] IRLR 682, EAT—see Chapter 3,
para. 3.45 *et seq.*
[72] [1995] IRLR 623, CA. In *Edinburgh Home-Link Partnership*, above n. 56, the EAT held that, on the facts
before it, the ET had been entitled to hold that the directors of a company were not assigned to its activities
of providing services to homeless people when they were transferred—within the scope of TUPE by way of
an inhousing to the relevant council—as it was put (at para. 16), their role was 'largely strategic, involved the
maintenance of the organisation itself and was not concerned with direct involvement with service delivery.'
[73] [2003] IRLR 28, CA.

4.48   *Skillbase Services Ltd v King*[74] concerned a council housing maintenance contract which constituted about 80 per cent of the work carried on by the relevant contractor's Grangemouth depot
of which Mr King was the branch manager. When the contract was brought back in-house,
TUPE applied but both the ET and EAT held that Mr King was not wholly or predominantly employed in the undertaking transferred. The basis for this decision, which the Court of
Session found to be sound, was that Mr King was not involved directly in the daily operational
aspects of the contract, did not have regular contact with the client council, and managed the
other functions conducted at the depot for which he was responsible. The proper approach had
been applied, which was to consider a wide range of circumstances. Relevant considerations
could include the amount of time spent in the relevant business, the terms of the employee's
contract, and the allocation within the business of the costs of the employee's employment.

4.49   In *Williams v Advance Cleaning Services (1) Engineering & Railway Solicitors Ltd (In liquidation)*[75] between 60 and 70 per cent of a manager's work related to one particular contract but
he was not assigned to that part undertaking when it was awarded elsewhere—his job related
to several contracts and not just the one lost by the transferor. The EAT made the point that
'it is not sufficient for an employee to show that he was substantially involved in the part
transferred—he has to show that he was effectively assigned to the part transferred'[76] and that
the factors set out in *Duncan Web Offset* were 'neither an exhaustive list nor a mandatory one
that a tribunal has to recite and consider item by item'.[77]

4.50   In *Onwuka v Spherion and others*[78] the employee in question worked for a particular business
unit which was sold pursuant to a transaction falling within the scope of TUPE. The ET's
decision—to the effect that the employee had, by the time of transfer, ceased to work for
the relevant part of the business and there was no more work for him in that business such
that his employment remained with his original employer—was upheld by the EAT as one
properly open to it. This was the case despite the fact that the employee's name had been on
the preliminary list of those to be transferred, he was circulated with the materials circulated
to those to be transferred, and had no other fixed employment with the employer as of the
date of transfer. The ET was nonetheless entitled to form 'the view on the totality of the facts
that at the transfer date the [employee] was not "on the bench" as an employee assigned to
the part of the [business transferred]'.[79]

7. Absence and assignment

4.51   The fact that an employee might not actually be in attendance at work at the point of transfer
does not necessarily exclude that person from being assigned to the relevant economic entity
or activity. In *Fairhurst Ward Abbotts v Botes*[80] the question arose of whether an employee
who had been absent from work because of sickness for the period prior to the transfer was
transferred to either transferee of the undertaking in which he had been employed and which
was split between two third parties on transfer. The ET had held that:

> Mr Salih had been off sick since January 1999. He had become detached from the remain-
> der of the workforce constituted by the applicants. Although on paper he was assigned to

---

[74] [2005] All ER (D) 106, CS.
[75] UKEAT/0838/04.
[76] Ibid. at para. 15.
[77] Ibid. at para. 13.
[78] UKEAT/0523/06.
[79] Ibid. at para. 34.
[80] [2004] IRLR 304, CA.

the part of the undertaking transferred to [Fairhurst], that was not the real situation. He was not in fact employed in the part transferred. He had a contract of employment with [Botes]. Therefore he remained in that employment until he was either transferred under TUPE or dismissed. He was not transferred to either area, and therefore the decision by [Botes] to treat him as no longer being employed by them was a dismissal of him, which was unfair.[81]

The Court of Appeal, however, took the view that it was an error of law to hold that, as **4.52** Mr Salih had been away sick since January 1999, he had become detached from the remainder of the workforce and was not in fact employed in the part transferred immediately before the date of the transfer. If he was in fact employed in that part of the undertaking for the purposes of TUPE, the fact that he was away from work because he was sick would not of itself prevent the transfer from including him. As Mummery LJ said:

> A person on sick leave, like a person on holiday, on disability leave or on maternity leave, remains a person employed in the undertaking, even though he is not actually at his place of work. The question is whether he was employed in the part transferred. That is a factual matter.[82]

In *Marcroft v Heartland (Midlands) Ltd*[83] the defendant served notice of resignation prior to **4.53** a relevant transfer and this notice expired after the sale of the business in which he worked. Following his resignation, the defendant's original employer agreed that he was not required to attend the office but was on call. There was no consultation with the defendant about any relevant transfer nor was the employee referred to in the relevant sale documentation. When the defendant subsequently commenced employment with a competitor, and the claimant (which had acquired the relevant business) instituted High Court proceedings for breach of the restrictive covenants to which the defendant was subject by soliciting clients, the defendant argued that he was not 'assigned' to the undertaking (the original employer's commercial insurance department) which had transferred to the claimant. Consequently, his employment had not transferred to the claimant and it could not enforce the relevant restrictive covenants against him.

At first instance the defendant was held to have remained assigned to the relevant undertak- **4.54** ing (i.e. the commercial insurance department) notwithstanding his having handed in his notice—even while only on call, the defendant had remained part of the commercial insurance team. The Court of Appeal upheld this conclusion, making clear that it cannot be right, in principle, that an employee becomes automatically assigned on a temporary rather than permanent basis to an undertaking or relevant activities, and therefore loses the protection of TUPE, simply by virtue of handing in his notice. The first instance judge was also held to have been entitled to hold that the reduction in volume of, and the change to the nature of, the work which the defendant did once it had been confirmed that he would only be on call did not take the defendant outside the scope of TUPE.

8. Redeployment and temporary or artificial assignments

For an employer to utilize a mobility clause to redeploy employees so as to avoid their transfer **4.55** to the transferee as a consequence of a relevant transfer may not be legally effective. This was

---

[81] At para. 61 of the ET's decision.
[82] [2004] IRLR 304, CA at para. 40.
[83] [2011] IRLR 599, CA.

the finding of HHJ Pugsley in *Jones v Darlow Estate Agency*[84] a view upon which Elias J commented as follows in *Royal Mail Group v Communication Workers Union*:

> Our view is that it is at least arguable that the approach in *Jones* is correct, so that where a mobility clause is used for the very purpose of ensuring that employees who would otherwise transfer are precluded from doing so, this is inconsistent with the policy underlying the Directive.[85]

4.56 Conversely, one of the issues which may concern a transferee in relation to a TUPE transfer is the quality of the workforce which it will inherit. If the test of assignment is applied as a snapshot at the point of transfer, then a transferee may be exposed to the risk that the transferor may, in the period prior to a TUPE transfer, seek to redeploy staff within its organization in order to assign to the transferring undertaking or activities, and therefore to pass to the transferee, employees of lesser skills and experience than would otherwise have transferred.

4.57 Similarly, if an employee works in an operation for a short period on, for example, a one-off project basis, it can be argued that he or she does not form part of the human stock of the undertaking or activities in question and should therefore not fall within the scope of TUPE on the basis of the coincidental occurrence of a TUPE transfer during the duration of that temporary engagement. Commercial agreement, identifying the transferring employees, and seeking to control the degree to which a workforce can be varied in the run-up to transfer, is the preferable solution to these issues if practicable and acceptable.

4.58 As noted above, the 2006 Regulations introduced the concept of assignment into TUPE expressly for the first time, thereby codifying the *Botzen* approach. Regulation 2(1) also specifically addresses the issue of temporary involvement in the relevant undertaking or activities by providing that for these purposes assignment means that the relevant employee is 'assigned other than on a temporary basis'.

4.59 The 2005 Consultation noted that the qualification to the concept of assignment, excluding those who are temporarily assigned to an undertaking or activities from the scope of TUPE, reflects the EAT decision in *Securiplan v Bademosi*.[86] A security guard had been temporarily transferred from his regular place of work to work at a magistrates' court for a period of one year. He was found not to have been assigned to the magistrates' court for the purposes of TUPE on the basis that the assignment was temporary (which thereby took his position outside the scope of the *Botzen* principle).

4.60 There may therefore be difficult distinctions to be drawn in practice between temporary redeployments and specific consecutive assignments as part of an overall contractual engagement. The substance of the matter will need to be addressed carefully by the ET as a matter of fact. The 2009 Guidance suggests that:

> [w]hether an assignment is 'temporary' will depend on a number of factors, such as the length of time the employee has been there and whether a date has been set by the transferor for his return or re-assignment to another part of the business or undertaking.[87]

---

[84] UKEAT/1038/97.
[85] [2009] IRLR 108 at para. 120.
[86] [2003] All ER (D) 435, EAT, discussed at 2005 Consultation para. 40.
[87] At p. 10.

As Lady Smith observed in *Seawell Ltd v Ceva Freight (UK) Ltd and anor*,[88] an employee **4.61** might be working full time on an activity at the point of transfer but not be assigned to that activity for the purposes of TUPE 'since he normally did other work and was only helping out, on a temporary basis e.g. to cover another employee's annual leave'.[89]

In *Carisway Cleaning Consultants Ltd v Richards & anor*[90] the ET had found that the employee **4.62** in question had been deceived—'gulled' as the ET put it—into agreeing to moving to a new location in circumstances where the employer knew that its contract at that location was coming to an end and therefore the employee (with whom it had been having some difficulties) would then transfer away from its employment pursuant to TUPE to a third party. The ET considered that the employee was persuaded to relocate by fraud and what is fraudulent is void. The EAT accepted that the ET was entitled to find that the employee was not part of the undertaking which was transferred—he had only been part of the undertaking because he had been defrauded into going there.

It has been argued that it is difficult to reconcile the analysis deployed in *Carisway* with the **4.63** provisions of TUPE since there is no apparent basis in either the European or the domestic case law for the specific reasons for the actual assignment of an individual employee to be relevant to the question of fact as to whether the individual is or is not assigned to the transferring business or activities. Critics of the *Carisway* decision argue that it might be possible to argue that an assignment made for ulterior motives was actually temporary and therefore ineffective to assign the employee to the undertaking or activities (or part thereof) transferred. This analysis, it can be argued, would achieve the same result—in terms of ensuring that only those properly to be transferred and protected by TUPE fall within its scope—but in a way which is more consonant with the scheme of the legislation. On the basis of either approach, it appears that ETs are entitled to be astute to tackle avoidance of the protective effect of TUPE by way of artificial assignments.

9. Appeals against dismissal and interim relief

In *G4S (Justice Services) Ltd v Anstey and others*[91] the issue was addressed of the application **4.64** of TUPE to employees who had been dismissed for gross misconduct prior to a relevant transfer (i.e. not for a reason connected with the transfer) but whose internal appeals were still outstanding as at that transfer. The question was whether, when their appeals (heard by the transferor) against the dismissal were successful, the employees were to be treated as employed by the transferor immediately before the transfer such that their employment transferred to the transferee under TUPE. The EAT held that the successful appeal effectively 'expunged' the original dismissal and that the employees should have been treated as in effect having been employed by the transferor as at the point of the transfer and accordingly within the scope of TUPE.

The fact that the appeals had not been heard prior as at the date of the relevant transfer **4.65** did not affect this result. In *Anstey*, by reference to the decision of the Court of Appeal in *Roberts v West Coast Trains Ltd*,[92] the EAT based its decision on the concept of the

---

[88] [2012] IRLR 802, EAT.
[89] Ibid. at para. 18.
[90] UKEAT/629/97.
[91] [2006] IRLR 588, EAT.
[92] [2005] ICR 254, EAT.

'vanishing' dismissal. A successful appeal means that the original dismissal is, albeit assessed retrospectively, a nullity. That the appeals had not been heard before the transfer date made no difference to the EAT's analysis that G4S, which now operated the contract on which the employees had been employed, was bound to reinstate the employees in question once their reinstatement had been decided upon by the transferor in accordance with their contracts of employment. The employees' employment was preserved in the meantime for the purposes only of determining their appeals following the transfer. Once their appeals had succeeded and the dismissals were set aside, viewed retrospectively the employees were employed by the transferor immediately before the transfer such that they fell within the scope of TUPE. Regulation 5(3)—which requires an employee, in order to be in scope for the purposes of TUPE, to be employed immediately before the transfer—therefore provided no bar to the employees transferring to G4S.

4.66 HHJ Peter Clark explained the correct analysis of the position in relation to the then current provision[93] as follows:

> In my judgment the principle in *Litster* applies in this way. The Claimants would have been employed by GSL immediately before the transfer if their successful appeals had been heard and determined before the transfer date. The Claimants' rights to have their appeals heard arose under or in connection with their contracts of employment. Thus, the employment was preserved for the purposes only of determining their appeals. They were to be treated as being 'suspended' without pay, to apply the approach in *Savage*,[94] approved in *Tipton*.[95] If the appeal succeeded and the dismissals were set aside, they continued in employment but with G4S as a result of the transfer. Viewed retrospectively, they were employed by GSL immediately before the transfer and Regulation 5(3) provides no bar to the obligation to reinstate transferring to G4S. If not, the original dismissals by GSL stood and the Claimants' employment was not to be treated as transferred, applying the reasoning in *Roberts*.[96] They would not then have been employed by GSL immediately before the transfer.

4.67 By contrast, in *Dowling v ME Ilic Haulage & anor*[97] Burton J held that a continuation order made by an ET—which preserves an individual's relationship with his employer by way of interim relief—does not continue the contract of employment for the purposes of TUPE because it is a purely statutory and unilateral step pursuant to which the employee continues to be employed and be entitled to receive his remuneration but is not obliged to work. As a former employee, an individual who obtains interim relief does not fall within the scope of TUPE or indeed the principle established in *Litster* protecting an individual who would have been employed in the undertaking immediately before the transfer but for a dismissal connected with it. Burton J held that interim relief entails a liability towards the individual employee which does not pass to the transferee pursuant to TUPE.

10. Knowledge of transfer and collective consultation

4.68 There is no express requirement imposed by TUPE on the transferor or the transferee to notify the relevant employees on an individual, as opposed to collective, basis of the fact of their impending or actual transfer to the transferee either generally or in order for the transfer of their employment to the transferee to be effective. There is nonetheless a collective

---

[93] Regulation 5(3) of TUPE 1981, now regulation 4(3).
[94] *Sainsbury v Savage* [1981] ICR 1, CA.
[95] *West Midlands Co-Operative Society Ltd v Tipton* [1986] ICR 192, HL.
[96] *Roberts v West Coast Trains* [2004] IRLR 789, CA.
[97] [2004] ICR 1176, EAT.

obligation to provide information to and consult with appropriate representatives of the affected employees in advance of a TUPE transfer.[98]

In *Photostatic Copiers (Southern) Ltd v Okuda*[99] it was suggested that TUPE could not operate **4.69** to transfer an employee's employment to the transferee unless the employee was informed of the transfer and of the identity of the transferee. This analysis was not followed in *Secretary of State for Trade & Industry v Cook*.[100] As Morison J put it in *Cook*, 'if the employee needs to know, in advance, the identity of the transferee before the contract is transferred, unscrupulous employers would simply refuse to disclose what was happening'.[101]

The principle that transfer of employment pursuant to TUPE is automatic and is not depend- **4.70** ent on collective or individual notification to affected employees was reiterated in *Marcroft v Heartland (Midlands) Ltd*.[102] Mummery LJ indicated that 'there is no basis in fact or law for the suggested implied term in the contract of employment that would render transfer of it ineffective unless the employee has been provided with information about the transfer'.[103] In *Marcroft* it was also held that a failure to comply with the collective information and consultation obligations of TUPE does not prevent an employee from transferring. The remedy for breach of the collective information and consultation obligations of TUPE is an award under regulations 15 and 16 and not an avoidance of a transfer that has taken place. As Mummery LJ put it:

> 40. . . . there is no legal basis for saying that the transfer of his contract of employment was, on the facts found, ineffective. There is a duty under Regulation 13 to provide the representatives of the affected workers with certain information (which does not, however, include the right to object). It is not an obligation to provide the information to Mr Marcroft personally. But even if such a duty could somehow be spelled out of that regulation, the duty rests with the PMI, not Heartland since they are not his employer. The remedy for breach of the Regulation 13 duty is a claim in the Employment Tribunal under Regulations 15 and 16, not an avoidance of the transfer that has taken place.

> 41. Further, compliance with Regulation 13 is not a condition precedent to an effective transfer of a contract of employment. If it were, there would be no point in TUPE conferring the right to object, since the transferor employer in the position of PMI could always prevent a transfer by the simple device of not providing the employee's representative with information in compliance with Regulation 13. Such a construction would undermine the protective purpose of TUPE and the Directive implemented by it.

C. Electing not to Transfer and Consequent Claims

1. Introduction

In implementing into domestic legislation the provisions of Article 4.2 of the Directive, TUPE **4.71** provides[104] three routes by which an employee can elect not to transfer to the transferee:

- an objection to the transfer—which leads to the employee in question having no claim against transferor or transferee;

---

[98] See Chapter 9.
[99] [1995] IRLR 11, EAT.
[100] [1997] IRLR 150, EAT.
[101] Ibid. at para. 12.
[102] [2011] IRLR 599, CA.
[103] Ibid. at para. 42.
[104] By way of regulations 4(7), 4(9) and 4(11).

- resignation in response to a substantial change in working conditions to the employee's material detriment. This enables the employee to bring an unfair dismissal claim but does not enable the employee to a breach of contract claim to be brought against the employer (or indeed the employee);
- resignation without notice in response to a repudiatory breach of contract. This entitles the employee to treat himself or herself as constructively dismissed, and therefore potentially to bring wrongful and unfair dismissal claims as appropriate.

2. Objection to transfer

4.72 That an employee has the right to object to transfer was established by the ECJ in *Katsikas v Konstantinidis*[105] in which the ECJ held as follows:

> 31. In fact, if the Directive, which is intended to achieve only partial harmonisation of the subject-matter (see judgment of *Daddy's Dance Hall* [1988] IRLR 315, cited above, point 16), allows an employee to remain in employment with a new employer on the same conditions as those agreed with the transferor it cannot be interpreted as obliging the employee to continue his employment relationship with the transferee.

> 32. Such an obligation would undermine the fundamental rights of the employee who must be free to choose his employer and cannot be obliged to work for an employer that he has not freely chosen.

> 33. It follows from that that the provisions of Article 3(1) of the Directive do not prevent an employee from objecting to the transfer of his contract of employment or of his employment relationship and, thus, from not benefiting from the protection provided to him by the Directive.

> 34. Nevertheless, as the Court has held (in its judgment in *Berg and Busschers* [1989] IRLR 447, cited above, point 12), the purpose of the Directive is not to ensure that the contract of employment or the employment relationship with the transferor is continued where the undertaking's employees do not wish to remain in the transferee's employ.

> 35. It follows from that that the Directive does not oblige Member States to provide that the contract of employment or employment relationship be continued with the transferor in a case where an employee freely decides not to continue the contract of employment or the employment relationship with the transferee. In such cases, it is for the Member States to determine the fate of the contract of employment or of the employment relationship.

4.73 Regulation 4(7) provides that the contract of employment of an employee and its associated rights, powers, duties, and liabilities which would otherwise transfer to the transferee by virtue of a relevant transfer do not transfer to the transferee if the employee 'informs the transferor or the transferee that he objects to becoming employed by the transferee'. Regulation 4(8) provides that, where an employee objects to his or her employment transferring to the transferee as a result of a relevant transfer in accordance with regulation 4(7), the relevant transfer operates to terminate the employee's contract of employment with the transferor and that, in such circumstances, the employee shall 'not be treated, for any purpose, as having been dismissed by the transferor'. No specific time frame is explicitly identified with regard to when an employee is entitled to object to transfer pursuant to regulation 4(7).

---

[105] [1993] IRLR 179, ECJ.

The right to object to transfer, if exercised, therefore operates to avoid the automatic trans- **4.74** fer of employment from transferor to transferee of an employee assigned to the relevant undertaking or grouping of employees. The fact that exercise of the right to object to transfer pursuant to regulation 4(7) leads to the employee not being treated for any purpose as having been dismissed by the transferor[106] leaves the employee with no claim against either transferor or transferee in relation to the termination of his or her employment, absent a claim under regulation 4(9) or regulation 4(11).[107] Regulations 4(7) and 4(8) therefore provide a simple statutory right to opt out of transferring to the transferee and to leave the business without notice, compensation, or any claim against transferor or transferee.

It is important to note that exercise of the right to object under regulation 4(7) simply **4.75** operates to terminate the employee's employment. An objection does not of itself establish a statutory ability to remain with the transferor as Lady Smith made clear in *Capita Health Solutions Ltd v BBC and McLean*.[108] As HHJ McMullen QC said in *Chambers v QCR Motors Ltd (in voluntary liquidation) & others*,[109] '[w]hen an employee objects to a relevant transfer, the contract does not carry over but the employee can continue to be employed by the transferor'. In terms of the correct legal analysis (as opposed to what happens in practice), an agreement to remain with the transferor needs to be agreed, coupled with an objection, if both transferor and employee wish the employee not to transfer automatically to the transferee. This is the structure adopted in the Retention of Employment Model deployed in relation to certain National Health Service (NHS) Private Finance Initiative Projects.

The termination of employment occasioned by an objection to transfer pursuant to regula- **4.76** tion 4(7) does not of itself free the employee from any restrictive covenants to which he or she may be contractually subject following the termination of employment. However, a number of points should be noted. First, the transferee will have acquired the relevant business but will not have inherited the employment of the employee in question and the contractual benefit of any relevant covenants. The transferee will therefore arguably have no contractual privity with regard to the employee entitling it to enforce any restrictive covenants in the contract of employment of an employee whose employment would otherwise have transferred to the transferee but whom it never employed.

Second, the transferor can be argued no longer to have a legitimate business interest to **4.77** protect (to the extent that it has disposed of the business to which the employee's restrictive covenants apply) upon which it would have to base a contention that the restrictive covenants are enforceable. Any restrictive covenants contained in the employee's contract of employment may therefore be difficult to enforce against the employee by either transferor or transferee.

Third, an objection to transfer pursuant to regulation 4(7) does not need to be justified or **4.78** reasonable to be valid. No breach of contract nor change to working conditions need be established in contrast to the right to terminate employment established by, respectively, regulations 4(10) and 4(9). Exercising the statutory right to object to transfer therefore enables employees to depart with immediate effect on the transfer ignoring the notice period

---

[106] Regulation 4(8).
[107] See para. 4.122 *et seq.*
[108] [2008] IRLR 595, CA at para. 42.
[109] UKEAT/0549/09 at para. 39.

which they would otherwise be required to serve in order lawfully to terminate their employment. An event as apparently anodyne as an internal group reorganization may provide employees with an opportunity to exercise the right to object to transfer in order to be able to terminate their employment with immediate effect. The availability of a right to object to transfer can be particularly relevant if at the particular time the employees in question wish to join a competitor.[110]

4.79 The point was made in *Hay v George Hanson (Building Contracts) Ltd*[111] that TUPE does not require the employer to inform the employee of the 'draconian' consequences—of immediate termination without notice or any claim—of his or her objection (which situation the EAT viewed as 'singularly unfortunate' and which the amendments to the legislation made in 2006 left unchanged).

3. Effecting the objection

4.80 Simply to complain about the transfer is not sufficient to avoid the automatic transfer of the employee's employment. In *Hay v George Hanson (Building Contracts) Ltd*[112] it was held that an employee's objection to transfer must be communicated to the transferor or transferee before the transfer by way of an actual refusal. As Lord Johnston said:

> it seems to us that the scheme of this particular piece of legislation is clear, and does not require to be approached in any artificial or purposive way. What is intended is to protect the right of an employee not to be transferred to another employer against his will, and it is 'against his will' that is the necessary part of the process. We therefore construe the word 'object' as effectively meaning a refusal to accept the transfer, and it is equally clear from reg. 5(4A) that that state of mind must be conveyed to either the transferor or the transferee. But we do not consider it necessary to lay down any particular method whereby such a conveyance could be effected. In our opinion, it could be by either word or deed, or both, and each case must be looked at on its own facts to determine whether there was a sufficient state of mind to amount to a refusal on the part of the employee to consent to the transfer, and that that state of mind was in fact brought to the attention of either the transferor or the transferee.[113]

4.81 The objection must be real. In *Senior Heat Treatment Ltd v Bell*[114] employees completed forms stating that they did not wish to transfer employment to the transferee but wished to receive details of the redundancy payments available to them. Having received the relevant redundancy payments on termination of their employment with the transferor, the individuals took up employment with the transferee pretty much immediately thereafter. Despite the fact that the individuals had completed a form which specifically stated that they did not wish to transfer, the fact that they did start employment with the transferee immediately after the transfer was considered to be inconsistent with an objection to transfer for the purposes of TUPE.

4.82 The importance for transferors of understanding the potential consequences of an employee's exercise of his or her right to object to transfer is demonstrated by *Hope v PGS Engineering*.[115]

---

[110] One way, albeit untested, in which this concern could be addressed would be by the transferor assigning the benefit of the relevant restrictive covenants to the transferee—see Goulding, *Employee Competition*, 2nd Edition, Oxford: OUP, 2012 at para. 5.337.

[111] [1996] IRLR 427, EAT at para. 9.

[112] Above, n. 110.

[113] Ibid. at para. 10.

[114] [1997] IRLR 614, EAT.

[115] UKEAT/0267/04.

The employee notified the transferee of the business in which he worked that he did not wish to transfer to its employment. Had that action been treated as the exercise of the right to object to transfer, the employee would have had no claim as the termination of his employment would not have constituted a dismissal.[116] However, the transferor placed the employee on garden leave for his notice period after his objection. The employee's employment therefore came to an end by virtue of the dismissal taking effect on expiry of the notice period as opposed to the exercise of the right of objection. Being transfer-related, the dismissal was automatically unfair. Since the employee objected to transfer, the liability for this dismissal remained with the transferor.[117]

4. Secondment or objection?

That the factual matrix must be consistent with a genuine objection to transfer for such **4.83** objection to be valid is demonstrated by *Capita Health Solutions Ltd v BBC and McLean*.[118] In that case the BBC outsourced various functions to Capita including the occupational health function in which the claimant employee worked. The employee raised a grievance, which was rejected, about her concerns relating to her role and early retirement entitlements after the transfer. Subsequent to this the BBC proposed that the employee be seconded to Capita for six weeks following the transfer. The employee responded with her resignation and acceptance of the six-week secondment. During the secondment period the employee's salary and benefits continued to be provided by the BBC. The EAT concluded that the test of whether an employee has in fact objected to transfer is an objective one in relation to which the parties' stated intentions are relevant but not determinative.[119] Lady Smith was not convinced that on a valid objection the employee's employment could automatically continue after the transfer itself—as she put it:

> If...it had been intended that objecting employees be required or able to work out notice periods that ran on after the date of transfer, it is more than reasonable to have expected that to be provided for in the Regulations...That is not to say that an objecting employee cannot be employed by the transferor employer after the transfer date, but the transferor is not obliged to retain such an employee in his employment. Any such employment would be under a new contract.[120]

On the facts of this case, despite the parties' use of the term 'secondment' to describe the **4.84** arrangement put in place, the agreement that the employee should work for Capita for six weeks, there being no job for her with the BBC at the end of that period, meant that the employee could not be held validly to have objected to transfer in circumstances where her employment had not terminated but had continued. For the employee to accept the secondment proposal and work for Capita was inconsistent with a valid objection to the transfer of her employment to Capita under TUPE. As Lady Smith put it:[121]

> The claimant does not, of course, insist that she effectively objected. She accepts that her employment transferred. Further, not only did she set out in writing that she was prepared to accede to the first respondents' proposal that she 'proactively work with Capita' but she did so. The use of the word 'secondment' does not, in my view, change matters. What happened

---

[116] Per TUPE 1981, regulation 5(4B); now regulation 4(8).
[117] Per TUPE 1981, regulation 5(4A); now regulation 4(7).
[118] [2008] IRLR 595, CA.
[119] Ibid. at para. 40.
[120] Ibid. at para. 41.
[121] Ibid. at para. 44.

was not secondment in its proper sense, which connotes a temporary assignation regarded, at least at its outset, as being on the basis that the employee will return to work directly for the seconding employer. It was never intended that that would happen.

5. Ignorance of transfer and subsequent objection

4.85 TUPE is silent as to the timing of an objection pursuant to its provisions and the question therefore arises of whether the right to object to transfer can be exercised after the transfer has occurred as well as before that point in time. If this were not permissible, it would disable an employee who only learned of the transfer on or after the occurrence of the event itself from relying on the right to object.

4.86 In *New ISG Ltd v Vernon and others*[122] it was held that, in circumstances where an employee does not know the identity of the transferee prior to a relevant transfer, the employee can potentially exercise the right to object to the transfer after the transfer takes place. This issue arose in the context of an attempt by a transferee to enforce post-termination restrictive covenants against certain executives previously employed in the business which it acquired by way of a relevant transfer. The employees in question were not advised of the identity of the purchaser before completion of the transfer and it was not suggested that they were advised that they had the right to object to being employed by the transferee.

4.87 The transferee argued that the employees' objections to transfer, delivered when they became aware of the transfer after it had been completed, were ineffective. The transferee contended that the wording of regulation 4(7) was plain and that on any ordinary construction the notification by the employee must take place before the date of the transfer on the basis that the objection is framed in the relevant provisions as being an objection to the future state of 'becoming employed by the transferee' as opposed to 'having become employed by the transferee'.

4.88 In two prior EAT decisions a literal interpretation of the corresponding provisions in TUPE 1981 was adopted such that to be effective the right to object could only be exercised prior to the relevant transfer. Lord Johnston took the view in *Hay v George Hanson (Building Contracts) Ltd*[123] that the objection must be:

> so brought to the transferor's or transferee's attention before the date of the transfer because, under reg. 5(4B), the transfer itself automatically terminates the contract. Accordingly, if the terms of reg. 5(4A) are not satisfied in fact, there is an automatic transfer on the appropriate date.

4.89 In *Secretary of State v Cook*,[124] albeit obiter, Morison J said as follows:

> In relation to the employee who, had he known what was happening, would have objected to being transferred, it seems to us that he has lost nothing of value. Had he objected in time he would have lost his employment without an opportunity of claiming compensation, since he would not have been dismissed (reg. 4B). It is to be noted that Parliament provided that an objector could give notice either to the transferor or to the transferee. If the objector, through concealment, found himself employed by the transferee before he could raise an objection, then it seems to us that the moment he discovered what had happened and that his employer was not the transferor but the transferee, he could leave his employment without liability; at

---

[122] [2008] IRLR 115, Ch.
[123] [1996] IRLR 427, EAT at para. 10.
[124] UKEAT/582/96.

the least, the parties to the transfer would be estopped from denying that the employee had exercised his right to object timeously. Further, it may well be the case that it would be a breach of the employer's duty of good faith to employees to conceal from them a transfer which has taken place. Whether any such breach would give the employees valuable claims for damages would need examination. Further, an employee has an express right to terminate his contract in the circumstances provided by reg. 5(5).

Nonetheless, in *Vernon* it was accepted that the court should adopt a purposive construc- **4.90** tion to regulation 4(7) so that in appropriate circumstances an objection to transfer can validly be made after the occurrence of the relevant transfer in question. The analysis of the court was that 'in a case such as this where the employee does not know the identity of the transferee before the date of the transfer [the transferee's] construction undermines the fundamental freedom of the employee to choose his employer'.[125] The transferee objected that this approach would render it uncertain precisely when (i.e. how long after the relevant transfer) the right to object to transfer is lost. However, HHJ Behrens QC took the view that the assessment of this issue would be 'likely to be no more difficult than determining if an employee has affirmed the contract in a constructive dismissal case'.[126]

In reaching this decision, HHJ Behrens QC adopted the following analysis of the preceding **4.91** authorities which were inconsistent with his conclusions. In his view in *Hay* Lord Johnston did not have in mind a case such as this where the employee was not informed of the identity of the transferee until after the date of the transfer.[127] Also, he considered that Morison J's analysis in *Cook* failed to appreciate that the right to object can have value—as the *Vernon* case itself demonstrated, by reference to the avoidance of restrictive covenants which objection to transfer can effect.

6. Changes to working conditions

(a) TUPE 1981

TUPE 1981, regulation 5(5) provided that its provisions with regard to automatic transfer **4.92** of employment and the right to object to transfer[128] were:

> without prejudice to any right of an employee arising apart from these Regulations to termi-
> nate his contract of employment without notice if a substantial change is made in his work-
> ing conditions to his detriment; but no such right shall arise by reason only that, under that
> paragraph, the identity of his employer changes unless the employee shows that, in all the
> circumstances, the change is a significant one and is to his detriment.

TUPE 1981, regulation 5(5) and its successor, regulation 4(9), derive from Article 4.2 which **4.93** provides that:

> If the contract of employment or the employment relationship is terminated because the
> transfer involves a substantial change in working conditions to the detriment of the employee,
> the employer shall be regarded as having been responsible for termination of the contract of
> employment or the employment relationship.

---

[125] Ibid. at para. 70.
[126] Ibid.
[127] Ibid. at para. 72.
[128] Per TUPE 1981 regulations 5(1) and 5(4A) respectively.

4.94   In *Rossiter v Pendragon plc and Crosby-Clarke v Air Foyle Ltd*[129] the EAT held that constructive dismissal could be established in the TUPE context without a breach of contract on the part of the employer. As HHJ Wilkie QC saw it:

> in the context of a transfer of undertakings, section 95(1)(c) has to be construed so as to give effect to the Directive as incorporated into English law by the Regulations [and] this calls for a different construction from that which applies in the purely domestic context, In particular, it does not require the tribunal to find a breach of contract in order to give rise to the entitlement to resign and claim constructive dismissal under [ERA] 1996.[130]

4.95   However, the Court of Appeal in *Rossiter*[131] held that TUPE 1981, regulation 5(5) only permitted an employee to bring a constructive dismissal claim in the context of a TUPE transfer where the traditional common law test of a repudiatory breach of contract by the employer was satisfied. A change to working conditions, even if detrimental, was not sufficient to give rise to a constructive dismissal claim unless there were a repudiatory breach of contract on the part of the employer. The Court of Appeal considered it unlikely that Article 4.2 could create a form of constructive dismissal based on a threshold lower than repudiatory breach of contract. Accordingly, it was held that TUPE 1981, regulation 5(5) was not intended to create a right to claim constructive dismissal based on detrimental changes to working conditions falling short of a repudiatory breach of contract, in addition to and distinct from the right to claim constructive dismissal arising in relation to a repudiatory breach of contract. Regulation 5(5) could entitle an employee to elect not to transfer to the transferee but the employee would not have a consequent claim in the absence of a constructive dismissal on traditional common law principles.

4.96   As Peter Gibson LJ put it:

> When one turns to the language of reg. 5(5), in my judgment it is made quite clear that no new right was thereby intended to be created. The Regulation preserves rights which arise 'apart from these Regulations'. The only right to claim constructive dismissal which arises apart from TUPE is the right of the employee to resign when faced with a repudiatory breach of contract by the employer. If there were to be a right to claim constructive dismissal by reason only of a substantial change in working conditions to the employee's detriment, without there being a breach of contract, that would be a new right. That right would not arise apart from TUPE, but only by reason of TUPE. The language of reg. 5(5) was plainly chosen so as to implement Article 4(2) of the Directive. It was also, in my judgment, intended to be consistent with s. 95(1)(c) of the [ERA 1996]. Only conduct by the employer amounting to a repudiation of the contract would entitle the employee to terminate the contract 'without notice'.[132]

(b) Regulation 4(9)[133]

4.97   *Rossiter* was effectively reversed by virtue of the restatement in the 2006 Regulations by regulation 4(9) of the right on the part of an employee to terminate his or her employment in response to a substantial change to working conditions to the employee's material detriment.

---

[129] UKEAT/243/00.
[130] Ibid. at para. 29.
[131] [2002] IRLR 483, CA.
[132] Ibid. at para. 33.
[133] See Wynn-Evans, 'Substantial Changes and the Right not to Transfer' (February 2009) ELJ 9.

Regulation 4(9) provides that where a relevant transfer: **4.98**

> involves or would involve a substantial change in working conditions to the material detriment of a person whose contract of employment is or would be transferred under paragraph 1(1), such an employee may treat the contract of employment as having been terminated, and the employee shall be treated for any purpose as having been dismissed with notice by the employer.

Regulation 4(9) therefore potentially provides employees affected by a relevant transfer with **4.99** rights of action additional to the simple right to object to transfer if their position is prejudiced, even if the change made by the new employer falls short of a repudiatory breach of contract. As the 2005 Consultation put it, a substantial change of working conditions to the detriment of an employee 'may not be sufficiently serious to amount to repudiatory breach of contract by the employer, entitling the employee to resign and claim constructive dismissal'.[134] For example, the transferee may act entirely lawfully (i.e. without breach of contract) by relying on an express contractual power to vary bonus or benefit arrangements or to relocate staff. However, if this results in a substantial change to working conditions to the employee's material detriment, regulation 4(9) will be engaged.

Any concern that employees could exercise the right provided by regulation 4(9) on the basis **4.100** of trivial concerns is met by two elements of the provision—that the change must be substantial and that its detrimental effect must be material for the right provided by regulation 4(9) to be available. In terms of what constitutes a 'substantial change in working conditions to the material detriment' of the relevant employee, the 2009 Guidance states that:

> [t]his will be a matter for the courts and the tribunals to determine in the light of the circumstances of each case. What might be a trivial change in one setting might constitute a substantial change in another. However, a major relocation of the workplace which makes it difficult or much more expensive for an employee to transfer, or the withdrawal of a right to a tenured post, is likely to fall within this definition.[135]

The requirement that the relevant detriment be material was introduced into the drafting of regulation 4(9) as a result of the consultation process over what became the 2006 Regulations. No such materiality threshold appears in the Directive. However, in *Tapere v South London & Maudsley NHS Trust*[136] the EAT took the view that this qualification of materiality was not inconsistent with the Directive—'although "*material*" is added to the rubric of the Directive, we do not think that the addition is at all at odds with the meaning of the Directive, so long as the purpose of the adjective is regarded as an emphasis that the trivial or fanciful cannot be accepted as "*detriment*"'.[137]

In any event there needs to be a causal connection between the transfer and the changes to **4.102** working conditions in question for regulation 4(9) to engage given that it explicitly requires it to be the case that the transfer 'involves or would involve' the requisite substantial changes.

(c) Dismissal claims and regulation 4(9)

Regulation 4(9) therefore creates the possibility of a claim effectively of constructive dismissal **4.103** based on substantial and materially detrimental changes to working conditions separate to

---

[134] At para. 46.
[135] At p. 16.
[136] [2009] IRLR 972, EAT.
[137] Ibid. per HHJ Hand QC at para. 52.

the 'traditional' common law test based on repudiatory breach of contract. Whereas TUPE 1981, regulation 5(5) only provided a right to terminate employment, regulation 4(9) expressly determines there to be a dismissal in these circumstances. That 'traditional' constructive dismissal is specifically and separately referred to in regulation 4(11) only reinforces the point that regulation 4(9) creates, in the TUPE context, a separate claim based on a less demanding test than the repudiatory breach of contract on the part of the employer required to make out a traditional constructive dismissal claim.

4.104 Notwithstanding the fact that regulation 4(9) deems there to be a dismissal when the employee exercises the right which it provides, regulation 4(9) denies the employee a wrongful dismissal damages claim against the employer in those circumstances. Regulation 4(10) provides that '[n]o damages shall be payable by an employer as a result of a dismissal falling within [regulation 4(9)] in respect of any failure by the employer to pay wages to an employee in respect of a notice period which the employee has failed to work'.[138] That said, regulation 4(9) does not deny the employee his or her contractual right to payment should the employee continue actually to be employed during his or her notice period.

4.105 In the 2005 Consultation[139] the formulation that the deemed dismissal created by regulation 4(9) would not lead to a contractual claim in respect of the employee's notice period was justified on the basis that it was not 'right for an employer to be penalized for failing to give notice of termination in a situation where the employment contract was terminated in [such] circumstances'. Why an unfair dismissal claim can ensue when the regulation 4(9) right is exercised but not a wrongful dismissal claim was not articulated.

4.106 Since regulation 4(9) deems there to be a dismissal when an employee exercises the right which it provides, an unfair dismissal claim can be founded on an employee's election to terminate his or her employment pursuant to regulation 4(9). That exercise of the right afforded by regulation 4(9) leads to a potential unfair dismissal claim is supported by the answer in the 2009 Guidance to the question of whether it is unlawful for the transferee to make such substantial changes in working conditions and whether it is automatically unfair when an employee resigns because such a change has taken place. The 2009 Guidance indicates that:

> The Regulations merely classify such resignations as 'dismissals'. This can assist the employee if he subsequently complains of unfair dismissal because he does not need to prove he was 'dismissed'. However, to determine whether the dismissal was unfair, the tribunal will still need to satisfy itself that the employer had acted unreasonably, and there is no presumption that it is unreasonable for the employer to make changes.[140]

4.107 It would appear that the dismissal which is deemed to occur on exercise of the right conferred by regulation 4(9) will be transfer related and therefore automatically unfair for the purposes of regulation 7(1) unless saved by the existence of an ETOR and the dismissal not being otherwise unfair.[141]

---

[138] The first draft of what was to become TUPE 2006 deemed the dismissal resulting from the exercise of the regulation 4(9) right to be 'with notice'.

[139] At para. 46.

[140] At p. 16.

[141] See Chapter 7 for discussion of transfer-related dismissals.

(d) The Directive

The consistency of regulation 4(9) with the Directive has been rendered less than clear by the   **4.108**
ECJ decision in *Juuri v Amica Oy*[142] on the issue of substantial changes to working conditions under the Directive, albeit in relation to the Finnish transfer legislation. The employee
in question worked at a staff canteen which transferred to a third party within the scope of
the Directive. Because the new employer indicated that her employment would now be
governed by the applicable accommodation and catering sector collective agreement, rather
than the metal industry agreement which had applied to her employment prior to transfer,
the employee terminated her contract of employment with immediate effect having failed
to change her new employer's decision. Her argument was that her working conditions had
become substantially worse as a result of the transfer of the undertaking because her income
had fallen significantly and she was required to work at different locations. The employee's
claim was not only for the compensation in respect of the applicable four-month notice
period but also for the equivalent under Finnish law of unfair dismissal.

The relevant legislation, reflecting Article 4(2) more closely than TUPE 2006 does, provides   **4.109**
that the employer is responsible for the termination of employment of an employee who
elects not to transfer to the transferee on the basis of substantial changes to the employee's
working conditions. However, it makes no explicit provision with regard to the consequent
compensation payable to an employee who exercises this right.

The employee's claim was rejected by the domestic court on the basis that Article 4(2) could   **4.110**
not be construed as supplementing the national rules on dismissal compensation. The questions which were referred to the ECJ for a preliminary ruling were:

> 1. Is Article 4(2) of the ARD to be interpreted as meaning that a Member State must, where
> an employee has given notice to terminate their contract of employment after their working
> conditions become substantially worse following the transfer of an undertaking, in its law
> guarantee the employee the right to obtain financial compensation from the employer in
> the same way as in the case where the employer has unlawfully (i.e. unfairly) terminated the
> employment contract?
>
> 2. If the employer's responsibility is not that extensive, is it nevertheless obliged to provide
> compensation for pay and other benefits in respect of the employee's notice period?[143]

The ECJ concluded that in essence the precise consequences of the termination of employ-   **4.111**
ment in these circumstances must be established by each Member State under its national
law.[144] That said, the ECJ also observed that:

> the national court is required, in a case within its jurisdiction, to ensure that, at the very least,
> the transferee employer in such a case bears the consequences that the applicable national law
> attaches to termination by an employer of the contract of employment or the employment
> relationship, such as the payment of the salary and other benefits relating, under that law, to
> the notice period with which an employer must comply.[145]

Juuri can be therefore be interpreted as requiring the employer to pay contractual notice pay   **4.112**
and other benefits relating to the notice period (as would be the case under contract law if
a summary dismissal were effected in breach of contract). This clearly raises a question as to

---

[142] [2009] 1 CMLR 33, ECJ.
[143] Ibid. at AG18.
[144] Ibid. at para. 35.
[145] At para. 30.

the validity of regulation 4(10) to the extent that it precludes an employee from being able to bring a wrongful dismissal claim in respect of the applicable notice period. The counter-argument is that regulation 4(10) is part of the applicable national law and therefore valid since Article 4(2) does not require a particular level of compensation in respect of termination of employment in these circumstances.

(e) Applying regulation 4(9)

4.113 *Tapere v South London and Maudsley NHS Trust*[146] considered the operation of regulation 4(9) in a situation where an employee had been required to relocate to a new place of work which she considered detrimental not least in terms of increased travel time. The EAT identified two components to regulation 4(9)—first there must be a 'substantial change in working conditions'; second that change must be to the material detriment of the person whose contract of employment is transferred pursuant to TUPE.

4.114 In relation to the concept of 'working conditions' HHJ Hand QC commented as follows:

> In our judgment Parliament did not intend '*working conditions*' in regulation 4(9) to be confined to a physical state of affairs as might be the case if the matter were being looked at from the point of view of health and safety or environmental considerations. It seems to us obvious that the regulation implements the decision of the European Court of Justice in *Merckx and Neuhuys v Ford Motors Belgium SA* [1996] IRLR 467, where salesmen were transferred to a new dealership at a different workplace without any guarantee as to client base or sales figures, so that there was potential for an adverse impact on commission. All these components were regarded by the European Court of Justice as 'working conditions' and it follows that the phrase applies to contractual terms and conditions as well as physical conditions.[147]

4.115 With regard to the need for there to be a substantial change to those working conditions the view of HHJ Hand QC was that:

> Whether or not there is a change in working conditions will be a simple question of fact. Whether or not it is a change of substance will also be a question of fact and the Employment Tribunal will need to consider the nature as well as the degree of the change in order to decide whether it is substantial. In the sense that the employee will not be the arbitrator of whether the change is substantial, it might be said that the approach is objective but, as the case of *Merckx and Neuhuys v Ford Motors Belgium SA* illustrates, the character of the change is likely to be the most important aspect of determining whether the change is substantial. There, the European Court of Justice regarded the change as substantial because it was a change in remuneration. No doubt, in such cases there will be endless scope for argument as to the degree of change; the employer will assert that the money will be the same in the end result; the employee will protest that cannot be so; but the focus, in our judgment must be on the nature of the change.[148]

4.116 In *Tapere* the reference in regulation 4(9) to 'material detriment' was viewed[149] as seeking to exclude the trivial or fanciful as a recognition of the analysis of Lord Hope in *Shamoon v Royal Ulster Constabulary*,[150] albeit in the discrimination field, that the word detriment connotes materiality. In that decision Lord Hope described the question to be answered as

---

[146] [2009] IRLR 972, EAT.
[147] Ibid. at para. 44.
[148] Ibid. at para. 45.
[149] Ibid. at para. 52.
[150] [2003] IRLR 285, HL.

follows—'Is the treatment of a kind that a reasonable worker would or might take the view that in all the circumstances it was to his detriment?'[151]

The EAT also disagreed with the ET's assessment that the test of whether a detriment is material was an objective one, i.e. that the competing arguments of employee and employer should, as the EAT described the ET's analysis, be 'contrasted, weighed and arbitrated upon'.[152] As HHJ Hand QC put it: **4.117**

> [w]hat has to be considered is the impact of the proposed change from the employee's point of view.... The questions which ought to have been asked were whether the employee regarded those facts as detrimental and, if so, whether there was a reasonable position for the employee to adopt? In determining the matter by weighing the employee's position against that of the employer and deciding that the employer's position was reasonable, the employment tribunal looked at the matter from the wrong standpoint and thus misdirected itself as to the correct approach to regulation 4(9).[153]

In *Nationwide Building Society v Benn and others*[154] following the transfer of the undertaking in which they were employed from the Portman Building Society to the Nationwide Building Society, the claimant employees contended that the terms of their employment were altered to their detriment by the new employer. Job roles and responsibilities were downgraded as they were assimilated into their new roles. The new bonus scheme in which the employees in question participated post transfer was substantially less beneficial than their previous scheme. The ET's decision was upheld that the diminutions in the job which the claimants were to perform and in one employee's case a significant reduction in bonus 'rightly led to the conclusion that the Claimants had been dismissed by application of regulation 4(9)'.[155] **4.118**

(f) Other points

Certain aspects of TUPE 1981, regulation 5(5) were not carried over into regulation 4(9). First, although it is implicit in the provision that the employee's employment is terminated with immediate effect by the employer if the employee terminates his or her employment on that basis, regulation 4(9) does not expressly state that the employee can in such circumstances terminate his employment without notice. Second, there is no equivalent of the proviso to TUPE 1981, regulation 5(5). This provided that the right to terminate employment in response to a substantial detrimental change to working conditions did not arise by reason only that the identity of the employer would change, unless the employee could show that in all the circumstances the change of employer was a significant change and was to his or her detriment. Whether the change to the identity of the employer consequent upon a TUPE transfer can lead to regulation 4(9) being engaged is presumably dependent on the factual issues of the consequent detriment (which, importantly, must be to working conditions) and its materiality. **4.119**

The ability to terminate employment based on a substantial and materially detrimental change to working conditions presumably does not apply where contractual variations are agreed by the employee in connection with the transfer under regulations 4(4) and 4(5). Since regulation 4(9) is stated expressly to be subject to regulation 9, an affected employee **4.120**

---

151 Ibid. at para. 35.
152 *Tapere*, above n. 136, at para. 53.
153 Ibid. at para. 54.
154 UKEAT/0273/09.
155 Ibid. at para. 65.

cannot invoke regulation 4(9) in relation to a permitted variation agreed in an insolvency situation by appropriate representatives.

4.121   The interaction of regulation 4(9), enabling an employee to object to transfer and claim unfair dismissal based on a substantial change to his material detriment to his working conditions, with changes to pension rights is not addressed explicitly in TUPE 2006. On the face of it, it might be argued that a change to an employee's pension entitlements could be a substantial change to working conditions to the employee's material detriment. However, this analysis does not sit well with the provisions of TUPE which exclude from its protection certain occupational pension rights on a relevant transfer.[156] For a change to those non-preserved pension rights to enable an employee to rely on regulation 4(9) would not be consistent with regulation 10(3) which provides that a transferring employee is not be entitled to bring a claim against the transferor for breach of contract or constructive unfair dismissal 'arising out of a loss or reduction in his rights under an occupational pension scheme in consequence of the transfer, save insofar as the alleged breach of contract or dismissal (as the case may be) occurred prior to the date on which these Regulations took effect'.

7. Constructive dismissal

4.122   Regulation 4(11) states that the 'automatic transfer' provisions[157] of and the rights to object to transfer[158] provided by TUPE are 'without prejudice to any right of an employee arising apart from these Regulations to terminate his contract of employment without notice in acceptance of a repudiatory breach of contract by his employer'. This preserves the ability of an employee to claim constructive dismissal by reason of the transferor's or transferee's fundamental breach of contract on the basis of the traditional test of a repudiatory breach of contract. Regulation 10(3) precludes a breach of contract or constructive unfair dismissal claim where the transferee fails to honour, after a relevant transfer, those occupational pension scheme entitlements which regulation 10 excludes from transfer to the transferee.[159]

4.123   In order for an employee to be able to claim damages for wrongful dismissal in circumstances where he has objected to transfer, the individual will have to establish a repudiatory breach of contract on the part of the employer which the employee accepted—a constructive dismissal claim will therefore remain available, in such circumstances pursuant to regulation 4(11), as distinct from being unavailable pursuant to regulation 4(9).

4.124   An example of a transfer-related constructive dismissal is *Euro-Die (UK) Ltd v Skidmore*[160] where the employer's failure to assure an employee of the security of his position post transfer constituted a breach of the implied duty to maintain mutual trust and confidence. Lindsay P said as follows:

> Where an employer, in answer to a concerned employee, fails at a crucial juncture to give an assurance which asks no more than for the true employment position to be recognised on a subject as essential to the employee's ease of mind as continuity of employment it cannot be said, in our view, that that failure cannot represent so fundamental a breach of the implied

---

[156]   See regulation 10(3) and Chapter 11.
[157]   Regulation 4(1).
[158]   Regulations 4(7), 4(8), 4(9), and 4(10).
[159]   See Chapter 11.
[160]   UKEAT/1158/98.

terms as to trust and confidence as to entitle the employee to treat himself as constructively dismissed. If, accordingly, such a failure could be such a breach, it was open to the Tribunal as masters of fact to hold, as they did, that it was such a breach.

8. Claims against the transferor

The 2006 Regulations do not expressly address or overrule the principle established in **4.125** *University of Oxford v Humphreys*[161] in which an employee terminated his contract in advance of a relevant transfer because the terms of employment which the transferee intended to impose upon him would have been significantly to his detriment. The Court of Appeal held that the right to object to transfer[162] is entirely separate from the free-standing right to terminate employment without notice in response to a substantial detrimental change to working conditions.[163] The Court of Appeal's analysis was that the (common law) constructive dismissal claim which was being made by the employee prior to transfer could only lie against the employer at the relevant time (i.e. the transferor). Moreover, TUPE 1981, regulation 5(4A) specifically stated that, as a consequence of an objection of the kind under consideration, no 'rights, powers, duties or liabilities' would transfer to the transferee under TUPE (as an exception to the general principle of transfer of employment-related liabilities). The remedy against the transferor was specifically stated not to transfer to the transferee.

Potter LJ explained the analysis as follows: **4.126**

> it is clear that to the extent that the common law right of the employee to terminate and sue for constructive dismissal is preserved by paragraph (5), it is a right which exists and must be asserted against the transferor employer. The reason is twofold. First, it is the nature of the common law right and remedy that both exists in respect of the employer who wrongly terminates the employee's contract of employment, and cannot be asserted against a proposed transferee. Second, it is because the introductory wording of paragraph (4A) excludes the statutory novation under paragraph (1) and the comprehensive transfer of rights and obligations under paragraph (2); thus the remedy against the transferor employer is not transferred.[164]

This principle was applied in *Thomas v Ewar Stud Farm Ltd (1) the Lord Tryon (2)*[165] in which **4.127** it was made clear that the *Litster*[166] principle of transfer to the transferee of liability for a pre-transfer dismissal does not apply in relation to a resignation/objection to transfer in accordance with what was for the purposes of that case regulation 5 TUPE 1981.

TUPE 2006 does nothing to remove liability from the transferor in such circumstances **4.128** (where it is arguably the transferee which creates the problem). Regulation 4(7) repeats the provisions of TUPE 1981 considered in *Humphreys*. This interpretation is supported by the rejection of suggestions during the consultation process that references in regulation 4(9) should be to the transferor or transferee depending on the timing, As the Consultation Response put it,[167] the view was taken that 'an employee can use draft Regulation 4(9) and 4(10) to seek redress against the transferor or the transferee, depending on the identity of his employer at the material time'. It therefore appears still to be the case (however

---

[161] [2000] IRLR 183, CA.
[162] Under TUPE 1981, regulations 5(4A) and 5(4B); now regulations 4(7) and 4(8).
[163] TUPE 1981, regulation 5(5); now, as amended, regulation 4(9).
[164] *Humphreys*, above n. 161, at para. 39.
[165] UKEAT/934/01.
[166] See para. 4.25 *et seq*.
[167] At para. 3.11.

counter-intuitive it may seem) that an employee can object to transfer on the grounds of an anticipatory constructive dismissal on the part of (or even arguably an anticipatory change to his or her employment terms to be implemented by) the transferee and yet have an unfair dismissal claim against the transferor rather than the transferee. The *Humphreys* decision reinforces the need for transferors where possible to seek appropriate indemnities from transferees to protect themselves against the financial consequences of such claims.

4.129   In contrast, in *Sita (GB) Ltd v Burton*,[168] the transferee's conduct towards the relevant employees prior to transfer was not found capable of leading to a constructive dismissal. As the relevant issues arose prior to transfer when the employees were employed by the transferor, the transferee's conduct could not lead to a breach of a contract to which the transferee was not yet party nor did it create a breach of trust and confidence in the transferor as the employer at the material time. Being based on an alleged breach of the implied duty to maintain trust and confidence rather than the right to object to transfer or a substantial change to working conditions to their detriment, the employees' claims failed. The *SITA* decision, it should be noted, was not based on an argument of anticipatory breach of contract.

9. Change of location

4.130   That a change of location associated with a TUPE transfer can potentially enable employees to object to transfer under regulation 4(9) and, depending upon the circumstances, give rise to a constructive unfair dismissal claim pursuant to regulation 4(11) was demonstrated by *Abellio London Ltd v Musse et al (1) Centrewest London Buses Ltd (2)*.[169] The employees in question were bus drivers employed originally by CentreWest at its Westbourne Park depot. When the bus route which they worked on was transferred to Abellio by way of what was accepted to be a SPC, Abellio intended to relocate the drivers to its Battersea depot. This change of location entailed between one and two hours' additional travel each day for the affected staff. The employees were held by the ET to be entitled to terminate their employment pursuant to regulation 4(9) on the basis that the change to their location was a substantial change to their working conditions to their material detriment.

4.131   The EAT considered that the ET had been entitled to conclude on the basis of the evidence before it that the extension of the working day of about two hours was material. The change was also a repudiatory breach of contract. The employees' contract of employment folder identified the other work locations to which employees could be moved and Battersea was not stated to be one of them. Nor was there a valid variation of this provision. Consequently, the employees were constructively dismissed for the purposes of regulation 4(11) and, being by reason of the transfer, their dismissals were automatically unfair. The EAT rejected the argument that regulation 4(2)—which transfers to the transferee the transferor's rights and powers—could, in the context of these specific contractual arrangements, make 'a location that was not that of the employer at the time into one which had become a depot of the employer'.[170]

4.132   In *Holis Metal Industries Ltd v GMB (1) Newell Ltd (2)*[171] the EAT noted the potential application of regulation 4(9) in the context of a change of location relating to an overseas

---

[168] [1997] IRLR 501, EAT.
[169] [2012] IRLR 360, EAT.
[170] Ibid. para. 35.
[171] [2008] IRLR 187, EAT. See Chapter 12, para. 12.24 *et seq*. See Chapter 5, para. 5.54.

transfer. If a transferor plans to implement a relevant transfer entailing the relevant under-taking or activities being taken offshore, that transferor faces the risk of employees who would otherwise transfer to the transferee (and presumably be made redundant) exercising the right provided by regulation 4(9) ahead of the transfer on the basis that the relocation overseas would constitute a substantial change to their working conditions to their mate-rial detriment. On the basis of *University of Oxford v Humphreys*[172] the employees' unfair dismissal claims would then presumably lie against the transferor. Given that redundancy might well in such circumstances have been inevitable, the compensation recoverable by the employees might not be significant but it is of concern in any event to transferors that they can be liable in such circumstances for the consequences of what will happen post transfer in terms of working conditions as well as for more traditional constructive dismissal claims.

---

[172] See para. 4.125 *et seq.*

5

WHAT TRANSFERS?

A. **Individual Rights**	5.01	12. Mobility clauses	5.51
1. General position	5.01	13. Collectively determined terms	5.55
2. What is transferred?	5.08	B. **Collective Agreements**	5.73
3. What is not transferred?	5.13	1. The Directive and TUPE	5.73
4. Discretionary entitlements	5.17	2. Collective agreements and recognition	
5. No improvement of employee's position	5.21	defined	5.81
6. Employer's liability compulsory		3. Legal enforceability	5.84
insurance	5.25	C. **Trade Union Recognition**	5.88
7. Restrictive covenants	5.29	1. Transfer of recognition	5.88
8. Difficulties in replicating entitlements	5.31	2. Continuation of recognition	5.92
9. Share options	5.35	3. Statutory recognition	5.95
10. Changes to statutory rights	5.39	D. **Other Representative Structures**	5.96
11. Continuity of employment	5.45		

A. Individual Rights

1. General position

5.01 TUPE has been described as having a 'Worzel Gummidge' effect whereby '[t]he head is swapped but the body (the business) continues'.[1] In *Carisway Cleaning Consultants Ltd v Richards and anor*[2] Maurice Kay J described the effect of the transfer legislation as follows:

> It is as if, for legal purposes, the old employer and the new employer had got together with the employee and said: 'do you agree to your contract being transferred with all its terms, advantages and liabilities to the new employer?' and the employee had said to both of them: 'yes, I do agree.' That would be a novation of the contract, as it would be called legally. Article 5 has that effect where there is a relevant transfer.

5.02 Subject to the specific provisions of TUPE relating to insolvency situations,[3] employees' rights to object to their transfer to the transferee and the exclusion of criminal liabilities and certain occupational pension rights from those liabilities which the transferee inherits, the transferee effectively sits in the shoes of the transferor following the relevant transfer as regards the employment of the employees, including responsibilities for the past acts and

---

[1] Pollard, 'Pensions and TUPE' (2005) 34 ILJ 127.
[2] UKEAT/629/97.
[3] Regulations 8 and 9—see Chapter 10.

omissions of the transferor. Subject to these important exceptions, on a relevant transfer the transferor ceases to be responsible for any employment obligations in respect of the transferring employees—these all transfer to the transferee.

The precise rights and obligations which transfer to the transferee depend on national law as **5.03** indicated by the ECJ in *Daddy's Dance Hall*[4] where it was said that:

> The Directive is intended to achieve only partial harmonisation, essentially by extending the protection guaranteed to workers independently by the laws of the individual Member States to cover the case where an undertaking is transferred. It is not intended to establish a uniform level of protection throughout the Community on the basis of common criteria. Thus, the Directive can be relied on only to ensure that the employee is protected in his relations with the transferee to the same extent as he was in his relations with the transferor under the legal rules of the Member State concerned.

More specifically, the operation of TUPE attaches to the relevant employees' contracts of **5.04** employment. Regulation 4(2) provides that:

(a) all the transferor's rights, powers, duties and liabilities under or in connection with any such contract shall be transferred by virtue of this regulation to the transferee; and

(b) any act or omission before the transfer is completed, of or in relation to the transferor in respect of that contract or a person assigned to that organised grouping of resources or employees shall be deemed to have been an act or omission of or in relation to the transferee.

When the 2006 Regulations were introduced the specific clarification was made in regula- **5.05** tion 4(2) that the transferee inherits any 'act or omission' of the transferor as distinct from anything done by it.[5] This change was made 'for completeness'.[6]

To summarize the position ahead of detailed consideration of the case law on the issues **5.06** which arise in this context, and the separate discussions which follow of the position in relation to collective agreements[7] and collective information and consultation,[8] the following pre-transfer liabilities pass to transferees under TUPE:

- liability for breaches of contract arising prior to transfer;
- liability in respect of statutory employment claims;
- liability in tort—for example, an employee's claim for personal injury[9] or misrepresentation;[10]
- continuous employment for statutory purposes;[11]
- the transferor's compulsory employers' liability insurance.[12]

---

[4] [1988] IRLR 315, ECJ at para. 17.
[5] As was the formulation in TUPE 1981 and the first draft of what became the 2006 Regulations.
[6] Consultation Response para. 3.8.
[7] See para. 5.55 *et seq.* in relation to individual entitlements deriving from collective agreements and para. 5.73 *et seq.* in relation to collective agreements generally.
[8] See Chapter 9.
[9] See para. 5.25.
[10] See *Hagen v ICI Chemicals and Polymers Ltd* [2002] IRLR 31, QBD, discussed in more detail with regard to misrepresentation in relation to TUPE transfers and in particular pensions at Chapter 11, para. 11.48 *et seq.*
[11] *D36 Ltd v Castro* EAT/0853/03. See para. 5.45 *et seq.*
[12] See para. 5.25.

5.07 The following liabilities do not transfer:

- criminal liability;
- liabilities relating to occupational pension scheme benefits for old age, invalidity, or survivors;
- failure to comply with TULRCA, s. 188.

2. What is transferred?

5.08 Save where otherwise expressly provided by TUPE,[13] the transferee is liable for everything the transferor has done in relation to the transferring employees[14] in terms of 'powers, rights, duties and liabilities'. The matters for which the transferee becomes responsible are those which arise 'under or in relation to' the relevant contract and therefore the transferee becomes responsible for the consequences of the transferor's conduct whether in connection to failure to pay wages, acts of discrimination, or otherwise. That the transferee is liable for pre-transfer actions of the transferor is exemplified by *DJM International Ltd v Nicholas*.[15] An act of discrimination against an employee on the part of the transferor was inherited by the transferee even though that claim related to a contract which had expired prior to the employment the termination of which led to the proceedings in question. Similarly, in *Gutridge and others v Sodexo Ltd and anor*[16] rights to equal pay which crystallized during the employees' employment with the transferor transferred under TUPE to the transferee and remained extant until validly terminated or varied.

5.09 *Unicorn Consultancy Services v Westbrook*[17] demonstrates that the transferee can inherit rights which employees had against the transferor and which crystallized prior to transfer. In that case, the transferor operated a profit-related pay (PRP) scheme in respect of employees whose employment transferred to a new contractor pursuant to TUPE. The transferor failed to make to the employees' payments due under the PRP scheme when they fell due shortly before the relevant transfer. The EAT held that the liability to make the relevant PRP payments transferred under the legislation to the transferee. This was the case even though the liability arose prior to transfer. The EAT explained the position as follows:[18]

> In reaching this conclusion we have not forgotten that in other situations...practical problems would arise that do not arise on the facts of this case...[I]n our judgment the correct approach to the application of TUPE in respect of transferred contracts of employment is to construe and apply the relevant package of rights and obligations of the employees and employer...in the circumstances that exist and the result is not simply a result of construction of the original contract and related documents...[I]n a different factual situation...the alternative argument of the employees that the [transferee] company was under an obligation to provide a replacement scheme or make payments equivalent to those 'earned' under the [transferor's] scheme could be relevant and provide a solution that accords with the underlying purpose of TUPE.

5.10 Notwithstanding the general transfer of obligations from transferor to transferee, the decision in *The Procter & Gamble Company v Svenska Cellulosa Aktiebolagetsca SCA Hygiene*

---

[13] See para. 5.13 *et seq.*
[14] Save where TUPE expressly provides otherwise.
[15] [1996] IRLR 76, EAT.
[16] [2009] IRLR 721, CA.
[17] [2000] IRLR 80, EAT.
[18] Ibid. at para. 50.

Products Manchester Ltd (formerly known as SCA Hygiene Investments Ltd),[19] indicates that a transferee cannot be responsible for liabilities which would otherwise transfer to it pursuant to TUPE but have already been satisfied by the transferor or some other person, As Hildyard J put it, regulation 4(2)(a) and (b):

> should be construed together so as to confine the rights, powers, duties and liabilities to be transferred by statutory process to those rights, powers, duties and liabilities under or in respect of a continuing contract of employment that have not already been substantially satisfied, performed, exercised or discharged by the transferor, whether in cash or kind.[20]

5.11 The transferee will (unless it reverses the decision) be bound by any decision by the transferor to terminate an employee's employment on notice and by the reason for it. In *BSG Property Services v Tuck*[21] the transferor and transferee incorrectly concluded that TUPE did not apply to the transfer of a local authority activity. The transferee inherited the relevant employees who had been given notices of termination by the transferor which had not expired as at the date of the transfer. As the actions of the transferor were deemed by TUPE to be those of the transferee, the transferee was bound by the transferor's (redundancy) reason for dismissal. That reason for dismissal, being incorrectly predicated on TUPE not applying, was untenable. Consequently the dismissals were unfair.

5.12 A transferring employee transfers subject to his obligations to the employer—as was indicated in *Marcroft v Heartland (Midlands) Ltd*,[22] '[o]nce the protection [of TUPE] is provided to the employee then it must be right that the protection he has does not only protect him as to his rights but it must carry with it any burdens he has under the contract'.[23] However, this principle may not be straightforward to apply in the context of particular provisions such as mobility clauses and restrictive covenants as the case law analysed below demonstrates.[24]

3. What is not transferred?

5.13 The transferee does not inherit responsibility for occupational pension entitlements falling within the subject matter of the 'pensions exclusion'.[25]

5.14 Criminal liabilities are also excluded from the scope of the transferee's inheritance and the transfer does not remove the transferor's responsibility for the relevant offence. Regulation 4(6) provides that regulation 4(2) 'shall not transfer or otherwise affect the liability of any person to be prosecuted for, convicted of and sentenced for any offence'. Therefore, whilst a transferee may inherit contractual and tortious liabilities in respect, for example, of a pre-transfer breach of the transferor's health and safety responsibilities to the transferring employees, it will not inherit any liability to prosecution if the default committed by the transferor also constituted a criminal offence. The transferor will remain liable for the criminal offence.

---

[19] [2012] IRLR 733, Ch, discussed in more detail in Chapter 11, para. 11.30 *et seq.*
[20] Ibid. at para. 122.
[21] [1996] IRLR 134, EAT.
[22] [2011] IRLR 599, CA.
[23] Ibid. at para. 27 per Mummery LJ.
[24] See para. 5.29 *et seq.* with regard to restrictive covenants and para. 5.51 *et seq.* in relation to mobility clauses.
[25] i.e. old age, invalidity, and survivors' benefits under occupational pension schemes—see Chapter 11 for detailed discussion of the pensions exclusion.

5.15 *Jowett (Angus) & Co Ltd v National Union of Tailors and Garment Workers*[26] confirmed that liability for failure to comply with the obligation to consult with a recognised trade union or employee representatives in relation to a redundancy situation required by TULRCA 1992, s. 188 does not transfer to the transferee. The possibility was raised in the 2005 Consultation of making liability for such a protective award joint and several on the transferor and transferee where the relevant redundancies were transfer related.[27] As the consultation process produced no consensus on the issue, the position was not changed by TUPE 2006.[28]

5.16 That the Directive (and therefore by extension TUPE) only operates to transfer-employment-related rights and obligations in accordance with its terms and does not extend to wider categories of contractual arrangement was demonstrated by *Vigano v Red Elite de Electrodomesticos SA*.[29] The ECJ held that the Directive did not, in relation to a transfer of an undertaking falling within its scope, operate to transfer a commercial lease held by the transferor with a third party. This was the case even though the termination of the lease in question was likely to lead to the termination of the employment contracts of the relevant employees whose employment transferred to the transferee. There had been a transfer of an undertaking from the transferor, an electrical retailer, to the transferee following the transferor's entering into voluntary insolvency comprising a number of the transferor's outlets. The owners of the premises argued that they had to give consent before the lease in question could be assigned and there was no obligation in them to accept the assignment of the relevant lease from the transferor to the transferee. If the lease were not assigned the transferee would have to cease operations at the relevant outlet which would clearly affect the employment of the relevant staff. The ECJ noted that the wording of Article 3(1) only operates to transfer to the transferee those of the transferor's rights and obligations which arise from a contract of employment or employment relationship. A lease setting out the legal relationship between a landlord and a tenant could not be said to derive from a contract of employment or employment relationship and therefore was not within the scope of the automatic transfer of rights and obligations effected by the Directive.

4. Discretionary entitlements

5.17 Changes to matters which do not have the status of fixed contractual entitlements may be relevant to the ability of a transferring employee to terminate his or her employment by reason of a substantial change to his or her working conditions to his or her material detriment[30] but the question also arises of whether TUPE operates to transfer non-contractual matters to the transferee.

5.18 Whether the rights and obligations which transfer pursuant to TUPE are only those which are contractual, as distinct from those which are non-contractual, was considered by Peter Gibson LJ in *Bernadone v Pall Mall Services Group and others*:[31]

> It would seem to me to be surprising if the rights and obligations were to be limited to contractual claims and to exclude claims in tort. Why should there be such a dividing line (in accordance with the distinction in English law pertaining to torts and contracts) in a directive? It is

---

[26] [1985] IRLR 426, EAT.
[27] 2005 Consultation para. 85.
[28] Consultation Response para. 7.8.
[29] [2009] 1 CMLR 428, ECJ.
[30] Pursuant to regulation 4(9). See Chapter 4, para. 4.93 *et seq.*
[31] [2000] IRLR 487, CA.

the more surprising when the language used in the Directive is broad 'arising from' and when it is not only a contract of employment but also an employment relationship (which is plainly something different) from which 'the rights and obligations must arise'. The fact that the rights and obligations of the transferor which transfer are those arising from an employment relationship clearly gives force to the argument that non-contractual working conditions do pass to the transferee but only on the same terms by way of their status as applied prior to transfer.[32]

Similarly, in the context of the transfer or non-transfer of pension-related rights and obli- **5.19** gations under TUPE Hildyard J observed as follows in *The Procter & Gamble Company v Svenska Cellulosa Aktiebolagetsca SCA Hygiene Products Manchester Ltd (formerly known as SCA Hygiene Investments Ltd)*:[33]

> In my judgment, the phrase 'rights and obligations' in Article 3(1) and in TUPE is to be liberally interpreted without regard to domestic distinctions between a discretionary entitle- ment and a legally enforceable right. The entitlement of the transferring employees, and its concomitant obligation, though discretionary, are such as to transfer by operation of TUPE accordingly.[34]

Consistent with this appraisal of the width of the scope of TUPE, but noting the need to **5.20** analyse properly the nature of the right being transferred, Hildyard J also made the following observations about the approach to be adopted when applying TUPE in this context and assessing the precise legal status of what is transferred:

> 117. More generally, the fulfilment of the purposes and intent of TUPE requires a flexible and pragmatic, rather than literal and 'black letter', approach. Indeed, as it seems to me, a more than ordinary flexibility is often required: for that is the price, or at least a necessary concomitant, of the conclusion that every sort of right, even an expectation which is subject to the exercise of a discretionary power, is to be transferred pursuant to TUPE. Rights that in other circumstances would be considered either too personal, or spectral or uncertain, or which call for benefits that as a matter of fact the transferee has not the power to provide, can only be treated as transferable if, when circumstances require, something more flexible than their literal replication is permitted.
>
> 118. Further, what is important throughout is not the label but the substance of the right, power, duty and liability concerned: to satisfy the objectives of TUPE, it is necessary in each case to unpack the economic components, with a view to providing for substantial identity (or failing which substantive equivalence) of economic benefit after the transfer as before.

5. No improvement of employee's position

The fact of transfer from transferor to transferee of an employee's contract of employment **5.21** cannot, as a matter of law, operate to improve the position of the employee. In *Whitehouse v Charles A Blatchford and Sons Ltd*[35] Buxton LJ made the point that 'the Directive does not create new rights for the employee but only ensures that a transfer of the undertaking employing him does not destroy his rights'.

An example of this principle in operation is *Jackson v Computershare Investor Services plc*.[36] **5.22** The employee in question commenced work with the transferor, which did not operate any

---

[32] Ibid. at para. 34.
[33] [2012] IRLR 733, Ch.
[34] Ibid. at para. 68.
[35] [1999] IRLR 492, CA at para. 41.
[36] [2008] IRLR 70, CA.

severance scheme, in 1999 and transferred to the transferee pursuant to TUPE in 2004. When she was made redundant in 2005 she sought to argue that she should benefit from the scheme applying to those joining the transferee prior to 2002 rather than the less generous scheme for those commencing employment with the transferee subsequently. As TUPE deemed her employment with the transferee as having commenced in 1999 for statutory purposes, the employee argued that this should be considered to be her start date for the purposes of determining from which severance scheme she should benefit.

5.23 Mummery LJ stated that the objective of the Directive and TUPE is not 'to confer additional rights on the employee or to improve the situation of the employee'[37] and that 'the true effect of the deeming provision in regulation 4(1) . . . is not to give a transferred employee access to employment benefits other than those to which the employee was entitled before the transfer of the undertaking'.[38] Mummery LJ rejected what he saw as:

> the attempt to make artificial use of TUPE in a contextual fashion for the purposes of interpreting CIS's contract for enhanced severance pay terms in a way which displaces [the] ET's undoubtedly correct finding of fact that Mrs Jackson joined CIS after 1 March 2002 and miraculously transforms her from being a post-2002 new entrant into a pre-2002 joiner.[39]

5.24 A further example of this point is *Small and others v The Boots Co plc and anor*.[40] When certain employees transferred pursuant to TUPE from Unipart back to the employment of Boots (by whom they had previously been employed prior to transferring to Unipart), they claimed to be entitled to participate in a bonus scheme for the relevant year, 2007. However, to be eligible to participate in the relevant bonus arrangement an employee was required to have commenced employment prior to 1 January 2007 whereas the employees in this case only transferred to the employment of Boots on 1 April 2007 so were ineligible for the bonus scheme under its strict terms. The employees' claim was that, by virtue of their transferring to the employment of Boots pursuant to TUPE, they should be deemed effectively always to have been employed by Boots and therefore employed for the purposes of the bonus scheme on 1 January rendering them eligible to participate. This argument was rejected on the basis that the situation was 'indistinguishable'[41] from *Jackson*—the employees were not, as Slade J put it,[42] 'seeking to preserve rights they had with Unipart which they claim to retain on the TUPE transfer to Boots'. The proper analysis was as follows: '[the employees] had no such rights when they were employed by Unipart. They are seeking to use the provisions of TUPE which are designed to preserve rights not to create them.'[43]

6. Employers' liability compulsory insurance

5.25 In *Bernadone v Pall Mall Services Group and others*[44] the Court of Appeal held that liabilities to employees for personal injury or disease arising from their employment by the transferor prior to a TUPE transfer are automatically inherited by the transferee. Peter Gibson LJ held

---

[37] Ibid. at para. 30.
[38] Ibid. at para. 31.
[39] Ibid. at para. 33.
[40] [2009] IRLR 328, EAT.
[41] Ibid. at para. 49.
[42] Ibid.
[43] Ibid.
[44] [2000] IRLR 487, CA which decision the 2005 Consultation described (at para. 86) as according with 'the Government's own view of the legal position under the Directive and the Regulations'.

that there was sufficient connection between the alleged liability and the employee's contract of employment for that liability to be transferred.[45] Rather more intriguingly, given the common law concept of privity of contract, the Court of Appeal also held that the benefit of any compulsory employers' liability insurance taken out by the transferor similarly passes to the transferee on a transfer. The result of this transfer of the benefit of the transferor's arrangements means that the transferee may[46] rely on the transferor's pre-transfer insurance cover as against the transferor's insurer to meet any liabilities incurred pre-transfer but for which it becomes responsible by virtue of the operation of TUPE. This is the case even though it was not a party to that insurance contract. As Peter Gibson LJ put it:

> 48. The transferor employer's right is to recover from the insurers an indemnity in respect of the transferor's liability arising from or in connection with the contract of employment. That is the very liability which the transferor was required to insure under the 1969 [ECLIA]. True it is that that right is under the contract of insurance with third parties, the insurers. But the important point is that the right arises from and is in connection with the contract of employment, because the liability insured under the contract is such a liability.

> 49. Such a solution is, in my judgment, consistent with the purpose of the Directive and of the Regulations. Moreover it is just, because the transferor's insurers have received a premium in respect of this very liability and there is no good reason why the Regulations should be construed in a way as to enable the insurers to keep the premium but avoid liability.

The *Bernadone* decision affects private sector employers that have the statutory obligation to **5.26** arrange appropriate employers' liability insurance.[47] In its deliberations prior to the enactment of the 2006 Regulations, the Government considered the position established by *Bernadone* in relation to transfers between private sector employers to be satisfactory[48]—'the transfer of the benefit of the insurance cover bought by the transferor ensures that the transferee can comply with [employers' liability compulsory insurance] requirements in relation to liabilities incurred pre-transfer'.[49]

However, in the context of transfers from the public sector to the private sector, the **5.27** Government considered the situation to be unsatisfactory. Public sector employers are generally not covered by, or are exempt from, the requirement to put employers' liability insurance cover in place.[50] Since in such circumstances no insurance is in place prior to the relevant transfer the benefit of which can transfer to the transferee, regulation 17(2) renders

---

[45] Ibid. at para. 39.

[46] Subject to the terms of the insurance cover itself.

[47] ECLIA 1969, s. 1(1) provides that: '[e]xcept as otherwise provided by this Act, every employer carrying on any business in Great Britain shall insure, and maintain insurance, under one or more approved policies with an authorised insurer or insurers against liability for bodily injury or disease sustained by his employees, and arising out of and in the course of their employment in Great Britain in that business, but except in so far as regulations otherwise provide not including injury or disease suffered or contracted outside Great Britain'.

[48] 2005 Consultation para. 87.

[49] Ibid.

[50] ECLIA 1969, s. 3 provides exemptions pursuant to which the legislation does not require any insurance to be effected by certain specified authorities, anybody corporate established by or under any enactment for the carrying on of any industry or part of an industry, or of any undertaking, under national ownership or control and any employer exempted by regulations. Examples of specified authorities for the purposes of this exemption include health service bodies as defined in National Health Service and Community Care Act 1990, s. 60(7), National Health Service trusts established under Part 1 of that Act, the Common Council of the City of London, district and county councils, the councils of London boroughs, the London Fire and Emergency Planning Authority, and any police authority.

the transferor and the transferee jointly and severally liable for liabilities to employees where compulsory insurance does not apply.[51]

5.28 This joint and several liability arises 'on completion of a relevant transfer'[52] in respect of the prescribed category of liability but only where the transferor is not required or is exempted from the requirement to effect employers' liability insurance.[53] A transferee entering into a TUPE transaction with a public sector employer may therefore wish in such circumstances to seek an indemnity from the transferor in respect of such pre-transfer liabilities.

7. Restrictive covenants

5.29 The concerns which may arise in relation to restrictive covenants in the contracts of employment of the transferring employees are demonstrated by *Morris Angel & Son Ltd v Hollande*.[54] The relevant restrictive covenants precluded the employee in question from soliciting or doing business with customers who had dealt with the transferor in the previous year. The employee was dismissed immediately after a relevant transfer. When the transferee sought to enforce the restrictive covenants against the employee, at first instance the covenant was construed as having effectively been amended[55] so that references to the transferor were replaced by references to the transferee. Accordingly, the covenant's provisions identifying the protected category of customers whom the employee should not approach or deal with was construed as referring to any person who had done business with the transferee in the previous year. So construed, since during the previous year the employee had been engaged by and the relevant business conducted by the transferor, rather than the transferee, no person fell within the scope of the covenant. However, the Court of Appeal permitted a purposive interpretation which enabled enforcement of the covenant on the basis that it should be construed as referring to those who dealt with the undertaking[56] in the year prior to the termination of the employee's employment.

5.30 In reaching this conclusion the Court of Appeal noted[57] the observation of Lord Templeman in *Litster v Forth Dry Dock & Engineering Co Ltd*[58] as to the effect of the Directive which was summarized as 'as being that upon the transfer of a business from one employer to another, the benefit and burden of a contract of employment between the transferor and a worker in the business should devolve on the transferee'. The Court of Appeal concluded that to apply TUPE such that the contract of employment in question should be read as if it were made

---

[51] Article 3(1) permits such a provision (as noted in the 2005 Consultation at para. 88). Regulation 17 provides that:
   (1) Paragraph (2) applies where:
      (a) by virtue of section 3(1)(a) or (b) of the Employers' Liability (Compulsory Insurance) Act 1969 ('the Act'), the transferor is not required by that Act to effect any insurance; or
      (b) by virtue of section 3(1)(c) of the 1969 Act, the transferor is exempted from the requirement of that Act to effect insurance.
   (2) Where this paragraph applies, on completion of a relevant transfer the transferor and the transferee shall be jointly and severally liable in respect of any liability referred to in section 1(1) of the 1969 Act, in so far as such liability relates to the employee's employment with the transferor.
[52] Regulation 17(2).
[53] Regulation 17(1)(a) and (b) by reference to ECLIA 1969 s. 3(1)(a), (b), (c).
[54] [1993] IRLR 169, CA, in which the leading judgment was given by Dillon LJ.
[55] By virtue of the TUPE transfer.
[56] As opposed to the transferor or transferee.
[57] *Morris Angel & Son Ltd v Hollande*, above n. 54 at para. 23.
[58] [1989] IRLR 161, HL.

ab initio with the transferee—thus limiting the scope of the relevant restrictive covenant to the transferee's customers to the exclusion of the transferor's—would turn the relevant covenant 'into a quite different and possibly much wider obligation than the obligation which bound [the employee] before the transfer'.[59] In the Court of Appeal's view, '[s]uch an obligation was not remotely in contemplation when the services agreement was entered into' and Dillon LJ could see no reason why TUPE should have 'sought to change the burden on the employee'.[60] Dillon LJ took the view that the 'more reasonable construction' was that 'the words "the transfer shall have effect..." are to be read as referring to the transferee as the owner of the undertaking transferred or in respect of the undertaking transferred'.[61]

8. Difficulties in replicating entitlements

Bonus schemes and other benefit arrangements may also cause difficulties in terms of post-transfer replication. If a transferee acquires part of an undertaking, it may find it difficult precisely to replicate bonus or other benefit arrangements which are specific to the transferor's group.[62] For example, the criteria applying, for example, to a bonus scheme operated by the transferor may be entirely irrelevant to the business of the transferee and yet may form terms of the contract of employment by which the transferee is in principle bound pursuant to regulation 4(1). Subject to the ability to agree changes to employees' terms and conditions of employment provided by regulations 4(4) and 4(5),[63] a continuing concern is the fact that the literal application of TUPE operates to transfer all contractual obligations to the transferee regardless of the fact that, as a consequence of the change to the identity of the employer, the transferring entitlements might be rendered inappropriate or meaningless. **5.31**

Mitie Managed Services Ltd v French[64] addressed the extent to which a transferee could be required to replicate a profit-sharing or bonus arrangement which was operated by the transferor and therefore which was tailored to its particular circumstances rather than those of the transferee. A number of employees participated in a profit-sharing scheme operated by the transferor prior to their transfer to the transferee. The employees argued that they remained contractually entitled to participate in the scheme operated by the transferor after the transfer even though they were no longer employed by that company. In establishing the obligation placed by TUPE on transferees in such a situation, the EAT adopted a test of 'substantial equivalence' in these particular circumstances where exact replication of the relevant benefit was in effect unjust, absurd or impossible. As the EAT put it:[65] **5.32**

> [i]t would make it difficult if not impossible to contend that a profit related pay entitlement could not be the subject of transfer but it is not conclusive as to precisely what has transferred by way of contractual entitlement in relation to a particular scheme. So far as that is concerned it is our view that the entitlement of the transferred employees in the case such as this, which has complications absent from, say Unicorn, is to participation in a scheme of substantial equivalence but one which is free from unjust, absurd or impossible features.

---

[59] *Morris Angel & Son Ltd v Hollande,* above n. 54 at para. 23.
[60] Ibid. at para. 23.
[61] Ibid. at para. 24.
[62] Such as group travel, health, and concessionary purchase arrangements.
[63] See Chapter 6.
[64] [2002] IRLR 521, CA.
[65] Ibid. at para. 16.

5.33 It is therefore clear that transferees may to some extent be able to modify the entitlements of transferring employees which cannot exactly be replicated in their organizations, provided that the employees are not thereby prejudiced. Whilst the substantial equivalence approach enables a transferee to deal with a benefit which it cannot replicate in the context of its business, that principle is not capable of permitting replacement on an equivalence basis of benefits which can be continued but that the transferor would prefer to vary in some way. As the EAT indicated in *Tapere*,[66] substantial equivalence is not relevant to a contractual provision which is entirely clear and capable of continuation practically and sensibly.

5.34 *Small and others v The Boots Co plc and anor*[67] addressed whether claims based on substantial equivalence could be enforced in the ET as distinct from in the High Court or County Court. In this case warehousemen employed by Boots were in receipt of performance bonuses until their employment transferred to Unipart pursuant to a relevant transfer. They received no bonuses while employed by Unipart—although in respect of two of the relevant three years warehousemen remaining with Boots did receive such payments—and some three years later returned to the employment of Boots following a further relevant transfer. The EAT held that a claim for a bonus by way of substantial equivalence following a relevant transfer is for an unquantified amount and cannot therefore be brought in the ET as an unlawful deduction from wages claim,[68] although such a claim can be brought in the ET as a breach of contract claim provided the relevant conditions apply.[69]

9. Share options

5.35 Unless an ongoing contractual entitlement to receive further benefits can be established, it is strongly arguable that share option rights granted to transferring employees prior to a relevant transfer are not inherited by the transferee. One argument in support of this analysis is that the share option arrangement is a separate contract additional to the employment contract and therefore not an obligation which transfers to the transferee 'under or in connection' with the relevant employee's employment contract in accordance with regulation 4(2)(a).[70] This argument[71] is bolstered by the fact that share option schemes often state[72] that they and entitlements awarded under them form no part of the employees' contracts of employment.

5.36 In any event, a share option can often be construed as a historic entitlement whose own terms determine what happens on the occurrence of a relevant transfer. The relevant share option scheme rules may trigger the ability to exercise the option on the employee leaving the employment of the grantor of the option or its group.[73] In such circumstances, the relevant scheme rules will often require exercise of the share option during a specified period

---

[66] See para. 5.51 *et seq.*

[67] [2009] IRLR 328, EAT.

[68] Pursuant to ERA 1996, s. 23.

[69] Under Article 3(c) of the Employment Tribunals (Extension of Jurisdiction) (England and Wales) Order 1994 SI 1994/1623, i.e. the claim, inter alia, arises or is outstanding upon termination of employment.

[70] See *Chapman and Elkin v CPS Computer Group plc* [1987] IRLR 462, CA, discussed below at para. 5.37 *et seq.*

[71] Which faces the difficulty that share option grants are often parasitic and conditional upon continued employment.

[72] In order to seek to exclude their benefits from the scope of a wrongful damages claim by the relevant employee if dismissed in breach of contract.

[73] As will be the consequence of a relevant transfer other than by way of an internal group reorganization.

following termination of employment, failing which the option will lapse. The benefit of the option in such circumstances is 'self-determining' and delivered in accordance with its original terms. Requiring the transferee to replicate the benefit would lead to a (counter-intuitive) windfall for the relevant employees, who would then potentially be able both to exercise their options under the express rules applying to their entitlements as against the transferor and to demand replacement share option entitlements from the transferee. The position, however, would be different in relation to a contractually binding obligation to continue regular option grants by which the transferee could, subject to its terms, be bound and in relation to which the 'substantial equivalence' test described above might well come into play.

Chapman and Elkin v CPS Computer Group plc[74] concerned whether a share option was cap- **5.37**
able of exercise following a relevant transfer. By virtue of a relevant transfer the employment of the claimant employees transferred outside the group of companies whose parent, CPS, had granted them options to purchase shares in CPS under its stock option scheme. After the transfer and the cessation of their employment with the relevant transferor group company, the employees sought to exercise their options. However, CPS took the view that they were not entitled to do so on the basis that the circumstances in which their employment with the transferor company terminated did not constitute redundancy, which was the only one of the provisions enabling the options to be exercisable after the termination of their employment within the transferor's group on which the employees could rely in this particular situation.

The Court of Appeal rejected the argument that TUPE had the consequence that the **5.38**
employees' employment with the transferor had not terminated by reason of redundancy for purposes of the option scheme. The option contract, being between the option holder employee and CPS as opposed to the transferor employer, was viewed as not concerned with the employee's contract of employment but rather as a separate contract. TUPE was seen as having no relevance to the question of whether the employees' employment with the transferor did or did not cease by reason of redundancy. As May LJ put it,[75] 'the Regulations are not to be construed so as to amend the definition of redundancy which can be extracted from s. 81(2) of the [Employment Protection (Consolidation)] Act [1978]. The Regulations only provide that in certain circumstances the transfer of an employer's undertaking to another, even in what can shortly be described as a 'redundancy situation' shall not have the effect of determining the contracts of service of the employees of the erstwhile transferor'. On these particular facts the fact that the transferor ceased to conduct its business constituted a redundancy situation for the purposes of the rules of the relevant scheme notwithstanding the fact that the employees' employment transferred to the transferee pursuant to TUPE.[76]

10. Changes to statutory rights

Whilst addressing legislation which has now been repealed, *Cross v British Airways plc*[77] **5.39**
made, inter alia, the points that, first, the rights of transferring employees are preserved by TUPE regardless of the understanding of the parties at the time of the relevant transaction and, second, that statutory employment rights are to be applied at the time when the employees seek their enforcement and the occurrence of a TUPE transfer has no bearing on the application of those rights.

---

[74] [1987] IRLR 462, CA.
[75] Ibid. at para. 30.
[76] Ibid. at paras 24–5.
[77] [2005] IRLR 423, EAT.

5.40   British Airways had a contractual retirement age of 55 from 1971. Employees of British Caledonian, which merged with British Airways in 1988, enjoyed a retirement age of 60. TUPE was not considered by the parties to apply to the merger of the two companies at the time of the relevant transaction. Nonetheless, the ET concluded that the merger did constitute a relevant transfer. Accordingly, despite their having accepted British Airways' employment terms[78] in 1988 and British Airways paying substantial monies to fund full pension entitlements at 55, the employees retained their contractual retirement age of 60 by virtue of TUPE's preservation of their contractual rights.[79]

5.41   The issue then arose as to the effect of TUPE on 'normal retirement age' for the purposes of the then relevant legislation. Contending that 55 was its normal retirement age, British Airways argued that, even if the British Caledonian contractual retirement age of 60 were preserved by TUPE, the dismissal of the relevant employees could not lead to unfair dismissal claims on the basis of the provisions of ERA 1996, s. 109 which were in force at the time but have now been repealed. ERA 1996, s. 109 disapplied the right in ERA 1996, s. 94 to claim unfair dismissal where an employee has attained normal retirement age on or before the effective date of termination of employment. Normal retirement age for these purposes was the normal retiring age for an employee holding the position held by the employee or, if there were none, 65.

5.42   Despite finding that the normal retiring age of 55 was well known throughout the business, the ET concluded that the former British Caledonian staff had a normal retirement age of 60. On appeal, the EAT found 55 to be the normal retirement age based on the proper test.[80]

5.43   Against this, the employees had argued that to permit a new normal retirement age for statutory purposes coming into effect post-transfer would contravene the provisions of TUPE 1981 regulation 5(2)[81] which transferred all rights, powers, duties, and liabilities in relation to the transferring employees to the transferee. This provision was argued to preserve the pre-transfer normal retirement age for statutory purposes as well as contractually. The ET agreed, holding that the right to claim unfair dismissal was a right, power, duty, or liability within the scope of TUPE 1981, regulation 5 for the protective purposes of TUPE and the Directive.

5.44   The EAT rejected the argument that TUPE rendered impermissible an altered normal retirement age for statutory purposes introduced after a relevant transfer. The statutory unfair dismissal jurisdiction should be applied as at the time of dismissal.[82] It is therefore clear that TUPE does not preserve employees' statutory (as distinct from contractual) rights as they are as at the point of transfer. Statutory entitlements must be determined by reference to the relevant legislation at the particular time when an issue of eligibility or otherwise arises.

---

[78]   Including a contractual retirement age of 55.

[79]   The principle established in *Daddy's Dance Hall* and *Wilson* meant that any purported or alleged consent to the variation of retirement age was invalid—see Chapter 6.

[80]   Which was 'to ascertain what would be the reasonable expectation or understanding of the employees holding that position at the relevant time' per Lord Fraser in *Waite v GCHQ* [1983] 2 AC 714, HL.

[81]   Now regulation 4(2).

[82]   Rather than by reference to the position obtaining at some earlier point in time such as the employee becoming employed by the dismissing employer as a consequence of a TUPE transfer.

11. Continuity of employment

Regulation 4(2)(a) preserves on a relevant transfer 'all the transferor's rights, powers, duties **5.45** and liabilities under or in connection with any [transferred] contract of employment' and thereby preserves the continuity of employment of the transferring employees for statutory purposes. The EAT confirmed this to be the case in *D36 Ltd v Castro*[83] (which approved the position agreed by the parties by the Court of Appeal in *Astley v Celtec*[84]).

In *D36*[85] two grounds of appeal were of relevance to this issue. First, it was argued that the **5.46** meanings of the term 'transfer' as deployed in ERA 1996, s. 218(2) and TUPE were separate and distinct concepts.[86] The contention was that the ET erred in holding that TUPE and the Directive should 'be treated as part of a single scheme for the protection of employees' rights and should be interpreted consistently with an identical interpretation of the concept of a transfer of undertaking in line with ECJ decisions'.[87] Second, it was argued that TUPE does not, of itself, preserve statutory continuity for the purposes of eligibility to bring an unfair dismissal claim under ERA 1996.[88] The ET's judgment was held to be sound, HH Judge Birtles making the following observations:

> 23. The Court of Appeal has recently held that, where it has direct affect, the Acquired Rights Directive preserves continuity of employment upon a relevant transfer: Astley v Celtec [2002] IRLR 629. It would appear that the conclusion was reached with the agreement of the parties rather than by the Court of Appeal having heard argument from both sides. However, that conclusion is consistent with two recent decisions of the European Court of Justice: Sanchez Hidalgo v Asociacion de Servicios Aser [1999] IRLR 136 and Collino and Chiappero v Telecom Italia SpA [2000] IRLR 788.

> 24. Those cases all concern the preservation of continuity of employment in cases where the transfer is from one state authority to another provided that the transfer is the transfer of an undertaking or a part of an undertaking for the purposes of the Directive. We can see no difference in the case of a TUPE transfer. TUPE must be interpreted consistently with the Directive and the decisions of the ECJ on the equivalent provisions of the Directive. In our judgment there can be no logical difference between the preservation of continuity between state authorities under the Directive and the transfer of private undertakings covered by TUPE. If academic support for that proposition is needed we find it in Harvey on Industrial Relations and Employment Law Vol. 1, paragraph 472 (Issue 166).

ERA 1996, s. 218(2) addresses the issue more directly by providing that: **5.47**

> If a trade or business, or an undertaking (whether or not established by or under an Act), is transferred from one person or another:
>   (a) the period of employment of an employee in the trade or business or undertaking at the time of the transfer counts as a period of employment with the transferee; and
>   (b) the transfer does not break the continuity of the period of employment.[89]

---

[83] UK/EAT/0853/03.
[84] [2002] IRLR 629, CA.
[85] Above, n. 83.
[86] Ibid. at para. 13.
[87] Ibid. at para. 15.
[88] And indeed other rights dependent on statutory continuity of employment such as the right to a statutory redundancy payment.
[89] In *Oakland v Wellswood (Yorkshire) Ltd* [2010] IRLR 82, CA, the Court of Appeal held that ERA 1996, s. 218(2) operated to preserve statutory continuity of employment on acquisition of a business out of administration, thereby rendering it unnecessary for the Court of Appeal (at that stage of the litigation) to determine the then extant uncertainty as to the application of TUPE to such transactions—see Chapter 10, para. 10.24 *et seq.*

5.48 Other provisions governing the preservation of continuity of employment in circumstances which could, depending upon the circumstances, constitute or which are similar to a TUPE transfer are ERA 1996, s. 218(3),[90] s. 218(4),[91] s. 218(5),[92] s. 218(6),[93] s. 218(7),[94] and s. 218(8), (9).[95]

5.49 *Senior Heat Treatment Ltd v Bell*[96] demonstrates the operation of the statutory provisions with regard to continuity of employment in slightly unusual circumstances. The relevant employees opted to object to transfer and received redundancy payments. Their signing new contracts and becoming employed by the transferee soon thereafter meant not only that they did not object validly to the transfer of their employment to the transferee under what was then TUPE 1981, regulation 5(4).[97]

5.50 Moreover, receipt by the employees in question of a statutory redundancy payment did not operate to break their continuity of employment as provided for by ERA 1996, s. 214(2). As the employees were neither dismissed (nor for that matter redundant) because their employment transferred to the transferee under TUPE, the payment they received was not a statutory redundancy payment. ERA 1996, s. 214(2) therefore did not apply to break continuity of employment for statutory purposes. On termination of employment with the transferee, employment with both the transferor and transferee applied to entitle the employees to a statutory redundancy payment taking into account pre-transfer employment. The employees therefore received payment twice in respect of their pre-transfer employment.

12. Mobility clauses

5.51 In *Tapere v South London and Maudsley NHS Trust*[98] the contract of employment of the employee in question permitted her to be required to work in locations 'within the NHS Trust' for which she worked. Her employment transferred on a relevant transfer to a different NHS Trust which had a wider and different geographical scope and the new transferee employer proposed that her place of employment be moved to a new location within the wider area of the transferee as soon as possible after the transfer. This new location would increase the employee's journey time but was within the scope of the mobility clause if it was construed by reference to the geographical area of the new transferee employer as opposed to the previous transferor employer.

5.52 The ET had held that the benefit of the mobility clause transferred to the respondent and therefore entitled the transferee to require the employee to transfer her place of work to any of the locations at which it operated, i.e. to any place within the transferee's as distinct from the transferor's NHS Trust area. However, as a matter of construction, the EAT considered that the provision that the employee could be required to work at locations 'within the Trust' confined the scope of the ability of the employer to relocate the employee rather than, as the ET had considered, being a provision which added nothing to the construction of the

---

[90] Change of employer as a result of an Act of Parliament.
[91] Transfer of employment to personal representatives on death of the employer.
[92] Change in the composition of a partnership.
[93] Transfer of employment between associated employers.
[94] Local education transfers.
[95] Transfer of employees between health service employers.
[96] [1997] IRLR 614, EAT.
[97] Now regulation 4(7).
[98] [2009] IRLR 972, EAT.

agreement.[99] Moreover, the employee's contract of employment was to be construed as at the time when it was entered into. To apply the mobility clause to the area of operation of the transferee (rather than the transferor) would be to widen the geographical scope of the employee's contract to her disadvantage and to reduce her protections contrary to the purposes of the transfer of undertakings legislation. Substantial equivalence[100] had no relevance where the contractual provision was entirely clear.[101]

As the EAT put it: **5.53**

What the Employment Tribunal did here was to increase the scope of the geographical area in which the employee could be required to work. This altered the terms of her contract to her disadvantage and resulted in her employment being less protected after the transfer than it was before. Such an interpretation is the antithesis of the purpose of the Directive 2001/23/EC and, thus, of TUPE 2006, which is the domestic implementation of it. There was no difficulty about either construing the clause or as to its practical implementation. That there was a practical difficulty caused by the nature of the transaction cannot alter the meaning of the clause. The Appellant was based at Burgess Park. Her contract only empowered her employer to require her to move to other locations within the area of the Community Health South London NHS Trust. It was an inherent part of the transaction that the geographical location of the undertaking must move from Burgess Park to Bethlem Hospital and no doubt that created a practical difficulty but such a difficulty cannot invoke the concept of 'substantial equivalence'. If it could, then the whole purpose of the Directive and TUPE, which is achieved by preserving terms and conditions of employment, would be undermined.[102]

In similar vein, in *Abellio v Musse and others*[103] Langstaff J analysed an attempt by a transferee   **5.54**
to have transferring employees work at its depot rather than their original base on the basis merely of the change to the identity of the employees' employer as follows:

For our part, there is a distinction to be drawn between the continuation of a contract of employment, which is preserved by TUPE, and the identity of the employer, which plainly changes. If it were otherwise, there would be no need to distinguish between transferor and transferee, for instance. At the time, 17 September 2009, CentreWest was the employer subject to the contract that CentreWest had with the Claimants. The fact that there has been a transfer since does not mean that one may substitute 'Abellio' for 'CentreWest'. The provisions of Regulation 4(2) provide that, '[CentreWest's] acts or omissions shall be deemed to have been an act or omission of or in relation to the transferee', but that does not make, in our view, a location that was not that of the employer at the time into one which had become a depot of the employer.[104]

13. Collectively determined terms

In *Alemo-Herron and others v Parkwood Leisure Ltd*,[105] the issue to be determined was   **5.55**
the scope of the protection provided by TUPE to transferring employees whose terms of employment are, prior to the relevant transfer, determined, in accordance with a collective

---

[99] Ibid. at para. 33.
[100] Ibid. at paras 34 and 35, referring to *Mitie Managed Services v French and others* and *Morris Angel and Son Ltd v Hollande*, respectively discussed at para. 5.32 *et seq.* and 5.29 *et seq.*
[101] Ibid. at para. 37.
[102] Ibid. at para. 38.
[103] [2012] IRLR 360, EAT.
[104] Ibid. at para. 35.
[105] [2010] IRLR 298, CA; [2011] IRLR 696, SC. See, for discussion of the decision of the Court of Appeal, Wynn-Evans, 'TUPE, Collective Agreements and the Static-Dynamic Debate' (2010) 39 ILJ 275.

agreement, by a third party negotiating body—and in particular whether, after a transfer of an undertaking, a transferee can remain bound by a pay determination method established by a collective agreement in which the transferor was directly involved but to which the transferee is, after the transfer in question, not a party.

5.56 The claimant employees were originally employed by the London Borough of Lewisham on standard contracts which provided that their terms and conditions were to be determined in accordance with collective agreements negotiated by the National Joint Council for Local Government Services (NJC), a body which included representatives of local authority employers and trade unions. As a result of a transfer of an undertaking falling within the scope of the applicable legislation, the employment of the employees in question transferred from the London Borough of Lewisham to a private-sector transferee, CCL Ltd, in 2002. The employees continued to receive pay increases in line with pay settlements determined by the NJC until a further transfer of the undertaking in which they were employed to Parkwood Leisure Ltd in 2004. The dispute which arose in this litigation was whether Parkwood was bound by pay settlements determined by the NJC in respect of the period from 2006 to 2008, when it was not a direct party to the NJC nor involved in its deliberations.

5.57 Article 3 provides that the transferee is required to comply with any collective agreement applying to the transferor until the date of the termination or expiry of the collective agreement or the entry into the application of another collective agreement. Member States have the ability in their implementing legislation to limit to one year the period for which compliance with collective agreements can be required by their domestic transfer of undertakings legislation.

5.58 Regulation 5(1) of TUPE 1981, the legislation applicable in this case, provided that 'all the transferor's rights, powers, duties and liabilities under or in connection with any such contract [of employment] shall be transferred by virtue of this Regulation to the transferee'. Its regulation 6 operated to transfer applicable collective agreements to the transferee subject to the important qualification that this transfer of collective agreements was without prejudice to the presumption of their unenforceability under the separate domestic legislation governing the legal status of collective agreements.

5.59 In *Alemo-Herron*, the EAT had,[106] reversing the ET's decision, held that the employees were indeed entitled to pay settlements as determined by the NJC in respect of the period in question and therefore to benefit from changes to the collective agreement which came into effect following the date of the relevant transfer. In so doing, the EAT adopted what had become known as the 'dynamic' approach adopted in domestic cases such as *Whent v T Cartledge Ltd*[107] rather than the 'static' approach adopted by the ECJ in *Werhof v Freeway Traffic Systems Gmbh*.[108]

5.60 The analysis which the dynamic approach adopts is based on the principle that the transfer of undertakings legislation operates to preserve the contractual terms of the transferring employees. As a corollary of that protection, on a relevant transfer the transfer of undertakings legislation is therefore interpreted as preserving contractual provisions which provide for the determination of employees' terms and conditions by third parties, such as negotiating

---

[106] [2009] IRLR 322, EAT.
[107] [1997] IRLR 153, EAT.
[108] [2006] IRLR 400, ECJ.

bodies, even if the transferee employer is, after the transfer in question, no longer involved in or party to the external mechanic in question. Such provisions determining terms and conditions of employment are therefore preserved in the same way as any other contractual provision and this ensures that the contracts of employment of the transferring employees are to be operated after the transfer in the same evolving and 'dynamic' way as before the relevant transfer.

In *Whent* HHJ Hicks QC had made the point that 'there is simply no reason why parties should not, if they choose, agree that matters such as remuneration be fixed by processes in which they do not participate'.[109] A similar approach was adopted in *Glendale Managed Services v Graham*[110] where the relevant contractual provision was that the rate of remuneration would 'normally' be in accordance with the NJC. The Court of Appeal held that there was an implied term that the employer was obliged to inform the employees if money was to be a departure from the norm. Whilst *Whent* was not cited, the *Graham* decision was consistent with it. **5.61**

In *Werhof* the ECJ held that the rights of the employees to continue to benefit from collectively agreed terms and conditions are static (and therefore preserved as at the transfer date) rather than dynamic. Consequently, in that decision the ECJ held that the transferee was found to be bound by the terms of employment determined in accordance with the relevant collective agreement only as they were in force as at the date of the relevant transfer, but not by the fruits of subsequent collective agreements to which the transferee was not a party. **5.62**

Despite this ECJ authority, the EAT considered that it could not alter the domestic law as settled in cases such as *Whent*. In adopting this approach, the EAT found particular comfort in the fact that Article 3(2), which explicitly addresses the effect of collective agreements, was not transposed into the domestic implementing legislation. *Alemo-Herron* was viewed by the EAT as, in essence, being on all fours with *Whent* given that in the earlier decision it was held that a collective agreement which was, as a matter of contract, incorporated into the employees' contracts was valid after a contracting out to the private sector, even though the transferee employer was not a party to the collective agreements in question. **5.63**

The EAT was also unswayed by the argument (to which the ECJ had regard in *Werhof*) that holding the transferee to the results of a collective agreement to which it was not a direct party constituted a breach of the employer's right to freedom of association under Article 11 of the European Convention on Human Rights[111] and, in particular, the right not to join an employer's association. In the EAT's view, an employer could terminate or negotiate collective bargaining arrangements if it so wished. This argument did not detain the Court of Appeal.[112] **5.64**

Before the Court of Appeal, similar arguments were run to those which had been deployed below. In essence, Parkwood argued that *Werhof*, as a decision of the ECJ, should be considered to be the binding authority in situations such as this, not least as the fact pattern in *Alemo-Herron* was virtually indistinguishable. Its argument was that *Werhof* established the **5.65**

---

[109] *Whent*, above n. 107, at para. 16.
[110] [2003] IRLR 465, CA.
[111] As, in the domestic context, set out in Schedule 1 to the Human Rights Act 1998.
[112] Which in essence approached the matter as one of the interpretation of the domestic implementing legislation.

proper interpretation not just of the Directive but also of the domestic legislation.[113] Such an approach was said to be consistent with the 'the duty of the court to give to reg[ulation] 5 a construction which accords with the decisions of the European Court upon the corresponding provisions of the Directive to which the regulation was intended to give effect'.[114]

5.66 Against this, the employees argued that *Werhof* did no more than rule that the Directive did not require Member States to establish domestic transfer of undertakings legislation under which transferees are bound by collective agreements to which they are not parties and likewise did not prohibit such a structure. Given the absence in TUPE of provisions equivalent to Article 3(2) expressly limiting the potential enforceability of collective agreements, it was argued that TUPE simply preserved the provisions of the transferring employees' employment contracts and made no distinction in respect of the enforcement of provisions deriving from collective agreements from those individually agreed. The employees also argued that, whatever *Werhof* decided, it did not preclude the United Kingdom, in its domestic implementation of the Directive, from giving employees more favourable rights and that the correct interpretation of TUPE required the conclusion that it did just that, in particular by enabling enforcement by transferred employees of their contractual rights in accordance with conventional principles of the domestic law of the contract of employment. Domestic law permitted the contractually binding determination of matters such as pay by third parties and TUPE operated to preserve that domestically uncontroversial contractual structure.

5.67 The Court of Appeal accepted that, but for the ECJ's decision in *Werhof*, the employees' case would have been 'unanswerable' and acknowledged that the dynamic interpretation was the 'conventional application of ordinary principles of contract law to the statutory consequences [of TUPE]'.[115] Nonetheless, Rimer LJ acknowledged[116] that it could 'readily be regarded as unsatisfactory, at any rate from the employer's viewpoint, that an employer should find itself committed to employment terms negotiated from time to time by bodies in whose collective bargaining negotiations it is entitled to no voice or representation, perhaps bodies in which it wishes to have no voice or representation' and it was held that *Werhof* had established the proper interpretation of the Directive, rejecting the dynamic approach in favour of the static interpretation. The Court of Appeal could also see nothing in TUPE to justify a more expansive interpretation than that adopted by the ECJ in *Werhof*.

5.68 When the matter reached the Supreme Court, the questions to be determined were,[117] first, whether the relevant provisions of TUPE were intended to be more generous than Article 3(1) as interpreted by the ECJ in *Werhof* and, second, whether it is open to the national court to construe those provisions more generously because to do so is not precluded by Article 3(1). It was held that there was no evidence to support the contention that regulations 5(1) and 5(2) of TUPE 1981 and regulations 4(1) and 4(2) of TUPE 2006 had been drafted with any purpose other than to give effect to Article 3(1). The domestic legislation was not intended to be more generous in substance than its European parent despite some minor differences in the drafting.[118]

---

[113] Which should be interpreted in a manner consistent with the Directive which it implements.

[114] The principle identified by Lord Keith in *Litster and others v Forth Dry Dock & Engineering Co Ltd* and other decisions—see Chapter 1, para. 1.18 *et seq.*

[115] *Alemo-Herron and others v Parkwood Leisure Ltd* [2010] IRLR 298, CA per Rimer LJ at para. 46.

[116] Ibid. at para. 50.

[117] [2011] IRLR 696, SC per Lord Hope at para. 26.

[118] Ibid. at para. 28 per Lord Hope.

Nonetheless, the Supreme Court considered that the answer to the question of whether **5.69** the Directive precludes a national court from adopting the dynamic approach was not *acte clair*. First, the factual matrix in *Werhof* was materially different, concerning as it did a different system of employment law in Germany which assumed membership on the part of the employer of the relevant employer's federation which leads to the collective agreement in question being binding. In the United Kingdom, neither is there an equivalent legal obligation nor is membership of the negotiating body a prerequisite for the collective agreement to be binding, as the domestic position is governed by individual contracts. Second, the question in *Werhof* was effectively whether the proper approach to the interpretation of the Directive was to adopt the static approach. *Werhof* did not decide whether domestic legislation was permitted to be more favourable to employees than required by the Directive by adopting the dynamic interpretation. Consequently, the Supreme Court considered that the answer to the question of whether Article 3(1) precludes national courts from giving a dynamic interpretation to the relevant provisions of TUPE should be the subject of a reference to the CJEU for a preliminary ruling under Article 267 TFEU.[119] The position therefore remains uncertain pending clarification from the CJEU.

Even though TUPE operates to preserve collective agreements it does not, however, entrench **5.70** those agreements in the face of subsequent statutory changes affecting their substance. *Worrall and others v Wilmott Dixon Partnerships Ltd and anor*[120] considered a provision relating to redundancy entitlements contained in a collective agreement entered into by the Council from whose employment the relevant employees transferred under TUPE to the transferee employer by way of a number of relevant transfers. In the relevant collective agreement it was recorded that the Council would, with regard to the pension entitlements of those made redundant, award at least five added years' pensionable service when exercising its discretion under the Local Government (Early Termination of Employment) (Discretionary Compensation) (England and Wales) Regulations 2000. The power to award added years' pensionable service in this way was abolished in 2006 and the employer therefore contended that it did not have the power in question when the claimant employee subsequently applied for voluntary redundancy and sought added years' service to be awarded for the purposes of his pension benefits.

The EAT upheld the ET's decision, inter alia, that the employee did not retain the right to **5.71** be awarded added years pensionable service by virtue of TUPE because the statutory power to make such an award had been abolished. Even if the static approach applied to preserve rights determined by collective agreements only as at the point of transfer, this did not mean that subsequent statutory changes should be ignored—on the contrary they should be taken to be effective. The EAT rejected the contention that:

> the terms of the employment contract are frozen as at the date of the transfer and if some provisions which were valid at the time of the first transfer later become unlawful, the court would still be obliged to enforce the contractual rights considered as at the date of the transfer and ignore the subsequent legislation.[121]

---

[119] Ibid. per Lord Hope at paras 46–8.
[120] UKEAT/0521/09 in which the *Parkwood* decision (at the Court of Appeal stage) was considered.
[121] At para. 28.

5.72 By way of explanation, and indicating that the *Parkwood* case addressed a different point, Silber J commented as follows:[122]

> the *Parkwood* case, following as it does the *Werhof* case, goes no further than preventing parties from being bound by 'future changes to collective agreement', which are very different from statutory prohibitions on making payments...(and)...there is no reason of principle why an employer who is a transferee under TUPE is outside the scope of statutory provisions and immune from such provisions...(and) the mere fact that the *Parkwood* decision is based on an EU Directive is not an acceptable excuse for ignoring statutory provisions[123]

B. Collective Agreements

1. The Directive and TUPE

5.73 Article 3.3 provides that:

> [f]ollowing the transfer, the transferee shall continue to observe the terms and conditions agreed in any collective agreement on the same terms applicable to the transferor under that agreement, until the date of termination or expiry of the collective agreement or the entry into force or application of another collective agreement. Member States may limit the period for observing such terms and conditions with the proviso that it shall not be less than one year.

5.74 Regulation 5 implements this provision into the domestic legislation with the effect that on a relevant transfer the transferee inherits any collective agreement made by or on behalf of the transferor with a trade union that is recognised by the transferor in respect of any employee whose contract transfers to the transferee pursuant to regulation 4(1). Regulation 5 provides as follows:

> Where at the time of a relevant transfer there exists a collective agreement made by or on behalf of the transferor with a trade union recognised by the transferor in respect of any employee whose contract of employment is preserved by regulation 4(1) above, then:
> (a) without prejudice to sections 179 and 180 of the 1992 Act (collective agreements presumed to be unenforceable in specified circumstances) that agreement, in its application in relation to the employee, shall, after the transfer, have effect as if made by or on behalf of the transferee with that trade union, and accordingly anything done under or in connection with it, in its application in relation to the employee, by or in relation to the transferor before the transfer, shall, after the transfer, be deemed to have been done by or in relation to the transferee; and
> (b) any order made in respect of that agreement, in its application in relation to the employee, shall, after the transfer, have effect as if the transferee were a party to the agreement.

5.75 TUPE does not take advantage of the ability in Article 3 to limit the period for which a transferee is required to observe the terms and conditions of a collective agreement relating to the transferring employees. As noted above, the minimum obligation, if this option had been taken up, would have been to require applicable collective agreements to be complied with for one year post-transfer.

---

[122] At para. 29.

[123] In similar vein, in the context of the variation of employees' terms and conditions of employment, the ECJ held in *Boor v Ministre de la Fonction Publique* [2005] IRLR 61, ECJ that the Directive did not preclude the application of national legislation to reduce an employee's salary on transfer from a private sector to public sector employer in order to comply with applicable legislation, see Chapter 6, para. 6.17.

Regulation 5(a) provides that: **5.76**

> [w]here at the time of a relevant transfer there exists a collective agreement made by or on behalf of the transferor with a trade union recognised by the transferor in respect of any employee whose contract of employment is preserved by regulation 4(1) above, then:
>
> (a) without prejudice to sections 179 and 180 of the 1992 Act[124] that agreement, in its application in relation to the employee, shall, after the transfer, have effect as if made by or on behalf of the transferee with that trade union, and accordingly anything done under or in connection with it, in its application in relation to the employee by or in relation to the transferor before the transfer, shall, after the transfer, be deemed to have been done by or in relation to the transferee; and
>
> (b) any order made in respect of that agreement, in its application in relation to the employee, shall, after the transfer, have effect as if the transferee were a party to the agreement.

Accordingly, in the same way that employment contracts transfer under TUPE to the trans- **5.77**
feree with all associated rights, powers, duties, obligations, and liabilities, collective agreements satisfying the relevant requirements and which are applicable to the transferring employees (or some of them) transfer to the transferee. Also, any order made in respect of the collective agreement shall, after the transfer, have effect as if the transferee were a party to the agreement.[125]

The principal elements of the application of regulation 5 are: **5.78**

- there must have been an agreement made by or on behalf of the transferor;
- the agreement must have been with a recognised trade union;
- the agreement must satisfy the statutory test of what constitutes a collective agreement;
- the agreement must have been in existence at the time of transfer;
- whether the agreement was legally enforceable is irrelevant.

The transferee is not bound by an agreement reached with a trade union which is not recog- **5.79**
nised by the transferor. That a collective agreement made 'on behalf of' the transferor falls within the scope of regulation 5 extends its protection to industry-wide collective agreements agreed by employers' organizations (on behalf of their member organizations) and recognised trade unions to which the transferor may not be a direct party.

The relevant collective agreement must also have been in place at the time of the relevant **5.80**
transfer. This raises the possibility, subject to the potential industrial relations consequences, of the agreement being terminated prior to the relevant transfer in order to avoid its transfer to the transferee. Termination of a collective agreement with a trade union in order to evade the effect of regulation 5 may not, depending on the circumstances, be practicable.[126]

2. Collective agreements and recognition defined

Unless an agreement with a recognised trade union constitutes a collective agreement for **5.81**
these purposes, it does not fall to transfer to the transferee under regulation 5. Regulation 2(1) provides that the term 'collective agreement' bears the same meaning in regulation 5 as in TULRCA 1992, s. 178(1), i.e. 'any agreement or arrangement by or on behalf of one or

---

[124] Which provide for collective agreements to be presumed to be unenforceable in specified circumstances.
[125] Regulation 5(b).
[126] Especially if such termination is precluded by virtue of the currency of an award of statutory recognition.

more trade unions and one or more employers or employers' associations and relating to one or more of the matters mentioned in TULRCA, Section 178(2)'.

5.82 To fall within the scope of regulation 5, a collective agreement must be with a recognized trade union. Pursuant to regulation 2(1) 'recognised' has the meaning given to it by TULRCA 1992, s. 178(3), i.e. 'recognition of the union by an employer or two or more associated employers, to any extent, for the purpose of collective bargaining'. The matters prescribed by TULRCA 1992, s. 178(2), to at least one of which a collective agreement must relate in order for it to satisfy the statutory test for these purposes, are:

- terms and conditions of employment or the physical conditions in which legal workers are required to work;
- engagement or non-engagement or termination or suspension of employment or the duties of employment of one or more workers;
- allocation of work or the duties of employment as between workers or groups of workers;
- matters of discipline;
- the membership or non-membership of the trade union on the part of a worker;
- facilities for officials of trade unions;
- machinery for negotiation or consultation, and other procedures, relating to any of the foregoing matters including the recognition by employers or employees' associations of the right of a trade union to represent workers in any such negotiation or consultation or in the carrying out of such procedures.

5.83 Only if one of the above matters is addressed will an agreement qualify as a collective agreement for the purposes of regulation 5 and so be susceptible to transfer to the transferee by virtue of TUPE as a consequence of a relevant transfer.

3. Legal enforceability

5.84 A collective agreement made with a recognised trade union is inherited by the transferee regardless of whether the collective agreement in question is legally enforceable and regardless of whether its provisions have been incorporated into individual employees' contracts of employment. That said, the fact of transfer does not of itself render the relevant collective agreement any more or less legally enforceable. Regulation 5(a) provides for the transfer of a (qualifying) collective agreement 'without prejudice to sections 179 and 180 of the 1992 [TULRCA] Act (collective agreements pursuant to be enforceable in certain circumstances)'.

5.85 TULRCA 1992, s. 179(1) and (2) provides that a collective agreement entered into before 1 December 1971 or after 15 September 1974 is presumed not to be legally enforceable. Pursuant to TULRCA 1992, s. 179(3), if a written collective agreement contains an express statement that the parties intend the agreement to be a legally enforceable contract then this presumption is displaced.

5.86 It might be argued that, if a collective agreement is not legally enforceable and therefore can effectively be ignored by the transferee in contractual (if not industrial relations) terms, regulation 5 provides little meaningful protection for a recognized trade union or its members in relation to a relevant transfer. However, the provision does have the benefit of subjecting the transferee to the collective agreements by which the transferor was bound, breach or termination of which by the transferee could lead to lawful industrial action (subject to the applicable balloting and requirements being satisfied).

If particular terms of a collective agreement have already been incorporated into the terms of **5.87** an individual's contract of employment, no reliance need be placed by an affected employee (as opposed to the relevant trade unions) on regulation 5.

C. Trade Union Recognition

1. Transfer of recognition

Article 6.1 provides that: **5.88**

> [if] the undertaking, business or part of an undertaking or business [subject to a transfer] pre-serves its autonomy, the status and function of the representatives or of the representation of the employees affected by the transfer shall be preserved on the same terms and conditions and subject to the same conditions as existed by virtue of law, regulation, administrative provision or agreement, provided that the conditions necessary for the constitution of the employees' representation are fulfilled.

Regulation 6 implements this principle into the domestic legislation and applies only where, **5.89** after a relevant transfer, the organised grouping of resources or employees which is transferred to the transferee maintains an identity distinct from the remainder of the transferee's under-taking. Whether the relevant transfer occurs by way of a transfer of an undertaking within regulation 3(1)(a) or an SPC within regulation 3(1)(b), the crucial requirement is that the pre-transfer grouping must maintain an identity distinct from the remainder of the transferee's operation after the transfer. Regulation 6(1) provides that the provisions of regulation 6 apply 'where after a relevant transfer the transferred organised grouping of resources or employees maintains an identity distinct from the remainder of the transferee's undertaking'.

Assuming that the requisite distinct identity of the relevant grouping of resources or employ- **5.90** ees is maintained, regulation 6(2) provides that:

> [w]here before such a transfer an independent trade union is recognised to any extent by the transferor in respect of employees of any description who in consequence of the transfer become employees of the transferee, then, after the transfer—
> (a) the trade union shall be deemed to have been recognised by the transferee to the same extent in respect of employees of that description so employed; and
> (b) any agreement for recognition may be varied or rescinded accordingly.

Accordingly, only if the relevant trade union is independent and recognised by the transferor in **5.91** respect of the transferring staff can recognition transfer to the transferee automatically under regulation 6. Recognition will only be continued on the same basis as it applied pre-transfer (i.e. in respect of the relevant employees and substantive issues with regard to which the trade union was recognised). The trade union will not acquire recognition rights in respect of any wider category of employees or a wider scope of collective bargaining rights simply by virtue of the transfer. It should also be noted that there is no requirement as to the scope of pre-transfer recognition for regulation 6 to apply. The pre-transfer recognition does not have to be com-prehensive in its scope or substance. There is no minimum threshold of recognition for these purposes. All that is required by regulation 6(2) is recognition 'to any extent'.

2. Continuation of recognition

No special transfer-related protection is provided with regard to the continuation of trade **5.92** union recognition following its initial preservation in accordance with regulation 6. Since regulation 6(2)(b) expressly provides that a transferring collective agreement can be varied or rescinded, the relevant trade union's rights to continued recognition are only those which were enjoyed pre-transfer. This lack of protection for continued recognition raises the possibility (albeit as yet untested) of, in appropriate circumstances, the removal of recognition entitling an employee to resign and make a claim based on the ability established by regulation 4(9) for a transferring employee to terminate his or her employment in response to a substantial change to his or her working conditions to his or her material detriment related to the relevant transfer.

5.93 The provisions providing for the continuation of trade union recognition do not apply in circumstances where the relevant undertaking transferred is integrated into the transferee's business and loses its identity. Absent agreement with the transferee, the trade union in those circumstances would not retain recognition in respect of the transferred employees whom it represented pre-transfer. This is a potentially significant limitation on the operation of regulation 6 where transferring operations are integrated into the transferee's existing activities. The transferring employees will retain their employment terms but potentially not the recognized status of their trade union.

5.94 If recognition is lost because the organised grouping of resources or employees in question does not retain an identity distinct from the remainder of the transferee's undertaking by virtue of a process of post-transfer integration, recognition could then only be reinstated by way of industrial relations pressure or the statutory recognition process. In either case, attempts to re-establish recognition would be conducted by reference to the transferee's wider workforce with all that entails in terms of timing and the feasibility of a recognition claim (in terms, for example, of levels of trade union support and the relevant workforce constituency being different).

3. Statutory recognition

5.95 It appears, even absent specific regulations, that the concept of recognition in TUPE is wide enough to cover recognition awarded under the statutory recognition procedure as much as it does voluntarily agreed recognition. Nonetheless, when the 2006 Regulations were enacted it was indicated that regulations were planned in due course pursuant to TULRCA 1992, s. 169(b) to ensure that declarations made by the CAC and outstanding applications made to the CAC under the statutory trade union recognition procedure are preserved in the event of a change in the identity of the employer including by reason of a relevant transfer. It was considered appropriate[127] to implement such measures 'to make explicit' the transfer of CAC declarations of trade union recognition. No such regulations have yet been adopted.

D. Other Representative Structures

5.96 Unless they fall within the scope of trade union recognition or the specific definition of collective agreements, other employee consultative or representative arrangements relating to the transferring of employees, such as consultation fora and staff consultative committees, do not fall within the scope of regulation 6. Accordingly, such arrangements are therefore

---

[127] 2001 Consultation para. 105 *et seq*. See also 2005 Consultation para. 48.

arguably not required by TUPE to be complied with by the transferee unless necessary or appropriate for industrial relations or human resource management reasons.

The lack of express provision in TUPE catering for the consequences of a TUPE trans- **5.97** fer for other statutory representative structures, and most particularly on information and consultation arrangements put in place to comply with the Information and Consultation of Employees Regulations 2004 and European Works Councils would appear to have the consequence that such arrangements can only be continued or re-established post-transfer by reference to the transferee's operations.

6

CHANGES TO EMPLOYEES' CONTRACTS

A. Invalidity of Transfer-related		2. Categories of variation	6.30
Contract Changes	6.01	3. Compatibility with EU law	6.33
1. Introduction	6.01	4. Connection with the transfer	6.35
2. The case law	6.06	5. ETORs and contract changes	6.45
3. Practical issues	6.18	6. Beneficial changes	6.52
B. Permissible Contract Changes	6.27	7. Pension changes	6.61
1. TUPE 2006	6.27		

A. Invalidity of Transfer-related Contract Changes

1. Introduction

6.01 One of the most controversial aspects of the transfer of undertakings legislation is the extent to which it confers mandatory and inderogable protection on the terms and conditions of employment of transferring employees. Whilst the precise scope of this protection is open to some debate, TUPE seeks in the domestic context to establish a framework for some degree of valid transfer-related contract variation to be permissible.

6.02 In situations where TUPE does not apply, employers may in the normal course of events seek to vary the terms and conditions of the employment of their employees in a number of ways. To avoid the risk of constructive dismissal or a refusal to accept a unilaterally imposed change to terms and conditions, agreement may be sought to the contractual change in question. In more extreme circumstances, where employees will not agree to changes that an employer wishes to introduce, the employer may seek to serve notice of termination on the relevant employees coupled with an offer of re-engagement on the revised terms. This risks a refusal of the offer of continued employment and consequent unfair dismissal claims. In such circumstances, an unfair dismissal claim can be defended if the employer can demonstrate a sufficient business reason for needing to implement the change and has conducted itself in a way which the tribunal accepts constituted fair dismissal for the purposes of ERA 1996, s. 98(4). A variety of factors are taken into account in assessing the fairness of such a dismissal.[1]

---

[1] Relevant cases on this issue, detailed treatment of which falls outside the scope of this work, include *St. John of God (Care Services) Ltd v Brooks* [1992] IRLR 546, EAT and *Catamaran Cruises Ltd v Williams* [1994] IRLR 386, EAT.

It should also be noted that dismissals or proposed dismissals connected with an exercise **6.03** seeking to change employees' terms and conditions of employment can trigger the application of the collective redundancy information and consultation obligations prescribed by TULRCA 1992, s. 188, where twenty or more redundancy dismissals are proposed in a ninety-day period at one establishment.

The case law in relation to the Directive and TUPE provides that, in the transfer of undertak- **6.04** ings context, employees enjoy inderogable mandatory protection in relation to their contractual terms and conditions of employment save with regard to certain occupational pension rights.[2] Whilst a contractually valid change to an employee's contract which is entirely unconnected with a relevant transfer will be effective, a transfer-related change will not be effective even where the employee consents to the variation. This principle was codified into TUPE in the 2006 Regulations by the provisions of regulations 4(4) and 4(5)[3] subject to two exceptions—first, pursuant to regulation 4(4) where there is an ETOR for the contractual variation which validates the change;[4] and, second, in insolvency situations where permitted variations can be agreed.[5]

In the context of TUPE transfers, particularly where the viability of a particular transaction **6.05** may to an extent depend on changing employees' terms, the principle that transfer-related contract changes cannot be made (or at least can only be made in very limited circumstances) has been viewed from the commercial perspective as a significant obstacle as it makes more difficult transactions whose feasibility may depend to a material extent on reductions in employment costs or harmonization of the terms of employment of the transferring employees with those of the transferee's existing workforce. This may hamper the avoidance of dismissals by way of variations to the employees' contracts.

2. The case law

Whilst TUPE 2006 codified the position with regard to transfer-related contract changes, it **6.06** is worth reviewing the European and domestic case law background. The principle that an employee may not waive the rights established by the Directive—and that the transferee cannot justify contract changes which are detrimental to the employee on the basis that they are compensated for by other favourable amendments—was established in *Daddy's Dance Hall*.[6] In that case, the employee was dismissed by his employer when the lease held by his employer of the premises where he was employed as a manager was determined. Following what was held to be a transfer of an undertaking for the purposes of the Directive, the employee was then engaged by the new lessee, on the basis of fixed rather than commission-based remuneration and a three-month trial period during which his employment could be terminated on fourteen days' notice.

In considering the issue of whether an employee can waive the rights established by the **6.07** Directive, the ECJ made the following observations:

> 14. . . . Directive 77/187/EEC aims at ensuring for workers affected by the transfer of an undertaking the safeguarding of their rights arising from the employment contract or relationship.

---

[2] As to the detail of this 'pensions exclusion' see Chapter 11.
[3] See para. 6.27 *et seq.*
[4] And even this provision has its uncertainties—see para. 6.33 *et seq.*
[5] See Chapter 10, para. 10.54 *et seq.*
[6] [1988] IRLR 315, ECJ.

As this protection is a matter of public policy, and, as such, outside the control of the parties to the employment contract, the provisions of the Directive, in particular those relating to the protection of workers against dismissal because of the transfer, must be considered as mandatory, meaning that it is not permissible to derogate from them in a manner unfavourable to employees.

15. It follows that the workers concerned do not have the option to waive the rights conferred on them by the Directive and that it is not permissible to diminish these rights, even with their consent. This interpretation is not notwithstanding the fact that, as in the instant case, the worker, to offset disadvantages arising for him from a change in his employment relationship obtains new advantages so that he is not, overall, left in a worse position than he was before.

18. Consequently, insofar as national law allows, apart from the assumption of a transfer of an undertaking, the employment relationship to be altered in a way which is unfavourable to the workers, in particular as regards their protection against dismissal, such alteration is not excluded purely because the undertaking has in the meantime been the subject of a transfer and that as a consequence the agreement has been made with the new proprietor of the undertaking. As the second lessee has in fact been substituted for the first lessee pursuant to Article 3(1) of the Directive in respect of rights and obligations arising from the employment relationship, this relationship may be altered with regard to the second lessee within the same limits as for the first lessee, on the understanding that in no case the transfer of the undertaking itself can constitute the reason for this alteration.

19. . . . a worker cannot waive the rights conferred upon him by the mandatory protections of Directive 77/187 even if the disadvantages for him of such a course of action are offset by advantages so that overall he is not left in a worse position. Nevertheless, the Directive must not preclude an alteration in the working relationship agreed with the new proprietor of the undertaking insofar as such an alteration is permitted by the applicable national law in cases other than transfers of undertakings.

6.08 Employee protection in this context requires that the transfer itself cannot be the reason for a contract change. To that (potentially very significant) extent the traditional common law ability of parties to vary their contractual relations by agreement is overridden. What is particularly challenging for those unfamiliar with the operation of the transfer legislation is the fact that this protection of employees' contractual rights is mandatory and inderogable. That a transferring employee's terms and conditions of employment are preserved on a relevant transfer and that the transfer itself may never constitute the reason for a change to those terms and conditions of employment was again confirmed in *Rask and Christensen v ISS Kantineservice A/S*,[7] in which the ECJ stated that:

> Article 3 of the Directive must be interpreted as meaning that, on the transfer, the terms of the contract of employment or of the employment relationship relating to salary, in particular to its date of payment and composition may not be varied, notwithstanding that the total amount remains unchanged. The Directive does not, however, preclude a variation of the employment relationship with the new employer insofar as national law allows such a variation independently of the transfer of an undertaking.[8]

6.09 These principles were considered in the domestic context in relation to TUPE in the associated decisions in *Wilson v St. Helen's Borough Council*[9] and *Meade and Baxendale v British*

---

[7] [1993] IRLR 133, ECJ.
[8] Ibid. at para. 31.
[9] [1996] IRLR 320, EAT; [1997] IRLR 505, CA; [1998] IRLR 706, HL.

Fuels Ltd,[10] the facts of which can be summarized in brief as follows.[11] In *Wilson*, management of the operation of a care home transferred from a county council to a borough council and the transferring employees agreed to being employed on the borough council's inferior terms. Some time later, the employees sought to rely on their old terms of employment as against the transferee. In *Meade* employees were dismissed and re-engaged on new terms in connection with a relevant transfer and similarly sought at a later stage to rely on the terms they had enjoyed prior to transfer.

Whilst this litigation covered a variety of issues and legal analyses during its progress, the **6.10** principles which it established—subject to the subsequent statutory provisions of the regulations 4(4) and 4(5) —can be summarized as follows. If an employer agrees changes to terms and conditions of employment with employees by reason of a relevant transfer then, even if these changes are agreed by the employees, they are invalid. The invalidity of transfer-related changes to employees' contracts of employment was reiterated in *Martin v South Bank University*[12] where it was held that acceptance by transferring employees of new terms of employment harmonizing their terms with those of the transferee's existing staff was invalid. More particularly, the ECJ stated that:[13]

> . . . Article 3 of the directive precludes the transferee from offering the employees of a transferred entity terms less favourable than those offered to them by the transferor in respect of early retirement, and those employees from accepting those terms, where those terms are merely brought into line with the terms offered to the transferee's other employees at the time of the transfer, unless the more favourable terms previously offered by the transferor arose from a collective agreement which is no longer legally binding on the employees of the entity transferred, having regard to the conditions set out in Article 3(2).
>
> As the ECJ indicated,[14] '[s]ince the transfer of undertaking is indeed the reason for the unfavourable alterations of terms of early retirement offered to the employees of that entity, any consent given by some of those employees to such an alteration is invalid in principle'.

However, if an employee is dismissed and re-engaged on new terms, even though this course **6.11** of action is adopted to achieve the same result as a simple agreement, the new terms agreed in respect of the employee's re-engagement are valid in the context of the transfer of undertakings legislation.[15] The dismissal is not, as had been argued, a nullity. As Lord Slynn put it in *Wilson v St. Helen's Borough Council*,[16] 'neither the Regulations nor the Directive nor the jurisprudence of the Court create a Community law right to continue employment which does not exist under national law'.

It has been argued that contract changes should only be invalid if the transfer is the sole **6.12** reason for them and that accordingly post-transfer changes for which there are other reasons (which may be nonetheless to a greater or lesser extent transfer-related) should be permitted. *Daddy's Dance Hall* and the associated decisions have been described as 'point of entry' cases

---

[10] [1996] IRLR 541, EAT; [1997] IRLR 505, CA; [1998] IRLR 706, HL.

[11] A more detailed discussion of the extensive twists and turns of the litigation is unnecessary in view of the introduction in 2006 of regulations 4(4) and 4(5) which effectively codify the relevant principles.

[12] [2004] IRLR 74, ECJ.

[13] Ibid. at para. 8.

[14] Ibid. at para. 45.

[15] Although an unfair dismissal claim may result from the dismissal.

[16] [1998] IRLR 706, HL at para. 71.

where changes to the terms of employment of the transferring employees are introduced by the transferee at the point of the transfer rather than at some later stage. To apply the principle that changes by reason of the transfer cannot be agreed after the point of entry is argued to fail properly to recognize the ability to change terms to the extent permitted by applicable national law which was explicitly referenced in *Daddy's Dance Hall*.

6.13 As *Daddy's Dance Hall* considered changes made at the point of (rather than after) transfer, this argument seeks to confine the prohibition of transfer-related changes to variations made at the point of transfer. A contract change at the time of transfer for no other reason than the transfer would be invalid as an attempt to contract out of the protection of the Directive. An example would be dismissals effected to enhance the saleability of the relevant operation. However, once the employee has transferred to the transferee with his or her employment rights intact, this analysis contends that the purpose of the Directive has been achieved.[17] The relevant employees have not been prejudiced by the fact of transfer. A post-transfer change to the employees' contracts which is transfer-related because it would not have occurred had there not been a transfer may not solely be by reason of the transfer if there are other reasons for it. The parties should (it is then argued) be free to agree subsequent contract changes, subject to the usual protections of domestic law, consistent with the point made in *Daddy's Dance Hall*[18] that the employment relationship may be altered with regard to the transferee to the same extent that it could have been with regard to the transferor, provided that the transfer of the undertaking may never constitute the reason for that amendment. This would be consonant with the (limited) function of the Directive which, as *Daddy's Dance Hall* confirms, is to ensure protection of the employee as against the transferee to the same extent as applied in respect of the transferor. It also accords with the important proviso that the transfer itself can never constitute the reason for a valid contract change.[19]

6.14 These observations highlight one difficulty which can arise from the *Daddy's Dance Hall* principle—the degree of causal link or connection between the transfer in question and the contract changes which are sought to be challenged which is required for the amendments to be invalid.[20] As noted above, in *Daddy's Dance Hall* the ECJ indicated that changes permitted by national law would be valid provided that the transfer of the undertaking itself may never constitute the reason for the amendment.[21] Where the transfer is not the reason for contract changes, because they are prompted by some other economic or organisational reason, they will be valid; by contrast, transfer-related changes can still be invalid even if agreed some time after the transfer. As Lord Slynn of Hadley said in *Wilson*:[22]

> The question as to whether and in what situations, where there has been a transfer and employees have accepted the dismissal, claimed compensation based on it and worked for a long period after the transfer, there can be a valid variation by conduct is not an easy one. I do not accept the argument that the variation is only invalid if it is agreed on or as a part of the transfer itself. The variation may still be due to the transfer and for no other reason even if it comes

---

[17] In terms of the protection of employment and contractual rights on transfer.

[18] *Daddy's Dance Hall*, above n. 6, at para. 18.

[19] See also, in relation to this argument, Deakin and Morris, *Labour Law*, 6th Edition, Oxford: Hart, 2012, pp. 246–7.

[20] See para. 6.38 *et seq.* for discussion of some cases addressing this issue.

[21] *Daddy's Dance Hall*, above n. 6, at para. 18.

[22] Above n. 6, at 1166.

later. However, it seems that there must, or at least may, come a time when the link with the transfer is broken or can be treated as no longer effective …

Although on a transfer, the employees' rights previously existing against the transferor are enforceable against the transferee and cannot be amended by the transfer itself, it does not follow there cannot be a variation of the terms of the contract for reasons which are not due to the transfer either on or after the transfer of the undertaking. It may be difficult to decide whether the variation is due to the transfer or attributable to some separate cause. If, however, the variation is not due to the transfer it can, in my opinion on the basis of the authorities to which I have referred, validly be made.

The jurisprudence does not provide particularly clear guidance on the nature of the connec- **6.15**
tion between the transfer and the contract change which will invalidate the amendment. In *Wilson* Lord Slynn referred to contract changes being invalid if 'due to the transfer and no other reason'[23] whereas in *Ralton v Havering College of Further Education*[24] the EAT described such invalidity arising where the transfer is the 'sole cause'. In *Martin*, the Advocate General's view was that a contract change would be valid if the reason or at least the main reason for the change was not the transfer. Various factors could be taken into account in this assessment including the proximity of the change to the transfer and whether the change was part of a process of harmonization of employees' terms of employment. The ECJ ultimately held that offering less favourable terms was precluded by the Directive. Relatively little assistance was provided with regard to the causal link between the transfer and the potentially invalid term other than to indicate that a process of harmonization of the terms of employment of the transferring employees with those of the transferee's existing employees would be connected with the transfer and therefore invalid. A material connection with the transfer appears to be sufficient to invalidate the contract changes regardless of the fact that there might be other reasons for their introduction.

It has been suggested that employees' positions are adequately protected if their overall pack- **6.16**
age of employment terms and benefits is no less favourable after than before a relevant trans-fer. Quite apart from the difficulty of applying such a test and the uncertainty which it might create, it is not consistent with the current state of the law. It was made clear in *Daddy's Dance Hall*[25] that an employee cannot waive the rights conferred on him or her even if the disad-vantages of a particular change are offset by other favourable changes such that he or she is in no worse position overall. This point arose in the domestic context in *Credit Suisse First Boston (Europe) Ltd v Lister*[26] where it was noted that:

The effect of the decision in the *Daddy's Dance Hall* case is that the agreement is ineffective insofar as it purports to impose on the employee an obligation to which he was not previously subject. To that extent it is disadvantageous to him and it is no answer to say that in the instant case it also gave him a compensating benefit which more than made up for it.[27]

The *Daddy's Dance Hall* principle cannot override domestic legislation with regard to terms **6.17**
and conditions of employment. In *Boor v Ministre de la Fonction Publique*[28] on transfer from a private sector to public sector employer the relevant employee's salary was reduced in order

---

[23] *Wilson*, above n. 16, at 1166.
[24] [2001] IRLR 738, EAT.
[25] Above n. 6 at para. 15.
[26] [1998] IRLR 700, CA.
[27] Ibid. at para. 34. See also *Power v Regent Security Services Ltd* [2007] IRLR 226, EAT at para. 60.
[28] [2005] IRLR 61, ECJ.

to comply with applicable legislation but in apparent conflict with the *Daddy's Dance Hall* principle against transfer-related changes to employees' contracts, whether or not voluntary. The ECJ indicated that the Directive did not preclude the application of national legislation to reduce an employee's salary in such circumstances. The salary reduction was not invalidated by the Directive but the relevant employees were nonetheless left with the ability to terminate employment on grounds of a substantial change in working conditions to their detriment pursuant to Article 4.2.[29]

3. Practical issues

(a) Retrospective claims

6.18 That transfer-related changes to employees' contracts of employment can be invalidated by TUPE even where implemented with the agreement of the employee in question is particularly problematic for transferees who wish to agree transfer-related variations. The fact that the employee's consent is effectively negated by the change being transfer-related enables an employee to bring retrospective claims in respect of benefits which have ostensibly been freely and voluntarily bargained away. Where a contract change can be treated as invalid, employees can bring breach of contract claims in respect of the preceding six years. Claims can extend over a potentially longer period by way of a claim in respect of unlawful deductions from wages based on a series of deductions where the applicable time limit is three months from the last of the series of deductions unless it was not reasonably practicable for a complaint to be presented within such period and the claim is presented within such further period as the ET considers reasonable.[30]

(b) Compromise agreements and contracting out

6.19 One way in which employers have sought to address the issue of the inability of employees to agree valid changes to their contracts of employment in relation to a relevant transfer is by proceeding to terminate the employment of the employees, re-engaging them on the desired revised terms and conditions of employment and dealing with the potential consequent unfair dismissal and other statutory claims by requiring the employees to enter into statutory compromise agreements waiving those statutory employment claims. That this approach is of doubtful efficacy has not specifically been addressed in the case law. However, *Solectron Scotland Ltd v Roper*[31] suggests that it may be.

6.20 In *Solectron*, compromise agreements entered into by employees on termination of their employment settling all claims, including a dispute about the validity of certain contractual changes made in relation to a TUPE transfer were valid, notwithstanding the contracting-out provisions of the transfer legislation. What the employees were doing by entering into the compromise agreements in question was to compromise disputes with regard to their entitlements on the termination of their employment. The employer was not seeking to vary the employees' contracts as the employees were being made redundant.

6.21 As there was no change in terms and conditions for the future, because the relevant contracts came to an end, the compromise agreements did not arise solely or even mainly by reason of

---

[29] For a similar result in relation to the application of collective agreements affected by post transfer changes to applicable legislation, see *Worrall and others v Wilmott Dixon Partnerships Ltd and anor* UKEAT/0521/09 discussed at Chapter 5, para. 5.70.

[30] See ERA 1996, s 23.

[31] [2004] IRLR 4, EAT.

the transfer. Accordingly, the prohibition of transfer-related changes established by *Daddy's Dance Hall* and the related cases was not breached. As Elias J said:

> It is, however, to be noted in this case that the effect of the compromise agreement is solely to compromise a financial claim that the employee has on the termination of his employment contract. The employer is not purporting to vary the contract but merely compromise a dispute as to its value. Moreover, there is no change in the terms and conditions of the future by reason of the obvious fact that the contract has come to an end.

> Accordingly, if one looks at the policy line behind *Daddy's Dance Hall* and related cases it is not infringed, it seems to us, by a compromise agreement made in such circumstances as arise here. We think that, properly analysed, it cannot be said that these particular compromise agreements arise solely or even mainly by reason of the transfer.[32]

The implication of these observations is that compromise agreements entered into as part of **6.22** an arrangement implementing changes to employees' terms as a result of or in connection with a relevant transfer could fall foul of the prohibition on transfer-related changes and therefore be ineffective.

(c) Continuity of employment

Even if the use of a compromise agreement to waive unfair dismissal claims in connection **6.23** with a transfer-related dismissal and re-engagement on new terms were valid, it would not be effective to break continuity of employment for the purposes of statutory employment rights.[33] Continuity for these purposes may well be preserved on the basis of ERA 1996, s. 218(2) where the cessation of employment and re-engagement arise at the point of transfer. Even where the dismissal precedes and the re-engagement occurs subsequent to a TUPE transfer, continuity may be preserved, especially in the light of the presumption of continuity established by ERA 1996, s. 210(5), on the basis of there not being a week in which the employee's relations with his employer were not governed by a contract of employment[34] or of there being effectively an agreed cessation of work.[35]

(d) Restrictive covenants

The consequences of the rule invalidating transfer-related contract changes can be signifi- **6.24** cant. Not only can employees who agree to salary reductions subsequently bring proceedings to recover the amounts they had agreed to forgo; other terms agreed in connection with a relevant transfer as part of the process of the transferring employees joining the transferee can potentially be evaded, such as restrictive covenants.

In *Credit Suisse First Boston (Europe) Ltd v Padiachy*[36] three employees entered into new **6.25** employment agreements with Credit Suisse which had agreed to acquire the business in which they worked from Barclays de Zoete Wedd. It was argued that the new terms represented an improvement to their terms and conditions of employment but they did include a new covenant precluding them from working for a competitor for three months should

---

[32] Ibid. at paras 44–5.
[33] See Chapter 4, para. 4.81 and Chapter 5, para. 5.49 for discussion of *Senior Heat Treatment Ltd v Bell* [1997] IRLR 614, EAT which related to the effect on continuity of employment for statutory purposes of the making of redundancy payments when the employees' employment transferred to the transferee for the purposes of TUPE.
[34] ERA 1996, s. 212(1).
[35] ERA 1996, s. 212(3).
[36] [1998] IRLR 504, QBD.

they voluntarily terminate their employment. The *Daddy's Dance Hall*[37] principle described above[38] was applied, enabling the employees to avoid the new restrictive covenant to which they agreed, on the basis that 'the transfer was more than merely the occasion for the change; it was the reason for the change'.[39] The argument that the employees were better off overall was rejected as irrelevant by statement in *Daddy's Dance Hall*[40] to the effect that the disadvantages of a new contractual arrangement cannot be offset by its advantages. As Longmore J put it:

> I do not think that a court either can, or should, start to weigh the competing advantages and disadvantages of new terms of employment which have arisen by reason of the transfer of the undertaking. [Counsel] emphasised the negative in the phrase 'so that overall he is not left in a worse position' and submitted that it would be absurd if the employee is in fact in a better position, and the Court could still not enforce the new terms. That, however, seems to me to be the effect of the judgment of the European Court.[41]

6.26 *Padiachy* was a first instance decision but the result was the same in the Court of Appeal when the issue was litigated again shortly afterwards in *Credit Suisse First Boston (Europe) Ltd v Lister*.[42] The employee in question had received significant financial benefits under retention arrangements put in place in connection with a transfer which also imposed new restrictive covenants upon him. By reference to the *Daddy's Dance Hall* principle,[43] he was found not to be bound by those new restrictive covenants as their introduction was related to the relevant transfer. The transferee had argued that 'if, on a fair view of the new contract as a whole, the employee is better off than he was before, it cannot properly be said that the new contract has derogated from [the employee's] rights in an unfavourable manner'[44] and that any other view led to 'absurdity, or at least to injustice'.[45] The Court of Appeal considered that *Padiachy* was correctly decided and that *Daddy's Dance Hall*, which it was required to follow, did effectively invalidate the new covenants.

B. Permissible Contract Changes

1. TUPE 2006

6.27 In the 2001 Consultation, the DTI made clear[46] that it believed that the approach of the ECJ in *Daddy's Dance Hall* was in line with the employment protection aims of the Directive and the principle that employees cannot contract out of the rights afforded to them.[47] In the light, however, of what was considered to be the uncertainty in the domestic case law as to the circumstances in which a change in terms and conditions can validly be made, the DTI proposed to 'improve the operation of the regulations by making clear that they do not preclude transfer-related changes to terms and conditions that are made for an ETOR—that

---

[37] Above n. 6.
[38] See para. 6.06 *et seq.*
[39] *Padiachy*, above n. 36, at para. 19 per Longmore J.
[40] *Daddy's Dance Hall*, above n. 6, at para. 19, quoted at para. 6.07 above.
[41] *Padiachy*, above n. 36, at para. 21.
[42] [1998] IRLR 700, CA.
[43] See para. 6.06 *et seq.*
[44] *Lister*, above n. 42, at para. 27.
[45] Ibid. at para. 28.
[46] At para. 78.
[47] TUPE 1981, regulation 12—as redrafted, now regulation 18.

is, an economic, technical or organisational reason entailing changes in the workforce'.[48] Accordingly, the validity of such changes would then depend only on the normal contractual principles applying in circumstances other than a transfer of an undertaking.

Regulations 4(4) and 4(5) seek to clarify the operation of TUPE in this context and to **6.28** establish some flexibility in relation to transfer-related changes to terms and conditions of employment. Despite reference in the 2005 Consultation[49] to the possibility of valid contractual variations being agreed between the parties or their representatives, contract changes pursuant to regulations 4(4) and 4(5) can only be validly agreed by the employees themselves and not by a trade union or elected employee representatives on their behalf.[50]

It can be argued, by reference to Article 3, that the category of contractual variations caught **6.29** by the provisions of regulation 4(4) is in any event wider than strictly necessary to ensure compliance with the Directive by extending not only to changes which are, by reason of the transfer but also to those connected with it, a wider and potentially less predictable formulation. Regulations 4(4) and 4(5) nevertheless make the domestic position clear at least with regard to the fact that changes by reason of a transfer are void and those connected with a transfer potentially so, save where there is an ETOR for the change.

2. Categories of variation

The effect of regulations 4(4) and 4(5) is that there are three categories of contractual vari- **6.30** ation, the key element of the application of which is the 'sole or principal reason' for the relevant change:

• Variations for which the sole or principal reason is 'the transfer itself'[51] or 'a reason connected with the transfer that is not an economic, technical or organisational reason entailing changes in the workforce'.[52] Such variations are void and ineffective regardless of the employee's consent. This provision reflects the principle established in *Daddy's Dance Hall*.[53]

• Variations for which the sole or principal reason is unconnected with the transfer.[54] These are valid, since *Daddy's Dance Hall* does not apply to them, subject to the normal rules of contractual variation. To adopt the example given in the 2006 Guidance,[55] '[a] reason unconnected with a transfer could include the sudden loss of an expected order by a manufacturing company or a general upturn in demand for a particular service or a change in a key exchange rate'.

• Variations for which the sole or principal reason is 'a reason connected with the transfer that is an economic, technical or organisational reason entailing changes in the workforce'.[56] These variations are valid and it is this provision that sought to clarify and expand the ability to agree contract changes in relation to a relevant transfer.

---

[48] At para. 83.
[49] At para. 44.
[50] In contrast to the permitted variations provided for in the insolvency context by regulation 9 which can only be agreed by recognised trade unions or elected employee representatives—see Chapter 10, para. 10.54 *et seq.*
[51] Regulation 4(4)(a).
[52] Regulation 4(4)(b).
[53] See para. 6.06 *et seq.*
[54] Regulation 4(5)(b).
[55] At p. 17.
[56] Regulation 4(5)(a).

6.31 Regulation 4(5) provides that employees are not prevented from agreeing to variations falling within the latter two categories. This provision effectively preserves the need for variations to be valid under the applicable contractual principles in any event if they are to be binding.

6.32 Causation and connection are therefore crucial aspects of regulations 4(4) and 4(5). If there is no connection between the contract change and the relevant transfer then the change is not invalid.[57] A contract change is invalid if the sole or principal reason for the variation is the transfer itself.[58] If the contract change is transfer-related but the reason for it is not an ETOR, the amendment remains invalid.[59] If there is an ETOR justifying the change, then the changes will not be invalid.[60] The reason for the contract change in question and the nature of that reason are therefore central to whether it can validly be agreed for the purposes of regulations 4(4) and 4(5).

3. Compatibility with EU law

6.33 It was acknowledged in the 2005 Consultation[61] that the Directive contains no specific provision allowing for otherwise valid variations to employees' terms and conditions of employment to be potentially effective where the sole or principal reason for them is a transfer-related ETOR. Nonetheless in terms of compatibility with EU law, the Government based its argument that the provisions of regulations 4(4) and 4(5) are legitimate on Article 4.1, which permits dismissals on the basis of an ETOR. The view of the DTI (as it then was) was that it was illogical for ARD 2001 to permit employers to dismiss employees on the basis of an ETOR but for them not to be able (perhaps as an alternative to dismissal) to agree changes to terms and conditions for the very same category of reason. Otherwise, there would be what was described as a 'perverse incentive' for employers to dismiss employees and then offer to re-engage them (with potential loss of continuity) or to recruit new staff on different terms and conditions. This would be contrary to the employment protection aims of the legislation and was considered not to have been the intention of the Directive.

6.34 In the light of the *Daddy's Dance Hall* principle that the employee cannot agree to a waiver of his or her rights where the change is transfer-related, the compatibility with the Directive of this ability to agree contract changes occasioned by an ETOR can be argued to be questionable. The possibility therefore remains of employees retrospectively challenging changes to which they have agreed pursuant to regulations 4(4) and 4(5) by reference to *Daddy's Dance Hall*. Their argument would be that TUPE 2006 is *ultra vires* the Directive because it seeks to permit what *Daddy's Dance Hall* prohibits by legitimizing transfer-related contract changes.

4. Connection with the transfer

6.35 The basis for a contractual variation and whether it is by reason of the transfer, for a reason connected with the transfer, unconnected with the transfer, or indeed is for an ETOR is a central issue to the operation of regulations 4(4) and 4(5).

---

[57] Regulation 4(5)(b).
[58] Regulation 4(4)(a).
[59] Regulation 4(4)(b).
[60] Regulation 4(5)(a).
[61] At para. 45.

The 2009 Guidance[62] addresses the issue of the difference between an action that is by reason **6.36**
of the transfer itself and an action which is for a reason which 'is connected with' the transfer
and indicates that:

> [w]here an employer changes terms and conditions simply because of the transfer and there
> are no extenuating circumstances linked to the reason for that decision, then such a change
> is prompted by reason of the transfer itself. However, where the reason for the change is
> prompted by a knock-on effect of the transfer—say, the need to re-qualify staff to use the dif-
> ferent machinery used by the transferee—then the reason is 'connected to the transfer'.

Connection with the transfer can be established some time after the transfer occurs. As the **6.37**
2006 Guidance put it,[63] echoing the comments of Lord Slynn in *Wilson*:[64]

> [t]here is likely to come a time when the link with the transfer can be treated as no longer effec-
> tive. However, this must be assessed in the light of all the circumstances of the individual case,
> and will vary from case to case. There is no 'rule of thumb' used by the courts or specified in
> the Regulations to define a period of time after which it is safe to assume that the transfer did
> not impact directly or indirectly on the employer's actions.

In terms of timing, the decisions in the context of transfer-related dismissals in *Taylor v* **6.38**
Connex South Eastern Ltd[65]—in which the employee was dismissed two years after a relevant transfer but nonetheless the dismissal was held to be transfer-related—and in *London
Metropolitan University v Sackur and others*[66]—where the relevant transfer was in August
2002 but dismissals arising from a harmonization exercise conducted during 2004 were held
to be transfer-related—demonstrate the possibility of changes being transfer-related some
time after the event.

With regard to connection with the transfer, in *Smith and others v Trustees of Brooklands* **6.39**
College[67] the ET's finding was upheld that the consensual variation of certain employees'
pay rates was not void pursuant to regulation 4(4)—the sole or principal reason for the
variation was not the transfer itself or a reason connected with the transfer which is not an
ETOR. Some two years after a merger of two colleges, the new employer considered that the
employees in question were being overpaid in error—their salary was calculated as if they
worked on a full-time (thirty-six-hour) basis even though they were actually only working
twenty-five or twenty-two hours per week. After negotiation, a phased reduction to the
employees' salaries was agreed.

The ET concluded that the original arrangements were not a mistake and that the reason for **6.40**
the subsequent variation was not connected to the transfer but was the erroneous belief on
the part of the transferee's human resources director that the salary levels in question were
paid in error and were higher than those warranted in the sector. In reaching this conclusion
the ET took into account the fact that the changes occurred some two years after the relevant
transfer and found that the changes were not intended to achieve harmonization of salaries
across the two merged colleges (which would have entailed the changes being connected
with the prior transfer). Regulation 4(4) therefore did not engage.

---

[62] At p. 13.
[63] At p. 18.
[64] See para. 6.09 above.
[65] UK EAT/1243/99; see Chapter 7 para. 7.22.
[66] UKEAT/0286/06; see Chapter 7 para. 7.23.
[67] UKEAT/028/11.

6.41 The EAT dismissed an appeal and made the point that regulation 4(4) does not entail the application of a 'but for' test.[68] The question is the reason for the variation which is a question of fact for the ET to assess. A legal assessment then has to be made of whether that reason was connected with the transfer. The ET had reached a decision open to it—the steps taken by the transferee could have been taken at any time irrespective of TUPE.

6.42 HHJ McMullen QC expressed the position as follows:[69]

> 28. It is common ground that this is not a 'but for' jurisdiction; the answer to that is obvious: 'but for' the four employees coming within the bailiwick of Ms Hopkins [the HR Director] at Brooklands, she would not have sought to reduce their pay. But that is not the test. The question is, what was the reason? What caused her to do it? It was her view that they were overpaid by reason of a mistake. The mistake was in awarding these Claimants the pay they were on. That was determined against the Respondent; Ms Hopkins was wrong, there was no error, the parties agreed it. But the second sense in which an error arises is that this method of payment does not conform to any other within the sector, where there is to be a diminution in the pay of part time workers according both to the number of weeks they work and the hours in which they work in those weeks. So, in a sense, they were paid in a way which might be described as an error but probably more realistically it was that they were not paid in accordance with standard practice.
>
> 29. The Judge cited the issue correctly, cited the regulation correctly and made the findings of fact which were open to him. These included an assessment of the period of time that had elapsed from the transfer to the variation and what was going on in Ms Hopkins' mind. Those are both objective and subjective circumstances. But the real issue here is what was in her mind and why did she decide to do it? Although she got the premise wrong, there was no doubt what her reason was. Once those findings were made, a legal assessment has to be made as to whether or not they were connected with the transfer. In my judgement the Judge made the correct decision as a matter of law, that these were not reasons falling within regulation 4(4).

6.43 In *Enterprise Managed Services Ltd v Dance*[70] Enterprise Managed Services Ltd provided appliance maintenance services to Modern Housing Solutions while another contractor provided building maintenance services to the same client. Following the client warning its contractors of the need to improve performance, Enterprise Managed Services agreed with its own employees' changes to their terms of employment including amended hours of work and the introduction of performance-related pay. Some time later Enterprise Managed Services took over the building maintenance contract conducted by another contractor and subsequently decided to harmonize the terms of the employees who transferred to it as a result of the relevant transfer with those of its existing employees. This entailed extending to the transferring employees the changes which Enterprise Managed Services had agreed with its existing employees with regard to productivity some time previously. Whilst most employees agreed to the harmonized terms, some twenty did not, were dismissed and re-engaged on the new terms, and claimed that their dismissals were automatically unfair contrary to regulation 7.

6.44 The ET had, by a majority, held that the reason for the changes to the transferring employees' terms was harmonization with the terms of employment of the transferee's existing employees and that the changes were driven by the productivity gains which the changes delivered

---

[68] i.e. would the change not have occurred but for the transfer.
[69] At paras 28–9.
[70] UKEAT/0200/11.

when agreed with the transferee's existing staff. The EAT allowed an appeal and remitted the case to a fresh ET for the issue again to be addressed indicating[71] that '[s]ince it is open to an employer to effect productivity changes in accordance with the ordinary law, this does not become unlawful when there has been a relevant transfer if the reason is connected to that drive for productivity changes'.

5. ETORs and contract changes

If an employer wishes validly to make changes to an employee's terms and conditions of employment for the purposes of regulations 4(4) and 4(5) and these changes are connected with the transfer, then the employer needs to jump two hurdles. The employer needs to demonstrate that the amendment is valid in general contractual terms. In addition, it needs to demonstrate that the reason for the change constitutes an ETOR. **6.45**

In light of the detailed definition of an ETOR and the case law which has clarified the operation of that concept,[72] establishing that the reason for proposed contract amendments is an ETOR may be a significant challenge for an employer which seeks to implement what, absent a relevant transfer, would otherwise be valid changes to terms and conditions of employment. Economic, technical, or organisational reasons (in general terms) may exist for changes to employees' contracts of employment. For example, changes may need to be made to salary, overtime, or commission levels and other working practices to reflect commercial challenges facing the business in question. Technical changes may require amendments to terms of contract as to working methods. Relocation, integration, and restructuring can constitute organisational reasons for changes. **6.46**

However, an ETOR for these purposes is not merely an economic, technical, or organizational reason for the proposed contractual variation—the relevant economic, technical, or organisational reason must also entail changes in the workforce. In *Berriman v Delabole Slate Ltd*[73] no change occurred to the workforce as there were no dismissals and there was no reduction of the number of staff. There was simply a change to the employees' terms and conditions. It was held that the concept of a change in the workforce required either a change in the numbers involved or, possibly, a change in their job functions which did not result in any overall reduction in numbers. This principle was subsequently followed in *Crawford v Swinton Insurance Brokers Ltd*[74] where there was a significant change to the employee's job function which constituted an ETOR. **6.47**

Unless the employer can establish an ETOR in the sense of its economic, technical or organisational reason entailing changes in the workforce, justifying changes to the contracts of employment of transferring employees by reference to changes to the workforce (construed as it is by reference to changes in workforce numbers or functions) may therefore be challenging. A transferee may need to reduce salaries or benefits and to reduce headcount in order to make viable an undertaking which it is contemplating acquiring. Subject to appropriate implementation, there will be in such circumstances an ETOR which can validate the contract changes as well as provide a defence to unfair dismissal claims. But what if the contract changes which are agreed (as they may often be intended to) enable the employer to avoid **6.48**

---

[71] Ibid. at para. 20.
[72] See Chapter 7, para. 7.42 *et seq.*
[73] [1985] IRLR 305, CA. See Chapter 7, para. 7.51 *et seq.*
[74] [1990] IRLR 42, EAT.

entirely the very dismissals and/or changes to the workforce which regulations 4(4) and 4(5) require in order to render permissible the changes proposed to the contracts of those employees who remain? The changes then appear to be impermissible despite the consequences for the workforce overall being less severe.

6.49 It therefore appears that cost-saving measures which do not accompany or entail changes in job numbers or functions will not validate transfer-related changes to employees' terms and conditions of employment, however justified they might otherwise be in economic, technical, or organisational terms, because the definition of an ETOR will not be satisfied by virtue of there being associated changes in the workforce. Only if the changes are associated with changes in workforce numbers or functions will the changes be valid and effective in accordance with regulations 4(4) and 4(5).

6.50 The limited scope of the ability validly to agree transfer-related contract changes provided by regulations 4(4) and 4(5) was reflected in the answer provided in the 2006 Guidance to the question of whether this freedom to vary contracts permits the transferee employer to harmonize the terms and conditions of the transferred workers with those of the equivalent grades and types of employees which it already employs:

> No. According to the way the courts have interpreted the Acquired Rights Directive, the desire to achieve 'harmonisation' is by reason of the transfer itself. It cannot therefore constitute 'an ETO reason connected with a transfer entailing changes in the workforce'.[75]

6.51 The Government made its position clear in the Consultation Response.[76] It saw great merit in permitting agreement to vary terms to achieve greater harmonization as long as the employees were left no worse off overall. It considered that damaging cost and human resources consequences can arise from groups of employees being on different sets of terms and conditions. The Government effectively concluded (with regret) that it could go no further than regulations 4(4) and 4(5) whilst (in its view) ensuring compatibility with the Directive. Only after amendment of the Directive, which the then administration indicated that it supported and would pursue, would any greater ability to harmonize terms be permissible.

6. Beneficial changes

6.52 *Power v Regent Security Services Ltd*[77] considered the validity of a change agreed to the contract of employment of an employee in connection with a relevant transfer for the purposes of the transfer of undertakings legislation and which was to the advantage of that employee. The issue was whether transfer-related changes to the advantage of employees are unenforceable such that the employer can argue that those changes are void in the same way that employees can argue that detrimental changes cannot be enforced. The contractual amendment in question was held to be binding on the employer, notwithstanding the prohibition on transfer-related contract variations established by the case law on TUPE and the Directive.[78]

6.53 In *Power*, the employee was employed to manage a particular estate under a contract of employment which provided for a retirement age of 60. After a relevant transfer for the

---

[75] At p. 17.
[76] At paras 3.4–3.7.
[77] [2007] IRLR 226, EAT.
[78] See Wynn-Evans, 'The Ongoing Saga of TUPE and Contractual Variations' (2007) 36 ILJ 480.

purposes of what was then TUPE 1981, the employee agreed a contractual retirement age of 65. Whether this was a valid amendment was germane to the issue of whether the employee was able, when compelled to retire at 60, to claim unfair dismissal on the basis that he had not reached the normal retirement age for the purposes of the then applicable ERA 1996, s. 109.[79]

The ET accepted the employer's argument that the variation to the employee's contractual **6.54** retirement age was made by reason of the relevant transfer and was therefore invalid. The ET considered the nullification of transfer-related changes pursuant to the *Daddy's Dance Hall* principle[80] to be neutral as between employer and employee and not to be limited to those changes which are detrimental to the employee. In so concluding the ET relied up regulation 12 of what was TUPE 1981, which rendered unenforceable any attempt to contract out of its provisions. In reaching this conclusion, the ET was presumably influenced by the fact that the ECJ's comments in *Daddy's Dance Hall* referred ostensibly to all transfer-related variations and drew no distinction between variations which are to the advantage of employees and those which are to their detriment.

Before the EAT, the employee argued that nothing in the Directive sought to protect the **6.55** interests of the employer (although this is questionable since the legislation operates to transfer powers and rights, as well as duties and obligations, from transferor to transferee). He also contended that there was no reason why the employer should be able to resile from an agreement which it had reached and that the current case was distinguishable from decisions such as *Daddy's Dance Hall*[81] and *Credit Suisse (First Boston) Ltd v Lister*,[82] in which employees sought to avoid detrimental (as opposed to favourable) variations even where they formed part of a package of changes to terms of conditions which were neutral or positive for the employee overall.

In allowing an appeal and upholding the validity of the advantageous contractual variation **6.56** of a later retirement age, Elias P referred to the recitals to the Directive and to comments in *P Bork v Foreningen af Arbejdslere i Danmark*[83] confirming the objective of the legislation of safeguarding employees' rights in the event of a transfer as well as to Clarke LJ's observation in *Credit Suisse (First Boston) Ltd v Lister*[84] that the relevant case law 'contain[s] many statements to the effect that the purpose of the Directive is to ensure that a transfer of a business "has no prejudicial effects" on the employees of the transferor and that it "does not subject them to less favourable treatment"'. Elias P concluded that 'it would be inconsistent with the aim of protecting the workforce to refuse them benefits contractually conferred by the transferee'.[85] Elias P analysed the invalidity of transfer-related contractual variations as optional on the part of the employee and made the following observations:

> 53. In our view *Daddy's Dance Hall* and *Credit Suisse* merely establish that if the employee wishes to rely upon a term originally found in the agreement with the transferor (but which will have transferred to the transferee) rather than relying upon a term in the varied or new

---

[79] A now repealed provision which prevented unfair dismissal claims being brought in relation to dismissal after that normal retirement age.

[80] For further discussion see para. 6.06 *et seq*.

[81] Ibid.

[82] [1998] IRLR 700, CA.

[83] [2001] IRLR 51, ECJ.

[84] [1998] IRLR 700, CA at para. 16.

[85] *Power*, above n. 77, at para. 51.

agreement with the transferee, he will be entitled to do so. It is not a question whether objectively viewed the original term is more beneficial or not. It is simply a question whether the employee wishes to rely upon it, although no doubt he will only do so where he thinks that it is beneficial. He must be the best judge of his own interests. If he perceives it to be beneficial to seek to rely on the original term, he can seek to do so in preference to the inconsistent later term. (There is a powerful argument why it should sometimes be a condition of so doing that he gives credit for benefits derived under the new contract, but that is not an issue that arises here.)

54. However, in our judgment there is no reason why he should not be permitted to hold the employer to the new term if he considers it to be more favourable. Again, it is immaterial whether, objectively viewed, it is more favourable....

61.... There is nothing in the case law of the ECJ, nor in the Regulations, nor in the public policy which they are designed to enshrine, which would require that the transferee employer be allowed to resile from a voluntarily agreed variation to the contract, even where the transfer is the reason for the variation, as it admittedly was in this case.

6.57 This analysis allows favourable variations to stand if the employee so chooses without offending against the *Daddy's Dance Hall* principle. What Elias P described[86] as 'compensating advantages' by way of new benefits do not save detrimental variations and the argument was also rejected that regulation 12 of TUPE 1981—now regulation 18 of the 2006 Regulations—could operate to render ineffective a beneficial but nonetheless transfer-related change.

6.58 What this analysis leaves unresolved, however, is whether, if transfer-related contract changes can be invalidated effectively at the employee's option, the employee can pick and choose between the pre- and post-transfer terms of employment and retain any 'compensating advantages' received whilst avoiding detrimental variations. As Clarke LJ noted in *Credit Suisse First Boston (Europe) Ltd v Lister*,[87] although they did not fall to be decided in that particular case, a number of issues arise in relation to the situation where such compensating advantages have been agreed in consideration for contractual variations which an employee subsequently avoids, including whether the new contract is void in its entirety and whether principles of estoppel or change of position can be relevant where the contract has been wholly or partly performed. In *Credit Suisse First Boston (Europe) Ltd v Padiachy*[88] Longmore J commented, in relation to the consideration which the employee had received in respect of his agreement to restrictive covenants by which he was not bound pursuant to the *Daddy's Dance Hall* principle, that he could 'see no answer to that £2,000 being repayable'.[89]

6.59 In *Power*, Elias P also gave (albeit fleeting and *obiter*) credence to the argument that employers can seek recompense for the compensating advantages rendered in return for detrimental changes which an employee subsequently avoids. He indicated that an employee who utilizes his right to argue that detrimental transfer-related contractual variations are invalid may have to 'give up any benefits obtained under the varied contract as a condition of so doing'[90] and that there was a 'powerful argument'[91] that an employee should give credit for the benefits

---

[86] Ibid. at para. 60.
[87] Above n. 84, at para. 39.
[88] Above n. 36.
[89] Ibid. at para. 22.
[90] *Power*, above n. 77, at para. 60.
[91] Ibid. at para. 53.

received in consideration for the detrimental transfer-related variation which the employee seeks to avoid. An ability on the part of employers to be able to reclaim benefits conferred on employees as consideration for the detrimental variations which they agree but subsequently seek to avoid not only lacks as yet a clear jurisprudential basis, although it could presumably be based on principles of unjust enrichment if nothing else; it also raises potentially difficult issues of enforcement. Detrimental changes may be challenged a considerable period after the relevant transfer—for example, as was the case in *Lister*—when restrictive covenants agreed in relation to a relevant transfer are sought to be enforced by the employer on eventual termination of employment. Recovery of the relevant benefits may well not be enforceable in practice or equitable at that stage in terms of an employee's resources or change of position. Where the compensating advantages for the void detrimental changes are not directly monetary, recompense may not easily be quantifiable.

The *Power* decision was made by reference to the provisions of TUPE 1981. Regulations **6.60** 4(4) and 4(5), which expressly render void all transfer-related changes which are not saved by an ETOR, regardless of whether or not they are beneficial, were introduced after that decision. It has therefore been argued that the principle established in *Power* did not survive the introduction of the 2006 Regulations. It has also been suggested that employees may only be able to enforce beneficial transfer-related changes to their contracts of employment, if the employer seeks to withdraw them, on the basis of some form of estoppel. Notwithstanding this debate, the 2009 Guidance states that 'changes to terms and conditions agreed by the parties which are entirely positive are not prevented by the regulations'.[92]

7. Pension changes

Changes to occupational pension scheme arrangements fall outside the scope of the issues **6.61** discussed in this Chapter both with regard to the invalidity in principle of transfer-related changes and the limited ability provided by TUPE to make valid transfer-related amendments to the terms and conditions of employment of transferring employees. This is a consequence of regulation 10 which excludes certain occupational pension scheme benefits from the entitlements preserved on a relevant transfer.[93] Transferring employees are entitled to insist on the levels of pension provision required by the combined effect of the PA 2004 and the PPR 2005 as against the transferee but only if they enjoyed membership of or were (actually or contingently) eligible to participate in an occupational pension scheme operated by the transferor.

Since the relevant category of occupational pension scheme entitlements do not survive **6.62** a relevant transfer, a transferee's changes to the pre-transfer pension arrangements for the transferring employees do not constitute changes to those employees' contracts which require employee consent or fall within the scope of regulation 4 so as potentially to be void as transfer-related. This is the case even if compliance with the pension protection regime established by PA 2004 and PPR 2005 involves the introduction of a materially inferior

---

[92] At p. 13.
[93] See Chapter 11 for discussion of the 'pensions exclusion'.

level of pension provision. The transferee therefore has, subject to PA 2004 and PPR 2005, considerable scope to amend the level of pension provision for transferring employees who previously enjoyed occupational pension scheme entitlements without their consent and without concern about those pension changes subsequently being found to be invalid, provided that the relevant pension arrangements are not preserved by TUPE because they fall outside the scope of the pensions exclusion.

6.63   The pensions exclusion extends only to the limited category of old age, invalidity, and survivors' benefits falling within its scope. Other benefits provided under occupational pension schemes (such as early retirement and redundancy entitlements), as well as pension arrangements which do not fall within the scope of the pensions exclusion (such as contributions to employees' personal pension arrangements), cannot be varied with the impunity which, subject to PA 2004 and PPR 2005, regulation 10 affords to transferees. Changes to such pension benefits as do transfer to the transferee under regulation 4 because they do not fall within the scope of regulation 10 will (outside the scope of the specific insolvency provisions of TUPE) fall to be covered by the regime established by regulations 4(4) and 4(5) and therefore, if transfer-related, will need to be justified by an ETOR if they are to be valid.

6.64   In this context, it is also worth noting that PA 2004, s. 258(6) permits transfer-related changes to the pension benefits required to be provided by PA 2004 and PPR 2005. Such changes can validly be agreed post-transfer subject to the normal contractual rules. No further requirements need to be satisfied.

7

TRANSFER-RELATED DISMISSALS

A. Introduction	7.01	2. Statutory redundancy payments	7.45
B. Automatic Unfairness	7.10	3. What can be an ETOR?	7.46
1. Regulation 7(1)	7.10	4. The workforce	7.60
2. Protected persons	7.12	5. Whose ETOR?	7.65
3. Exceptions	7.16	D. Liability and Fairness	7.72
4. Reason for dismissal	7.19	1. General	7.72
5. No transfer or transferee in		2. Lack of sufficient service to claim	
contemplation	7.24	unfair dismissal	7.74
6. Whose reason for dismissal?	7.35	3. Assertion of a statutory right	7.75
C. Economic, Technical, or Organisational		4. Redundancy pooling and TUPE	7.79
Reasons Entailing Changes in the		5. Enforcement issues	7.83
Workforce	7.43	6. Summary	7.86
1. Regulations 7(2) and 7(3)	7.43		

A. Introduction

A crucial element of the protection which the Directive and TUPE provide for employees **7.01**
affected by an event or transaction falling within their scope is the remedy available if the
transferee fails to honour its obligation to continue the employment of the relevant employees or if either the transferor or the transferee effects dismissals which are connected with the
transfer. The remedy provided by TUPE, in conjunction with the ERA 1996, is (in addition
to any wrongful dismissal damages available) an unfair dismissal claim.[1] That an injunction
cannot be sought to restrain dismissals alleged to be transfer-related was confirmed in *Betts
v Brintel Helicopters Ltd & anor*.[2]

Article 4.1 provides that: **7.02**

> the transfer of an undertaking, business or part of the undertaking or business shall not in itself
> constitute grounds for dismissal by the transferor or the transferee. This provision shall not
> stand in the way of dismissals that may take place for economic, technical or organisational
> reasons entailing changes in the workforce.

The Directive and by extension TUPE do not invalidate transfer-related dismissals but **7.03**
national law provides the remedy for such a dismissal in breach of the protection of the

---

[1] Detailed discussion of the unfair dismissal regime more generally falls outside the scope of this work.
[2] [1997] IRLR 361, HC.

legislation. Describing this principle in the context of TUPE Lord Slynn said as follows in *Wilson and others v St. Helen's Borough Council*:[3]

> Where the transferee does not take on the employees who are dismissed on transfer the dismissal is not a nullity though the contractual rights formerly available against the transferor remain intact against the transferee. For the latter purpose, an employee dismissed prior to the transfer contrary to Article 4(1), i.e. on the basis of the transfer, is to be treated as still in the employment of the transferor at the date of transfer.[4]

7.04 In terms of his methodology of the personal work contract, Freedland describes the fact that a dismissal prior to a relevant transfer remains legally effective but may result in liabilities transferring to the transferee as a 'contractual sub-transfer' rather than as a 'contractual full transfer'—a pre-transfer dismissal takes the contract of employment into 'post-employment mode, giving rise only to post employment obligations, if any, and liabilities for wrongful dismissal or earlier breaches of contract. The transfer of the undertaking operate[s] to transfer the contract of employment to the transferee of the undertaking only in that limited sense'.[5]

7.05 Regulation 7(1) implements Article 4.1 into domestic law, establishing the protection provided to employees dismissed in connection with a relevant transfer by deeming an offending dismissal automatically unfair for the purposes of the ERA 1996, Part X.[6] TUPE does not itself provide the remedy for an impermissible transfer-related dismissal—it creates a specific category of automatically unfair dismissal for the purposes of the domestic unfair dismissal jurisdiction. This formulation therefore incorporates by reference the eligibility requirement of the requisite period of continuous employment under ERA 1996.[7] This limitation on the eligibility of employees to claim the protection against transfer-related dismissal established by TUPE is permissible as a result of Article 4(1) which permits Member States to provide that the protection against dismissal provided by that Article 'shall not apply to certain specific categories of employees who are not covered by the laws and practice of the Member States in respect of protection against dismissal'.

7.06 A crucial element of the operation of the protection of employees in relation to transfer-related dismissals is the concept of an 'economic, technical or organisational reason entailing a change in the workforce' (ETOR). Where a dismissal which is transfer-related is nonetheless by reason of an ETOR, the dismissal is not automatically unfair but is tested for its fairness in the normal way under ERA 1996. The concept of an ETOR, which applies only where there are legitimate reasons for a dismissal based upon the operation of the relevant business, therefore provides the gateway for the avoidance of automatic unfairness in respect of a transfer-related dismissal.

---

[3] [1998] IRLR 706, HL.

[4] Ibid. at para. 73.

[5] Freedland, *The Personal Employment Contract*, Oxford: OUP, 2003 p. 511.

[6] Regulation 7(1)—'that employee shall be treated for the purposes of Part X of the 1996 Act (unfair dismissal) as unfairly dismissed'.

[7] Which, in relation to those employees whose continuous employment began on or after 6 April 2012, is two years pursuant to the Unfair Dismissal and Statement of Reasons for Dismissal (Variation of Qualifying Period) Order 2012 SI 2012/989 and, in respect of those whose continuous employment began before 6 April 2012, is one year pursuant to the Unfair Dismissal and Statement of Reasons for Dismissal (Variation of Qualifying Period) Order 1999 SI 1999/1436.

Regulation 7 in effect establishes four different categories of dismissal: **7.07**

- dismissals for which the sole or principal reason for the dismissal is the transfer itself.[8] An example would be dismissal of employees to facilitate sale of the business in which they work;
- dismissals for which the sole or principal reason is a reason connected with the transfer that is not an ETOR.[9] An example would be dismissals resulting from a transfer related contract harmonization exercise not entailing a change in the workforce (and therefore not fulfilling the requirements of an ETOR);
- dismissals for which the sole or principal reason is not the transfer itself but is a reason connected with the transfer that is an ETOR of either the transferor or transferee before the transfer.[10] An example would be dismissals by reason of a genuine redundancy situation arising from the acquisition of a business and a consequent rationalization conducted by the transferee;
- dismissals for which the sole or principal reason is unconnected with the transfer.[11] An example would be dismissals for gross misconduct or consequent upon a relocation which would have been necessary regardless of the relevant transfer.

This categorization in part seeks to address a concern which had arisen in relation to TUPE **7.08**
1981. TUPE 1981, regulation 8(1) deemed transfer-related dismissals automatically unfair.[12]
TUPE 1981, regulation 8(2) then proceeded to disapply TUPE 1981, regulation 8(1) and to apply the usual test of unfair dismissal where there was an ETOR justifying the dismissal.[13]
Some decisions had indicated that this structure meant that, once a dismissal was found to be transfer-related, the ET could not then consider whether an ETOR excepted the dismissal from automatic unfairness.[14] Regulation 7 makes the position clear.[15]

To summarize, therefore: **7.09**

- Dismissals for which the reason is a relevant transfer or which are connected with a relevant transfer but for which there is no ETOR potentially justifying the dismissal are automatically unfair.
- If a dismissal is transfer-related but is nonetheless for an ETOR, then the dismissal is potentially unfair subject to the normal test of unfair dismissal pursuant to ERA 1996.

---

[8] Regulation 7(1)(a).
[9] Regulation 7(1)(b).
[10] Regulation 7(2).
[11] This implicit category is not explicitly identified by TUPE 2006.
[12] 'where either before or after a relevant transfer, any employee of the transferor or transferee is dismissed, that employee shall be treated ... as unfairly dismissed if the transfer or a reason connected with it is the reason or principal reason for his dismissal'.
[13] where an economic, technical or organisational reason entailing changes in the workforce of either the transferor or the transferee before or after a relevant transfer is the reason or principal reason for dismissing an employee:
    (a) paragraph (1) above shall not apply to his dismissal; but
    (b) without prejudice to the ... test of fair dismissal ... the dismissal shall ... be regarded as having been for a substantial reason of a kind such as to justify the dismissal of an employee holding the position which that employee held.
[14] See *Trafford v Sharpe and Fisher (Building Supplies) Ltd* [1994] IRLR 325, EAT; *Warner v Adnet* [1998] IRLR 394, CA; *Kerry Foods Ltd v Creber* [2000] IRLR 10, EAT. The point was also considered in the 2001 Consultation at para. 75.
[15] The categorization of dismissals adopted in regulation 7 is based on the Government's view of the 'correct interpretation of the Directive's requirements in this regard' and 'mirrors the approach taken in draft regulation 4 in relation to changes to terms and conditions'—see 2005 Consultation para. 51.

- Where a dismissal is not connected with a relevant transfer, then TUPE's prohibition on transfer-related dismissals does not engage and the fairness of dismissal will again be assessed under the normal principles of unfair dismissal. Even if contemporaneous with a relevant transfer, a dismissal based on misconduct, capability, or redundancy unconnected with the transfer falls to be assessed under the usual unfair dismissal principles rather than regulation 7.

B. Automatic Unfairness

1. Regulation 7(1)

7.10   Regulation 7(1) provides as follows:

> Where either before or after a relevant transfer, any employee of the transferor or transferee is dismissed, that employee shall be treated for the purposes of Part X of the 1996 [ERA] (unfair dismissal) as unfairly dismissed if the sole or principal reason for his dismissal is:
>
> (a) the transfer itself; or
> (b) a reason connected with the transfer that is not an economic, technical or organisational reason entailing changes in the workforce.

7.11   Accordingly, those who are eligible to claim unfair dismissal[16] are in principle able to claim automatic unfair dismissal where they can show that a transfer-connected reason is the reason for dismissal and no ETOR applies to 'save' the dismissal from automatic unfairness. It is clear that regulation 7 extends to cases of constructive dismissal as well as express dismissal, not least by virtue of the fact that regulation 4(11) expressly records the right of an employee to terminate his or her employment on grounds of repudiatory breach of contract.[17]

2. Protected persons

7.12   Regulation 7 applies to protect employees who are dismissed in connection with a relevant transfer regardless of whether their employment is such that it should transfer to the transferee under regulation 4. Employees who are dismissed by reason of the transfer can still claim automatic unfair dismissal under regulation 7 even if they would not have transferred in the normal course of the operation of TUPE. This is the effect of regulation 7(4) which provides that regulation 7 applies 'irrespective of whether the employee in question is assigned to the organised grouping of resources or employees that is, or will be, transferred'.

7.13   Accordingly, if an employee of the transferor whose employment does not fall to transfer to the transferee pursuant to TUPE (because the employee is not assigned to the relevant undertaking or the organised grouping of employees which is the subject of an SPC), or if an existing employee of the transferee is dismissed, and the relevant dismissal is for a reason connected with the transfer, then the employee will be able to claim automatic unfair dismissal under regulation 7. The consequent unfair dismissal claim lies against the actual employer (the transferor or transferee, as the case may be). An employee whose employment should not transfer under TUPE to the transferee because he or she does not fall within the scope of

---

[16] By virtue of being employees for the purposes of ERA 1996 and having completed the requisite qualifying period of service.
[17] See Chapter 4, para. 4.122 *et seq.*

the legislation cannot bring a claim against the transferee if dismissed by the transferor even if that reason is connected with the transfer.[18]

As amended in 2006, TUPE also expressly incorporates into the legislation the principle **7.14** established in *Litster v Forth Dry Dock & Engineering Co Ltd*,[19] which ensured that the protection of the legislation extends beyond those whose employment actually transfers to the transferee by virtue of regulation 4 or who were employed immediately before the transfer. Accordingly, TUPE's protections apply to those who would have so transferred but were dismissed prior to the transfer (other than where an ETOR applies)—such employees are protected by regulation 7 even though they were not employed immediately before the transfer so as to be within the scope of regulation 4 and therefore to transfer to the employment of the transferee.

The inheritance by the transferee of these liabilities is effected by regulation 4(3) which defines **7.15** those employees whose contracts of employment and associated liabilities transfer to the transferee on a relevant transfer as those employed immediately before the transfer or who would have been so employed if they had not been unfairly dismissed in the circumstances described in regulation 7(1).[20] As noted above, in the absence of an ETOR, regulation 7(1) deems transfer-related dismissals automatically unfair whether they are effected before or after a relevant transfer. The combination of these two provisions ensures that an employee whose employment is dismissed by reason of a relevant transfer but in the absence of an ETOR, even if that occurs some time before the transfer occurs,[21] can claim automatic unfair dismissal under regulation 7(1) and can pursue that claim against the transferee pursuant to regulation 4(3).

3. Exceptions

Two particular exceptions to regulation 7 provided by regulations 7(5) and 7(6). First, regula- **7.16** tion 7(5)[22] provides that the deeming of a dismissal automatically unfair by regulation 7(1):

> shall not apply in relation to the dismissal of any employee which was required by reason of the application of section 5 of the Aliens Restriction (Amendment) Act 1919 to his employment.[23]

Second, regulation 7(6) provides that regulation 7(1): **7.17**

> shall not apply in relation to a dismissal of an employee if the application of section 94 of the 1996 [Employment Rights] Act to the dismissal of the employee is excluded by or under any provision of the 1996 [Employment Rights] Act, the 1996 [Employment] Tribunals Act or [the Trade Union and Labour Relations (Consolidation) Act (TULRCA)] 1992.

Consequently, employees cannot rely on regulation 7(1) in support of a claim of automa- **7.18** tically unfair dismissal if, for example, a claim for unfair dismissal cannot be made because:

- the employee has not satisfied the requirement of continuous service imposed by ERA 1996, s. 94;[24]

---

[18] Regulation 4(3) only operates to transfer to the transferee liabilities in respect of those assigned to the relevant undertaking or organised grouping of employees.
[19] [1989] IRLR 161, HL.
[20] See Chapter 4, para. 4.22 *et seq.*
[21] For example, see *Spaceright Europe Ltd v Baillavoine* [2012] IRLR 111, CA discussed at para. 7.30.
[22] Which repeats verbatim TUPE 1981, regulation 8(4).
[23] Space constraints preclude a detailed examination of this maritime-related provision.
[24] See above n. 7.

- an unfair dismissal claim is barred by virtue of his or her having been engaged in unlawful industrial action as provided by TULRCA 1992, s. 237 *et seq.*;
- conciliation has taken place under the Employment Tribunals Act 1996, s. 18.

4. Reason for dismissal

7.19 To recap, under regulation 7(1), a dismissal will be automatically unfair where the 'sole or principal' reason for the transfer is 'the transfer itself' or 'a reason connected with the transfer' that is not an ETOR. Even where it can be shown that the transfer is not the 'sole or principal' reason for the dismissal, regulation 7 will still be engaged where the reason is 'connected with the transfer'. If the dismissal is connected with the transfer but is by reason of an ETOR then automatic unfairness pursuant to regulation 7(1) is avoided pursuant to regulation 7(2). Factual disputes may therefore arise as to whether a dismissal is by reason of a relevant transfer itself, connected with a relevant transfer, connected with a relevant transfer but by reason of an ETOR, or unconnected with the relevant transfer in question.

7.20 As the Court of Appeal put it in *Abernethy v Mott*,[25] 'a reason for dismissal is a set of facts known to the employer or beliefs held by him which cause him to dismiss the employee'. Connecting that reason for dismissal with the transfer need not necessarily be based on the employer appreciating or considering that its knowledge of facts or beliefs which cause the decision to dismiss has anything to do with the transfer. Factual or causal connection can be established independently of the employer's view of whether the transfer was anything to do with the dismissal. There is no time limit upon the period during which dismissal can be deemed to be transfer-related and therefore automatically unfair. A dismissal may be transfer-related even if it occurs some considerable time after the transfer itself. A review of some of the case law in this area illustrates the arguments upon which the ETs and courts are called upon to adjudicate.

7.21 In *Warner v Adnet*[26] the reason for dismissals effected by receivers was the attempt to continue to trade rather than the transfer in question. Accordingly, the dismissals were not transfer-related. Similarly, in *Norris v Brown and Root Ealing Technical Services Ltd*,[27] an ET's decision was upheld by the EAT to the effect that a dismissal caused by financial difficulties relating to underfunding was not for a reason connected with a relevant transfer. In *Longden and anor v Ferrari Ltd and anor*[28] the EAT held by a majority that the ET had been entitled to find that neither the transfer nor a reason connected with it was the reason or principal reason for the dismissal of the claimant employees. Whilst the purchaser of the relevant business had identified the staff whom it considered that it was essential be retained, this did not necessarily entail a request to dismiss other staff and the dismissals in question were found, legitimately by the ET, to have been effected because of financial constraints and pressure from the transferor's bank.[29] In *Page and anor v Lakeside Collection Ltd and anor*[30] employees were dismissed by administrative receivers on their appointment and those dismissals were found to be for an ETOR because fewer managerial staff were required during the period of administrative receivership. The ET rejected the argument that the dismissals

---

[25] [1974] IRLR 213, CA at para. 13.
[26] [1998] IRLR 394, CA.
[27] UKEAT/386/00.
[28] [1994] IRLR 157, EAT.
[29] Ibid. at paras 39–41.
[30] UKEAT/0216/10.

were the consequence of a conspiracy to prevent the transfer of the relevant employees' employment. The administrative receiver's evidence to this effect was accepted and the ET's finding was held by the EAT to be one which it was entitled to reach as a consequence.

That an employee's dismissal can be 'connected with' the transfer even though the dismissal **7.22** occurs some time after the relevant transfer is demonstrated by *Taylor v Connex South Eastern Ltd*,[31] in which the employee was dismissed two years after a relevant transfer. Nonetheless, the dismissal was held to be transfer-related. The employee was dismissed for refusing to accept a new contract removing contractual holiday and redundancy entitlements which he had enjoyed with his previous employer. That the majority of staff had accepted the changes in question was of no relevance—the reasonableness of either party's position is not relevant to the process of identifying the causative reason for the dismissal. The ET had entirely properly found the reason for the dismissal to have been the relevant transfer, without which the contractual changes would not have been demanded.

London Metropolitan University v Sackur and others[32] further demonstrates that dismissal **7.23** some considerable time after a relevant transfer can nonetheless be shown to be connected to that transfer. Following the merger of London Guildhall University and the University of North London to form London Metropolitan University on 1 August 2002, the employer sought to move staff on to contracts of employment emanating from the University of North London by way of a harmonization exercise in a process conducted during 2004. The ET held that the reason for the relevant employees' dismissal—which was designed to compel harmonization of the relevant employment terms—was the original transfer pursuant to which the dismissed employees became employed by London Metropolitan University. Despite the suggestion that there were various reasons for the proposed contract changes, including a desire to retain students, maintaining two sets of contracts being impracticable and the relevant union having agreed to the contracts when they were originally introduced pre-transfer at the University of North London, the ET's finding was upheld by the EAT. The ET's conclusions, based as they were on its primary factual findings and the inferences which it drew from the evidence before it, could not be impeached.

5. No transfer or transferee in contemplation

With regard to the issue of establishing the connection of a dismissal with a subsequent **7.24** transfer, problems can arise whereas at the point of dismissal there is no transfer or definite or likely transferee in contemplation. This can be a particularly acute problem in the context of receiverships and administrations, where employees seek to bring claims against a solvent transferee rather than an insolvent transferor and therefore contend that their earlier dismissal was related to a subsequent transfer.

Dismissals may be effected to make the relevant business more attractive to potential acquir- **7.25** ers (which would point towards the dismissals being transfer-related). They may, however, be needed to preserve the viability of the business (pointing towards the dismissal either not being transfer-related at all or being connected to the transfer but by reason of an ETOR). The situation is further complicated if at the time of dismissal a transaction is not in the process of being devised, a specific potential acquirer is not in the course of negotiations with the eventual transferor, or there are a number of parties interested in acquiring the business.

---

[31] UKEAT/1243/99.
[32] UKEAT/0286/06.

7.26   In *Harrison Bowden Ltd v Bowden*[33] connection of the dismissal in question with the transfer was established, rendering the dismissal automatically unfair, even though no specific transferee had been identified at the time of dismissal. Dismissal could be transfer-related even in the absence of an identifiable specific transferee at the time of dismissal. In determining that TUPE did operate to protect an employee in circumstances where a transferee had not been identified at the point of dismissal, Tuckey J said as follows:

> We think that the reference to 'the transfer' is a reference to a transfer which actually takes place which these regulations contemplate by the definition of 'the relevant transfer'. Regulation 8(1) is directed to the situation both before and after such a transfer. We cannot see that it is of importance that the transferee has been identified at or before the moment of dismissal. *P Bork International A/S v Foreningen of Arbejdsleddene i Danmark* which is the decision of the European Court of Justice which prompted and informed the decision of the House of Lords in *Litster* suggests that the approach in considering cases such as these is to look back in time to see what actually happened. In that case there was no question of the transferee being identified at the moment of dismissal and yet it was a case in which the workers concerned were protected by the Directive.[34]

7.27   In *Ibex Trading Co Ltd v Walton*[35] employees were dismissed before any approach had been made to the administrator of the relevant business with regard to its disposal. As a relevant transfer was a mere 'twinkle in the eye' at the point of dismissal, liability did not pass to the ultimate transferee. The approach adopted in *Harrison Bowden* was rejected—to fall within the scope of TUPE's protection, a dismissal needed to be connected with *the* transfer as distinct from *a possible* transfer. As Morison J put it:

> Contrary to what was said in the *Harrison Bowden* case, we attach significance to the definite article in regulation 8(1) 'that employee shall be treated ... as unfairly dismissed if the transfer or a reason connected with it is the reason or the principal reason for the dismissal'. The link, in terms of time, between the dismissals and the transfers will vary considerably. In *Litster* the time difference was one hour; often it will be more. A transfer is not just a single event: it extends over a period of time culminating in a completion. However, here, the employees were dismissed before any offer had been made for the business. Whilst it could properly be said that they were dismissed for a reason connected with a possible transfer of the business, on the facts here we are not satisfied that they were dismissed by reason of the transfer or for a reason connected with the transfer. A transfer was, at the stage of the dismissal, a mere twinkle in the eye and might never have occurred. We do not say that in every case. It is necessary for the post active transferee to be identified; because sometimes one purchaser drops out at the last minute and another purchaser replaces him.[36]

7.28   In *Morris v John Grose*[37] the EAT preferred the *Harrison Bowden* approach to that adopted in *Ibex*. As Bell J said:[38]

> In our view, however, the words 'the transfer' towards the end of regulation 8(1) do not by necessary construction have to refer to the relevant particular transfer which has actually taken place. If that was the necessary meaning of regulation 8(1) it could have been made quite clear by the use of the words such as 'that transfer' or 'the particular transfer'. Although 'the' is described as a definite article, it is not always used as such in ordinary English, and in our view

---

[33] [1994] ICR 186, EAT.
[34] Ibid. at para. 191.
[35] [1994] IRLR 564, EAT.
[36] Ibid. at para. 25.
[37] [1998] IRLR 499, EAT.
[38] Ibid. at paras. 41 and 43.

the words 'the transfer', as they are used in regulation 8(1), could perfectly well mean 'transfer' or 'a transfer'. In our judgment this view of the meaning of regulation 8(1) is more consistent with the broad scope of the Directive.

Moreover, to decide otherwise would lead to quite unfair anomalies as the Appeal Tribunal in *Harrison Bowden* pointed out. Why, for instance, should employees who are dismissed by reason of a particular anticipated transfer which does not go through but which is promptly replaced by another comparable transfer in circumstances where a transfer to someone was inevitable, not have the benefit of regulation 8(1), subject to regulation 8(2), when they would have had that protection if the original transfer had gone through? Yet this would be the result of a restrictive construction of 'the transfer' in regulation 8(1).

In *CAB Automotive Ltd v Blake and others*[39] the EAT held that, where an administrator was **7.29** 'slimming down' a business with a view to sale, the ET was entitled to conclude that the reason or principal reason for the dismissal was the transfer or a reason connected with it despite the fact that no potential buyer had at that stage been identified. In relation to the conflict between *Ibex* and *Harrison Bowden* Beatson J said as follows:

> First we would have rejected the invitation to rule that the decision in *Morris*'s case was wrong. It is the most recent decision of this Tribunal on this issue. It decided to follow *Harrison Bowden Ltd v Bowden* [1994] ICR 186 rather than *Ibex Trading Co Ltd v Walton* [1994] ICR 907 and did so after reviewing the relevant authorities with the exception of *Sidney Smith v Hill* EAT 17 February 1998. (See page 666D). The approach taken in *Morris*'s case is also more consistent than that in *Ibex*'s case with the broad scope of *Directive 77/187/EEC* which the 1981 regulations implement.[40]

In *Spaceright Europe Ltd v Baillavoine*[41] the Court of Appeal considered this issue—whether, **7.30** for an employee to be able to claim that his dismissal is connected to the transfer and therefore that his dismissal is one that is potentially automatically unfair and for which the transferee is liable, the transfer—or indeed the identity of the transferee—needs to have been identified or be in contemplation at the time of dismissal and resolved the conflict in the EAT authorities. The Court of Appeal upheld the decision of the ET that the dismissal of the chief executive officer of the relevant business, on the same day as his employer went into administration, was for a transfer-connected reason and was automatically unfair, even though the business and assets were sold a month later and the identity of the transferee, and indeed the specific transaction itself, was not in the administrators' contemplation at the time of the dismissal.

The administrators' evidence was that the chief executive's dismissal was decided upon because **7.31** the employer did not need the chief executive after the appointment of the administrator. However, this evidence was rejected. The dismissal was found to have been effected in order to facilitate the sale of the business—and therefore transfer-connected—and dismissal was found to be automatically unfair as it was not justified as being for an ETOR. The Court of Appeal was satisfied that the dismissal was connected to the transfer on the basis that achieving a sale of the business was the real motivation for the chief executive's dismissal, not the ongoing conduct of the business. Moreover, as the role of chief executive continued to exist post-transfer, the dismissal was not for an ETOR. The ETOR defence as the Court of Appeal put it, 'is not available in the case of dismissing an employee to enable the administrators to

---

[39] UKEAT/0298/07.
[40] At para. 32.
[41] [2012] IRLR 111, CA.

make the business of the company a more attractive proposition to perspective transferees of the going concern'.[42]

7.32 The Court of Appeal took the view that a dismissal can be connected with a transfer even though the particular transfer or transferee is not named, identified, or contemplated at the date of dismissal. As Mummery LJ put it, '[t]he natural and ordinary meaning of the language of reg. 7(1) does not require a particular transfer or transferee to be in existence or contemplation at the time of dismissal'.[43] The analysis adopted in *Harrison Bowden* was held to be more consistent with the broad scope of the Directive than the analysis in *Ibex*. Nonetheless, the Court of Appeal made clear that the ET must, when considering the reason for dismissal, assess the evidence and determine the reason for dismissal or whether that reason was connected to the transfer.

7.33 As Mummery LJ put it:

> 44. The exercise under regulation 7(1) only has to be carried out if there has been both a dismissal, which is claimed to be automatically unfair, and a relevant transfer. If, on the one hand, no relevant transfer ever takes place, there is no basis for making a claim for automatic unfair dismissal for a transfer-related reason. The regulation would simply not be engaged.
>
> 45. If, on the other hand, a dismissal and a relevant transfer do take place, the regulation could be engaged. The ET is then required by the regulation to look to the fact of dismissal and, as a matter of the objective assessment of the evidence, to determine the reason for it and whether that reason was 'connected with' the transfer. As a matter of ordinary English and of plain common sense a dismissal prior to the transfer could have been for a reason 'connected with the transfer', even though that particular transfer or transferee was not known, identified or contemplated at the date of dismissal. It is a common experience of life that an event (A) may sensibly be considered to be 'connected with' a later event (B), even though it was not known, contemplated or foreseen at the time of event (A) that event (B) would happen. This approach gives straightforward effect to the words 'the transfer' in regulation 7(1), rather than requiring the substitution of other words such as 'transfer' simpliciter, or 'a transfer', or 'any transfer'. It puts the weight of the analysis instead on the breadth of the words 'connected with'. Subject to that possible difference in analysis, however, the approach is the same as that in *Harrison Bowden* and *Morris* which, as Beatson J said in *CAB Automotive* at paragraph 32, is more consistent than that in *Ibex*'s case with the broad scope of the Directive which TUPE implements.

7.34 As this test can be seen as potentially in effect being applied retrospectively, the *Spaceright* decision demonstrates the scope for transferees to be liable for pre-transfer dismissals and their need to conduct careful and potentially extensive due diligence about what liabilities they might inherit in respect of those dismissed pre-transfer. The connection of the dismissal with the subsequent relevant transfer will of course need to be established.[44] The fact that a dismissal can be transfer-related where the identity of the acquirer is not known nor a specific transfer contemplated when a dismissal is effected unavoidably increases the risk that transferees will be liable for pre-transfer dismissals, particularly those effected by administrators, where it cannot be established that the dismissal truly relates to the conduct of the business rather than the facilitation of its sale.

---

[42] Ibid. at para. 47.
[43] Ibid. at para. 43.
[44] For an example of where such a connection was not established, see the discussion of *KLT Water Engineering Ltd v Irvine and others* UKEATS/0005/09 at para. 7.84 *et seq.*

6. Whose reason for dismissal?

In *Dynamex Friction Ltd and anor v Amicus and others*[45] the Court of Appeal addressed the   **7.35**
question of whether an ET had been justified in concluding that employees had been dismissed for an economic reason rather than for a reason connected with a relevant transfer
in circumstances where it was argued that the dismissals of a number of employees had
been stage managed prior to transfer so that the ultimate transferee could evade employing these employees or being liable for their dismissals. The employees contended that they
were dismissed not because there were no funds available to pay them but by reason of the
transfer. Even if there had been no collusion with a director of the original business and its
purchaser of the business with whom he was associated, it was contended that the administrator had been the 'unwitting tool' of that director in dismissing the relevant staff and that
this rendered the dismissals transfer-related. The allegation was that it should have been
inferred from the evidence that the director in question had stage managed the placing of
the employer in administration, knowing that the dismissals were inevitable and that a sale
of a business to the purchaser was likely, harbouring the hope (if not the expectation) that he
would soon take over the purchaser.

In *Dynamex* the transferor employer was declared insolvent on 7 August 2003 and passed   **7.36**
into administration. The administrators dismissed the relevant employees on grounds of
redundancy on the same day. The relevant employees were advised to apply to the Secretary
of State for payment of unpaid wages or redundancy payments out of their national insurance fund. On 12 August 2003 financial information was circulated about the business to
a variety of interested parties. On 15 August 2003 the plant and machinery of the relevant
business was sold to a company owned by a Mr Craig Smith, who had been the sole director
of the original employer prior to its insolvency, and the assets comprising its production line
were bought by a new company set up with Mr Craig Smith's assistance and in which he later
acquired a 60 per cent shareholding. Some sixty of the originally dismissed employees were
taken on and given new contracts of employment and other employees argued that their
dismissals were automatically unfair pursuant to TUPE.

The ET had held that there was a relevant transfer but that the dismissals in question were not   **7.37**
effected by reason of the transfer or for a reason connected with it and consequently were not
automatically unfair. The employees had sought to argue that the administration itself, or at
the very least the timing of the administration and its associated dismissals, were controlled
by the group of companies in which the sole director of the company prior to the transfer was
involved and that there was consequently collusion between him and the transferee. They
argued that the structure of the company, the timing, and order of events were stage managed
in order to bypass the operation of the transfer legislation, albeit that the administrator may
have been an unwitting tool of Mr Smith's machinations.

The argument that TUPE's protection against transfer-related dismissals should engage on   **7.38**
the basis that the dismissals were stage managed failed primarily on the basis that the controlling mind of the employer was found to be the administrator who took the decision
to dismiss based on the cash flow position of the business. In the absence of collusion, the
motivations, whatever they might have been, of a former director of the original employer
who nonetheless was associated with the acquisition of the relevant business was held to be a

---

[45] [2008] IRLR 515, CA.

factor which should not be taken into account. As a matter of fact it was held that there was no collusion between the employer which effected the dismissals and the eventual purchaser which would require a connection to be found between the dismissals and the eventual transfer. Rather, the dismissals were for genuine economic reasons given the fact, as the administrator made clear to the employees at the time of dismissal, the employer had no money to pay out unpaid wages or redundancy payments.

7.39 The ET's decision was upheld by the Court of Appeal. As Ward LJ put it, emphasizing the need to focus on the reason of the relevant decision maker for the decision to dismiss:

> In deciding whether the reason for dismissal was an economic one or a transfer-related one, one has to identify whose thought process is the subject of this analysis. It has to be he who took the decision. It has to be [the administrator's] decision that comes under the microscope. The Employment Tribunal found as a fact that he decided that he had no option but to dismiss the employees because he had no money with which to pay them. That is an economic reason. True it was that at the time when that decision was taken there was a need to sell the business and there was the possibility that a sale could be achieved. But no purchaser had been identified. No purchaser was identified until a week later. There is nothing to suggest that the administrator took the view that he had to dismiss the staff in order to have a better prospect of selling the business. There is no suggestion . . . of the dismissal of the existing workforce being engineered specifically with a view to avoiding liabilities to the employees. There is no suggestion of a calculated disregard for the obligations imposed by the regulations. This is not a device, transparent or otherwise, on [the administrator's] part to escape the legitimate claims of the workforce. He was not acting at the behest of or in collusion with either Craig Smith or Dynamex. As the Tribunal found, the administrator dismissed the employees in spite of any transfer not with a view to effecting it. That finding destroys any argument that the transfer had anything to do with the dismissals.[46]

7.40 Even though there was a suggestion that a third party had a hand in the decision to dismiss, this was of no moment—again, as Ward LJ explained:

> the critical question is whose decision was it? Once the answer is that it was the administrator's decision, then nothing done by Craig Smith before that decision was taken nor after it could have any bearing on the reasons why [the administrator] acted as he did. The facts may give rise to the inevitable conclusion that Craig Smith cynically manipulated the insolvency of Friction, saw the opportunity of the August holidays as the best time to place the company in administration and did so not simply with a hope but with every expectation that by reason of Realty's [the transferee's] close association with Dynamex, Dynamex itself would soon fall into his palm. That is what happened. It is not an attractive story. It brings no credit to Craig Smith. But Craig Smith did not decide to dismiss the employees even though he knew that would happen and wanted it to happen. [The administrator] dismissed them. He did so for economic reasons.[47]

7.41 Whilst *Dynamex* makes clear that the motives of those who actually take the decision to dismiss will be crucial to establishing the reason for a particular dismissal and whether it was connected with a relevant transfer, Lawrence Collins LJ took the view, albeit dissenting, that the argument to the effect that the national court should not look solely at the motive of the legal entity which in law effected dismissal and therefore can look at the wider factual matrix was respectable. In his view:

> It seems to me that the approach to the Directive taken in the rulings of the European Court and the opinions of the Advocates General do not shut out the argument which the respondents

---

[46] Ibid. at para. 59.
[47] Ibid. at para. 61.

make in this case, namely that the national court should not look solely at the motives of the legal entity which in law effects the dismissal. I do not say that they are bound to win if they can show stage-management by Mr Smith. What I do say is that this is not a proper case for their claim to be, in effect, struck out on a point which has not been raised below and which has not been the subject of adequate findings of fact. It is a point which is of sufficient general importance to justify the further findings of fact which the EAT thought necessary, perhaps followed, at the appropriate stage, by a reference to the European Court.[48]

The true basis for the decision to dismiss the relevant employees will therefore be the cen- **7.42** tral factual issue where the employees seek to argue that their dismissal is transfer related. In *Honeycombe 78 Ltd v Cummins and anor*[49] the ET was found[50] to have erred in not concluding:

> ...that the principal reason for dismissal was economic, not one connected with the transfer. On the facts of that case, the administrator concluded on the day after his appointment that he would have to dismiss the staff *because* there were no assets to pay them at that stage and that is what he did. Although the possibility of the sale of the business to a Mr and Mrs Goodman existed, he reached his decision to dismiss the workforce *irrespective* of their offer to provide funding and their outline proposals to purchase the business.

C. Economic, Technical, or Organisational Reasons Entailing Changes in the Workforce

1. Regulations 7(2) and 7(3)

The automatic unfairness which flows from a dismissal being by reason of a relevant transfer **7.43** or for a reason connected with it is avoided regulation 7(2):

> where the sole or principal reason for the dismissal is a reason connected with the transfer that is an economic, technical or organisational reason entailing changes in the workforce of either the transferor or the transferee before or after a relevant transfer.

Regulation 7(3) then establishes the effect of an ETOR (i.e. the avoidance of automatic **7.44** unfairness of the dismissal and the application of the normal test of unfair dismissal) by virtue of a potentially fair reason for dismissal being deemed to have been established. Regulation 7(3) provides that:

> Where paragraph [7](2) applies:
> (a) paragraph [7](1) shall not apply;
> (b) without prejudice to the application of section 98(4) of the 1996 [Employment Rights] Act (test of fair dismissal), the dismissal shall, for the purposes of sections 98(1) and 135 of that Act (reason for dismissal), be regarded as having been for redundancy where section 98(2)(c) of that Act applies, or otherwise for a substantial reason of a kind such as to justify the dismissal of an employee holding the position which that employee held.

2. Statutory redundancy payments

Regulation 7(3)(b) confirms that a transfer-related dismissal which is for an ETOR can **7.45** also, for statutory purposes, be by reason of redundancy, thereby entitling the dismissed

---

[48] Ibid. at para. 68.
[49] UKEAT/100/99.
[50] To adopt the summary of the case in the judgment of Ward LJ in *Dynamex Friction and anor v Amicus and others*, above n. 45, at para. 51.

employee (if otherwise eligible) to a statutory redundancy payment. The predecessor provision in TUPE 1981, regulation 8(2)(b), deemed a transfer-related dismissal which was by reason of an ETOR to be for 'a substantial reason of a kind such as to justify the dismissal of an employee holding the position which that employee held' as distinct from being by reason of redundancy.[51] This potentially led to a paradoxical position. The employer could avoid automatic unfairness of a transfer-related dismissal if it could demonstrate that the dismissal was by reason of redundancy (clearly an economic reason satisfying the concept of an ETOR). However, that employee would not be entitled to a statutory redundancy payment because the reason for the dismissal was deemed by TUPE 1981 to be for 'some other substantial reason' rather than redundancy. Since dismissal by reason of redundancy is a pre-requisite of entitlement to the statutory redundancy payment, the drafting of TUPE 1981 potentially denied dismissed employees' payments which would have been expected to be due given the nature of the reason for dismissal. The inclusion in the 2006 Regulations of the wording in regulation 7(3)(b), which effectively confirms that a transfer-related dismissal by reason of an ETOR can also be by reason of redundancy where applicable, was seen as correcting a 'longstanding error'.[52] Where the relevant statutory test is satisfied, an employee who is dismissed by reason of an ETOR which constitutes a dismissal by reason of redundancy can claim the statutory redundancy payment. As the dismissal by reason of an ETOR is then to be assessed for its fairness on the usual principles of ERA 1996, s. 98(4) this does not prevent the employee seeking to establish unfair dismissal by reason, for example, of unfair selection for redundancy.

3. What can be an ETOR?

7.46 The concept of an ETOR is not defined in detail in TUPE. As the 2006 Guidance put it:[53]

> there is no statutory definition of [the] term, but it is likely to include:
> (a) a reason relating to the profitability or market performance of the transferee's business (ie an economic reason);
> (b) a reason relating to the nature of the equipment or production processes which the transferee operates (ie a technical reason); or
> (c) a reason relating to the management or organisational structure of the transferee's business (ie an organisational reason).

7.47 An ETOR needs to relate to the conduct of the business. In *Whitehouse v Charles A Blatchford & Sons Ltd* Beldam LJ observed as follows:

> It seems to me that the words 'economic technical or organisational reason entailing changes in the workforce', clearly support the conclusion that the reason must be connected with the future conduct of the business as a going concern.[54]

7.48 The concept of an economic reason for dismissal can relate only to the conduct of the relevant business rather than wider issues such as a wish of the transferee to sell the business

---

[51] In *McGrath v Rank Leisure Ltd* [1985] IRLR 323, EAT the EAT had held that under TUPE 1981 a dismissal which was found to be by reason of an ETOR was automatically to be treated as for 'some other substantial reason' for the purposes of what is now ERA 1996, s. 98(2)(b).

[52] 2005 Consultation para. 52 referring to *Canning v (1) Niaz (2) McLaughlin* [1983] IRLR 431, EAT.

[53] At p. 17.

[54] [2000] ICR 542, EAT at 548F.

(which otherwise could be used to legitimate dismissals simply to facilitate a sale). As the EAT put it in *Wheeler v Patel & anor*:[55]

> The economic reasons apt to bring a case within paragraph (2) must, in our view, be reasons which relate to the conduct of the business. If the economic reason were no more than a desire to obtain an enhanced price, or no more than a desire to achieve a sale, it would not be a reason which relates to the conduct of the business. It would not in our judgment, be an 'economic' reason for the purposes of para (2). We think that an ejusdem generis approach to construction justifies giving a limited meaning to the adjective 'economic' in para (2). We think the need to leave a sensible scope para (4) similarly requires a limited meaning to be given to the adjective 'economic' in para (2).[56]

Likewise, as Mummery LJ put it in *Spaceright Europe v Baillavoine*:[57]   **7.49**

> [f]or an ETO reason to be available there must be an intention to change the workforce and to continue to conduct the business, as distinct from the purpose of selling it. It is not available in the case of dismissing an employee to enable the administrators to make the business of the company a more attractive proposition to prospective transferees of a going concern.

A technical reason might arise from changes in processes, technologies, and the like. In terms   **7.50**
of what can constitute an organisational reason entailing changes in the workforce, *Porter and Nanayakkara v Queens Medical Centre*[58] indicates that changes to job functions can fall within the concept of an ETOR. In this particular case, an entirely new organization was introduced with regard to the provision of paediatric services.

It is not, however, sufficient to show an economic, technical, or organisational reason for   **7.51**
the dismissal in order to avoid a transfer-related dismissal being automatically unfair. That economic, technical, or organisational reason must also entail a change in the workforce. As *Berriman v Delabole State Ltd*[59] demonstrated, where there is no change in the workforce but simply changes to terms and conditions of employment, then an ETOR is not established. In this particular case, a (constructive) dismissal relating to changes to rates of remuneration was not associated with any change to the workforce as the same number of employees remained employed. There was therefore no change to the workforce as required for there to be an ETOR for the purposes of TUPE and, accordingly, since the constructive dismissal was transfer-related, it was automatically unfair.

As the Court of Appeal put it: **7.52**

> [t]he phrase 'economic, technical or organisational reason entailing changes in the workforce' in our judgment requires that the change in the workforce is part of the economic, technical or organisational reason. The employers' plan must be to achieve changes in the workforce. It must be an objective of the plan, not just a possible consequence of it.

> Secondly, we do not think that the dismissal of one employee followed by the engagement of another in his place constitutes a change in the 'workforce'. To our minds, the word 'workforce' connotes the whole body of employees as an entity: it corresponds to the 'strength' or the 'establishment'. Changes in the identities of the individuals who make up the workforce

---

[55] [1987] IRLR 211, EAT.
[56] Ibid. at para. 21 per Scott J.
[57] [2012] IRLR 111, CA at para. 47.
[58] [1993] IRLR 486, QBD.
[59] [1985] IRLR 305, CA.

do not constitute changes in the workforce itself so long as the overall numbers and functions of the employees looked at as a whole remain unchanged.[60]

7.53 For the ETOR 'defence' to the otherwise automatic unfairness of a transfer-related dismissal to be available, there must be a change in the numbers of the workforce or a change in their job functions as a result of the economic, technical, or organisational reason for the dismissal. An example of where a change in job functions was, even in the absence of a change in workforce numbers, found to constitute an ETOR is *Crawford v Swinton Insurance Brokers Ltd*.[61] In connection with a relevant transfer, the role of the employee in question was changed from being that of a secretary to being an insurance saleswoman. In relation to her constructive and unfair dismissal claims, the EAT acknowledged that a change in job function could satisfy the concept of an ETOR without there being a change in the identity or numbers of the workforce.

7.54 As the EAT put it:

> What, in our judgment, has to be looked at, is the workforce as an entity, as a whole, separate from the individuals who make it up and it then has to be seen whether the reason in question is one which involves a change in that workforce, strength or establishment and we are satisfied that there can well be a change in a workforce if the same people are kept on but they are given entirely different jobs to do. We would regard a workforce that was engaged in a different occupation as being, for the purposes of regulation 8(2), changed if that happened as a result of an organisational change on a relevant transfer.[62]

7.55 The interpretation of what is now regulation 7(2) adopted in *Berriman* has been viewed by some commentators as an unnecessary and inappropriate gloss on the provisions of the Directive which in its equivalent provisions in Article 4.1 does not provide that an economic, technical or organisational reason entailing changes in the workforce can only be satisfied by changes to the number or roles of the workforce. Nonetheless, that *Berriman* is correct was reiterated by the EAT in *London Metropolitan University v Sackur and others*[63] in which *Crawford* was seen as attenuating the *Berriman* principle—the combined effect of *Berriman* and *Crawford* is that, for an employer to be able to establish an ETOR on which it can rely, it must establish that there are changes in the workforce either by way of reductions to staff numbers or changes to job functions. The EAT in *Sackur* saw no basis upon which *Berriman* or *Crawford* could be viewed as incorrect. Consistent with this, in *Nationwide Building Society v Benn and others*,[64] it was conceded, 'rightly' as the EAT put it,[65] that 'a desire of a transferee to harmonise roles of transferred employees is a potential organisational reason for dismissal within the meaning of reg. 7(2). Changes in roles amount to a change in function and that is a change in the workforce.'[66]

7.56 *Whitehouse v Chas A Blatchford and Sons Ltd*[67] provides an illustration of the need to establish the connection of the reason for dismissal with the running of the relevant operation for the ETOR 'defence' successfully to be relied upon and the fact that narrow distinctions may

---

[60] Ibid. at paras 15 and 16.
[61] [1990] IRLR 42, EAT.
[62] Ibid. at para. 92.
[63] UKEAT/0286/06.
[64] [2010] IRLR 922, EAT.
[65] Ibid. at para. 52.
[66] Ibid.
[67] [1999] IRLR 492, CA.

need to be drawn between dismissals by reason of a transfer and those for an ETOR. The transferee of a contract to supply prosthetic appliances to a hospital body had been informed during a retendering process (in which it was successful) that the award of the contract was conditional upon staffing costs being lowered by the number of technicians being reduced by one. The employee selected for redundancy complained that his dismissal was automatically unfair but the ET held that the dismissal was for an ETOR on the basis that a redundancy was inevitable.

The Court of Appeal upheld the ET's decision. The argument was rejected that there was **7.57** no difference between a dismissal designed to facilitate the sale of a business and a dismissal which was necessary to secure a contract. That the transferor and transferee agreed that dismissals would take place was not decisive—the question was whether the decision to terminate was to facilitate the transfer or was for an ETOR. The reason for the employee's dismissal was the fact that the transferee would operate the undertaking with one fewer employee—the transfer was merely the occasion for the dismissal rather than the reason for it. The requirement for fewer technicians was directly connected with the provision of the relevant services and therefore could constitute an ETOR.

It has been argued—and some ET decisions[68] have proceeded on the basis—that the **7.58** *Berriman* principle means that an ETOR is not established where there is a relocation of the undertaking or activities which are the subject of the relevant transfer but no change in staff numbers or functions.

The Manchester College v Hazel and anor[69] demonstrates the need carefully to analyse the **7.59** reason for and timing of the employer's actions when considering whether the employer can argue successfully that there is an ETOR for a dismissal enabling it to evade automatic unfairness under regulation 7(1). Some six months after a relevant transfer, the respondent sought voluntary redundancies and pay cuts from amongst its workforce. The claimants, who had been informed that their jobs were not at risk, were dismissed and following their refusal to sign new contracts but were re-engaged on new terms. The EAT held that the ET was entitled to find that the dismissals were effected to achieve harmonization, since the time for reducing staff numbers had passed by the time they were implemented. Consequently, whilst the dismissals were transfer connected and for an economic, technical or organisational reason, there was no ETOR for the purposes of TUPE since the change, at the stage when it was implemented, did not entail any change to the workforce in terms of its numbers.

4. The workforce

In *Meter U Ltd v Ackroyd and others*[70] the issue arose of whether a transferee could utilize the **7.60** ETOR defence provided by regulation 7(2) to avoid dismissals being automatically unfair under TUPE in circumstances where it replaced directly employed staff with corporate franchisees. The ET had held that for the transferee to dismiss the meter readers who had been employed by the transferor because its business model in relation to the relevant meter reading functions entailed the use of franchisees rather than employees for reasons of competitiveness was not by reason of an ETOR.

---

[68] *Royden and others v Barnetts Solicitors*, ET case number 2103451/07; *Tapere v South London and Maudsley NHS Trust*, ET case number 2329562/07.
[69] UKEAT/0642/11.
[70] [2012] IRLR 367, EAT.

7.61 The EAT disagreed although certain of these claims were nonetheless remitted to the ET for consideration of the issue of whether the transferee's franchise business model was a sham and, if not, whether the dismissals were fair or unfair. The concept of workforce deployed in regulation 7(2) was held (provided that the new arrangements were not a sham) not to include corporate franchisees. Hence to remove employees and replace them with franchisees did constitute a change to the workforce rather than a change within (but not to) that workforce. The change to the model of utilizing corporate franchisees to perform the relevant activities therefore entailed a reduction in the workforce.[71] As Slade J put it:

> [a]pplying an ordinary common sense use of the word 'workforce' it does not include limited companies. These have an identity separate from their directors or controlling shareholders. They are not people, workers or employees although they will engage them. Employees of corporate franchisees are part of their employer's workforce.[72]

7.62 *Spaceright Europe Ltd v Baillavoine*[73] addressed, amongst other things, an argument about the transferee's workforce changes to which are required as a consequence of the employer's economic, technical, or organisational reason in order to establish an ETOR. The chief executive of the transferor employer was dismissed by its administrators on the day on which it went into administration. Just over a month later, the business was sold by way of a relevant transfer. The ET held the dismissal to be unfair. First, the sole or principal reason for dismissal was connected with the transfer because the employee was dismissed to enable a purchaser to require the business without the burden of its chief executive. Second, even if there had been an economic or organisational reason for the employee's dismissal, the employer, as a holding company, had no workforce and therefore the dismissal could not be an ETOR—as there was no workforce there could not be changes to it as required for there to be an ETOR. The EAT upheld an appeal. There was no inherent reason why an employer should not be considered to have a workforce constituted by just one person.

7.63 In *Nationwide Building Society v Benn & others*[74] the question arose as to whether an ETOR can be established in relation to only part of the workforce. Unfair dismissal claims were brought by employees following the transfer of the undertaking in which they were employed from the Portman Building Society to the Nationwide Building Society. The employees contended that the terms of their employment were altered to their detriment by the new employer. Job roles and responsibilities were downgraded as they were assimilated into their new roles. The new bonus scheme in which the employees in question participated post-transfer was substantially less beneficial than their previous scheme. The employees argued that the new employer had committed fundamental breaches of the employees' contracts of employment entitling them to resign.

7.64 The ET's decision that the employees had been dismissed constructively or by virtue of regulation 4(9) was upheld by the EAT as was the finding that the dismissals were for an organisational reason entailing changes in the workforce for the purposes of regulation 7(2), by virtue of the integration process which the transferee conducted. This was the case even though the changes affected only a section of the workforce, i.e. the transferred employees. The changes

---

[71] The EAT also held that the dismissal of the employees was for reason of redundancy—see ibid. paras 51 and 52.

[72] Ibid. at para. 38. Regrettably, it was not necessary for the EAT to decide whether a change in status, for example from employee to independent contractor, is a change in the workforce within the meaning of reg. 7—see para. 40.

[73] [2012] IRLR 111, CA.

[74] UKEAT/0273/09.

in question did not have to affect the whole of the workforce in order to fall within the scope of an ETOR for the purposes of regulation 7(2). As the EAT put it:

[r]egulation 7(2) does not state that the organisational reason must entail changes in the entirety of the workforce. In this case the organisational change affected a body of transferring employees. In our judgment the ET did not err in concluding that organisational reasons entailed changes in the workforce. It did not err in concluding that the dismissals of the Claimants were for an ETO reason.[75]

5. Whose ETOR?

BSG Property Services v Tuck[76] held that the relevant reason for dismissal to be assessed for its **7.65** potential unfairness (whether automatic or otherwise) is that of the employer who dismisses the employee or employees in question. The transferee inherited employees at the point of transfer who were serving out notice of termination of employment which had prior to transfer been served by the transferor on the erroneous assumption that TUPE did not apply in the particular circumstances and therefore the employees were redundant. The transferee was bound by the reason the transferor had for making redundancies. As Mummery J put it:

The fallacy in the decision of the Industrial Tribunal and in the arguments of BSG is that BSG itself did not actually dismiss the applicants for any reason of its own, let alone for an economic or organisational reason. It had no reason in mind. It did not believe it was the employer.[77]

Regulation 7(2), if satisfied in relation to a pre-transfer dismissal, causes liability for the dismissal **7.66** to remain with the transferor, even if in general terms the dismissal is unfair. Consequently, whether a transferor can rely on the transferee's ETOR can have important practical and commercial implications. That the transferor cannot rely on the transferee's reduced need for staff in order to establish an ETOR for the purposes of regulation 7(2), and thereby avoid a dismissal prior to the transfer being unfair pursuant to regulation 7(1), was confirmed by the Inner House of the Court of Session in *Hynd v Armstrong*.[78] As Lord Reed put it, the right to terminate for an ETOR arises 'where the employer dismisses the employee for a reason of its own, relating to its own conduct of the business and entailing a change in its own workforce . . . and not where the employer dismisses the employee for reasons unrelated to the conduct of its own business'.[79]

In this case, a solicitor was made redundant by the firm by which he was employed on the **7.67** day of its dissolution, being the day before its business recommenced in the form of a different partnership. The ET found that this dismissal was for an ETOR and was fair, being a straightforward redundancy. The Inner House of the Court of Session construed what is now regulation 7(2), and was then TUPE 1981, regulation 8(2), as referring to the reason of the employer effecting dismissal when providing that a dismissal by reason of an ETOR is not automatically unfair. As Lord Reed put it:

for regulation 8(2) to apply where an employee is dismissed by the transferor, the transferor's reason for dismissal must relate to the transferor's future conduct of the business: a

---

[75] Ibid. at para. 72. In *Miles v Insitu Cleaning Limited* UKEAT/0157/12, the EAT confirmed that it was an error of law for an ET to fail to consider whether the ETOR relied upon by the employer applied to the employee in question and whether the change was more than minimal, both of which questions would need to be answered in the affirmative for the ETOR 'defence' to be available.

[76] [1996] IRLR 134, EAT.

[77] Ibid. at para. 31(6).

[78] [2007] IRLR 338, CSIH.

[79] Ibid. at para. 44.

condition which cannot be met where the transferor has no intention of continuing the business.[80]

7.68 The Inner House of the Court of Session took the view that to construe what is now regulation 7(2) 'to entitle an employer to dismiss his employees prior to a transfer of the undertaking, on the ground of redundancy, where the employees are surplus to the requirements of the transferee ... would not ... be consistent with the intention of the Directive'.[81] Moreover, to allow otherwise would allow employees lawfully to be dismissed pre-transfer without the employer being required to consider the wider pool of employees to which those employees would transfer, for the purposes, for example, of redundancy selection. This would not be consistent with the objective of the Directive of protecting the employees and ensuring that they are not placed in a less favourable position solely as a result of the transfer. In addition, if dismissal were permitted prior to transfer in such circumstances, employees' ability to recover their entitlements on dismissal would be prejudiced in an insolvency situation because the commercial incentive would be for the insolvent company, from whom dismissal entitlements would be less easily recoverable, to effect dismissal.[82]

7.69 The employee could potentially have been dismissed fairly after the transfer by the transferee whose conduct at that point of the business in question would entail the need for fewer employees. Post-transfer, the employee could have been made redundant by the employer to whose requirements he was surplus. As Lord Reed commented:

> [a]n unfair dismissal could readily have been avoided, on that hypothesis, if the dismissal had been effected at a time when the appellant was actually redundant, by the employer to whose requirements the employee was actually surplus, rather than being effected in advance of that date, by a different employer, in anticipation of those circumstances.[83]

7.70 This argument might operate to limit the compensation recoverable by a dismissed employee but does not avoid the unfairness of a pre-transfer dismissal which is effected by the transferor but the reason for which is the transferee's ETOR.

7.71 The principle that the transferor cannot rely on the transferee's reason for dismissal in order to establish an ETOR for the purposes of regulation 7(2) is an especially acute problem if the parties' commercial objectives would have been for any necessary redundancies to be effected at or by the point of transfer. For dismissal by the transferor prior to transfer on the basis of the transferee's redundancy reason to lead to automatically unfair dismissal for which the transferee will be liable constrains the parties' ability to effect redundancies based on the transferee's future requirements in the period leading up to the transfer itself. In practice, a pragmatic solution may be for the transferor and the transferee to conduct effectively joint collective consultation in advance of the transfer in question so that the requisite redundancy consultation (including collective consultation, if required, pursuant to TULRCA 1992, s. 188) can be completed prior to the transferee dismissing on or shortly after the date of transfer. This approach enables the transferee to terminate at an early stage without falling foul of the inability of the transferor to rely on the transferee's ETOR. Any argument that the transferee, as the dismissing employer, has not complied with its obligations under TULRCA 1992, s. 188 would be met by the contention (albeit untested) that

---

80 Ibid. at para. 43.
81 Ibid. at para. 31.
82 Ibid. at para. 32.
83 Ibid. at para. 45.

the consultation conducted by the transferor as the pre-transfer employer is deemed to have been conducted by the transferee by virtue of regulation 4(2)(b) which provides in effect that any act of the transferor in respect of the relevant employees is deemed by virtue of TUPE to be an act of the transferee.

D. Liability and Fairness

1. General

Save where a transferor terminates the employment of an employee who would otherwise **7.72** transfer to the transferee on a relevant transfer by reason of an ETOR, or for a reason unconnected with the transfer, liability for pre-transfer obligations is transferred entirely to the transferee as is permitted by the Directive. That said, Article 3(1) does permit Member States to provide in their national legislation that both transferor and transferee should be jointly liable for pre-transfer liabilities, an option which TUPE does not take up. The current position is certainly the most straightforward and in theory ensures, especially where a transferor is insolvent or has no material assets, that employees have an effective remedy against the transferee. However, a transferee may consider that it is unjust for it to be responsible for liabilities which it did not actually create. On this basis it can be argued that it would be appropriate for the legislation to allow ETs to apportion awards as between transferors and transferees in their discretion having regard to their relative culpability or responsibility for the relevant breach of the transfer legislation.

In respect of dismissals effected by the transferor prior to a relevant transfer, the transferee **7.73** only becomes liable for unfair dismissal liabilities pursuant to TUPE where the dismissal is automatically unfair pursuant to regulation 7(1) and is not by reason of an ETOR for the purposes of regulation 7(2). *Thompson v SCS Consulting Ltd*[84] demonstrates this point. Mr Thompson was dismissed some eleven hours before a transfer agreed by receivers. His dismissal, at the behest of the transferee, was held to be for an ETOR on the basis that the dismissal was decided upon as part of a reduction to the size of the workforce of an overstaffed, inefficient, and insolvent business. This was held not to be a case of collusion between transferor and transferee to effect dismissal in order to secure a sale or enhance the sale price. Accordingly, even though it was transfer-related, the dismissal was not automatically unfair—because it was by reason of an ETOR—and liability for the dismissal, even if unfair on normal principles, remained with the transferor.

2. Lack of sufficient service to claim unfair dismissal

Even if a dismissal is transfer-related, the requisite continuity of service is still required for an **7.74** employee to be able to claim unfair dismissal pursuant to regulation 7.[85] An employee who does not have the requisite period of qualifying service[86] cannot claim unfair dismissal unless dismissal is for one of the specific reasons in respect of which a qualifying period of service is not required. Where such a claim of unfair dismissal is available, the transferee may still be liable even where the dismissal is effected by the transferor before the transfer.

---

[84] [2001] IRLR 801, EAT.
[85] *Milligan v Securicor* [1995] IRLR 288, EAT.
[86] See above, n. 7.

3. Assertion of a statutory right

7.75 ERA 1996, s. 104 provides that the rights conferred by TUPE are rights dismissal by reason of the assertion of which can lead to an unfair dismissal claim without the need for any period of qualifying service. ERA 1996, s.104 deems an employee's dismissal unfair without the need for completion of a period of qualifying service where the reason or, if more than one, the principal reason for dismissal is, inter alia, that the employee brought proceedings against the employer in respect of one of the statutory rights to which the section applies—the right not to be unfairly dismissed being such a right.

7.76 *Perry's Motor Sales Ltd & anor v Lindley*[87] concerned a situation where an individual had not completed the then requisite one year's qualifying service needed to be eligible to claim unfair dismissal, whether such a claim was made generally or by reference to regulation 7(1). However, the claim was of dismissal by reason of an assertion of a statutory right pursuant to ERA 1996, s. 104. The EAT held that where, in connection with a transfer, the transferee had directed the transferor to dismiss the employee because the employee had brought previous ET proceedings against the transferee, the employee had a claim against the transferee for automatic unfair dismissal under ERA 1996, s. 104. In this case, the employee had previously been employed by the transferee but resigned claiming constructive dismissal and subsequently agreed to a settlement of the resulting ET proceedings. She subsequently became employed by the transferor, the parent company of which was acquired by the first appellant. The transferor was instructed by the transferee to dismiss the employee and this was done a month or so before a transfer of an undertaking from the transferor to the transferee falling within the scope of regulation 3(1)(a).

7.77 The ET considered that regulation 4(2)(b) deemed any act by the transferor prior to the transfer in respect to the employee's contract of employment with the transferor to have been done by the transferee. Consequently, the actual dismissal of the employee by the transferor was deemed to have been an act of the transferee. The EAT agreed with this analysis—regulation 4(2)(b) operated to deem the transferee as having dismissed the employee. Regulation 4(2)(a) did not affect that analysis, being an entirely separate provision which transfers all the rights, duties, and powers of the transferor to the transferee in respect of a contract of employment that does transfer.

7.78 The transferee, deemed as it was by regulation 4(2)(b) to have been the dismissing employer, was found to have dismissed the employee by reason of the employee's earlier attempt to enforce relevant statutory rights against it and therefore the employee was unfairly dismissed for the purposes of ERA 1996, s. 104. This conclusion was, in the EAT's view, consistent not only with the literal interpretation of the legislation but also its purpose of the safeguarding of employees' rights on a relevant transfer. This result was not considered to be, as had been argued before the EAT, an illegitimate and artificial extension of the ambit of TUPE.

4. Redundancy pooling and TUPE

7.79 *Barnes and others v Brush Transformers Ltd and anor*[88] concerned a redundancy exercise conducted in relation to the transfer of the fabrication work of one sister company, Brush

---

[87] UKEAT/0616/07.
[88] UKEAT/256/99.

Transformers, to another sister company, Brush Electrical. Of the staff employed by Brush Transformers, nine were redeployed within its remaining business, nineteen were found employment with Brush Electrical, and twenty-six were dismissed by reason of redundancy. The ET found that there was a relevant transfer, that the dismissals were connected with that transfer, but that the dismissals were not automatically unfair, an ETOR for the purposes of regulation 8(2) being made out. In terms of the fairness of the dismissal for the purposes of ERA 1996, s. 98(4) the ET held that it was not unfair to treat the Brush Transformer's employees as the pool for redundancy selection.

7.80 On appeal, the employees argued that this approach was inappropriate as it was contended to result in the employees of Brush Transformers being denied the protection of TUPE—the employer then might be permitted to 'discriminate' between 'old' and 'new' employees of Brush Electrical whereas it should have operated a combined redundancy selection pool across both businesses. The EAT rejected an appeal, highlighting the general difficulty as a matter of principle in challenging an employer's determination of the selection pool where the employer has genuinely applied its mind to the problem.

7.81 In reaching this decision, the EAT maintained the orthodox position with regard to redundancy pooling and, consistent with the principle that a dismissal connected with a transfer but saved from automatic unfairness by an ETOR is assessed for its fairness on the usual principles established pursuant to ERA 1996, s. 98(4), did not create a TUPE-specific rule for redundancy exercises conducted in conjunction with a relevant transfer. Nor indeed did it make any difference to the result that the employer had erroneously believed that TUPE did not apply to the particular situation. As HHJ Peter Clark put it:

> 21. Applying the general approach to selection of the pool it is well established that it will be difficult for an employee to challenge the pool for selection where the employer has genuinely applied his mind to the problem. [Counsel] submits that these employers did not, since they believed that there was here no relevant transfer. As to that, the evidence before the Employment Tribunal indicated that whereas the Respondents believed that no transfer would arise they were uncertain of the position and sought to establish a procedure which would be fair if they were wrong in their assumption. Certainly there was no finding by the Employment Tribunal that had the Respondents firmly believed that a relevant transfer would occur, they would have dealt with the matter any differently.
>
> 22. . . . We find ourselves in a similar position of that of Lord McDonald's Employment Appeal Tribunal sitting in *Green -v- Fraser* [1985] IRLR 55, to which Mr Linden has referred us. This is a case in which two reasonable employers might follow a different course of action. One would opt for a combined pool; the other would not.

7.82 The EAT also addressed the issue of redundancy selection in the context of a transfer-related redundancy exercise in *First Scottish Searching Services Ltd v McDine & anor*.[89] The ET found that the employees' dismissals following a relevant transfer were unfair. In its view, whilst the selection pools were ones which it was open to a reasonable employer to select, there was a risk of unfairness in the absence of 'some system of moderation' moderating two separate sets of scores for two separate groups of employees—the transferees' existing workforce and the employees who transferred to it from two transferors. An appeal to the EAT was successful on the basis that the ET did not explain what it meant by moderation, did not make any findings as to the risk of unfairness which it identified having given rise to any

---

[89] UKEATS/0051/10.

inconsistency or how a system of moderation would have altered the results of the process. The ET had 'fallen into the trap of engaging in microscopic "over-minute" examination of the type warned against by Waite LJ in *British Aerospace plc* and Lord Johnston in *John Brown Engineering*'.[90] The ET effectively held that the process was fatally flawed but did not identify adequately or assess the extent of the risk of unfairness caused by the lack of moderation. The EAT considered that in doing so the ET had impermissibly substituted its own view for that of the employer. Care nonetheless needs to be taken in ensuring that the relevance in application of redundancy selection criteria applied across groups of employees comprising the transferee's pre-existing employees and those who have transferred into its employment on a relevant transfer can be justified.

5. Enforcement issues

7.83   On occasion employees who succeed in a claim of unfair dismissal will find that the employer against whom the claim was brought has been party to a subsequent relevant transfer such that it no longer has assets sufficient to meet the successful employee's award of compensation. The actual or contingent claims of an ex-employee dismissed for reasons unconnected with a subsequent relevant transfer do not transfer to the transferee on that relevant transfer by virtue of TUPE.[91] TUPE does not provide a remedy where a transfer of a business occurs or is engineered after a dismissal which is not connected with that subsequent transfer—the relevant award of compensation is only enforceable against the (now potentially insolvent) entity which has disposed of its business.

7.84   This point is demonstrated by *KLT Water Engineering Ltd v Irvine and others*[92] where the claimants, who resigned alleging constructive and unfair dismissal, were unable to bring their claims against a company to which their employer's business was transferred some ten months later by virtue of a relevant transfer. If the contracts of employment of the relevant employees and/or the associated liabilities do not transfer to the transferee under regulation 4, and no claim can be made under regulation 7 against the transferee based on the pre-transfer dismissal being related to the transfer to the eventual transferee of the relevant undertaking or activities, then TUPE provides no further protection. In *KLT Water Engineering Ltd* no relevant transfer was in contemplation at the time of the employees' alleged constructive dismissals. In contrast to *Spaceright*,[93] and despite alleging collusion designed to engineer the removal to the transferee of the assets against which they could enforce their unfair dismissal claims absent a relevant transfer, the employees could not establish the connection with the relevant transfer which by virtue of regulation 7 would enable them potentially to claim unfair dismissal against the transferee of the business in which they had worked. Subsequent chicanery with regard to the ownership of the business cannot 'revive' the dismissed employees' terminated contracts so as to render their earlier dismissals connected to the subsequent transfer.

---

[90]   Ibid. at para. 45, referring to *British Aerospace v Green* [1995] IRLR 433, CA and *John Brown Engineering Ltd v Brown & others* [1997] IRLR 90, EAT.

[91]   *Tsangacos v Amalgamated Chemicals* [1997] IRLR 4, EAT. This assumes that the subsequent transfer is not part of a series of transactions—see regulation 3(6)(a) and Chapter 2, para. 2.127 *et seq*.

[92]   UKEATS/0005/09.

[93]   Above, n. 41.

As Lady Smith put it,[94] the proper approach to the interpretation of TUPE in this context **7.85** is as follows:

> employers cannot effectively dismiss employees (or cause their resignation) because of the anticipation of a transfer or the fact of a transfer. That is not the same as saying that if employers decide to transfer their business because employees have, at some earlier stage, been dismissed and/or resigned the effect is to revive contracts of employment which were previously brought to an end at a stage when there was no question of any transfer being in contemplation. That is not the purpose of TUPE and there is no indication either in the Regulations or in any of the authorities referred to that it is so. We agree…that the implications of such an approach would be wide reaching and could cause real difficulties for those entering into legitimate transactions for business transfers. The employee protection would be quite different from that which underlies TUPE.

6. Summary

By way of conclusion to this Chapter, the scheme of TUPE with regard to transfer-related **7.86** dismissals can be summarized as follows:

- Regulation 4 is the operative provision which transfers to the transferee the employment contracts (and associated liabilities) of employees falling within the scope of TUPE by virtue of being assigned other than on a temporary basis to the economic entity or activities which are the subject of the relevant transfer in question.
- Regulation 4(3) extends regulation 4 not just to those employed as at the point of transfer but also those who would have been so employed had they 'not been unfairly dismissed in the circumstances described in regulation 7(1)'.
- Regulation 4(2)(a) transfers to the transferee all the liabilities of the transferor in respect of the employees covered by regulation 4(3).
- If an employee is dismissed before the transfer and the dismissal is automatically unfair under regulation 7(1)[95] then regulations 4(2)(a) and (b) render the transferee liable for that automatically unfair dismissal.
- If the transferee inherits liability under the combination of regulations 7(1), 4(2), and 4(3), it inherits not only unfair dismissal liability but also potentially other liabilities arising prior to transfer such as for unpaid wages and wrongful dismissal.
- If an employee is dismissed for a transfer-related reason but there is an ETOR for that dismissal satisfying regulation 7(2), then the dismissal is not automatically unfair for the purposes of regulation 7(1).
- Where regulation 7(2) applies to a pre-transfer dismissal by virtue of there being an ETOR, then liability for the dismissal, and any consequent unfairness, rests with the transferor— since regulation 4(2) only transfers to the transferee liabilities relating to dismissals which are automatically unfair for the purposes of regulation 7(1).
- Regulation 7(3)(a) provides that, where there is an ETOR, regulation 7(1) does not apply (so as to render the dismissal automatically unfair). However, pursuant to regulation 7(3)(b), this avoidance of automatic unfair dismissal is without prejudice to the ability of

---

[94] At para. 21.
[95] Because the transfer or a connected reason is the sole or principal reason for the transfer and there is no ETOR.

the employee (assuming that the individual has completed the requisite period of continuous service) to claim unfair dismissal on the basis of ERA 1996, s. 98, with the issue of the fairness of the dismissal being assessed in accordance with the normal principles of ERA 1996, s. 98(4).

• Provided that it can establish there to be an ETOR which avoids a transfer-related dismissal being automatically unfair, an employer will be deemed to have dismissed the employee for the potentially fair reason of either redundancy (if the statutory criteria in that regard are satisfied) or 'some other substantial reason' justifying dismissal.

8

EMPLOYEE LIABILITY INFORMATION

A. **Introduction**	8.01	D. **Delivery and Updating**	8.30
1. The Directive	8.01	E. **Instalments**	8.34
2. TUPE 2006	8.03	F. **Indirect Provision**	8.35
B. **Employees**	8.07	G. **Timing**	8.37
C. **Information**	8.09	H. **Remedy**	8.41
1. Prescribed information	8.09	1. Award	8.41
2. Employment particulars	8.11	2. Principles of award	8.44
3. Disciplinary and grievance		3. Minimum award	8.48
procedures	8.14	4. Mitigation	8.51
4. Claims	8.15	I. **Due Diligence Exercises**	8.52
5. Data protection	8.19	J. **Contracting Out**	8.61
6. Former employees	8.28		

A. Introduction

1. The Directive

Article 3.2 permits Member States, if they wish to do so, to introduce into their domestic legislation implementing the Directive provisions requiring the transferor to notify the transferee of all rights and obligations in relation to the employees whose employment is to transfer to the transferee on a transfer of undertaking insofar as those matters are (or ought to be) known to the transferor at the time of the transfer. This obligation operates independently from the other protections provided by the Directive so failure to comply does not affect the transfer of employees and associated rights otherwise effected by the legislation.

8.01

Specifically, Article 3.2 provides that:

8.02

> Member States may adopt appropriate measures to ensure that the transferor notifies the transferee of all the rights and obligations which will be transferred to the transferee under this Article [3], so far as those rights are or ought to have been known to the transferor at the time of transfer. A failure by the transferor to notify the transferee of any such right or obligation shall not affect the transfer of that right or obligation and the rights of any employees against the transferee and/or transferor in respect of that right or obligation.

2. TUPE 2006

In the 2001 Consultation, the Government confirmed its intention to take advantage of the option provided by Article 3.2. The benefit of an obligation on the transferor to provide what

8.03

TUPE 2006 defines as 'employee liability information'[1] was considered to be that transferees would be entitled to full and accurate information about the liabilities which they would inherit as a result of a TUPE transfer and therefore would be 'well placed to meet them'.[2] This obligation would ensure transparency and avoid what was described as 'sharp practice'[3] such as where, just before transfer, terms and conditions of employment or the composition of the workforce assigned to the particular undertaking or activities are varied to the disadvantage of the transferee. That said, an obligation to provide information does not of itself prevent the mischiefs in question being committed. If complied with, it simply alerts the transferee to any such development. Changes to the employment situation at a late stage simply trigger the obligation to update the original notification of employee liability information.

8.04   The obligation to notify the transferee of employee liability information was also perceived as promoting competitiveness. Smaller businesses with lesser bargaining power were considered to be less able than others to negotiate contractual safeguards with regard to employee information, which disadvantage this new notification obligation would (to an extent) remedy. The obligation to provide employee liability information no doubt makes it more likely that transferees will be given by transferors the information which they need to operate the employment contracts of those employees whom they inherit as a consequence of a relevant transfer. However, it may not necessarily have any material effect on the relative bargaining strengths of the parties in relation to the negotiation of more detailed, specific and protective warranties, indemnities, and contract pricing, not least in light of the fact that the obligation is only in principle required to be complied with fourteen days prior to the transfer itself as opposed to the (potentially earlier) time at which the contract binding the parties into the relevant contract is entered into.

8.05   Regulation 11 does not remove the need for transferees to consider seeking detailed due diligence, backed by appropriate warranties and indemnities, in the process of negotiation of a transfer. Its assistance to a transferee who commercially cannot secure such protections is limited by the scope of the information required to be provided. Nonetheless, in the absence of comprehensive contractual protection, disclosure in accordance with regulation 11 will assist not just logistically in ensuring that the transferee knows what terms and conditions it needs to continue in respect of the transferring employees but also evidentially in relation to any dispute with employees concerning their contractual entitlements. It will not, however, necessarily give adequate commercial protection. While considerable substantive detail must be provided, the information required to be disclosed is not comprehensive enough for the commercial purposes of many due diligence exercises. Examples of information which does not fall within the scope of the employee liability information required to be provided pursuant to regulation 11 but which might be of assistance to a transferee in readying itself for the transfer to its employment of the relevant employees are enhanced redundancy and severance entitlements, confidentiality and restrictive covenant obligations, details of any trade union and other recognition arrangements in place in relation to the transferring employees and compliance with the requirements of immigration legislation.

8.06   Regulations 11 and 12 set out the requirements and applicable conditions of the obligation to provide employee liability information in detail. It should be appreciated that these are obligations

---

[1] Regulation 11(2)(a)–(e).
[2] 2001 Consultation para. 69; 2005 Consultation para. 80.
[3] 2005 Consultation para. 80.

triggered by the fact of an impending relevant transfer. No request from the transferee is required for the obligation to provide employee liability information to arise—it is an automatic obligation.

B. Employees

The obligation imposed upon the transferor to provide employee liability information to **8.07** the transferee relates only to those who are employees for the purposes of TUPE. That said, particularly in view of the potential uncertainty concerning the issue of what constitutes employee status, not least in the context of agency workers, ensuring compliance with regulation 11 may on occasion be far from straightforward in terms of assessing in respect of which individuals information needs to be collated and disclosed to the transferee.

Regulation 11(1) provides that the employees about whom the relevant information must **8.08** be supplied by the transferor to the transferee are those who are 'assigned to the organised grouping of resources or employees that is the subject of a relevant transfer'. Care therefore needs to be taken to ensure that the proper (i.e. transferring) group of employees is identified for the purposes of complying with the obligation to provide the requisite employee liability information. The wording adopted in regulation 11(1) mirrors the wording used to identify those employees who transfer.[4] The assessment of which employees are the subject of the obligation to provide employee liability information needs to be conducted on the basis of the guiding principle of assignment (other than on a temporary basis) to the relevant undertaking or organized grouping of employees.[5]

C. Information

1. Prescribed information

Regulation 11(2) prescribes the employee liability information to be disclosed by the trans- **8.09** feror to the transferee which is to be disclosed in respect of the relevant employees as:

- the identity and age of the employee;[6]
- those particulars of employment that an employer is obliged to give to an employee pursuant to ERA 1996, s. 1;[7]
- information of any:
  - disciplinary procedure taken against the employee to which a relevant Code of Practice applies,[8]
  - grievance procedure taken by the employee to which a relevant Code of Practice applies,[9]
- information of any court or tribunal case, claim, or action:
  - brought by an employee against the transferor, within the previous two years,[10]

---

[4] Regulation 4(1).
[5] See Chapter 4, para. 4.36 *et seq.*
[6] Regulation 11(2)(a).
[7] Regulation 11(2)(b).
[8] Regulation 11(2)(c)(i).
[9] Regulation 11(2)(c)(ii).
[10] Regulation 11(2)(d)(i).

- that the transferor has reasonable grounds to believe that an employee may bring against the transferee, arising out of the employee's employment with the transferor;[11]
- information of any collective agreement which will have effect after the transfer, in its application in relation to the employee, pursuant to regulation 5(a).[12] Accordingly, only collective agreements which fall to transfer to the transferee in respect of the transferring employees pursuant to regulation 5 need to be disclosed in accordance with the requirements of regulation 11.

8.10 Regulation 11 does not extend to criminal liabilities generally so these need not be disclosed by the transferor in respect of the transferring employees, even if foreseeable, if they do not entail claims against the transferor or transferee by an employee as envisaged by regulation 11(2)(d). The fact that the matters within the scope of the obligation to provide written particulars of employment must be disclosed means that occupational pension entitlements must be notified even though they do not, in principle, transfer to the transferee pursuant to regulation 10. Claims in respect of accrued pension rights presumably need not be disclosed if (as is likely save in cases of claims based on the *Beckmann/Martin* cases) the transferor can reasonably conclude that, by virtue of regulation 10, no claim in that regard can be brought against the transferee.

2. Employment particulars

8.11 Rather than define the contractual entitlements of transferring employees by reference to generic concepts of remuneration, benefits, entitlements, and liabilities, the contractual aspects of the transferor's relationship with the assigned employees must be disclosed to the transferee by reference to those written particulars of employment which an employer is obliged to provide to an employee pursuant to ERA 1996, s. 1. That no such, or incomplete, particulars might have been provided to the relevant employee by the transferor is presumably irrelevant as the reference to the ERA 1996, s. 1 obligation is deployed to identify the types of information to be disclosed in order to comply with regulation 11. If written particulars have been provided (in a contract or formal statement), the transferor will need to ensure that up-to-date and comprehensive details are provided. If no such particulars have been provided to the employees, they will need to be compiled for the purposes of complying with regulation 11.

8.12 The written particulars which are listed in ERA 1996, s. 1 and are therefore the items which fall within the scope of the employee liability information to be disclosed pursuant to regulation 11(2) are:

- the names of the employer and employee;[13]
- the date when the employment began;[14]
- the date on which the employee's period of continuous employment began (taking into account any employment with a previous employer which counts towards that period);[15]
- the scale or rate of remuneration or the method of calculating remuneration;[16]

---

[11] Regulation 11(2)(d)(ii).
[12] Regulation 11(2)(e).
[13] ERA 1996, s. 1(3).
[14] Ibid.
[15] Ibid.
[16] ERA 1996, s. 1(4)(a).

- the intervals at which remuneration is paid (that is, weekly, monthly, or other specified intervals);[17]
- any terms and conditions relating to hours of work (including any terms and conditions relating to normal working hours);[18]
- any terms and conditions relating to any of the following:
  - entitlement to holidays, including public holidays, and holiday pay (the particulars given being sufficient to enable the employee's entitlement, including any entitlement to accrued holiday pay on the termination of employment, to be precisely calculated);
  - incapacity for work due to sickness or injury, including any provision for sick pay;
  - pensions and pension schemes;[19]
- the length of notice which the employee is obliged to give and entitled to receive to terminate his contract of employment;[20]
- the title of the job which the employee is employed to do or a brief description of the work for which he is employed;[21]
- where the employment is not intended to be permanent, the period for which it is expected to continue or, if it is for a fixed term, the date when it is to end;[22]
- either the place of work or, where the employee is required or permitted to work at various places, an indication of that and of the address of the employer;[23]
- any collective agreements which directly affect terms and conditions of the employment including, where the employer is not a party, the persons by whom they were made;[24]
- where the employee is required to work outside the United Kingdom for a period of more than one month:
  - the period for which he is to work outside the United Kingdom,
  - the currency in which remuneration is to be paid while he is working outside the United Kingdom,
  - any additional remuneration payable to him, and any benefits to be provided to or in respect of him, by reason of his being required to work outside the United Kingdom,
  - any terms and conditions relating to his return to the United Kingdom.[25]

8.13 The obligation to provide employee liability information under regulation 11 only extends, in relation to employees' contractual terms and conditions of employment, to the specific written particulars of employment required to be provided under ERA 1996, s. 1 and does not require the transferor to provide the transferee with details of further contractual terms and conditions of employment. Whilst full disclosure may well be good practice, the obligation to provide employee liability information is limited to employees' specific written particulars rather than the full contractual position. Full copies of all contractual documentation are not required to be disclosed by regulation 11.

---

[17] ERA 1996, s. 1(4)(b).
[18] ERA 1996, s. 1(4)(c).
[19] ERA 1996, s. 1(4)(d).
[20] ERA 1996, s. 1(4)(e).
[21] ERA 1996, s. 1(4)(f).
[22] ERA 1996, s. 1(4)(g).
[23] ERA 1996, s. 1(4)(h).
[24] ERA 1996, s. 1(4)(j).
[25] ERA 1996, s. 1(4)(k), subject to ERA 1996, s. 1(5).

3. Disciplinary and grievance procedures

8.14 The requirement to disclose information about disciplinary and grievance procedures conducted in relation to the transferring employees is confined to those matters to which a relevant code of practice applies. For these purposes the relevant code of practice is the ACAS Code of Practice on Disciplinary and Grievance Procedures.[26] With regard to disciplinary and grievance procedures, the 2009 Guidance suggests[27] that the relevant category of grievances are 'grievances which could give rise to any subsequent complaint to an employment tribunal about a breach of a statutory entitlement'. It also indicates, perhaps surprisingly, that the disciplinary action which must be notified to the transferee is 'action taken under the ACAS Code of Practice on disciplinary and grievance procedures [and does] not include oral or written warnings or suspensions on full pay'.[28]

4. Claims

8.15 The transferor is subject to two obligations with regard to actual and potential claims on the part of the transferring employees. The first obligation is to provide information about court or tribunal claims or actions brought against the transferor in the period of two years prior to the relevant transfer in respect of the transferring employees.[29] The second obligation—to provide information effectively about potential claims—is less straightforward. The obligation is to provide 'information of any court or tribunal case, claim or action . . . that the transferor has reasonable grounds to believe that an employee may bring against the transferee, arising out of the employee's employment with the transferor'.[30]

8.16 What constitutes 'reasonable grounds' for belief of the likelihood of a claim being brought is necessarily fact-sensitive. In addition, regulation 11(2)(d)(ii) could have identified the disclosable claims as those which the transferring employees potentially have against the transferor and which the transferee would inherit under TUPE. It did not do so—while to be disclosable a claim or potential claim must arise from the employee's employment with the transferor, it must also be the case that the transferor reasonably believes that the claim may be brought against the transferee.

8.17 The formulation adopted in regulation 11(2)(d)(ii) with regard to potential claims can therefore be interpreted to cover not just claims which the transferee inherits as a result of the acts or omissions by the transferor in respect of the transferring employees' pre-transfer employment. Regulation 11(2)(d)(ii) potentially requires the transferor to inform the transferee of claims which the transferring employees might make against the transferee arising out of the transferee's pre-transfer conduct. If an employee is in a position, as a result of the transferee's actions, where he or she is able to exercise the right to terminate employment in response to changes to working conditions[31] or to claim constructive dismissal[32] and this possibility comes to the (reasonable) attention of the transferor, it arguably falls within the scope of regulation 11(2)(d)(iii), which is not limited to claims created by or lying only against the transferor. So construed, regulation 11 would require the transferor to inform the transferee

---

[26] ACAS Code of Practice 1—Disciplinary and Grievance Procedures (April 2009).
[27] At p. 19.
[28] At p. 20.
[29] Regulation 11(2)(d)(i).
[30] Regulation 11(2)(d)(ii).
[31] Regulation 4(9).
[32] Regulation 4(11).

of the claims to which it was potentially exposing itself. It is not clear that this was the intention behind the formulation adopted in regulation 11(2)(d)(iii).

The 2009 Guidance[33] provides some further guidance on the issue of assessing when a potential claim can fall within the scope of regulation 11(2)(d)(ii). In answer to the question of how the transferor can decide whether it is reasonable to believe that a legal action could occur, it is suggested that: **8.18**

> [t]his is a matter of judgment and depends on the characteristics of each case. So, where an incident seems trifling—say, where an employee slipped at work but did not take any time off as a result—then there is little reason to suppose that a claim for personal injury damages would result. In contrast, if a fall at work led to hospitalisation over a long period or where a union representative raised the incident as a health and safety concern, then the transferor should inform the transferee accordingly.

5. Data protection

It is expressly provided that the age and identity of every relevant employee must be provided as part of the employee liability information which the transferor is required to deliver to the transferee.[34] **8.19**

In order to avoid breach of the provisions of the DPA 1998 with regard to the processing of 'personal data', it is often considered prudent only to supply anonymized information about the transferring employees as part of due diligence processes. DPA 1998 requires, if the processing of personal data such as employees' names is to be lawful, either consent of the data subject (in this context a transferring employee) or a legal obligation to effect the processing. Delivery of employees' names to a third party transferee clearly constitutes 'processing' for the purposes of DPA 1998. Therefore, save as required by regulation 11, such disclosure is only permissible under the DPA with employee consent. **8.20**

Since the requirement to provide the employee liability information is legally required pursuant to regulation 11, there is no breach of the data protection legislation in providing personal details about transferring employees to the transferee in advance of their transfer from the transferor to the transferee provided that the information falls within the scope of regulation 11(2). DPA 1998, Schedule 2, paragraph 3 provides that processing of personal data (which transfer to a third party of employee names constitutes) is permitted where the processing is 'necessary for compliance with any legal obligation to which the data controller is subject, other than an obligation imposed by contract'.[35] **8.21**

That regulation 11 imposes a legally binding obligation also ensures that disclosure to the transferee by the transferor of 'sensitive personal data'[36] about transferring employees is not **8.22**

---

[33] At p. 20.
[34] Regulation 11(2)(a).
[35] In this context the transferor is the data controller and the legal obligation is that imposed by regulation 11(2).
[36] DPA 1998, s. 2 defines sensitive personal data as:
  personal data consisting of information as to:
  (a) the racial or ethnic origin of the data subject;
  (b) his political opinions;
  (c) his religious beliefs or other beliefs of a similar nature;
  (d) whether he is a member of a trade union (within the meaning of the Trade and Labour Relations (Consolidation) Act 1992),
  (e) his physical or mental health or condition,

in breach of DPA 1998, again provided that it falls within the scope of regulation 11(2). DPA 1998, Schedule 3, paragraph 2(1) provides that one of the conditions permitting the processing of sensitive personal data is that '[t]he processing is necessary for the purposes of exercising or performing any right or obligation which is conferred or imposed by law on the data controller in connection with employment'. Information relating, for example, to a potential employment claim the central facts of which related to an employee's sexual orientation would appear to be disclosable pursuant to regulation 11 (and would need to be so disclosed to ensure compliance) without breach of the DPA 1998.

8.23 Nonetheless, careful consideration may still need to be given to whether disclosure of information containing personal data can be given without being anonymized during a pre-contract due diligence process. Only if information falls within the scope of regulation 11(2) will the DPA 1998 condition (for permissible data processing) of compliance with a legal obligation be satisfied. The supply of information wider than that specified in regulation 11(2) will still be covered by the relevant DPA protections.

8.24 The other protections prescribed by DPA 1998 (in terms of the data protection principles set out in its Schedule 1) will still need to be considered when complying with the obligation to provide employee liability information with regard to all 'personal' aspects of the information disclosed and not just employee names. Examples of the applicable data protection principles which may be particularly relevant in this context are that:

- personal data shall be accurate and, where necessary, kept up to date;[37]
- appropriate technical and organisational measures shall be taken against unauthorized or unlawful processing of personal data and against accidental loss or destruction of, or damage to, personal data;[38]
- personal data shall not be transferred to a country or territory outside the European Economic Area unless that country or territory ensures an adequate level of protection for the rights and freedoms of data subjects in relation to the processing of personal data.[39]

8.25 The Information Commissioner has issued a Good Practice Note on disclosure of employee information under TUPE.[40] Amongst other things, this guidance reminds employers of the need carefully to assess whether disclosure is permitted under TUPE without regard to the provisions of the DPA 1998. As the guidance indicates, there are various scenarios in which the provisions of regulation 11 do not engage to disapply the usual protections of the DPA 1998 with regard to the processing of personal data and sensitive personal data. These include transfers which are outside the scope of TUPE (such as share takeovers), the proposed transferee requesting information wider in scope than the prescribed employee liability information and there being a number of potential bidders, only one of whom will

---

(f) his sexual life,

(g) the commission or alleged commission by him of any offence, or

(h) any proceedings for any offence committed or alleged to have been committed by him, the disposal of such proceedings or the sentence of any court in such proceedings.

[37] DPA 1998, Sch. 1, principle 4.
[38] DPA 1998, Sch. 1, principle 7.
[39] DPA 1998, Sch. 1, principle 8.
[40] Dated 21.05.08. Accessible via www.ico.gov.uk.

become the eventual new employer but all of whom need the information to assess whether to pursue the purchase. As this guidance puts it:

> Wherever possible, the employer should release information that is anonymous or, at the very least, should remove obvious identifiers such as name. Employers should only disclose this extra information with the consent of the individuals concerned, or put in place appropriate safeguards to make sure that the information will only be used in connection with the proposed business transfer and will not be kept once it has been used for this purpose.

In terms of the transfer of employment records on completion of a relevant transfer the **8.26** Information Commissioner's guidance states as follows:

> It is likely that once the transfer has taken place the new employer will need a large proportion of an individual's employment record to manage the workforce and run the business. The former employer would not need the employees' consent to the transfer of their personal information if it was necessary for the purpose of the transfer and business needs of both parties. The new employer should consider whether all the information in the personnel files is needed and delete or destroy securely any unnecessary information.

It is assumed, although TUPE does not expressly address the point, that the obligation to **8.27** provide employee liability information only applies when there is a likely or definite transferee. On this analysis (and consistent with the Information Commissioner's Guidance) provision of employee information to bidders in a tender process before a final decision is made on the tender would fall outside the scope of regulation 11 and therefore be subject to the data protection considerations described above.

6. Former employees

Regulation 11(4) provides that: **8.28**

> [t]he duty to provide employee liability information...shall include a duty to provide employee liability information of any person who would have been employed by the transferor and assigned to the organised grouping of resources or employees that is the subject of a relevant transfer immediately before the transfer if he had not been dismissed in the circumstances described in regulation 7(1), including, where the transfer is effected by a series of two or more transactions, a person so employed and assigned or who would have been so employed and assigned immediately before any of those transactions.

Accordingly, if an employee is dismissed prior to the transfer in circumstances where there **8.29** is no ETOR avoiding automatic unfair dismissal,[41] that employee falls within the scope of the obligation imposed upon the transferor to provide the prescribed employee liability information in accordance with regulation 11(2). Careful consideration of the nature of pre-transfer dismissals will be needed to ensure appropriate notification to the transferee in order to comply with regulation 11.

D. Delivery and Updating

The transferor is obliged to notify the transferee of the requisite employee liability infor- **8.30** mation either in writing[42] or 'by making it available to him in a readily accessible form'.[43]

---

[41] In which case, pursuant to regulation 4(3), liability for the dismissal does not transfer to the transferee.
[42] Regulation 11(1)(a).
[43] Regulation 11(1)(b).

Presumably, whilst a written report may be required as to matters of which there is no documentary record, provision of copy documentation (such as contracts, handbooks, benefit scheme documentation, ET documentation, etc.) or access to an electronic data room will suffice where appropriate as part of the process of complying with regulation 11.

8.31 As the 2009 Guidance put it:[44]

> The information must be provided in writing or in other forms which are accessible to the transferee. So, it may be possible for the transferor to send the information as computer data files as long as the transferee can access that information, or provide access to the transferor's data storage. Likewise, in cases where a very small number of employees are transferring and small amounts of information may be involved, it might be acceptable to provide the information by telephone. However, it would be a good practice for the transferor to consult the transferee first to discuss the methods which he can use.

8.32 If there is 'any change in the employee liability information', then the transferor must notify the transferee in writing of the change.[45] The transferor therefore needs to ensure that its systems are such that, and that the management of the transfer process is conducted on the basis that, the employee liability information disclosed about employees, salary, and other remuneration, details of claims made and so on, is reviewed and updated on a regular basis in order to ensure at all times that up-to-date information has been provided.

8.33 This aspect of regulation 11 can be particularly important in a detailed tendering process where bidders may have been provided with outline employee information at the outset in order to assist them with formulating their bids. It is not sufficient for the transferor to assume that it has discharged its obligations simply by providing what does constitute full disclosure as at the outset of a negotiation or contracting process but which subsequently becomes incomplete or inaccurate.

E. Instalments

8.34 The employee liability information required to be notified to the transferee may be delivered 'in more than one instalment'.[46] The transferor will wish to keep a clear record of what information was provided when in order to be able to deal with any subsequent argument about the adequacy of its compliance with regulation 11. That said, it is clear that provision of employee liability information from a variety of sources (for example, through the due diligence process handled by lawyers for the commercial parties in the course of the negotiation of a transaction and the direct provision of information from human resources departments) may cumulatively satisfy the requirements of regulation 11. Careful coordination and management of the information provision process will nonetheless be needed to avoid confusion and dispute.

---

[44] At p. 19.
[45] Regulation 11(5).
[46] Regulation 11(7)(a).

F. Indirect Provision

The requisite employee liability information can be provided 'indirectly, through a third party'.[47] This delivery option was included, inter alia, to reflect the fact that, where contracts are reassigned or retendered, the ultimate client may well be responsible for passing employee liability information to bidders and the successful contractor and indeed may be the only party in direct contact with bidders and an incoming contractor during a tender process or contract reassignment.

8.35

Incumbent contractors will wish to ensure that any client wishing to be responsible for providing information to bidders as part of a retendering process does indeed pass the information on in a timely fashion. On an outsourcing, therefore, whilst a client may wish to include in the relevant contract provisions requiring an initial contractor to provide employee liability information as and when required (and particularly in advance of retendering or termination), the contractor itself will want protection from the client with regard to timely provision of information to new contractors (as well as compliance by the client with the protections of DPA 1998). This is especially relevant if the retendering is, as can often be the case, a process in which the transferor is not involved, over which it has no control, and of whose precise timing (apart from the ultimate end of its contract with the client) it is ignorant. Incumbent contractors will wish to avoid the situation where, because they have no control over the retendering process, they have inadequate information as to when the obligation to provide employee liability information arises (and in respect of what transferee) and consequently inadvertently become exposed to a potentially significant penalty for breach of the requirements of regulation 11.

8.36

G. Timing

In terms of the date at or by reference to which the information is given, regulation 11(3) requires disclosure of the information 'as at a specified date not more than 14 days before the date on which the information is notified to the transferee'. If special circumstances render this not reasonably practicable the information should be disclosed as soon as reasonably practicable. There is no obligation to provide the information any earlier, as might be of assistance to the transferee in preparing to take on the transferring employees.

8.37

A requirement of notification in any event no later than the 'completion' of the relevant transfer was contained in the draft regulation but was omitted from the final version of regulation 11. Where special circumstances apply, notification can presumably therefore be provided after the transfer as long as this still constitutes disclosure as soon as reasonably practicable.

8.38

The 2009 Guidance[48] addresses the circumstances where it may not be reasonably practicable to provide the information fourteen days in advance of the transfer occurring and indicates that:

8.39

> [t]hese would be various depending on circumstances. But, clearly, it would not be reasonably practicable to provide the information in time, if the transferor did not know the identity

---

[47] Regulation 11(7)(b). The 2001 Consultation had considered making it a requirement to provide the information through the client in a retendering situation (i.e. a service provision change involving the reassignment of a service contract) but this was not adopted since it was considered not always to be appropriate—see 2005 Consultation para. 78 and 2001 Consultation para. 72.

[48] At p. 20.

of the transferee until very late in the process, as might occur when service contracts are re-assigned from one contractor to another by a client, or, more generally, when the transfer takes place at very short notice.

8.40 The delivery of the requisite information is not calibrated by reference to the entry by the commercial parties into a binding contract to effect the transaction which constitutes a TUPE transfer. If (as will very often be the case) the relevant contract giving rise to a transfer of an undertaking is agreed some time before the transfer takes place, the obligation to provide employee liability information, which only has to be complied with by fourteen days prior to the actual transfer, will not assist a transferee in terms of ascertaining employment-related liabilities for the purposes of the commercial negotiation of contract terms.

H. Remedy

1. Award

8.41 The ET determines complaints of failure to comply with regulation 11. Awards of compensation are based on loss rather than by way of a penalty.[49] The complaint must be presented:

- before the end of the period of three months beginning with the date of the relevant transfer;[50] or
- within such further period as the tribunal considers reasonable in a case where it is satisfied that it was not reasonably practicable for the complaint to be presented before the end of that period of three months.[51]

8.42 Where an ET finds a complaint under paragraph (1) well founded, it:

- shall make a declaration to that effect;[52]
- may make an award of compensation to be paid by the transferor to the transferee.[53]

8.43 The amount of the compensation to be awarded by the ET where breach of regulation 11 is established is prescribed by regulation 12(4) as:

> such as the tribunal considers just and equitable in all the circumstances, . . . having particular regard to:
> (a) any loss sustained by the transferee which is attributable to the matters complained of; and
> (b) the terms of any contract between the transferor and the transferee relating to the transfer under which the transferor may be liable to pay any sum to the transferee in respect of a failure to notify the transferee of employee liability information.[54]

2. Principles of award

8.44 This very general power to award compensation based on loss has no statutory maximum in contrast to the remedies for breach of the collective information and consultation regimes applying to relevant transfers[55] and redundancy exercises of the requisite scale.

---

[49] Regulation 12(1). Regulation 12(7), combined with Employment Tribunals Act 1996, s. 18, establishes the ET as the forum for such complaints.
[50] Regulation 12(2)(a).
[51] Regulation 12(2)(b).
[52] Regulation 12(3)(a).
[53] Regulation 12(3)(b).
[54] Regulation 12(4)(a) and (b).
[55] Regulations 13–6.

Whilst loss may be straightforward to identify in relation, for example, to an undisclosed **8.45** discrimination claim which the transferee inherits, the fact that an award for breach of regulation 11 is determined by reference to what is just and equitable in all the circumstances gives ETs considerable flexibility in the awards which they may make. It appears possible that transferees will be able to mount compensation claims analogous to breach of warranty claims. Transferees may well seek to base arguments for compensation on what they would have done, the value of what they would have acquired, and what they would have paid for the relevant business had accurate and comprehensive employee liability information been provided.

Regulation 12(4) provides that the terms of a commercial agreement between transferor and **8.46** transferee will be relevant to the award under regulation 12 where that contract provides for the transferor to pay 'any sum' to the transferee 'in respect of a failure to notify the transferee of employee liability information'. If warranty and indemnity provisions in a transfer agreement provide for compensation for breach of the disclosure obligations imposed by the agreement, they can presumably be taken into account in assessing the loss by reference to which the just and equitable award of compensation for breach of regulation 11 is to be assessed. Presumably, *de minimis* provisions can also be taken into account.

The relevance of compensation or damages payable by the transferor to the transferee pursu- **8.47** ant to their commercial arrangements is defined by reference to the obligation to provide employee liability information. Construing the position strictly, compensation for breach of warranties as to matters of wider scope than the employee liability information as defined by regulation 11(2) is irrelevant to the ET's consideration of the level of award to be made (unless considered to be just and equitable in the circumstances).

3. Minimum award

The assessment of the compensation capable of being awarded by the ET in respect of breach **8.48** of the regulation 11 obligation is subject to important further provisions. First, regulation 11(5) provides that, regardless of the issues of loss described above, the minimum award shall be £500 per employee in respect of whom the transferor has failed to comply with its obligations. This minimum award need not, however, be made if the ET considers it 'just and equitable in all the circumstances, to award a lesser sum'.

The nature of the transferor's breach will be relevant to the number of employees in respect **8.49** of whom such a minimum award can or should be made by the ET. Unlike regulation 15, which provides for compensation for breach of regulation 13 of up to thirteen weeks' pay per affected employee (as that term is defined in regulation 13(1)), regulation 12(5) limits the application of the minimum award to those employees in respect of whom the transferor has breached its regulation 11 obligations. By way of example, strictly construing this provision, if the transferor complied with all its regulation 11 obligations save for the provision to the transferee of the relevant employment particulars of one employee, the regulation 11 breach would only relate to one employee and presumably the £500 minimum award could only be made in respect of that one employee. By way of contrast, a failure by the transferor to notify the transferee of a collective agreement covering a workforce of thousands would constitute a breach of the regulation 11 obligation in respect of all those employees in relation to all of whom the £500 minimum award should in principle be made unless ET considers that it is not just and equitable to do so.

8.50 The 2009 Guidance makes one specific observation in relation to the issue of when the tribunal would not make the minimum award of compensation because to do so would be unjust or inequitable. It indicated that 'it might be fair to assume that trivial or unwitting breaches of the duty may lead to the ET waiving what would otherwise be a minimum award of compensation'.[56]

4. Mitigation

8.51 Regulation 12(6) provides a further principle for the ET to consider in exercising its jurisdiction to award compensation in respect of breach of regulation 11. The principle of mitigation of loss under common law must also be taken into account in assessing the loss in respect of which (to the extent just and equitable and subject to the parties' commercial terms) an award can be made under regulation 12.

I. Due Diligence Exercises

8.52 The parties involved in a relevant transfer will therefore need to consider a variety of issues in relation to the provision of information about those employees who will transfer from transferor to transferee under TUPE. Clients awarding contracts will wish to oblige their contractors contractually to provide the requisite information to them as and when requested for onward transmission to potential bidders in order to ensure that subsequent retendering processes can be managed effectively and to reassure transferees that an incumbent contractor is bound contractually to provide the information which is required by statute to be disclosed and which they may often wish to see earlier than the statute actually requires to assist in the formulation of bids. Transferors will wish to ensure that they take proper steps, by way of investigation of the liabilities which have arisen in respect of the transferring employees, to comply with the (albeit limited) obligation imposed by regulation 11. Incumbent contractors will wish to ensure that on a retendering no dispute arises about the timely provision of information and that the client is contractually required to do all that is reasonably necessary to enable them to comply with their obligations.

8.53 Notwithstanding the obligation to notify employee liability information and the availability of compensation in respect of breach, transferees will still wish, where feasible, to ensure that appropriate warranties and indemnities provide more extensive protection when compared with that supplied by regulation 11.

8.54 That said, whether or not commercial indemnity protection can be obtained, transferees may often wish to utilize the obligation imposed by TUPE to provide employee liability information to put pressure on transferors promptly to provide full employee information. Transferees may well wish to make specific and detailed requests and argue that the request simply reflects the transferor's obligations under regulation 11 in any event.

8.55 In formulating due diligence requests by reference to the obligation on the transferor to provide employee liability information, it needs to be borne in mind that the obligation imposed by regulation 11 is limited to the specific items referred to in regulation 11(2). Basic contractual obligations and responsibilities, claims, and debts can be seen clearly to

---

[56] At p. 30.

fall within the scope of the employee liability information which is to be notified by the transferor to the transferee. That said, there may well also be information which a transferee will wish to seek, depending upon the nature of the business in question, as part of a due diligence process but which will fall outside the strict scope of the concept of employee liability information for the purposes of regulation 11. By way of example, information about the industrial relations history of the operation in question, whether any regulatory or governmental body has ever investigated the business, staff turnover, any restrictive covenants to which the transferring employees are subject pursuant to their contracts of employment and other matters may need to be sought for important commercial reasons but would be outside the scope of regulation 11.

Whilst space constraints preclude a detailed treatment of all the due diligence issues which **8.56** can arise when negotiating and documenting relevant transfers, there are a number of crucial categories of information that a transferee will wish wherever possible to obtain.

A list of all potential employees who might transfer employment following the transaction **8.57** should be sought including those who have not yet commenced employment. Relevant details about those employees would include, in respect of each employee, the employer, the name of the employee, the date on which the employee's continuous employment for statutory purposes began, the job title, the notice period, salary, any overtime entitlements, and any pay increases awarded.

Full details should be sought of any share option bonus, profit sharing, or commission **8.58** arrangements in which the transferring employees participate, including the applicable scheme rules. Not least in order to be able to assess employment costs and the arrangements needing to be replicated post-transfer, details should be sought of all other employment benefits offered or provided to the transferring employees. Examples of the arrangements about which information should be sought include life assurance schemes, private and permanent health insurance arrangements, company car and travel policies, enhanced redundancy arrangements, retirement policies, relocation policies, and long service award schemes.

Employment documentation itself is of course crucial and copies should be sought of all **8.59** standard terms and conditions of employment, of all employment contracts with directors and other transferring employees whose employment is terminable on greater than, say, three months' notice, of any employment handbooks and similar policy documents, all applicable disciplinary and grievance procedures, and details of any pension schemes. Pension details sought should extend to early retirement entitlements, eligibility requirements, and which transferring employees are eligible to participate in the scheme.

An appreciation of the collective and industrial relations framework in which the transfer- **8.60** ring undertaking operates can be invaluable. Accordingly, details should be sought of all agreements with trade unions, of works councils arrangements and other employee representative structures, of trade union membership, and of the industrial relations history of the business. Full details should also be sought of past, outstanding, and anticipated applications to ETs or courts by any existing or past employees as well as historic dismissals, not least given the risk of an employee dismissed prior to transfer alleging that the dismissal was transfer-related and therefore that the transferee inherits any liability for any consequent unfair dismissal claim.

J. Contracting Out

8.61 In the first draft of what became the 2006 Regulations, the prohibition on contracting out of the provisions of TUPE referred to a number of provisions of TUPE 2006 other than regulation 11. The omission of regulation 11 from the scope of the anti-avoidance provisions of TUPE would presumably have meant that, as between themselves, the transferor and transferee could have agreed to disapply regulation 11. This position was reversed in the final version of the 2006 Regulations on the basis that it would have disadvantaged the employees. The prohibition of contracting out in regulation 18 applies equally to the obligation imposed upon the transferor to provide employee liability information to the transferee.[57]

---

[57] See Chapter 12, para. 12.01 *et seq.*

9

COLLECTIVE INFORMATION AND CONSULTATION

A. **Overview**	9.01	E. **Representation of Employees**	9.61
B. **Affected Employees**	9.06	1. Appropriate representatives	9.61
C. **Information**	9.14	2. Electing employee representatives	9.70
1. Prescribed information	9.14	3. Protection of employee representatives	9.75
2. Legal, economic, and social implications	9.18	F. **Remedies for Breach**	9.89
3. Measures	9.20	1. Complaints	9.89
4. Accuracy of information	9.30	2. Compensation	9.104
5. Timing	9.34	3. Joint and several liability	9.119
6. Delivery	9.37	4. Individual enforcement	9.128
7. Transferee measures	9.39	5. Special circumstances defence	9.130
8. Information where consultation is not		6. Confidentiality	9.135
compulsory	9.43	7. Injunctions	9.138
D. **Consultation**	9.48	G. **Interaction with Other Consultation**	
1. When consultation is required	9.48	**Requirements**	9.139
2. Whose obligation?	9.51	1. Collective redundancy consultation	9.139
3. Nature and timing of consultation	9.53	2. Other statutory obligations	9.142
4. Post-transfer consultation	9.59	H. **Planning for Compliance**	9.153

A. Overview

Regulation 13 (as supplemented by regulations 14-16) imposes on transferors and trans-   **9.01**
ferees specific obligations with regard to the provision of information to, and the conduct
of consultation with, representatives of those employees who are affected by a relevant
transfer.

By way of overview, TUPE 2006 requires that, long enough before a relevant transfer to   **9.02**
enable the employer of any affected employees to consult appropriate representatives of
those affected employees, the employer shall provide specified information to those representatives[1] and shall consult with them with a view to reaching agreement in relation to
any measures which are envisaged.[2] Appropriate representatives for these purposes will be
representatives of a recognized trade union or, if there is none, employee representatives who
either constitute an existing representative body with competence to deal with TUPE issues
or who are elected in accordance with the requirements of regulation 14. The penalty for

---

[1] Regulation 13(2).
[2] Regulation 13(6).

217

failure to comply with these obligations is potentially significant—an award of up to thirteen weeks' pay per affected employee.[3]

9.03   These are therefore material obligations which can complicate any transfer process and which necessitate careful planning to ensure compliance, given their detailed technical requirements with regard not only to the information and consultation obligations themselves but also the identity and election of the representatives of the affected employees with whom the parties must deal in order to satisfy the requirements of the legislation.

9.04   With regard to these information and consultation obligations, TUPE 2006 largely repeats the provisions of TUPE 1981. As it was put in the 2005 Consultation, other than with regard to the issue of joint and several liability for awards in respect of breach of their requirements, these provisions essentially mirror TUPE 1981, regulations 10 and 11 'with only a couple of minor amendments to reflect more closely the wording of the current Directive'.[4] Accordingly, the case law prior to 2006 remains relevant.

9.05   The principal amendment which the 2006 Regulations made to this information and consultation regime was to provide that the liability for any penalty awarded in respect of any failure to provide information to and consult with appropriate representatives of the affected employees as required by regulation 13 is borne jointly and severally between transferor and transferee. This resolved some previous case law uncertainty as to whether liability for this penalty for non-compliance rested only with the transferor or could transfer to the transferee along with other employment-related liabilities (on the basis that it constituted a liability in connection with an employee's employment).[5]

B. Affected Employees

9.06   The information and consultation obligations imposed by regulation 13 apply only in respect of employees affected by the transfer. The definition of employee set out in regulation 2(1) therefore needs to be considered carefully in this context to ensure that the relevant obligations are complied with.[6] Whilst those who are not employees in terms of their legal status are irrelevant for these purposes, this is a broader category of person than the employees whose contracts will (or should) actually transfer to the transferee pursuant to regulation 4.[7] As regulation 13(1) makes clear, the references in the information and consultation provisions to 'affected employees' are to:

> any employees of the transferor or the transferee (whether or not assigned to the organised grouping of resources or employees that is the subject of a relevant transfer) who may be affected by the transfer or may be affected by measures taken in connection with it; and references to the employer shall be construed accordingly.

---

[3]   Regulation 15(15).

[4]   At para. 81.

[5]   See 2005 Consultation paras 82 and 83 as well as *Alamo Group (Europe) Ltd v Tucker and anor* [2003] IRLR 266, EAT; *TGWU v James McKinnon, JR Haulage Ltd and others* [2001] IRLR 597, EAT; *Kerry Foods Ltd v Creber* [2000] IRLR 10, EAT.

[6]   See Chapter 4, para. 4.10 *et seq.* for further discussion.

[7]   The transferring employees are those employees who, pursuant to regulation 4(1), are assigned (other than on a temporary basis) to the relevant organised grouping of resources or employees and whose contracts of employment therefore transfer from the transferor to the transferee as a result of the relevant transfer.

Employees of the transferor who do not transfer under TUPE to the transferee because they **9.07** are not assigned to the relevant undertaking or activities may nonetheless be affected by a relevant transfer. For example, a business disposal conducted by way of a relevant transfer may lead to redundancies amongst the transferor's remaining workforce, perhaps, for example, in relation to a central services function. Careful consideration needs to be given to what effects the transfer may have and therefore whether constituencies of employee wider than just those who fall within the scope of TUPE (such that their employment transfers from the transferor to the transferee) need to be addressed by the transferor or the transferee in an information and consultation process complying with the requirements of regulation 13.

The obligations imposed by regulation 13 apply in relation to any transfer of an undertak- **9.08** ing regardless of the number of employees involved. This is in contrast to the threshold in respect of collective consultation obligations relating to redundancies which are only triggered where twenty or more employees are proposed to be made redundant at one establishment in a ninety-day period.[8]

UNISON v Somerset County Council and others[9] considered the scope of regulation 13 in **9.09** terms of the affected employees in respect of whom it applies. The affected employees are those who will or may be transferred or whose jobs are in jeopardy by reason of the proposed transfer. Those who have applications within the organization pending at the time of transfer may also be affected employees. The obligation does not extend to the whole workforce nor indeed to those whose future prospects, in terms of career opportunities, might be affected by change in the recruitment arrangement in the part transferred.

UNISON arose as a result of the formation of a joint venture vehicle which was to employ **9.10** staff previously employed by Somerset County Council and Taunton Deane Borough Council in the provision of transactional and corporate support services. A staffing agreement dealing with how the joint venture should advertise and process vacancies in the future was agreed just before the joint venture arrangements were finalized. Staff had been given the choice of transferring under TUPE to or, as an alternative, being seconded to the joint venture vehicle. No consultation took place with the relevant recognized trade union with regard to the staffing agreements and it complained of a breach of regulation 13 because the staffing arrangement entailed a change to the treatment of the wider workforce remaining with the relevant councils—they would now only be notified of vacancies at the same time as those vacancies were externally advertised.

The ET and the EAT held that regulation 13 did not engage in relation to employees outside **9.11** the relevant business areas which were the subject of the relevant transfer—they were not employees who were immediately affected by the transfer. The EAT rejected the contention that employees in the wider workforce who were not in scope for the purposes of TUPE were nonetheless affected employees for these purposes because their job prospects in the future (in the sense of the opportunity to move to perhaps a more congenial or better paid post than their existing one) would be affected by the fact that the recruitment advertisement process was being changed. Consequently, the changes made to the staffing agreement were not measures relating to affected employees which would trigger the obligation to conduct consultation as required by regulation 13(6).

---

[8] TULRCA 1992, s. 188.
[9] [2010] IRLR 207, EAT.

9.12   As Bean J put it:

> the 'affected employees' are those who will be or may be transferred or whose jobs are in jeopardy by reason of the proposed transfer, or who have job applications within the organisation pending at the time of transfer. We do not think that the definition extends to the whole of the workforce, nor to everyone in the workforce who might apply for a vacancy in the part transferred at some point in the future.[10]

9.13   To hold otherwise would, in the view of the EAT, have:

> very dramatic consequences. It would mean, for example, that where on a transfer of part of an undertaking the majority of the workforce transferred on identical terms, but a small number of managers had their numbers reduced or their pay and terms and conditions adversely affected, then any employee of the company or authority concerned at a more junior level who might, in future, aspire to seek promotion to managerial level would be on [counsel's] argument an 'affected employee' within reg. 13. Thus there would be an obligation on the authority to consult employee representatives of the rank and file, if we may so describe them, even if the union concerned had no representation whatever in managerial ranks. This would, we think, be a very surprising conclusion. It is very common in workforces in both public and private sectors for vacancies to be advertised internally before they are advertised externally and if part of the undertaking is then transferred under TUPE, it would lead to the conclusion in many if not most cases that every employee of the organisation concerned is potentially an 'affected employee'.[11]

C. Information

1. Prescribed information

9.14   Regulation 13 prescribes the information which must be provided by the transferor to the appropriate representatives of the affected employees. The obligation is to provide the prescribed information and not all background materials—as Millett J put it in *Institution of Professional Civil Servants v Secretary of State for Defence*:[12]

> insofar as any information is not factual but is based upon appraisal and judgement, as in the case of manpower forecasts for example (assuming for this purpose, without deciding, that such forecasts constitute information at all within the subsection), it does not include the calculations and assumptions on which the appraisal or judgement is based, nor are the unions entitled to demand such calculations and assumptions in order to challenge their validity.

9.15   The information which the employer of employees affected or to be affected by a relevant transfer is obliged to provide to appropriate representatives of those employees in advance of a relevant transfer is as follows:

- the fact that the relevant transfer is to take place, the date or proposed date of the transfer, and the reasons for it;[13]
- the legal, economic, and social implications of the transfer for any affected employees;[14]

---

[10] Ibid. at para. 21.
[11] Ibid. at para. 19.
[12] [1987] IRLR 373, Ch.
[13] Regulation 13(2)(a).
[14] Regulation 13(2)(b).

- the measures which the employer envisages it will, in connection with the transfer, take in relation to any affected employees or, if he envisages that no measures will be so taken, that fact;[15]
- if the employer is the transferor, the measures, in connection with the transfer, which it (i.e. the transferor) envisages that the transferee will take in relation to any affected employees who will become employees of the transferee after the transfer by virtue of regulation 4 or, if it envisages that no measures will be so taken, that fact;[16]
- the information about agency workers described in para. 9.17 below.

Regulation 13(2)(a), following the amended provisions of the ARD 2001, requires confirmation of 'the date or proposed date of the transfer'. The equivalent provision in TUPE 1981 required the less precise disclosure of 'when, approximately, [the transfer] is to take place'.[17] **9.16**

Following amendments made by the Agency Workers Regulations 2010[18] the transferor **9.17** and/or the transferee as the case may be, if required to provide information to the appropriate representatives pursuant to regulation 13(2), must include specific prescribed information about its use of agency workers pursuant to regulation 13(2A). This is the case even though it does not appear that any consultation is then explicitly required about that aspect of the conduct by the transferor or the transferee of its business or how the consequences of a TUPE transfer for affected employees might be influenced by the use of agency workers or any change thereto. Nonetheless, the appropriate representatives will acquire information which may be of value to them in any consultation process which ensues, especially where redundancies are proposed in conjunction with the TUPE transfer in question. The requirement to disclose the use of agency workers is not calibrated by reference to the undertaking or activities which are the subject of the relevant transfer but must relate to all those agency workers engaged by the transferor or the transferee, as the case may be. Regulation 13(2A) provides that the transferor or transferee, as the case may be, must supply to the appropriate representatives 'suitable information relating to the use of agency workers (if any) by that person'.[19] For these purposes, such suitable information means:[20]

(a) the number of agency workers working temporarily for and under the supervision and direction of the employer;
(b) the parts of the employer's undertaking in which those agency workers are working; and
(c) the type of work those agency workers are carrying out.

2. Legal, economic, and social implications

The concept of the 'legal, economic and social implications' of the transfer for the affected **9.18** employees of which the appropriate representatives must be informed pursuant to regulation 13(2)(b) needs to be considered carefully in order to avoid breach of the relevant obligations. The legal consequences of a relevant transfer are usually clear (in terms of the change to the identity of the employer and the retention of statutory and contractual employment rights other than in relation to the occupational pension scheme benefits).

---

[15] Regulation 13(2)(c).
[16] Regulation 13(2)(d).
[17] TUPE 1981, regulation 10(2)(a).
[18] SI 2010/93, regulation 25, Sch. 2, Pt 2, paras 28, 29. These amendments came into effect as from 1 October 2010.
[19] Regulation 13(2A)(a).
[20] Regulation 13(2A)(b)(i)–(iii).

9.19   The economic and social consequences of a relevant transfer (in terms of issues such as the human resources and industrial relations philosophy, working environment, financial stability, and other characteristics of the transferee) may be somewhat more difficult to assess and convey succinctly, objectively, and comprehensively than the legal consequences. These consequences cannot, however, be ignored in formulating the notification to be given to appropriate representatives of the employees affected by a relevant transfer in accordance with regulation 13(2).

3. Measures

9.20   The term 'measures' is generally assumed to cover dismissals or changes to terms and conditions or other variations in terms of working patterns, working methods, or location which affect the employees in question but is a wide concept. In *Institution of Professional Civil Servants v Secretary of State for Defence*[21] Millett J described the term 'measures' as:

> a word of the widest import, and includes any action, step or arrangement, while 'envisages' simply means 'visualises' or 'foresees'. Despite the width of these words, it is clear that manpower projections may not be measures; though positive steps to achieve planned reductions in manpower levels otherwise than through natural wastage would be.[22]

9.21   In Millett J's assessment the obligation to disclose measures which are envisaged does not extend to 'mere hopes or possibilities' and it is 'not enough that there should be some possibility in contemplation; the company must have formulated some definite plan or proposal which it has in mind to implement, if necessary after appropriate negotiation with the unions'.[23]

9.22   It is generally considered that the concept of measures being envisaged does require some relatively clear (if not finalized or definite) plan or proposal to have been formulated or which the employer has in mind to implement. General and unspecific intentions to review the situation post-transfer will arguably not be measures which the employer envisages and therefore will not give rise to the obligation to consult (not least since there would then be very little to discuss by way of consultation). The act of entering into a transaction whose consequence is the transfer of employees from the transferor to the transferee in accordance with TUPE is not a measure about which consultation is required as it constitutes a matter of 'business policy'.[24] The description of measures for these purposes set out by Millett J also suggests that the steps which an employer can envisage which will fall within the scope of the information and consultation obligations of regulation 13 can extend to actions which are lawful and contractually valid. Reliance by an employer on a contractual power, for example, to vary an employee's place of work or bonus entitlements is capable of falling within this concept of measures if the relevant step is connected with the transfer.

9.23   *Todd v Strain and others*[25] concerned the sale of a care home which led to a claim by thirty-two of the sixty-four affected employees complaining of a breach of the TUPE information and consultation regime. The transferor had not arranged the election of employee representatives

---

[21] [1987] IRLR 373, Ch.
[22] Ibid. at para. 12.
[23] Ibid.
[24] Ibid. at para. 13.
[25] [2011] IRLR 11, EAT. See Wynn-Evans, 'Measuring up for TUPE Consultation' (2010) 17(9) ELA Briefing 4.

but had informed a group of approximately one-third of the affected employees of the impending sale and confirmed that their jobs were safe, the intention being that they would inform their colleagues of the position. In a decision in which it found that the transferee had not been at fault, the ET made the maximum permissible award against the transferor. The ET held, inter alia, that the transferor should have consulted representatives of the affected employees with regard to certain administrative changes which related to the employees' remuneration arrangements post-transfer, one of which was a change to the employees' pay date, and which the tribunal considered to be a measure for these purposes.

In upholding the ET's decision, the EAT made clear that the fact that the change which was **9.24** envisaged with regard to pay dates was not to the disadvantage of the employees in question and was irrelevant to the issue of whether it constituted a measure for TUPE purposes. As Underhill P put it:

> the Regulations do not prescribe that any effect must be disadvantageous in order to trigger the requirement to consult. We have considered whether the effect in question was so trivial as to be *de minimis*, but we do not think that such a conclusion could be justified in view of the Tribunal's express finding, at least in relation to the 'tax rebate', that the changes in their payment arrangements caused worry among the staff concerned. It is not difficult to imagine how any change to the payment arrangements with which employees are familiar, and all the more so in the context of a change of employer, is liable to be unsettling; and part of the purpose of the duty to consult must surely be to enable transitional arrangements of the kind adopted here to be explained to employees and for them to be reassured, if this be the case, that they will not in any way be prejudiced by them. The sums involved were no doubt small, but it must be borne in mind that many of the employees in question were low-paid.[26]

The EAT also drew a distinction between two types of consequence of a relevant transfer **9.25** in assessing whether measures are envisaged and therefore whether the collective duty to inform and consult arises under TUPE. Despite the width of the concept of a measure, 'it must nevertheless be something deliberately done by the transferor over and above what necessarily occurs as a consequence of the transfer itself'.[27] Changes that are an inevitable consequence of the transfer will not attract the information and consultation duties— an example would be the simple fact that the new employer's organization will, by virtue of the transfer, be responsible for making salary payments post-transfer. However, where post-transfer administrative arrangements depart from the normal pre-transfer practice then information and consultation about those measures will be required under TUPE.

Todd therefore alerts transferors to the point that practical and administrative matters can **9.26** constitute measures just as much as more dramatic actions such as relocations, redundancies, and changes to benefits and terms and conditions of employment, and therefore will also trigger the consultation obligation. Issues which may need to be considered as potentially constituting measures, in addition to dismissals and contract changes, could, depending on the context, include matters as diverse as changes of reporting line, uniform changes, internal management reorganizations, and job title changes.

Todd therefore encourages careful analysis of the detailed practical and logistical aspects of **9.27** the implementation of the transaction in question to assess the extent to which they attract the duty to inform and consult. In light of their obligation to notify the transferor of any

---

[26] Ibid. at para. 20.
[27] Ibid. at para. 18.

measures which they envisage making,[28] and the liability which they may incur if breach of that obligation causes any failure by the transferor to comply with its obligations,[29] transferees will also need to be mindful of *Todd* when seeking to comply with regulation 13(4) by notifying the transferor of the measures which they envisage implementing.

9.28 The specific position with regard to pensions is also worth considering. Although the precise scope of regulation 10 is complex,[30] rights in relation to occupational pension schemes, generally speaking, do not transfer to the transferee on a relevant transfer. Subject therefore to the minimum standards of post-transfer pension preservation established by the combined effect of the PA 2004 and the PPR 2005 and the commercial and human resources imperatives of the situation, the transferee therefore has free rein with regard to the pension arrangements which it puts in place for transferring employees who have previously enjoyed pension benefits falling within the scope of the pensions exclusion.

9.29 It might be thought that the changes to transferring employees' pension rights which a transfer often entails do not constitute 'measures' because they do not affect contractual rights which the transferee inherits. Especially in the light of Millett J's comments, it is thought that pension changes connected with a transfer do constitute measures and therefore trigger the information and consultation obligations of regulation 13, even though the transferring employees' post-transfer rights may be limited to the entitlements conferred by the combined effect of PA 2004 and PPR 2005.

4. Accuracy of information

9.30 *Royal Mail Group Ltd v Communication Workers Union*[31] concerned a complaint of a breach of regulation 13 in relation to the transfer of a large number of post offices from Post Office Ltd to WH Smith. The relevant trade union had been concerned that the transfers were proceeding on an (in its view) erroneous assumption by the employer that the transfers did not fall within the scope of TUPE not least because, due to a combination of redeployment and a voluntary redundancy exercise, no staff would actually transfer to WH Smith. This is what the employees were told, there being no direct consultation with the trade union. As it transpired, in actual fact some employees did remain in the relevant functions at the time of transfer rather than by them having been redeployed or made redundant.

9.31 The question before the Court of Appeal was whether the obligation to provide the appropriate representatives with information was an objective or subjective one, i.e. did the employer have to provide objectively accurate information or information that it believed was accurate. It was accepted that the obligation with regard to the accuracy of the information provided to appropriate representatives was subjective.

9.32 The Court of Appeal's analysis was that, in order to achieve the consultation which is the objective of regulation 13, it is necessary for the appropriate representatives to understand the employer's position with regard to the transfer—which necessarily depends on what the employer believes the legal position to be in relation to the employees. The provision of information is only the 'commencement point' for the consultation exercise.[32] The employer

---

[28] Under regulation 13(4)—see para. 9.40 *et seq.*
[29] Under regulation 15(5)—see para. 9.41.
[30] See Chapter 11.
[31] [2009] IRLR 1046, CA.
[32] Ibid. at para. 69.

had argued that it is by no means necessarily the case that the legal implications of a transfer are clear-cut or even readily predictable and, as Waller LJ noted, '[a]n obligation to warrant accuracy seems to make it impossible for an employer to say that the answer is not clear'[33] and '[w]hat representatives should be informed of is a considered view as to the legal implications and an employer will not be able simply to say without considering the point "this is what I believed"'.[34]

A general defence of ignorance—on the basis that the employer failed to appreciate that the circumstances in question constituted a relevant transfer—is unlikely to be effective. As Elias J said at the EAT stage in *Royal Mail Group Ltd v Communication Workers Union*:[35] **9.33**

> We strongly suspect—although the issue was not argued before us—that it would not be a defence for an employer to say that he did not inform or consult because he did not realize that there was a transfer at all, or because he genuinely believed that there was not. We also think that he would be liable for failing to inform and consult with respect to persons who are affected by the transfer although he had genuinely not thought that they were. In these contexts, therefore, an objective interpretation of the law is probably required.

5. Timing

That an anticipated TUPE transfer does not ultimately take place does not avoid its information and consultation obligations engaging. As Popplewell J said in *Banking Insurance and Finance Union v Barclays Bank plc*:[36] **9.34**

> [i]t would be quite contrary to the whole spirit of the legislation and to the Directive if there were to be no sanction for failure to consult in relation to a proposed transfer which happened not to take place. It is true that the word 'proposed' does not appear as it does, for instance, in section 101 of the Employment Protection Act 1975, but the Regulations are clearly designed to deal with consultation before any transfer has taken place and to give the union the right to complain if they are not informed or consulted about the proposed transfer. The Regulations say nothing as to when the complaint can be presented and industrial common sense dictates that an actual transfer is not an essential part of the bringing of a complaint.

Regulation 13 requires information and consultation in advance of a potential transfer. Precisely when the obligation to provide information to employee representatives arises will inevitably be a question of fact, given the lack of any more specific prescribed requirement in the legislation than that information be provided 'long enough before' the transfer to enable consultation to take place.[37] Again, this contrasts with the collective redundancy consultation regime established by TULRCA 1992, s. 188 with its prescribed minimum thirty- and ninety-day consultation periods prior to any dismissals taking effect by reference to which the proper time for the provision of the requisite information can be assessed (because the information must be provided before that consultation commences). **9.35**

What constitutes provision of the required information long enough before the transfer to enable consultation to take place is a particularly nebulous concept if no 'measures' are envisaged to be taken in relation to the transfer by either the transferor or transferee. In that **9.36**

---

[33] Ibid. at para. 67.
[34] Ibid. at para. 66.
[35] [2009] IRLR 108, EAT at para. 130.
[36] [1987] ICR 495, EAT at 504H.
[37] Regulation 13(2)—'[l]ong enough before a relevant transfer to enable the employer of any affected employees to consult the appropriate representatives of any affected employees…'.

scenario there is no consultation formally required by reference to which the appropriate timing of the provision of information can be determined. A transfer may occur on completion of a contract or transfer of actual management responsibility so careful assessment needs to be made of when the obligation arises.

6. Delivery

9.37 The provision of the requisite information to appropriate representatives is not expressly required to be in writing although common sense, good practice, and the clear implication of the wording of regulation 13(5) all suggest that this is the proper method of delivery.

9.38 Regulation 13(5) states that the information to be given to the appropriate representatives 'shall be given to each of them by being delivered to them, or sent by post to an address notified by them to the employer, or (in the case of representatives of a trade union) sent by post to the union at the address of its head or main office'. As a practical matter, in order to ensure certainty and avoid subsequent disputes, how and where information is to be delivered needs to be determined (presumably by agreement if possible with the appropriate representatives).

7. Transferee measures

9.39 The transferor is required by regulation 13(2)(d) to inform the appropriate representatives of the affected employees whom it employs of the measures (if any) which it, the transferor, envisages that the transferee will take in connection with the transfer in relation to its employees who will transfer to the transferee. In line with the objective of ensuring that employees (through their representatives) are adequately informed about the transfer and consulted about related changes, the relevant representatives are therefore to be informed in advance of what (if anything) the transferee plans to do after the transfer in relation to the employment of those affected employees—at least to the extent that the transferor envisages that the transferee will be taking measures in connection with the transfer.

9.40 TUPE makes this obligation practicable by requiring the transferee to notify the transferor prior to the transfer of such intentions as it may have with regard to measures which it may take in relation to the transferring employees. More specifically, regulation 13(4) requires the transferee to 'give the transferor such information at such a time as will enable the transferor to perform' its duty to inform the appropriate representatives of the measures which the transferee envisages taking in respect of the transferring employees (or, if there are none, of that fact).[38]

9.41 Compliance with this obligation requires a careful assessment by the transferee of whether it has plans for the workforce which can be construed as being measures and are sufficiently definite to have the status of being envisaged. The transferee is incentivized to comply with this obligation to inform the transferor of any measures which it envisages taking by the fact that regulation 15(5) enables the transferor to join the transferee into any proceedings complaining of breach of these obligations.

---

[38] The transferor's duty to provide details of the measures anticipated by the transferee is imposed by regulation 13(2)(d).

Regulation 13(2)(d) is formulated differently from the equivalent provision in TUPE 1981[39] **9.42**
in that it is based on the transferor's anticipation of what the transferee will do, a change to
the legislation which went without detailed comment from the Government as to the rationale for its introduction. TUPE 1981 required provision by the transferor of information as
the measures which the transferee envisaged taking. However, regulation 13(2)(d) refers to
what the transferor envisages the transferee will do by way of measures. In complying with
this duty, the transferor is assisted by the obligation imposed on the transferee by regulation 13(4) to confirm its measures. To calibrate the obligation by reference to the transferor's state of mind also provides the transferor with some degree of protection from claims.
Nonetheless, regulation 13(2)(d) arguably requires greater consideration by the transferor of
what it considers the transferee might do than reliance only on the transferee's notification
by way of compliance with regulation 13(4).

8. Information where consultation is not compulsory

Cable Realisations Ltd v GMB Northern[40] addressed the transferor's obligation under regula- **9.43**
tion 13 to provide information to appropriate representatives, in this case a recognized trade
union, even in the absence of measures being envisaged which would give rise to an obligation
of compulsory consultation under regulation 13(6). The ET had held that, in the particular
circumstances of the case, whilst to provide the requisite information on 15 August 2007 was
on the face of it sufficient time prior to a relevant transfer on 3 September 2007, there was
nonetheless a breach of regulation 13(2). The information was provided only two days before
a factory shutdown which entailed 99 per cent of staff being on holiday and 85 per cent
being away from home, including union site representatives and members (although not the
full-time official). Even though there was no breach of regulation 13(6) since on the facts
no duty to consult arose, there was very little time for meaningful consultation even though
any such consultation would have been voluntary. The ET held that the transferor was in a
position to provide the information required on 13 August 2007 and could have deferred
the transfer date. The ET awarded three weeks' pay per affected union member employee in
respect of the employer's breach of its obligation to provide the requisite information to the
appropriate representatives.

It had been argued that nothing in the Directive or otherwise extended the scope of regula- **9.44**
tion 13(2) to voluntary consultation and that therefore there was no breach of regulation 13
if no compulsory consultation was required and the requisite information was not provided.
The EAT rejected the suggestion that the reference in regulation 13(2) to consultation is only
to the compulsory consultation required pursuant to regulation 13(6) because measures are
envisaged and not to voluntary consultation which is not specifically required by that provision. The requisite information must be provided dven if there is no obligation to consult.

In reaching this decision the EAT had regard to the views expressed by Millett J in *Institution* **9.45**
of Professional Civil Servants v Secretary of State for Defence[41] when considering the fact
that TUPE obliges the employer to provide information about the various matters specified but only requires consultation about one of them—the measures envisaged. Millett
J had indicated his view that the reference to consultation referred to in the preamble to

---

[39] TUPE 1981, regulation 10(2)(d).
[40] UKEAT/0538/08.
[41] [1987] IRLR 373, Ch.

what is now regulation 13[42]—which requires the provision of the requisite information long enough before the transfer to allow for consultations—is to 'voluntary consultations which the unions may seek on any topic once they have their requisite information, but which the transferring employer is not compelled to grant if he chooses not to do so'.[43]

9.46 Whilst in *Cable Realisations* the EAT noted that the Directive gave no assistance either way on the issue, its view was consistent with that of Millett J in *Institution of Professional Civil Servants v Secretary of State for Defence*. Based on the industrial relations rationale behind TUPE, the EAT held that regulation 13(2) was designed to allow the representatives of the affected employees the opportunity to engage in a consultation process with the employer on an informal basis whether or not the employer is required to consult, an issue which is determined by the separate provision of regulation 13(6). The fact that consultation is not required by regulation 13(6) because in the particular circumstances no measures are envisaged does not negate the obligation to provide the requisite information under regulation 13(2).

9.47 HHJ Peter Clark summarized the issue and the answer to it as follows:

> 29. . . . The question . . . is whether 'consult' in Regulation 13(2) of the 2006 Regulations means consult as required by Regulation 13(6), no such requirement arising in the present case or can it refer equally to voluntary consultation, as Millett J though in IPCS?
>
> 30. In support of the former construction [Counsel] submits that since Regulation 13(6) only requires consultation concerning measures which the employer envisages he will take in relation to the affected employees (provided for in Regulation 13(2)(d)) the requirement to provide information under Regulation 13(2) is not dependent on the purpose of consultation. That is expressly provided for in respect of the information required under Regulation 13(2)(d) by Regulation 13(6).
>
> 31. Whilst we see the logic of that submission as a matter of pure construction we think and here this Tribunal enjoys the benefit of the vast practical experience of its industrial members, that it overlooks the industrial relations rationale behind TUPE and in turn the Directive. [Counsel] contends that the purpose behind the requirement to provide information under Regulation 13(2) is to put at rest the minds of affected employees as far as possible at a time of impending changes. We think that it goes further than that; it is designed to allow the representatives of those employees to engage in a consultation process with the employer on an informed basis. Whether the employer is obliged to engage in such a consultation exercise is dependent on Regulation 13(6).

D. Consultation

1. When consultation is required

9.48 Regulation 13(6) imposes an obligation on the employer of any employees affected by a relevant transfer to consult with appropriate representatives if it envisages that it will, in connection with the transfer, be taking measures in relation to any of the affected employees. Regulation 13(6) provides that '[a]n employer of any affected employees who envisages that he will take measures in relation to an affected employee, in connection with the relevant

---

[42] And was at the time regulation 10 of TUPE 1981.
[43] Ibid. at para. 13.

transfer, shall consult the appropriate representatives of that employee with a view to seeking their agreement to the intended measures'.

That the obligation to consult is framed by reference to the affected employees means, as **9.49** noted above,[44] that the collective consultation obligation under regulation 13 may, depending upon the circumstances, arise in respect of non-transferring employees of the transferor and the transferee's existing employees as well as those who do transfer. Those of the transferor's workforce whose roles and position may be affected by specific measures to be taken as a consequence of the transfer of the relevant undertaking, and those of the transferee's workforce in relation to whom measures are envisaged connected with or prompted by the transferring employees joining the transferee's operation, can therefore constitute affected employees for these purposes.

The trigger for consultation is therefore the employer envisaging taking measures. Only **9.50** measures to be taken 'in connection with the transfer' fall within the scope of this obligation. There therefore needs to be a causal connection or clear link between the measures being envisaged and the relevant transfer in question for these provisions to be engaged such that details of the measures envisaged must be provided to employee representatives under regulation 13(2) and consultation about them conducted pursuant to regulation 13(6). Measures entirely unconnected with the transfer do not trigger these obligations. So, for example, a relocation or changes to benefits not prompted by, connected to, or forming part of the process of a transfer may not trigger the obligation to provide information to and to conduct consultation with appropriate representatives. However, depending on the numbers involved and whether dismissals could potentially result, the collective redundancy consultation obligations of TULRCA 1992, s. 188 could nonetheless be triggered.

2. Whose obligation?

The obligation to inform and consult appropriate representatives pursuant to regulation **9.51** 13 is imposed on the employer of the affected employees. It is important, if measures are envisaged, to identify upon whom the obligation to consult is imposed. A transferor that is simply disposing of a business in circumstances where it is the transferee that proposes to take measures in relation to those employees whom it inherits will not envisage taking any measures while it is the employer of the affected employees.

Whilst the transferor has an obligation to deliver to the appropriate representatives the **9.52** requisite information about the measures which it envisages that the transferee will take pursuant to regulation 13(2)(d), it can therefore be argued that the transferor does not have a consultation obligation with regard to those (transferee's) measures—that obligation should, it is submitted, fall to the transferee. That said, in practical terms, pre-transfer consultation with regard to measures which the transferee wishes to implement (such as a change of location, redundancies, etc.) may well need to occur prior to transfer in order that the relevant measures can be implemented at the required point in time. Such consultation therefore, for human resources and industrial relations reasons, as well as to avoid breach of TUPE, may be conducted jointly by the transferor and the transferee.

---

[44] See para. 9.06 *et seq.*

3. Nature and timing of consultation

9.53 For these purposes, consultation is expressly required to be conducted 'with a view to seeking ... agreement'.[45] Regulation 13(7) makes clear the basis upon which this dialogue should be conducted. The employer is required 'in the course of those consultations' to:

- consider any representations made by the appropriate representatives;[46]
- reply to those representations;[47]
- if it rejects any of those representations, state its reasons for doing so.[48]

9.54 It can be important, substantively and evidentially, for employers to engage in and record the consultation conducted in order to reduce the scope for disputes either during the process itself or subsequently by a complaint of breach of regulation 13.

9.55 The inclusion in regulation 13 of this specific statutory formulation as to the meaning of consultation indicates the continued relevance in this particular context of the guidance as to the meaning of consultation in *R v British Coal Corporation and Secretary of State for Trade and Industry ex parte Price*:[49]

> fair consultation involves giving the body consulted a fair and proper opportunity to understand fully the matters about which it is being consulted and to express its views on those subjects with the consultor thereafter considering those views properly and genuinely.[50]

9.56 Nothing specific is said in regulation 13 about a minimum duration of consultation. As already noted, in contrast to the collective redundancy consultation regime prescribed by TULRCA 1992, s. 188, there are no prescribed minimum periods for TUPE consultation. The period of time for which consultation should be conducted will therefore need to be determined by reference to the complexity of the matter, the significance and seriousness of any measures envisaged by the transferor or transferee, the extent to which dialogue continues and is necessary with appropriate representatives, and good human resources practice in order to minimize the risk of it being argued that, by failing to engage in the process for long enough or in sufficient detail, the relevant employer has failed to consult as required 'with a view to seeking agreement'. If the TULRCA 1992 collective redundancy consultation obligations also arise because of a redundancy exercise relating to the TUPE transfer in question, those separate consultation obligations and their specific timing requirements will also need to be considered with additional consequences for the timing and detail of the consultation process.

9.57 In relation to the appropriate length of consultation for the purposes of regulation 13, it was argued in *Baxter v Marks and Spencer*[51] that a ninety-day period would have been appropriate, analogous with the period required in respect of collective redundancies affecting a similar number of employees. The EAT rejected this argument and held that:[52]

> [t]he Tribunal correctly stated that there is no judicial or statutory authority as to what is long enough. ... Whilst in some cases the 90 day period may be useful by way of analogy, it does

---

[45] Regulation 13(6).
[46] Regulation 13(7)(a).
[47] Regulation 13(7)(b).
[48] Ibid.
[49] [1994] IRLR 72, CA, a decision in an entirely different context but which is often cited as providing a useful description of what consultation means in the context of collective employment law generally.
[50] Ibid. at para. 25.
[51] UKEAT/162/05.
[52] Ibid. at para. 30.

not provide an answer as to whether there has been sufficient consultation.... what matters is not the time span but what happens in the time span.

In *Todd v Strain and others*[53] the EAT observed that 'part of the purpose of the duty to consult must surely be to enable transitional arrangements...to be explained to employees and for them to be reassured, if this be the case, that they will not in any way be prejudiced by them'.[54] This interpretation of the application of TUPE's collective information and consultation regime is presumably intended to avoid the 'needless worry', as the ET had put it,[55] which had been caused to the employees in *Todd*, many of whom were low paid, by the lack of communication as to the changes to be made to their pay arrangements.

9.58

4. Post-transfer consultation

In *Amicus v City Building (Glasgow) LLP*[56] the EAT held that the transferee is not required to conduct consultation under regulation 13(6) about the measures which it envisages taking in respect of the transferring employees once the transfer has taken place. That the obligation to consult over measures which are related to the transfer ceases on the date of transfer was seen as consistent not only with TUPE but also the Directive in light of the drafting of Article 7(3) which provides that the consultation which is required must take place before the change in the business is effected.

9.59

The EAT took the view that consultation about post-transfer measures could not have been intended to be required by the Directive, not least as contract changes by reason of the transfer are not possible, even by agreement.[57] This is perhaps an unduly robust view of Article 7(2) and TUPE—measures need not affect terms which are contractual[58] and regulations 4(4) and 4(5) do seek to legitimate transfer-related contract changes for which there is an ETOR. However, this authority does establish the position that post-transfer consultation is not required by regulation 13.[59] The analysis that post-transfer consultation is not required by regulation 13 was seen as consistent with the time limit provision of regulation 15(12) which provides for complaints of breach of the information and consultation provisions to be presented to the ET within three months of the relevant transfer. It was considered that, if the information and consultation obligation imposed by regulation 13 continued beyond the transfer, the three-month time limit running from the date of that transfer provided for by regulation 15(12) would not have been appropriate. To interpret the Directive and TUPE as requiring ongoing post-transfer consultation about transfer-related measures was also seen as unduly burdensome and potentially unworkable as an entirely open-ended and unreasonable burden.[60]

9.60

---

[53] [2011] IRLR 11, EAT.

[54] Ibid. at para. 20.

[55] Ibid. at para. 25.

[56] [2007] IRLR 253, EAT.

[57] Ibid. at paras 60–3.

[58] See *Todd v Strain and others*, above n. 25.

[59] Which, as the EAT noted, is consistent with all the previous European and practitioner commentaries on the Directive and TUPE.

[60] *Amicus v City Building (Glasgow) LLP*, above n. 56, at para. 64.

E. Representation of Employees

1. Appropriate representatives

9.61 The obligation imposed on the relevant employer by regulation 13, both with regard to the provision of information and the conduct of consultation concerning measures, is to deal with 'appropriate representatives'. Regulation 13(3) defines appropriate representatives as either:

- representatives of an independent trade union which is recognised by the employer in respect of the relevant employees;[61]

or in any other case at the employer's election:

- employee representatives appointed or elected by the affected employees otherwise than for the purposes of regulation 13, who (having regard to the purposes for and the method by which they were appointed or elected) have authority from those employees to receive information and to be consulted about the transfer on their behalf;[62] or
- employee representatives elected by any affected employees, for the purposes of regulation 13, in an election satisfying the requirements of regulation 14(1).[63]

9.62 In the absence of a recognized independent trade union, the employer can choose to deal with either representatives elected in accordance with the specific requirements set out in regulation 14[64] or representatives elected or appointed as representatives on another occasion but who nonetheless have authority to receive information and to be consulted about the transfer on behalf of the relevant employees.

9.63 If an independent trade union is recognized in respect of some or all of the employees affected by the relevant transfer, the employer is obliged to deal with that trade union in respect of the employees in respect of whom it is recognized. The employer cannot choose to disregard the recognized independent trade union and instead elect to deal with elected employee representatives.[65]

9.64 It is immaterial whether all the employees in respect of which the recognized trade union is recognized are or are not members of that trade union. What matters in establishing the obligation on the employer to deal with a trade union when complying with regulation 13 is the scope of that trade union's recognition. If the trade union is recognized in respect of a particular undertaking, it constitutes the appropriate representative for all employees within the scope of its recognition whether or not they are members. There is no duty to provide information to or to consult with a trade union which is not recognized.

9.65 For the purposes of regulation 13, a trade union representative is defined by regulation 2(2) as 'an official or other person authorised to carry on collective bargaining with that employer by that trade union'. A trade union representative for these purposes therefore need not be employed by the transferor nor a transferring employee and can be an external official.

---

[61] Regulation 13(3)(a).
[62] Regulation 13(3)(b)(i).
[63] Regulation 13(3)(b)(ii).
[64] See para. 9.70 *et seq.*
[65] The ability of the employer to elect to deal with employee representatives instead of a recognized trade union was removed from TUPE 1981 by the Collective Redundancies and Transfer of Undertakings (Protection of Employment) (Amendment) Regulations 1999 SI 1999/1925.

If there is no recognized independent trade union in respect of the affected employees or **9.66** there are affected employees or categories of affected employee in respect of which there is no independent recognized trade union, then 'employee representatives' of those employees must be dealt with by the employer which is subject to the regulation 13 consultation obligation. Even where the workforce is heavily unionized, the relevant union or unions may not, for example, have recognition in respect of management. In that eventuality appropriate employee representatives will need to be dealt with on behalf of that category of staff in order to ensure compliance with the requirements of regulation 13.

In the absence of a recognized trade union, appropriate representatives of the affected **9.67** employees will either be specifically elected in accordance with regulation 14 or be existing representatives with appropriate authority. A standing committee of employee representatives or consultative forum will only suffice as a body of employee representatives for the purposes of regulation 13 if, 'having regard to the purposes for and the method by which they were appointed or elected',[66] they have the authority from those employees to receive information and to be consulted about the transfer. In order to constitute appropriate representatives with whom an employer can deal in order to comply with the obligations imposed by regulation 13, an employee consultative forum therefore needs not only to have been constituted by an election or nomination process which gives it representative legitimacy but also for its terms of reference clearly to encompass receipt of information about and consultation in relation to TUPE transfers.

Given these fact-sensitive requirements, care needs to be taken in this regard if an existing **9.68** employee representative body or members of it are to be utilized for the purposes of the information and consultation required by regulation 13. That regulation 15(3) places the burden of proof—to establish that an employee representative or representatives satisfy the relevant requirements—on the employer reinforces the need for care in this regard.

Regulation 13(8) requires the employer to provide the appropriate representatives with 'such **9.69** accommodation and other facilities as may be appropriate'. Office, typing, and meeting facilities may therefore need to be provided. The ACAS Code of Practice on Time Off for Trade Union Duties and Activities refers to facilities which may be appropriate for trade union representatives and which could by analogy be relevant for appropriate representatives.[67]

2. Electing employee representatives

Regulation 14 sets out the requirements for the election of employee representatives with **9.70** whom the employer can deal in order to satisfy its obligations under regulation 13 in the absence of a recognized trade union or of existing employee representatives who satisfy the requirements of regulation 13(3)(b)(i). Only if these requirements are complied with do such elected employee representatives qualify as appropriate representatives for the purposes of compliance with regulation 13.

---

[66] Regulation 13(3)(b)(i).

[67] Para. 46 of the ACAS Code on time off for trade union duties and activities—see n.109—indicates that, 'where resources permit', facilities should include matters such as use of notice boards, email, and intranet/internet facilities, accommodation for meetings, confidential space for meetings to discuss disciplinary, grievance, and other confidential matters, access to members who work at a different location and access to e-learning tools where computer facilities are available.

9.71 The prescribed election requirements pursuant to regulation 14 are that:

- the employer shall make such arrangements as are reasonably practicable to ensure that the election is fair;[68]
- the employer shall determine the number of representatives to be elected so that there are sufficient representatives to represent the interests of all affected employees having regard to the number and classes of those employees;[69]
- the employer shall determine whether the affected employees should be represented either by representatives of all the affected employees or by representatives of particular classes of those employees;[70]
- before the election the employer shall determine the term of office as employee representatives so that it is of sufficient length to enable information to be given and consultation under regulation 13 to be completed;[71]
- the candidates for election as employee representatives are affected employees on the date of the election;[72]
- no affected employee is unreasonably excluded from standing for election;[73]
- all affected employees on the date of the election shall be entitled to vote for employee representatives;[74]
- the employees entitled to vote shall be entitled to vote for as many candidates as there are representatives to be elected to represent them or, if there are to be representatives for particular classes of employee, may vote for as many candidates as there are representatives to be elected to represent their particular class of employee;[75]
- the election shall be conducted so as to secure, so far as reasonably practicable, that those voting do so in secret[76] and that the votes at the election are accurately counted.[77]

9.72 If one of the representatives elected in accordance with regulation 14 ceases so to act, then the employees should be asked to elect a replacement essentially in the same manner.[78]

9.73 If the employer needs to elect employee representatives for the purposes of compliance with the required information and consultation process, then, in timing terms, the employer will comply with regulation 13 if it provides the prescribed information as soon as is reasonably practicable after the election of the representatives (provided that the employer has invited the affected employees to elect employee representatives and that information was issued long enough before the time for provision of information to allow for an election).[79] Careful thought therefore needs to be given to the time required to be committed to the election process in order to ensure that the representatives are in place long enough before the transfer for the information to be provided and for adequate consultation, where relevant, to be conducted.

---

[68] Regulation 14(1)(a).
[69] Regulation 14(1)(b).
[70] Regulation 14(1)(c).
[71] Regulation 14(1)(d).
[72] Regulation 14(1)(e).
[73] Regulation 14(1)(f).
[74] Regulation 14(1)(g).
[75] Regulation 14(1)(h).
[76] Regulation 14(1)(i)(ii).
[77] Regulation 14(1)(i)(i) and (ii).
[78] Regulation 14(2). The requirements of regulation 14(1)(b), (c), (d), (g), and (h) do not apply in relation to an election for a replacement employee representative.
[79] Regulation 13(10).

If there is no recognized independent trade union in respect of relevant affected employees, **9.74** and the employer seeks to arrange an election for employee representatives, but the employees fail to elect representatives within a reasonable time, then the employer can comply with its information provision obligation by providing the relevant information directly to each affected employee. Regulation 13(11) provides that '[i]f, after the employer has invited any affected employees to elect appropriate representatives, they fail to do so within a reasonable time, he shall give to any affected employees the information set out in [regulation 13](2)'.[80] In *Howard v Millrise Ltd (1) SG Printers (2)*[81] it was confirmed that the employer does have an obligation to initiate an election for representatives and, if an election process fails to produce employee representatives, the employer is entitled to inform and consult with employees directly.

3. Protection of employee representatives

(a) Introduction

Employee representatives for the purposes of the information and consultation obligations **9.75** of regulation 13 are afforded specific statutory protections designed to enable employees to become involved in the collective information and consultation aspects of transfers of undertakings without fear or favour.[82] These protections are similar to the protections afforded to trade union representatives in the performance of their duties.

(b) Detriment

ERA 1996, s. 47(1) provides protection for employees from being subjected by their employer **9.76** to a 'detriment' as a result of any functions or activities which they perform (or propose to perform) as employee representatives. The right is 'not to be subjected to any detriment by any act, or any deliberate failure to act'.

The same protection is afforded to candidates standing for election as employee representa- **9.77** tives. ERA 1996, s. 47(1A) provides protection to employees who participate in the election of employee representatives (for example, by casting their vote in the election). ERA 1996, s. 47(1A) differs slightly from ERA 1996, s. 47(1), however, in that there is no protection against proposed participation. This could technically prevent an employee from seeking redress where he or she suffered a detriment as a result of his or her proposed (as opposed to actual) participation in an election for employee representatives. It is generally considered[83] that a purposive construction should be applied to the interpretation of this provision and that participation should be widely construed to include proposed participation. The term

---

[80] This provision derives from Article 7.6 which provides that:
Member States shall provide that, where there are no representatives of the employees in an undertaking or business through no fault of their own, the employees concerned must be informed in advance of:
- the date or proposed date of the transfer,
- the reason for the transfer,
- the legal, economic and social implications of the transfer for the employees,
- any measures envisaged in relation to the employees.

[81] UKEAT/0658/04.

[82] See the comments of Otton J in *R v Secretary of State for Trade and Industry ex parte Unison* [1996] IRLR 439 where he indicated at para. 40 that representatives must be 'independent of and not beholden to the employer'.

[83] See *Harvey on Industrial Relations and Employment Law*, Division DII, Victimisation, para. 336.

'detriment' is not given a statutory definition although it clearly means prejudicial treatment short of actual dismissal and has been held to mean 'putting under a disadvantage'.[84]

9.78 A detriment can therefore arise by way of failure to promote or offer training facilities or other unfavourable treatment. In order to attract the statutory protection applicable in this context, the detrimental act or omission must be taken on the ground of the employee's activities as an actual or potential employee representative. This factual issue therefore needs to be addressed by reference to the employer's reason for action. It is not strictly necessary to show an intention to penalize an employee for becoming involved in the representative process.

9.79 The compensation to be awarded by the ET (which hears complaints in this regard) in relation to an employee being subjected to such a detriment (in addition to a declaration to that effect)[85] is based upon what is just and equitable in all the circumstances, taking into account the nature of the infringement and any loss suffered by the employee.[86] In determining compensation the ET is entitled to take into account whether or not the employee has mitigated his or her loss[87] and the extent to which the employee contributed to the events giving rise to the complaint of detriment.[88] The loss for which compensation is to be awarded can cover expenses incurred as a result of the relevant act or omission and the loss of any benefit otherwise reasonably expected.[89]

9.80 Where the detriment in question amounts to dismissal, the provisions of ERA 1996, s. 47 do not apply.[90] The separate protection against dismissal must then be considered.

(c) Dismissal

9.81 Where an employee has been dismissed by virtue of involvement in the employee representative process, protection is provided by way of a claim for unfair dismissal. ERA 1996, s. 103 provides that where an employee has been dismissed (including, for these purposes, selected for redundancy) due to any functions or activities which he performed (or proposed to perform) as an employee representative or candidate, that dismissal will be automatically unfair. If the employee is dismissed as a result of his or her involvement in the election of employee representatives, this too will constitute an automatically unfair dismissal pursuant to ERA 1996, s. 105.

9.82 The normal qualifying period of service required for an employee to be eligible to claim unfair dismissal[91] does not apply in these circumstances.[92] Similarly, the exclusion of unfair dismissal claims in relation to dismissals connected with industrial action does not apply in such circumstances.[93]

---

[84] *Ministry of Defence v Jeremiah* [1979] IRLR 436, CA at para. 637.

[85] ERA 1996, s. 49(1)(a).

[86] ERA 1996, s. 49(1)(b), (2).

[87] ERA 1996, s. 49(4).

[88] ERA 1996, s. 49(5).

[89] ERA 1996, s. 49(3)(a), (b).

[90] ERA 1996, s. 47(2).

[91] Which, in relation to those employees whose continuous employment begins on or after 6 April 2012, is two years pursuant to the Unfair Dismissal and Statement of Reasons for Dismissal (Variation of Qualifying Period) Order 2012 SI 2012/989 and, in respect of those whose continuous employment began before 6 April 2012, is one year pursuant to the Unfair Dismissal and Statement of Reasons for Dismissal (Variation of Qualifying Period) Order 1999 SI 1999/1436.

[92] ERA 1996, s. 108(3)(f).

[93] TULRCA 1992, ss 237(1A), 238(2A).

In order to seek to preserve his or her position, an employee dismissed in these circumstances **9.83** can seek interim relief (pursuant to which the ET may order continuation of the employment contract).[94] Whilst the compensatory award for unfair dismissal is assessed on the usual basis, the unfair dismissal basic award in these circumstances will be a minimum of £5,300.[95]

Protection is also provided to trade union representatives against action short of dismissal or **9.84** dismissal related to their trade union activities.[96]

(d) Time off

ERA 1996, s. 61 provides an employee representative with the right to be permitted by his **9.85** or her employer to take reasonable time off during working hours in order to perform his or her functions as a candidate for election as or as an employee representative or in order to undergo training to perform such functions.[97] There is no statutory obligation on an employer to train employee representatives in relation to what can be quite complex issues. This time off is paid.[98] Complaints of unreasonable refusal of time off or failure to make the required payments in respect of such time off to an employee are made to the ET.[99]

A complaint of breach is to be presented to the ET[100] within three months from the relevant **9.86** event or, if not reasonably practicable, as soon as possible.[101] If an employee succeeds in a complaint then the ET effectively must make a declaration to that effect,[102] can order payment to the employee in respect of any time off where the employer has breached its payment obligations[103] and can, in cases where time off has been unreasonably refused, order payment of the amount which would have been payable had the time off been taken.[104]

TULRCA 1992, s. 168 provides that an employee who is an official of a recognized trade **9.87** union has the right to paid time off during working hours for the purpose of carrying out his or her duties as such an official concerned with the provision of information and the consultation required under TUPE 2006.[105] Detailed provisions[106] address the employee's entitlement to pay in respect of such time off. Time off is also required to be permitted for relevant training approved by the Trades Union Congress or relevant trade union.[107]

---

[94] ERA 1996, s. 120. But see *Dowling v ME Ilic Haulage and anor* [2004] ICR 1176, EAT, discussed further at Chapter 4, para. 4.67, in which Burton J held that the making of a continuation order by an ET does not render the employee assigned to the relevant undertaking for the purposes of regulation 4.

[95] Pursuant to Employment Rights (Increase of Limits) Order 2011 SI 2011/3006.

[96] TULRCA 1992, ss 146, 152. No period of qualifying service is required for an unfair dismissal claim on these grounds pursuant to TULRCA 1992, s. 154.

[97] ERA 1996, s. 61(1).

[98] ERA 1996, s. 61(2) sets out the detailed provisions establishing the appropriate hourly rate payable to an employee who exercises his or her right to paid time off in those circumstances. The right is only to be paid in respect of hours required to be worked under the employee's contract. Time spent on representative duties outside the employee's contracted hours do not attract the right to be paid—see *Hairsine v Kingston upon Hull C.C.* [1992] ICR 212, EAT.

[99] ERA 1996, s. 63.

[100] As to permitting time off to be taken or payment in respect of such time off—ERA 1996, s. 63(1)(a) and (b).

[101] ERA 1996, s. 63(2)(a) and (b).

[102] ERA 1996, s. 63(3).

[103] ERA 1996, s. 63(5).

[104] ERA 1996, s. 63(4).

[105] TULRCA 1992, s. 168(1)(c).

[106] TULRCA 1992, s. 169.

[107] TULRCA 1992, s 168(2).

9.88 The amount of time which can be taken off and the appropriate occasions for time to be taken off must be reasonable having regard to any relevant ACAS Code.[108] Presumably ACAS guidance in respect of trade union representatives will be relevant by analogy in relation to employee representatives.[109] Factors to be taken into account in determining whether proposed time off is reasonable include potentially the amount of time already taken off, the size of the organization, the number of workers, the need to maintain safety and security, and the nature (if applicable) of the employer's production process.[110] Employers are also encouraged to consider the issues which arise in the context of ensuring proper representation as a result of factors such as shift and part-time working.[111]

F. Remedies for Breach

1. Complaints

(a) Who can complain and on whose behalf?

9.89 Failure to inform or consult as required by regulation 13 can lead to a complaint to the ET pursuant to regulation 15.[112] Complaints can only be brought before the ET (and by way of appeal the EAT) by virtue of regulation 16(1) and regulation 16(2).

9.90 Regulation 15 identifies which persons can bring a complaint in respect of what nature of default. With regard to other breaches of regulation 13, a complaint may be brought:

- by any of the affected employees employed by him if the failure relates to the election of employee representatives[113] (for example, a failure to comply with the election requirements of regulation 14);
- by the employee representatives to whom the failure related in relation to any other failure relating to them[114] (such as timely provision of information to or failure properly to consult with the elected representatives);
- by a trade union if the failure relates to trade union representatives[115] (such as failure to provide adequate or timely information to them or to consult with them where required);
- by any of the affected employees employed by the employer in any other case[116] (such as a complete failure to comply with the TUPE information and consultation regime).

9.91 In terms of standing to bring a complaint of breach of regulation 13, the principle established in relation to the collective redundancy information and consultation obligations of TULRCA 1992 by *Northgate HR Ltd v Mercy*[117] applies equally to TUPE. In *Mercy*, the

---

[108] TULRCA 1992, s. 168(3).

[109] See ACAS Code of Practice 3: Time off for trade union duties and activities (2010), brought into force by the Employment Protection Code of Practice (Time Off for Trade Union Duties and Activities) Order 2009 SI 2009/3223.

[110] Ibid. paras 25 and 32.

[111] Ibid. para. 26.

[112] Pursuant to regulation 16(1) ERA 1996, s. 205(1) and Employment Tribunals Act 1996, s. 18 render a complaint to the ET the sole route by which compensation can be obtained under regulation 15. Pursuant to regulation 16(2), appeals are to the EAT (on questions of law only).

[113] Regulation 15(1)(a).

[114] Regulation 15(1)(b).

[115] Regulation 15(1)(c).

[116] Regulation 15(1)(d).

[117] [2008] IRLR 222, CA.

Court of Appeal upheld the view of the EAT that TULRCA 1992, s. 189(1) limits the ability to bring complaints of inadequate provision of information to or consultation with appropriate representatives to those representatives. A purposive interpretation, allowing an individual employee to complain about an employer's inadequate dealings with the appropriate representatives actually in place, was rejected—TULRCA 1992, s. 189(1) was viewed as a 'carefully devised provision defining and restricting standing to bring a complaint' and a statutory provision which 'deals with the complaint as a collective rather than an individual matter and limits standing, no doubt so as to prevent the possibility of numerous individual challenges which are not supported by appropriate representatives'.[118] Given the structure adopted for the bringing of complaints there was seen to be 'no protection gap in the legislation which results from according the statutory language its obvious and natural meaning'.[119]

This analysis was approved in relation to regulation 13 in *Nationwide Building Society v Benn and others*[120] where Slade J said that 'the principle relied upon in *Mercy* is equally applicable to the right to bring a claim for breach of the information and consultation provisions of TUPE'. **9.92**

The EAT decision in *Independent Insurance Company Ltd v Aspinall*[121] considered, albeit in the context of a complaint of breach of TULRCA 1992, s. 188, the extent to which the ET is entitled to award compensation for breach of collective information and consultation requirements where such a claim is brought by an individual claimant as distinct from a trade union or elected employee representative. Since the wording of regulation 15 with regard to complaints of breach of regulation 13 mirrors the corresponding provisions of TULRCA 1992,[122] it is to be assumed that the approach adopted in *Independent Insurance* applies equally to complaints in relation to regulation 15. **9.93**

The EAT held that, in such proceedings, the ET can only make an award in respect of the individual claimant and cannot make an award in respect of other employees whereas trade union or employee representatives can obtain protective awards only for those whom they represent in the relevant litigation. The EAT[123] approved the analysis of the Editors of *Harvey* which was as follows:[124] **9.94**

> TULRCA 1992 says that a protective award is 'an award in respect of … employees … in respect of whose dismissal or proposed dismissal the employer has failed to comply with a requirement of section 188' (section 189(3)). On a purely literal construction, that provision might be read as giving *any* claimant the right to seek a protective award covering *every* employee in respect of whom the employer has failed to consult. But that is not so. The provision must be read in its context: a personal claimant may obtain a protective award for himself; a representative claimant may obtain a protective award for those whom he represents in the litigation. So, in the typical case, a trade union may obtain a protective award for all the employees in its bargaining unit (whether they are members of the union or not). But the award it obtains may not be stretched to cover those outside its bargaining unit, whether the outsiders are members

---

[118] Ibid. at para. 15.
[119] Ibid.
[120] [2010] IRLR 922, EAT at para. 60.
[121] [2011] IRLR 716, EAT.
[122] TULRCA 1992, s. 189(1).
[123] *Independent Insurance*, above n. 121, at paras 35 and 36. Reference was also made by the EAT to *Transport & General Workers Union v Brauer Coley* [2007] ICR 226, EAT.
[124] *Harvey on Industrial Relations and Employment Law* at para. 2757.

of the union or not, and whether the outsiders are represented by some other person or union or not. It is a case of each to his own.

9.95 As the EAT put it:

> We note the descriptions of the constituencies of the trade union and the employee representatives to which we have referred. It would be an amazing sea change in the legislation if a right of an individual gave that individual greater representative status than the trade union or elected representatives so that he could effectively make a claim for all persons affected by the redundancy in a wider pool than the constituency without any debate.[125]

9.96 Moreover, if a trade union cannot make a claim in respect to those who are not represented in a particular workplace but are similarly affected, the EAT could not see how it could be right that an individual could, without notice, bring claims on behalf of other claimants in respect of whom he owes no duties and has no authority to act. Any other finding could lead to potentially absurd results where, for example, an individual claimant might be able to bring successful proceedings which would benefit other employees whose claims had been dismissed, struck out, or not even brought.

(b) Burden of proof

9.97 Whilst the burden of proof generally rests with the complainant to show failure to comply with the requirements of regulation 13, the burden of proof is nonetheless specifically placed on the employer in relation to certain specific issues.

9.98 First, where a question arises as to whether or not it was reasonably practicable for an employer to perform a particular duty or what steps it took towards performing it, it is for the employer to show special circumstances which rendered it not reasonably practicable for it to perform the duty[126] and that it took all such steps towards its performance as were reasonably practicable in those circumstances.[127]

9.99 Second, where a question arises as to whether or not an employee representative constituted an appropriate representative for the purposes of regulation 13, it is for the employer to show that the employee representative had the necessary authority to represent the affected employees.[128] This will be particularly relevant where the employer seeks to deal with an existing staff representative body.

9.100 Third, if there is a complaint with regard to the election of employee representatives (i.e. that the election of employee representatives was in some way defective), then it is for the employer to demonstrate that the applicable requirements have been satisfied.[129]

(c) Transferee's breach

9.101 A transferor may breach its information provision obligations under regulation 13 if it is unaware prior to the transfer of the measures which the transferee envisages taking and therefore fails to comply with its obligation to notify the relevant representatives of those measures which it envisages that the transferee will take. If the transferor fails to comply with its information provision obligations because the transferee does not provide it with the

---

[125] *Independent Insurance*, above n. 121, at para. 49.
[126] Regulation 15(2)(a).
[127] Regulation 15(2)(b).
[128] Regulation 15(3).
[129] Regulation 15(4).

requisite information with regard to its envisaged measures in advance of the transfer,[130] then the transferor may put forward a defence that it was not reasonably practicable for it to perform the duty in question by reason of that failure on the part of the transferee.[131] However, this argument cannot be put forward unless the transferor gives the transferee notice of its intention to show that fact and thereby joins the transferee as a party to the proceedings.[132] Where a complaint is made out in such circumstances, the ET is required to make a declaration to that effect and may order the transferee to pay appropriate compensation 'to such descriptions of affected employees as may be specified in the award'.[133]

(d) Timing of complaint

9.102 A complaint of breach of the information and consultation obligations imposed by regulation 13 must be presented to the ET within three months of the date of the relevant transfer[134] or, in the case of an attempt to enforce against the transferee an order made against the transferor on the basis of joint and several liability, three months from the date of the relevant order.[135] The ET is entitled to permit late lodging of a complaint within such further period as the ET considers reasonable in a case where it is satisfied that it was not reasonably practicable for the complaint to be presented before the end of the three-month period.[136]

9.103 A claim of breach of regulation 13 can be presented to the ET before the transfer has actually concluded. As Mummery J put it in *South Durham Health Authority v UNISON*[137] in relation to the corresponding provisions of TUPE 1981:

> Read in its ordinary and natural meaning, the regulation only specifies an *end date* for the presentation of a complaint to the tribunal, ie before the end of the period of three months beginning with the date on which the transfer is completed.... The regulation does not in terms specify a *start date* or prohibit an industrial tribunal from considering a complaint presented to the tribunal before any particular date. In other words, it is a limitation provision which prohibits the [employment] tribunal from considering complaints presented *after* a certain date. It is not a provision concerned with the accrual of a cause of action necessary to entitle a person to present a complaint to a tribunal.[138]

2. Compensation

9.104 If a breach of regulation 13 is established the ET is obliged to make a declaration to that effect and award compensation to the affected employees against the transferor[139]—subject to the defence available to the transferor in respect of a breach by the transferee breach of regulation 13(4)[140]—or the transferee[141] as the case may be.

9.105 Pursuant to regulation 16(3) the 'appropriate compensation' to be paid in relation to failure to comply with the information and consultation obligations imposed by regulation 13 is

---

[130] As required by regulation 13(4).
[131] Regulation 15(5).
[132] Ibid.
[133] Regulation 15(8)(b).
[134] Regulation 15(12)(a).
[135] Regulation 15(12)(b).
[136] Regulation 15(12).
[137] [1995] IRLR 407, EAT.
[138] Ibid. at para. 13.
[139] Regulation 15(8)(a).
[140] See para. 9.40 *et seq.*
[141] Regulation 15(7).

'such sum not exceeding thirteen weeks' pay for the employee in question as the tribunal considers just and equitable having regard to the seriousness of the failure of the employer to comply with his duty'. This is payable in respect of 'such descriptions of affected employees as may be specified in the award'.[142] In the light of the width of the definition of an affected employee, it can be appreciated that these liabilities can, depending upon the circumstances, be significant. The tax treatment of an award made pursuant to regulation 15 is not addressed explicitly in the tax legislation, TUPE or any case law. As it does not arise from employment or its termination *per se* such an award can be argued neither to constitute (income taxable) earnings pursuant to the Income Tax (Earnings and Pensions) Act 2003 nor a termination payment exempt from income tax but only to the extent of £30,000 pursuant to s. 401 of that Act. It is therefore thought that such an award should be calculated and awarded by the ET on a gross basis.

9.106 A week's pay is calculated by reference to the following dates:[143]

- if an employee is dismissed by reason of redundancy,[144] then a week's pay for the purposes of compensation for failure to comply with the TUPE information and consultation regime is calculated by reference to the date by reference to which the statutory redundancy payment is calculated or would have been calculated had the employee been entitled to a redundancy payment;[145]
- if the employee is dismissed for any other reason,[146] the effective date of termination of the employment;[147]
- in any other case, the date of the relevant transfer.[148]

9.107 A week's pay is calculated in accordance with the provisions of ERA 1996[149] but is not subject to the statutory cap (of, at the time of writing, £430[150]) which applies in respect of certain other statutory entitlements such as the weekly wage taken into account when calculating the statutory redundancy payment. In *Zaman and others v Kozee Sleep Products Ltd t/a Dorlux Beds UK*[151] it was clarified that the cap on 'a week's pay' for the purposes of ERA 1996, s. 227 does not apply to awards of compensation under regulation 15 in respect of breaches of regulation 13. As Underhill P put it:

> the structure of section 227(1) is that it identifies specifically each kind of award or payment which the cap applies. It does not apply to every kind of payment under the Act defined by reference to a week's pay. If the intention had been to apply the cap to a payment under regulation 15 it seems to us that it would have been necessary either to amend section 227 to include a specific reference to such payments or to make an express provision in TUPE itself to the application of the cap.[152]

---

[142] Ibid.

[143] Regulation 16(4).

[144] Within the meaning of ERA 1996, ss 139 and 155.

[145] Regulation 16(4)(a).

[146] Regulation 16(4)(b).

[147] As determined in accordance with ERA 1996, ss 95(1) and (2), 97.

[148] Regulation 16(4)(c).

[149] ERA 1996, ss 220–8 per regulation 16(4).

[150] Employment Rights (Increase of Limits) Order 2011 SI 2011/3006, increasing to £450 per week with effect from 1 February 2013 pursuant to the Employment Rights (Increase of Limits) Order 2012 SI 2012/3007.

[151] [2011] IRLR 196, EAT.

[152] Ibid. at para. 10.

Sweetin v Coral Racing[153] confirmed that the approach to be adopted in assessing compensa-   **9.108**
tion for breach of regulation 13 is the same as that to be applied in respect of the collective
redundancy consultation regime under TULRCA 1992. Whilst in that case the respondent
submitted that the circumstances of a failure to comply with the information and consultation obligations imposed by TUPE would not necessarily fall to be regarded in as serious
a light as in the case of failure to conduct collective redundancy consultation, the EAT
disagreed.

In the view of the EAT, the respective drafting of TUPE 1981, regulation 11[154] and of   **9.109**
TULRCA 1992, s. 188 reflect each other and both underline the importance of compliance
with the duty to consult. Although it was accepted that the consequences of redundancy
(loss of employment) could be more serious than of failure to consult in relation to a TUPE
transfer (where employment should in principle be preserved), the imposition of a consultation requirement by the Directive and the use of the same terminology in both statutes
displaced the possibility of an inference that the approach to compensation should be any
different. Both TUPE and TULRCA 1992 focus on the nature and extent of the employer's
default, and accordingly it was clear that both awards were 'penal in nature, rather than solely
compensatory'.[155]

The ET's decision in *Sweetin* was therefore flawed as it had focused on what amounted to   **9.110**
'appropriate compensation' rather than recognized the need to focus on the punitive and
deterrent nature of the award and any mitigating factors.

Accordingly, the approach to be adopted in determining compensation for breach of regula-   **9.111**
tion 13 is that applying to breaches of TULRCA 1992. The relevant principles were set out
by Peter Gibson LJ in *Susie Radin v GMB and others*[156] as follows:

- the purpose of the award is to provide a sanction for breach not to compensate employees
  for consequential loss;
- the ET has a wide discretion as to what is just and equitable;
- the employer's default may vary from the technical to a complete failure to inform and
  consult;
- the deliberateness of the failure and any advice taken may be relevant;
- the proper approach is to start with the maximum award and reduce the award only where
  mitigating circumstances are judged appropriate to justify a reduction.

Arguments to the effect that consultation would have been futile are viewed as irrelevant as   **9.112**
Longmore LJ confirmed in *Susie Radin*:

> It may at first sight seem surprising to say that the fact that consultation would have been futile
> is something which an employment tribunal should not take into account when assessing the
> length of time for which a protective award should be made. But the argument that took place
> has convinced me (1) that there is nothing in the statutory wording which requires such futil-
> ity to be taken into account and (2) that in a collective claim brought by a union it would be
> impossible to take such futility into account in a fair and practical way.[157]

---

153 [2006] IRLR 252, EAT.
154 Now regulation 15.
155 *Sweetin*, above n. 153, at para. 30.
156 [2004] ICR 893, CA. See also *Smith and anor v Cherry Lewis Ltd* [2005] IRLR 86, EAT.
157 *Susie Radin*, n. 156 at para. 49.

9.113   *Transport and General Workers Union v Morgan Platts Ltd (in administration)*[158] also indicates the penal nature of such awards. Again in the context of collective redundancy consultation, the EAT indicated that the maximum ninety-day period should be the starting point in calculating an award in respect of breach. The ET should then consider whether it can be argued that a lesser award should be made. In this particular case, the employer's failures had been serious in that there was no consultation at all and there was accordingly no justification for an award lower than the maximum penalty.

9.114   The ET nonetheless has a wide discretion to do what is just and equitable as the EAT confirmed in *Amicus v GBS Tooling Ltd (in administration)*.[159] An appeal was rejected against the ET's decision in determining a protective award to take into account, by way of mitigating circumstances, steps which had been taken to keep the relevant trade union informed of developments. These steps indicated that the employer had not deliberately, recklessly, or negligently failed to comply with its obligations. The ET had not erred in awarding a protective award of a period of seventy days (as opposed to the maximum permissible period of ninety days). Mitigating factors, in terms of previous informal discussions with the trade union, pre-dating the decision which triggered the consultation obligation, could properly be taken into account in determining the appropriate penalty.

9.115   In *Todd v Strain and others*,[160] the EAT reduced the ET's award for breach of regulation 13 from the maximum of thirteen weeks' pay per employee to seven weeks' pay per employee on the basis that the failure was not at the most 'extreme end of the scale, so as to justify a maximum award'.[161] The EAT specifically contrasted the employer's conduct in *Sweetin* where there had been no information or consultation at all—the first that the employees knew about the transfer was when the representative of the new owners announced himself at the premises on the day that it took place—with that in *Todd*. Whilst in *Todd* the process followed and information given was inadequate and therefore the breach more than merely technical, the employer had at least held a meeting with a significant proportion of the workforce, had given some basic information out, and had made clear that the transferee would not be reducing staff numbers or changing terms and conditions.

9.116   In reinforcing the ET's discretion as to the appropriate level of an award under regulation 16—and the need not to apply the approach adopted in *Sweetin* and *Susie Radin* 'mechanically'[162]—*Todd* therefore highlights the potential relevance and importance of two particular issues—the nature of the subject matter of the requisite consultation and the extent of any attempts at consultation. The EAT's view of the appropriate level of award was influenced by the fact that the matters about which there should have been consultation—transitional pay arrangements—whilst not so trivial as not to constitute measures were nonetheless 'not of any great significance'.[163] The EAT also placed a potentially important qualification on the starting point for consideration of an award in case of breach being the maximum award with discounting if applicable for mitigating circumstances. In the EAT's view, this aspect of the *Susie Radin* guidance was 'directed at the case where the employer has done nothing at all,

---

[158] UKEAT/0646/02.
[159] [2005] IRLR 683, EAT.
[160] [2011] IRLR 11, EAT.
[161] Ibid. at para. 28.
[162] Ibid. at para. 29.
[163] Ibid. at para. 28.

and it should not be applied mechanically in a case where there has been some information given and/or some consultation but without using the statutory procedure'.[164]

Peter Gibson LJ made clear in *Susie Radin* that the ET has a wide discretion in determining **9.117** the relevant awards as to what is just and equitable, that the employer's default may vary from a technical to a complete failure to inform and consult, and that the deliberateness of the failure and any advice taken may be relevant. To that extent, therefore, *Todd* is a valuable reminder that the *Susie Radin* guidance is more nuanced than establishing in every case a presumption, albeit rebuttable, of a maximum award in cases of breach of TUPE's information and consultation obligations.

As a reminder of the breadth of the tribunal's discretion, the *Todd* decision indicates that a **9.118** maximum award is not automatic and that such efforts at information and consultation as may have been attempted, even if inadequate, are relevant to the level of any award, as is the substantive significance of the matters about which there should have been consultation. An example of a similar approach to that adopted in *Todd*, albeit in the context of collective redundancy consultation, is *National Coal Mining v NUM*,[165] where the EAT held that ordinarily the ET should award less than a maximum protective award where the employer undertakes 'more than minimal' consultation.

3. Joint and several liability

Regulation 15(9) renders the transferee jointly and severally liable with the transferor in **9.119** respect of certain awards of compensation in respect of breach of the information and consultation obligations imposed by regulation 13. Regulation 15(9) identifies the compensation for which liability is joint and several as that payable under regulation 15(8)(a)—an order against the transferor for breach of its regulation 13 obligations—and regulation 15(11)—an order to pay compensation which has previously been ordered to be paid by the transferor or transferee but which has not been satisfied.

As the 2005 Consultation noted,[166] there had been conflicting case law as to whether liability **9.120** for failure to comply with the information and consultation obligations could be inherited by the transferee. The argument that the transferee should inherit liability for the transferor's failure to comply with its information and consultation obligations was that the obligations in question and the associated financial penalties for breach relate to transferring employees' employment and therefore should be inherited by the transferee on the same basis that it inherits other pre-transfer obligations and liabilities.

The counter-argument was that to pass the liability for breach of TUPE's information and **9.121** consultation obligations to the transferee would not only be unfair on a transferee (which would often have no control over the transferor's conduct) but would also remove any incentive on the transferor to comply with the obligations imposed upon it. On this analysis, these liabilities should be an exception to the rule that employment liabilities generally transfer to the transferee on a relevant transfer.

To make the transferor and transferee jointly and severally liable for the compensation pay- **9.122** able for breach of the regulation 13 information and consultation obligations is permitted by

---

[164] Ibid. at para. 29.
[165] UKEAT/0397/06.
[166] 2005 Consultation paras 83–5.

Article 3.1 and was perceived as enabling employee representatives to choose whether to take action against either or both of the relevant parties in order to enforce awards made in respect of breaches of the obligations imposed by regulation 13.[167] The Government acknowledged that, in making a choice as to who to sue, the employee representatives would be strongly influenced by the relative ability to pay of transferor and transferee. Joint and several liability therefore makes it more likely (particularly in insolvency situations) that employees and their representatives will be able to find respondents against whom they can bring claims which can economically be enforced.

9.123 However, where the transferor is insolvent and the transferee has been unable to insist on compliance by the transferor with its obligations or to secure protection against the consequent compensation exposure by way of a worthwhile indemnity or retention, joint and several liability in this context leaves the transferee in practice liable for potentially significant compensation awards. In order to facilitate recovery by the affected employees or representatives of the compensation due for breach of regulation 13, the risk is allocated to the transferee in respect of breach of obligations over compliance with which it may have no control or influence.

9.124 This provision reinforces the need (where possible) for transferees to obtain adequate warranty and indemnity protection in respect of those information and consultation obligations for which it is not directly responsible. Likewise, the transferor may wish to seek reciprocal protection as it is jointly and severally liable for compensation payable by the transferee as a result of its defaults, particularly where it fails to provide information as to the measures which it envisages to the transferor as required by regulation 13(4).

9.125 One interpretation of the operation of the joint and several liability of provisions of regulation 15(9) which is thought not to have been intended suggests that, if a transferee fails to conduct the required information and consultation in respect of its own existing workforce who will be affected by an impending transfer and an award is made against it for breach of regulation 13, the transferor will be jointly and severally liable for the award made against the transferee.

9.126 With regard to the proper approach to be adopted by the ET procedurally in dealing with the issue of joint and several liability pursuant to regulation 15(9) the EAT made the following observations in *Dillon v Todd*:

> If a party is to be made liable as a result of the order of a tribunal, which is the effect of para (9), it is right in principle that he should be a party to the proceedings in question, so that he can have the opportunity to contest his liability: If he is not joined by the Claimant, he can be joined by the primary Respondent or by the tribunal—see r 10(2)(k) of the Employment Tribunal Rules of Procedure. It is true that in a TUPE case like the present the transferee's liability will depend on the acts or omissions of the transferor, of which the transferee may in practice have little knowledge. But that makes no difference in principle; and the reality is that in TUPE cases the transferor is often unwilling or unable to defend the claim and the transferee is the only person who can even if he is at some disadvantage in doing so. If, therefore, the transferee has been a party to the proceedings, as Care Concern was here, on the basis that

---

it would be jointly and severally liable for any award made against the transferor, it would be very odd if any eventual order were not made against it.[168]

The ET is not entitled to make any order as to apportionment of the relevant liability as between the transferor and transferee or as to contribution as between the transferor and transferee based on their relative culpability in relation to the breach or breaches of regulation 13 that led to the relevant award being made. In *Todd v Strain and others*,[169] the EAT upheld the argument that the ET in that case had erred by finding that the transferee was not liable for any compensation awarded under regulation 15 and therefore should be dismissed from the proceedings. The EAT held that the transferee is jointly and severally liable with the transferor in respect of compensation awarded under regulation 15(8)(a). Counsel for the transferee was recorded as acknowledging that the issue of appointment of liability in respect of an award under regulation 15 as between transferor and transferee '(if not addressed in the sale agreement) fell to be determined, if necessary, in the ordinary courts'.[170] This approach is consistent with two decisions from the discrimination context. In *London Borough of Hackney v Sivanandan*[171] the practice of apportioning liability as between those jointly liable for acts of unlawful discrimination was disapproved of. In *Brennan and others v Sunderland City Council and others*[172] the EAT held that the ET has no jurisdiction to determine claims for contribution under the Civil Liability (Contribution) Act 1978 between persons jointly or concurrently liable for damage caused by an act of unlawful discrimination, nor indeed does that Act create such a right between such persons.[173] **9.127**

4. Individual enforcement

As Underhill P put it in *Dillon and others v Todd and anor*[174] 'the original award of the ET, which is made in favour of a class of employee rather than of individuals as such, is not enforceable in its own right'. Regulation 15(10) provides that an employee may present a complaint to an ET on the ground that he is an employee of the description to which an order under regulation 15(8) relates and that the transferor or transferee, as the case may be, has failed, wholly or in part to pay the relevant compensation to him.[175] The applicable time limit for making such a complaint is three months from the date of the ET's order under regulation 15(8) or within such other period as the ET considers reasonable in a case where it is satisfied that it was not reasonably practicable for the complaint to be presented before the end of that three-month period.[176] **9.128**

In *Dillon* the issue arose of how this time limit operated when, on appeal, an order under regulation 15(8) was made by the EAT either in circumstances where the ET had made no **9.129**

---

[168] UKEATS/0010/11 at para. 12 per Underhill J.
[169] [2011] IRLR 11, EAT.
[170] Ibid. para. 35.
[171] [2011] IRLR 740, EAT.
[172] UKEAT/0286/11.
[173] Amongst the various reasons for its decision was the EAT's conclusion (at para. 24) that the Civil Liability (Contribution) Act 1978 'is concerned only with claims justiciable in the ordinary courts' and (at para. 25) that the legislature had 'simply failed to consider the question of contribution in the context of liability for unlawful discrimination, and since the right to contribution is a creature of statute [the EAT] cannot repair that omission'.
[174] UKEAT/0010/11 at para. 4.
[175] Regulation 15(10) (a) and (b).
[176] Regulation 15(12).

order or where the EAT made an order on different terms from that of the ET. The EAT held that the time limit prescribed by regulation 15(12) runs from the date of the order of the EAT rather than that of the ET. As the original ET judgment had not contained an order against the transferee, to hold that time ran from the original ET judgment would, in the view of Underhill J, produce a nonsensical result so far as concerns that transferee, who could not be then said to have failed to pay compensation in pursuance of the relevant order. The EAT considered that the reference to the 'tribunal', in regulations 15(10)(b) and 15(12)(b) could be taken to refer where relevant to the EAT as opposed to the ET.[177]

5. Special circumstances defence

9.130 Regulation 13(9) provides that if there are 'special circumstances which render it not reasonably practicable for an employer to perform a duty imposed on him by any of [regulation 13] paragraphs (2) to (7) he shall take all such steps towards performing that duty as are reasonably practicable in the circumstances'. Regulation 13(9) essentially requires the employer to act to the extent it can as soon as it can.

9.131 With regard to complaints of breach of the obligations imposed by regulation 13, the 'special circumstances' defence mirrors regulation 13(9). Regulation 15(2) states that, if there is a question of reasonable practicability, the burden of proof is on the employer to show that there were special circumstances which rendered it not reasonably practicable for it to perform the duty[178] and that it took all such steps towards its performance as were reasonably practicable in those circumstances.[179] The matter is one of fact for the ET to assess.

9.132 The case law on the equivalent provisions in the context of the collective redundancy consultation obligation imposed by TULRCA 1992, s. 188 is again of assistance in this regard. To adopt Bean J's summary of that decision,[180] in *Bakers Union v Clarks of Hove Ltd*[181] the Court of Appeal held that, in order for an employee to be able to establish a special circumstances defence, the circumstances must be special in the sense of being something unforeseen or unexpected, something out of the ordinary run of commercial or financial events and must be special to the facts of the particular case. Examples of such events would be a disruption of the plant or sudden withdrawal of supplies by a major supplier. Insolvency, precipitating a fire sale of assets, may not be sufficient to constitute special circumstances.[182] In *H Rooke and Sons Ltd*[183] the EAT held that the employer has to show that there were special circumstances which rendered it not reasonably practicable for him to perform the (information and consultation) duty and that he took all steps towards its performance as were reasonably practicable in the circumstances.

9.133 It is also clear that a parent company's decision that results in a transfer triggers the regulation 13 information and consultation obligations. That a parent took the relevant decision is no excuse for failure by the subsidiary transferor or transferee to comply with its obligations under regulation 13. Lack of internal group communication is no excuse for

---

[177] Where the EAT exercises its powers under the Employment Tribunals Act 1996, s. 35 to make appropriate orders.

[178] Regulation 15(2)(a).

[179] Regulation 15(2)(b).

[180] In *UNISON v Somerset County Council and others* [2010] IRLR 207 at para. 25.

[181] [1978] IRLR 366, CA.

[182] See *Re Hartlebury Printers Ltd (in liquidation)* [1992] IRLR 516, HC.

[183] [1978] IRLR 204, EAT.

non-compliance. Regulation 13(12) provides that 'the duties imposed on an employer by this regulation shall apply irrespective of whether the decision resulting in the relevant transfer is taken by the employer or a person controlling the employer'.[184] This provision derives from Article 7.4 which states that:

> [t]he obligations laid down in this Article shall apply irrespective of whether the decision resulting in the transfer is taken by the employer or an undertaking controlling the employer. In considering alleged breaches of information and consultation requirements laid down by this Directive, the argument that such a breach occurred because the information was not provided by an undertaking controlling the employer shall not be accepted as an excuse.

In *UNISON v Somerset County Council and others*[185] the EAT rejected an appeal against the **9.134** finding of the ET that the employer had satisfied the special circumstances defence in the context of 'fast moving events and the approaching deadline . . . [and] the situation in the negotiations [being] pressured'.[186] As fast-moving negotiations and pressured deadlines might be seen as part of the normal run of commercial matters viewed by the Court of Appeal in *Bakers Union v Clarks of Hove Ltd*[187] as insufficient to make out the special circumstances defence, this decision demonstrates its open-textured and fact-sensitive nature.

6. Confidentiality

One issue which may concern parties to transfers of undertakings in the context of employee **9.135** consultation is confidentiality. This is a particular concern for companies listed on stock exchanges which may as a consequence of their listing be reluctant to elect representatives and provide information to them if the transaction which would then be discussed is price-sensitive and accordingly highly confidential. In *Institution of Professional Civil Servants v Secretary of State for Defence*,[188] Millett J made the point that in his view 'it is implicit that [the transferee] will also give the requisite information to [the transferor] in a form which will enable him to perform his statutory duty, and he is not entitled to supply it under cover of commercial confidentiality so as to disable him from complying with his duty'.[189] The case law on the collective redundancy consultation obligations of TULRCA 1992, whose collective information and consultation principles are substantially similar to those of TUPE, also indicates that arguments based on commercial confidentiality seeking to excuse an employer from full compliance may well receive short shrift from the ET.

In *MSF v Refuge Assurance plc*[190] the employer contended that the requirement for secrecy **9.136** in the Takeover Code amounted to special circumstances legitimately preventing disclosure of a potential merger until it was completed. Lindsay J made the following observations on the issue:

> At the Employment Tribunal the companies argued that the requirements of secrecy imposed by the Takeover Code (to which the merger was subject) were a special circumstance. The

---

[184] Regulation 13(12) is a similar provision to TULRCA 1992, s. 188(7). which deems a parent's failure to inform an employer of decisions leading to redundancies not to constitute special circumstances rendering compliance with the statutory obligation not reasonably practicable.
[185] [2010] IRLR 207, EAT.
[186] Ibid. at para. 26.
[187] Above, n. 181.
[188] [1987] IRLR 373, Ch.
[189] Ibid. at para. 11.
[190] [2002] IRLR 324, EAT.

Employment Tribunal made no finding on this issue. The Takeover Code has not been put before us...in these circumstances we express no view on either part of S188(7) save to say that in our view it cannot be simply assumed that disclosure to, say, a senior union official on the like terms of confidence as would be applicable to the companies' directors would necessarily be so restrictive that it would be completely useless to him and that it would therefore represent a step that need not be taken by the employer, or that such an official would necessarily decline to accept information on such terms. It is to be noted that *Hamish Armour v ASTMS* [1979] IRLR 24, at paragraph 11, contemplates (without proposing) disclosure to responsible union officials on a confidential basis.[191]

9.137 These observations suggest that an employer should make every effort to disclose what it can to appropriate representatives and to consider what confidentiality protections will facilitate that disclosure process.

7. Injunctions

9.138 *Amicus v Dynamex Friction Ltd*[192] addressed the potential use of injunctions in the context of the enforcement of a complaint of breach of TUPE's collective information and consultation obligations. The relevant trade union, which had commenced ET proceedings alleging breach of what are now the regulation 13 information and consultation requirements, sought an injunction against the two transferees of the business in question ordering them not to dispose of their assets. An injunction was granted prohibiting the disposal of, dealing with, or other diminution of the value of the transferees' assets up to a value of £325,000 pending determination of the ET claims. Such a freezing order is only available in respect of proceedings which exist at the time of the application for the order. A pre-existing cause of action in respect of which ET proceedings had been issued could be protected by such an order to avoid the dissipation of assets and consequent removal of the possibility of enforcement of any compensation awarded by the ET. There was sufficient evidence to support the award of a freezing order in this case.[193]

G. Interaction with Other Consultation Requirements

1. Collective redundancy consultation

9.139 A detailed treatment of the collective redundancy consultation requirements of TULRCA 1992, s. 188 is beyond the scope of this work. Suffice it to say, where an employer proposes to make redundant twenty or more employees in a ninety-day period at one establishment, an obligation arises to consult with recognized unions or employee representatives with a view to seeking agreement, as does an obligation to provide certain specified information to those representatives in writing as a precursor to that consultation. The protective penalty for breach is an award of up to ninety days' pay per affected employee. The principles with regard to the election of employee representatives and the nature of the consultation to be

---

[191] [2002] IRLR 324, EAT at para. 55.
[192] [2005] IRLR 724, QBD.
[193] The TUC proposed during the consultation on the changes which led to the 2006 Regulations that the legislation should include an ability for those affected to seek an injunction to prevent completion of a relevant transfer until the requisite collective information and consultation obligations have been fulfilled. The Government concluded that the remedy (of compensation) already provided was adequate—see Consultation Response para. 7.7.

conducted, as well as the special circumstances defence to claims of breach, are very similar to the requirements of the 2006 Regulations.

The information and consultation obligations imposed by TUPE and TULRCA 1992, s. 188 **9.140** are separate. Complaints of breach lead to separate and therefore potentially cumulative awards of compensation. Whilst there may be some degree of overlap, particularly in relation to redundancy situations arising in connection with a transfer, both sets of obligations need to be considered carefully for compliance where they apply. It may be that collective redundancy and TUPE consultation need to be conducted in tandem where redundancies are being effected, for example, on a relocation as part of the transfer process. Conversely, where the TULRCA 1992 collective redundancy consultation requirements do not apply on the basis that fewer than twenty employees are being made redundant during the relevant period, consultation with appropriate representatives will still be required with regard to those redundancies under regulation 13 on the basis that the redundancies constitute 'measures'.

The principal differences between the two regimes which can be of practical importance are **9.141** the timing of the commencement of the required process and the duration of the requisite consultation. Whereas TUPE requires, under regulation 13, the requisite information be given to the appropriate representatives long enough before a transfer to enable the employer to consult, under TULRCA 1992 the corresponding obligation is to provide the information in good time and in any event not less than thirty or ninety days before the first proposed dismissal takes effect depending on whether twenty or more or one hundred or more redundancies are envisaged in a ninety-day period at one establishment.[194]

2. Other statutory obligations

(a) Information and Consultation of Employees Regulations 2004

Consideration may also need to be given to the relevant employer's obligations under ICE, **9.142** the penalty for breach of which is an award by the CAC of a penalty up to £75,000.

Under ICE, an employer may be required to establish information and consultation arrange- **9.143** ments in relation to which a variety of information provision and consultation obligations arise. Any specific obligations contained in a negotiated agreement will of course be relevant. Otherwise, under ICE, regulation 20, the 'standard information and consultation provisions' apply and the employer will be required to provide a variety of information to those ICE representatives including information regarding:

- the recent and probable development of the undertaking's activities and economic situation;[195]
- the situation, structure, and probable development of employment within the undertaking;[196]
- decisions likely to lead to substantial changes in work organization or in contractual relations including those referred to in regulations 10 to 12 TUPE 1981.[197]

---

[194] TULRCA 1992, s. 188(1A).
[195] ICE, regulation 20(1)(a).
[196] ICE, regulation 20(1)(b).
[197] ICE, regulation 20(1)(c). These are the TUPE provisions with regard to 'measures'. So decisions which could lead to a business sale or other relevant transfer or to measures trigger the obligation to consult with ICE representatives under ICE, regulation 20(1)(c).

9.144   This information must be given at such time, in such fashion, and with such content as is appropriate to enable, in particular, the ICE representatives to conduct an adequate study and, where necessary, to prepare for consultation.[198]

9.145   Consultation is required in relation to the second and third of the categories above. This consultation is, inter alia, to be conducted with a view to seeking agreement on decisions within the scope of the employer's power.[199]

9.146   All this would indicate that a separate and additional obligation to consult with ICE representatives would be required in relation to a proposed transfer of an undertaking were it not for ICE, regulation 20(5)(b). ICE, regulation 20(5)(b)[200] brings to an end any obligation to deal with ICE representatives from the point when the collective information and consultation obligations under regulation 13 arise. Provided that the employer notifies the ICE representatives in writing that it is doing so, the employer can then proceed to comply with the TUPE information and consultation obligations without reference to the ICE information and consultation obligations and the ICE representatives. If it does not notify the ICE representatives of a decision only to conduct TUPE consultation, the employer remains bound by the obligations imposed both under ICE and under TUPE. This notification must be 'given on each occasion on which the employer has become or is about to become subject to the [regulation 13] duty'.

9.147   If there is a recognized trade union which must be dealt with in accordance with regulation 13, then the ICE process cannot be used to avoid that obligation. Absent a recognized trade union, ICE representatives may constitute appropriate representatives for TUPE 2006 purposes but the employer is free if it chooses, once the TUPE 2006 obligations arise, to cease to deal with the ICE representatives and to elect or deal with a separate body of representatives which satisfies the requirements of regulation 14.

9.148   It is worth noting that ICE, regulation 20(5) only permits an employer to cease consultation under ICE and to follow only the TUPE collective consultation route in relation to its ICE, regulation 20(1)(c) obligation, i.e. as to decisions likely to lead to substantial changes in work organization or in contractual relations including those referred to in TUPE 1981, regulations 10 to 12. The obligation imposed by ICE, regulation 20(1)(b) (to consult about the situation, structure, and probable development of employment within the undertaking) must still be complied with by way of dealing with the ICE representatives in relation to what is after all a decision-making stage earlier than that which triggers TUPE collective consultation requirements. Considerations as to the general future of the relevant undertaking or activities will therefore still be covered by ICE, regulation 20(1)(b).

---

[198]   ICE, regulation 20(2).
[199]   ICE, regulation 20(4)(d).
[200]   ICE, regulation 20(5) provides that:

[t]he duties in this regulation to inform and consult the information and consultation representatives on decisions falling within paragraph (1)(c) cease to apply once the employer is under a duty under … (b) regulation 10 of the Regulations referred to in paragraph 1(c)(ii) (duty to inform and consult representatives), and he has notified the information and consultation representatives in writing that he will be complying with his duty under the legislation referred to in sub-paragraph (a) or (b), as the case may be, instead of under these Regulations, provided that the notification is given on each occasion on which the employer has become or is about to become subject to the duty.

This framework applies to standard ICE arrangements implemented under ICE. The inter-action between regulation 13 and pre-existing agreements and negotiated agreements for the purposes of ICE will depend on the terms of the relevant agreements. **9.149**

What this all means in short is that an employer which has in place a standard information and consultation arrangement under ICE must inform and consult the relevant ICE repre-sentatives about matters which may lead to a transfer of an undertaking falling within the scope of TUPE. Once a potential transaction is sufficiently advanced, the employer must deal with a recognized trade union if there is one as required by regulation 13 but otherwise is able to elect to switch to the TUPE 2006 regime, or to deal with the ICE representatives, or indeed to address the issues under both sets of arrangement. This distinction between consideration of matters which may lead to a TUPE transfer and a TUPE transfer process which engages regulation 13 will require careful consideration. **9.150**

(b) European Works Council obligations

Whilst the detailed rules and regulations relating to the establishment of EWCs is beyond the scope of this work, the domestic legislation[201] implementing into UK law the requirements of the EU Directive on the establishment of EWCs[202] should not entirely be ignored in this context. This legislation establishes the requirement with which undertakings or groups of undertakings with at least 1,000 employees in EU Member States and at least 150 employees in two of those States can be made to comply. **9.151**

While the parties to an EWC arrangement may determine (through the 'Special Negotiating Body') the details of how their EWC mechanism is to work, there is a default model which applies if agreement is not reached. For these purposes it is worth noting that of the matters which must be considered with an EWC and which may be relevant in the TUPE context are the structure, economic, and financial situation of the business, the probable trend of employment, investments and substantial changes affecting the organization, and closures. Accordingly, developments which may lead to TUPE transfers may in any event fall for consideration in the context of an applicable EWC arrangement if transnational in scope or effect. **9.152**

H. Planning for Compliance

The fact that liability for failure to comply with the information and consultation regime is now joint and several places transferees in a difficult situation if they lack a commercial or contractual position which enables them to require the transferor to comply with its obliga-tions and/or provide suitable indemnity protection in relation to any liability which may arise in respect of the relevant requirements. In view of the potentially significant exposure involved, commercial contracts recording outsourcings and other similar arrangements will often need to impose specific obligations on the relevant parties to comply with their obli-gations and to provide appropriate financial protection by way of reliable indemnities in respect of the liabilities arising on breach. **9.153**

---

[201] The Transitional Information and Consultation of Employees Regulations 1999 SI 1999/3323.
[202] Directive 94/45/EC.

9.154 Assuming that the parties are able and prepared to comply with their obligations, careful planning also needs to take place with regard to what can be a complex process in terms of, for example:

- identifying the constituencies from whom employee representatives should be elected;
- conducting an election for employee representatives at a potentially sensitive time;
- identifying what if any measures the transferee envisages taking and whether any plans are sufficiently definite and formulated to constitute proposals which the transferee envisages making;
- analysing whether employees other than those directly transferring are sufficiently affected to need to be drawn into the consultation process;
- whether different categories of employees need to be consulted with separately depending on the nature of their involvement and the effects upon them of the transfer;
- the logistical and practical issues involved in running a fair and secret election, whether or not with the participation of an independent scrutineer;
- potentially conducting a collective redundancy process in parallel with the transfer of undertakings consultation process if a redundancy or relocation programme of the requisite scale is being implemented in conjunction with the transfer;
- assessing whether ICE or EWC obligations are triggered and need to be addressed.

9.155 The 2009 Guidance[203] provides the following commentary on these issues:

> The legislation does not specify how many representatives must be elected or the process by which they are to be chosen. An employment tribunal may wish to consider, in determining a claim that the employer has not informed or consulted in accordance with the requirements, whether the arrangements were such that the purpose of the legislation could not be met. An employer will therefore need to consider such matters as whether:
>
> - the arrangements adequately cover all the categories of employees who may be affected by the transfer and provide a reasonable balance between the interests of the different groups;
> - the employees have sufficient time to nominate and consider candidates;
> - the employees (including any who are absent from work for any reason) can freely choose who to vote for;
> - there is any normal company custom and practice for similar elections and, if so, whether there are good reasons for departing from it.

---

[203] At p. 23.

10

TUPE AND INSOLVENCY

A. **Introduction**	10.01	E. **Opening/Instituting Insolvency**	
1. The Directive	10.01	**Proceedings**	10.50
2. TUPE 2006	10.09	F. **Permitted Contract Variations**	10.54
B. **Bankruptcy and Analogous Insolvency**		1. Introduction	10.54
Proceedings	10.18	2. Which employees?	10.60
C. **Administration**	10.24	3. Appropriate representatives	10.62
D. **Transferor's Debts**	10.37	4. Agreement of employment representatives	10.71
1. Relevant insolvency proceedings	10.37	5. The nature of permitted variations	10.75
2. Relevant employees	10.40	6. Issues of interpretation	10.78
3. Excluded debts	10.41	G. **Misuse of Insolvency Proceedings**	10.84
4. Timing	10.48	H. **Hiving Down**	10.85

A. Introduction

1. The Directive

The case law on the Directive prior to the adoption of ARD 2001 established that its provisions did not apply to transfers of undertakings where, to paraphrase, the relevant business had been declared insolvent in what has become known as a 'terminal insolvency', i.e. with the purpose of the liquidation of the assets of the business. In *Abels v Administrative Board of the Bedrijfsvereniging voor de Metaalindustrie en de Electrotechnische Industrie*[1] the distinction was drawn by the ECJ between terminal insolvencies (i.e. liquidation proceedings where the individual protections of ARD would not apply) and other forms of insolvency procedure to which ARD would apply—in that case the Danish SvB procedure over which there was lesser judicial supervision than that jurisdiction's liquidation proceedings and where the objective was primarily to safeguard the relevant assets and, where practicable, to continue the business.[2] The justification for excluding terminal insolvencies from the full application of the transfer legislation was summarized by the EAT in *OTG*,[3] reflecting the distinction drawn

10.01

---

[1] [1987] 2 CMLR 406, ECJ.

[2] See also *D'Urso and others v Ercole Marelli Elettromeccanica Generale SpA (in special administration) and others* [1992] IRLR 136, ECJ.

[3] *OTG Ltd v Barke and others; Olds v Late Editions; Key2Law (Surrey) Ltd v Antiquis and others; Secretary of State for Business, Innovation and Skills v Coyne and others; Head Entertainment Ltd v Walker and others* [2011] IRLR 272, EAT at para. 11. See Wynn-Evans, 'TUPE, Administration and the Rescue Culture' (2011) 40 ILJ 451.

in *Abels* and ARD between terminal and other insolvencies. A liquidation has the objective of the disposal of the relevant assets. The collective interests of the employees are seen as best served in such circumstances by disapplying the protection of the transfer legislation on the basis that the obligation to take on the entire workforce on the same terms might operate as a disincentive to potential purchasers of the business as a going concern. On this analysis, the risk of the dismissal of some employees and the diminution of terms for others who are retained is preferable to the relevant staff all losing their jobs.

10.02 In *Abels* the ECJ took the view that 'if the directive had been intended to apply also to transfers of undertakings in the context of [liquidation and analogous insolvency proceedings], an express provision would have been included for that purpose'[4] and held as follows:

> 23. It cannot...be concluded that Directive 77/187 imposes on the Member States the obligation to extend the rules laid down therein to transfers of undertakings, businesses or parts of businesses taking place in the context of insolvency proceedings instituted with a view to the liquidation of the assets of the transferor under the supervision of the competent judicial authority.
>
> 24. It must nevertheless be made clear that, even though, in view of the considerations set out above, transfers of that kind do not fall within the scope of the above-mentioned directive, the Member States are at liberty independently to apply the principles of the directive, wholly or in part, on the basis of their national law alone.

10.03 That insolvency proceedings which do not constitute such terminal insolvency situations would fall within the scope of the Directive was based on the fact that:

> the object of the proceedings is primarily to safeguard the assets of the insolvent undertaking and, where possible, to continue the business of the undertaking by means of a collective suspension of the payment of debts with a view to reaching a settlement which will ensure that the undertaking is able to continue operating in the future.[5]

10.04 The distinction between terminal insolvencies to which the Directive would not apply with its full rigour and other insolvencies to which it would was therefore to be based on the purpose of the insolvency procedure in question. Consequently, as the ECJ said in *Jules Detlier Equipement v Dassy and Sovramspral (in liquidation)*:[6]

> [I]n deciding whether the Directive applies to the transfer of an undertaking subject to an administrative or judicial procedure, the determining factor is the purpose of the procedure in question although account should also be taken of the form of the procedure, insofar as it means that the undertaking continues or ceases trading, and of the Directive's objectives.[7]

10.05 ARD 1998[8] incorporated the principle established by *Abels* explicitly into the Directive, the current incarnation of which provision, Article 5(1), provides as follows:

> Unless Member States provide otherwise, Articles 3 [transfer of the employment relationship] and 4 [prohibition of dismissals on ground of the transfer] shall not apply to any transfer of an undertaking, business or part of an undertaking or business where the transferor is the subject of bankruptcy proceedings or any analogous insolvency proceedings which have been instituted with a view to the liquidation of the assets of the transferor and are under the supervision

---

[4] *Abels*, above n. 1, at para. 17.
[5] Ibid. at para. 28.
[6] [1998] IRLR 266, ECJ.
[7] Ibid. at para. 25.
[8] By way of Article 4A of ARD 1998.

of a competent public authority (which may be an insolvency practitioner authorised by a competent public authority).

Further flexibility was introduced in ARD 2001 whose Article 5.2 provides two options for Member States in certain insolvency contexts. The options introduced by Article 5.2 were to: **10.06**

- provide that the transferor's pre-existing debts towards the transferring employees do not pass to the transferee where protection is provided in relation to these debts for those employees which is at least equivalent to that provided for by the EC Insolvency Directive;[9]
- permit employers and employee representatives to agree changes to terms and conditions of employment which are made by reason of the transfer itself, provided that these changes are made in accordance with national law and practice and with a view to ensuring the survival of the business and thereby preserving jobs.

These options apply, pursuant to Article 5.2, in relation to 'insolvency proceedings which have been opened in relation to a transferor whether or not these proceedings have been instituted with a view to the liquidation of the assets of the transferor and provided that such proceedings are under the supervision of a competent public authority'. These variations to the effect of the Directive can therefore be applied to those insolvency situations which are not 'terminal'.   **10.07**

It is therefore important to distinguish between the differential application of the Directive in different types of insolvency situation. Unless a Member State's implementing legislation provides otherwise, transactions occurring in the context of terminal insolvencies (bankruptcies and liquidations) do not attract the employment protection provisions of the Directive in terms of transfer of employment and prohibition of transfer-related dismissal in the absence of an ETOR. Other insolvency proceedings (which are not instituted with a view to the liquidation of the transferor's assets) can still attract the application of the a Member State's transfer of undertakings legislation where transactions falling within their scope occur but their application can be moderated by the limitation of the debts inherited by the transferee and the ability to agree what TUPE styles[10] 'permitted variations' to the contracts of employment of transferring employees. In the light of this distinction, the crucial issue in this context is therefore the nature of the insolvency procedure being conducted.   **10.08**

2. TUPE 2006

Prior to the introduction of the 2006 Regulations, there had been some doubt as to whether *Abels* did actually operate to disapply TUPE 1981 from terminal insolvencies.[11] That there was no specific mention of insolvency in TUPE 1981 was argued potentially to indicate that TUPE was not intended to extend to insolvency situations. In *Belhaven Brewery v Berekis*,[12] Lord Coulsfield considered that TUPE applied in cases of insolvency on the basis that there was no explicit exclusion of the application of the domestic legislation in insolvency   **10.09**

---

[9] AT/987/EEC.
[10] In regulation 9.
[11] See Pollard, 'Insolvent Companies and TUPE' (1996) 25 ILJ 191.
[12] UKEAT/724/92.

situations and that the European jurisprudence was of no interpretative assistance in that regard. In his view:

> As the [employment] tribunal pointed out, the Directive does not prevent a Member State from conferring greater rights on employees than those which are laid down in the Directive and although it has been held that it may be appropriate to refer to a Directive in order to extend a scope of regulations made, ostensibly in order to give effect to that Directive, we were not referred to any authority in which the clear meaning of Regulations has been restricted by reference to a Directive.

10.10 Moreover, subsequent to *Abels*, amendments were made to TUPE 1981 in 1993[13] and at that stage no amendments were made to the legislation to reflect the principle which that case established in relation to the Directive. It was argued that the failure to make any such amendment could 'by implication, be taken to have confirmed the statutory authority of all TUPE'[14] on the basis that the option by then presented in *Abels* to disapply the transfer legislation in cases of terminal insolvency was not taken up, thereby indicating that TUPE applied fully in such situations. Nonetheless, the possibility that *Abels* did not apply to the domestic transfer legislation was rejected by the EAT decision in *Perth & Kinross Council v Donaldson and others*[15] which took the view that TUPE 1981 did not apply to a case of 'irretrievable insolvency'.

10.11 Nonetheless, in *TGWU v Swissport (UK) Ltd (in administration) and an or*,[16] the transaction which was contended to constitute a transfer of an undertaking occurred in the context of what was described as 'a fairly catastrophic or "terminal" insolvency'.[17] The EAT indicated in effect that the same principles apply as in any other case to determine whether a transaction out of insolvency constitutes a transfer of an undertaking—TUPE 1981 was not to be 'answered in such a way as to exclude cases of transfers in insolvency situations, even where the administrators have neither carried on the business in question nor transferred any part of it as a going concern'.[18] There was

> no reason why TUPE cannot apply where the facts are such as to justify a finding that there has been a transfer of a stable economic entity, even where the transferor has not continued trading and there has been no sale or transfer of part of the transferor's undertaking as a growing concern.[19]

10.12 To disapply the automatic transfer and dismissal protection provisions of the legislation in cases of terminal insolvency is not mandatory under ARD. As Collins had noted in relation to a previous incarnation of the legislation, ARD 'deliberately left to member states the allocation of liability in the event of insolvencies followed by sales of the assets of businesses in liquidation'.[20] Article 5.1 provides for the terminal insolvency exception save where national law provides otherwise. TUPE could thus have been applied in full to terminal insolvencies. However, when the domestic transfer legislation was recast in the 2006 Regulations, the

---

[13] These amendments related principally to the collective information and consultation obligations now contained in regulations 13–15—see Chapter 9.
[14] Pollard, above n. 11.
[15] [2004] IRLR 121, EAT.
[16] [2007] ICR 1593, EAT.
[17] Ibid. at para. 59.
[18] Ibid. at para. 78.
[19] Ibid. at para. 66.
[20] Collins, 'Transfer of Undertakings and Insolvency' (1989) 18 ILJ 144.

option to apply TUPE in cases of terminal insolvency provided by Article 5.1 was not taken up and the disapplication of TUPE's provisions as to automatic transfer and transfer-related dismissals was made express resolving the previous uncertainties in the case law. The relevant implementing provision, regulation 8(7), was not intended to change the legal position but rather to make explicit what was previously implicit.[21]

This approach was adopted as being 'in line with the "rescue culture" that the Government aims to promote'.[22] The rescue culture has the objective of facilitating business survival in insolvency situations with consequent potential preservation of employment to a greater or lesser extent. As Davies described it, reference to the rescue culture is 'to a shift in emphasis on the part of insolvency practitioners, appointed to take over the management of ailing companies, away from the sale of the company's assets on a break up basis and towards continuing to trade with a view to disposing of the business, or at least parts of it, as a going concern'.[23]   **10.13**

The 2006 Regulations also adopted both options provided by Article 5.2. The provisions of regulations 8 and 9, which record the modified application of TUPE in the insolvency context, apply to relevant transfers for the purposes of regulation 3 and therefore in relation both to transfers of undertakings for the purposes of regulation 3(1)(a) and SPCs for the purposes of regulation 3(1)(b). In short, therefore, the specific protection for employees (in terms of transferring their employment to the transferee automatically with their terms and conditions preserved, other than in respect of occupational pension scheme rights, and deeming transfer-related dismissals potentially automatically unfair) provided by TUPE does not apply in relation to transactions entered into in the context of 'terminal insolvencies'. In certain other insolvency situations, TUPE provides that the transferee does not inherit certain debts owed to the transferring employees by the transferor which are met by the Government. The employer may also, in certain insolvency situations, agree changes to the terms and conditions of employment of the transferring employees with appropriate representatives of those employees.   **10.14**

In implementing Article 5.1 and adopting the provisions permitted by Article 5.2, TUPE was not drafted directly by reference to domestic insolvency law and its various specific forms of insolvency procedure. Rather the Directive's formulations (which are framed by reference to the purpose of the relevant procedure) were adopted instead.   **10.15**

Regulation 8, which sets out the insolvency-related provisions of TUPE, therefore adopts the distinction between 'terminal' and other insolvency proceedings by use of two specific concepts—those of, first, 'bankruptcy and other analogous insolvency proceedings' and, second, 'relevant insolvency proceedings'. More specifically, regulation 8(7) incorporates the principle established by Article 5.1 by providing that the automatic transfer of employees and protection against transfer-related dismissals provided by regulations 4 and 7 respectively are disapplied in relation to 'bankruptcy proceedings or other analogous insolvency proceedings'. Pursuant to regulation 8(2), the relaxation of TUPE's effects in relation to the transferor's debts and the ability of employee representatives to agree variations to employees' contracts apply in relation to 'relevant insolvency proceedings'.   **10.16**

---

[21] 2005 Consultation para. 65.
[22] See 2001 Consultation para. 87.
[23] Davies, 'Employee Claims in Insolvency: Corporate Rescues and Preferential Claims' (1994) 23 ILJ 141.

10.17 By way of summary, Elias P provided the following overview of the structure and operation of regulation 8 in *Secretary of State for Trade and Industry v (1) Slater and others and (2) CGF Nationwide Site Services Ltd*:

> 13. The scheme of the TUPE Regulation broadly is this. Typically where there is a transfer of an undertaking, regulation 4 provides that the employees are automatically transferred to the transferee with the latter taking over all the liabilities of the transferor.
>
> 14. Regulation 7 provides that any dismissal will be automatically unfair unless it is for an economic, technical or organisational reason connected with the transfer. However, it is recognised that to apply these principles to insolvent businesses would discourage potential purchasers of the business from acquiring the business. That would be to the detriment of the employees.
>
> 15. Regulation 8 therefore aims to relieve transferees of the burdens which would otherwise apply in certain defined circumstances.
>
> 16. Essentially this is done in two quite distinct ways. The most extensive exception from the effect of TUPE is created by regulation 8(7) (which is intended to reflect the provisions of Article 5.1 of the Directive). This provides that where the insolvency proceedings are analogous to bankruptcy proceedings and have been instituted with a view to liquidation of the assets, then neither regulations 4 nor 7 apply at all. There is no transfer of staff to the transferee and no claim for unfair dismissal against him (although other provisions of TUPE, such as the information and consultation regulations, continue to operate).
>
> 17. A narrower exception is carved out where regulation 8(6) applies. This applies to insolvency proceedings where the purpose is not with a view to liquidation of assets. This does not altogether exclude, but it does modify, the effects of regulations 4 and 7. It means that the transferee does not pick up all of the liabilities which would otherwise transfer to him.[24]

B. Bankruptcy and Analogous Insolvency Proceedings

10.18 Regulation 8(7) provides that regulations 4 and 7, being the provisions establishing the protections of TUPE in terms of the transfer of employees and the ability to claim unfair dismissal in relation to transfer-related dismissals, do not apply 'to any relevant transfer where the transferor is the subject of bankruptcy proceedings or any analogous insolvency proceedings which have been instituted with a view to the liquidation of the assets of the transferor and are under the supervision of an insolvency practitioner'. This effectively repeats the exclusion from the scope of the Directive pursuant to Article 5.1 of transactions effected as part of a terminal insolvency.

10.19 The Insolvency Act 1986, Part XIII provides the definition of an individual's acting as an insolvency practitioner which applies for the purposes of regulations 8 and 9. Capacities in which an individual acts as an insolvency practitioner in respect of companies include those of liquidator, administrative receiver, administrator, and supervisor of a voluntary arrangement.[25] Other sections of IA 1986, Part XIII[26] set out the relevant provisions applicable to the qualifications required for a person to act as an insolvency practitioner.

10.20 The wording of regulation 8(7) adopts the generic description set out in Article 5.1 of the nature of the insolvency procedures to which regulations 4 and 7 do not apply. Despite

---

[24] [2007] IRLR 928, EAT.

[25] IA 1986, s. 388(1)(a) and (b); IA 1986, s. 389(2) identifies the situations in which a person acts as an insolvency practitioner in relation to individuals.

[26] IA 1986, ss 390–8.

the inevitable uncertainty which this 'copying out' approach entailed—as demonstrated by the litigation which ensued over the application of regulation 8(7) to administrations—the justification for its adoption was that it (supposedly) ensures a simple provision, 'future proofs' the provision against subsequent changes in insolvency procedures, and ensures that TUPE 2006 goes no further in derogating from its normal protections for employees than the Directive permits.[27]

In terms of the application of this generic wording to the current domestic insolvency regime, the Government's view[28] was that regulation 8(7) applies 'in particular [to] compulsory winding up and bankruptcy' and 'that relevant transfers are most unlikely to occur in these cases in any event, as it is very rare that a business or part of a business, survives in the wake of such a procedure'. The 2005 Consultation acknowledged[29] a degree of uncertainty with regard to whether a creditors' voluntary winding up falls within the scope of Article 5.1's exclusion of the Directive's normal application (as well as whether the exclusion by Article 5.2 of the transfer to the transferee of the relevant category of debts applies in such a situation). Although Elias P declined to express a view as to whether a creditors' voluntary winding up fell within regulation 8(6) or regulation 8(7) when expressly invited to do so in *Secretary of State for Trade and Industry v (1) Slater and others and (2) CGF Nationwide Site Services Ltd*,[30] it is thought that proceedings such as creditors' involuntary liquidation and compulsory liquidation/winding up would fall within the scope of regulation 8(7). **10.21**

It should be noted that regulation 8(7) only disapplies regulations 4 and 7 from applying to relevant transfers arising in relation to bankruptcy and analogous insolvency proceedings. The regulation 13 collective information and consultation obligations would still apply to a relevant transfer in such a scenario. **10.22**

Charlton and Charlton Thermosystems (Romsey) Ltd[31] concerned a situation where insolvency procedures were on foot in relation to the relevant business but TUPE still applied. In this case under the legislation prior to the introduction of the explicit provisions of regulation 8(7), the argument that TUPE did not apply to compulsory winding-up proceedings on the grounds of insolvency did not engage since in that case all that had happened was that the relevant company had been struck off the register. As the EAT put it: **10.23**

> no insolvency proceedings exist in consequence of the registrar's act in striking off the name of the company from the register. All that has happened is that the company has ceased to exist, without being wound up, and its assets are vested in the Crown unless and until an order is made declaring the dissolution void or restoring the name of the company to the register.[32]

C. Administration

Whether administration pursuant to Schedule B1 to the IA 1986 constitutes bankruptcy or other analogous insolvency proceedings—and therefore a terminal insolvency to which regulations 4 and 7 do not apply—has caused particular uncertainty in the period after the **10.24**

---

[27] 2005 Consultation paras 58 and 64.
[28] Ibid. at para. 64.
[29] At para. 64 footnote 8.
[30] Above n. 24 and see para. 10.17.
[31] [1995] IRLR 79, EAT.
[32] Ibid. at para. 16.

adoption of the 2006 Regulations. Whether TUPE applies with its full rigour to transactions out of administration is of considerable importance not only to the employees affected but also to those devising, structuring, and negotiating such transactions. The increased use of pre-pack administration—in which the intended administrator is involved prior to appointment in 'planning in advance an arrangement under which the business of the company is to be sold immediately after his appointment, bypassing the statutory procedure of the creditors meeting, and without any direction from the court'[33]—brought this issue into particular focus. That said, it is important to note that in the litigation addressing this issue, no distinction has been drawn between pre-packs and other administrations for the purposes of considering the proper application of TUPE 2006.

10.25 The issue of the status of administration for the purposes of regulation 8 was first addressed in *Oakland v Wellswood (Yorkshire) Ltd* by both the EAT[34] and (albeit only in passing) the Court of Appeal.[35] As it was put by the editors of *Harvey*,[36] the EAT in *Oakland* defied the assumption—based on the view that 'the purpose of administration generally is not to put the company into liquidation but to rescue its business'—that regulations 4 and 7 do apply to administration and are not disapplied by regulation 8(7). As a rescue rather than a liquidation strategy, administration had been assumed not to constitute an insolvency procedure instituted with a view to the liquidation of the assets of the transferor. Consistent with that assumption, the Insolvency Service had indicated in its guidance its view that 'TUPE does apply to insolvencies where the intention is to rescue the business. If your employer is in administration . . . you will be protected by TUPE'.[37]

10.26 In *Oakland* the EAT held that whether regulation 8(7) operated to exclude the application of regulations 4 and 7 was a question of fact for the ET to determine on the particular facts of the specific insolvency procedure in question. On the facts of the case the ET found as a matter of fact that the administrators had considered that, of the three statutory objectives of administration set out in Schedule B1, the first (rescuing the company as a going concern) was not achievable, the second (achieving a better result for creditors as a whole than would be likely on a winding up) would be prejudiced by the losses consequent upon further trading and that therefore they should pursue the third objective of an administration (to realize property to make a distribution to creditors). The administrators had anticipated a move in due course from administration to creditors' voluntary liquidation. As the objective of the administration in these circumstances was found to be the realization of the assets of the business it was held to have been instituted for the purposes of its eventual liquidation such that regulation 8(7) engaged. This administration was therefore on its facts a terminal insolvency by way of bankruptcy or other analogous insolvency proceedings to which regulations 4 and 7 did not apply.

10.27 The EAT upheld the judgment of the ET that the appointment of the joint administrators was, as a matter of fact, made with a view to the eventual liquidation of the assets of the transferor and that therefore regulation 8(7) was engaged. HHJ Peter Clark considered this result to accord with the policy behind Article 5.1 and of regulation 8(7), 'namely the

---

[33] As described by the EAT in *OTG Ltd v Barke and others*, above n. 3.
[34] [2009] IRLR 250, EAT.
[35] [2010] IRLR 82, CA.
[36] *Harvey on Industrial Relations and Employment Law* Division FH [167.06].
[37] Insolvency and Redundancy—a Guide for Employees, URN 09/1558, para. 39.

"rescue culture" whereby a purchaser ... is not put off by the effects of TUPE protection. The outcome, as demonstrated by the case, was that some jobs were preserved and the creditors benefited from the best available option.' The EAT accepted that, where the joint administrators continued to trade with a view to a sale as a going concern, a relevant transfer would attract the protection of regulation 4. However, where, as in this case, the administrators took immediate steps to dispose of the assets of the business, the EAT held that the ET was entitled to hold that the appointment of the administrators was with a view to the eventual liquidation of the assets of the relevant business.

When *Oakland* reached the Court of Appeal, the primary issue for consideration was whether **10.28** those employees who were in the event engaged by the relevant purchaser retained continuity of employment for statutory purposes pursuant to ERA 1996, s. 218(2).[38] The Court of Appeal declined to determine the proper interpretation of regulation 8(7) as it considered it unnecessary to do so for two reasons—first, the continuity of employment issue was resolved on the basis of ERA 1996, s. 218(2) rather than TUPE 2006; second, it had not heard full argument on the proper interpretation of regulation 8(7). Nonetheless, Moses LJ[39] expressed the view that there were 'strong grounds for thinking that both the employment tribunal and the employment appeal tribunal took the wrong approach to their construction of both Article 5 of the Directive and to regulation 8'.

When the regulation 8(7) issue came before the EAT again in *OTG*, the EAT concluded that **10.29** as a matter of principle administration can never fall within the scope of regulation 8(7) and therefore always falls within the protective scope of regulations 4 and 7. This analysis was described as the 'absolute approach' in contrast to the 'fact based approach' adopted by the EAT in *Oakland*. This debate as to whether and how administration should or should not be categorized as a terminal insolvency procedure to which the individual protections of TUPE would not apply had been anticipated by Pollard. He noted that it was unclear from the drafting of regulation 8(7) whose view as to the purpose of an administration would determine whether regulation 8(7) would apply and when that view would be assessed.[40] Neither the Notice of Appointment statutory declaration (which only confirms that appointment is in accordance with Schedule B1) nor the Statement of Proposed Administration states the purpose of the particular administration. That said, Pollard's view was that the use in regulation 8(7) of the concept of proceedings being instituted with a view to the liquidation of assets implied 'looking at what happened when the process started'.[41] The crux of the debate as to the proper interpretation of regulation 8(7) was whether the test is, on the one hand, of the legal nature of the process in principle when it starts—its generic purpose as an insolvency procedure—or, on the other hand, of the factual nature of the process when it is implemented or indeed as it develops—its specific purpose in the particular situation in which the insolvency procedure of administration is deployed.

The EAT was clearly alive to the general and specific commercial context of this litigation— **10.30** that transferees seeking to avoid employment liabilities would favour the fact-based approach whilst employees would favour the absolute approach (as it would ensure their protection by

---

[38] As to which issue see for further discussion, Chapter 5, para. 5.45 *et seq.*
[39] *Oakland*, above n. 34, at para. 10.
[40] Pollard, *Corporate Insolvency: Employment and Pension Rights*, London: Tottel, 2007 at paras 13.67–13.69.
[41] Ibid. at para. 13.69.

TUPE). For TUPE to apply in full to administrations would also reduce the liabilities faced by the Secretary of State pursuant to the guarantees established by ERA 1996, Chapter VI, Part XI (in respect of redundancy payments) and Chapter XII of the same legislation (in respect of various other prescribed payments).

10.31 The fact-based approach was rejected in *OTG* in favour of the absolute approach on a number of grounds. An analysis based on the general objective of the relevant type of insolvency procedure, rather than the intention of the administrator in the particular factual matrix, was seen as producing legal certainty and avoiding the risk of difficult and unpredictable disputes about the administrator's intentions upon which it would be undesirable for employment protection rights to depend. As the EAT put it,[42] 'a bright-line rule has clear advantages'. More particularly, Article 5.1 was interpreted as expressly identifying terminal insolvencies by reference to the object of the procedure when instituted. At the outset of an administration, the primary objective is to rescue the company as a going concern, rather than a liquidation of assets, and the administrator is not required to identify by that stage which of the three objectives set out in paragraph 3 of Schedule B1 (and set out above) he is intending to pursue. Consequently, administration (properly assessed at the point of its being instituted rather than by reference to how it might subsequently develop) was viewed by the EAT in *OTG* as having the objective of rescue of the company as a going concern, not liquidation of its assets, and therefore as falling outside the scope of the regulation 8(7) exemption. The legislator was seen as drawing a distinction between liquidation and other proceedings based on their legal character rather than the intentions of the relevant insolvency practitioner.

10.32 That said, certainty was not the only basis for this decision. The EAT viewed the insolvency provisions of the Directive and TUPE as derogations from the overall employee protection objective of the transfer legislation. Consequently, any uncertainty as to the application of regulation 8(7) should be resolved against the background of that objective. The EAT therefore took the view that the primary purpose of the transfer legislation of employment protection 'in any doubtful case must prevail'.[43] This view supported the adoption of the absolute approach over the fact-based approach.

10.33 In *OTG* the EAT acknowledged that the distinction between terminal and other insolvency proceedings is 'debatable'[44] and is 'somewhat blunt'.[45] Nonetheless, the EAT preferred the restrictive interpretation of the absolute approach, which produces certainty and favours employee protection, over the less predictable fact-based approach. The EAT preferred to resolve the question of the proper application of regulation 8(7) as one of principle based on a precise reading of the purpose of administration as prescribed by Schedule B1 rather than by reference to potentially unpredictable transaction-specific practice. A further argument advanced in favour of the absolute approach is that the situation of a business (in terms of its viability and sale prospects) where administration is the chosen insolvency procedure is as a general rule arguably likely to be not so serious as to warrant the disapplication of the

---

[42] *OTG*, above, n. 3, at para. 22.
[43] Ibid. at para. 21.
[44] Ibid. at para. 12.
[45] Ibid. at para. 24.

protections of TUPE in contrast to a liquidation where this is seen as permissible to facilitate the salvage of the business or part of it.

When the matter reached the Court of Appeal in *Key2Law LLP v d'Acquis*[46] the absolute **10.34** approach was again preferred over the fact-based approach. Rimer LJ, in the leading judgment, considered it 'unsatisfactory in principle that the determination of whether or not administration proceedings are, in any particular case, to be characterized as "analogous insolvency proceedings" should depend on the evidence leading up to the making of the appointment of the administrators'.[47] Determining the objective or predominant objective of the administrators' appointment will often be uncertain. Longmore LJ, in concurring with Rimer LJ, was persuaded that:

> [t]he framers of the EC directive on which regulation 8(7) is based, could not have contemplated the kind of complex and uncertain factual inquiry which would in many cases have to be conducted if it were necessary to decide what 'view' the institutor of the administration had in mind when the administration began.[48]

Moreover, the fact-based approach was viewed as being premised on an erroneous inter- **10.35** pretation of the scheme of Schedule B1. An administration order is made for the purpose of Schedule B1, as Rimer LJ put it, to keep the administrators' options open. An administrator may need to make decisions different from those anticipated prior to appointment. It was considered odd to seek to decide whether or not the transfer legislation applies to a particular administration by reference to expectations of the likely outcome prior to its making which may not be fulfilled and indeed may be entirely reversed.[49] The proper test was the purpose of the administration order when made—and the legal duties to which the administrator is thereby subjected—rather than what the applicants for an administration order might have hoped for from the administration or indeed any preconceived ideas the administrator may have had as to how he was going to perform his functions.[50] Rimer LJ considered it to be:

> in principle anyway wrong to identify the purpose of an appointment of administrators by reference to pre-appointment considerations as to the particular objective or objectives that it is foreseen that an appointment is reasonably to achieve. The present case shows that an appointment that is made with the intention, hope or expectation of—or, perhaps, 'with a view to'—the achieving of a particular objective may not achieve it. The fallacy of the 'fact-based' approach is that it proceeds on the erroneous basis that the factual considerations that conclusively identify the objective 'with a view' to which the appointment is made. That involves a misinterpretation of the scheme of Schedule B1.[51]

Rimer LJ therefore approved[52] of the EAT's analysis that, given the alternatives open to the **10.36** administrator upon the making of an administration order, it is not possible rationally to

---

[46] [2011] IRLR 272, CA. At the time of writing, it is understood that this case is on appeal to the SC.
[47] Ibid. at para. 96.
[48] Ibid. at para. 111 per Longmore J.
[49] Ibid. at para. 98.
[50] Ibid. at para. 101.
[51] Ibid. at para. 97.
[52] Ibid. at para. 102.

conclude that an administrator's appointment is made with a view to the liquidation of the transferor's assets, whatever his 'pre-conceived ideas'.[53]

D. Transferor's Debts

1. Relevant insolvency proceedings

10.37 Were it not for the regime established by regulation 8, all the debts owed by the transferor to the transferring employees would transfer to the transferee on a relevant transfer not falling within the scope of the exemption from the application of regulations 4 and 7 established by regulation 8(7).[54] However, where the business in question is the subject of 'relevant insolvency proceedings', regulation 8(1) provides that the provisions of regulations 8(2)–(6) apply to exclude certain of the debts owed by the transferor to the transferring employees from the liabilities inherited by the transferee.

10.38 As is the case with regulation 8(7), the approach of TUPE 2006 in defining the insolvency proceedings to which its provisions relating to the transferor's debts apply is to repeat the wording of the Directive.[55] Following Article 5.2, relevant insolvency proceedings are defined by regulation 8(6) as 'insolvency proceedings which have been opened in relation to the transferor not with a view to the liquidation of the assets of the transferor and which are under the supervision of an insolvency practitioner'. This reflects the provisions of Article 5.2 and the focus of the relevant ECJ decisions on the purpose of the relevant insolvency regime.[56] Accordingly, where the insolvency procedure is not 'terminal', then TUPE still applies although modified in its effect insofar as concerns those transferor's debts addressed by regulations 8(2)–(6).

10.39 The 2005 Consultation indicated the view that administration, company and individual voluntary arrangements, and creditors' voluntary winding up, but not administrative or other receivership or any other voluntary winding up, are covered by the provisions of regulation 8(2)–(6) with regard to the transferor's debts.[57] The 2009 Guidance considers that relevant insolvency proceedings will include:

> [a]ny collective insolvency proceedings in which the whole or part of the business or undertaking is transferred to another entity as a going concern. That is to say it covers insolvency proceedings in which all creditors of a debtor may participate and in relation to which the insolvency office-holder owes a duty to all creditors. The Department considers that 'relevant insolvency proceedings' does not cover winding up by either creditors or members where there is no such transfer.[58]

---

[53] Ibid. para. 98.
[54] Under what is now regulation 4—see 2005 Consultation para. 59—and save with regard to other matters specifically excluded from transfer such as those pension entitlements falling within the 'pensions exclusion' described in Chapter 11.
[55] 2005 Consultation para. 58.
[56] See *D'Urso v Ercole Marelli Elettromeccanica Generale SpA* [1992] IRLR 136, ECJ; *Spano v Fiat Geotech* [1995] ECR 1-4321; *Jules Detlier Equipement v Dassy* [1998] IRLR 266, ECJ.
[57] At para. 58.
[58] At p. 26.

2. Relevant employees

Pursuant to regulation 8(2), the 'relevant employees' who are covered by TUPE's specific **10.40** provisions with regard to the transfer of the transferor's debts in relation to relevant insolvency proceedings are those employees of the transferor:

- whose contract of employment transfers to the transferee pursuant to TUPE.[59] Transfer by agreement where TUPE does not actually engage to effect the automatic transfer of the relevant employee's contract of employment will not suffice. TUPE must actually operate to transfer (or apply to the transfer of) the relevant employee's employment since regulation 8(2)(a) requires the relevant employee's employment to transfer 'by virtue of these Regulations';
- whose employment with the transferor is terminated 'before the time of the transfer in the circumstances described in regulation 7(1)'.[60] This extends the limitation of the transfer of the transferor's debts to the transferee to those owed to an employee who is automatically unfairly dismissed prior to the relevant transfer (i.e. an employee who was unfairly dismissed before or after the transfer by reason of the transfer itself or a reason connected with the transfer that is not an ETOR).

3. Excluded debts

Regulation 8(5) provides that regulation 4 'shall not operate to transfer liability for the sums **10.41** payable to the relevant employee under the relevant statutory schemes'. Regulation 8 therefore excludes from the scope of the liabilities which the transferee inherits under regulation 4 those sums which are payable to relevant employees under the 'relevant statutory schemes'. These schemes are specified in regulation 8(4) and are the state-guaranteed payment schemes from the National Insurance Fund.

In *Secretary of State for Trade and Industry v (1) Slater and others and (2) CGF Nationwide Site* **10.42** *Services Ltd*,[61] Elias P summarized the position with regard to the transfer of liabilities pursuant to regulation 8(6) as follows:

18. Regulation 8(3) has the effect of making the Secretary of State liable for the obligations still outstanding at the date of transfer which are caught by Part XII of the 1996 Act. There is a deemed dismissal at that stage for purposes of fixing those liabilities even although there has been no actual dismissal. However, to the extent that these liabilities exceed the statutory limits, liability transfers to the transferee.

19. Regulation 8(5) has the effect of making the insolvency fund rather than the transferee liable to meet any redundancy liabilities.

Whilst a detailed treatment of the statutory guarantee payment schemes, and in particular **10.43** the limitations to which they are subject, is outside the scope of this work, they are:

- the payments to be made by the Secretary of State under ERA 1996, ss 166–70.[62] These include statutory redundancy payments and payments in accordance with conciliation or

---

[59] Regulation 8(2)(a).
[60] Regulation 8(2)(b).
[61] [2007] IRLR 928, EAT.
[62] Regulation 8(4)(a).

compromise agreements made by way of an agreement to refrain from bringing a claim for the statutory redundancy entitlement;

- the payments to be made by the Secretary of State under ERA 1996, ss 182–90 on the insolvency of an employer where the relevant employee's employment has been terminated.[63] These payments relate to matters such as arrears of pay, notice pay, holiday pay, and guarantee payments, subject to detailed eligibility requirements and limitations.

10.44 The award for failure to comply with the obligations imposed by regulation 13 to effect collective information and consultation does not fall within the scope of ERA 1996, ss 184–6 in contrast to awards in respect of breach of the collective redundancy information and consultation obligations of TULRCA 1992, s. 188. In *Connor and anor v the Secretary of State for Trade & Industry*[64] Burton J took the opportunity to speculate, as he put it, on why that was the case. In his view:

> [i]t may be that this is because in many cases, if not in the majority, the party who will be liable in respect of the TUPE protective award will not be at any rate, in the first instance, the employer of the employee and it is, of course, the insolvent employee, as specifically stated by the heading to Part XII of ERA, whose obligation in legislation is dedicated to guaranteeing.[65]

10.45 This adaptation of the effects of TUPE in relation to relevant insolvency proceedings applies not only to employees dismissed in relation to the transfer but also to those whose employment has transferred to the transferee by virtue of TUPE (as opposed to a transfer of employment by agreement in circumstances where the employee falls outside the scope of TUPE).[66] This leads to a variation of the usual position under ERA 1996, s. 102(b), which applies the statutory guarantee payment provisions only to those who have actually been dismissed. Regulation 8(3) provides that the date of the relevant transfer is treated as the date of the termination of employment for the purposes of the relevant statutory payments and the transferor is treated as the employer.[67] A transferring employee can therefore claim the statutory redundancy payment and other relevant payments from the state calculated as at the point of transfer. In response to concerns raised by consultees, the DTI[68] (as it then was) confirmed its view that payment to a transferring employee of the statutory redundancy payment by the Government pursuant to a relevant statutory scheme has the effect of ensuring 'that the transferred workers have to build up their future entitlement to redundancy payments with the new employer from zero'.

10.46 The overall effect of these provisions is therefore that those whose employment by a transferor in relation to which relevant insolvency proceedings are ongoing transfer to the transferee in accordance with TUPE, or who are automatically unfairly dismissed in connection with the transfer, are entitled to receive payments from the Secretary of State in respect of the relevant debts in the same way as they would have been had they been dismissed by the insolvent employer. The transferee does not, as would otherwise be the case, inherit liability for those debts for which the Secretary of State is liable.

---

[63] Regulation 8(4)(b).
[64] UKEAT/0589/05.
[65] Ibid. at para. 37.
[66] Regulation 8(2)(b).
[67] Regulation 8(3).
[68] Consultation Response paras 5.5 and 5.7.

The transferee is only excused from liability for the debts specifically excluded from transfer **10.47** by regulations 8(2)–(6). Debts not covered by the relevant statutory schemes or the excess of any debts owed by the transferor to the transferring employees over the applicable statutory limits are still inherited by the transferee in the normal course under regulation 4. As the 2005 Consultation noted,[69] liabilities for debts owed to employees other than those who transfer under TUPE to the transferee remain with the transferor. Debts owed to those dismissed prior to transfer for an ETOR remain with the transferor. In addition, this modified insolvency regime in relation to relevant insolvency proceedings only deals with debts. Transferees are not excused from liabilities for automatically unfair pre- or post-transfer dismissals under TUPE.

4. Timing

Pressure Coolers Ltd v Molloy[70] addressed an important timing point in relation to the state **10.48** guarantee payment schemes established by Part XII of ERA 1996 as they are applied in relation to relevant transfers by regulation 8(2)–(6)—the relevant debt must arise before the relevant transfer. Regulations 8(2)–(6) were held not to change that position, to the extent that those provisions provide that the debts of the transferor which are within scope of the guarantee provided by the ERA 1996 are 'frozen' at the point of transfer. This interpretation was held to be consistent not only with Article 5(2)(a)—which refers to the relevant debts as those which are payable before the transfer—but also the effect of regulation 8(3)—which amends the relevant provisions of ERA 1996 so as to disapply the requirement that there be a termination of employment and to deem the transferor to be the employer for these purposes.

Post-transfer liabilities (such as, in *Molloy*, those arising from a post-transfer unfair dismissal) **10.49** did not constitute a liability of a transferring employer for the purposes of the insolvency provisions of regulation 8(2)–(6) as there is no such liability as at transfer. These liabilities were therefore to be borne by the transferee and did not pass to the state. To have held otherwise was seen as contrary to the policy of TUPE to minimize the burden on transferees of the liabilities transferring with those employees who are within its scope. The EAT rejected the argument that there was a policy justification, by way of providing incentives for 'pre-pack' administrations, for widening the scope of the state guarantee beyond the debts payable as at transfer given that the usual application of TUPE was in any event modified in relation to the insolvency situations to which Part XII of ERA 1996 applies.

E. Opening/Instituting Insolvency Proceedings

One question which arises in relation to both regulation 8(6) and regulation 8(7) is the **10.50** precise time at which they engage. As already noted, in regulation 8(6) relevant insolvency proceedings are defined as insolvency proceedings which have been 'opened' in relation to the transferor. Regulation 8(7) refers to bankruptcy proceedings or any analogous insolvency proceedings which have been 'instituted' with a view to the liquidation of assets of the transferor. Regulations 8(6) and 8(7) both require that the proceedings in question are under the supervision of an insolvency practitioner. Therefore, since proceedings have to be both

---

[69] At para. 59, footnote 5.
[70] [2011] IRLR 630, EAT.

opened/instituted and under the supervision of an insolvency practitioner, it is irrelevant whether insolvency proceedings have been instituted until an insolvency practitioner has been appointed in accordance with IA 1986, s. 388.

10.51 In *Secretary of State for Trade and Industry v (1) Slater and others and (2) CGF Nationwide Site Services Ltd*[71] the EAT considered there to be no particular distinction to be drawn between proceedings being opened under regulation 8(6) or instituted under regulation 8(7) and held that when any type of insolvency proceedings commences will depend on the statutory provisions relating to the particular proceedings. Following a decision to place the company by which the relevant employees were employed into voluntary liquidation, a vehicle formed by certain executives of the original employing entity acquired what they believed only to be the assets of the business by way of what was found actually to be an acquisition of the business within the scope of TUPE. The company was only formally put into voluntary liquidation after the acquisition. The employees remained in employment with the transferee and claimed from the transferee payments of back pay and holiday pay relating to the period before transfer. The transferee denied liability, arguing that regulation 8 operated to place liability for these payments with the Secretary of State and to relieve the transferee of these liabilities which it would otherwise have inherited under TUPE.

10.52 The EAT held that on any view the transfer occurred before the relevant proceedings were under the supervision of the insolvency practitioner as required in respect of both regulation 8(6) and regulation 8(7). TUPE's specific insolvency provisions therefore did not apply to the transaction in question and TUPE applied in full. The earlier involvement in an advisory capacity of the individual who was subsequently appointed as the relevant insolvency practitioner did not constitute insolvency proceedings under the supervision of an insolvency practitioner prior to the individual's appointment as liquidator. Put shortly, Elias P's view was that the issue of whether insolvency proceedings have been 'opened' or 'instituted' depends on the statutory provisions governing the applicable form of insolvency procedure and that, in order to be under the supervision of an insolvency practitioner, the relevant practitioner needs actually to have been appointed.[72]

10.53 The EAT did not consider it necessary to determine when proceedings commence in relation to a creditors' voluntary liquidation i.e. whether proceedings commence at the point of the resolution of the members or the creditors' meeting.

F. Permitted Contract Variations

1. Introduction

10.54 Utilizing the option provided by Article 5.2, where relevant insolvency proceedings are on foot in relation to the transferor, regulation 9 establishes the ability of employers and appropriate representatives of the transferring employees validly to agree changes connected with or caused by a relevant transfer to the terms and conditions of employment of these transferring employees. For such changes to be valid, certain specific requirements must be satisfied.

---

[71] [2007] IRLR 928, EAT.
[72] Ibid. at paras 25–32.

It was considered that the consequences of taking up this option would be entirely positive **10.55** provided that adequate safeguards were provided for employees.[73] Employers and appropriate representatives of the transferring employees would then have the same freedom to negotiate in transfer scenarios as in other situations where changes to terms and conditions might need to be agreed with a view to securing the survival of an insolvent business and the consequent saving of jobs.

This ability to change terms not only evades the prohibition on transfer-related contract **10.56** changes established by cases such as *Daddy's Dance Hall* and *Wilson*[74] but is also less constrained, and therefore wider in scope, than the ability introduced by regulations 4(4) and 4(5) to agree transfer-related contract changes—primarily because no ETOR need be established in order to take advantage of this derogation from the general principles of TUPE.[75]

Regulation 9 only applies in relation to 'relevant insolvency proceedings', i.e. to the same **10.57** types of insolvency procedure as the provisions as to the transferor's debts set out in regulation 8(2)–(6).[76] Regulation 9(7) provides that 'relevant insolvency proceedings' has the meaning given to the expression by regulation 8(6), i.e. 'insolvency proceedings which have been opened in relation to the transferor not with a view to the liquidation of the assets of the transferor and which are under the supervision of an insolvency practitioner'.

Regulation 9(1) provides that '[i]f at the time of a relevant transfer the transferor is subject to **10.58** relevant insolvency proceedings these Regulations shall not prevent the transferor or transferee (or an insolvency practitioner) and appropriate representatives of assigned employees agreeing to permitted variations'. These permitted variations can be agreed between the transferor or transferee (or an insolvency practitioner) and 'appropriate representatives'. The period during which permitted variations can be agreed is not expressly addressed by regulation 9. Presumably, although it is not expressly stated, the transferee must agree the changes prior to or at the point of transfer—it can be surmised that this special regime is intended only to operate while the relevant business or undertaking is the subject of the relevant insolvency proceedings in order to facilitate its whole or partial sale as a going concern.

Regulation 9 also only makes reference to permitted variations being agreed by appropriate **10.59** representatives of the transferring employees. This indicates that employees cannot individually agree contract changes under regulation 9. Consequently, it must be presumed that changes agreed by employees individually which are connected with a relevant transfer must satisfy regulations 4(4) and 4(5) in order to be valid, even if relevant insolvency proceedings have been instituted in respect of the relevant business.[77]

2. Which employees?

Permitted variations can only be agreed by appropriate representatives of 'assigned employ- **10.60** ees'. For these purposes 'assigned employees' are 'those employees assigned to the organised grouping of resources or employees that is the subject of a relevant transfer'.[78] Permitted

---

[73] 2001 Consultation para. 93.
[74] See Chapter 6, para. 6.06 *et seq.*
[75] Ibid.
[76] See para. 10.37 *et seq.*
[77] See Chapter 6, para. 6.27 *et seq.*
[78] Regulation 9(7).

variations therefore can only be agreed in relation to those employees whose employment transfers to the transferee by virtue of TUPE on the relevant transfer in question.

10.61 This limitation on the scope of regulation 9 therefore means that those of the transferor's employees who do not transfer to the transferee by virtue of the particular relevant transfer cannot agree permitted variations under this regime. This is perhaps unsurprising as they do not fall to transfer to the transferee as a consequence of the transaction which the ability to agree permitted variations is intended to facilitate.

3. Appropriate representatives

10.62 Regulation 9(2) defines (and provides protection for) the 'appropriate representatives' of the transferring employees who can act to agree permitted variations pursuant to regulation 9. Regulation 9(2) provides that:

> [f]or the purposes of this regulation 'appropriate representatives' are:
> (a) if the employees are of a description in respect of which an independent trade union is recognised by their employer, representatives of the trade union; or
> (b) in any other case, whichever of the following employee representatives the employer chooses:
>   (i) employee representatives appointed or elected by the assigned employees (whether they make the appointment or election alone or with others) otherwise than for the purposes of this regulation, who (having regard to the purposes for, and the method by which they were appointed or elected) have authority from those employees to agree permitted variations to contracts of employment on their behalf;
>   (ii) employee representatives elected by assigned employees (whether they make the appointment or election alone or with others) for these particular purposes, in an election satisfying requirements identical to those contained in regulation 14 except those in regulation 14(1)(d).

10.63 The provisions of regulation 9 relating to employee representation are in essence the same as those applying in relation to the information and consultation 13.[79] That said, the appropriate representatives for the purposes of regulation 9 are identified by reference to 'assigned' rather than 'affected' employees. As only those who fall to transfer to the transferee—by virtue of being assigned to the relevant undertaking or organized grouping of employees—can be the subject of permitted variations, only their representatives can agree them.

10.64 Accordingly, if a trade union is recognized in respect of the relevant employees, it can negotiate valid transfer-related changes on behalf of those employees in a qualifying insolvency context.[80] Despite suggestions from consultation respondents that a specific provision be enacted confirming a recognized trade union's authority to agree permitted variations generally, no such provision was included in the 2006 Regulations. Nor was the suggestion of the Law Society of England and Wales taken up that there should be a requirement that agreements with trade unions be notified to the employees concerned in order to allow them to

---

[79] See Chapter 9. The only difference between regulation 9 and regulations 13–15 in this regard is the omission from regulation 9 of an equivalent of regulation 14(1)(d)—the employer being required to determine the term of office of a representative. This provision was presumably not considered relevant in the (likely to be short-term) context of a transaction out of insolvency.

[80] Regulation 9(2)(a).

question the changes.[81] Where non-union representatives are involved, such an obligation applies.[82]

If there is no recognized trade union in respect of the relevant undertaking or activities or there are categories of employee outside the scope of a recognized trade union's recognition, employee representatives can negotiate transfer-related changes provided that they are either elected in accordance with the relevant requirements or have the requisite authority to act.[83] As is the case with the regulation 13 information and consultation obligation, if there is a recognized union, only that union is empowered to agree permitted variations with regard to employees falling within the scope of its recognition. Separately elected employee representatives cannot in such circumstances be utilized for these purposes. **10.65**

Regulation 9(3) confirms that an individual may be an appropriate representative for the purposes of both the regulation 9 insolvency regime and the regulation 13 information and consultation obligations 'provided that where the representative is not a trade union representative he is either elected by or has authority from assigned employees (within the meaning of this regulation [9]) and affected employees (as described in regulation 13(1))'. Employee representatives for the purpose of a regulation 13 information and consultation process can agree permitted variations in the insolvency context but only if their authority and competence extends to the agreement of permitted variations. **10.66**

Specific authority is therefore required for employee representatives to be able validly to agree permitted variations. In this regard, regulation 9(2)(b)(i) provides that, where no election is conducted specifically for the purposes of appointing employee representatives competent to agree permitted variations, the representatives must '(having regard to the purposes for and the method by which they were appointed or elected) have authority from those employees to agree permitted variations to contracts of employment on their behalf'. It is not possible simply to take representatives elected only for regulation 13 information and consultation purposes or an existing employee forum and agree permitted variations with them unless it is possible to establish that they have the requisite authority for the purposes of regulation 9. **10.67**

The speed of completion of many transactions in insolvency situations may make it difficult to utilize this ability to introduce permitted variations if election of employee representatives needs to be conducted. That said, it may well be that, if employee representatives are being elected by employees engaged in a business which is or is likely to be in insolvency, it will be sensible for the employer or relevant insolvency practitioner in arranging the requisite elections specifically to establish the authority of the elected employee representatives to agree regulation 9 permitted variations as well as to participate in regulation 13 information and consultation. **10.68**

It is specifically provided that the protections provided under ERA 1996 for the purposes of the regulation 13 information and consultation obligations similarly apply to employee representatives for the purposes of permitted variations in the insolvency context.[84] **10.69**

---

[81] See Consultation Response para. 5.5.
[82] Regulation 9(5)(b).
[83] Regulation 9(2)(b)(i) and (ii).
[84] TUPE 2006, Schedule 2, para. 10. See Chapter 9, para. 9.75 *et seq.*

10.70 Similarly, regulation 9(4) makes consequential amendments to TULRCA 1992, s. 168 to ensure that trade union representatives have the rights to time off in this context similar to those which apply in relation to the regulation 13 information and consultation obligations. Time off is specifically permitted in respect of:

- negotiations with a view to entering into an agreement for the purposes of regulation 9;
- the performance on behalf of employees of the employer of functions related to or connected with the making of an agreement under that regulation.

4. Agreement of employee representatives

10.71 For permitted variations to be valid under regulation 9, specific additional requirements must be complied with in situations where the transferring employees are represented by employee representatives as opposed to being represented by a recognized trade union.[85] These additional safeguards are intended to recognize the fact that non-union representatives are not normally involved in negotiating changes to employees' terms and conditions and are therefore less likely to be experienced and knowledgeable than trade union representatives.[86] Variations agreed by union representatives are valid without these requirements needing to be satisfied. No particular requirements are specified in relation to the agreement by recognized trade unions of permitted variations.

10.72 First, the agreement recording the permitted variations must be in writing and signed by each of the employee representatives who have made it or, where that is not reasonably practicable, by a duly authorized agent of that employee representative.[87]

10.73 Second, the employer must, before the agreement is made available for signature, provide all employees to whom it is intended to apply on the date on which it is to come into effect with copies of the text of the agreement and such guidance as those employees might reasonably require in order to understand it fully.[88] The extent to which detailed guidance will need to be given as to the effects of changes will presumably depend upon their complexity. This is a requirement which will need to be addressed with care, especially since failure to comply with it presumably invalidates an otherwise effective permitted variation.

10.74 That the agreement must in these circumstances be signed by the employee representatives or their authorized agent raises two issues. First, it is arguably implicit (but not specifically stated) that the employee representatives must act unanimously (which may provide some further protection for minority groups of employees). Second, what constitutes a duly authorized agent is not specified. Clear, preferably written, evidence of the authorization of an agent who signs an agreement recording what are intended to be permitted variations for the purposes of regulation 9 (for example, one representative being appointed to act on behalf of the entire body of representatives) will be needed to ensure their validity, assuming all the other requirements are satisfied.

---

[85] Regulations 9(5)(a) and (b).
[86] 2005 Consultation, para. 70.
[87] Regulation 9(5)(a).
[88] Regulation 9(5)(b).

5. The nature of permitted variations

10.75 Regulation 9(6) provides that a permitted variation 'shall take effect as a term or condition of the assigned employee's contract of employment in place, where relevant, of any term or condition which it varies'. It is of immediate binding contractual effect.

10.76 To be valid, a permitted variation must also be 'designed to safeguard employment opportunities by ensuring the survival of the undertaking, business or part of the undertaking or business that is subject of the relevant transfer'.[89] This is a potentially important requirement necessitating establishment of the purpose of a permitted variation for it to be valid and proof of this purpose if the validity of the variation in question is subsequently challenged. Contemporaneous evidence on this point may be crucial in this regard.

10.77 Moreover, the scope of permitted variations is circumscribed—they cannot legitimate changes for which there is an ETOR.[90] The sole or principal reason for the permitted variation must be 'the transfer itself or a reason connected with the transfer that is not an economic, technical or organisational reason entailing changes in the workforce'. An example would be a transfer-related pay cut with no attendant workforce changes. If an ETOR exists for a proposed change—i.e. there is a change in the workforce by way of job losses or function changes—the permitted variation route cannot be used, although the ability for the employees themselves (as distinct from their representatives) to agree contract changes pursuant to regulation 4(4) and 4(5)[91] would then be available. The permitted variation route need not (and cannot) be used where the changes are not by reason of or related to the transfer. In such a case, pursuant to regulation 4(5)(b), TUPE does not engage to regulate contractual validity and the normal common law contractual rules apply.

6. Issues of interpretation

10.78 A number of issues remain untested in relation to the operation of regulation 9 with regard to permitted variations. The fact that trade union or (in the absence of a recognized trade union) employee representatives are empowered to agree permitted variations appears to give the affected employees no ability, in legal or process terms, individually to object to a change or changes which those representatives agree on their behalf. These changes are deemed contractual by regulation 9(6) if the representatives are appointed and act in accordance with the applicable requirements.

10.79 TUPE provides no specific framework for employees to be able to object to the decision of their representatives with regard to the detail of permitted variations or to opt out of the effect of the powers which regulation 9 confers. Accordingly, it appears that an employee's contract can, in contrast to the common law position, be amended without his or her agreement or authority with regard to the particularity of the change. In cases where a recognized union constitutes the appropriate representatives, the employees may not have given the union authority to agree such changes in the normal course of events but may find it conferred by statute in the insolvency context if a broad interpretation is applied to regulation 9. The representatives would seem able effectively to impose on the relevant workforce amendments to

---

[89] Regulation 9(7).
[90] Ibid.
[91] See Chapter 6.

their contracts of employment without those affected being required to validate (as distinct from being informed of) the detailed results of the negotiations conducted by their representatives. There is no apparent prohibition on differential treatment of different classes of or particular employees.

10.80 These (admittedly untested) issues arguably increase the exposure of employee representatives to the possibility of claims by employees against their representatives of negligence in the performance of their duties and the negotiation of contract changes. A representative's potential predicament in this regard may be exacerbated by the fact that, despite requests that such an obligation be introduced, nothing in TUPE requires the disclosure by the employer of any information to the representatives engaged in negotiating permitted variations.[92] These issues are put in even starker relief by the fact that regulation 9 (as is the case with regulation 13) does not expressly require elected employee representatives to be informed of their responsibilities, or indeed potential liabilities, nor does it specify their responsibilities to the employees whom they represent.

10.81 The 2005 Consultation did not address these concerns to any material extent. The role of appropriate representatives was likened to that of similarly elected persons under regulation 13[93] (even though appropriate representatives in relation to the collective information and consultation process do not, by virtue of TUPE, have the power to commit their constituency to legally binding agreements). The requirement, where the appropriate representatives are not union representatives, to circulate the proposed agreement and appropriate guidance was described as being based on the 'established precedent' of the Working Time Regulations 1998 where similarly structured 'workforce agreements' are permitted. Such workforce agreements are, however, limited in scope to a narrow category of working time issues in contrast to permitted variations, which could cover any aspect of the relevant employees' contracts of employment and benefit packages.

10.82 Objecting to transfer does not appear to be a route to compensation for employees whose rights are overridden by the collective permitted variation process. The fact that regulation 4(9) is expressly made subject to regulation 9 means that affected employees cannot exercise the right to terminate their employment by reason of a substantial change to their working conditions to their material detriment where the change has been agreed by their appropriate representatives in an insolvency situation under regulation 9. A traditional constructive dismissal claim pursuant to regulation 4(11) would appear to be unavailable because a permitted variation is deemed contractually valid and effective by regulation 9(6).

10.83 Employees who find themselves unhappy with changes which have been agreed on their behalf pursuant to regulation 9 may therefore have little room for manoeuvre. In terms of challenge to the validity of a permitted variation, employees would appear to have two particular avenues to consider in terms of arguing that a change is not valid and effective because it does not satisfy the definition of a permitted variation. It may be possible to argue that the change was not designed to safeguard employment opportunities. That said, the purposive aspect of a permitted variation appears to require only an intention or objective of safeguarding employment opportunities. Accordingly, it would appear that a permitted variation should not be capable of being rendered invalid on the basis that it was not objectively

---

[92] Consultation Response, para. 5.6.
[93] At para. 68.

required in order to (as opposed to being intended to) safeguard employment. Alternatively, it could be argued that inadequate guidance was given to the employees in order to enable them to understand the changes.

G. Misuse of Insolvency Proceedings

Article 5.4 requires Member States to 'take appropriate measures with a view to preventing **10.84** misuse of insolvency proceedings in such a way as to deprive employees of the rights provided for'. In its deliberations prior to the introduction of the 2006 Regulations, the Government considered that the existing safeguards set out in the Insolvency Act 1986 remain adequate for these purposes and therefore that no amendment to TUPE was required in that regard.[94] Essentially, protection against misuse of insolvency proceedings is provided by the limitation of the control and supervision of insolvency proceedings to those authorized to act as insolvency practitioners together with the other regulatory provisions of the Insolvency Act 1986 and the Company Directors' Disqualification Act 1986 establishing the regime of potential investigations and prosecutions following the cases of malpractice.

H. Hiving Down

TUPE 1981, regulation 4(1) provided that, where the receiver of property or an administra- **10.85** tor or liquidator in a creditors' voluntary winding up transferred the company's undertaking or part of the company's undertaking to a wholly owned subsidiary, the relevant transfer should be deemed for the purposes of the legislation not to have been effected until immediately before whichever was first to occur of:

- the transferee company ceasing (otherwise than by reason of its being wound up) to be a wholly owned subsidiary of the transferor company;
- the relevant undertaking being transferred by the transferee company to another person.

For the purposes of TUPE 1981, the transfer was then taken to have been effected imme- **10.86** diately before the final transaction in the process thereby leaving the employees employed by the insolvent company unprotected. This provision addressed what is known as 'hiving down' but was not replicated in TUPE 2006 on the basis that it no longer served any useful purpose.[95] Historically, hiving down was used as a mechanism to seek to avoid the application of TUPE. However, following *Litster*,[96] pre-transfer dismissals can lead to liability on the part of the transferee in any case, thereby rendering the TUPE 1981 provisions redundant. These provisions were not continued into the 2006 Regulations.

---

[94] 2001 Consultation paras 98–100; 2005 Consultation para. 73.
[95] 2001 Consultation, paras 101–3.
[96] [1989] IRLR 161, HL.

11

TUPE AND PENSIONS

A. Overview	11.01	F. Pension Communications	11.48
B. The Pensions Exclusion	11.06	1. Misrepresentation	11.48
C. TUPE Pension Provisions	11.10	2. Separate pension promises	11.54
D. Occupational Pension		G. PA 2004 and PPR 2005	11.56
Schemes	11.14	1. Introduction	11.56
		2. Eligibility requirements	11.61
E. The Limits of the Pensions		3. The minimum standard of pension	
Exclusion	11.21	provision	11.65
1. *Beckmann* and *Martin*	11.21	4. Enforcement	11.74
2. *Procter & Gamble*	11.30	5. Consultation	11.78
3. Practical issues	11.45	6. Auto-enrolment	11.79

A. Overview

11.01 The Directive permits Member States' domestic legislation to exclude membership of and benefits under occupational pension schemes from those rights of transferring employees which are preserved on a transfer falling within its scope.[1] For ease of reference, this can be styled the 'the pensions exclusion'. Regulation 10(1)[2] incorporates into domestic law this permissible exclusion of occupational pension rights from the scope of the entitlements of transferring employees which the transferee inherits and is required to honour after a TUPE transfer. In very general terms, occupational pension schemes for these purposes are defined benefit or defined contribution schemes established and operated by employers (as distinct from obligations to contribute to personal pension arrangements which do transfer to the transferee on a relevant transfer).

11.02 The pensions exclusion has proved over time to be a particularly controversial aspect of TUPE, particularly in the context of the contracting out of services from the public sector with the consequent potential loss of valuable pension rights more favourable than those generally offered in the private sector. To an extent this lack of pension protection was in more recent times mitigated in the public sector context by Government practice and contracting requirements.[3]

---

[1] By virtue of Article 4 (whilst also permitting Member States to provide that occupational pension rights do transfer).

[2] Previously regulation 7 of TUPE 1981.

[3] See Chapter 1, paras 1.57 *et seq*.

More generally, in practical terms, the consequences from the human resources and indus-   **11.03**
trial relations perspectives of failure to provide pension benefits post-transfer often impel
transferees to put in place some form of pension benefit in order to avoid potentially disas-
trous effects on staff morale and retention. However, until 6 April 2005, the only impetus
in the private sector to continue any pension provision for those who enjoyed pre-transfer
occupational pension arrangements falling within the scope of the pensions exclusion was
either the commercial imperative of maintaining staff relations or a requirement on the part
of a client awarding an outsourcing contract that pension provision be maintained for its
former employees after transfer to the new contractor.

The combined effect of the Pensions Act 2004 (PA 2004) and the Transfer of Employment   **11.04**
(Pension Protection) Regulations 2005 (PPR 2005) establishes a minimum level of pension
provision for transferring employees who enjoyed (or were eligible for) pension benefits in
their pre-transfer employment with the transferor. It is important to note that the pension
protection regime established by PA 2004 and PPR 2005 only requires transferees to extend
pension benefits to those transferring employees who enjoyed or were eligible (actually or
contingently) for pre-transfer occupational pension entitlements. For those who had no
such pension entitlements prior to transfer, no specific provision is made beyond the general
obligation to offer stakeholder pension arrangements and (as and when applicable) to operate auto-entitlement. Employment costs may be increased for transferees as a consequence of
the requirement to maintain a minimum level of pension benefit for transferring employees,
but this pension preservation regime was introduced with the objective of creating a 'level
playing field' for those competing for the award of contracts.

However, the pensions aspects of a relevant transfer may not simply consist of complying   **11.05**
with PA 2004 and PPR 2005. The ECJ case law on the extent of the pensions exclusion
means that certain pension-related benefits provided by the transferor which are available
to transferring employees may still need to be replicated post-transfer if they fall outside the
narrowly construed scope of the pensions exclusion. For example, if a transferee assumes that
it can simply offer a money purchase scheme complying with PA 2004 and PPR 2005 but
discovers that it is nonetheless, post-transfer, bound by certain aspects of the transferor's final
salary scheme of whose precise details it was unaware and which it erroneously assumed to
fall within the scope of the pensions exclusion (such as an entitlement to early retirement in
certain circumstances), there could be extremely significant cost in replicating those aspects
of a pension scheme which, *ex hypothesi*, the transferee will have decided not to continue.
Challenging commercial and liability allocation issues can therefore arise.

B. The Pensions Exclusion

Article 4 provides that: **11.06**

  (a) Paragraphs 1 and 3[4] shall not apply in relation to employees' rights to old age, invalidity
      or survivors' benefits under supplementary company or intercompany pension schemes
      outside the statutory social security schemes in Member States.

---

[4] Which are the operative provisions of the Directive requiring domestic legislation to transfer to the transferee all obligations, rights, powers, and duties in relation to the transferring employees.

(b) Member States shall adopt the measures necessary to protect the interests of employees and of persons no longer employed in the transferor's business at the time of the transfer in respect of rights conferring on them immediate or prospective entitlement to old age benefits, including survivors' benefits, under supplementary schemes referred to in sub-paragraph (a).

11.07 Put shortly, Article 4(a) excludes occupational pension scheme rights from the benefits which the transferee inherits under the Directive. Article 4(b) requires the Member States to ensure that the accrued pension benefits of the transferring employees are adequately protected but does not require Member States in their domestic implementing legislation to impose any mandatory obligation on transferees to continue those existing occupational pension benefits after transfer.

11.08 That the obligation in the predecessor provision of Article 4(b) to preserve pension rights could not be interpreted to require transferees to provide after a relevant transfer occupational pension benefits equivalent to those provided pre-transfer was confirmed in *Walden Engineering Co Ltd v Warrener*.[5] In that case it was argued that a scheme operated to replace the State Earnings Related Pension Scheme pension arrangement did not fall within the scope of the pensions exclusion because the relevant company scheme did not fall outside the statutory social security scheme—it was a replacement for it. The EAT made clear that the requirement in the Directive that Member States take measures to protect employees' and former employees' interests was simply a requirement to protect pension scheme rights accrued at the point of transfer—the UK has a separate statutory protection regime in this regard.[6]

11.09 In *Adams v Lancashire County Council and BET*,[7] the Court of Appeal held that a transferor Council was not in breach of the Directive by failing to secure the ongoing benefit of its occupational pension scheme when the employees transferred to the transferee. The argument was rejected that TUPE 1981, regulation 7 was of wider scope than permitted by the Directive. It was held that the Directive did not require occupational pension benefits to be continued post-transfer.

C. TUPE Pension Provisions

11.10 Regulation 10(1) provides that regulations 4 and 5 (which provide for the contracts of employment of the relevant employees and their associated rights and for collective agreements to transfer from the transferor to the transferee) shall not apply:

(a) to so much of a contract of employment or collective agreement as relates to an occupational pension scheme within the meaning of the Pensions Schemes Act 1993; or
(b) to any rights, powers, duties or liabilities under or in connection with any such contract or subsisting by virtue of any such agreement relating to such a scheme or otherwise arising in connection with that person's employment and relating to such a scheme.

---

[5] [1993] ICR 967, EAT.
[6] Pension Schemes Act 1993, Pensions Act 2004, and other protective legislation outside the scope of this work.
[7] [1997] IRLR 436, CA. See also *Eidesund v Stavanger Catering A/S* [1996] IRLR 684, ECJ.

Regulation 10(2) further provides that 'any provisions of an occupational pension scheme **11.11** which do not relate to benefits for old age, invalidity or survivors shall be treated as not being part of the scheme'.

One specific change to the operation of TUPE in relation to pension entitlements was made **11.12** in the 2006 Regulations. Regulation 10(3) provides that:

> An employee whose contract of employment is transferred in the circumstances described in regulation 4(1) shall not be entitled to bring a claim against the transferor for:
> (a) breach of contract; or
> (b) constructive unfair dismissal under Section 95(1)(c) of the 1996 [Employment Rights] Act arising out of a loss or reduction in his rights under an occupational pension scheme in consequence of the transfer, save insofar as the alleged breach of contract or dismissal (as the case may be) occurred prior to the date on which these Regulations took effect.

Some commentators had argued in relation to TUPE 1981 that a failure by the transferee **11.13** to confirm that it would continue to make pension provision equivalent to that enjoyed pre-transfer could constitute constructive dismissal or at least entitle an employee to terminate his or her employment in accordance with what was TUPE 1981, regulation 5(5)[8] on the basis of a substantial change to his or her detriment in his or her working conditions. Liability for such a claim would remain with the transferor pursuant to the pensions exclusion.[9] The possibility of such a claim was removed by way of the introduction in the 2006 Regulations of the provisions of regulation 10(3).

D. Occupational Pension Schemes

There are two principal aspects of the pensions exclusion set out in ARD 2001. The first is **11.14** that it is limited in its scope to 'old age, invalidity or survivors' benefits'. As well as pension related benefits that do not qualify as old age benefits, transferees need therefore to be alert to the risk of inheriting responsibilities for entitlements such as death-in-service benefits and incapacity early retirement pensions on the basis that they are survivors' or invalidity benefits. Other benefits do transfer to and are inherited by the transferee. As discussed below, this formulation presents some potentially difficult issues. Second, the arrangements which the pension exclusion covers are 'supplementary company or inter-company pension schemes'.

TUPE does not refer to the concept of supplementary company or intercompany pension **11.15** schemes. Rather, it provides that 'occupational pension schemes' fall outside the scope of the transfer of contractual entitlements to the transferee.[10]

PSA 1993, s. 1 provided the following definition of an occupational pension scheme: **11.16**

> 'occupational pension scheme' means any scheme or arrangement which is comprised in one or more instruments or agreements and which has, or is capable of having effect in relation to one or more descriptions of categories of employments so as to provide benefits, in the

---

[8] Now regulation 4(9).
[9] Following the analysis, confirmed in *Hagen v ICI Chemicals and Polymers Ltd* [2002] IRLR 31, EAT, that occupational pension scheme-related liabilities do not transfer to the transferee and *Humphreys* (discussed in Chapter 4, para. 4.125 *et seq.*), pursuant to which the transferor is liable in respect of the termination of the employee's employment in such circumstances prior to a relevant transfer even though it is caused by the transferee's actions.
[10] Regulation 10.

form of pensions or otherwise, payable on termination of service, or on death or retirement, to or in respect of earners with qualifying service in an employment of any such description or category.

11.17 PA 2004, s. 239 now provides the following definition of an occupational pension scheme as follows:

'occupational pension scheme' means a pension scheme:
(a) that:
    (i) for the purpose of providing benefits to, or in respect of, people with service in employments of a description, or
    (ii) for that purpose and also for the purpose of providing benefits to, or in respect of, other people, is established by, or by persons who include, a person to whom subsection (2) applies when the scheme is established or (as the case may be) to whom that subsection would have applied when the scheme was established had that subsection then been in force, and
(b) that has its main administration in the United Kingdom or outside the Member States, or a pension scheme that is prescribed or is of a prescribed description.

11.18 The issue arises of whether there is any practical or other distinction between these two definitions of what constitutes an occupational pension scheme. As Pollard noted,[11] the requirement of qualifying service by reference to which benefits must be payable no longer applies but the main administration of the scheme must now be in the United Kingdom or outside the EU. A pension arrangement which would otherwise constitute an occupational pension scheme would therefore fall outside the PA 2004, s. 239 definition (and therefore outside the scope of the pensions exclusion) if administered outside the UK but within the EU.

11.19 These definitions of what constitutes an occupational pension scheme are considered to cover defined contribution and defined benefit schemes established and operated by employers (which therefore fall outside the scope of the legislation and need not be continued post-transfer by the transferee) and not to contractual obligations to make a financial contribution to an individual's externally operated and managed personal pension arrangement (which the transferee therefore does inherit). An employer's obligation to make a financial contribution to an employee's own personal pension arrangement simply constitutes a cash contribution and therefore does not fall within the scope of the pensions exclusion—it is preserved on transfer like any other contractual benefit. Similarly, a stakeholder pension[12] arrangement, even if it has been established by the employer, is thought not to constitute an occupational pension scheme and will be inherited by the transferee on a relevant transfer.

11.20 A group personal pension scheme is akin to a personal pension arrangement falling outside the scope of pension exclusion because it entails the making of contributions by the employer to be invested on behalf of the employee by a pension provider. The fact that there are now (consequent upon amendments made by PA 2004) separate definitions of occupational pension schemes and personal pension schemes in the PSA 1993, s. 1 bolsters this argument. However, the fact that a group personal pension scheme is to an extent operated by the employer does provide some basis for arguing that it is an occupational pension scheme within the meaning of the legislation. The fact that such arrangements can, in administrative terms, be transferred relatively easily to a transferee and entail specific and finite contribution

---

[11] Pollard, 'Pensions and TUPE' (2005) 34 ILJ 127.
[12] Established pursuant to the requirements of the Welfare Reform and Pensions Act 1999.

liabilities (as well as the advantage of external administration) means that in practice this debate is rarely relevant. It is, however, generally accepted that group personal pensions do not constitute occupational pension schemes on the basis that they are by their nature akin to a grouping of individual personal pension arrangements.

E. The Limits of the Pensions Exclusion

1. *Beckmann* and *Martin*

The litigation surrounding the precise scope of the pensions exclusion makes clear that trans- **11.21** ferees cannot simply ignore occupational pension schemes in their entirety. The pensions exclusion is expressly confined in its scope to old age, survivors', and invalidity benefits. Therefore, other entitlements which are on occasion provided under occupational pension schemes (such as enhanced redundancy and early retirement entitlements) may fall outside the scope of the pensions exclusion and accordingly constitute benefits to which transferring employees remain entitled post-transfer as against the transferee.

Franklin v BPS Public Sector Ltd was an early consideration of the pensions exclusion.[13] **11.22** Employees who had been employed by an NHS Trust, and whose employment transferred to a new employer when their activities were outsourced, had been engaged originally under the Whitley Council terms and conditions of employment. These terms and conditions made special provision for early payment of superannuation and compensation benefits if the employees were made redundant. These entitlements effectively constituted accelerated pension benefits payable in a redundancy situation. The transferee argued that these specific entitlements fell within the scope of the pensions exclusion under TUPE 1981, regulation 7 so that it was accordingly not legally bound to honour them.

The EAT held that, as the entitlements were payable under legislation, they did not consti- **11.23** tute a contractual liability which would transfer under TUPE 1981, regulation 5. The EAT also took the view that the relevant entitlements constituted benefits for old age, invalidity, or survivors and therefore fell within the scope of the pensions exclusion. The basis for this finding was the characterization of the relevant benefits as related to retirement, even though the retirement in relation to which they were payable was earlier than normal retirement age. Pension benefits were held not to change their character simply because they were triggered early by redundancy.

However, this approach to the interpretation of the pensions exclusion was rejected by the **11.24** ECJ in *Beckmann v Dynamco Whicheloe Macfarlane Ltd*.[14] Again, under the Whitley Council rules, employees were entitled to an enhanced lump sum redundancy payment and to early retirement pension entitlements upon dismissal by redundancy after the age of 50. The ECJ applied a strict interpretation of the pensions exclusion which it considered should be construed narrowly. In terms of old age (i.e. pension) benefits, only benefits which are pay- able on conclusion of the employee's working life are excluded from transfer. Benefits which become due earlier, even if they are provided as part of and are payable in accordance with the rules of a pension scheme, fall outside the scope of the pensions exclusion and are inherited

---

[13] [1999] IRLR 212, EAT.
[14] [2002] IRLR 578, ECJ.

by the transferee. That the relevant entitlements derived from statutory obligations made no difference to this analysis.

11.25 As the ECJ put it:

> only benefits paid from the time when an employee reaches the end of his normal working life as laid down by the general structure of the pension scheme in question, and not benefits paid in circumstances such as those in point in the main proceedings (dismissal for redundancy) that can be classified as old-age benefits, even if they are calculated by reference to the rules for calculating normal pension benefits did not fall within the pensions exclusion and therefore were inherited by the transferee.[15]

11.26 Accordingly, rights going beyond the strict ambit of old age, invalidity, and survivors' benefits survive a TUPE transfer and remain part of the employee's transferring contractual entitlements as against the transferee. This analysis can extend not just to entitlements which can easily be characterized as not being pension-related (such as enhanced redundancy payments) but also to benefits which are to a degree pension-related but which arise earlier than at normal retirement age such as early retirement entitlements.

11.27 *Martin and others v South Bank University*[16] again concerned the issue of whether a transferee was bound to honour Whitley Council conditions of service with regard to enhanced retirement pension entitlements and other compensation payable on cessation of work by reason of redundancy, efficiency, or organizational change. The ECJ held that early retirement benefits and benefits intended to enhance the conditions of such retirement are not old age, invalidity, or survivors' benefits within the meaning of the Directive.

11.28 The ECJ considered that there was no basis upon which entitlements arising on dismissal or early retirement agreed with the employer should be treated differently from entitlements arising after the age of 50 (which in *Beckmann* had been held not to constitute old-age benefits and therefore to fall outside the scope of the pensions exclusion). Accordingly, these benefits did fall within the scope of the contractual entitlements passing to the transferee on a relevant transfer. Any consent to an unfavourable alteration of the applicable early retirement terms was accordingly invalid in principle.[17]

11.29 As the ECJ put it in *Martin*:

> Rights contingent upon dismissal or the grant of early retirement by agreement with the employer fall within the 'rights and obligations' referred to Article 3(1) of Business Transfers Directive 77/187. It is clear from the wording of Article 3 that all the transferor's rights and obligations arising from the contract of employment, except in the cases mentioned in Article 3(3), are transferred to the transferee, regardless of whether or not their implementation is contingent upon the happening of a particular event, which may depend on the will of the employer.

> Early retirement benefits arising by agreement between the employer and the employee to employees who have reached a certain age are not old-age, invalidity or survivors' benefits under supplementary company or inter-company pension schemes falling within the exception provided for by Article 3(3) of the Business Transfers Directive and therefore obligations arising upon early retirement are transferred to the transferee.

---

[15] Ibid. at para. 30.
[16] [2004] IRLR 74, ECJ.
[17] See Chapter 6.

In light of the decision in the *Beckmann* case that only benefits paid from the time when an employee reaches the end of his or her working life can be classified as old-age benefits, there was no reason to treat benefits applied for upon dismissal by reason of redundancy, as in *Beckmann*, any differently from those applied for upon early retirement which does not correspond to the departure of an employee at the end of his or her normal working life, as in the present case.

Article 3 of the Business Transfers Directive precludes the transferee from offering the employees of a transferred entity less favourable terms than those offered to them by the transferor in respect of early retirement, and those employees from accepting those terms, where those terms are merely brought into line with the terms offered to the transferee's other employees at the time of transfer unless the more favourable terms previously offered by the transfer law arose from a collective agreement which is no longer legally binding on the employees of the entity transferred.

Where, contrary to Article 3 of the Business Transfers Directive, employees have accepted early retirement on terms less favourable than that to which they were entitled under their employment relationship with the transferor, it is for the transferee to ensure that those employees are accorded early retirement on the terms to which they were entitled under their employment relationship with the transferor.[18]

2. *Procter & Gamble*

(a) Introduction

11.30 It had been suggested that, since both *Beckmann* and *Martin* address NHS pension arrangements, it was not certain that the principles they establish apply in the private sector context. Against this view, it was argued that there is little apparent support for that view to be found in the decisions themselves. That said, there is similarly little indication in the two decisions as to whether they are of general application. The cases both related to a specific public sector context not normally found in the private sector. The relevant public sector arrangements comprised not only a pension payable from normal retirement but also a pension payable until that point.

11.31 The nature of the liabilities which the *Beckmann* and *Martin* decisions operate to transfer to the transferee on a relevant transfer where those occupational pension liabilities are contingent on employer consent was further considered in *The Procter & Gamble Company v Svenska Cellulosa Aktiebolagetsca SCA Hygiene Products Manchester Ltd (formerly known as SCA Hygiene Investments Ltd)*.[19] This case concerned a purely private sector context and therefore appears to dispel any view that *Beckmann* and *Martin* only apply to cases of public sector pensions. *Procter & Gamble* concerned a dispute which arose in the context of contractual provisions for adjustments to the purchase price for the purchase of a business according to whether or not certain accrued pension liabilities transferred pursuant to TUPE. In summary, Hildyard J held that a right to enhanced early retirement pension entitlements which was contingent on employer approval did transfer under TUPE in accordance with the terms of the particular arrangements—in this case to have the application properly considered—but only to the extent that those entitlements were not satisfied pursuant to the transferor's scheme in any event and not in respect of any benefits payable after normal retirement age.

---

[18] Ibid. at para. 55.
[19] [2012] IRLR 733, Ch. This is a complex case to which the brief analysis required by space constraints cannot do justice.

11.32   Procter & Gamble (P&G) operated a pension scheme whose defined benefit section made provision for certain enhanced 'early retirement benefits' (ERBs) for employees who were active members of the scheme and, albeit with employer consent, retired at age 55. These ERBs entailed a favourable actuarial reduction factor and the payment of a bridging pension until the state retirement age.

11.33   P&G sold its European tissue towel business to SCA and, since SCA did not wish to inherit any UK pension liability, specific provisions were agreed in the relevant asset sale agreement to address the principles established by the *Beckmann* and *Martin* decisions. Rather than a '*Beckmann* indemnity',[20] which would deal with liabilities as and when they might fall due, the asset sale agreement provided for an actuarial valuation of any liabilities in respect of the scheme 'for and in respect of each Transferring Employee in respect of accrued pensionable service' which transferred to SCA, and for P&G in effect to pay SCA for such liability (by way of adjustment to the purchase price). This adjustment to the relevant purchase price 'might or might not prove sufficient to meet the transferred liabilities as they perceive them to be, but . . . drew the line once and for all'.[21]

11.34   The dispute which arose was two-fold—first, whether the provision for ERBs in the P&G scheme constituted an obligation of such a nature that it transferred to SCA pursuant to TUPE; and, second, if so, whether the obligation so transferred constituted a liability for the purposes of the provision of the sale agreement providing adjustments to the purchase price referable to such pension liabilities.[22]

(b) Was there a right apt to transfer?

11.35   P&G had argued that the provision for ERBs in its scheme was not a right or obligation falling within Article 3(1), nor a right, power, duty, or liability within the meaning of regulation 4 and that therefore neither the benefit nor the burden of the obligation to provide ERBs transferred to the transferee, SCA, under TUPE. In effect the argument was that the ERBs did not transfer under TUPE because they were not contained within the employees' contracts of employment but were set out in the relevant trust deed and pension scheme rules and therefore were not the subject of contractual commitments by P&G as the employees' employer. In the event, it was conceded, however, that the ERBs were entitlements arising in connection with the contracts of employment subject to the transfer. Consequently, P&G modified its position to argue (effectively in the alternative) that the ERBs were not an accrued liability at the point of transfer because they were discretionary, and that in any event a zero value should be attributed to those rights, because it makes no sense to value a duty only to consider granting a benefit. The entitlement in question was therefore argued to be:

> never a right to be given ERBs but rather was a right to apply for ERBs, and to have that application properly considered by P&G (and after transfer by SCA) in its discretion (which is unfettered, and exercisable having regard to the company's own financial and other interests, subject only to the implied obligation of good faith.[23]

---

[20]   As the indemnities often agreed in business sale agreements to deal with the pensions issues arising from the *Beckmann* and *Martin* cases are called.

[21]   *Procter & Gamble*, above n. 19, at para. 12.

[22]   Space constraints do not permit detailed consideration of this second issue.

[23]   *Procter & Gamble*, above n. 19, at para. 70, referring to the '"*Imperial* duty", as explained by Sir Nicolas Browne-Wilkinson V-C (as he then was) in *Imperial Group Pension Trust Ltd and Others v Imperial Tobacco Ltd and Others* [1991] 1 WLR 589 at 597'.

Having thus reformulated its argument, P&G effectively argued that the entitlement to an **11.36** ERB with employer consent was not a right susceptible to transfer under TUPE. As Hildyard J put it,[24] P&G contended that:

> P&G had no duty or liability in respect of early retirement pensions that had not yet come into payment. It did not promise its employees that they would be available in the future, or that they would take any particular form, or that the Fund would continue at all, or that even if it continues unamended it would give its consent to a member taking early retirement. The only effective promise was that once a pension had been earned, it would not be taken away. But P&G has kept this promise, because the members remain entitled to the pensions that have been earned to the date of the transfer of employment in the shape of their deferred pensions. Ex hypothesi they had not by then acquired any right to early retirement pensions (as if they had they would not have transferred); and P&G had made no promises that they ever would.

These arguments were rejected. First, the entitlement, even if discretionary in the sense of **11.37** being subject to employer consent, was apt for transfer pursuant to TUPE. Hildyard J held that the fact that an entitlement is discretionary, and may be varied or even terminated unilaterally by the employer, does not take it outside the scope of Article 3(1):

> In my judgment, the phrase 'rights and obligations' in Article 3(1) and in TUPE is to be liberally interpreted without regard to domestic distinctions between a discretionary entitlement and a legally enforceable right. The entitlement of the transferring employees, and its concomitant obligation, though discretionary, are such as to transfer by operation of TUPE accordingly.[25]

Second, the right which the transferring employees retained as against the transferee was **11.38** analysed to be an entitlement to good faith consideration for ERBs. Hildyard J put it as follows:[26]

> It seems to me that in the absence of any suggestion of a long standing and settled practice adopted by the relevant company and such as to confer some greater right on an employee . . . for the purposes of English domestic law at any rate what relevant employees had was not a contractual right subject to a contingency, but only the expectation of being fairly treated (in accordance with the 'Imperial duty') in exercising their entitlement to be considered for ERBs. The question then is what difference this characterisation of the 'rights' makes.

(c) What obligation did transfer?

The question therefore then arose of for what precise liabilities SCA became responsible as a **11.39** result of the transfer to it of the entitlement to ERBs under the scheme. In the judgment of Hildyard J what was important to this question was:

> not the label but the substance of the right, power, duty and liability concerned: to satisfy the objectives of TUPE, it is necessary in each case to unpack the economic components, with a view to providing for substantial identity (or failing which substantive equivalence) of economic benefit after the transfer as before.[27]

This approach required careful analysis of how the various elements of the ERBs were dealt **11.40** with (whether by way of deferred pensions or otherwise) to ensure that responsibility for

---

[24] *Procter & Gamble,* above n. 19, at para. 63.
[25] Ibid. at para. 67.
[26] Ibid. at para. 75.
[27] Ibid. at para. 118.

specific entitlements were allocated correctly as between P&G and its scheme trustees on the one hand and SCA on the other. Hildyard J considered that regulation 4(2)(a) and (b):

> should be construed together so as to confine the rights, powers, duties and liabilities to be transferred by statutory process to those rights, powers, duties and liabilities under or in respect of a continuing contract of employment that have not already been substantially satisfied, performed, exercised or discharged by the transferor, whether in cash or kind.[28]

11.41 More particularly, he considered that:

> regulation 4(2)(a) should be construed as referable only to liabilities which have not been substantively satisfied in economic terms.... [and] regulation 4(2)(b) should be construed as treating the deferred pension provided as an act in relation to the transferor which is treated as an act of or in relation to the transferee such as to meet that element of the package of benefits that ERBs comprise.[29]

11.42 Consequently, only the transferred rights or benefits comprised within the ERBs which had not already been met 'in economic substance by virtue of transferring members becoming entitled to deferred pensions in the P&G Fund' transferred to SCA.[30] In effect, this meant that the only liability which transferred to SCA was that in relation to specific enhancements provided under the scheme.[31] From the wider perspective of the purpose of the transfer of undertakings legislation, Hildyard J took the view that this result 'accord[ed] with, and [gave] effect to, the objectives of TUPE and the Directive which it is intended to implement'.[32] In his view it could not:

> have been the intended effect of TUPE or the Directive that further to the transfer there should be a dual liability to ensure the funding of the scheme, which (given the lack of any basis or mechanism for extinguishing the obligations of P&G to the trustees of the P&G Fund) is what would result if the funding obligation were to be treated as transferred.[33]

(d) ERBs after normal retirement age

11.43 In identifying the proper approach to the issue of to whom responsibility passes for transferring entitlements Hildyard J indicated that:

> [w]hat is required to achieve the safeguarding of the rights of transferring employees is to ensure the provision from some source of an equivalent result in respect of the individual benefits comprised in the bundle. What to my mind is plainly required is to unpack the rights comprised in the package marked "ERB", forget nomenclature, and split out rights which have already been fulfilled, are already vested and will remain exercisable against the P&G Fund trustees, from the remainder (which transfer to SCA).[34]

11.44 One further point considered in *Procter & Gamble* was the status of any payments of the ERBs after an individual's normal retirement age. The instalments of the pension payable under the scheme after normal retirement age fell within the scope of the pensions exclusion. SCA had argued that a pension which provides a 'unitary benefit' payment of which commences prior to the normal retirement age cannot be an old-age benefit for the purposes

---

[28] Ibid. at para. 122.
[29] Ibid. at paras 122–3.
[30] Ibid. at para. 124.
[31] Ibid.
[32] Ibid. at para. 111.
[33] Ibid.
[34] Ibid. at para. 121.

of the principles established by *Beckmann* and *Martin*.[35] P&G sought to distinguish the position in this case, arguing that *Beckmann* and *Martin* dealt with entitlements triggered by redundancy and relating to the period prior to the normal retirement age as opposed to ERBs which continued on past normal retirement age.[36] As Hildyard J put it:

> Unless persuaded that the CJEU has indicated such a rule, I would consider it plain and obvious that instalments of pensions paid to someone after NRA, where the characteristic of the benefit and its obvious and only purpose has always been to support the recipient after retirement having attained a specified age and without any other trigger, fall to be characterised as old-age benefits, and none the less so simply because the pension had first come into payment before NRA.[37]

3. Practical issues

Transferees accordingly need to appreciate the limited scope of the pensions exclusion and the possibility that they will have to honour pension benefits payable earlier than normal retirement. Due diligence as to what the transferee will or might arguably inherit in terms of ongoing occupational pension obligations is therefore crucial for those engaging in transfers of undertakings since transferees need to establish what liabilities they do inherit, what pre-transfer entitlements do not transfer, and to what extent new pension arrangements may need to be implemented to comply with PA 2004 and PPR 2005. **11.45**

As the potential liabilities arising under the principles established by these cases can be very significant, the transferee may, where the commercial circumstances permit, wish to seek to extract an indemnity from the transferor in respect of any claims made by transferring employees post-transfer to benefits preserved by *Beckmann/Martin*. Employees may seek to rely on the *Beckmann/Martin* decisions a considerable time after the relevant transfer took place. Alternatively, an adjustment may need to be negotiated to the purchase price where a business sale is affected by the issue. **11.46**

Quite apart from the need to analyse carefully what the transferor's obligations are and whether they transfer to the transferee on a relevant transfer under the *Beckmann/Martin* decisions, actuarial advice may need to be obtained to assess the potential exposure if the transferee proposes not to continue the relevant benefits and it is arguable that they may nonetheless transfer under TUPE. The unpredictability and potential scale of the liabilities which may arise as a result of *Beckmann* and *Martin* may make it unlikely that a transferor will readily agree to an open-ended indemnity liability, as may the availability of ways in which the liabilities associated with this issue can be mitigated. If the employer's consent is required to the taking of early retirement pension benefits covered by the *Beckmann/Martin* decisions then the employer may be able to decline to give this consent. This may of course lead an employee to argue that the decision to withhold the required consent when taken by the transferee is in breach of contract as a capricious or entirely unjustifiable exercise of that discretion.[38] This argument may have particular force if the transferor had a specific practice in relation to the grant of consent in relation to early retirement pensions. Deviation from **11.47**

---

[35] Ibid. at para. 135.
[36] Ibid. at para. 135.
[37] Ibid. at para. 147.
[38] With reference to the 'Imperial duty' referred to in *Procter & Gamble*—above n. 23 and under the principles established in decisions such as *Clark v Nomura International plc* [2000] IRLR 766, QBD and *Horkulak v Cantor Fitzgerald International* [2004] IRLR 942, CA.

that practice without good reason may be difficult to justify as not being capricious. There is also an argument, dependent upon the factual matrix, that under regulation 4 the transferee may be bound by the transferor's approach if that can be characterized as effectively contractual by virtue of being a custom and practice.

F. Pension Communications

1. Misrepresentation

11.48 In *Hagen v ICI Chemicals and Polymers Ltd*[39] Elias J held that employees could bring claims of negligent misstatement against a transferor which had inaccurately indicated that the post-transfer pension arrangements which the transferee would operate would be broadly comparable to their pre-transfer entitlements. The employees had suffered a detriment as a result of this misrepresentation. In the light of their bargaining position, it was held that the employees would have been able to secure more advantageous pension entitlements with the transferee had they been aware of the true position.

11.49 It was held that it was 'just, fair and reasonable' to impose a common law duty of care on the transferor when making statements to employees in a transfer situation in circumstances where it had assumed responsibility for the information it chose to provide to the relevant employees. The transferor knew and intended that the statements that it made would be drawn to the attention of the employees, who were a limited and identifiable number of individuals. In addition, the statements in question were made at least in part to encourage the relevant staff to transfer to the employment of the transferee to the extent that reassurance was provided to the employees about their employment terms. Further, the transferor was found to have been in a good position to assess the accuracy of what it was telling staff given that it was a party to the relevant transfer agreement. This duty of care was imposed notwithstanding the collective information and consultation obligations imposed by TUPE, which did not displace or make it unnecessary or inappropriate to impose a duty of care since they are limited in scope, are only owed to the relevant appropriate representatives rather than the directly affected employees themselves and provide no remedy for negligent misstatement.[40]

11.50 However, there was found to be no legal duty imposed on the transferor to take care when giving advice to the affected employees to the effect that it was in their best interests to transfer to the employment of the transferee. In any event the advice given by the transferor that the employees were likely to have better employment prospects with the transferee was held not to be negligent, being found to have been based on reasonable grounds even if expressed on occasion with some over-enthusiasm.[41]

11.51 It was also held that the transferee, as the employees' prospective employer, was under a duty to take reasonable care to ensure that any information given was accurate and that any statements of intentions were capable of being fulfilled. Nonetheless, the employees' allegations of breach—in relation to representations that there were no plans to make redundancies,

---

[39] [2002] IRLR 31, QBD, a detail-heavy case only very briefly addressed here.
[40] Ibid. at paras 84–7.
[41] Ibid. at paras 255–7.

that there would be no changes to terms and conditions, and that pension rights would be broadly similar—were rejected on the evidence.[42]

In terms of whether it was the transferor or the transferee who bore liability for the mis-representations which were established to have been made by the transferor, Elias J made it clear that liability in tort is, as a matter of general principle, capable of transferring to the transferee under TUPE as a liability arising in connection with a contract of employment.[43] However, the misrepresentations which were established by the employees to have made by the transferor only related to the benefits conferred under the relevant pension scheme. As the subject matter of the transferor's misrepresentations was the applicable occupational pension arrangements, Elias J held that the liability for the relevant representations remained with the transferor on the basis of regulation 7 of TUPE 1981, the predecessor of regulation 10 excluding from transfer to the transferee the prescribed category of pension liability. Put simply, pension-related misrepresentations fell within the scope of the pensions exclusion now contained in regulation 10. Elias J described the relevant provision as follows:

> This is framed in very broad terms. Its effect is that no liabilities transfer where they arise under or in connection with so much of the contract as relates to an occupational pension scheme. In my judgment, given the wide meaning given to the words 'in connection with' in *Bernadone*, a liability which arises from a misrepresentation about pension benefits under an occupational pension scheme gives rise to a potential liability 'in connection with' that part of the contract relating to the scheme. Accordingly it is caught by Reg. 7 and does not transfer. It follows that the liability remains with ICI.[44]

In addition to the concerns it raises about pension promises, this decision does remind trans-ferees of the risk of their becoming liable for a transferor's pre-transfer (and non-contractual) representations outside the pensions context in cases where detrimental reliance on the rep-resentations by affected employees can be established. Protection against such liabilities can only be obtained by the transferee by an appropriate contractual indemnity.

11.52

11.53

2. Separate pension promises

Whitney v Monster Worldwide Ltd[45] demonstrates the potential, notwithstanding the pensions exclusion, for pension-related obligationsto be created by transferees by way of separate promises. In this case, the employee was employed by MSL Holdings until his employment was transferred to Monster pursuant to a relevant transfer after the acquisition of his original employer by Monster's parent. The employee was able to establish that, when the original employer decided to wind up the defined benefit pension scheme in which the employee then participated and replaced it with a defined contribution plan, he and other key employees were given a contractual 'no detriment' guarantee. This guarantee was to the effect that they would suffer no loss if the benefits provided by the defined contribution plan ultimately were lower in value than would have been the case under the defined benefit scheme.

11.54

It was common ground that the pensions exclusion meant that there was no statutory trans-fer of the no detriment guarantee from MSL Holdings to Monster under TUPE. However,

11.55

---

[42] Ibid. see para. 258 *et seq.*
[43] Ibid. at para. 330, referring to *Bernadone v Pall Mall Services Group* [2000] IRLR 487, CA—see Chapter 5, para. 5.25.
[44] Ibid. at para. 332.
[45] [2011] Pens LR 1, CA.

Monster was liable to honour the no detriment guarantee by virtue of the assurances which Monster had given that it would replicate the pension entitlements of the transferred employees and these assurances were found to extend to the no detriment guarantee. The ultimate owner of Monster had indicated that Monster would honour every commitment of the original employer including 'pay and benefits'. That these assurances were given by the parent company which initially acquired the employee's employer rather than the subsidiary to which his employment was subsequently transferred under TUPE made no difference to the analysis. The assurances were seen as given on behalf of the parent, whichever company became the employee's employer in due course. The Court of Appeal was satisfied that Monster intended to honour the no detriment guarantee when the assurances in question were given, assumed the defined contribution plan in which the employee participated (and through which any additional benefits needed to honour the no detriment guarantee had been planned to be delivered), and gained access to a surplus under the defined benefit scheme which was to fund the no detriment guarantee. The assurances were 'meant to be relied upon and were relied upon'[46] even though they were given some months before the employee was transferred to his eventual employer.

G. PA 2004 and PPR 2005

1. Introduction

11.56 The debate with regard to the protection of employees' occupational pension rights following a TUPE transfer has in recent years been particularly acute with regard to public sector pension provision. In its reforms of the transfer of undertakings legislation, the Government proceeded to require all transferees, whether in the private or the public sector, and regardless of whether the transferor operated a defined benefit, defined contribution, or stakeholder occupational pension scheme, to make a minimum level of pension provision for transferring employees who were active members of occupational pension schemes when employed by the transferor to which the employer made a contribution, were eligible to become active members of such schemes, or would have become eligible to do so had they been employed for a longer period of time.[47]

11.57 The obligation on transferees to preserve some level of pension benefits post-transfer for transferring employees is imposed by the combined effect of PA 2004, ss 257 and 258 and of PPR 2005. These pension provisions operate independently from and in addition to TUPE and therefore do not affect its exclusion of the transferor's pre-transfer provision of old age, invalidity, and survivors' benefits under occupational pension schemes from those contractual rights which are inherited by the transferee.

11.58 PA 2004 and PPR 2005 establish a minimum level of pension benefits to be provided by the transferee to transferring employees for or in respect of whom an occupational pension scheme was provided prior to transfer. This may of course constitute a reduction (or even, although perhaps less likely, an increase) to the pre-transfer level of pension benefits enjoyed by transferring employees whilst they were employed by the transferor. Whilst pensions law more generally, which is outside the scope of this work, establishes a detailed regulatory

---

46 Ibid. at para. 31.
47 See 2001 Consultation paras 36–59 for detailed discussion of the options considered for pension protection both in the public sector context and otherwise.

regime, PA 2004 and PPR 2005 do not prescribe in detail the rules and other administrative provisions of the pension arrangements to be put in place and do not require continuation of early retirement or ill-health aspects of the transferor's pension arrangements (to which the *Beckmann/Martin* decisions described above may nonetheless apply). The transferee can elect, without regard to the nature and value of the pension benefits which the transferor afforded to the transferring employees, to provide defined contribution or defined benefit arrangements of its choosing to those employees who enjoyed pre-transfer pension benefits provided that they comply with the basic standards required by PA 2004 and PPR 2005.

PA 2004 and PPR 2005 were not greeted with unanimous approval. That the provisions **11.59** require a basic level of pension provision for transferring employees does nothing to protect valuable defined benefit pension arrangements which employees enjoy prior to a TUPE transfer. It has also been argued that employees with low earnings are particularly prejudiced by PA 2004 and PPR 2005 because the employer's obligation to make pension contributions is parasitic upon the employee's contributions which low earners may find more difficult to make than higher earners.

In passing it is worth noting that, whilst PA 2004 and PPR 2005 only afford their protections **11.60** to those employees who actually do transfer under TUPE to the transferee, the pensions protection regime will presumably also be relevant to dismissal claims related to a transfer. An employee who enjoyed pension benefits with the transferor and who succeeds in a claim of automatically unfair dismissal against the transferee on the basis that he or she was dismissed in connection with the relevant transfer will presumably be able to recover compensation for that unfair dismissal incorporating a pension element based on the requirements of PA 2004 and PPR 2005. After all, those regulations prescribe the minimum level of pensions benefits which the employee should have enjoyed with the transferee had he or she not been unfairly dismissed, which thereby form a potential head of loss in an unfair dismissal (and potentially a wrongful dismissal) claim.

2. Eligibility requirements

(a) Transfer

A number of requirements need to be satisfied for the protective regime of PA 2004 and PPR **11.61** 2005 to apply:

- there must be a relevant transfer to which TUPE applies;[48]
- as a result of this TUPE transfer, the employee in question must cease to be employed by the transferor of the relevant business/undertaking and become employed by the transferee;[49]
- the transferor must have been the employer for the purposes of an occupational pension scheme.[50]

There therefore appears to be nothing to prevent PA 2004 and PPR 2005 from applying to an intra-group transfer falling within the scope of TUPE.

---

[48] PA 2004, s. 257(1)(a).

[49] PA 2004, s. 257(1)(b). Under PA 2004, s. 257(8) this includes employment with an associate of the transferor.

[50] PA 2004, s. 257(1)(c)(i). The relevant occupational pension scheme of which a transferring employee was an actual or potential member must be one for the purpose of which the transferor was the employer—this must presumably be taken, in a group context, to cover occupational pension schemes in respect of which the transferor is one of several participating employers.

(b) Eligible employees

11.62 The following categories of employee qualify for the protection of the pensions protection regime established by PA 2004 and PPR 2005:

- employees who immediately before the transfer were active members of the transferor's occupational pension scheme;[51]
- employees who immediately before transfer were not members but were eligible to become members of the transferor's occupational pension scheme[52]—those who had not taken up pension scheme membership but are still entitled to do so at the point of transfer are therefore protected. There is no definition of eligibility, raising therefore the issue of whether an employee whose participation in the transferor's occupational pension scheme is at the employer's discretion qualifies for the protection afforded by PA 2004 and PPR 2005;[53]
- employees who immediately before the transfer would have been active members or eligible to be active members of an occupational scheme had they been employed for a longer period.[54] Those who as at the date of transfer had yet to complete a waiting period of employment required before they could become members of the relevant pension scheme therefore also enjoy the entitlements conferred by PA 2004 and PPR 2005.

11.63 In relation to all these categories of protected employee, the employee's actual or potential entitlement to occupational pension benefits is to be assessed immediately before the relevant transfer. Employees' contractual rights and the eligibility rules of the relevant pension scheme therefore need to be considered as at the point of transfer to determine whether the regime established by PA 2004 and PPR 2005 applies in each particular case.

11.64 In relation to defined contribution arrangements operated by a transferor prior to a TUPE transfer, an employee will not qualify for the pensions entitlements conferred by PA 2004 and PPR 2005 unless the transferor employer either did or was required to make contributions for that employee (or would have been so required had the otherwise eligible employee joined the relevant scheme).[55]

3. The minimum standard of pension provision

(a) The entitlement

11.65 The pensions preservation regime established by PA 2004 and PPR 2005 incorporates into protected employees' contracts of employment a contractual entitlement[56] either:

- to become a member of an occupational pension scheme provided by the transferee employer[57] which satisfies the specific requirements prescribed by PA 2004 and PPR 2005; or

---

[51] PA 2004, s. 257(2)(a). An active member for the purposes of PA 2004 is an employee in pensionable service for the purposes of pension benefits under the relevant scheme. PA 2004, s. 318(1) cross-refers to this definition in the Pensions Act 1995, s. 124(1). A deferred member or pensioner is therefore not within the scope of these provisions.

[52] PA 2004, s. 257(3)(a).

[53] See Pollard, n. 11 above, at p. 132: 'The better view seems to be that such an employee is not "eligible" for this purpose. But it is not as clear as it might be.'

[54] PA 2004, s. 257(4)(a).

[55] PA 2004, ss 257(2)(b), (3)(b), (4)(b). Pursuant to PA 2004, s. 257(7) minimum payments required to be made pursuant to PSA 1993 do not satisfy this requirement. These minimum payments arise in relation to schemes which are contracted out of the state second pension.

[56] PA 2004, s. 258(1).

[57] PA 2004, s. 258(1) and (2).

- to 'relevant contributions'[58] by the transferee to a stakeholder pension scheme of which the employee is a member.[59]

The obligation to provide the prescribed level of pension provision commences with immediate effect from the employee's employment transferring from the transferor to the transferee or (if later) the date on which the employee would have become eligible to join the transferor's pension scheme had he or she remained with the transferee.[60] Accordingly, transferring employees must still complete any waiting period for pension benefits which applied to them in relation to the transferor's pension scheme before being able to insist on their entitlements under PA 2004 and PPR 2005 being provided to them by the transferee. Even though the pension benefit which the transferee provides by way of compliance with PA 2004 and PPR 2005 may, depending upon the circumstances, constitute an inferior level of pension provision than that afforded by the transferor, PA 2004 and PPR 2005 do not, by virtue of the relevant employees transferring to the transferee, accelerate or vary the existing eligibility requirements under the arrangements operated by the transferor. **11.66**

As the application of PA 2004 and PPR 2005 is based on eligibility to participate in an occupational pension scheme (as opposed to actual membership), it would also appear that the transferee must make pension provision for those who did not take such membership up whilst employed by the transferor (even though entitled to do so) but who choose to exercise their eligibility rights post-transfer. There appears to be no time limit to that obligation. Accordingly, employees who were eligible to join the transferor's occupational pension scheme but did not do so will have the right to insist on the minimum standard of provision required by PA 2004 and PPR 2005 as and when they elect to insist on that right. **11.67**

The eligibility rules of the transferor's occupational pension scheme may well repay careful attention to determine if such a contingent entitlement needs to be catered for effectively in perpetuity. It may be the case, depending on the particular scheme rules, that if an employee does not exercise his or her right to join a pension scheme within a certain time after he or she becomes eligible to participate in it, participation is at the employer's discretion. In this situation, as noted above, it may be doubtful whether the employee qualifies for the protection afforded by PA 2004 and PPR 2005. **11.68**

(b) Level of benefit

It is for the transferee to decide what sort of occupational pension benefit to provide post-transfer in order to comply with PA 2004 and PPR 2005 (i.e. a defined benefit or defined contribution or stakeholder arrangement). The statutory criteria governing the value of the arrangement which the transferee is required to provide depend on what type of scheme is offered. **11.69**

If the scheme which the transferee offers is a defined contribution or stakeholder scheme, then the transferee employer must, in respect of each period for which the employee is paid, at least match the employee's contributions up to a maximum contribution of 6 per cent of **11.70**

---

[58] PA 2004, s. 258(7).
[59] PA 2004, s. 258(1) and (3). A stakeholder pension scheme for these purposes is, pursuant to PA 2004 s. 258(7), a pension scheme registered under the Welfare Reform and Pensions Act 1999, s. 2.
[60] PA 2004, s. 258(7) (definition of 'the relevant time').

remuneration (regardless of the level of pre-transfer contribution).[61] Remuneration for these purposes only includes the employee's basic rate of pay and excludes bonuses, commissions, overtime, and any similar payments or deductions in respect of tax, national insurance, or pension contributions.[62] No guidance is provided by the legislation with regard to how relevant contributions are to be fixed.[63] Employees therefore appear able to increase and vary contributions. There is no express provision limiting the number and amount of such changes.

11.71 If the transferee does not offer a defined contribution, money purchase, or stakeholder scheme, then the benefits which it provides must satisfy one of the following requirements. The transferee's scheme must satisfy either the 'reference scheme' test or 'such other test as may be prescribed in regulations'.[64]

11.72 The reference scheme test is satisfied if the relevant pension scheme meets the statutory standard referred to in PSA 1993, s. 12A. The reference scheme test is the test that applies if a pension scheme is to be contracted out of the second state pension. Its key elements[65] are, inter alia:

- a normal pension age of 65 for both men and women;
- a pension payable from normal retirement age in respect of each year of pensionable service of 1/80 of average qualifying earnings calculated over the last three tax years;
- specified spouse's pension entitlements;
- prescribed annual pension increases;
- revaluation of deferred pension.

11.73 PPR 2005 establishes the alternative basis on which a defined benefit scheme which does not satisfy the reference scheme test will nonetheless comply with the obligation to provide post-transfer pension benefits to those who enjoyed them prior to a relevant transfer. Pension arrangements will satisfy PPR 2005 if the employer establishes an arrangement which satisfies either of the following:

- the arrangement provides a value of benefits of at least 6 per cent of pensionable pay for each year of employment[66] together with the total amount of any contributions made by the employee (which employee contributions may not exceed 6 per cent of pensionable pay)[67]—there is no prescribed mechanism for calculating this value;
- the employer makes 'relevant contributions' which match the employee's contributions up to a maximum of 6 per cent of basic pay in respect of each period in relation to which the employee is paid.[68]

---

[61] PPR 2005, regulation 3(1)(a) and (b).

[62] PPR 2005, regulation 3(2)(a) and (b). The minimum payments required to be made in respect of money purchase schemes which are contracted out of the state second pension are also ignored pursuant to PA 2004, s. 257(7) and PPR 2005, regulation 3(3).

[63] See Pollard, above n. 11, at p. 133.

[64] PA 2004, s. 258(2)(c).

[65] See Occupational Pension Schemes (Contracting-Out) Regulations 1996 SI 1996/1172.

[66] 'Pensionable pay' is defined (PPR 2005, regulation 2(2)) as that part of the remuneration payable to a member of a scheme by reference to which the amount of contributions and benefits are determined under the rules of the scheme.

[67] PPR 2005, regulation 2(1)(a).

[68] PPR 2005, regulation 2(1)(b).

4. Enforcement

(a) *Contractual status*

PA 2004 renders the prescribed minimum level of pension benefits a contractual right for **11.74** employees.[69] This arguably places transferring employees in a better position than those of the transferee's employees who participate in its existing pension arrangements. Those employees may well not have a contractual right to a specific level of benefit which cannot be varied without the employee's consent. The pension benefits of the transferee's existing employees may be capable of being changed or even discontinued unilaterally by the employer if the rules of the relevant pension arrangements so permit (subject of course to the ability to vary entitlements being contractually valid and subject to any challenge to the exercise of that power on grounds of irrationality, perversity, or breach by the employer of the implied duty to maintain trust and confidence). It therefore may well be desirable for the transferee to seek, if feasible, to agree with transferring employees[70] that their post-transfer pension provision is specifically subject to and in accordance with the rules of the relevant scheme, thereby incorporating an ability to change or discontinue pension arrangements in the future.

(b) *Pensions Regulator*

Failure to provide pension benefits of the required standard not only leaves employees with **11.75** direct claims against the transferee. The Pensions Regulator has the following powers in respect of breaches of PA 2004 (which extends therefore to breaches of these minimum pension obligations) which could be used to penalize employers who fail to comply with their obligations:

- fines of up to £5,000 can be imposed on individuals or £50,000 otherwise;[71]
- where an employer contribution to an occupational pension scheme is not paid, the Pensions Regulator has the power to exercise such powers as the trustees or manager of the scheme has to recover the contribution.[72]

(c) *Anti-avoidance*

PA 2004, s. 257(5) makes clear that an employee who is an active, eligible, or contingent **11.76** member of an occupational pension scheme will still qualify for the protection of PA 2004 and PPR 2005 where the relevant requirement 'would have been satisfied but for any action taken by the transferor by reason of the transfer'. Steps taken by an employer to terminate a pension scheme or amend eligibility or other conditions prior to transfer in order to remove or limit the obligations which a transferee will inherit will therefore be open to challenge, subject to the ability on the part of the affected employees to demonstrate (in terms of causation) that the relevant action was taken by reason of the transfer.

(d) *Changing benefits*

It is open to transferring employees and the transferee to agree that the entitlements estab- **11.77** lished by PA 2004 and PPR 2005 be varied or disapplied[73] but this appears only to be

---

[69] PA 2004, s. 258(1).
[70] But only after transfer, as permitted by PA 2004, s. 258(6).
[71] PA 2004, ss 7 and 10.
[72] PA 2004, s. 17.
[73] PA 2004, s. 256(6).

permitted post-transfer. In contrast to other transfer-related changes to employees' contractual terms and conditions, a change to the basic entitlements established by PA 2004 and PPR 2005 appears not to require satisfaction of any specific criteria or requirements. An otherwise contractually valid change to pension entitlements derived from PA 2004 and PPR 2005, provided that it is effected post-transfer, is therefore permissible and effective.

5. Consultation

11.78 Amendment to the pension entitlements of transferring employees, even if this simply entails the replacement of pre-transfer occupational pension entitlements with the minimum level of pension provision required by PA 2004 and PPR 2005, will engage the information and consultation requirements of regulation 13. Occupational pension matters are not excluded from the scope of those information and consultation requirements in the way that they are by regulation 10 from the provisions relating to transfer of individual and collective obligations under regulations 4 and 5. Consultation obligations in this regard will presumably fall primarily on the transferee as it will be the party which will be implementing 'measures' by way of pension changes. However, the transferor may also need to consider what steps it needs to take and what consultations are thereby necessitated with regard to the pension scheme in which the transferring (or its remaining) employees participate, for example if the scheme is to be terminated as a consequence of or in connection with a relevant transfer.[74]

6. Auto-enrolment

11.79 Whilst a detailed treatment of the auto-enrolment requirements being phased in from October 2012 is outside the scope of this work, the requirements imposed on employers to enrol eligible individuals into a pension arrangement complying with the applicable criteria may be relevant for those engaged in TUPE transfers.[75] In the period from 1 October 2012, at a time which will be determined by reference to its size—a so called "staging date"[76]—an employer will be required to auto-enrol eligible workers into a qualifying pension scheme complying with prescribed statutory requirements and to make a minimum level of pension contributions on their behalf into that scheme. Unless the relevant individual already participates in an occupational or personal pension arrangement which satisfies the relevant criteria or is enrolled in the Government's NEST arrangements the employer will have to utilize an 'automatic enrolment scheme'.

11.80 These auto-enrolment provisions operate separately from the provisions with regard to minimum levels of pension provision following a relevant transfer set out in the PA 2004 and PPR 2005. This can in theory mean that those transferring into a transferee's employment will be entitled to a higher level of pension provision pursuant to the PA 2004 and PPR 2005 than under the auto-enrolment legislation in light of the fact that the required employer contribution is being phased in over time and may, at the time of transfer be lower than the level prescribed by PA 2004 and PPR 2005.

---

[74] Subject to compliance, if applicable, with the Occupational and Personal Pension Schemes (Consultation by Employers and Miscellaneous Amendment) Regulations 2006 SI 2006/349.

[75] See generally the Pensions Act 2008 and supplementary secondary legislation.

[76] PA 2008, s. 29; Employers Duties (Implementation) Regulations 2010 SI 2010/4, regulation 5.

The Pensions Regulator has issued guidance[77] as to how employers should approach auto-enrolment in the context of a relevant transfer as follows:[78]   **11.81**

- Where a worker changes employer as a result of a TUPE transfer, the new employer will be responsible for complying with the employer duties that arise in relation to that worker. This means they will have to assess the worker with effect from the transfer date and where appropriate, automatically enrol them. In effect, they are treated as a new joiner for that employer.
- Scheme requirements under TUPE operate in parallel to the employer duties and both must be complied with as necessary. If the transferred worker was in a pension scheme on the transfer date, the new employer must place them into a scheme that complies with TUPE provisions when they are transferred. If the worker is assessed as an eligible jobholder on the transfer date, they must be automatically enrolled into a qualifying scheme.... However, if the scheme the employer used to meet the TUPE requirements is also a qualifying scheme, the employer would not need to automatically enrol the worker. If the scheme used to meet TUPE provisions is not a qualifying scheme, the employer must use a different qualifying scheme to meet their automatic enrolment duties.
- If the transferred worker was not in a pension scheme at the transfer date but was still entitled to become a member, on transfer, the entitlement to a TUPE-compliant scheme remains and must be honoured by the new employer. If the new employer assesses that the worker is an eligible jobholder on the transfer date, they can use postponement... as long as the worker is still able to opt in to a TUPE-compliant and qualifying scheme during the postponement period.

The requirements of a qualifying scheme and the ability to postpone enrolment are outside   **11.82** the scope of this work but this guidance would appear to indicate that an individual who is eligible for auto-enrolment must automatically be enrolled by the transferee into a scheme satisfying the relevant criteria following a relevant transfer if the individual is at that time eligible for auto-enrolment. This would appear to be the case even if the employee had, prior to transfer, opted out of the applicable scheme as is the individual's statutory right[79] and notwithstanding the rule which applies otherwise to the effect that an employer is not obliged to enrol an individual afresh if he or she has opted out in the previous 12 months.

As has been noted by other commentators, the requirement following a relevant transfer   **11.83** to re-enrol those who have opted out and the possibility of transferring employees being entitled to higher levels of pension benefit from the transferee by virtue of PA 2004 and PPR 2005 than the pension provision required to be afforded to the transferee's existing workforce by virtue of the auto-enrolment provisions are issues which apply equally to intragroup reorganizations effected by way of relevant transfers as to transactions with external third parties.

---

[77] Pensions Regulator—Guidance Note 2—Workplace Pensions Reform, Guidance Note 2, Getting Ready, section 4 accessed at http://www.thepensionsregulator.gov.uk/docs/pensions-reform-getting-ready-v4.pdf.

[78] Ibid. at para. 57 *et seq.*

[79] PA 2008, s. 8.

12

MISCELLANEOUS

A. Contracting Out	12.01	**E. Equal Pay**	12.43
1. Prohibition	12.01	1. Time limits for bringing claims	12.44
2. Compromise agreements	12.05	2. Genuine material factor defence	12.48
B. Territoriality	12.12	**F. Drafting and Commercial Issues**	12.51
1. Introduction	12.12	1. Introduction	12.51
2. TUPE 2006	12.16	2. Due diligence	12.52
3. Continental shelf	12.23	3. Warranties	12.55
4. Cross-border transfers	12.24	4. Indemnities	12.60
C. Tax and Employee Transfer	12.38	5. Outsourcing	12.64
D. Immigration	12.41		

A. Contracting Out

1. Prohibition

12.01 Any attempt to contract out of the effect of and protections provided by TUPE is unlawful. Regulation 18 provides that:

> Section 203 of the 1996 [Employment Rights] Act (restrictions on contracting out) shall apply in relation to these Regulations as if they were contained in that Act, save for that section shall not apply in so far as these Regulations provide for an agreement (whether a contract of employment or not) to exclude or limit the operation of these Regulations.

12.02 ERA 1996, s. 203 provides that:

> Any provision in an agreement (whether a contract of employment or not) is void insofar as it purports:
> (a) to exclude or limit the operation of any provision of this Act; or
> (b) to preclude a person from any proceedings under this Act before an [employment tribunal].

12.03 There are limited circumstances in which the prohibition against contracting out in ERA 1996 does not apply.[1] These include agreements where an ACAS conciliation officer has

---

[1] ERA 1996, s. 203(2).

taken action under the Employment Tribunals Act 1996, s. 18[2] and compromise agreements satisfying the relevant statutory requirements.[3]

Regulation 16(10) provides that the Employment Tribunals Act 1996, s. 18 shall apply to the rights conferred by regulation 15 and associated proceedings. An ACAS Conciliation Officer can therefore act to settle or exclude claims for breach of the collective information and consultation requirements of regulation 13.

12.04

2. Compromise agreements

In the TUPE context, compromise agreements are relevant to more than just the settlement of actual or potential unfair dismissal claims. Such agreements have regularly been deployed in relation to transfer-related changes to employees' terms and conditions of employment in order to avoid associated unfair dismissal claims. The *Wilson* and *Meade* decisions established that transfer-related contract changes to employees' terms and conditions of employment, even if agreed by the affected employees, are invalid.[4] Accordingly, prior to the introduction in the 2006 Regulations of the ability to agree transfer-related changes to employees' terms and conditions of employment for which there is an ETOR,[5] the only way in which employees could validly agree to the amendment of their terms and conditions of employment would be by agreeing new contracts after a dismissal. Dismissal and re-engagement would not invalidate the new terms and conditions of employment whereas a simple agreement during continued employment would be void.

12.05

Since to adopt this route, when seeking to implement valid transfer-related changes, would entail a dismissal upon which an unfair dismissal claim could be based, the practice arose of employers seeking to agree compromise agreements with individuals where transfer-related changes were being implemented. On this basis, the employer could argue that the transfer-related change was valid because it was introduced in a new employment following a dismissal and could take comfort from the fact that the compromise agreement, provided it was otherwise valid, would sign away any employment-related claims arising from the dismissal. The concern inevitably arose as to whether such an arrangement would constitute contracting out of the effect or operation of TUPE and therefore be invalid.

12.06

To an extent this problem may have diminished in importance given the ability introduced by regulations 4(4) and 4(5) for employees to agree transfer-related changes and for appropriate representatives of transferring employees to agree permitted variations in certain insolvency situations pursuant to regulation 9. That said, as a result of the confined scope of the

12.07

---

[2] ERA 1996, s. 203(2)(d).

[3] ERA 1996, s. 203(2)(e) and equivalent provisions in the Sex Discrimination Act 1975, s. 77, Race Relations Act 1976, s. 72, Trade Union and Labour Relations (Consolidation) Act (TULRCA) 1992, s. 288, Disability Discrimination Act 1995, s. 9, Working Time Regulations 1998 (SI 1998/1833), regulation 35, National Minimum Wage Act 1998, s. 49(3), Transnational Information and Consultation of Employees Regulations 1999 (SI 1999/3323), regulation 41, Part-time Workers (Prevention of Less Favourable Treatment) Regulations 2000 (SI 2000/1551), regulation 9, Information & Consultation of Employees Regulations 2004 (SI 2004/3426), regulation 9, Fixed-Term Employees (Prevention of Less Favourable Treatment) Regulations 2002 (SI 2002/2034), regulation 10, Employment Equality (Sexual Orientation) Regulations 2003 (SI 2003/1661), regulation 35, Employment Equality (Religion or Belief) Regulations 2003 (SI 2003/1660), regulation 35 and Equality Act 2010, s. 147.

[4] See Chapter 6, para. 6.06 *et seq.*

[5] By virtue of regulations 4(4) and 4(5)—see Chapter 6, para. 6.27 *et seq.*

ability to change terms under regulations 4 and 9, employers may still seek to utilize the compromise agreement route but need to appreciate that its efficacy remains doubtful.

12.08 The EAT decision in *Solectron Scotland Ltd v Roper and others*[6] dealt with a slightly different point—the extent to which a compromise agreement can be valid in relation to the settlement of termination-related claims based on TUPE. The employees had signed compromise agreements when made redundant. They subsequently argued that they were nonetheless entitled to enhanced redundancy terms which they had enjoyed in a previous employment from which they had transferred pursuant to the transfer legislation to the employer by whom they were dismissed. The ET held that the employees were entitled to the enhanced redundancy terms. Inter alia, the ET relied on the then applicable prohibition on contracting out, TUPE 1981, regulation 12, which provided that 'any provision of any agreement (whether a contract of employment or not) shall be void insofar as it purports to exclude or limit the operation of regulation 5'.[7]

12.09 The EAT held that the ET was wrong to find that the compromise agreement was invalidated by TUPE 1981, regulation 12. The compromise agreement did not arise solely or even mainly by reason of the transfer. It compromised the claims which the employees had on termination of their employment. This was not an agreement varying the employment contract (or, for that matter, the effect of TUPE) but one settling a dispute with regard to the consequences of its termination. The compromise agreement did not therefore fall foul of the prohibition on contracting out. The implicit risk nonetheless remains that a termination and re-engagement coupled with a compromise agreement designed to validate otherwise void transfer-related contract changes may fall foul of the prohibition on contracting out.

12.10 *Thompson and others v Walton Car Delivery and BRS Automotive*[8] demonstrates an important point of privity of contract in the context of compromise agreements. An agreement entered into by an employee with the transferor did not operate to protect the transferee from claims under TUPE. A tripartite agreement between employee, transferor, and transferee may therefore be necessary. Alternatively, the benefit of the compromise agreement could be extended to the desired persons by use of the Contracts (Rights of Third Parties) Act 1999. *Tamang v Act Security Ltd*[9] also demonstrates the importance of the scope of and parties to a settlement agreement addressing claims arising under TUPE which may lie against various parties. The claimants bought various claims under TUPE and their original employer, Reliance, was released from those proceedings by way of a settlement agreement entered into through the offices of ACAS. The agreement did not, however, expressly extend to the two other respondents in the proceedings. The ET had reached the conclusion that the settlement agreement reached with Reliance constituted a release of all three tortfeasors on the basis that a release of one debtor releases the others. However, the EAT held that the proper construction of the settlement agreement was that it constituted a covenant not to sue the original employer (who was a party to the settlement agreement) rather than a release of the other respondents. Extension of the benefit of the agreement to those other parties could not be implied. The respondents other than Reliance could not rely on the settlement agreement.

---

[6] [2004] IRLR 4, EAT. See Chapter 6, para. 6.19 for further discussion of *Solectron*.
[7] Regulation 18 has the equivalent effect.
[8] [1997] IRLR 343, EAT.
[9] UKEAT/0046/12.

Despite concerns about the position being raised at the time,[10] the 2006 Regulations do not expressly address whether a compromise agreement can validly be utilized to exclude claims for breach of the collective information and consultation obligations imposed by regulation 13. The lack of reference to TUPE in the operative provisions establishing the ability to waive statutory rights under a compromise agreement[11] suggests that a compromise agreement cannot be valid to waive any claims in that regard.[12]

12.11

B. Territoriality

1. Introduction

ARD 2001 contains certain territorial limitations even if the interaction between domestic Member States' implementing legislation is unclear. Article 1.2 provides that the Directive applies 'where and insofar as the undertaking, business or part of the undertaking or business to be transferred is situated within the territorial scope of the Treaty [of Rome]'. The key to the application of the Directive is physical location of the relevant operations as opposed to their ownership, company registration, or overall control and direction.

12.12

However, the Directive provides no further guidance on or assistance in relation to transfer of undertakings issues as between Member States. The Directive cannot of course straightforwardly be relied on per se. It is the Member State's implementing legislation that confers direct rights on employees. Regard therefore needs to be had to that domestic legislation with regard to the territorial scope of each Member State's transfer protections.

12.13

TUPE 1981 contained specific provisions as to its territorial scope. TUPE 1981, regulation 13(1) provided that its principal provisions did not apply to an employment in respect of which the employee ordinarily worked outside the United Kingdom. Thus, the protection against dismissal because of a relevant transfer,[13] the obligation to inform and consult representatives,[14] and the ability to bring claims for compensation for breach of those information and consultation obligations[15] did not extend to those ordinarily working outside the United Kingdom. Also, TUPE 1981, regulation 13(2) deemed a person working on board a ship registered in the United Kingdom to be ordinarily working in the United Kingdom unless the employment was wholly outside the United Kingdom or the employee was not ordinarily resident in the United Kingdom.

12.14

The 2006 Regulations contain no such territoriality provisions. As the 2005 Consultation noted,[16] similar territoriality provisions were removed from other employment rights legislation in 1999. Whether an employee working abroad is able to bring a claim under TUPE depends in part on the wider principles of employment law.[17]

12.15

---

[10] See *TUPE, Draft Revised Regulations, Government Response to the Public Consultation*, Department of Trade and Industry, February 2006 at para. 8.6.

[11] ERA 1996, s. 203 and Employment Tribunals Act 1996, s. 18.

[12] As is the case also in relation to claims of breach of TULRCA 1992, s. 188.

[13] TUPE 1981, regulation 8.

[14] TUPE 1981, regulation 10.

[15] TUPE 1981, regulation 11.

[16] At paras 92 and 93.

[17] See *Serco Ltd v Lawson* [2006] IRLR 289, HL and the cases which follow it, detailed discussion of which falls outside the scope of this work, which give guidance on the circumstances in which those working outside

2. TUPE 2006

12.16 TUPE 2006 does nonetheless contain some provisions addressing certain specific aspects of its territorial application with regard to the undertakings and activities which it covers. There can only be a relevant transfer under regulation 3(1)(a) where the relevant undertaking is situated in the United Kingdom immediately before the transfer—within regulation 3(1)(a) is the requirement that the undertaking be 'situated immediately before the transfer in the United Kingdom'.

12.17 The provisions of regulation 3(1)(b) are contingent on there being, prior to the putative SPC, an organised grouping of employees situated in Great Britain pursuant to regulation 3(3)(a)(i).[18] In *Argyll Coastal Services Ltd v Stirling and others*[19] the EAT commented that regulation 3(3)(a)(i):

> clearly requires that group to be based in Great Britain. Whilst regulation 3(4)(c) makes it clear that, of itself, the fact that a person or persons who are part of that organised grouping of employees work outside the United Kingdom does not prevent the provisions of regulation 3(3)(a)(i) being satisfied, it does not… in any way detract from it being a fundamental pre-requisite of a 'service provision change' transfer that there be an organised grouping of employees situated in Great Britain.[20]

12.18 The 2009 Guidance provides[21] the following example in relation to SPCs:

> the test is whether there is an organised grouping of employees situated in the UK (immediately before the service provision change). For example, where a contract to provide website maintenance comes to an end and the client wants someone else to take over the contract, if in the organised grouping of employees that has performed the contract, one of the IT technicians works from home, which is outside the UK, that should not prevent the Regulations applying to the transfer of the business. However if the whole team of IT technicians worked from home which was outside the UK, then a transfer of the business for which they work would not fall within the Regulations as there would be no organised grouping of employees situated in the United Kingdom.

12.19 One potential consequence of the requirement that the undertaking or activities in question be situated in the United Kingdom immediately before the transfer is that an employee based in the United Kingdom who works in relation to an undertaking or activity situated outside the United Kingdom is not protected by TUPE if that business is disposed of unless either he or she falls within the protective scope of the transfer legislation of the Member State in which the relevant undertaking or activity is located, or the UK operation of itself can be argued to be the subject of a transfer of an undertaking or part thereof or an SPC.

12.20 Regulation 3(4)(b) expressly provides that a transfer of an undertaking or SPC falls within the scope of TUPE 2006 regardless of certain international aspects. That the relevant transfer is governed or effected by the law of a country or territory outside the United Kingdom

---

Great Britain may enjoy domestic unfair dismissal and other statutory rights. See Merrett, *Employment Contracts in Private International Law*, Oxford: OUP, 2011.

[18] Regulation 3(3)(a)(i). The SPC concept established by regulation 3(1)(b) does not apply in Northern Ireland pursuant to the combined effect of regulation 2(3) and Schedule 1 para. 2.

[19] UKEATS/0012/11.

[20] Ibid. at para. 18.

[21] At p. 9, apparently eliding the United Kingdom and Great Britain.

does not disapply TUPE.[22] That a business sale or outsourcing contract may be governed by foreign law makes no difference to the application of TUPE.

Similarly, that the persons employed in the undertaking, business, or part transferred or in **12.21** relation to the activities which are the subject of an SPC ordinarily work outside the United Kingdom does not take what would otherwise be a transfer of an undertaking or an SPC outside the scope of TUPE provided that the other requirements for there to be a relevant transfer are met.[23] Employees assigned to a business located in the United Kingdom but who work outside that jurisdiction can still be covered by TUPE. To quote from the 2009 Guidance:[24]

> the Regulations may still apply notwithstanding that persons employed in the undertaking ordinarily work outside the United Kingdom. For example, if there is a transfer of a UK exporting business, the fact that the sales force spends the majority of its working week outside the UK will not prevent the Regulations applying to the transfer, so long as the undertaking itself (comprising, amongst other things, premises, assets, fixtures & fittings, goodwill as well as employees) is situated in the UK.

Finally, TUPE can apply to employees otherwise qualifying for its protection even if their **12.22** employment is governed by the law of a country or territory outside the United Kingdom.[25] By way of example, employees who have been transferred from overseas to a business or undertaking situated in the United Kingdom can still be covered by TUPE even if they themselves have contracts governed by foreign law which they signed when they first joined the employer outside the United Kingdom.

3. Continental shelf

Whether TUPE applies to the United Kingdom sector of the continental shelf has been a **12.23** moot point. In *Addison and others v Denholm Ship Management (UK) Ltd*[26] the EAT held that the phrase 'in the United Kingdom'[27] did not include the United Kingdom sector of the continental shelf. The Government's own view[28] was that *Addison* was wrongly decided and that TUPE applies in cases where the transferor's business is situated in the United Kingdom sector of the continental shelf. The combination of this view and the provisions of the TUPE described above relating to the geographical location of the relevant undertaking or service provision activity made it unnecessary in the Government's opinion (when it considered the matter as part of the deliberations which led to the 2006 Regulations) for there to be any explicit provision in TUPE 2006 addressing the application of the legislation to the continental shelf.

4. Cross-border transfers

The trend towards international outsourcing, particularly in the fields of information tech- **12.24** nology support and call centre operations, has increased the importance of the international aspects of transfer of undertakings legislation. How the domestic and European transfer of

---

[22] Regulation 3(4)(b((i) (Great Britain in the case of an SPC).
[23] Regulation 3(4)(c).
[24] At pp. 8–9.
[25] Regulation 3(4)(b)(ii).
[26] [1997] IRLR 389, EAT.
[27] Required of the relevant individual's employment under regulation 13 of TUPE 1981 for TUPE 1981 to apply to that person.
[28] 2005 Consultation, para. 93.

undertakings legislation interact has caused considerable uncertainty which has not yet fully been resolved, partly through lack of case law decisions. As HHJ Ansell speculated in *Holis Metal Industries Ltd v GMB (1) Newell Ltd (2)*:[29]

> The lack of cases in this area may suggest that companies proceed on the basis that the 2006 Regulations do not apply either because of extra-territoriality or because of the identity issue and they prefer to treat the UK based workforce as redundant with the unions and employees preferring to concentrate efforts on securing the best financial deal for their future.[30]

12.25 Space constraints do not permit a detailed analysis of the interaction of Member States' transfer of undertakings regimes. A review commissioned by the Directorate-General for Employment Social Affairs and Equal Opportunities in this regard[31] drew the distinction between an 'ownership transfer'—where the undertaking does not change location but is acquired by a transferee from a different Member State to that in which it is location—and a 'relocation transfer' where the transferee relocates the business to a new place of work in a different Member State and considered that:

> The Directive applies to both Ownership and Relocation Transfers from one Member State to another Member State or to a third country but does not apply where the undertaking is situated outside the EU originally, even if the Transferor, Transferee or both of them are domiciled in the EU.[32]

12.26 This review concluded that:

> Cross-border transfers are caught by the ARD where and insofar as the business transferred is situated within the European Union. Under the Directive the transfer of a business results in the automatic assumption of the employment relationship by the transferee on the same terms and conditions. Dismissals because of the business transfer are explicitly prohibited. These issues (and others) concern the individual employment relationship of the employees employed in the business. If the transferee is situated in another Member State, the employee can generally rely on the Jurisdiction Regulation[33] in order to enforce his rights in the country of his regular workplace. The Rome Convention[34] is the legal instrument which governs the question of which law is to be applied in such a case.
>
> On the other hand, the ARD also contains provisions aiming at the preservation of the employee representatives (art 6). If employee representatives want to enforce their rights under the ARD they can rely on the Jurisdiction Regulation provided the business ('economic entity') transferred has not been relocated to the transferee's country. In the latter case the international jurisdiction is determined by national law. Equally, there is no Community instrument regulating which law is applicable if the business has been relocated across the borders.

12.27 In *Holis* the EAT addressed the issue of the territorial application of TUPE in relation to transfers abroad from the United Kingdom. A manufacturing business in Tamworth was closed and the assets of a part of the business were disposed of to a purchaser based in Israel.

---

[29] [2008] IRLR 187, EAT. See Wynn-Evans, 'Does TUPE apply to Offshoring?' (March 2008) ELJ 6.
[30] Ibid. at para. 9.
[31] CMS Employment Practice Area Group, 'Study on the Application of Directive 2001/23/EC to Cross Border Transfers of Undertakings', study no VT/2005/101 (September 2006) at p. 66. See also Hepple, 'The Legal Consequences of Cross Border Transfers of Undertakings within the European Union—A Report for the European Commission DG-V' (1998).
[32] Ibid. at p. 61.
[33] EC Regulation 44/2001 on jurisdiction and the recognition and enforcement of judgments.
[34] The Convention on the Law Applicable to Contractual Obligations (1980) see Merrett, *Employment Contracts in Private International Law*, Oxford: OUP, 2011.

Whilst some plant and machinery were transferred to Israel, no staff transferred. The GMB brought a claim against both the original employer and the purchaser, alleging breaches of the collective information and consultation obligations imposed by regulation 13 and the collective redundancy consultation obligations imposed by TULRCA 1992, s. 188. The preliminary issue before the ET and which was the subject of the appeal to the EAT was limited to whether TUPE could apply to an alleged transfer of an undertaking to a jurisdiction outside the EU.

The EAT identified two issues which need to be addressed in such circumstances. The first **12.28** issue is whether TUPE can apply to transfers to jurisdictions outside the United Kingdom and, in particular, to jurisdictions outside the EU. The second issue, in circumstances such as these where the putative transfer is argued to be a transfer of an undertaking rather than an SPC, was whether the economic entity has retained its identity after transfer such that TUPE applies.

In *Holis*, the overseas respondent argued that, if TUPE applied to a transfer outside the **12.29** EU, workers would need to make claims against a foreign employer (the transferee) in a jurisdiction which might well not recognize the relevant concepts such as unfair dismissal or collective consultation. The basic policy of TUPE and the Directive was the protection of workers, but to apply TUPE to international transfers would leave them significantly worse off than if they retained rights against the transferor. On this analysis, TUPE should therefore only apply within the EU, where at least there was an attempt to have a uniform system of protection for employees. Moreover, it argued that application of the Directive should be limited to transfers within the territorial scope of the Treaty of Rome—in other words, applying between businesses situated within the EU and not to transfers to non-member states.

The overseas respondent also sought to limit the extraterritorial application of TUPE by **12.30** reference to wider principles than the policy behind the transfer legislation. An analogy was drawn with the Posted Workers Directive[35] which is limited to postings within the EU. It was therefore argued that it would be surprising for the transfer of undertakings legislation, as another form of European employment law protection, to have wider scope in protecting employees' rights. Reliance was also placed on the general principles of United Kingdom law that it does not have extraterritorial effect unless clearly provided for, that the courts are reluctant to impose obligations in respect of conduct outside the jurisdiction,[36] and that domestic legislation does not, unless there is an express intention to the contrary, apply to foreign persons outside the United Kingdom.[37] It was argued that the drafting of TUPE did not reverse any of these presumptions.

The claimant employee sought to deal with these objections to applying TUPE to trans- **12.31** fers outside the EU in a number of ways, including criticizing the overseas respondent for confusing the application of the legislation (the transactions which it covers) with its extent (its territorial limits). The claimant argued that TUPE could and should apply to transfers outside the EU, in light of the absence of explicit provision on the issue in the Directive

---

[35] 96/71/EC.
[36] *Mackinnon v Donaldson, Lufkin & Jenrette* [1986] 1 All ER 613.
[37] *Arab Bank plc v Mercantile Holdings Ltd* [1994] 2 All ER 74.

and in TUPE 2006, there being no distinction drawn in the Directive between internal and cross-border transfers, the removal of provisions governing territoriality from original drafts of the Directive and the DTI's statement (in its consultation on the 2006 legislation) that whether claims could be brought under TUPE 2006 would depend on the normal principles of international law. The claimant also relied on the fact that the transfer of assets and the associated redundancies arising in this case occurred, and therefore the complaints raised in the proceedings arose, within the United Kingdom.

12.32 The EAT concluded that TUPE can apply to an international transfer. It held that the legislation is precise in establishing its application to undertakings and activities situated in the UK immediately before the transfer and that a purposive approach to the legislation requires employee protection even in relation to transfers to outside the EU.[38] HHJ Ansell was 'satisfied that the pre-transfer requirement of location in the UK acts as a significant limitation which should not offend against the comity of nations'.[39] Whilst enforcing employees' rights might prove difficult when bringing claims against overseas respondents, this of itself should not be a bar to this interpretation of TUPE. The fact that the overseas transferee had participated in these particular proceedings demonstrated that enforcement might not always be a problem.[40] The weight of judicial, academic, and practitioner commentary was considered to be in favour of this interpretation.

12.33 *Holis* does not conclusively resolve the question of whether an overseas transfer operates to transfer the employees in question automatically to the new overseas location or rather simply to the transferee at their current work location—from which they will be relocated or at which they will be geographically redundant (in the later case thereby potentially enabling the transferee to avoid automatic unfairness by way of an ETOR). The latter analysis is arguably the more consistent with the principles of TUPE which operates to transfer the relevant employees to the transferee on the basis that they are otherwise unaffected by the transfer. Were employees automatically to transfer to the new location overseas that could potentially take them outside the scope of the protection of domestic employment legislation as (then) overseas employees.[41]

12.34 It therefore now appears likely that, if an undertaking is transferred or an SPC occurs from the United Kingdom to outside the EU, TUPE will apply. Consequently, the likelihood is increased that the transferor will be subject to the requisite collective information and consultation obligations under regulation 13 (as will the transferee as it will be taking measures of which it is bound to inform the transferor under regulation 13(4)).

12.35 Moreover, as it is the transferee who has the reason for dismissal on an offshoring (i.e. the relocation), the application of TUPE to offshorings makes it risky for the transferor to dismiss the relevant employees. Only the transferee has the ETOR which avoids a transfer-related dismissal being automatically unfair under regulation 7.[42]

---

[38] Ibid. at para. 41.
[39] Ibid.
[40] Ibid. at para. 43.
[41] And presumably therefore not within any of the categories of overseas employees covered by domestic employment protection legislation in accordance with *Serco Ltd v Lawson* [2006] IRLR 289, HL.
[42] The inability of the transferor to rely on the transferee's ETOR is discussed further at Chapter 7, para. 7.64 *et seq.*

As the EAT noted in *Holis*,[43] there is one other potential claim that should be borne in mind **12.36** in the context of overseas transfers. Employees may be able to bring a claim against the transferor based on *University of Oxford v Humphreys*[44] if, prior to an overseas transfer, they claim constructive dismissal under regulation 4(11) on the basis of an anticipatory breach of contract or object to the transfer under regulation 4(9) on the basis that the transfer overseas would involve a substantial change to working conditions to their detriment.[45] In the *Humphreys* case, it was held that an objection to the transfer meant that the transferee avoided inheriting any rights, powers, or duties relating to the relevant staff, who could only bring claims against the transferor.

The international dimension of TUPE inevitably interacts with the issue of whether the **12.37** requirements for a relevant transfer are satisfied in any event and the move of a business or functions abroad may lead to arguments that the offshoring of the relevant undertaking or activities entails changes to the relevant operation which take the transfer outside the scope of TUPE. It may be argued that regulation 3(1)(a) does not apply on the basis that the economic entity does not retain its identity in its overseas incarnation.[46] A similar argument may be attempted in relation to regulation 3(1)(b) if the transaction in question could be an SPC—to the effect that the activities conducted after the putative SPC are not fundamentally or essentially the same as beforehand.[47]

C. Tax and Employee Transfer

Kuehne and Nagel Drink Logistics Ltd and others v the Commissioners for Her Majesty's Revenue **12.38** *and Customs*[48] concerned the proper tax treatment of payments made to transferring employees in order to facilitate the transfer process. Payments of £4,800 each were made to a number of employees on their transfer from Scottish & Newcastle UK Ltd (S&N) to Kuehne & Nagel Drink Logistics Ltd (KNDL) pursuant to a relevant transfer for the purposes of TUPE whereby Kuehne Nagel and S&N created KNDL as a joint venture vehicle to which their respective drinks distribution businesses were transferred. The relevant payments were negotiated between S&N and the recognized trade union which represented the relevant employees and addressed the employees' concerns that the pension scheme operated by KNDL which the staff would join on transfer from S&N was inferior to the scheme in which they participated whilst employed by S&N. The transfer proceeded smoothly without the industrial action which had been threatened in relation to the issue of post-transfer pensions.

The First Tier Tribunal and Upper Tribunal held that these payments were liable to tax as **12.39** 'earnings . . . from an employment' for the purposes of the Income Tax (Earning and Pensions) Act 2003 and also liable to national insurance contributions, as 'earnings . . . derived from an employment' for the purposes of the Social Security Contribution and Benefits Acts 1992, s. 6. At the First Tier Tribunal, the payments were held to have been made to avoid disruption and to secure the continued and willing services of the employees. The threat of strike action

---

[43] *Holis*, above n. 29, at para. 23, with reference to McMullen, 'International Outsourcing and Transnational Transfers of Undertakings: United Kingdom Perspective' (2005) The Company Lawyer 296.
[44] [2000] IRLR 183, CA and see Chapter 4, para. 4.125 *et seq.*
[45] See Chapter 4, para. 4.92 *et seq.*
[46] See Chapter 2 generally.
[47] See Chapter 3 generally.
[48] [2012] EWCA Civ 34, CA.

was not merely the means by which payment was secured—it was a substantial cause of the payment. As a reward or inducement for future willing service, the payment was taxable and the employees' argument was rejected that the payment was made for loss of pension rights which were not taxable emoluments and that therefore the payments should not be taxable. The appellants had sought, as Mummery LJ put it, to reformulate the question to be determined in a way which he considered was not appropriate—the statutory question required the connection between the payments and the employment to be determined rather than the question which the appellants sought to be answered of whether

> a payment made to an employee to compensate him or her for the loss of pension rights has been secured in part by the threat of industrial action, making it necessarily an emolument from the employment when it would not otherwise be an emolument from the employment had it been paid without the threat of an industrial actions being needed to secure it?[49]

12.40 In upholding the inferior tribunals' decisions, Mummery LJ noted that the provision in the legislation that the relevant earnings be or derived from an employment requires there to be 'in actual fact, . . . a relevant connection or a link between the payments to the employees and their employment'.[50] This was the statutory language whose application fell to be determined in these proceedings. The Court of Appeal held that the decision of the First Tier Tribunal was not wrong in law. The circumstances of and reasons for the payments had been correctly considered. The First Tier Tribunal had addressed the proper statutory question in its findings that the threat of industrial action was a substantial cause of the payments. That finding was not cancelled out or diminished by the presence of another factor—compensation for loss of pension rights—unrelated to any emolument.

D. Immigration

12.41 It is a criminal offence knowingly to employ an individual without permission to work in the United Kingdom.[51] An employer can also be liable for a civil penalty where an employer negligently employs someone without permission to work in the United Kingdom.[52] It is understood that transferees do not need to make individual document checks on transferring employees provided that they can demonstrate that the employees were inherited by virtue of a relevant transfer for the purposes of TUPE.

12.42 With regard to the steps which need to be taken in respect of notifications to the UK Border Agency of TUPE transfers insofar as they relate to those who are licensed sponsors for the purposes of the United Kingdom's immigration control arrangements, the UKBA's guidance provides in summary as follows. If a licensed sponsor takes over an employer which is not a licensed sponsor, the transferee sponsor must inform UKBA within 28 calendar days. If a licensed sponsor is taken over by a company which is not a licensed sponsor, the existing sponsor is required to inform the UKBA of this occurrence. The new organization must apply for a sponsor licence within twenty-eight calendar days. Failure to do so means that the permission to remain in the United Kingdom which applies to those sponsored migrants who have transferred as a consequence of the relevant transfer is likely to be reduced to sixty

---

[49] Ibid. at para. 25.
[50] Ibid. at para. 33.
[51] Immigration, Asylum and Nationality Act 2006.
[52] Ibid.

calendar days to allow them time to find a new sponsor (on the basis that they will then no longer be working for a licensed sponsor). If both transferor and transferee are licensed sponsors, then *both* must inform of the change of employer within twenty-eight calendar days of it occurring. The employer which was the subject of the transfer must inform the UKBA as to who now has responsibility for the relevant individuals. The transferee is required to inform the UKBA of the individuals for whom it has taken responsibility.

E. Equal Pay

While a detailed examination of the equal pay legislation and its interaction with TUPE is **12.43** outside the scope of this work, it is worth noting in passing the interaction of TUPE with the equal pay legislation in two particular respects—the time limit which applies in relation to equal pay claims made in respect of pre-transfer employment, and the extent to which pay differentials can be justified in equal pay terms by reference to the historic derivation of the relevant terms from different employers prior to a TUPE transfer bringing the relevant individuals within the employment of the same employer. Space constraints permit a review of only two cases on these points.

1. Time limits for bringing claims

Gutridge and others v Sodexo Ltd and others[53] addressed the issue of the commencement **12.44** point of the six-month limitation period for bringing equal pay claims under what was the EqPA 1970 and is now the EA 2010. The claimant employees were female domestic cleaners whose employment transferred pursuant to TUPE from an NHS Trust to Sodexo under a contracting-out arrangement. Their equal pay claims against Sodexo identified as comparators colleagues who had not transferred from the transferor employer to Sodexo. The employees' claims against Sodexo therefore in part related to equal pay entitlements in respect of a period of employment prior to transfer with the transferor for which entitlements the transferee was liable consequent upon having become the employees' employer pursuant to TUPE. The time limit for bringing equal pay claims is six months from the termination of employment and the question which arose was whether these claims against the transferee had to be brought within six months of the date of transfer—being the date when the employees ceased employment with the transferor by virtue of the transfer—or six months from the end of their employment with the transferee.[54]

Relying on *Powerhouse Retail v Burroughs*[55] Sodexo argued that the applicable six-month **12.45** time limit ran from the date of the transfer, which was when the claimants' employment with the employer—the transferor—with whose other employees they claimed equal pay had come to an end. This contention was rejected by the ET which held the termination of employment with the transferee to be the point at which the limitation period commenced. The EAT overturned this decision in part on the basis that the date of the transfer did indeed start the limitation period in relation to any equal pay claims deriving from the period of

---

[53] [2009] IRLR 721, CA.

[54] The applicable legislation for the purposes of this case, Equal Pay Act 1970, s. 2ZA, effectively provided that the date by which a claim should be brought is 'the date falling six months after the last day on which the woman was employed in the employment'.

[55] [2006] IRLR 381, HL.

employment with the transferor.[56] Claims against the transferee for failing to respect the employees' transferred rights in respect of the period after the transfer could, however, be brought within six months of termination of employment with the transferee.

12.46 The Court of Appeal upheld the EAT's analysis—the six-month time limit ran from the date of transfer in respect of the transferor's breach of the equal pay legislation. With regard to the transferee's breach of the equal pay legislation, the time limit ran from the end of the employee's employment with the transferee. This decision was considered not only to accord with justice and common sense but also to be consistent with the position that an employee cannot have greater rights against the transferee than the employee had against the transferor—to find otherwise would have extended the time limit beyond what would have been the position had the employees ceased employment with the transferor in the absence of a relevant transfer.[57] Consequently, claims in respect of the arrears of (equal) pay which the employees could seek in respect of their period of employment with the transferor could only be brought in the six months from transfer, whilst claims in respect of the transferee's direct (as opposed to inherited) liability for such arrears in respect of the period from the point of transfer could be brought in the six months following termination.

12.47 It was also held that the equal pay claims which the employees had in respect of their employment by the transferor prior to the relevant transfer were inherited by the transferee pursuant to what was then regulation 5 of TUPE 1981 and is now regulation 4. The rights to equal pay which crystallized during the employees' employment with the transferor transferred under TUPE to the transferee and remained extant until validly terminated or varied.[58]

2. Genuine material factor defence

12.48 In *Skills Development Scotland Co Ltd v Buchanan and anor*[59] the issue addressed by the EAT was the reliance by the employees' employer on the 'genuine material factor' defence under EqPA 1970, s. 1(3) in circumstances where the employer contended that TUPE was explanatory of the significant pay differential between the claimants and their male comparator. Having joined the respondent's employment consequent upon TUPE transfers the differential in the employees' pay was broadly maintained. The ET found that TUPE was 'an explanation for the disparity in pay after the event as opposed to the when the payments were made'.[60] Nonetheless, it held that the material factor defence was made out but only in respect of the specific period from 2002 to 2004 and not thereafter. The genuine material factor defence was rejected in respect of the period from when the employer operated a new PRP scheme which permitted the salary of those overpaid for their current position to be frozen, a step which could have eradicated the differential treatment in question but which the employer did not take in relation to the higher paid comparator over the subsequent years prior to the claims being commenced.

12.49 As the EAT identified, the key issue is causation—'[i]f the employer establishes a subsisting causal link between a non gender related explanation and the difference in pay complained

---

[56] [2008] IRLR 752, EAT.
[57] See *Gutridge,* above n. 53, at paras 81 and 97 per Lady Justice Smith.
[58] Ibid. see para. 101.
[59] UKEATS/0042/10.
[60] Ibid. para. 7, quoting para. 81 of the ET judgment.

of, the defence is made out'.[61] Reference was made to the earlier EAT authority in *King's College v Clark*,[62] where, to adopt Lady Smith's summary that decision,[63] the ET had held that there was no causal connection between TUPE and the employee's disparate pay because when the employer had carried out a grading review, it could have brought her into line with her comparator's terms and conditions—the reason it did not do so was that it mistakenly and genuinely thought that her post was properly graded when it was not. The EAT allowed an appeal—'the grading review did not break the causative chain stretching back to the historical difference in pay due to the protection afforded by TUPE to [the comparator's] terms and conditions of employment'.[64]

The EAT in *Buchanan* therefore allowed an appeal on the basis, put shortly, that the employer's application of its 'standard approach to pay increases…did not break the causal chain that emanated from the gender-neutral fact of the effect of TUPE'.[65] The mere effluxion of time could not, by way of what was described as an 'evaporation principle', cause a gender-neutral explanation to lose its 'non-sex character'.[66] **12.50**

F. Drafting and Commercial Issues

1. Introduction

A comprehensive study of the drafting and other issues which can arise when structuring **12.51** and documenting a TUPE transfer is outside the scope of this work. The level of complexity, scale of potential employment problems, commercial imperatives, and relative bargaining strengths of the parties will vary depending on the particular transaction in question, all of which makes generalization relatively unhelpful, but there are certain key issues that transferors and transferees and indeed those awarding contracts by way of outsourcing and retendering need to bear in mind.

2. Due diligence

The issue of due diligence is often important for both parties. A purchaser of a business or **12.52** potential contractor will need to understand the terms upon which employees are engaged and the potential liabilities which it may inherit for a variety of reasons. Principal amongst these are the pricing of the contract, the extent to which the transferee will wish to pass back to the transferor liability in respect of particular issues and liabilities which already exist, and the extent to which the transferee may be able to introduce cost savings, flexible working practices, and other changes in order to extract greater value from the relevant business.

The obligation requiring transferors to provide employee liability information to transferees **12.53** is of some assistance in bolstering the ability of a transferee to insist on disclosure from the transferor. The compensation payable for breach is intended to incentivize transferors to comply with an obligation which smaller business contractors might not be able to extract

---

[61] Ibid. at para. 22.
[62] UKEAT/1049/02.
[63] *Buchanan*, above n. 59, at paras 23–5.
[64] *King's College*, above n. 62, at para. 29.
[65] *Buchanan*, above n. 59, at para. 39.
[66] Ibid. at para. 40.

by commercial negotiation from a powerful transferor. However, the lateness of the required delivery and the limited scope of the information to be provided means that the obligation may be of limited value. Accordingly, transferees will still seek, where appropriate and possible, full due diligence from transferees and to have these reinforced by warranties.

12.54 In any case, issues which a due diligence request should consider potentially go wider than the scope of the employee liability notification obligation imposed by regulation 11. Information may be sought about those who are not (or may not be) employees such as consultants and agency workers in order to be able to assess their status, whether they automatically transfer, and if not what steps need to be taken to secure their continued involvement in the business if they are key.

3. Warranties

(a) Commercial context

12.55 The issues arising in relation to warranties concerning employment matters in business sale and similar arrangements often interrelate with wider commercial considerations with regard to qualifications and limitations on warranties in the relevant contract generally. The ultimate value to a transferee of an employment warranty may be affected by issues such as thresholds for the aggregate value of liabilities arising by reason of breach of warranty and qualifications to the warranties themselves based on knowledge (for example, by reference to the belief of the warrantors as opposed to objective fact).

12.56 Whilst the employee notification obligation imposed by regulation 11 does require updating of details which change between initial provision and the actual transfer, it will be important to ensure warranties are accurate at all material times, especially with regard to ongoing issues to be addressed in the lead-up to transfer (in particular, compliance with the collective information and consultation obligations).

(b) Transferor warranties

12.57 By way of brief summary, the warranties which a transferee will expect from a transferor will (in addition to any specific concerns which arise from the due diligence process) address issues such as confirmation that:

- the disclosed employees are the only employees who will transfer to the transferee by virtue of TUPE as a consequence of the transfer;
- all disclosed employee details are accurate and complete;
- full details of all actual or potential employment-related disputes and claims (both collective and individual) have been disclosed;
- all trade union, recognition, and other employee representation details have been fully disclosed and all such collective agreements and related obligations have been fully complied with;
- save as disclosed, no contract changes or pay rises have been agreed of contracted for;
- the transferor has complied with its obligations under regulation 11 with regard to collective information and consultation obligations;
- full details have been disclosed of all agency workers and all employees on maternity terms or absent by reason of sickness;
- no agreements exist for specific payments on termination of employment to transferring employees;

- full disclosure has been made of benefits such as sick pay entitlements, private medical insurance, company car benefits, relocation benefits, enhanced maternity leave and pay entitlements, and mortgage subsidies;
- full disclosure has been made of disciplinary rules and procedures (whose precise contractual status may be a separate issue);
- there have been no dismissals in connection with the transfer;
- the transferor has complied with all obligations (including orders and awards) to which it is subject in respect of the transferring employees;
- no investigations or enquiries have been threatened, or have been or are being indicated by any regulatory of governmental body under their respective statutory powers;
- all dismissals and grievances have been dealt with properly.

(c) Transferee warranties

In terms of the warranties which the transferor may seek to extract from the transferee, these will often be driven by commercial, industrial relations, or human resource management imperatives to maintain employee morale and loyalty, especially where there is an ongoing relationship between transferor and transferee (for example, on an outsourcing or by continued commercial supply of goods or services). It may be necessary to seek the transferee's commitment to continue the transferor's level of pension benefits or redundancy terms or to seek an undertaking that redundancies in respect of the transferring employees will not be effected for a period after the transfer. **12.58**

In terms of the legal liabilities which can arise under TUPE, the transferor may wish to seek warranties from the transferee that it does not propose any changes to terms and conditions of employment or working conditions. Undisclosed intentions in this regard could give rise to liabilities for breach of regulation 13 as well as individual claims based on *University of Oxford v Humphreys*.[67] **12.59**

4. Indemnities

Provided that the relevant party has the wherewithal to satisfy its obligations, indemnities are crucial in allocating economic responsibility between the parties in relation to employment liabilities. There may be a variety of qualifications to indemnities based on thresholds for the value of qualifying claims, the time period to which an indemnity extends, and with regard to whether the indemnity covers the entirety of the liability in question or a percentage of it. The types of liability which indemnities will seek to address will include claims in respect of: **12.60**

- wrongful dismissal;
- unfair dismissal;
- unlawful discrimination under the Equality Act 2010 and its predecessors;
- liabilities under the Working Time Regulations 1998;
- personal injury liabilities;
- unlawful deductions from wages pursuant to ERA 1996;
- claims against the transferor based on the *Humphreys* decision or regulation 4(9);
- failure to comply with the collective redundancy consultation requirements of TULRCA 1992, s. 188;

---

[67] See Chapter 4, para. 4.125 *et seq.*

- failure to comply with the information and consultation obligations of regulation 13. This is particularly important following the introduction by TUPE 2006 of the provision that liability for any penalty payable for breach of the regulation 13 requirements is now borne by the transferor and the transferee jointly and severally;
- any fines arising (for example, any penalty payable for failure to notify BIS of redundancies as required by TULRCA 1992);
- liabilities arising under TUPE generally;
- legal and other costs incurred in dealing with the above liabilities.

12.61 One starting point in drafting indemnities is that the transferor is responsible for liabilities arising up to the point of transfer and the transferee responsible for liabilities thereafter. Exceptions to that approach may arise. For example, if a transferor is required by the transferee to effect dismissals prior to dismissal, the transferee may agree to indemnify the transferor for any liability which the transferor inherits (even if as a matter of law, that liability may well transfer to the transferee).

12.62 Such indemnities may need to distinguish between fixed termination costs (such as notice payments and statutory redundancy payments) and those costs and liabilities which can be avoided, minimized, or mitigated, such as unfair dismissal liabilities and awards for failure to comply with applicable information and consultation obligations under TUPE or in relation to collective redundancies. These latter costs may be allocated on a fault basis (for example, if the transferor simply makes an error in the handling of a dismissal or the transferee fails to provide adequate information to ensure compliance with the applicable collective obligations).

12.63 A transfer agreement may also need to address the situation where employees other than those disclosed actually do transfer under the legislation to the transferee. In such circumstances it may be that it is commercially agreed that the transferor bears the liability for the dismissal of this employee. However, in order to mitigate its liabilities in that regard, the transferor may wish first to be informed of the situation and to be afforded the opportunity to offer continued employment to the affected employee. Alternatively, an adjustment may need to be made to the pricing of the contract—this will be particularly relevant in those outsourcings where employment costs are an explicit factor in contracting pricing.

5. Outsourcing

12.64 Many of the provisions used in business transfer agreements will be relevant to the commencement and cessation of outsourcing arrangements. Some specific issues which may arise in that context are as follows:

- the client will wish a contractor to be contractually obliged to provide employee information on request in order to facilitate any subsequent retendering process since bidders will expect and, if successful, be entitled to such information;
- contractors will wish the client to be required contractually to do all that is reasonably possible on a retendering or on termination of the contract more generally to ensure that the contractor can comply with its obligation to provide the prescribed employee liability information under regulation 11 to a replacement contractor;
- controls may need to be in place where the pricing of the contracting depends on staffing levels and related employment costs—these would require control on the part of the client over salary levels and terms and conditions of employment;

- the contractor may be required to comply with the client's employment policies;
- on termination of the contract the allocation of liability for employment costs needs to be considered if a new contractor will take on staff. The contractor may wish the client to ensure that a new contractor takes on staff falling within the scope of the transfer legislation on their existing terms or for an indemnity in this regard to be provided. The client may consider these liabilities to be the contractor's responsibility;
- notwithstanding the assignment test deployed in regulation 4(1) to identify which employees transfer on a relevant transfer, controls may be needed on staff allocation to avoid 'social dumping';
- an incoming contractor will often have no contractual or commercial relationship with the incumbent. The party awarding the contract may impose under the initial outsourcing agreement an obligation on the initial contractor to indemnify a new contractor in relation to compliance with its regulation 13 obligations and employment liabilities arising whilst the relevant employees are employed by the initial contractor.

Transfer of Undertakings (Protection of Employment) Regulations 2006

Made 6th February 2006
Laid before Parliament 7th February 2006
Coming into force 6th April 2006

The Secretary of State makes the following Regulations in exercise of the powers conferred upon him by section 2(2) of the European Communities Act 1972 (being a Minister designated for the purposes of that section in relation to rights and obligations relating to employers and employees on the transfer or merger of undertakings, businesses or parts of businesses) and section 38 of the Employment Relations Act 1999.

1 Citation, commencement and extent

(1) These Regulations may be cited as the Transfer of Undertakings (Protection of Employment) Regulations 2006.

(2) These Regulations shall come into force on 6 April 2006.

(3) These Regulations shall extend to Northern Ireland, except where otherwise provided.

2 Interpretation

(1) In these Regulations—

'assigned' means assigned other than on a temporary basis;

'collective agreement', 'collective bargaining' and 'trade union' have the same meanings respectively as in the 1992 Act;

'contract of employment' means any agreement between an employee and his employer determining the terms and conditions of his employment;

references to 'contractor' in regulation 3 shall include a sub-contractor;

'employee' means any individual who works for another person whether under a contract of service or apprenticeship or otherwise but does not include anyone who provides services under a contract for services and references to a person's employer shall be construed accordingly;

'insolvency practitioner' has the meaning given to the expression by Part XIII of the Insolvency Act 1986;

references to 'organised grouping of employees' shall include a single employee;

'recognised' has the meaning given to the expression by section 178(3) of the 1992 Act;

'relevant transfer' means a transfer or a service provision change to which these Regulations apply in accordance with regulation 3 and 'transferor' and 'transferee' shall be construed accordingly and in the case of a service provision change falling within regulation 3(1)(b), 'the transferor' means the person who carried out the activities prior to the service provision change and 'the transferee' means the person who carries out the activities as a result of the service provision change;

'the 1992 Act' means the Trade Union and Labour Relations (Consolidation) Act 1992;

'the 1996 Act' means the Employment Rights Act 1996;

'the 1996 Tribunals Act' means the Employment Tribunals Act 1996;

'the 1981 Regulations' means the Transfer of Undertakings (Protection of Employment) Regulations 1981.

(2) For the purposes of these Regulations the representative of a trade union recognised by an employer is an official or other person authorised to carry on collective bargaining with that employer by that trade union.

(3) In the application of these Regulations to Northern Ireland the Regulations shall have effect as set out in Schedule 1.

3 A relevant transfer

(1) These Regulations apply to—
  (a) a transfer of an undertaking, business or part of an undertaking or business situated immediately before the transfer in the United Kingdom to another person where there is a transfer of an economic entity which retains its identity;
  (b) a service provision change, that is a situation in which—
    (i) activities cease to be carried out by a person ('a client') on his own behalf and are carried out instead by another person on the client's behalf ('a contractor');
    (ii) activities cease to be carried out by a contractor on a client's behalf (whether or not those activities had previously been carried out by the client on his own behalf) and are carried out instead by another person ('a subsequent contractor') on the client's behalf; or
    (iii) activities cease to be carried out by a contractor or a subsequent contractor on a client's behalf (whether or not those activities had previously been carried out by the client on his own behalf) and are carried out instead by the client on his own behalf,
    and in which the conditions set out in paragraph (3) are satisfied.
(2) In this regulation 'economic entity' means an organised grouping of resources which has the objective of pursuing an economic activity, whether or not that activity is central or ancillary.
(3) The conditions referred to in paragraph (1)(b) are that—
  (a) immediately before the service provision change—
    (i) there is an organised grouping of employees situated in Great Britain which has as its principal purpose the carrying out of the activities concerned on behalf of the client;
    (ii) the client intends that the activities will, following the service provision change, be carried out by the transferee other than in connection with a single specific event or task of short-term duration; and
  (b) the activities concerned do not consist wholly or mainly of the supply of goods for the client's use.
(4) Subject to paragraph (1), these Regulations apply to—
  (a) public and private undertakings engaged in economic activities whether or not they are operating for gain;
  (b) a transfer or service provision change howsoever effected notwithstanding—
    (i) that the transfer of an undertaking, business or part of an undertaking or business is governed or effected by the law of a country or territory outside the United Kingdom or that the service provision change is governed or effected by the law of a country or territory outside Great Britain;
    (ii) that the employment of persons employed in the undertaking, business or part transferred or, in the case of a service provision change, persons employed in the organised grouping of employees, is governed by any such law;
  (c) a transfer of an undertaking, business or part of an undertaking or business (which may also be a service provision change) where persons employed in the undertaking, business or part transferred ordinarily work outside the United Kingdom.
(5) An administrative reorganisation of public administrative authorities or the transfer of administrative functions between public administrative authorities is not a relevant transfer.
(6) A relevant transfer—
  (a) may be effected by a series of two or more transactions; and
  (b) may take place whether or not any property is transferred to the transferee by the transferor.
(7) Where, in consequence (whether directly or indirectly) of the transfer of an undertaking, business or part of an undertaking or business which was situated immediately before the transfer in the United Kingdom, a ship within the meaning of the Merchant Shipping Act 1995 registered in the United Kingdom ceases to be so registered, these Regulations shall not affect the right conferred by section 29 of that Act (right of seamen to be discharged when ship ceases to be registered in the United Kingdom) on a seaman employed in the ship.

4 Effect of relevant transfer on contracts of employment

(1) Except where objection is made under paragraph (7), a relevant transfer shall not operate so as to terminate the contract of employment of any person employed by the transferor and assigned to the

organised grouping of resources or employees that is subject to the relevant transfer, which would otherwise be terminated by the transfer, but any such contract shall have effect after the transfer as if originally made between the person so employed and the transferee.

(2) Without prejudice to paragraph (1), but subject to paragraph (6), and regulations 8 and 15(9), on the completion of a relevant transfer—

    (a) all the transferor's rights, powers, duties and liabilities under or in connection with any such contract shall be transferred by virtue of this regulation to the transferee; and

    (b) any act or omission before the transfer is completed, of or in relation to the transferor in respect of that contract or a person assigned to that organised grouping of resources or employees, shall be deemed to have been an act or omission of or in relation to the transferee.

(3) Any reference in paragraph (1) to a person employed by the transferor and assigned to the organised grouping of resources or employees that is subject to a relevant transfer, is a reference to a person so employed immediately before the transfer, or who would have been so employed if he had not been dismissed in the circumstances described in regulation 7(1), including, where the transfer is effected by a series of two or more transactions, a person so employed and assigned or who would have been so employed and assigned immediately before any of those transactions.

(4) Subject to regulation 9, in respect of a contract of employment that is, or will be, transferred by paragraph (1), any purported variation of the contract shall be void if the sole or principal reason for the variation is—

    (a) the transfer itself; or

    (b) a reason connected with the transfer that is not an economic, technical or organisational reason entailing changes in the workforce.

(5) Paragraph (4) shall not prevent the employer and his employee, whose contract of employment is, or will be, transferred by paragraph (1), from agreeing a variation of that contract if the sole or principal reason for the variation is—

    (a) a reason connected with the transfer that is an economic, technical or organisational reason entailing changes in the workforce; or

    (b) a reason unconnected with the transfer.

(6) Paragraph (2) shall not transfer or otherwise affect the liability of any person to be prosecuted for, convicted of and sentenced for any offence.

(7) Paragraphs (1) and (2) shall not operate to transfer the contract of employment and the rights, powers, duties and liabilities under or in connection with it of an employee who informs the transferor or the transferee that he objects to becoming employed by the transferee.

(8) Subject to paragraphs (9) and (11), where an employee so objects, the relevant transfer shall operate so as to terminate his contract of employment with the transferor but he shall not be treated, for any purpose, as having been dismissed by the transferor.

(9) Subject to regulation 9, where a relevant transfer involves or would involve a substantial change in working conditions to the material detriment of a person whose contract of employment is or would be transferred under paragraph (1), such an employee may treat the contract of employment as having been terminated, and the employee shall be treated for any purpose as having been dismissed by the employer.

(10) No damages shall be payable by an employer as a result of a dismissal falling within paragraph (9) in respect of any failure by the employer to pay wages to an employee in respect of a notice period which the employee has failed to work.

(11) Paragraphs (1), (7), (8) and (9) are without prejudice to any right of an employee arising apart from these Regulations to terminate his contract of employment without notice in acceptance of a repudiatory breach of contract by his employer.

5 Effect of relevant transfer on collective agreements

Where at the time of a relevant transfer there exists a collective agreement made by or on behalf of the transferor with a trade union recognised by the transferor in respect of any employee whose contract of employment is preserved by regulation 4(1) above, then—

(a) without prejudice to sections 179 and 180 of the 1992 Act (collective agreements presumed to be unenforceable in specified circumstances) that agreement, in its application in relation to the employee, shall, after the transfer, have effect as if made by or on behalf of the transferee with that trade union, and accordingly anything done under or in connection with it, in its application in relation to the employee, by or in relation to the transferor before the transfer, shall, after the transfer, be deemed to have been done by or in relation to the transferee; and

(b) any order made in respect of that agreement, in its application in relation to the employee, shall, after the transfer, have effect as if the transferee were a party to the agreement.

6 Effect of relevant transfer on trade union recognition

(1) This regulation applies where after a relevant transfer the transferred organised grouping of resources or employees maintains an identity distinct from the remainder of the transferee's undertaking.

(2) Where before such a transfer an independent trade union is recognised to any extent by the transferor in respect of employees of any description who in consequence of the transfer become employees of the transferee, then, after the transfer—

(a) the trade union shall be deemed to have been recognised by the transferee to the same extent in respect of employees of that description so employed; and

(b) any agreement for recognition may be varied or rescinded accordingly.

7 Dismissal of employee because of relevant transfer

(1) Where either before or after a relevant transfer, any employee of the transferor or transferee is dismissed, that employee shall be treated for the purposes of Part X of the 1996 Act (unfair dismissal) as unfairly dismissed if the sole or principal reason for his dismissal is—

(a) the transfer itself; or

(b) a reason connected with the transfer that is not an economic, technical or organisational reason entailing changes in the workforce.

(2) This paragraph applies where the sole or principal reason for the dismissal is a reason connected with the transfer that is an economic, technical or organisational reason entailing changes in the workforce of either the transferor or the transferee before or after a relevant transfer.

(3) Where paragraph (2) applies—

(a) paragraph (1) shall not apply;

(b) without prejudice to the application of section 98(4) of the 1996 Act (test of fair dismissal), the dismissal shall, for the purposes of sections 98(1) and 135 of that Act (reason for dismissal), be regarded as having been for redundancy where section 98(2)(c) of that Act applies, or otherwise for a substantial reason of a kind such as to justify the dismissal of an employee holding the position which that employee held.

(4) The provisions of this regulation apply irrespective of whether the employee in question is assigned to the organised grouping of resources or employees that is, or will be, transferred.

(5) Paragraph (1) shall not apply in relation to the dismissal of any employee which was required by reason of the application of section 5 of the Aliens Restriction (Amendment) Act 1919 to his employment.

(6) Paragraph (1) shall not apply in relation to a dismissal of an employee if the application of section 94 of the 1996 Act to the dismissal of the employee is excluded by or under any provision of the 1996 Act, the 1996 Tribunals Act or the 1992 Act.

8 Insolvency

(1) If at the time of a relevant transfer the transferor is subject to relevant insolvency proceedings paragraphs (2) to (6) apply.

(2) In this regulation 'relevant employee' means an employee of the transferor—

(a) whose contract of employment transfers to the transferee by virtue of the operation of these Regulations; or

(b) whose employment with the transferor is terminated before the time of the relevant transfer in the circumstances described in regulation 7(1).

(3) The relevant statutory scheme specified in paragraph (4)(b) (including that sub-paragraph as applied by paragraph 5 of Schedule 1) shall apply in the case of a relevant employee irrespective of the fact that the qualifying requirement that the employee's employment has been terminated is not met and for

those purposes the date of the transfer shall be treated as the date of the termination and the transferor shall be treated as the employer.

(4) In this regulation the 'relevant statutory schemes' are—
   (a) Chapter VI of Part XI of the 1996 Act;
   (b) Part XII of the 1996 Act.

(5) Regulation 4 shall not operate to transfer liability for the sums payable to the relevant employee under the relevant statutory schemes.

(6) In this regulation 'relevant insolvency proceedings' means insolvency proceedings which have been opened in relation to the transferor not with a view to the liquidation of the assets of the transferor and which are under the supervision of an insolvency practitioner.

(7) Regulations 4 and 7 do not apply to any relevant transfer where the transferor is the subject of bankruptcy proceedings or any analogous insolvency proceedings which have been instituted with a view to the liquidation of the assets of the transferor and are under the supervision of an insolvency practitioner.

9 Variations of contract where transferors are subject to relevant insolvency proceedings

(1) If at the time of a relevant transfer the transferor is subject to relevant insolvency proceedings these Regulations shall not prevent the transferor or transferee (or an insolvency practitioner) and appropriate representatives of assigned employees agreeing to permitted variations.

(2) For the purposes of this regulation 'appropriate representatives' are—
   (a) if the employees are of a description in respect of which an independent trade union is recognised by their employer, representatives of the trade union; or
   (b) in any other case, whichever of the following employee representatives the employer chooses—
      (i) employee representatives appointed or elected by the assigned employees (whether they make the appointment or election alone or with others) otherwise than for the purposes of this regulation, who (having regard to the purposes for, and the method by which they were appointed or elected) have authority from those employees to agree permitted variations to contracts of employment on their behalf;
      (ii) employee representatives elected by assigned employees (whether they make the appointment or election alone or with others) for these particular purposes, in an election satisfying requirements identical to those contained in regulation 14 except those in regulation 14(1)(d).

(3) An individual may be an appropriate representative for the purposes of both this regulation and regulation 13 provided that where the representative is not a trade union representative he is either elected by or has authority from assigned employees (within the meaning of this regulation) and affected employees (as described in regulation 13(1)).

(4) In section 168 of the 1992 Act (time off for carrying out trade union duties) in subsection (1), after paragraph (c) there is inserted—
', or
   (d) negotiations with a view to entering into an agreement under regulation 9 of the Transfer of Undertakings (Protection of Employment) Regulations 2006 that applies to employees of the employer, or
   (e) the performance on behalf of employees of the employer of functions related to or connected with the making of an agreement under that regulation'.

(5) Where assigned employees are represented by non-trade union representatives—
   (a) the agreement recording a permitted variation must be in writing and signed by each of the representatives who have made it or, where that is not reasonably practicable, by a duly authorised agent of that representative; and
   (b) the employer must, before the agreement is made available for signature, provide all employees to whom it is intended to apply on the date on which it is to come into effect with copies of the text of the agreement and such guidance as those employees might reasonably require in order to understand it fully.

(6) A permitted variation shall take effect as a term or condition of the assigned employee's contract of employment in place, where relevant, of any term or condition which it varies.

(7) In this regulation—

'assigned employees' means those employees assigned to the organised grouping of resources or employees that is the subject of a relevant transfer;

'permitted variation' is a variation to the contract of employment of an assigned employee where—

(a) the sole or principal reason for it is the transfer itself or a reason connected with the transfer that is not an economic, technical or organisational reason entailing changes in the workforce; and

(b) it is designed to safeguard employment opportunities by ensuring the survival of the undertaking, business or part of the undertaking or business that is the subject of the relevant transfer;

'relevant insolvency proceedings' has the meaning given to the expression by regulation 8(6).

10 Pensions

(1) Regulations 4 and 5 shall not apply—

(a) to so much of a contract of employment or collective agreement as relates to an occupational pension scheme within the meaning of the Pension Schemes Act 1993; or

(b) to any rights, powers, duties or liabilities under or in connection with any such contract or subsisting by virtue of any such agreement and relating to such a scheme or otherwise arising in connection with that person's employment and relating to such a scheme.

(2) For the purposes of paragraphs (1) and (3), any provisions of an occupational pension scheme which do not relate to benefits for old age, invalidity or survivors shall not be treated as being part of the scheme.

(3) An employee whose contract of employment is transferred in the circumstances described in regulation 4(1) shall not be entitled to bring a claim against the transferor for—

(a) breach of contract; or

(b) constructive unfair dismissal under section 95(1)(c) of the 1996 Act, arising out of a loss or reduction in his rights under an occupational pension scheme in consequence of the transfer, save insofar as the alleged breach of contract or dismissal (as the case may be) occurred prior to the date on which these Regulations took effect.

11 Notification of Employee Liability Information

(1) The transferor shall notify to the transferee the employee liability information of any person employed by him who is assigned to the organised grouping of resources or employees that is the subject of a relevant transfer—

(a) in writing; or

(b) by making it available to him in a readily accessible form.

(2) In this regulation and in regulation 12 'employee liability information' means—

(a) the identity and age of the employee;

(b) those particulars of employment that an employer is obliged to give to an employee pursuant to section 1 of the 1996 Act;

(c) information of any—

(i) disciplinary procedure taken against an employee;

(ii) grievance procedure taken by an employee, within the previous two years, in circumstances where [a Code of Practice issued under Part IV of the Trade Union and Labour Relations (Consolidation) Act 1992 which relates exclusively or primarily to the resolution of disputes applies];

(d) information of any court or tribunal case, claim or action—

(i) brought by an employee against the transferor, within the previous two years;

(ii) that the transferor has reasonable grounds to believe that an employee may bring against the transferee, arising out of the employee's employment with the transferor; and

(e) information of any collective agreement which will have effect after the transfer, in its application in relation to the employee, pursuant to regulation 5(a).

(3) Employee liability information shall contain information as at a specified date not more than fourteen days before the date on which the information is notified to the transferee.

(4) The duty to provide employee liability information in paragraph (1) shall include a duty to provide employee liability information of any person who would have been employed by the transferor and assigned to the organised grouping of resources or employees that is the subject of a relevant transfer immediately before the transfer if he had not been dismissed in the circumstances described in regulation 7(1), including, where the transfer is effected by a series of two or more transactions, a person so employed and assigned or who would have been so employed and assigned immediately before any of those transactions.

(5) Following notification of the employee liability information in accordance with this regulation, the transferor shall notify the transferee in writing of any change in the employee liability information.

(6) A notification under this regulation shall be given not less than fourteen days before the relevant transfer or, if special circumstances make this not reasonably practicable, as soon as reasonably practicable thereafter.

(7) A notification under this regulation may be given—
    (a) in more than one instalment;
    (b) indirectly, through a third party.

12 Remedy for failure to notify employee liability information

(1) On or after a relevant transfer, the transferee may present a complaint to an employment tribunal that the transferor has failed to comply with any provision of regulation 11.

(2) An employment tribunal shall not consider a complaint under this regulation unless it is presented—
    (a) before the end of the period of three months beginning with the date of the relevant transfer;
    (b) within such further period as the tribunal considers reasonable in a case where it is satisfied that it was not reasonably practicable for the complaint to be presented before the end of that period of three months.

(3) Where an employment tribunal finds a complaint under paragraph (1) well-founded, the tribunal—
    (a) shall make a declaration to that effect; and
    (b) may make an award of compensation to be paid by the transferor to the transferee.

(4) The amount of the compensation shall be such as the tribunal considers just and equitable in all the circumstances, subject to paragraph (5), having particular regard to—
    (a) any loss sustained by the transferee which is attributable to the matters complained of; and
    (b) the terms of any contract between the transferor and the transferee relating to the transfer under which the transferor may be liable to pay any sum to the transferee in respect of a failure to notify the transferee of employee liability information.

(5) Subject to paragraph (6), the amount of compensation awarded under paragraph (3) shall be not less than £500 per employee in respect of whom the transferor has failed to comply with a provision of regulation 11, unless the tribunal considers it just and equitable, in all the circumstances, to award a lesser sum.

(6) In ascertaining the loss referred to in paragraph (4)(a) the tribunal shall apply the same rule concerning the duty of a person to mitigate his loss as applies to any damages recoverable under the common law of England and Wales, Northern Ireland or Scotland, as applicable.

(7) Section 18 of the 1996 Tribunals Act (conciliation) shall apply to the right conferred by this regulation and to proceedings under this regulation as it applies to the rights conferred by that Act and the employment tribunal proceedings mentioned in that Act.

13 Duty to inform and consult representatives

(1) In this regulation and regulations 14 and 15 references to affected employees, in relation to a relevant transfer, are to any employees of the transferor or the transferee (whether or not assigned to the organised grouping of resources or employees that is the subject of a relevant transfer) who may be affected by the transfer or may be affected by measures taken in connection with it; and references to the employer shall be construed accordingly.

(2) Long enough before a relevant transfer to enable the employer of any affected employees to consult the appropriate representatives of any affected employees, the employer shall inform those representatives of—

    (a) the fact that the transfer is to take place, the date or proposed date of the transfer and the reasons for it;

    (b) the legal, economic and social implications of the transfer for any affected employees;

    (c) the measures which he envisages he will, in connection with the transfer, take in relation to any affected employees or, if he envisages that no measures will be so taken, that fact; and

    (d) if the employer is the transferor, the measures, in connection with the transfer, which he envisages the transferee will take in relation to any affected employees who will become employees of the transferee after the transfer by virtue of regulation 4 or, if he envisages that no measures will be so taken, that fact.

[(2A) Where information is to be supplied under paragraph (2) by an employer—

    (a) this must include suitable information relating to the use of agency workers (if any) by that employer; and

    (b) 'suitable information relating to the use of agency workers' means—

        (i) the number of agency workers working temporarily for and under the supervision and direction of the employer;

        (ii) the parts of the employer's undertaking in which those agency workers are working; and

        (iii) the type of work those agency workers are carrying out.]

(3) For the purposes of this regulation the appropriate representatives of any affected employees are—

    (a) if the employees are of a description in respect of which an independent trade union is recognised by their employer, representatives of the trade union; or

    (b) in any other case, whichever of the following employee representatives the employer chooses—

        (i) employee representatives appointed or elected by the affected employees otherwise than for the purposes of this regulation, who (having regard to the purposes for, and the method by which they were appointed or elected) have authority from those employees to receive information and to be consulted about the transfer on their behalf;

        (ii) employee representatives elected by any affected employees, for the purposes of this regulation, in an election satisfying the requirements of regulation 14(1).

(4) The transferee shall give the transferor such information at such a time as will enable the transferor to perform the duty imposed on him by virtue of paragraph (2)(d).

(5) The information which is to be given to the appropriate representatives shall be given to each of them by being delivered to them, or sent by post to an address notified by them to the employer, or (in the case of representatives of a trade union) sent by post to the trade union at the address of its head or main office.

(6) An employer of an affected employee who envisages that he will take measures in relation to an affected employee, in connection with the relevant transfer, shall consult the appropriate representatives of that employee with a view to seeking their agreement to the intended measures.

(7) In the course of those consultations the employer shall—

    (a) consider any representations made by the appropriate representatives; and

    (b) reply to those representations and, if he rejects any of those representations, state his reasons.

(8) The employer shall allow the appropriate representatives access to any affected employees and shall afford to those representatives such accommodation and other facilities as may be appropriate.

(9) If in any case there are special circumstances which render it not reasonably practicable for an employer to perform a duty imposed on him by any of paragraphs (2) to (7), he shall take all such steps towards performing that duty as are reasonably practicable in the circumstances.

(10) Where—

    (a) the employer has invited any of the affected employee to elect employee representatives; and

    (b) the invitation was issued long enough before the time when the employer is required to give information under paragraph (2) to allow them to elect representatives by that time,

the employer shall be treated as complying with the requirements of this regulation in relation to those employees if he complies with those requirements as soon as is reasonably practicable after the election of the representatives.

(11) If, after the employer has invited any affected employees to elect representatives, they fail to do so within a reasonable time, he shall give to any affected employees the information set out in paragraph (2).

(12) The duties imposed on an employer by this regulation shall apply irrespective of whether the decision resulting in the relevant transfer is taken by the employer or a person controlling the employer.

14 Election of employee representatives

(1) The requirements for the election of employee representatives under regulation 13(3) are that—
   (a) the employer shall make such arrangements as are reasonably practicable to ensure that the election is fair;
   (b) the employer shall determine the number of representatives to be elected so that there are sufficient representatives to represent the interests of all affected employees having regard to the number and classes of those employees;
   (c) the employer shall determine whether the affected employees should be represented either by representatives of all the affected employees or by representatives of particular classes of those employees;
   (d) before the election the employer shall determine the term of office as employee representatives so that it is of sufficient length to enable information to be given and consultations under regulation 13 to be completed;
   (e) the candidates for election as employee representatives are affected employees on the date of the election;
   (f) no affected employee is unreasonably excluded from standing for election;
   (g) all affected employees on the date of the election are entitled to vote for employee representatives;
   (h) the employees entitled to vote may vote for as many candidates as there are representatives to be elected to represent them or, if there are to be representatives for particular classes of employees, may vote for as many candidates as there are representatives to be elected to represent their particular class of employee;
   (i) the election is conducted so as to secure that—
      (i) so far as is reasonably practicable, those voting do so in secret; and
      (ii) the votes given at the election are accurately counted.
(2) Where, after an election of employee representatives satisfying the requirements of paragraph (1) has been held, one of those elected ceases to act as an employee representative and as a result any affected employees are no longer represented, those employees shall elect another representative by an election satisfying the requirements of paragraph (1)(a), (e), (f) and (i).

15 Failure to inform or consult

(1) Where an employer has failed to comply with a requirement of regulation 13 or regulation 14, a complaint may be presented to an employment tribunal on that ground—
   (a) in the case of a failure relating to the election of employee representatives, by any of his employees who are affected employees;
   (b) in the case of any other failure relating to employee representatives, by any of the employee representatives to whom the failure related;
   (c) in the case of failure relating to representatives of a trade union, by the trade union; and
   (d) in any other case, by any of his employees who are affected employees.
(2) If on a complaint under paragraph (1) a question arises whether or not it was reasonably practicable for an employer to perform a particular duty or as to what steps he took towards performing it, it shall be for him to show—
   (a) that there were special circumstances which rendered it not reasonably practicable for him to perform the duty; and
   (b) that he took all such steps towards its performance as were reasonably practicable in those circumstances.
(3) If on a complaint under paragraph (1) a question arises as to whether or not an employee representative was an appropriate representative for the purposes of regulation 13, it shall be for the employer to show that the employee representative had the necessary authority to represent the affected employees.
(4) On a complaint under paragraph (1)(a) it shall be for the employer to show that the requirements in regulation 14 have been satisfied.

(5) On a complaint against a transferor that he had failed to perform the duty imposed upon him by virtue of regulation 13(2)(d) or, so far as relating thereto, regulation 13(9), he may not show that it was not reasonably practicable for him to perform the duty in question for the reason that the transferee had failed to give him the requisite information at the requisite time in accordance with regulation 13(4) unless he gives the transferee notice of his intention to show that fact; and the giving of the notice shall make the transferee a party to the proceedings.

(6) In relation to any complaint under paragraph (1), a failure on the part of a person controlling (directly or indirectly) the employer to provide information to the employer shall not constitute special circumstances rendering it not reasonably practicable for the employer to comply with such a requirement.

(7) Where the tribunal finds a complaint against a transferee under paragraph (1) well-founded it shall make a declaration to that effect and may order the transferee to pay appropriate compensation to such descriptions of affected employees as may be specified in the award.

(8) Where the tribunal finds a complaint against a transferor under paragraph (1) well-founded it shall make a declaration to that effect and may—
   (a) order the transferor, subject to paragraph (9), to pay appropriate compensation to such descriptions of affected employees as may be specified in the award; or
   (b) if the complaint is that the transferor did not perform the duty mentioned in paragraph (5) and the transferor (after giving due notice) shows the facts so mentioned, order the transferee to pay appropriate compensation to such descriptions of affected employees as may be specified in the award.

(9) The transferee shall be jointly and severally liable with the transferor in respect of compensation payable under sub-paragraph (8)(a) or paragraph (11).

(10) An employee may present a complaint to an employment tribunal on the ground that he is an employee of a description to which an order under paragraph (7) or (8) relates and that—
   (a) in respect of an order under paragraph (7), the transferee has failed, wholly or in part, to pay him compensation in pursuance of the order;
   (b) in respect of an order under paragraph (8), the transferor or transferee, as applicable, has failed, wholly or in part, to pay him compensation in pursuance of the order.

(11) Where the tribunal finds a complaint under paragraph (10) well-founded it shall order the transferor or transferee as applicable to pay the complainant the amount of compensation which it finds is due to him.

(12) An employment tribunal shall not consider a complaint under paragraph (1) or (10) unless it is presented to the tribunal before the end of the period of three months beginning with—
   (a) in respect of a complaint under paragraph (1), the date on which the relevant transfer is completed; or
   (b) in respect of a complaint under paragraph (10), the date of the tribunal's order under paragraph (7) or (8),
or within such further period as the tribunal considers reasonable in a case where it is satisfied that it was not reasonably practicable for the complaint to be presented before the end of the period of three months.

16 Failure to inform or consult: supplemental

(1) Section 205(1) of the 1996 Act (complaint to be sole remedy for breach of relevant rights) and section 18 of the 1996 Tribunals Act (conciliation) shall apply to the rights conferred by regulation 15 and to proceedings under this regulation as they apply to the rights conferred by those Acts and the employment tribunal proceedings mentioned in those Acts.

(2) An appeal shall lie and shall lie only to the Employment Appeal Tribunal on a question of law arising from any decision of, or arising in any proceedings before, an employment tribunal under or by virtue of these Regulations; and section 11(1) of the Tribunals and Inquiries Act 1992 (appeals from certain tribunals to the High Court) shall not apply in relation to any such proceedings.

(3) 'Appropriate compensation' in regulation 15 means such sum not exceeding thirteen weeks' pay for the employee in question as the tribunal considers just and equitable having regard to the seriousness of the failure of the employer to comply with his duty.

(4) Sections 220 to 228 of the 1996 Act shall apply for calculating the amount of a week's pay for any employee for the purposes of paragraph (3) and, for the purposes of that calculation, the calculation date shall be—

    (a) in the case of an employee who is dismissed by reason of redundancy (within the meaning of sections 139 and 155 of the 1996 Act) the date which is the calculation date for the purposes of any entitlement of his to a redundancy payment (within the meaning of those sections) or which would be that calculation date if he were so entitled;

    (b) in the case of an employee who is dismissed for any other reason, the effective date of termination (within the meaning of sections 95(1) and (2) and 97 of the 1996 Act) of his contract of employment;

    (c) in any other case, the date of the relevant transfer.

17 Employers' Liability Compulsory Insurance

(1) Paragraph (2) applies where—

    (a) by virtue of section 3(1)(a) or (b) of the Employers' Liability (Compulsory Insurance) Act 1969 ('the 1969 Act'), the transferor is not required by that Act to effect any insurance; or

    (b) by virtue of section 3(1)(c) of the 1969 Act, the transferor is exempted from the requirement of that Act to effect insurance.

(2) Where this paragraph applies, on completion of a relevant transfer the transferor and the transferee shall be jointly and severally liable in respect of any liability referred to in section 1(1) of the 1969 Act, in so far as such liability relates to the employee's employment with the transferor.

18 Restriction on contracting out

Section 203 of the 1996 Act (restrictions on contracting out) shall apply in relation to these Regulations as if they were contained in that Act, save for that section shall not apply in so far as these Regulations provide for an agreement (whether a contract of employment or not) to exclude or limit the operation of these Regulations.

19 Amendment to the 1996 Act

In section 104 of the 1996 Act (assertion of statutory right) in subsection (4)—

    (a) the word 'and' at the end of paragraph (c) is omitted; and

    (b) after paragraph (d), there is inserted—

', and

    (e) the rights conferred by the Transfer of Undertakings (Protection of Employment) Regulations 2006'.

20 Repeals, revocations and amendments

(1) Subject to regulation 21, the 1981 Regulations are revoked.

(2) Section 33 of, and paragraph 4 of Schedule 9 to, the Trade Union Reform and Employment Rights Act 1993 are repealed.

(3) Schedule 2 (consequential amendments) shall have effect.

21 Transitional provisions and savings

(1) These Regulations shall apply in relation to—

    (a) a relevant transfer that takes place on or after 6 April 2006;

    (b) a transfer or service provision change, not falling within sub-paragraph (a), that takes place on or after 6 April 2006 and is regarded by virtue of any enactment as a relevant transfer.

(2) The 1981 Regulations shall continue to apply in relation to—

    (a) a relevant transfer (within the meaning of the 1981 Regulations) that took place before 6 April 2006;

    (b) a transfer, not falling within sub-paragraph (a), that took place before 6 April 2006 and is regarded by virtue of any enactment as a relevant transfer (within the meaning of the 1981 Regulations).

(3) In respect of a relevant transfer that takes place on or after 6 April 2006, any action taken by a transferor or transferee to discharge a duty that applied to them under regulation 10 or 10A of the 1981 Regulations shall be deemed to satisfy the corresponding obligation imposed by regulations 13 and 14 of these Regulations, insofar as that action would have discharged those obligations had the action taken place on or after 6 April 2006.

(4) The duty on a transferor to provide a transferee with employee liability information shall not apply in the case of a relevant transfer that takes place on or before 19 April 2006.

(5) Regulations 13, 14, 15 and 16 shall not apply in the case of a service provision change that is not also a transfer of an undertaking, business or part of an undertaking or business that takes place on or before 4 May 2006.

(6) The repeal of paragraph 4 of Schedule 9 to the Trade Union Reform and Employment Rights Act 1993 does not affect the continued operation of that paragraph so far as it remains capable of having effect.

Gerry Sutcliffe
Parliamentary Under Secretary of State for
Employment Relations and Consumer Affairs
Department of Trade and Industry
6th February 2006
Note—Schedules and Explanatory Memorandum omitted.

APPENDIX 2

Pension Act 2004

Pension protection on transfer of employment

257 Conditions for pension protection

(1) This section applies in relation to a person ('the employee') where—

   [(a) there is a relevant transfer within the meaning of the TUPE regulations,]

   (b) by virtue of the transfer the employee ceases to be employed by the transferor and becomes employed by the transferee, and

   (c) at the time immediately before the employee becomes employed by the transferee—

      (i) there is an occupational pension scheme ('the scheme') in relation to which the transferor is the employer, and

      (ii) one of subsections (2), (3) and (4) applies.

(2) This subsection applies where—

   (a) the employee is an active member of the scheme, and

   (b) if any of the benefits that may be provided under the scheme are money purchase benefits—

      (i) the transferor is required to make contributions to the scheme in respect of the employee, or

      (ii) the transferor is not so required but has made one or more such contributions.

(3) This subsection applies where—

   (a) the employee is not an active member of the scheme but is eligible to be such a member, and

   (b) if any of the benefits that may be provided under the scheme are money purchase benefits, the transferor would have been required to make contributions to the scheme in respect of the employee if the employee had been an active member of it.

(4) This subsection applies where—

   (a) the employee is not an active member of the scheme, nor eligible to be such a member, but would have been an active member of the scheme or eligible to be such a member if, after the date on which he became employed by the transferor, he had been employed by the transferor for a longer period, and

   (b) if any of the benefits that may be provided under the scheme are money purchase benefits, the transferor would have been required to make contributions to the scheme in respect of the employee if the employee had been an active member of it.

(5) For the purposes of this section, the condition in subsection (1)(c) is to be regarded as satisfied in any case where it would have been satisfied but for any action taken by the transferor by reason of the transfer.

(6)...

(7)...

(8) In this section—

   the 'TUPE Regulations' means the [Transfer of Undertakings (Protection of Employment) Regulations 2006];

   references to the transferor include any associate of the transferor, and section 435 of the Insolvency Act 1986 (c 45) applies for the purposes of this section as it applies for the purposes of that Act.

258 Form of protection

(1) In a case where section 257 applies, it is a condition of the employee's contract of employment with the transferee that the requirements in subsection (2) or the requirement in subsection (3) are complied with.

(2) The requirements in this subsection are that—

   (a) the transferee secures that, as from the relevant time, the employee is, or is eligible to be, an active member of an occupational pension scheme in relation to which the transferee is the employer, and

   (b) in a case where the scheme is a money purchase scheme, as from the relevant time—

(i)   the transferee makes relevant contributions to the scheme in respect of the employee, or

(ii)   if the employee is not an active member of the scheme but is eligible to be such a member, the transferee would be required to make such contributions if the employee were an active member, and

(c)   in a case where the scheme is not a money purchase scheme, as from the relevant time the scheme—

(i)   satisfies the statutory standard referred to in section 12A of the Pension Schemes Act 1993 (c 48), or

(ii)   if regulations so provide, complies with such other requirements as may be prescribed.

(3)   The requirement in this subsection is that, as from the relevant time, the transferee makes relevant contributions to a stakeholder pension scheme of which the employee is a member.

(4)   The requirement in subsection (3) is for the purposes of this section to be regarded as complied with by the transferee during any period in relation to which the condition in subsection (5) is satisfied.

(5)   The condition in this subsection is that the transferee has offered to make relevant contributions to a stakeholder pension scheme of which the employee is eligible to be a member (and the transferee has not withdrawn the offer).

(6)   Subsection (1) does not apply in relation to a contract if or to the extent that the employee and the transferee so agree at any time after the time when the employee becomes employed by the transferee.

(7)   In this section—

'the relevant time' means—

(a)   in a case where section 257 applies by virtue of the application of subsection (2) or (3) of that section, the time when the employee becomes employed by the transferee;

(b)   in a case where that section applies by virtue of the application of subsection (4) of that section, the time at which the employee would have been a member of the scheme referred to in subsection (1)(c)(i) of that section or (if earlier) would have been eligible to be such a member;

'relevant contributions' means such contributions in respect of such period or periods as may be prescribed;

'stakeholder pension scheme' means a pension scheme which is registered under section 2 of the Welfare Reform and Pensions Act 1999 (c 30).

Transfer of Employment (Pension Protection) Regulations 2005

Made 10th March 2005
Laid before Parliament 16th March 2005
Coming into force 6th April 2005

The Secretary of State for Work and Pensions, in exercise of the powers conferred upon him by sections 258(2)(c)(ii) and (7), 315(2) and 318(1) of the Pensions Act 2004 and all other powers enabling him in that behalf, by this instrument, which contains regulations made before the end of the period of six months beginning with the coming into force of the provisions by virtue of which they are made, hereby makes the following Regulations:

1 Citation, commencement, application and interpretation

(1) These Regulations may be cited as the Transfer of Employment (Pension Protection) Regulations 2005 and shall come into force on 6th April 2005.

(2) These Regulations apply in the case of a person ('the employee') in relation to whom section 257 of the Act (conditions for pension protection) applies, that is to say a person who, in the circumstances described in subsection (1) of that section, ceases to be employed by the transferor of an undertaking or part of an undertaking and becomes employed by the transferee.

(3) In these Regulations 'the Act' means the Pensions Act 2004.

2 Requirements concerning a transferee's pension scheme

(1) In a case where these Regulations apply, and the transferee is the employer in relation to a pension scheme which is not a money purchase scheme, that scheme complies with section 258(2)(c)(ii) of the Act (alternative standard for a scheme which is not a money purchase scheme) if it provides either—

   (a) for members to be entitled to benefits the value of which equals or exceeds 6 per cent of pensionable pay for each year of employment together with the total amount of any contributions made by them, and, where members are required to make contributions to the scheme, for them to contribute at a rate which does not exceed 6 per cent of their pensionable pay; or

   (b) for the transferee to make relevant contributions to the scheme on behalf of each employee of his who is an active member of it.

(2) In this regulation—
   'pensionable pay' means that part of the remuneration payable to a member of a scheme by reference to which the amount of contributions and benefits are determined under the rules of the scheme.

3 Requirements concerning a transferee's pension contributions

(1) In a case where these Regulations apply, the transferee's pension contributions are relevant contributions for the purposes of section 258(2)(b) of the Act in the case of a money purchase scheme, section 258(3) to (5) of the Act in the case of a stakeholder pension scheme, and regulation 2(1)(b) above in the case of a scheme which is not a money purchase scheme, if—

   (a) the contributions are made in respect of each period for which the employee is paid remuneration, provided that the employee also contributes to the scheme in respect of that period, and

   (b) the amount contributed in respect of each such period is—

      (i) in a case where the employee's contribution in respect of that period is less than 6 per cent of the remuneration paid to him, an amount at least equal to the amount of the employee's contribution;

      (ii) in a case where the employee's contribution in respect of that period equals or exceeds 6 per cent of the remuneration paid to him, an amount at least equal to 6 per cent of that remuneration.

(2) In calculating the amount of an employee's remuneration for the purposes of paragraph (1)—

      (a) only payments made in respect of basic pay shall be taken into account, and bonus, commission, overtime and similar payments shall be disregarded, and

      (b) no account shall be taken of any deductions which are made in respect of tax, national insurance or pension contributions.

(3) In calculating the amount of a transferee's pension contributions for the purposes of paragraph (1) in the case of a scheme which is contracted-out by virtue of section 9 of the Pension Schemes Act 1993, minimum payments within the meaning of that Act shall be disregarded.

Signed by authority of the Secretary of State for
Work and Pensions
Malcolm Wicks
Minister of State,
Department for Work and Pensions
10th March 2005

COUNCIL DIRECTIVE 2001/23/EC of 12 March 2001

on the approximation of the laws of the Member States relating to the safeguarding of employees' rights in the event of transfers of undertakings, businesses or parts of undertakings or businesses

The Council of the European Union,

Having regard to the Treaty establishing the European Community, and in particular Article 94 thereof,Having regard to the proposal from the Commission,Having regard to the opinion of the European Parliament[2],Having regard to the opinion of the Economic and Social Committee[3],

Whereas:

(1) Council Directive 77/187/EEC of 14 February 1977 on the approximation of the laws of the Member States relating to the safeguarding of employees' rights in the event of transfers of undertakings, businesses or parts of undertakings or businesses[4] has been substantially amended[5]. In the interests of clarity and rationality, it should therefore be codified.

(2) Economic trends are bringing in their wake, at both national and Community level, changes in the structure of undertakings, through transfers of undertakings, businesses or parts of undertakings or businesses to other employers as a result of legal transfers or mergers.

(3) It is necessary to provide for the protection of employees in the event of a change of employer, in particular, to ensure that their rights are safeguarded.

(4) Differences still remain in the Member States as regards the extent of the protection of employees in this respect and these differences should be reduced.

(5) The Community Charter of the Fundamental Social Rights of Workers adopted on 9 December 1989 ('Social Charter') states, in points 7, 17 and 18 in particular that: 'The completion of the internal market must lead to an improvement in the living and working conditions of workers in the European Community. The improvement must cover, where necessary, the development of certain aspects of employment regulations such as procedures for collective redundancies and those regarding bankruptcies. Information, consultation and participation for workers must be developed along appropriate lines, taking account of the practice in force in the various Member States. Such information, consultation and participation must be implemented in due time, particularly in connection with restructuring operations in undertakings or in cases of mergers having an impact on the employment of workers'.

(6) In 1977 the Council adopted Directive 77/187/EEC to promote the harmonisation of the relevant national laws ensuring the safeguarding of the rights of employees and requiring transferors and transferees to inform and consult employees' representatives in good time.

(7) That Directive was subsequently amended in the light of the impact of the internal market, the legislative tendencies of the Member States with regard to the rescue of undertakings in economic difficulties, the case-law of the Court of Justice of the European Communities, Council Directive 75/129/EEC of 17 February 1975 on the approximation of the laws of the Member States relating to collective redundancies[1] and the legislation already in force in most Member States.

(8) Considerations of legal security and transparency required that the legal concept of transfer be clarified in the light of the case-law of the Court of Justice. Such clarification has not altered the scope of Directive 77/187/EEC as interpreted by the Court of Justice.

---

[1] '© European Union, http://eur-lex.europa.eu/'. Only European Union legislation printed in the paper edition of the Official Journal of the European Union is deemed authentic.

[2] Opinion delivered on 25 October 2000 (not yet published in the Official Journal).

[3] OJ C 367, 20.12.2000, p. 21.

[4] OJ L 61, 5.3.1977, p. 26.

[5] See Annex I, Part A.

[1] OJ L 48, 22.2.1975, p. 29. Directive replaced by Directive 98/ 59/EC (OJ L 225, 12.8.1998, p. 16).

(9) The Social Charter recognises the importance of the fight against all forms of discrimination, especially based on sex, colour, race, opinion and creed.

(10) This Directive should be without prejudice to the time limits set out in Annex I Part B within which the Member States are to comply with Directive 77/187/EEC, and the act amending it,

HAS ADOPTED THIS DIRECTIVE:

Chapter I   Scope and definitions

Article 1

1.
  - (a) This Directive shall apply to any transfer of an under-taking, business, or part of an undertaking or business to another employer as a result of a legal transfer or merger.
  - (b) Subject to subparagraph (a) and the following provisions of this Article, there is a transfer within the meaning of this Directive where there is a transfer of an economic entity which retains its identity, meaning an organised grouping of resources which has the objective of pursuing an economic activity, whether or not that activity is central or ancillary.
  - (c) This Directive shall apply to public and private undertakings engaged in economic activities whether or not they are operating for gain. An administrative reorganisation of public administrative authorities, or the transfer of administrative functions between public administrative authorities, is not a transfer within the meaning of this Directive.

2. This Directive shall apply where and in so far as the undertaking, business or part of the undertaking or business to be transferred is situated within the territorial scope of the Treaty.

3. This Directive shall not apply to seagoing vessels.

Article 2

1. For the purposes of this Directive:
  - (a) 'transferor' shall mean any natural or legal person who, by reason of a transfer within the meaning of Article 1(1), ceases to be the employer in respect of the undertaking, business or part of the undertaking or business;
  - (b) transferee' shall mean any natural or legal person who, by reason of a transfer within the meaning of Article 1(1), becomes the employer in respect of the undertaking, business or part of the undertaking or business;
  - (c) 'representatives of employees' and related expressions shall mean the representatives of the employees provided for by the laws or practices of the Member States;
  - (d) 'employee' shall mean any person who, in the Member State concerned, is protected as an employee under national employment law.

2. This Directive shall be without prejudice to national law as regards the definition of contract of employment or employment relationship.

   However, Member States shall not exclude from the scope of this Directive contracts of employment or employment relationships solely because:
  - (a) of the number of working hours performed or to be performed,
  - (b) they are employment relationships governed by a fixed-duration contract of employment within the meaning of Article 1(1) of Council Directive 91/383/EEC of 25 June 1991 supplementing the measures to encourage improvements in the safety and health at work of workers with a fixed-duration employment relationship or a temporary employment relationship[2], or
  - (c) they are temporary employment relationships within the meaning of Article 1(2) of Directive 91/383/EEC, and the undertaking, business or part of the undertaking or business transferred is, or is part of, the temporary employment business which is the employer.

---

[2] OJ L 206, 29.7.1991, p. 19.

Chapter II   Safeguarding of employees' rights

Article 3

1. The transferor's rights and obligations arising from a contract of employment or from an employment relationship existing on the date of a transfer shall, by reason of such transfer, be transferred to the transferee.

   Member States may provide that, after the date of transfer, the transferor and the transferee shall be jointly and severally liable in respect of obligations which arose before the date of transfer from a contract of employment or an employment relationship existing on the date of the transfer.

2. Member States may adopt appropriate measures to ensure that the transferor notifies the transferee of all the rights and obligations which will be transferred to the transferee under this Article, so far as those rights and obligations are or ought to have been known to the transferor at the time of the transfer. A failure by the transferor to notify the transferee of any such right or obligation shall not affect the transfer of that right or obligation and the rights of any employees against the transferee and/or transferor in respect of that right or obligation.

3. Following the transfer, the transferee shall continue to observe the terms and conditions agreed in any collective agreement on the same terms applicable to the transferor under that agreement, until the date of termination or expiry of the collective agreement or the entry into force or application of another collective agreement.

   Member States may limit the period for observing such terms and conditions with the proviso that it shall not be less than one year.

4.
   (a) Unless Member States provide otherwise, paragraphs 1 and 3 shall not apply in relation to employees' rights to old-age, invalidity or survivors' benefits under supplementary company or intercompany pension schemes outside the statutory social security schemes in Member States.

   (b) Even where they do not provide in accordance with subparagraph (a) that paragraphs 1 and 3 apply in relation to such rights, Member States shall adopt the measures necessary to protect the interests of employees and of persons no longer employed in the transferor's business at the time of the transfer in respect of rights conferring on them immediate or prospective entitlement to old age benefits, including survivors' benefits, under supplementary schemes referred to in subparagraph (a).

Article 4

1. The transfer of the undertaking, business or part of the undertaking or business shall not in itself constitute grounds for dismissal by the transferor or the transferee. This provision shall not stand in the way of dismissals that may take place for economic, technical or organisational reasons entailing changes in the workforce.

   Member States may provide that the first subparagraph shall not apply to certain specific categories of employees who are not covered by the laws or practice of the Member States in respect of protection against dismissal.

2. If the contract of employment or the employment relationship is terminated because the transfer involves a substantial change in working conditions to the detriment of the employee, the employer shall be regarded as having been responsible for termination of the contract of employment or of the employment relationship.

Article 5

1. Unless Member States provide otherwise, Articles 3 and 4 shall not apply to any transfer of an undertaking, business or part of an undertaking or business where the transferor is the subject of bankruptcy proceedings or any analogous insolvency proceedings which have been instituted with a view to the liquidation of the assets of the transferor and are under the supervision of a competent public authority (which may be an insolvency practioner authorised by a competent public authority).

2. Where Articles 3 and 4 apply to a transfer during insolvency proceedings which have been opened in relation to a transferor (whether or not those proceedings have been instituted with a view to the liquidation of the assets of the transferor) and provided that such proceedings are under the supervision

of a competent public authority (which may be an insolvency practioner determined by national law) a Member State may provide that:

(a) notwithstanding Article 3(1), the transferor's debts arising from any contracts of employment or employment relationships and payable before the transfer or before the opening of the insolvency proceedings shall not be transferred to the transferee, provided that such proceedings give rise, under the law of that Member State, to protection at least equivalent to that provided for in situations covered by Council Directive 80/987/EEC of 20 October 1980 on the approximation of the laws of the Member States relating to the protection of employees in the event of the insolvency of their employer[3], and, or alternatively, that,

(b) the transferee, transferor or person or persons exercising the transferor's functions, on the one hand, and the representatives of the employees on the other hand may agree alterations, in so far as current law or practice permits, to the employees' terms and conditions of employment designed to safeguard employment opportunities by ensuring the survival of the undertaking, business or part of the undertaking or business.

3. A Member State may apply paragraph 20(b) to any transfers where the transferor is in a situation of serious economic crisis, as defined by national law, provided that the situation is declared by a competent public authority and open to judicial supervision, on condition that such provisions already existed in national law on 17 July 1998.

The Commission shall present a report on the effects of this provision before 17 July 2003 and shall submit any appropriate proposals to the Council.

4. Member States shall take appropriate measures with a view to preventing misuse of insolvency proceedings in such a way as to deprive employees of the rights provided for in this Directive.

Article 6

1. If the undertaking, business or part of an undertaking or business preserves its autonomy, the status and function of the representatives or of the representation of the employees affected by the transfer shall be preserved on the same terms and subject to the same conditions as existed before the date of the transfer by virtue of law, regulation, administrative provision or agreement, provided that the conditions necessary for the constitution of the employee's representation are fulfilled.

The first subparagraph shall not supply if, under the laws, regulations, administrative provisions or practice in the Member States, or by agreement with the representatives of the employees, the conditions necessary for the reappointment of the representatives of the employees or for the reconstitution of the representation of the employees are fulfilled.

Where the transferor is the subject of bankruptcy proceedings or any analoguous insolvency proceedings which have been instituted with a view to the liquidation of the assets of the transferor and are under the supervision of a competent public authority (which may be an insolvency practitioner authorised by a competent public authority), Member States may take the necessary measures to ensure that the transferred employees are properly represented until the new election or designation of representatives of the employees.

If the undertaking, business or part of an undertaking or business does not preserve its autonomy, the Member States shall take the necessary measures to ensure that the employees transferred who were represented before the transfer continue to be properly represented during the period necessary for the reconstitution or reappointment of the representation of employees in accordance with national law or practice.

2. If the term of office of the representatives of the employees affected by the transfer expires as a result of the transfer, the representatives shall continue to enjoy the protection provided by the laws, regulations, administrative provisions or practice of the Member States.

---

[3] OJ L 283, 20.10.1980, p. 23. Directive as last amended by the 1994 Act of Accession.

Chapter III   Information and consultation

Article 7

1. The transferor and transferee shall be required to inform the representatives of their respective employees affected by the transfer of the following:
    — the date or proposed date of the transfer,
    — the reasons for the transfer,
    — the legal, economic and social implications of the transfer for the employees,
    — any measures envisaged in relation to the employees.
    The transferor must give such information to the representatives of his employees in good time, before the transfer is carried out.
    The transferee must give such information to the representatives of his employees in good time, and in any event before his employees are directly affected by the transfer as regards their conditions of work and employment.

2. Where the transferor or the transferee envisages measures in relation to his employees, he shall consult the representatives of this employees in good time on such measures with a view to reaching an agreement.

3. Member States whose laws, regulations or administrative provisions provide that representatives of the employees may have recourse to an arbitration board to obtain a decision on the measures to be taken in relation to employees may limit the obligations laid down in paragraphs 1 and 2 to cases where the transfer carried out gives rise to a change in the business likely to entail serious disadvantages for a considerable number of the employees.
    The information and consultations shall cover at least the measures envisaged in relation to the employees.
    The information must be provided and consultations take place in good time before the change in the business as referred to in the first subparagraph is effected.

4. The obligations laid down in this Article shall apply irrespective of whether the decision resulting in the transfer is taken by the employer or an undertaking controlling the employer.
    In considering alleged breaches of the information and consultation requirements laid down by this Directive, the argument that such a breach occurred because the information was not provided by an undertaking controlling the employer shall not be accepted as an excuse.

5. Member States may limit the obligations laid down in paragraphs 1, 2 and 3 to undertakings or businesses which, in terms of the number of employees, meet the conditions for the election or nomination of a collegiate body representing the employees.

6. Member States shall provide that, where there are no representatives of the employees in an undertaking or business through no fault of their own, the employees concerned must be informed in advance of:
    — the date or proposed date of the transfer,
    — the reason for the transfer,
    — the legal, economic and social implications of the transfer for the employees,
    — any measures envisaged in relation to the employees.

Chapter IV   Final provisions

Article 8

This Directive shall not affect the right of Member States to apply or introduce laws, regulations or administrative provisions which are more favourable to employees or to promote or permit collective agreements or agreements between social partners more favourable to employees.

Article 9

Member States shall introduce into their national legal systems such measures as are necessary to enable all employees and representatives of employees who consider themselves wronged by failure to comply with the obligations arising from this Directive to pursue their claims by judicial process after possible recourse to other competent authorities.

Article 10

The Commission shall submit to the Council an analysis of the effect of the provisions of this Directive before 17 July 2006. It shall propose any amendment which may seem necessary.

Article 11

Member States shall communicate to the Commission the texts of the laws, regulations and administrative provisions which they adopt in the field covered by this Directive.

Article 12

Directive 77/187/EEC, as amended by the Directive referred to in Annex I, Part A, is repealed, without prejudice to the obligations of the Member States concerning the time limits for implementation set out in Annex I, Part B.

References to the repealed Directive shall be construed as references to this Directive and shall be read in accordance with the correlation table in Annex II.

Article 13

This Directive shall enter into force on the 20th day following its publication in the *Official Journal of the European Communities*.

Article 14

This Directive is addressed to the Member States.

Done at Brussels, 12 March 2001.

For the Council

The President

B. RINGHOLM

Annex I

Part A

Repealed Directive and its amending Directive
(referred to in Article 12)

Council Directive 77/187/EEC (OJ L 61, 5.3.1977, p. 26)

Council Directive 98/50/EC (OJ L 201, 17.7.1998, p. 88)

Part B

Deadlines for transposition into national law
(referred to in Article 12)

Directive	Deadline for transposition
77/187/EEC	16 February 1979
98/50/EC	17 July 2001

Annex II

Correlation Table

Directive 77/187/EEC	This Directive
Article 1	Article 1
Article 2	Article 2
Article 3	Article 3
Article 4	Article 4

Directive 77/187/EEC	This Directive
Article 4a	Article 5
Article 5	Article 6
Article 6	Article 7
Article 7	Article 8
Article 7a	Article 9
Article 7b	Article 10
Article 8	Article 11
—	Article 12
—	Article 13
—	Article 14
—	ANNEX I
—	ANNEX II

INDEX

absence from work
  period prior to transfer 4.51
  post-resignation 4.53–4.54
  sickness 4.51–4.52
  TUPE 2006 4.37, 4.44, 4.58
ACAS conciliation officers
  contracting-out 12.03–12.04
Acquired Rights Directive
  1977 Directive 1.01–1.03, 1.18–1.20, 1.24–1.25,
    1.32–1.33
  1988 Directive 1.26–1.27
  2001 Directive 1.26–1.27
  changes to employment contracts 6.04, 6.06–6.07,
    6.10, 6.27, 6.29, 6.33
  changes to working conditions 4.108–4.110, *335*
  collective agreements 5.73, 5.75
  collective information provisions 9.04, *337*
  collectively determined rights 5.57, 5.61–5.63, 5.66,
    5.68–5.69
  compliance 1.18–1.19
  consultation provisions 9.04
  continuity of employment 5.46
  cross-border transfers 122.26
  definitions *334*
  dismissals *335 see also* **dismissals**
  economic, technical or organisational reason
    (ETOR) *335*
  employee liability information 8.01–8.02
  employee protection 1.01–1.03, 1.05
  final provisions *337–8*
  harmonization 1.24
  implementation 1.01, 1.05. 1.10
  insolvency
    allocation of liability 10.12
    business rescue *336*
    changes to employment contracts 10.06, 10.14
    exclusion of TUPE 10.02, 10.09
    insolvency practitioners *335–6*
    insolvency proceedings 10.02–10.05, 10.07–10.08
    opening of proceedings *335*
    purpose of procedure 10.04
    terminal insolvency 10.01, 10.03–10.04, 10.08,
      10.12
    transferee's liability 10.06, 10.08, 10.14
    transferor's outstanding debts 1.33, 10.06, *336*
  labour-intensive activities 2.95–2.97, 2.100–2.104,
    2.111
  more favourable national legislation 1.37
  pensions
    occupational pension schemes 11.01, 11.06, 11.14
    old age, invalidity or survivor's benefits *335*
    supplementary company or intercompany pension
      schemes *335*
  prescribed information 1.33
  public sector 1.45

  purpose 1.01, 1.24
  relevant transfers 2.01
  scope *334*
  ships 2.137
  territoriality 12.12–12.13
  trade unions
    recognition 5.88
    representation 1.33
  transferees liabilities *335 see also* **transferees'
    liabilities**
  transferors obligations *335 see also* **transferors**
actuarial advice
  occupational pension schemes 11.47
administration
  administration orders 10.35–10.36
  analogous insolvency proceedings 10.34
  automatically unfair dismissals 7.24, 7.27,
    7.29–7.31, 7.36, 7.38, 7.62
  business rescue 10.25, 10.27, *336*
  employee protection 10.32
  employment liabilities
    absolute approach 10.29–10.31, 10.34–10.35
    fact-based approach 10.29–10.31, 10.34
  liquidation of assets 10.27, 10.29
  pre-pack administration 10.24
  purpose of administration 10.33
  terminal insolvency 10.24, 10.29, 10.31, 10.33
  TUPE 2006 10.24–10.30
affected employees
  agency workers 9.17
  compensation 9.104 *see also* **compensation**
  complaints 9.90 *see also* **complaints**
  definition of employee 9.06
  information and consultation 9.06
  jobs in jeopardy 9.09, 9.12
  legal, economic and social implications 9.15,
    9.18–9.19
  number of employees involved 9.08
  organised grouping of employees 9.06
  organised grouping of resources 9.06
  outside relevant business area 9.10–9.11
  subject to relevant transfer 9.06, 9.09, 9.12
  unassigned employees 9.07
  wider workforce 9.10–9.13
agency workers
  collective information provisions 9.15, 9.17
  consultation provisions 9.15, 9.17
  employee status 8.07
  employment by transferees 4.13
  prescribed information 1.31
appropriate representatives
  accommodation and facilities 9.69
  consultation provisions 9.02, 9.05, 9.10, 9.18,
    9.37–9.38, 9.48, 9.52–9.53, 9.61, 9.68, 9.74,
    9.141

appropriate representatives (*cont.*):
  election 9.61, 9.67, 9.70–9.74
  employee representatives 9.61, 9.66
  insolvency-related contract changes 10.54–10.55,
    10.59–10.60, 10.62–10.70, 10.81
  provision of information 9.02, 9.61, 9.68, 9.74
  trade union representation 9.61–9.65
  TUPE 2006 *321*
asset transfer
  absence of transfer 2.74, 2.76–2.80, 2.83–2.85, 2.91
  asset-reliant activities 2.82–2.85, 2.79–2.80, 2.87,
    2.92
  contextual matter 2.89
  continuing use of previous assets 2.78–2.81
  continuity of customers 2.90
  fact-specific approach 2.92
  intangible assets 2.87, 2.90
  multifactorial approach 2.84, 2.93
  production and operating methods 2.75–2.77
  relevant transfer 2.74–2.76, 2.80, 2.91
  similarity of post/pre-transfer activities 2.87–2.88,
    2.90
  supply of same services 2,81, 2.87–2.88
  transfer of employees 2.74, 2.86, 2.88
assignment
  consecutive assignments 4.60
  continuity of employment 4.41
  contracts of employment 4.08–4.09, 4.36, 4.43
  employee deceived into relocation 4.62
  integration into relevant business 4.39
  organised grouping of employees 4.36–4.37
  organised grouping of resources 4.36
  percentage test 4.40
  redeployment 4.55–4.56, 4.60–4.61
  relevant activities 4.37, 4.40, 4.44, 4.51, 4.61
  relevant part of undertaking 4.38, 4.40, 4.42,
    4.47–4.50. 4.53–4.54
  service provision change 4.37
  short-term contracts 4.57
  splitting of employment 4.45, 4.51
  temporary assignment 4.58–4.63
  temporary transfer of employee 4.59
  test of assignment 3.50–3.51, 3.53, 4.36, 4.38–4.39,
    4.41–4.43, 4.46, 4.56
  transferor's employees, 4.36, 4.38
  TUPE 1981 4.36
auto-enrolment
  eligible individuals 11.79, 11.82
  employers' obligations 11.79
  level of pension provision 11.80, 11.83
  pension contributions 11.79
  Pensions Act 2004 11.80
  Pensions Regulator guidance 11.81–11.82
  postponement 11.82
  Transfer of Employment (Pension Protection)
    Regulations 2005 11.80
automatic transfer
  contracts of employment 4.01–4.03
  date of relevant transfer 4.05–4.07
  employees
    ignorance of transfer 4.05
    opt out provision 4.01–4.03

  multiple transactions 4.04, *318*
  objection to transfer 4.74, 4.80, 4.92
  trade union recognition 5.91
  transfer over time 4.04
automatically unfair dismissals
  basis of decision 7.38–7.39, 7.41
  collusion with transferee 7.35, 7.37–7.38
  connection with transfer 7.09–7.11, 7.19–7.23,
    7.26–7.32, 7.35,7.86
  cross-border transfers 12.33, 12.35
  economic reasons 7.35, 7.38–7.40
  employee protection 7.05, 7.12–7.15
  exceptions 7.16–7.18
  insolvency 7.24–7.27, 7.29–7.32, 7.34, 7.36–7.38,
    7.62, 10.46
  liability 7.73
  motivation 7.38, 7.41
  no transfer 7.24–7.29, 7.33
  pre-transfer dismissals 7.34
  protected persons 7.12–7.15
  sole of principal reason 7.10, 7.19, 7.43, 7.62
  stage-managed dismissals 7.35, 7.38, 7.41
  third party involvement 7.40

bankruptcy *see also* **insolvency**
  Acquired Rights Directive 10.05, *335–6*
  exclusion of TUPE 10.18, 10.20
  insolvency practitioners 10.19
  opening of proceedings 10.50
  transfer-related dismissals 10.18
  TUPE 2006 10.16–10.17
bonus schemes
  continuation of benefits 5.24
  pre-transfer schemes 5.32
  replicating entitlements 5.31–5.32, 5.34
  substantial equivalence 5.32, 5.34
  transfer of rights 5.24
break in activities
  interruption of relevant activity 2.61
  no relevant transfer 2.63–2.64
  reason for suspension 2.61
  re-engagement of employees 2.62
  resumption of activities 2.63–2.64
  retention of identity 2.61, 2.63–2.64
  temporary suspension 2.62, 2.64

career breaks
  employment by transferees 4.13
change of location *see* **relocation**
changes to employment contracts *see* **transfer-related
    contract changes**
changes to workforce
  economic, technical or organisational reasons (ETOR)
    6.47–6.49, 7.47, 7.49–7.58, 7.62, 7.64
changes to working conditions
  Acquired Rights Directive 4.108–4.110, *335*
  changes to employment contracts 6.17
  connection with transfer 4.102
  constructive dismissals 4.94–4.96, 4.103
  contractual claims 4.105–4.106
  contractual variations 4.120
  health and safety 4.114

material detriment 4.97–4.101, 4.113, 4.116–4.121, 5.17
objection to transfer 4.92–4.93, 4.109, 4.121
pension entitlements 4.121
relocation 4.113
repudiatory breach 4.95–4.96, 4.99, 4.103
substantial changes 4.92–4.93, 4.100, 4.102–4.103, 4.106, 4.113, 4.115, 4.120, 5.17
termination of employment 4.92–4.93, 4.97, 4.108–4.111, 4.119–4.120
TUPE 1981 4.92, 4.103
TUPE 2006 4.97–4.98
unfair dismissal 4.105–4.106, 4.108, 4.121
working conditions 4.114
Cheesman **guidance**
relevant transfers
autonomy 2.126
existence of undertaking 2.126
operating methods 2.126
structure 2.126
specific works contracts 2.126
collective agreements
Acquired Rights Directive 5.73, 5.75
employee liability information 8.09, 8.12
enforcement 5.73, 5.78, 5.84–5.86
existence at time of transfer 5.78, 5.80
incorporation into employment contracts 5.87
post-transfer duration 5.75
recognised trade unions 5.78–5.79, 5.81–5.82
statutory test 5.78, 5.82
transferee's liabilities 5.73–5.75, 5.76–5.77, 5.83
transferor's agreements 5.78 – 5.79
TUPE 2006 *319–20*
collective information and consultation
Acquired Rights Directive 9.04
affected employees
agency workers 9.17
compensation 9.104
complaints 9.90
definition of employee 9.06
information and consultation 9.06
jobs in jeopardy 9.09, 9.12
legal, economic and social implications 9.15, 9.18–9.19
measures relating to affected employees, 9.48–9.50
number of employees involved 9.08
organised grouping of employees 9.06
organised grouping of resources 9.06
outside relevant business area 9.10–9.11
subject to relevant transfer 9.06, 9.09, 9.12
unassigned employees 9.07
wider workforce 9.10–9.13
collective redundancy consultation 9.108–9.109, 9.113, 9.132, 9.139–9.141
compensation 9.104–9.118 *see also* **compensation**
complaints 9.89–9.103 *see also* **complaints**
compliance
failure to comply 9.02–9.03, 9.05, 9.153
indemnity protection 9.153
outsourced contracts 9.153
planning for compliance 9.153–9.155

compromise agreements 12.11
confidentiality
collective redundancy consultation 9.135
commercial confidentiality 9.135
disclosure process 9.136–9.137
mergers 9.136
price sensitive information 9.135
Takeover Code 9.136
consultation
appropriate representatives 9.02, 9.05, 9.10, 9.18, 9.37–9.38, 9.48, 9.52–9.53, 9.141
fair consultation 9.55
industrial relations rationale 9.46–9.47
joint consultation 9.52
length of consultation 9.56–9.57
material obligations 9.03
measures relating to affected employees, 9.48–9.50
minimum duration 9.56
nature of consultation 9.53
post-transfer consultation 9.59–9.60
record of consultation 9.54
redundancies 9.56–9.57
requirement 9.48–9.52
statutory definition 9.53, 9.55
transfer date deferred 9.43
transferee's obligations 9.01, 9.39–9.42, 9.52
transferor's obligations 9.01, 9.40, 9.42–9.46, 9.52
transitional arrangements 9.58
voluntary consultation 9.43–9.45, 9.47
contracting-out 12.04
cross-border transfers 12.34
enforcement 9.128–9.129
European Works Councils 5.97, 9.151–9.152
insolvency 10.22, 10.44
joint and several liability 9.04–9.05, 9.119–9.127
knowledge of transfer
collective consultation 4.68, 4.70
identity of transferee 4.69, 4.90–4.91
implied terms 4.70
notification provisions 4.68
refusal to disclose 4.69
measures to be taken
administrative changes 9.23–9.26
breach of obligation 9.23, 9.27
business policy 9.22
changes to employment contracts 9.20, 9.26
definite plans 9.21–9.22
dismissals 9.20
location 9.20, 9.26
pension rights 9.28–9.29
redundancies 9.26, 9.56–9.57
remuneration arrangements 9.23–9.25
working methods 9.20
misrepresentation 11.49
outsourced contracts 9.153
prescribed information
agency workers 9.15, 9.17
date of transfer 9.15–9.16
fact of transfer 9.15
legal, economic and social implications 9.15, 9.18–9.19

collective information and consultation (*cont.*):
  prescribed information (*cont.*):
    measures to be taken 9.15, 9.20–9.29
    reason for transfer 9.15
  provision of information
    accuracy of information 9.30–9.33
    appropriate representatives 9.02
    delivery of information 9.37–9.38
    material obligations 9.03
    specified information 9.02
    timing 9.02, 9.34–9.36
    transferee's obligations 9.01
    transferor's obligations 9.01
  redundancies 9.08
  remedies for breach
    compensation 9.104–9.118, 9.128–9.129
    complaints 9.89–9.103, 9.128
    injunctions 9.138
    joint and several liability 9.119–9.127
    time limits 9.129
  special circumstances defence 9.131–9.132, 9.139
  statutory obligations 9.142–9.150 *see also*
      Information and Consultation of Employee
      Regulations 2004
  transferees' measures
    adequate information 9.39
    definite measures 9.41
    obligation to inform 9.39–9.41
    plans for workforce 9.41
    transferor's anticipation of measures 9.42
    transferor's duty to inform 9.40
  TUPE 1981 9.04
  TUPE 2006 1.35, *323–7*
collective redundancy consultation
  compensation 9.108–9.109, 9.113
  confidentiality 9.135
  consultation 9.139–9.141
  employee representatives 9.139
  employer's obligation 9.139–9.140
  protective penalty 9.139
  recognised trade unions 9.139
  special circumstances defence 9.132, 9.139
  TUPE obligations distinguished 9.140–9.141
collectively determined rights
  Acquired Rights Directive 5.57, 5.61–5.63,
      5.65–5.66, 5.68–5.69
  collective agreements 5.55–5.56, 5.66, 5.70–5.71
      see also **collective agreements**
  dynamic interpretation 5.59–5.60, 5.67, 5.69
  entitlement 5.55–5.56, 5.60
  freedom of association 5.64
  public/private sector transfers 5.56
  static interpretation 5.59, 5.67, 5.71–5.72
  transferees' liability 5.57–5.58
  transferors' liability 5.58
common law
  contracts of employment 1.06–1.08
  employment transfers, 1.06–1.09
compensation awards
  affected employees 9.104
  amount 8.43
  appropriate compensation 9.105, 9.110

based on loss 8.41, 8.44–8.45
calculation 9.105, 9.108, 9.110–9.111
collective redundancy consultation 9.108–9.109,
    9.113
consultation
  failure to consult 9.108–9.109, 9.111, 9.115
  futility 9.112
de minimis provisions 8.45
declarations 8.42
defence available to transferor 9.104
determent nature 9.110
dismissals 4.108–4.110
employer's default 9.109, 9.111
flexibility 8.45
joint and several liability 9.119, 9.122, 9.125, 9.127
maximum award 9.111, 9.113, 9.115–9.118
minimum award 8.48–8.50
mitigation 8.51, 9.111, 9.114
penal nature 9.110, 9.113
purpose 9.111
statutory cap 9.107
tax treatment 9.105
terms of commercial agreements 8.45–8.47
tribunal discretion 9.111, 9.114, 9.116–9.118
week's pay 9.105–9.107
complaints
  burden of proof 9.97–9.100
  collective information and consultation
    failure to consult 9.89
    failure to inform 9.89
  eligible persons
    affected employees 9.90
    employee representatives 9.90, 9.94–9.95
    individual claimants 9.91–9.96
    standing 9.91–9.96
    trade unions 9.90, 9.94–9.96
  timing 9.102–9.103
  transferee's breach 9.101
compromise agreements
  changes to employment contracts 6.19–6.22,
      12.05–12.07 *see also* **transfer-related contract**
      changes
  collective information and consultation 12.11
  continued employment 12.05
  dismissals 12.05–12.06
  privity of contract 12.10
  redundancy terms 12.08
  re-engagement 12.05, 12.09
  termination-related claims 12.08–12.09
compulsory liability insurance
  joint and several liability 5.27–5.28
  pre-transfer liabilities 5.06
  public/private sector transfers 5.27
  statutory obligation 5.25–5.27
  TUPE 2006 *327*
confidentiality
  collective redundancy consultation 9.135
  commercial confidentiality 9.135
  disclosure process 9.136–9.137
  mergers 9.136
  price sensitive information 9.135
  Takeover Code 9.136

constructive dismissals
change of location 4.130–4.132
changes to working conditions 4.94–4.96, 4.103
claims against transferors 4.125–4.126, 4.128
common law right 4.126
cross-border transfers 12.36
objection to transfer 4.122
pension entitlements 4.122
pre-transfer claims 4.124
repudiatory breach 4.122–4.123
resignation 4.71
termination of contract 4.122
transfer-related claims 4.123–4.124
consultation
appropriate representatives 9.02, 9.05, 9.10, 9.18,
    9.37–9.38, 9.48, 9.52–9.53, 9.141
compensation awards 9.108–9.109, 9.111–9.112,
    9.115
contracts of employment 1.10
fair consultation 9.55
industrial relations rationale 9.46–9.47
joint consultation 9.52
length of consultation 9.56–9.57
material obligations 9.03
measures relating to affected employees, 9.48–9.50
minimum duration 9.56
nature of consultation 9.53
post-transfer consultation 9.59–9.60
record of consultation 9.54
redundancies 9.56–9.57
requirement 9.48–9.52
statutory definition 9.53, 9.55
transfer date deferred 9.43
transferee's obligations 9.01, 9.39–9.42, 9.52
transferor's obligations 9.01, 9.40, 9.42–9.46, 9.52
transitional arrangements 9.58
voluntary consultation 9.43–9.45, 9.47
continental shelf
territoriality 12.23
continuation orders
contracts of employment 4.67
interim relief 4.67
continuity of employment
Acquired Rights Directive 5.46
assignment 4.41
changes to employment contracts 6.23
employee liability information 8.12
objection to transfer 5.49
preservation of rights 5.45–5.48
pre-transfer liabilities 5.06
redundancy payments 5.49–5.50
share-based transactions 1.40, 1.42
timing of transfer 2.130–2.131
unfair dismissal claims 5.46
contracting out (TUPE)
ACAS conciliation officers 12.03–12.04
collective information and consultation 12.04
prohibition 12.01–12.04, 12.09, *327*
TUPE 2006 *327*
contracts of employment
assignment 4.08–4.09, 4.36
automatic transfer 4.01–4.03

changes to employment contracts *see* **transfer-related
    contract changes**
common law 1.06–1.08
consultation 1.10
continuation 4.08
continuation orders 4.67
definition 4.10
dismissals, 1.06
employment liabilities, 4.11–4.12, 4.14, 4.24–4.25
employment rights 5.04
employment transfers 1.06–1.09
insolvency-related changes *see* insolvency
liabilities, rights and powers 1.10
novation 4.12
termination 4.09, 4.32–4.35, 4.122, 4.125, 4.130,
    5.11, 5.16, 6.02
transferees
    employees opt out provision 4.01–4.03
    inherited obligations 1.10
    liabilities 5.08, 5.10, 5.25
    pre-transfer dismissals 4.01
transferors
    freedom to choose employer 4.02–4.03, 4.90
    pre-transfer dismissals 4.01
TUPE 2006 *318–9*
unfair dismissals 1.10
variation *see* **transfer-related contract changes**
corporate veil
piercing the corporate veil 4.19–4.20, 4.23
cross-border transfers
Acquired Rights Directive 12.26
automatically unfair dismissal 12.33, 12.35
collective information and consultation 12.34
constructive dismissal 12.36
dismissals 12.26
employee representation 12.26
information technology 12.24
international outsourcing 12.24
offshoring 12.35
ownership transfers 12.25
relocation transfers 12.25, 12.35
transfer of employees 12.33
transfers from UK 12.27–12.30, 12.34
transfers outside EU 12.27–12.29
TUPE provisions 12.27–12.32, 12.37

damages
breach of good faith 4.89
concealment of transfer 4.89
employee liability information 8.47
material detriment *319*
mitigation *323*
personal injury 8.18
wrongful dismissal 4.04, 4.112, 4.123, 7.01
data protection
accuracy of data 8.24
age of employees 8.20
consent of individuals 8.25
Good Practice Note 8.25–8.27
identity of employees 8.20
permissible data processing 8.23
personal data 8.20–8.25

data protection (*cont.*):
  sensitive data 8.22, 8.25
  sexual orientation 8.22
  transfer of data abroad 8.24
  unauthorized processing 8.24
dismissals *see also* **transfer-related dismissals**
  appeals outstanding 4.64–4.65
  changes to working conditions 4.94–4.96, 4.103
  collective information provisions 9.20
  compensation 4.108–4.110
  compromise agreements 12.05–12.06
  constructive dismissals 4.71, 4.94–4.96, 4.103,
    4.122–4.124, 12.36
  consultation provisions 9.20
  continuation orders 4.67
  contractual notice pay 4.112
  cross-border transfers 12.26
  damages claims 4.104, 4.112, 4.123
  gross misconduct 4.64
  insolvency 10.01, 10.05, 10.12, 10.17–10.18
  national rules 4.108, 4.110
  pre-transfer dismissals 4.64–4.65
  redundancy 6.03, 7.79, 7.81–7.82
  resignations 4.71, 4.106
  setting aside 4.65–4.66
  TUPE 2006 *320*
  unfair dismissals 4.71, 4.105–4.106, 4.108, 4.121,
    7.01, 7.05
  "vanishing" dismissals 4.65
  wrongful dismissals 4.104, 4.112, 4.123
drafting
  importance 12.51
  indemnities 12.61
due diligence
  claims-related information 8.60
  commercial indemnity protection 8.54
  commission arrangements 8.58
  employee liability information 8.05, 12.53–12.54
  employment documentation 8.59
  importance 12.52
  indemnities 8.53
  industrial relations history 8.55, 8.60
  investigation of liabilities 8.52
  list of transferring employees 8.57
  occupational pension schemes 11.45
  profit-sharing schemes 8.58
  regulatory investigations 8.55
  requests 8.54–8.55
  restrictive covenants 8.55
  share options 8.58
  staff turnover 8.55
  transferees' liabilities 12.52
  warranties 8.53

economic activity
  commercial exploitation 1.50–1.51
  consideration requirement 1.50
  definition 1.50
  public sector 1.49–1.51
  single specific events 2.42, 3.100, 3.104–3.105,
    3.107–3.108, 3.125
  TUPE 2006 *318*

  TUPE transfers 1.49, 2.02–2.03, 2.06–2.07,
    2.25–2.26
economic entities
  activity not in itself an entity 2.31
  ancillary activities 2.27
  asset reliant 2.29
  autonomy 2.28–2.29, 2.31, 2.38
  break in activities 2.61–2.64
  definition 2.02, 2.26–2.27
  discrete entity 2.65–2.66
  distinct cost centre 2.30
  fragmentation 2.69
  identifiable 1.13
  one-person undertakings 2.33–2.35
  operational changes 2.51–2.57
  organised group of resources 2.27–2.28, 2.31
  post-transfer integration 2.58–2.60
  relevant transfers 2.01–2.02, 2.06–2.07, 2.25–2.26
  retention of identity 2.43–2.50
  specific works contracts 2.36–2.40
  stability 1.13, 2.28, 2.31–2.32, 2.35–2.38, 2.40
  structure 2.31, 2.38, 2.32
  transfer of part 2.65–2.71
  TUPE 2006 *318*
  TUPE transfers 2.02, 2.06–2.07, 2.25–2.26
economic, technical or organisational reason
  (ETOR)
  Acquired Rights Directive *335*
  changes to employment contracts
    commercial challenges 6.46
    generally 6.45
    harmonizing terms and conditions 6.50–6.51
    organisational reasons 6.46
    technical reasons 6.46
  conduct of business 7.47–7.48
  corporate franchises 7.60–7.61
  cost-saving measures 6.48–6.49
  definition 6.46, 6.49, 7.46
  dismissals
    joint consultation process 7.71
    justification 2.60, 4.25, 4.28–4.29, 4.107
    post-transfer dismissals 7.69
    pre-transfer dismissals 7.65–7.68, 7.70–7.71,
      7.86
    transferee's liability 7.65–7.66, 7.70–7.71
    transferor's liability 7.66–7.67, 7.71, 7.86
    transfer-related dismissals 7.02, 7.06, 7.08–7.09
    unfair dismissal 1.10, 7.06, 7.08, 7.10–7.11, 7.31,
      7.43–7.44, 7.51, 7.53, 7.56, 7.59–7.61, 7.86,
      8.29
  economic reasons 7.46, 7.48
  insolvency-related issues
    contract variations 10.77
    transferor's debts 10.47
  management 7.46
  market performance 7.46
  organisational reasons 7.46
  production processes 7.46
  profitability 7.46
  redundancies 7.45, 7.67–7.69, 7.71, 7.86
  replacement of staff 7.60–7.61
  technical reasons 7.46, 7.50

workforce
  changes to workforce 6.47–6.49, 7.47, 7.49–7.58,
    7.62, 7.64
  concept 7.60–7.61
  part of workforce 7.63–7.64
employee liability information *see also* **due diligence**
  accuracy 8.24, 8.33
  Acquired Rights Directive 8.01–8.02
  applicable conditions 8.06
  competitiveness 8.04
  compliance 8.03–8.04, 8.41
  confidentiality 8.05
  contracting –out 8.61
  data protection 8.19–8.27 *see also* **data protection**
  delivery
    accessible form 8.30–8.31
    written information 8.30–8.32
  disclosure 8.05, 8.07, 8.13
  due diligence 8.05, 12.53–12.54
  employees' rights and obligations
  immigration requirements 8.05
  indirect provision 8.35–8.36
  information
    accrued pension rights 8.10
    age of employee 8.09, 8.20, *322*
    collective agreements 8.09, 8.12
    commencement of employment 8.12
    continuous employment 8.12
    criminal liabilities 8.10
    disciplinary information 8.09, 8.14, *322*
    employee identity 8.09, 8.20, *322*
    employment particulars 8.09–8.13
    former employees 8.28–8.29
    grievance procedures 8.09, 8.14, *322*
    holiday entitlement 8.12
    hours of work 8.12
    job title 8.12
    notice period 8.12
    occupational pension schemes 8.10
    overseas workers 8.12
    place of work 8.12
    prescribed information 8.09–8.10
    remuneration 8.12, 8.32
    sickness or injury 8.12
    tribunal claims 8.09, 8.15–8.18, 8.32
    up to date information 8.32–8.33, *322*
  instalments 8.34
  redundancy entitlements 8.05
  relative bargaining power 8.04
  requirements 8.06
  restrictive covenants 8.05
  severance entitlements 8.05
  timing 8.37–8.40
  trade union recognition 8.05
  transferor's obligation to notify 8.01–8.04, 8.06–8.07
  transparency 8.03
  TUPE 2006 1.35, 8.03, *322–3*
employee representatives
  Acquired Rights Directive *336*
  adequate consultation 9.73
  affected employees 9.71
  appropriate representatives 9.61, 9.66

collective redundancy consultation 9.139
complaints procedure 9.90, 9.94–9.95 *see also*
  complaints
cross-border transfers 12.26
detriment 9.76–9.80
dismissal 9.81–9.84
election 9.70–9.74, 9.77
failure to elect 9.74
number of representatives 9.71
protection 9.75–9.88
replacement 9.72
term of office 9.71
time off 9.85–9.88
TUPE 2006 *325*
employees *see also* **affected employees; employee
  liability information; employee representatives**
  age 8.09. 8.20
  collective information provisions 9.06–9.12, 9.23–9.25
  consultation provisions 9.06–9.12, 9.23–9.25
  commencement of employment 8.12
  data protection *see* **data protection**
  definition 9.06
  disciplinary information 8.09, 8.14
  employee status 8.07
  employment details 8.09–8.13
  identification 8.08
  identity 8.09, 8.20
  job title 8.12
  organised grouping of employees *see* **organised
    grouping of employees**
  organised grouping of resources *see* **organised
    grouping of resources**
  place of work 8.12
  remuneration details 8.12, 8.32, 9.23–9.25
  sickness or injury 8.12
  working abroad 8.12, 12.15, 12.21–12.22
employers' liability insurance
  claims 1.35
  TUPE 2006 1.35
Employment Relations Act 1999
  treatment of employees 1.37–1.38
equal pay
  equal pay claims
    genuine material factor defence 12.48–12.50
    pre-transfer employment 12.43, 12.47
    time limits 12.43–12.46
  pay differentials
    genuine material factor defence 12.48–12.50
    historical derivations 12.43
    justification 12.43
  TUPE interaction 12.43
European Works Councils
  default model 9.152
  establishment 9.151
  representation structures 5.97
  Special Negotiating Body 9.152
  TUPE transfers 9.152

fragmentation
  divided activities 3.43–3.47
  divided liabilities 3.49
  series of transactions 2.128

fragmentation (*cont.*):
  service provision change 3.52–3.58
  test of assignment 3.50–3.51, 3.53
  transfer of part 2.69

health and safety
  changes in working conditions 4.114
hiving down
  creditors' voluntary winding up 10.85
  employee protection 10.86
  TUPE 1981
human rights
  freedom of association 5.64

identity
  change of client identity 2.57
  retention of identity 2.43–2.50, 2.61, 2.63–2.64,
    2.67–2.68, 2.99, 2.101, 2.108
immigration
  civil penalties 12.41
  criminal offences 12.41
  document checks 12.41
  employee liability information 8.05
  immigration controls 12.42
  legislative compliance 8.05
  licensed sponsors 12.42
  notification of transfers 12.42
  transferring employees 12.41
  UK Border Agency 12.42
indemnities
  avoidable liabilities 12.62
  drafting 12.61
  due diligence 8.53
  fixed termination costs 12.62
  importance 12.60
  indemnity protection 8.53, 9.124, 9.153
  occupational pension schemes 11.46–11.47
  qualifications 12.60
  time period 12.60
  transferee's liabilities 12.61
  transferor's liabilities 12.61, 12.63
  types of liability 12.60
individual enforcement
  compensation 9.128–9.129
  complaints 9.91–9.96
  time limits 9.129
individual rights
  bonus schemes 5.24, 5.31–5.32, 5.34
  collectively determined terms 5.55–5.72 *see also*
    collectively determined terms
  compulsory liability insurance 5.06
  continuity of employment 5.45–5.50
  contracts of employment 5.04 *see also* **contracts of
    employment**
  employment benefits 5.22–5.23
  generally 5.01–5.07
  mobility clauses 5.51–5.54
  modification 5.33
  non-transferable liabilities
    criminal liabilities 5.07, 5.14
    occupational pension schemes 5.07, 5.13
    TULRCA compliance 5.07, 5.15

preservation of rights 5.21, 5.24, 5.39, 5.40, 5.44,
    5.53
  pre-transfer liabilities 5.06
  profit-sharing schemes 5.32
  representation *see* **representation**
  share options 5.35–5.38
  statutory employment rights
    enforcement 5.39
    preservation of rights 5.39–5.40, 5.44
    retirement age 5.40–5.44
  substantial equivalence test 5.32–5.34
  transferee's liabilities 5.02–5.03, 5.06, 5.08–5.12,
    5.16, 5.25, 5.30 *see also* **transferee's liabilities**
  transferors
    liabilities 5.02, 5.04
    omissions 5.02, 5.04–5.05
**Information and Consultation Employment
  Regulations 2004**
  contractual changes 9.148
  delivery of information 9.144
  employers' obligations 9.142–9.143, 9.146, 9.150
  ICE representatives 9.143–9.144, 9.146–9.148, 9.150
  information requirements 9.143–9.145
  negotiated agreements 9.143, 9.149
  pre-existing agreements 9.149
  recognised trade union 9.147, 9.150
  substantial organizational changes 9.148
information technology
  cross-border transfers 12.24
injunctions
  freezing orders 9.138
insolvency *see also* **insolvency practitioners**
  Acquired Rights Directive
    allocation of liability 10.12
    business rescue *336*
    changes to employment contracts 10.06, 10.14
    exclusion of TUPE 10.02, 10.09
    insolvency practitioners *335–6*
    insolvency proceedings 10.02–10.05, 10.07–10.08
    opening of proceedings *335*
    purpose of procedure 10.04
    terminal insolvency 10.01, 10.03–10.04, 10.08,
      10.12
    transferee's liability 10.06, 10.08, 10.14
    transferor's outstanding debts 1.33, 10.06, *336*
  administration 10.24–10.36 *see also* **administration**
  automatically unfair dismissals
    administration 7.24, 7.27, 7.29–7.31, 7.36, 7.38,
      7.62
    no transferee in contemplation 7.24–7.26,
      7.29–7.30, 7.34, 7.39
    receiverships 7.24
    transferors' debts 10.46
  bankruptcy 10.05, 10.16–10.20, 10.50 *see also*
    bankruptcy
  changes to employment contracts
    Acquired rights Directive 10.06, 10.14
    appropriate representatives 10.54–10.55,
      10.59–10.60, 10.62–10.70, 10.81
    assigned employees 10.60–10.61, 10.63
    changes to terms or conditions 10.54–10.56,
      10.75, 10.81

economic, technical or organisational reason
    (ETOR) 10.77
employee representation 10.63, 10.67–10.69,
    10.71–10.74, 120.78
freedom to negotiate 10.55
nature of changes 10.75–10.77
negligence claims 10.80
objecting to change 10.78–10.79, 10.82–10.83
point of transfer 10.58
pre-transfer 10.58
recognised trade unions 10.64–10.65
relevant insolvency proceedings 10.57–10.58
requirements 10.54
safeguards 10.55, 10.76
specific authority 10.67–10.68
TUPE 2006 6.04
collective information and consultation 10.22, 10.44
compulsory winding up 10.21, 10.23
creditors' voluntary liquidation 10.26
creditors' voluntary winding up 10.21
dismissals 10.01, 10.05
joint and several liability 9.123
judicial supervision 10.01
liquidation proceedings 10.01–10.02, 10.07
misuse of proceedings 10.84
non-terminal proceedings 10.02–10.04, 10.07
opening of proceedings
    relevant insolvency proceedings 10.50–10.51
    statutory provisions 10.51–10.52
    supervision 10, 50, 10.52
    timing 10.50
    transferee's liability 10.51
purpose of procedure 10.04
rescue culture 1.35
safeguarding assets 10.01
special circumstances defence 9.132
terminal insolvency 10.01, 10.03–10.04,
    10.08–10.09, 10.11, 10.29, 10.31, 10.33
transferee's liability
    Acquired Rights Directive 10.06, 10.08, 10.14
    opening of proceedings 10.51
    transferors' debts 10.46–10.47
transferors debts
    automatically unfair dismissals 10.46
    collective information and consultation
        10.44
    economic, technical or organisational reason
        (ETOR) 10.47
    excluded debts 10.41–10.47
    opening of proceedings 10.07
    post-transfer liabilities 10.49
    pre-existing debts, 1.33, 10.06
    protective awards 10.44
    relevant employees 10.40
    relevant insolvency proceedings 10.37–10.39,
        10.45–10.46
    statutory guarantee payment schemes 10.43,
        10.45–10.48
    timing 10.48–10.49
    transfer of liabilities 10.41–10.42
    transferees' liability 10.46–10.47
TUPE 1981 10.09–10.11

TUPE 2006
    administration 10.24–10.30
    automatic transfer 10.12, 10.14, 10.17
    bankruptcy 10.16–10.17
    changes to employment contracts 10.14
    employee protection 10.14
    insolvency proceedings 10.15–10.16
    protection from dismissal 10.12, 10.17
    rescue culture 1.35, 10.13
    terminal insolvency 10.09–10.12, 10.14, 10.16
insolvency practitioners
    administrative receivers 10.19
    bankruptcy proceedings 10.19
    liquidators 10.19
    qualifications 10.19
    supervision 10.19, 10.50, 10.52, *335–6*
    voluntary arrangements 10.19
intermediaries
    transfer of undertaking 2.15
internal reorganizations
    TUPE 2006 1.11, 1.13, 1.43

joint and several liability
    collective information provisions 9.04–9.05
    compensation awards 9.119, 9.122, 9.125, 9.127
    compulsory liability insurance 5.27–5.28
    consultation provisions 9.04–9.05
    relative culpability 9.127
    transferees
        inherited liability 9.120–9.121, 9.125–9.126
        warranty and indemnity protection 9.124
    transferors
        failure to inform or consult 9.120–9.121, 9.123
        insolvency 9.123

labour-intensive activities
    Acquired Rights Directive 2.95–2.97, 2.100–2.104,
        2.111
    asset transfer 2.99
    cleaning services 2.94–2.96, 2.100–2.101, 2.104, 2.109
    deployment of individual efforts 2.94
    multifactorial approach 2.105–2.106, 2.124
    retention of identity 2.99, 2.101, 2.108
    security services 2.94, 2.103
    similar services 2.98, 2.109
    Spijkers factors 2.97, 2.106–2.108
    transfer of employees 2.99–2.100, 2.102–2.106,
        2.108, 2.110
    transfer of service contracts 2.97, 2.99–2.100
    transfer of undertaking 2.94–2.95
location
    change of location
        constructive dismissals 4.130–4.132
        material detriment 4.131–4.132
        objection to transfer 4.130
        overseas transfers 4.132
        repudiatory breach 4.131–4.132
        termination of contract 4.130
        unfair dismissals 4.131
    changes to working conditions 4.113
    cross-border transfers 12.25, 12.35
    operational changes 2.51–2.54

location (*cont.*):
  physical location of relevant operations 12.12
  relocation *see* relocation
  territoriality 12.12 *see also* **territoriality**

misrepresentation
  collective information and consultation 11.49
  contractual indemnities 11.53
  duty of care 11.49–11.51
  employee detriment 11.48
  negligent misstatement 11.48
  post-transfer arrangements 11.48
  transferee's liability 11.51–11.53
  transferor's liability 11.52

mitigation
  compensation awards 8.51, 9.111, 9.114
  damages claims *323 see also* **damages**

mobility clauses
  benefit 5.52
  geographical scope 5.51–5.53
  preservation of rights 5.53
  redeployment 4.55
  relocation 5.51–5.52, 5.54
  substantial equivalence 5.53

objection to transfer
  absence of claim 4.71
  automatic transfer 4.74, 4.80, 4.92
  change of location 4.130
  changes to working conditions 4.92–4.93, 4.109, 4.121
  claims against transferors 4.125
  communication 4.80
  consequences 4.79, 4.82
  constructive dismissals 4.122
  continuity of employment 5.49
  departure with immediate effect 4.78
  freedom to choose employer 4.90
  genuine objection 4.81, 4.83
  ignorance of transfer 4.85–4.87, 4.89
  justification 4.78
  notice period 4.78
  post-transfer 4.85, 4.90
  pre-transfer 4.88
  remaining with transferor 4.75
  right to object 4.72–4.75, 4.85–4.86
  secondment 4.83–4.84
  termination of employment 4.75–4.76, 4.83, 4.88, 4.92
  timing 4.73, 4.85, 4.89
  transfer to transferees 4.73
  transferee's identity 4.90–4.91
  transferor's business interest 4.77

occupational pension schemes
  Acquired Rights Directive 11.01, 11.06, 11.14
  changes to employment contracts 6.04, 6.61–6.63
  collective information provisions 9.28–9.29
  consultation provisions 9.28–9.29
  definitions 11.16–11.20
  employee liability information 8.10
  employment costs 11.04
  group personal pension schemes distinguished 11.20

level playing field 11.04
money-purchase schemes 11.05
non-transferable liabilities 5.07, 5.13
outsourcing contracts 11.03
Pensions Act 2004 11.17 *see also* **Pensions Act 2004**
pensions exclusion
  accelerated pension benefits 11.22
  actuarial advice 11.47
  Beckmann decision 11.24–11.26, 11.29–11.31, 11.33, 11.46–11.47, 11.58
  controversial nature 11.01
  defined benefit schemes 11.01, 11.19, 11.32
  defined contribution schemes 11.01, 11.19
  due diligence 11.45
  employee's consent 11.74
  employer consent 11.28, 11.31–11.32, 11.36–11.37, 11.47
  indemnity liability 11.46–11.47
  limits 11.06, 11.14, 11.21–11.22, 11.45
  Martin decision 11.27–11.31, 11.33, 11.46–11.47, 11.58
  old age, invalidity or survivors' benefits 11.06, 11.14, 11.21–11.22, 11.25–11.29, *335*
  post-transfer benefits 11.03, 11.05, 11.21, 11.46
  pre-transfer arrangements 11.03–11.04, 11.08
  private sector pensions 11.02, 11.30–11.31
  Proctor & Gamble decision 11.31–11.42
  public sector pensions 11.02, 11.30, 11.56
  redundancy provisions 11.22, 11.24, 11.26–11.27
  retirement-related benefits 11.23–11.29, 11.31
  supplementary company or intercompany schemes 11.06, 11.14–11.15, 11.29, *335*
  transferee's liabilities 11.45–11.47
  transferring employees 11.01, 11.04–11.05
  TUPE provisions 11.10–11.13, 11.15
Proctor & Gamble decision
  accrued pension liabilities 11.31, 11.33, 11.35
  defined benefit scheme 11.32
  early retirement benefits 11.32, 11.34–11.36, 11.43–11.44
  employer consent 11.31–11.32, 11.36
  private sector pensions 11.31
  right apt to transfer 11.35–11.38
  transferee's liabilities 11.31, 11.33, 11.39–11.42
public sector pensions 1.61
transferee's liabilities 11.06–11.09, 11.14, 11.21, 11.26, 11.28, 11.31, 11.45–11.47
TUPE provisions
  loss or reduction in rights 11.12
  pension exclusion 11.10–11.13, 11.15
  pre-transfer arrangements 11.13
  TUPE 1981 11.13
one-off service contracts
  client's intention 3.104
  interlinked tasks 3.102
  larger projects 3.101
  project teams 3.99
  short-term duration 3.98, 3.100, 3.102–3.108, 3.125
  single specific events 3.100, 3.104–3.105, 3.107–3.108, 3.125
  SPC exemption 3.98, 3.100–3.101, 3.106
  successive contracts 3.100, 3.105–3.106

one-person undertaking
economic entity 2.33–2.35
operational changes
client identity 2.57
generally 2.51
location 2.51–2.54
manner of operation 2.55–2.56
similar activities 2.51
organised grouping of employees
assignment 4.36–4.37, 8.08
collective information provisions 9.06
consultation provisions 9.06
employee liability information 8.08
groupings of one 3.84–3.92
identity of transferred employees 3.80, 3.125
no identifiable group 3.79
not necessarily organised grouping 3.81–3.83
service provision change 3.03–3.04, 3.12, 3.28,
    3.30, 3.78–3.80, 3.125
territoriality 12.17–12.18
trade union recognition 5.89
organised grouping of resources
assignment 4.36, 8.08
collective information provisions 9.06
consultation provisions 9.06
economic entity 2.33–2.35
employee liability information 8.08
trade union recognition 5.89
outsourcing
business activities 1.11
collective information and consultation 9.153
contractual obligations 12.64
employee information 12.64
employment costs 12.64
employment liabilities 12.64
employment policies 12.64
occupational pension schemes 11.03
relevant transfer, 1.11
salary levels 12.64
service provision change 1.14
social dumping 12.64
staff allocation 12.64
staffing levels 12.64
terms and conditions of employment 12.64

Pension Act 2004
auto-enrolment 11.80
compliance 11.05, 11.45, 11.58
consultation requirements 11.78
eligibility requirements
    eligible employees 11.62–11.64
    intra-group transfers 11.61
    relevant transfer 11.61
employee protection 11.57–11.58, 11.60–11.64
enforcement
    anti-avoidance 11.76
    changing benefits 11.77
    claims 11.75
    contractual status 11.74
    Pensions Regulator 11.75
information requirements 11.78
minimum standard of provision

entitlement 11.65–11.68
level of benefit 11.69–11.73
reference scheme test 11.71–11.73
occupational pension schemes 11.17 *see also*
    occupational pension schemes
post-transfer benefits 11.57–11.59, 11.69
pre-transfer arrangements 11.59
protection regime 11.04, *329–30*
pensions *see also* **occupational pension schemes**
accrued pension rights 8.10
auto-enrolment
    eligible individuals 11.79, 11.82
    employers' obligations 11.79
    level of pension provision 11.80, 11.83
    pension contributions 11.79
    Pensions Act 2004 11.80
    Pensions Regulator guidance 11.81–11.82
    postponement 11.82
    Transfer of Employment (Pension Protection)
        Regulations 2005 11.80
changes to employment contracts
    exclusions 6.61–6.63
    occupational pension schemes 6.04, 6.61–6.63
    pension protection 6.62
    permissible changes 6.64
    transfer-related changes 6.64
    transferring employees 6.61
changes in working conditions 4.121
collective information provisions 9.28–9.29
communications
    misrepresentation 11.48–11.53
    separate pension promises 11.54–11.55
constructive dismissals 4.122
consultation provisions 9.28–9.29
employee liability information 8.10
old age, invalidity or survivors' benefits 11.06, 11.14,
    11.21–11.22, 11.25–11.29
supplementary company or intercompany
    schemes 11.106, 11.14–11.15, 11.29
TUPE 2006 1.36
percentage test
assignment 4.40
service provision change 3.96–3.97
post-transfer integration
functional links 2.60
organizational autonomy 2.59
organizational links 2.60
retention of identity 2.58–2.59
transferee's existing operations 2.58
professional business services
dedicated teams 3.123
distinguished from other services 3.121
legal protection 3.119, 3.121
quality and performance 3.120
service provision change 3.119–3.124
services meriting exceptional treatment 3.121
profit-sharing schemes
due diligence 8.58
employee liability information 8.58
transferees' liabilities 5.32
project teams
one-off service contracts 3.99

public sector
Acquired Rights Directive 1.45
changes to employment contracts 6.17
Codes of Practice 1.59–1.61
collectively determined rights 5.56
economic activity 1.49–1.51
employee protection 1.39
occupational pension schemes 1.61
public authorities 1.45, 1.48
public/private sector transfers 5.27, 5.56, 6.17
public procurement 1.46
reorganizations
  administrative reorganizations 1.52–1.54
  public administrative authorities 1.55–1.58
  transfer of administrative functions, 1.52–1.54
telecommunications sector 1.47
TUPE 2006 1.45, 1.49, 2.05

receivership *see also* **insolvency**
automatically unfair dismissals 7.24
redeployment
assignments 4.56
mobility clauses 4.55
temporary redeployment 4.60–4.61
redundancy
changes to employment contracts 6.03
collective information provisions 9.08, 9.26
collective redundancy consultation
  compensation 9.108–9.109, 9.113
  consultation 9.139
  employee representatives 9.139
  employer's obligation 9.139–9.140
  protective penalty 9.139
  recognised trade unions 9.139
  special circumstances defence 9.132, 9.139
  TUPE obligations distinguished 9.140–9.141
compromise agreements 12.08
consultation provisions 9.08, 9.26, 9.56–9.57
continuity of employment 5.49–5.50
dismissals 6.03, 7.79, 7.81–7.82
economic, technical or organisational
  reason (ETOR) 7.45, 7.67–7.69,
  7.71, 7.86
employee liability information 8.05
fairness 7.81–7.82
redundancy payments 5.49–5.50, 7.45
redundancy pooling 7.79–7.82
special circumstances defence 9.132, 9.139
transfer-related dismissals 7.45
relevant transfers *see also* **service provision change;**
  transfer of undertaking
classic transfers 1.12
determination 2.09–2.11
external services 1.11
identification
  Acquired Rights Directive 2.01
  economic activity 2.03, 2.07
  economic entities 2.01–2.02, 2.06–2.07,
  2.25–2.26
  legal transfers 2.01, 2.12–2.13
  size of transferred business 2.04
  TUPE 2006 2.02

intention of parties 2.11
internal reorganization 1.11, 1.13, 1.43
outsourcing 1.11
public sector reorganizations 1.52–1.58, 2.05
retendering 1.11
sale of assets 1.11
series of transactions 2.127
ships 2.136
supply of goods 3.110
timing of transfer 2.134
relocation
change of location
  constructive dismissals 4.130–4.132
  material detriment 4.131–4.132
  objection to transfer 4.130
  overseas transfers 4.132
  repudiatory breach 4.131–4.132
  termination of contract 4.130
  unfair dismissals 4.131
changes to working conditions 4.113
costs 3.10
cross-border transfers 12.25, 12.35
fraud 4.62
mobility clauses 5.51–5.52, 5.54
remedies
compensation awards *see* **compensation awards**
complaints *see* **complaints**
contractual notice pay 4.112
damages
  breach of good faith 4.89
  concealment of transfer 4.89
  employee liability information 8.47
  material detriment *319*
  mitigation *323*
  personal injury 8.18
  wrongful dismissal 4.04, 4.112, 4.123, 7.01
injunctions 9.138
reorganizations (public sector)
administrative reorganizations 1.52–1.54
public administrative authorities 1.55–1.58
relevant transfers 2.05
transfer of administrative functions, 1.52–1.54
representation *see also* **employee representatives; trade**
  union recognition
consultative arrangements 5.96–5.97
European Works Councils 5.97, 9.151–9.152
post-transfer representation 5.97
staff committees 5.96
transfer of employees 5.96
transferee's liabilities 5.96–5.97
repudiatory breach
change of location 4.131–4.132
changes to working conditions 4.95–4.96, 4.99,
  4.103
constructive dismissals 4.122–4.123
resignation 4.71
resignation
absence from work 4.53–4.54
breach of contract claims 4.71
change in working conditions 4.71
constructive dismissals 4.71
repudiatory breach 4.71

resignation without notice 4.71
unfair dismissal claims 4.71
restrictive covenants
benefit and burden 5.30
changes to employment contracts 6.24–6.26
employee liability information 8.05
enforcement by transferees 5.29
protected customers 5.29–5.30
purposive interpretation 5.29
retention of identity
asset-reliant activities 2.48
assignment of lease 2.49
break in activities 2.61, 2.63–2.64
business disposed as going concern 2.44
business linked to property 2.49
continued operation 2.44
factual circumstances 2.45–2.48
labour-intensive activities 2.48, 2.99, 2.101, 2.108
no relevant transfer 2.50
requirement 2.43
resumed operation 2.44
service change provision 3.30, 3.36
transfer of part 2.67–2.68
retirement age
change to employment contract 6.53–6.54, 6.56
statutory employment rights 5.40–5.44

secondment
objection to transfer 4.83–4.84
series of transactions
combinations of transactions 2.127
fragmentation 2.128 *see also* **fragmentation**
relevant transfers 2.127
sequential transactions 2.127
treated as single transfer 2.128
service provision change
activities
activities conducted by transferees 3.12, 3.15
activities must transfer 3.59–3.60
character and quality of work 3.29
different contractors 3.67–3.69
diminution in work 3.41
discrete pieces of work 3.59
division of activities 3.125
expectation of future work 3.61–3.62
materially different service 3.34–3.35, 3.37–3.38
nature of contracted service 3.28
new methods of working 3.25–3.27
reallocation 3.25
relevant activities 3.125
retention of identity 3.30, 3.36
retraining 3.25–3.26
similar activities 3.30–3.33, 3.39–3.41, 3.58, 3.125
technological changes 3.25–3.26
work in progress 3.61–3.62
assignment 4.37
cessation of services 3.17
change of provision 3.12–3.13, 3.15, 3.24
client
change of client 3.68, 3.73
client remains the same 3.67–3.77

identity 3.63–3.66, 3.75
specific client 3.70
commodity services 3.09
concept 1.35
contractor/client relationships 3.03, 3.14, 3.18
definition 3.11–3.18
fragmentation 3.42–3.47, 3.50–3.58, 3.125 *see also* **fragmentation**
in-housing 1.14
interpretation
multifactorial approach 3.22
purposive interpretation 3.19–3.20, 3.23–3.24, 3.80
relevant transfer 3.21–3.22
introduction 3.01–3.10
limited period service provision 1.15
multiple clients 1.15
multiple transferees 3.42–3.43, 3.48–3.49
occasional services 1.15
one-off service contracts *see* **one-off service contracts**
on-going contracts 3.04, 3.12
organised grouping of employees 3.03–3.04, 3.12, 3.28, 3.30, 3.78–3.80, 3.81–3.92, 3.125
outsourcing 1.14
principle purpose
percentage test 3.96–3.97
quantitative comparisons 3.94
relevant activities 3.93–3.95
procurement of goods 1.16
professional business services *see* **professional business services**
purpose 3.02, 3.05
reducing insecurity 3.05–3.08, 3.10, 3.12
redundancy liabilities 3.10
relocation costs 3.10
retendering 1.14
statutory concept 3.02
sub-contractors 3.16, 3.18
supply of goods *see* **supply of goods**
territoriality 12.17–12.18, 12.20–12.21
TUPE 2006 1.35
voluntary/involuntary transfers 3.14
share options
contractual entitlement 5.35
due diligence 8.58
employee liability information 8.58
exercise of option 5.36–5.38
historic entitlement 5.36
non-transferable 5.35
self-determining benefit 5.36
separate contractual basis 5.35, 5.38
share-based transactions
change of ownership 1.40–1.41
continuity of employment 1.40, 1.42
TUPE transfers 1.41, 1.43–1.44
ships
Acquired Rights Directive 2.137
relevant transfer 2.136
territoriality 12.14
TUPE 1981 2.136–2.137, 12.14
TUPE 2006 2.136–2.138, *318*
UK registration 2.138

single specific events
  economic activity 2.42
  one-off service contracts 3.100, 3.104–3.105,
    3.107–3.108, 3.125
social dumping
  outsourcing 12.64
special circumstances defence
  approaching deadline 9.134
  burden of proof 9.131
  collective redundancy consultation 9.132, 9.139
  fast moving negotiations 9.134
  insolvency 9.132
  parent company decisions 9.133
  reasonable practicability 9.131–9.132
specific works contracts
  lack of autonomy 2.38
  lack of stability 2.36–2.40
Spijkers factors
  asset-reliant activities 2.48
  asset transfer 2.46, 2.54, 2.82
  factual circumstances 2.46–2.47, 2.84
  labour-intensive activities 2.48, 2.97, 2.106–2.108
  period of suspension 2.46
  retention of identity 2.44
  similarity of activities 2.45
  transfer of customers 2.46
  type of activity 2.47, 2.55
  type of undertaking 2.46
statutory employment rights
  enforcement 5.39
  preservation of rights 5.39–5.40, 5.44
  retirement age 5.40–5.44
  statutory guarantee payment schemes 10.43,
    10.45–10.48
sub-contractors
  service provision change 3.16, 3.18
substantial equivalence test
  individual rights 5.32–5.34
  mobility clauses 5.53
substantive change
  dismissals 1.35
  employees working abroad 1.35
  employers' compulsory liability insurance 1.35
  insolvency situations 1.35
  service provision change 1.35
  terms of employment 1.35
supply of goods
  assembly of parts 3.116–3.117
  finished goods 3.118
  goods-only contracts 3.114
  procurement 3.115
  relevant transfer 3.116
  sourcing and acquisition of goods 3.116–3.118
  SPC exemption 3.112–3.115

taxation
  earnings from employment 12.39
  facilitating transfer process 12.38–12.40
  transferring employees 12.38
territoriality
  Acquired Rights Directive 12.12–12.13
  continental shelf 12.23

cross-border transfers 12.24–12.36 *see also* **cross-border transfers**
employees working abroad 12.15, 12.21–12.22
location of relevant operations 12.12
national laws 12.13
ships 12.14
territorial limitations 12.12
TUPE 1981 12.14
TUPE 2006
  employees working abroad 12.21–12.22
  governing law 12.20, 12.22
  organised grouping of employees 12.17–12.18
  service provision change 12.17–12.18,
    12.20–12.21
  undertakings situated in UK 12.16, 12.18–12.19,
    12.22
timing of transfer
  continuity of employment 2.130–2.131
  determination 2.135
  employment obligations 2.129, 2.133–2.134
  importance 2.129
  period of years 2.130–2.132
  relevant transfers 2.134
trade union recognition *see also* **trade unions**
  continuation of recognition 5.92–5.94
  employee liability information 8.05
  transfer of recognition
    Acquired Rights Directive 5.88
    automatic transfer
    identity of relevant group 5.88–5.90
    organised grouping of employees 5.89
    organised grouping of resources 5.89
    pre-transfer recognition 5.91
    statutory recognition 5.95
  TUPE 2006 *320*
trade unions *see also* **trade union recognition**
  collective information and consultation 9.139,
    9.147, 9.150
  collective redundancy consultation 9.139
  complaints procedure 9.90, 9.94–9.96 *see also*
    complaints
  insolvency-related representation 10.64–10.65
  trade union representation
    Acquired Rights Directive 1.33
    appropriate representatives 9.63–9.64
    collective bargaining 9.65
    definition 9.65
    recognised trade union 9.63–9.64, 10.64–10.65
Transfer of Employment (Pension Protection)
  Regulations 2005
  auto-enrolment 11.80
  compliance 11.05, 11.45, 11.58
  consultation requirements 11.78
  employee protection 11.57–11.59, 11.60–11.64
  information requirements 11.78
  interpretation *331*
  post-transfer benefits 11.57–11.60, 11.69
  pre-transfer arrangements 11.59
  protection regime 11.04, *331*
  transferees
    pension contributions *331*
    pension scheme *331*

transfer of part of undertaking
  discrete economic entity 2.65–2.66
  existence prior to transfer 2.70–2.73
  fragmentation 2.69 *see also* **fragmentation**
  lack of tangible asset transfer 2.71
  larger economic entity 2.66–2.67
  relevant transfer 2.65–2.66, 2.70
  retention of identity 2.67–2.68
  separate economic identity 2.66
transfer of undertaking
  actual transfer, 2.07–2.08
  automatic transfer *see* **automatic transfer**
  break in activities 2.61–2.64
  commissioning under statutory provisions 2.20
  components 2.06
  date of transfer 4.01
  definition 2.02, 2.06, 2.14, 2.43
  degree of change 1.13
  determination 2.09–2.11, 2.45
  economic activity 2.03
  economic entities 2.02, 2.06–2.07, 2.25–2.26
  identifiable economic entity 1.13
  identification 2.01–2.02, 2.07–2.08
  intention of parties 2.11
  intermediaries 2.15
  intra-group transfers 2.21
  labour-intensive activities 2.94–2.95 *see also*
      labour-intensive activities
  lack of formality 2.22
  multiple forms of employment 2.25
  nature of transfer
      change of natural/legal person 2.13
      legal transfer 2.01, 2.12–2.13
  one-person undertakings 2.33–2.35
  operational changes 2.51–2.57
  operative provision 4.08–4.09
  phases 2.18
  post-transfer identity 1.13
  post-transfer integration 2.58–2.60
  property transfers 2.24
  relationships
      contractual relationships 2.15–2.17
      transferors/transferees 2.14–2.19
  retention of control 2.23
  retention of identity 2.43–2.50
  sale of on-going business 1.13
  size of business 2.04
  specific functions 2.19
  specific works contracts 2.36–2.40
  Spijkers factors 2.44–2.48, 2.54, 2.82, 2.84, 2.94,
      2.97, 2.106–2.108
  stable economic entity 1.13
  staged transfers 2.15
  third parties 2.15
  unstable contracts 2.41
transferees *see also* **transferee's liabilities**
  collective information provisions 9.01, 9.39–9.42
  consultation provisions 9.01, 9.39–9.42
  contracts of employment
      assignment 4.08
      automatic transfer 4.01
      continuation 4.08

  employee opt out 4.01–4.03
  employment liabilities 1.10, 4.11–4.12, 4.14,
      4.24–4.25
  inherited obligations 1.10
  novation 4.12
  pre-transfer dismissals 4.01
employment-related issues
  agency workers 4.13
  career breaks 4.13
  contracts for services 4.12
  corporate veil 4.19–4.20, 4.23
  employment liabilities 1.10, 4.11–4.12, 4.14,
      4.24–4.25, 5.02–5.03, 5.06
  identity of employees 4.17–4.19
  non-employees 4.12
  pre-transfer employment 4.09
  service companies 4.21
knowledge of transfer
  collective consultation 4.68, 4.70
  identity of transferee 4.69, 4.90–4.91
  implied terms 4.70
  notification provisions 4.68
  refusal to disclose 4.69
motives 2.112–2.114, 2.120–2.121, 2.123–2.125
multiple transferees 3.42–3.43, 3.48–3.49
occupational pension schemes
  inherited obligations 11.06–11.09, 11.14, 11.21,
      11.26, 11.28, 11.45–11.47
  Proctor & Gamble decision 11.31, 11.33,
      11.39–11.42
pensions
  misrepresentation 11.51–11.53.
  specific minimum level 1.36
post-transfer integration 2.58
relationship with transferors 2.14–2.19
transfer of employees 2.115–2.119, 2.122
TUPE avoidance 2.113
transferee's liabilities
  Acquired Rights Directive 5.16, 5.30
  bonus schemes 5.24, 5.31–5.32, 5.34
  collective agreements 5.73–5.75, 5.76–5.77, 5.83
  collectively determined rights 5.57–5.58
  compulsory liability insurance
      joint and several liability 5.27–5.28
      public/private sector transfers 5.27
      statutory obligation 5.25–5.27
  consequences of transferor's conduct 5.08
  contracts of employment 1.10, 5.08, 5.10–5.11, 5.16,
      5.25
  discretionary entitlements
      flexible approach 5.20
      non-contractual matters 5.17–5.18
      pension-related rights 5.19
      tort claims 5.18
  discriminatory acts 5.08
  due diligence 12.52
  employment benefits 5.22–5.23
  employment liabilities 1.10, 4.11–4.12, 4.14,
      5.02–5.03, 5.06, 9.120–9.121, 9.125–9.126
  employment protection 5.12, 5.16
  indemnities 12.61
  indemnity protection 9.124

transferees' liabilities (*cont.*):
  insolvency proceedings 10.06, 10.08, 10.14,
    10.46–10.47, 10.51
  joint and several liability 5.27–5.28, 9.120–9.121,
    9.125–9.126
  matters not transferred
    criminal liabilities 5.07, 5.14
    occupational pension schemes 5.07, 5.13
    TULRCA compliance 5.07, 5.15
  misrepresentation 11.51–11.53
  occupational pension schemes
    inherited obligations 11.06–11.09, 11.14, 11.21,
      11.26, 11.28, 11.45–11.47
    Proctor & Gamble decision 11.31, 11.33,
      11.39–11.42
  pensions
    misrepresentation 11.51–11.53.
    specific minimum level 1.36
  preservation of rights 5.21, 5.24, 5.39, 5.40, 5.44
  pre-transfer actions 5.08
  pre-transfer dismissals 4.01
  pre-transfer liabilities
    breaches of contract 5.06
    compulsory liability insurance 5.06
    continuous employment 5.06
    statutory employment claims 5.06
    tortious liabilities 5.06
  pre-transfer rights 5.09
  profit-sharing schemes 5.32
  replicating entitlements
    bonus schemes 5.31–5.32, 5.34
    modification of entitlements 5.33
    profit-sharing schemes 5.32
    substantial equivalence test 5.32–5.34
  representation 5.96–5.97
  restrictive covenants 5.29–5.30
  share options 5.35–5.38
  statutory employment rights
    enforcement 5.39
    preservation of rights 5.39–5.40, 5.44
    retirement age 5.40–5.44
  transfer of obligations 5.08–5.10
  transfer-related dismissals 7.86
  warranties 12.58–12.59
transferors
  claims against transferors
    constructive dismissals 4.125–4.126, 4.128
    detrimental terms of employment 4.125
    objection to transfer 4.125
    pre-transfer dismissals 4.127, 4.129
    termination of contract 4.09, 4.32–4.35, 4.125
  collective agreements 5.78–5.79
  collective information provisions 9.01, 9.40,
    9.42–9.46, 9.52, 9.120–9.121, 9.123
  collectively determined rights 5.58
  consultation provisions 9.01, 9.40, 9.42–9.46, 9.52,
    9.120–9.121, 9.123
  contracts of employment
    assignment 4.09, 4.36
    automatic transfer 4.01–4.03
    continuation 4.08
    employment liabilities 4.11–4.12, 4.14, 4.24–4.25

    freedom to choose employer 4.02–4.03. 4.90
    pre-transfer dismissals 4.01
    termination 4.09, 4.32–4.35, 4.125
  debts
    Acquired Rights Directive *336*
    automatically unfair dismissals 10.46
    collective information and consultation 10.44
    economic, technical or organisational reason
      (ETOR) 10.47
    excluded debts 10.41–10.47
    joint and several liability 9.123
    opening of proceedings 10.07
    post-transfer liabilities 10.49
    pre-existing debts, 1.33, 10.06
    protective awards 10.44
    relevant employees 10.40
    relevant insolvency proceedings 10.37–10.39,
      10.45–10.46
    statutory guarantee payment schemes 10.43,
      10.45–10.48
    timing 10.48–10.49
    transfer of liabilities 10.41–10.42
    transferees' liability 10.46–10.47
  definition 4.17
  employee liability information 8.01–8.04,
    8.06–8.07
  employment-related issues
    definition of employee 4.10–4.11
    dismissals 7.66–7.67, 7.71
    employment liabilities 4.11–4.12, 4.14, 4.24–4.25,
      5.02, 5.04
    identity of transferred employees 4.18–4.19,
      4.22
    national laws 4.10
    omissions 5.02, 5.04–5.05
    pre-transfer employment 4.09, 4.18–4.22,
      4.24–4.31
    relevant transfer 4.14–4.16
    service companies 4.21
  indemnities 12.61, 12.63
  joint and several liability 9.120–9.121, 9.123
  knowledge of transfer
    collective consultation 4.68, 4.70
    identity of transferee 4.69, 4.90–4.91
    implied terms 4.70
    notification provisions 4.68
    refusal to disclose 4.69
  misrepresentation 11.52
  relationship with transferees 2.14–2.19
  transfer-related dismissals 7.66–7.67, 7.71, 7.86
  warranties 12.57
transfer-related contract changes
  Acquired Rights Directive 6.04, 6.06–6.07, 6.10,
    6.27, 6.29, 6.33
  beneficial changes
    employee advantage 6.52, 6.54–6.55, 6.57,
      6.59
    employees' right to choose 6.56–6.58
    enforceability 6.52, 6.60
    reliance on original term 6.56, 6.58
    retirement age 6.53–6.54, 6.56
    validity 6.56

change in working conditions 6.17
compromise agreements 6.19–6.22 *see also*
    compromise agreements
connection with transfer
    but for test 6.41–6.42
    by reason of transfer 6.36
    post-transfer 6.37
    reason connected with transfer 6.36, 6.39–6.41
    requirement 6.30, 6.32, 6.50
    timing 6.38
consultation 6.03
continuity of employment 6.23
contracting-out 6.20, 6.27
detrimental variations 6.56–6.59
economic, technical or organisational reason
    (ETOR) 6.27, 6.29–6.30, 6.33, 6.35,
    6.45–6.51 *see also* **economic, technical or**
    organisational reason (ETOR)
insolvency 6.04, 10.06, 10.14, 10.54–10.83 *see also*
    insolvency
justification 1.10, 6.02, 6.06
less favourable terms 6.10, 6.16, 6.56
link between transfer and change 6.14–6.15
mandatory protection 6.01, 6.04–6.05, 6.07–6.08,
    6.27
notice of termination 6.02
pensions
    exclusions 6.61–6.63
    occupational pension schemes 6.04, 6.61–6.63
    pension protection 6.62
    permissible changes 6.64
    transfer-related changes 6.64
    transferring employees 6.61
permissible changes
    categories of contractual variations 6.29–6.32
    causation 6.30, 6.32
    contractual principles 6.27–6.28, 6.31
    economic, technical or organisational reason
        (ETOR) 6.27, 6.29–6.30, 6.33, 6.35
    EU law compatibility 6.33–6.34
    flexibility 6.28
    harmonization of terms 6.38, 6.40, 6.43–6.44,
        6.50–6.51
    pensions 6.64
    productivity gains 6.43–6.44
point of entry cases 6.12–6.13
post-transfer changes 6.12–6.14
prejudicial effects 6.56
public/private sector transfers 6.17
reasons for change 6.12–6.14, 6.30–6.31, 6.33,
    6.45
reengagement 6.02, 6.09, 6.11, 6.19, 6.43
restrictive covenants 6.24–6.26
retrospective claims 6.18, 6.34
unfair dismissal claims 1.10, 6.02, 6.19, 6.43
validity 6.01, 6.04, 6.10–6.12, 6.14–6.15, 6.32–6.33,
    6.45
variation of terms 6.01–6.02, 6.04, 6.08–6.10
waiver of rights 6.06–6.07, 6.34
transfer-related dismissals
connection with transfer 7.07, 7.09
contractual rights 7.03

economic, technical or organisational reason
    (ETOR) 7.02, 7.06, 7.08–7.09, 7.45–7.48
    see also **economic, technical or organisational**
    reason (ETOR)
employee protection 7.05–7.06
insolvency 10.01, 10.05, 10.12, 10.17–10.18
liability
    collusion between transferor/transferee 7.73
    joint liability 7.72
    pre-transfer obligations 7.72–7.73
    relative culpability 7.72
    transferee's liability 7.65–7.66, 7.70–7.71,
        7.72–7.74, 7.86
    transferor's liability 7.66–7.67, 7.71, 7.86
    unfair dismissals 7.73–7.74
point of transfer 7.86
pre-transfer dismissals 7.03–7.04, 7.86
reason unconnected with transfer 7.07, 7.09
redundancy 7.74–7.75, 7.67–7.69, 7.71, 7.79–7.82
sole or principal reason 7.07, 7.10
unfair dismissals 7.01, 7.05, 7.73–7.78, 7.83–7.85
    see also **unfair dismissals**
validity 7.02–7.03
TUPE 1981
ambiguities 1.17
amendments 1.26
assignment 4.36
changes to working conditions 4.92, 4.103, 4.119
collective information provisions 9.04
consultation provisions 9.04
entry into force 1.26
Fairness at Work 1.26
hiving down 10.85
implementation 1.04
insolvency provisions 10.09–10.11
interpretation 1.17
occupational pension schemes 11.13
reform 1.26–1.27
ships 2.136–2.137, 12.14
territoriality 12.14
TUPE 2006
amendments 1.31
appropriate representatives *321*
business flexibility 1.34
changes to working conditions 4.97, 4.98, 4.109
collective agreements *319–20*
consultation stage 1.28–1.29
contracts of employment 1.10, *318–9 see also*
    contracts of employment
dismissals *320 see also* **dismissals**
DTI Guidance 1.29
economic activity *318 see also* **economic activity**
economic entities *318 see also* **economic entities**
employee liability information 8.03, *322–3 see also*
    employee liability information
employee protection 1.01–1.03, 1.05, 1.10, 1.35, 1.39,
    10.14
employee representatives *321 see also* **employee**
    representatives
freedom of contract 1.02
impact 1.05–1.16
identification of transferred employees 1.35

TUPE 2006 (*cont.*):
  information and consultation requirements 1.35,
    323–5
  insolvency
    administration 10.24–10.30
    automatic transfer 10.12, 10.14, 10.17
    bankruptcy 10.16–10.17
    changes to employment contracts 10.14, *321–2*
    employee protection 10.14, *321–2*
    insolvency proceedings 10.15–10.16
    protection from dismissal 10.12, 10.17
    rescue culture 1.35, 10.13
    terminal insolvency 10.09–10.12, 10.14, 10.16
  internal reorganizations 1.11, 1.13, 1.43
  interpretation *317*
  introduction 1.30
  multiple transactions 4.04, *318*
  objective 1.06
  pensions 1.36, *322 see also* **pensions**
  public sector transfers 1.45, 1.49, 2.05
  purposive interpretation
    ECJ jurisprudence 1.18–1.22
    limits 1.25
    national courts 1.23–1.24
    objection to transfer 4.90
  relevant transfers *see* **relevant transfers**
  repeals *327*
  service provision change *318 see also* **service
    provision change**
  share-based transactions 1.40–1.44
  ships 2.136, *318*
  substantive change
    dismissals 1.35
    employees working abroad 1.35
    employers' liability insurance 1.35
    insolvency situations 1.35
    service provision change 1.35
    terms of employment 1.35
  territoriality
    employees working abroad 12.21–12.22
    governing law 12.20, 12.22
    organised grouping of employees 12.17–12.18
    service provision change 12.17–12.18,
      12.20–12.21
    undertakings situated in UK 12.16, 12.18–12.19,
      12.22, *318*
  trade union recognition *320 see also* **trade union
    recognition**
  transitional provisions *327–8*

unfair dismissals
  assertion of statutory right 7.75–7.78
    automatically unfair dismissal
      basis of decision 7.38–7.39, 7.41
      collusion with transferee 7.35, 7.37–7.38
      connection with transfer 7.09–7.11, 7.19–7.23,
        7.26–7.32, 7.35,7.86
      cross-border transfers 12.33, 12.35
      economic reasons 7.35, 7.38–7.40
      employee protection 7.05, 7.12–7.15
      exceptions 7.16–7.18
      insolvency 7.24–7.27, 7.29–7.32, 7.34,
        7.36–7.38, 7.62, 10.46
      liability 7.73
      motivation 7.38, 7.41
      no transfer 7.24–7.29, 7.33
      pre-transfer dismissals 7.34
      protected persons 7.12–7.15
      sole or principal reason 7.10, 7.19, 7.43, 7.62
      stage-managed dismissals 7.35, 7.38, 7.41
      third party involvement 7.40
    change of location 4.131
    changes to working conditions 1.10, 4.105–4.106,
      4.108, 4.121
    economic, technical or organisational reason (ETOR)
      1.10, 7.06, 7.08, 7.10–7.11, 7.31, 7.43–7.44, 7.51,
      7.53, 7.56, 7.59–7.61, 7.86, 8.29
    enforcement issues 7.83–7.85
    justification 1.10, 2.60, 4.25, 4.28–4.29, 4.107
    liability 7.73–7.74
    resignation 4.71
    service
      continuity of service 7.74
      qualifying service 7.74–7.76
    transfer-related contract changes 6.02, 6.19, 6.43
    transfer-related dismissals 7.01, 7.05
UK Border Agency
  immigration controls 12.42
unstable contracts
  unpredictable or precarious work 2.41

variation of employment contract *see* **transfer-related
  contract changes**

warranties
  commercial context 12.55–12.56
  due diligence 8.53
  protection 9.124
  transferees 12.58–12.59
  transferors 12.57
week's pay
  compensation awards 9.105–9.107
wrongful dismissals
  damages claims 4.104, 4.112, 4.123, 7.01